FROMMER'S
DOLLARWISE GUIDE TO THE SOUTHEAST & NEW ORLEANS

by Susan Poole

1984-85 Edition

CONTENTS

Chapter I   **INTRODUCING THE SOUTHEAST AND NEW ORLEANS**   **1**

     1. About This Book   **2**

     How to Save Money on All Your Travels—The $25-a-Day Travel Club   **5**

     2. Getting There   **8**

     3. Getting Around   **11**

Chapter II   **INTRODUCTION TO VIRGINIA**   **13**

     1. By Way of Background   **13**

     2. Traveling to Virginia   **17**

     3. Traveling Within Virginia   **17**

Chapter III   **ALONG THE VIRGINIA COAST**   **19**

     1. Alexandria   **19**

     2. Williamsburg   **26**

     3. Tidewater Virginia and the Eastern Shore   **36**

Chapter IV   **THE BLUE RIDGE MOUNTAINS**   **49**

     1. The Skyline Drive (Virginia)   **50**

     2. The Blue Ridge Parkway (Virginia and North Carolina)   **57**

Chapter V   **INTRODUCTION TO NORTH CAROLINA**   **71**

     1. By Way of Background   **72**

     2. Traveling to North Carolina   **75**

     3. Traveling Within North Carolina   **76**

Chapter VI   **NORTH CAROLINA'S COASTAL PLAIN**   **78**

     1. Nags Head and the Outer Banks   **78**

	2. Morehead City and Atlantic Beach	86
	3. Wilmington and Wrightsville Beach	91
Chapter VII	**PIEDMONT NORTH CAROLINA**	**97**
	1. Raleigh, Durham, Chapel Hill	98
	2. Winston-Salem	108
	3. Pinehurst	114
	4. Charlotte	120
Chapter VIII	**INTRODUCTION TO SOUTH CAROLINA**	**124**
	1. By Way of Background	124
	2. Traveling to South Carolina	128
	3. Traveling Within South Carolina	129
Chapter IX	**"LOW COUNTRY" SOUTH CAROLINA**	**130**
	1. The Grand Strand	131
	2. Charleston	139
	3. Hilton Head Island	150
Chapter X	**SOUTH CAROLINA: THE MIDLANDS AND "UP COUNTRY"**	**155**
	1. Columbia	155
	2. Around Columbia	160
Chapter XI	**INTRODUCTION TO GEORGIA**	**162**
	1. By Way of Background	163
	2. Traveling to Georgia	166
	3. Traveling Within Georgia	166
Chapter XII	**GEORGIA'S COAST**	**168**
	1. Savannah	169
	2. Brunswick and the Golden Isles	184
	3. Cumberland Island	191
Chapter XIII	**CENTRAL AND WESTERN GEORGIA**	**194**
	1. Atlanta	195
	2. Pine Mountain	210
	3. Plains and Other Area Attractions	213

Chapter XIV   **INTRODUCTION TO FLORIDA**   **216**
     1. By Way of Background   **217**
     2. Traveling to Florida   **222**
     3. Traveling Within Florida   **223**

Chapter XV   **FLORIDA: DOWN THE EAST COAST**   **225**
     1. St. Augustine   **225**
     2. Daytona Beach   **233**
     3. Disney World and Epcot Center   **236**
     4. Palm Beach   **248**

Chapter XVI   **MIAMI AND MIAMI BEACH**   **253**
     1. Getting Your Bearings   **254**
     2. Where to Stay   **258**
     3. Where to Eat   **264**
     4. Nightlife   **268**
     5. Sports   **270**
     6. Shopping   **272**
     7. Tours   **272**
     8. Sightseeing   **273**

Chapter XVII   **THE FLORIDA KEYS AND THE EVERGLADES**   **281**
     1. From Key Largo to Key West   **281**
     2. Key West   **287**
     3. The Everglades   **295**

Chapter XVIII   **THE GULF COAST OF FLORIDA**   **299**
     1. Fort Myers   **299**
     2. Sarasota   **305**
     3. St. Petersburg–Tampa   **312**

Chapter XIX   **ALONG THE GULF FROM FLORIDA TO NEW ORLEANS**   **323**
     1. Florida's Panhandle (Panama City)   **324**
     2. Mobile, Alabama   **328**
     3. Mississippi's Gulf Coast (Pascagoula and Biloxi)   **330**

Chapter XX   **INTRODUCTION TO NEW ORLEANS**   **335**
       1. By Way of Background   336
       2. Traveling to New Orleans   338
       3. Traveling Within New Orleans   338

Chapter XXI   **NEW ORLEANS HOTELS AND RESTAURANTS**   **343**
       1. Hotels, Motels, and Guest Houses   343
       2. Restaurants   350

Chapter XXII   **NEW ORLEANS: THINGS TO SEE AND DO**   **359**
       1. Seeing the Sights   360
       2. Nightlife   371
       3. Festivals   374
       4. The Sporting Life   376
       5. Shopping   376

Chapter XXIII   **NEW ORLEANS: 1984 LOUISIANA WORLD EXPOSITION**   **379**
       1. The Site   380
       2. Entertainment   381
       3. The Practicalities   383

MAPS

Virginia   15
Old Town Alexandria   24
Eastern Virginia   37
Skyline Drive and Blue Ridge Parkway   56
North Carolina   73
The North Carolina Coast   80
South Carolina   127
The Grand Strand   132
Charleston   142
Georgia   164
Savannah   172
Downtown Atlanta   196
Florida   218–219
Historic St. Augustine   230
Orlando and Vicinity   237
Greater Miami   256
Broward County   279
The Florida Keys   282
St. Petersburg   313
The French Quarter   361
French Quarter and Environs   363

**To my mother and father,
who gave me my Southern heritage.**

INFLATION ALERT: We don't have to tell you that inflation has hit the United States as it has everywhere else. In researching this book we have made every effort to obtain up-to-the-minute prices, but even the most conscientious researcher cannot keep up with the current pace of inflation. As we go to press, we believe we have obtained the most reliable data possible. Nonetheless, in the lifetime of this edition—particularly its second year (1985)—the wise traveler will add 15% to 20% to the prices quoted throughout these pages.

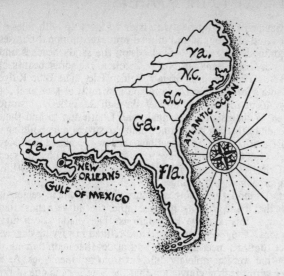

Chapter I

INTRODUCING THE SOUTHEAST AND NEW ORLEANS

1. About This Book
2. Getting There
3. Getting Around

ASK ALMOST ANYBODY about to set out on a visit south of the Mason-Dixon Line what they expect to find and you'll get an amazingly muddled reply. Margaret Mitchell's *Gone with the Wind* antebellum South; William Faulkner's Mississippi Deep South; Tennessee Williams's aging New Orleans southern belles or would-be belles; Atlanta's shiny, cosmopolitan image of the "new South"; tales of notorious speedtraps for out-of-state cars—all come together in a confused preconception of the region.

My own expectations were somewhat different. I was born and raised in the Southeast, and my travels to research this book were almost in the nature of a return pilgrimage. Having lived "up North" for some years now, I headed for the southern states that line this country's eastern coast with a little apprehension and the awareness that I would be seeing them from a new perspective. Periodic trips back home to visit relatives were different. This time I would be looking at *my* part of the country with the eyes of an "outsider." I would try to see it from the viewpoint of someone who hadn't grown up with tales of colonial heroes who lived and fought and argued over constitutional phrases right in the neighborhood—to see with fresh vision the sandy beaches and unspoiled, almost wild, Outer Banks of North Carolina, the softer beauty of South Carolina's Hilton Head, and Georgia's Golden Isles. The Blue Ridge Mountains and Atlanta's intriguing mix of old and new must be seen as if for the first time. It would be my task to wander through the orderly, historic streets of Alexandria, Williamsburg, Savannah, and Charleston to find their unique charm all over again. St. Augustine's ancient streets and buildings, southern Florida's frenetic sightseeing attractions, the low-key abandon of Key West, and that state's Gulf Coast would have to be looked at as if I hadn't seen them before. New Orleans's French Quarter, which I have loved all my life, would have to be approached as a stranger.

To my delight, I found that being a "tourist" in my home region is fun—the very things that made growing up there rather special were those that added zest and flavor to this odyssey. Expectations? They hadn't been high enough. Preconceptions? They were confirmed and refuted in varying degrees as I went from place to place, meeting people and places that hadn't changed in years and others that were completely different from my memories. As a visitor, I came away with the firm conviction that the Southeast is one of the most interesting and enjoyable sections of this country for the tourist. And, above all, I came back with a renewed appreciation for its people.

Meeting people is, in my book, one of the primary joys of travel. Certainly that is true in the Southeast. There is an unfailing courtesy and native friendliness that marks everyone you meet. I was not, of course, totally unprepared for that, having been taught from childhood that rudeness is an unforgivable sin (my grandmother once told me that a lady could tell anyone to "go to hell" if she did it politely!). But courtesy to the tourist seems to extend far beyond mere politeness to a real concern for comfort and convenience. Hospitality, that much-advertised attribute of Southerners, extends to today's paying guests as much as it ever did to house guests. Pride, another much-portrayed southern characteristic, extends to the South as a whole, one's native state, one's own part of that state, and especially to a hometown, all of which Southerners are eager to share with visitors. "I'll be proud to show you around," comes naturally to Southerners. They are equally proud of history, of which there is plenty, and "progress," evident everywhere you turn. They'll point with regional pride to a relic of the Civil War (which most now consider valiantly fought and fortunately lost), then direct your attention to a new industry or cultural center that makes it plain the South has a future as well as a past.

The Old South? The New South? They're both here in these five states, and New Orleans is its own special blend of the two. Whatever your preconceptions, come with an open mind, come prepared to relax and enjoy, and come secure in the knowledge that nowhere will you be more welcomed or go away more satisfied.

1. About This Book

These five southeastern states—Virginia, North and South Carolina, Georgia, and Florida—have a total area of some 243,830 square miles. That's a lot of ground to cover, and if you head south with no definite idea of what you want most to see and do, where to stay and eat, you can waste time, money, and temper getting around. It is to help in making your plans before you start out that this book has been written.

The hotels, restaurants, sightseeing attractions, and nightspots you'll read about have been carefully checked out, not within any specified maximum or minimum in price, but with the notion that you should get the *most* for your money whether you go luxury, moderate, or budget class. Because, however, most of today's travelers are in the medium-income group, you will find the emphasis throughout the book on prices that are neither in the highest nor lowest range. My own experience has taught me that there are times when price has little to do with quality: a "luxury" restaurant may serve mediocre, or even poor, food, and a budget establishment can be so loaded with charm that it would be a good buy at *any* price. The evaluations in this book were made with an eye on cost, of course (an expensive hotel or restaurant may, indeed, give you your money's worth but be well above the reach of most of us), but primarily with an eye on quality, and if you find a rave about an inexpensive place to stay or eat, it's because I found it exceptional as well as not costly. My judgments are, admittedly, entirely personal, and if the charm of a small hotel or restaurant means less to you than the sometimes colorless conveniences of large chains, the choice is yours to make (my choice is for the former). I hope that with these necessarily brief descriptions of what is available all along the way you'll be able to make that choice knowledgeably.

A WORD ABOUT PRICES QUOTED: Inflation, even with its occasional fluctuations, has become a part of the American scene. Thus, the prices shown here are *only those in effect at the time of writing.* Nowhere did I run into an establishment which promised to keep its prices stabilized or to give readers of this book any sort of price guarantee. Even if there is a variation in price by the time you reach a particular destination, however, the price *range* is likely to be the same, i.e., a medium-range hotel today will probably still be medium-priced for the area even with a hike in charges, although "medium" may be somewhat higher than at the time of this writing. In this sense, this is a *guide,* as the name says, to finding low-, medium-, and top-priced facilities.

HOTELS IN THE SOUTHEAST: Most of the medium-priced hotel and motel chains have branches in the states written about in this book. Some of the luxury chains, such as Hilton and Hyatt, are also represented in larger cities. In *all* of these, you will find air conditioning, color TV, and two double beds (unless noted otherwise in a description). Holiday Inns, Howard Johnson's, and other like chains tend to be pretty standard, and if a particular member is outstanding or differs in any respect, I've noted that for you. The higher-priced, luxury hotels will have additional features in rooms, such as separate dressing rooms, extra washbasins, etc.

The prices quoted throughout this book are for double-occupancy *rooms,* not per person. A money-saving technique when more than two people travel together is room-sharing. Instead of paying for two double rooms, three or more persons may rent one double room and pay a small extra fee for each additional *person,* which usually runs about $5 or $6 per night, much less than the cost of an extra room. If as many as five or six share a room, which will normally have two double beds, most motels will install rollaway cots for a small extra charge. Families, of course, often get a real price break when motels permit children under a certain age to occupy the same room as their parents at no additional charge. The age limit varies from 6 all the way up to 18, and unless you really can't stand having the kids underfoot at night, it will pay to look for these "family plan" establishments.

One further note about hotel accommodations: regardless of when you plan to travel—even if *you* consider it "off-season"—it is foolhardy to go without reservations. If your itinerary is not set and you cannot book for the entire trip before leaving home, it pays to call ahead just as soon as you know your next stopping point. Americans are on the road in increasing numbers even in these days of a strained economy, and there is *always* the possibility of being stranded without a room. Many motel chains have toll-free telephone numbers and some will teletype ahead for you if you'll be staying in another chain member in the next city.

A Dependable Budget Chain

A dependable, consistently good budget motel chain that proves the price-has-nothing-to-do-with-quality theory is **Days Inn,** which you will find throughout the Southeast. With double rooms seldom costing more than $38.88, and sometimes as little as $28.88, Days Inn is a real travel buy. Children from age 2 to 18 at various locations stay free with parents, and additional adults in the same room pay only $4 to $6. What's more, I have always found rooms to be as spacious as higher-priced accommodations (they're 12 × 24 feet), with thick shag carpeting, two double beds, color TV, a full bath, modern, comfortable furnishings, and tasteful, colorful decor. There is usually a Tasty World Restaurant attached, where breakfast can cost as little as $1.25, and a steak dinner will run about $6. There is always a pool, and sometimes a children's playground, coin-operated laundry facilities, and a service station. This same chain operates **Days Lodges,** with suites that sleep six, a completely equipped kitchen per suite, and open-air patio or private balcony, at prices of $44.88 and up.

For travelers over 55, membership in their September Days Club (with a small membership fee) has many benefits, including a 10% discount on food and lodging at some locations, rental car discounts, and special rates at many sightseeing attractions.

For a directory of Days Inns and Lodges in Southeast locations, as well as September Days Club information, write: Days Inns of America, Inc., 2751 Buford Hwy. NE, Atlanta, GA 30324 (tel. toll free 800/325-2525 or 404/320-2000).

A Dependable Luxury Chain

Actually, this heading is a bit misleading for the elegant **Guest Quarters Hotels**—luxury, they certainly are yet prices are in many instances on a par with or lower than luxury hotels that offer only a room. At each Guest Quarters location, what you'll get for those prices is: a designer-furnished living room with dining area, completely equipped kitchen, one or two bedrooms, spacious closets and bath, and all the services of a fine hotel. All those in the areas covered by this book have outdoor swimming pools, and each has a guest library, a notary public, and secretarial services for business travelers. Those completely equipped kitchens include coffee and tea for your first day (complimentary), and there's a grocery shopping service if you decide to make full use of the facilities. Not only is this an ideal way for families to take a break from the constant eat-out routine, but for executives, it offers an opportunity to entertain important clients (catering can be arranged through the excellent restaurants at each hotel). Extras that are available include 24-hour full-menu suite service at many locations, membership privileges at sports clubs, courtesy transportation to airports or inter-city destinations, a self-service guest laundry, and babysitting services. In the Southeast, you'll find Guest Quarters in Alexandria, Virginia; Greensboro, North Carolina; and Atlanta, Georgia; with another soon to be constructed in Tampa, Florida. Rates range from $85 for a one-bedroom suite to $172 for two bedrooms (rates vary from location to location, with some two-bedrooms as low as $97). I'll list addresses and rates for those along the way, but for a complete listing of Guest Quarters in other locations, write: Guest Quarters, 2550 M St. NW, Washington, DC 20037, or call 202/861-6600 (toll free, 800/424-2900).

A WORD ABOUT NIGHTLIFE: Nightlife in the Southeast, except for larger cities like Atlanta, Miami, and (of course!) New Orleans, tends to be concentrated in hotel lounges or to center around home entertaining. Where there are outstanding nightspots, you'll find them listed; otherwise, a friendly conversation or two with people who live in the locality will point you to the best current after-dark action.

. . . AND SHOPPING: Not being an avid shopper myself, I tend to overlook what may well be one of your primary interests. In the larger cities, I'll list major shopping centers for you, but all along the way, keep your eyes open for small, local shops—there are outstanding bargains to be found in small towns, where a little window-shopping during a lunch break may turn up a treasure. Look especially for locally made crafts, which will let you take a little of the regional charm home in your suitcase. In areas where such craft shops have been long established, I will tell you about them, but because they are sometimes transitory in nature and might have moved on while this book is still in print, a great many true artisans are no doubt omitted from our pages.

AN INVITATION TO READERS: Like all Dollarwise Guides, the *Dollarwise Guide to the Southeast and New Orleans* is our best effort to clue you in on how to get the most for your money. If, as a dollarwise traveler, you find we've missed an establishment that you find to be a particularly good value (or even one that's just fun and other readers ought to know about), we'd like to hear about it, and we invite you to write so it may be included in the next edition of this book. If, on the other hand, by the time you get to a particular destination you find a restaurant or hotel is *not* up to our description (chefs *do* change and hotels *do* deteriorate!), please write us about that, as well—the last thing we want in this book is misleading or untimely information. Any additional travel tips you may come up with (off days to visit attractions when they're less crowded, etc.) will also be appreciated. As you know, we update the Dollarwise Guides every two years, and if your suggestion or recommendation or comment is used in the next edition of this book, we'll send you a free copy. And, oh, yes, if you find this guide to be especially helpful, do drop us a line about *that*. Send whatever you have to say to Frommer/Pasmantier Publishers, 1230 Avenue of the Americas, New York, NY 10020.

How to Save Money on All Your Travels—the $25-a-Day Travel Club

In this book we'll be looking at how to get your money's worth in the Southeast and New Orleans, but you may want to learn about a "device" for saving money and determining value on *all* your trips by joining the popular, international $25-a-Day Travel Club, now in its 21st successful year of operation. The Club was formed at the urging of numerous readers of the $$$-a-Day and Dollarwise Guides, who felt that such an organization could provide continuing travel information and a sense of community to value-minded travelers in all parts of the world. And so it does!

In keeping with the budget concept, the membership fee is low and is immediately exceeded by the value of your benefits. Upon receipt of $14 (U.S. residents) or $16 (Canadian, Mexican, and other foreign residents) in U.S. currency to cover one year's membership, we will send all new members, by return mail (book rate), the following items:

(1) The latest edition of any *two* of the books except for *The Adventure Book*, which is available at only $7.50 to members (please designate in your letter which two you wish to receive):

Europe on $25 a Day
Australia on $25 a Day
England and Scotland on $25 a Day
Greece on $25 a Day
Hawaii on $35 a Day
Ireland on $25 a Day
Israel on $30 & $35 a Day
Mexico on $20 a Day
New Zealand on $20 & $25 a Day
Scandinavia on $25 a Day
South America on $25 a Day
Spain and Morocco (plus the Canary Is.) on $25 a Day
Washington, D.C. on $35 a Day

Dollarwise Guide to Canada
Dollarwise Guide to the Caribbean (including Bermuda and the Bahamas)
Dollarwise Guide to Egypt
Dollarwise Guide to England and Scotland
Dollarwise Guide to France
Dollarwise Guide to Germany
Dollarwise Guide to Italy
Dollarwise Guide to Portugal (plus Madeira and the Azores)
Dollarwise Guide to Switzerland and Austria (to be published March 1984)
Dollarwise Guide to California and Las Vegas
Dollarwise Guide to Florida
Dollarwise Guide to New England
Dollarwise Guide to the Southeast and New Orleans
(Dollarwise Guides discuss accommodations and facilities in all price categories, with special emphasis on the medium-priced.)

How to Beat the High Cost of Travel
(This practical guide details how to save money on absolutely all travel items—accommodations, transportation, dining, sightseeing, shopping, taxes, and more. Includes special budget information for seniors, students, singles, and families.)

The New York Urban Athlete
(The ultimate guide to all the sports facilities in New York City for jocks and novices.)

Museums in New York
(A complete guide to all the museums, historic houses, gardens, zoos, and more in the five boroughs. Illustrated with over 200 photographs.)

The Fast 'n' Easy Phrase Book
(The four most useful languages—French, German, Spanish, and Italian —all in one convenient, easy-to-use phrase guide.)

The Adventure Book
(From the Alps to the Arctic, from the Sahara to the Southwest, this stunning four-color showcase features over 200 of the world's finest adventure travel trips.)

Where to Stay USA
(By the Council on International Educational Exchange, this extraordinary guide is the first to list accommodations in all 50 states that cost anywhere from $3 to $25 per night.)

A Guide for the Disabled Traveler
(A guide to the best destinations for wheelchair travelers and other disabled vacationers in Europe, the United States, and Canada by an experienced wheelchair traveler. Includes detailed information about accommodations, restaurants, sights, transportation, and their accessibility. To be published March 1984.)

The Weekend Book
(This very selective guide covers the best mini-vacation destinations within a 175-mile radius of New York City. It describes special country inns and other accommodations, restaurants, picnic spots, sights, and activities— all the information needed for a two- or three-day stay. To be published May 1984.)

(2) A one-year subscription to the quarterly eight-page tabloid newspaper—**The Wonderful World of Budget Travel**—which keeps you up to date on fast-breaking developments in low-cost travel in all parts of the world bringing you the latest money-saving information—the kind of information you'd have to pay $25 a year to obtain elsewhere. This consumer-conscious publication also provides special services to readers: **The Traveler's Directory** (a list of members all over the world who are willing to provide hospitality to other members as they pass through their home cities); **Share-a-Trip** (offers and requests from members for travel companions who can share costs and help avoid the burdensome single supplement); and **Readers Ask ... Readers Reply** (travel questions from members to which other members reply with authentic firsthand information).

(3) A copy of **Arthur Frommer's Guide to New York,** a newly revised pocket-size guide to hotels, restaurants, nightspots, and sightseeing attractions in all price ranges throughout the New York area. (4) Your personal membership card which, once received, entitles you to purchase through the Club all Arthur Frommer publications for a third to a half off their regular retail prices during the term of your membership.

So why not join this hardy band of international budgeteers and participate in its exchange of travel information and hospitality? Simply send your name and address, together with your membership fee of $14 (U.S. residents) or $16 (Canadian, Mexican, and other foreign residents), in U.S. currency to:

$25-a-Day Travel Club, Inc., Frommer/Pasmantier Publishers, 1230 Avenue of the Americas, New York, NY 10020. And please remember to specify which *two* of the books in section (1) above you wish to receive in your initial package of members' benefits. Of, if you prefer, use the last page of this book, simply checking off the two books you select and enclosing $14 or $16 in U.S. currency.

2. Getting There

Many factors will determine how you get to the Southeast—budget, first of all; the amount of time you'll have for the trip; and just *where* you're headed in the Southeast. If your time is limited and you're coming from a long way off, say the West Coast, it would make sense to fly across country, then either rent a car or travel by public ground transportation. If your home is on the East Coast, you may be no more than a day or two of driving from your destination —or a train or bus ride of short duration. You'll find pertinent information about the public conveyances that reach each state in the introductory chapters for each. I'll let you in on some of my personal preferences (none of them based on solicitations or special considerations); however, remember that airlines, railroads, and bus companies *all offer frequent special fares, with substantial discounts and of limited duration,* that can save you considerable money. The fares shown are for regular, economy-class travel, but you should be *sure* to check on current details, schedules, and rates for all public carriers before figuring your costs. Remember, too, that public transportation can often turn out to be cheaper than driving, as well as letting you travel with the freedom to enjoy the scenery instead of constant map reading.

BY AIR: Flying is, of course, the quickest way to get where you're going. Figuring all costs, it may be no more expensive than some others, even cheaper than still others. And the smart traveler will, in addition to investigating any promotional fares offered by airlines at specific times, consider buying such standard, always-in-effect, money-saving tickets as the excursion plans. These usually entail such inconveniences as traveling on certain days of the week, staying a specified length of time, or other limiting conditions. However, it is possible to travel much less expensively just by planning your trip to meet those conditions.

The sample fares for air travel to major points in the five southeastern states and New Orleans that are shown here are for economy-class, roundtrip tickets *at the time of writing* (subject to almost certain change):

To	From New York	From Chicago	From Los Angeles
Alexandria, Va. (Washington, D.C.)	$130	$440	$758
Raleigh, N.C.	312	400	820
Charleston, S.C.	398	406	804
Atlanta, Ga.	408	374	758
Miami, Fla.	538	502	792
New Orleans, La.	584	448	714

A personal word here about airlines: most major airlines serve the Southeast and New Orleans, and you'll find those for specific destinations listed in each section of this book. For frequency of flights, quality of service, and general customer satisfaction, however, I have found Republic to be a leader—

and their fare structure is competitive, to say the least. A feature which can make a tremendous difference in your flight is the $10 additional fee which will move you from coach to Business Coach (equal, in my book, to first class on any line I've flown). There seems to be a special effort made by Republic crews to provide friendly, efficient service, and on some one-class flights, I have felt that it was an all-first-class operation in terms of comfort, although all fares were at the economy-coach level. Republic also offers exceptional tour packages in Florida and in other Southeastern states in conjunction with established land-tour operators. As I said earlier, this sort of endorsement has not been solicited by the airline and is a purely personal preference—but, then, recommendations based on my personal research are what this book is all about. For a current timetable at the time you plan to travel, or for package-tour information, write Republic Airlines, 7500 Airline Drive, Minneapolis, MN 55450.

Delta and Eastern also blanket the Southeast with frequent flights and attractive fly-drive packages are available to many resort areas such as Miami, St. Petersburg, and Disney World in Florida, and larger cities like New Orleans and Atlanta. You can save as much as 25% on airfare, have the convenience of a rental car (which will be waiting for you at the airport), and hotel arrangements are usually quite satisfactory, allowing enough flexibility in schedule and itinerary to permit comfortable travel. The airlines or your travel agent will have details and be able to make reservations.

Savings are also to be found by researching some of the newer, no-frills flights on airlines such as Air Florida (which flies to most major Eastern destinations, not just in that state), USAir, and Peoples Express. In short, depending on your needs, the times you must fly, etc., you will find a sort of airline supermarket that simply requires some astute shopping on your part.

BY TRAIN: The future of rail travel in the U.S. was very unclear for a time. Congress, in its infinite wisdom, had voted to cut back on many of Amtrak's cross-country routes, routes long established, but not especially profitable. With the advent of the gasoline shortage and a subsequent 60% to 70% increase in passenger load, a great many of these have now been reinstated, much to the relief of the traveling public. Of all modes of public transportation, rail represents the most economical use of fuel (Amtrak yields *twice* as many passenger miles per gallon as the next most economical, bus, and astonishingly higher percentages when compared to automobile and plane), and many travelers discovered a transportation method which became positively addictive. I am, personally, so enamored of the "romance of the rails" that not even the convenience of my own automobile sways me when a journey of any distance looms. And Amtrak has also come up with rail/car packages to many destinations that will provide a Hertz car to be picked up and returned to train depots, thus combining the best features of both.

On the whole, Amtrak has very good coverage along the eastern seaboard, rather spotty when you get away from the coast. My personal love of train travel is based both on economy and the fact that a train, unlike a plane or automobile travel along our superhighways, not only gives you a good look at the countryside, but some interesting backyards as well! In addition, today's trains are a pleasure to ride, with much more leg room than there used to be, wider seats, bar and restaurant (or snackbar) cars, and roomettes or compartments for longer trips. Diner-car meals suffered a bit during the cost cutbacks but have now come almost up to the high standards they've always met in the past.

As economical as regular coach fares are on Amtrak, there are frequent special rates which save even more. For example, the one-way fare from Los Angeles to Miami at the time of writing is $200—the excursion fare, round trip, is only $280! Also, there are periodic unlimited-travel passes available for specified time limits: in 1983, there was the "All Aboard, America" pass, and by the time you read this, there will probably be an "Anywhere" pass. The alert train traveler will keep abreast of Amtrak's latest offerings and try to schedule trips to take advantage of them. Incidentally, the popular U.S.A. RailPass is sold only outside the U.S. to residents of other countries—foreign visitors will also find available less expensive regional unlimited-travel passes, such as the Southern Region pass for about $200 which is good for two weeks. Those, too, must be bought before coming to the U.S.

The sample rail fares shown below to major points in the Southeast are regular, nondiscounted, round-trip coach costs at the time of writing.

To	From New York	From Chicago	From Los Angeles
Alexandria, Va.	$ 77	$196	$696
Raleigh, N.C.	115	202	468
Charleston, S.C.	151	274	504
Atlanta	252	230	501
Miami	302	286	654
New Orleans	380	228	400

Special Note: Amtrak has also put together package tours in the Southeast which are among the best travel bargains available in the country. All include transportation to your destination and accommodations—many add sightseeing admissions, entertainment, car rentals, etc. Contact your nearest Amtrak Tour Desk for details and prices. Any Amtrak office will direct you to its Tour Service. Also, a new service (via the Silver Palm) now connects Tampa and Miami with a link to Disney World, and Florida visitors will want to inquire about a new train/auto package (in the planning stage at the time of writing) which will transport passengers, along with their cars on the same train, nonstop from a point just south of Washington, D.C. to a central Florida destination (probably in the Orlando area). Fares will cover transportation and all meals.

BY BUS: Those two cover-the-country giants, Greyhound and Trailways, will get you to the Southeast from almost any starting point. Furthermore, although their standard fares are the cheapest way to travel, they both offer even greater bargains. Trailways' Eagle Pass, good for unlimited travel, costs $186.55 for seven days, $239.85 for 15 days, and $346.45 for 30 days. Greyhound's Ameripass costs about the same. Both companies also have periodic specials and you should always check for discounted fares in effect when you travel. A dramatic illustration of the savings available as this book is written is the difference between a discounted one-way fare of $99 between Los Angeles and Alexandria, Va. (Washington, D.C.), as opposed to the regular one-way fare of $275! The sample fares quoted below, however, are regular, non-discounted fares at the time of writing.

To	From New York	From Chicago	From Los Angeles
Alexandria, Va.	$ 80	$122	$550

Raleigh, N.C.	108	167	536
Charleston, S.C.	117	234	531
Atlanta, Ga.	240	192	523
Miami, Fla.	193	260	542
New Orleans	195	191	474

BY CAR: Although there was a time that automobile travel to the Southeast could be hazardous if you wandered down the eastern coast via U.S. 1, there are now Interstate highways leading into the region from every direction, connecting with well-planned, beautifully maintained state and federal road-ways within the several states with roadside rest areas at frequent intervals. Welcome Centers are at many state borders, providing special assistance to motorists as well as tons of tourist information. From a purely "easy to get around" point of view, driving is the most convenient way to come, particularly if you don't plan to stay in one of the metropolitan centers once you get there.

A Word About Car Rentals

You'll find all major car-rental companies throughout the Southeast. However, my own experience with most of them leads to this personal recom-mendation. You'll find **Thrifty Rent-A-Car** throughout the Southeast, and best of all, you'll find rates that are usually far below those of the major firms, primarily because of their very realistic policy of not paying for high airport rental space, but offering instead an airport pickup service (the same is true of your hotel or motel if you wish) and a two-rate structure, one which includes unlimited mileage, the other with a lower per-day (week, month, etc.) rate, but a per-mile charge. Thus, they can fit the charges to your needs. Most locations can furnish a wide range of car sizes (all the way up to a nine-passenger station wagon), and there are real money-saving specials offered from time to time at all locations. I'll list the locations in each state introductory chapter, but for a Thrifty world-wide directory and rate schedule, write Thrifty Rent-A-Car, 448 Exchange Center, P.O. Box 35250, Broken Arrow Expressway, Tulsa, OK 74135, or call toll free 800/331-4200.

READER'S TRANSPORTATION TIP: "In planning and executing a trip to several places on the East Coast, all by air, we found that in many locations renting a car for the days we were there was no more expensive for the four of us than simple transit back and forth to the airport would have been. In other locations, such as Washington, D.C., only because we had lived there did we know that the sensible choice was to avoid Dulles and Baltimore/Friendship airports, fly into National, and get ourselves into the city via the Metro for a few cents each. It pays to gather information on the relative convenience and cost of traveling via public transportation between tourist attractions in a particular location" (M. Aldrich, Minneapolis, Minn.).

3. Getting Around

BY AIR: There are several local airlines that fly within the region, and Delta, Eastern, Piedmont, and Southern have rather frequent air service to major points. We'll supply names of the most prominent local airlines as we go along.

BY TRAIN: Introductory chapters for each state have Amtrak stops listed, but it would pay to investigate thoroughly schedules between interstate points. Connections are not always easy to plan and time can be lost between trains.

The railroads offer very good access to the Southeast, not so good movement around it.

BY BUS: Greyhound, Trailways, and the local bus lines listed in each introductory chapter make it easy to get around and between states, and in most cases equipment is modern and quite comfortable.

BY CAR: As I said, highways in every Southeastern state are in good shape, and it is seldom, if ever, that you'll run into a badly paved roadway. The famed speedtraps that visitors once feared in Georgia and South Carolina have been virtually eliminated, although most state patrolmen keep a close eye on motorists to see that the 55-mile limit is not exceeded on state highways. There are frequent roadside picnic tables, some with outdoor grills, along both state and federal roads in this region, and picnicking can be a delightful way to save money, as well as a welcome break to enjoy the outdoors while you lunch or have a light supper. I have always found, too, that it's much easier when traveling by car to pack a small "hot pot" and cups for late-night or early-morning coffee. In fact, my family very often cuts down on eating costs by breakfasting in our room on sweet rolls or doughnuts bought the night before and served with instant coffee or hot chocolate, courtesy of the hot pot. Possible, of course, when you're traveling by other means, but most convenient when you can simply tuck a small box of eating supplies in the car.

Chapter II

INTRODUCTION TO VIRGINIA

1. By Way of Background
2. Traveling to Virginia
3. Traveling Within Virginia

THE COMMONWEALTH OF VIRGINIA, sometimes called "The Gateway to the South," is very much a part of my own growing up. I finished high school there, married and began my family on its coast, and somewhere along the line absorbed a love for its rich history that seems to imbue every native and is quick to hook most visitors. Virginia rightly claims "More America to the Mile" than any other part of the country (although New England states just might quarrel with that claim), and only the most complete dullard could travel the state and come away without a very real sense of this nation's beginnings.

1. By Way of Background

VIRGINIA PAST AND PRESENT: The Old Dominion, and this country, had its start in the London Company's small expeditionary force that settled at Jamestown on May 13, 1607. It was to become the first permanent English settlement, but for those first few years, it almost didn't make it. Ill-suited to deal with the primitive conditions in which they found themselves, those first colonists fell prey to dysentery, plague, fire, hunger that amounted to near starvation in 1609, and much internal bickering. Things picked up in 1610 when new settlers and fresh supplies arrived from England. Then, when John Rolf (who married the Indian princess Pocahontas) managed to convince enough farmers of the wisdom of growing tobacco as a "cash crop" and the first harvest was exported in 1614, they were off and running toward a sound economy. Two things happened in 1619 that would cast long shadows into the future: a representative legislative assembly was convened, and a Dutch man-of-war arrived carrying the first black indentured servants, the forerunner of a slave traffic that would later tear the nation apart.

Thus from its base of tobacco farming that spawned huge plantations along broad rivers and bays, an early democratic governing forum, and the use of slave labor, Virginia was a natural theater for the drama of history in which she would play a leading role. Bacon's Rebellion in 1676 was the first overt expression of dissatisfaction with British rule; it set the stage for events in the next century that sprang from the words and actions of Virginians such as Patrick Henry, Thomas Jefferson, George Washington, George Mason, James Madison, and John Marshall, and led eventually to full independence for all the American colonies. And from Virginians the new nation got its Constitution, Bill of Rights, and four of its first five presidents (Virginians held the presidency for 32 of our first 36 years!).

From the end of the Revolution until 1861 when it seceded from the Union, Virginia expanded its productive farms and busy ports until it became the richest state in the South. With the war against slavery that erupted in 1861, she became the very heart and soul of the Confederacy, with Richmond serving as its capital almost to the bitter end in 1865. In fact, the first major battle of that long, bloody struggle was fought in the state at Manassas, and the final act was played out at Appomattox.

After digging itself out from the debris of the postwar Reconstruction years, Virginia set out once more on a course of industrial growth. Today, you'll find it a harmonious blend of agriculture (tobacco, wheat, apples, corn, and hay), industry (not the least of which is tourism), and shipping. And following the philosophy that people who do not know their past can have no future, Virginia posts more than 1500 historical markers throughout the state to remind you of its important role in history.

You'll also find that there's much more than simply history to entertain the visitor. The east coast has some of the most popular beach resorts in the East and is a virtual sportsman's paradise, with excellent fishing, surf-riding, hunting, tennis, and golf. To the west are the Shenandoah Valley and the Blue Ridge Mountains, with horseback riding, hunting, and camping, as well as such natural wonders as Natural Bridge and the Luray Caverns.

VISITOR INFORMATION: For general information about Virginia, write: **Virginia State Travel Service,** 202 North 9th St., Suite 500, Richmond, VA 23219 (tel. 804/786-4484). If you're interested in golf, ask for "Golf in Virginia," their complete list of courses; in fishing, "Fresh Water Fishing in Virginia," a list of freshwater streams, lakes, and rivers, and "Salt Water Sport Fishing in Virginia," a guide to the annual saltwater sport-fishing tournament; in sightseeing with a historical bent, "Civil War Battlefield Parks," a guide to Civil War attractions, and "Historic Homes of Virginia," listing nearly 100 historic plantations, estates, and homes in the Old Dominion. Travelers with limited time or who wish to stick to the eastern part of the state should request

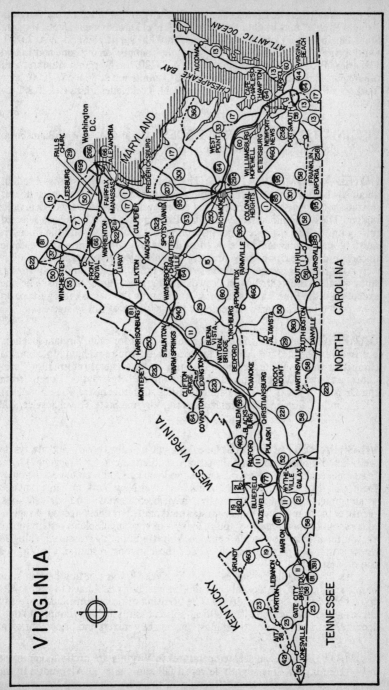

the excellent "Historic Chesapeake Bay Circle Tour." A brochure on "Virginia Annual Events" may be obtained from the Travel Development Dept., Virginia State Chamber of Commerce, 611 E. Franklin St., Richmond, VA 23219. Outdoorsmen will want to write the **Virginia Commission of Game and Inland Fisheries,** P.O. Box 11104, Richmond, VA 23220, for "Virginia Hunters" and other sports information or call the Game Commission at 804/257-1000. New Yorkers will find a Travel Service office at 11 Rockefeller Plaza (tel. 212/245-3080).

VIRGINIA TELEPHONE AREA CODES: Alexandria, 804; Williamsburg, 804; Virginia Beach, 804; Charlottesville, 804; Roanoke, 703.

HOTEL ACCOMMODATIONS: The large influx of tourists has brought about a generous supply of hotels, motels, campgrounds, and a few guest houses in some locations. As for prices, they cover everything from super-deluxe to budget. The accommodations you'll find listed in this book have been selected purely on the basis of a personal inspection and evaluation, and the prices, it must be said again, are those in effect *at the time of writing*—and in these uncertain days of rising costs, are very much subject to change.

As a rule, reservations will be less tight in fall, winter, and early spring, since Virginia draws its largest crowds during the summer months. The one exception is the Blue Ridge section, where literally thousands throng the parkway in October and early November for a last look at fall foliage.

CAMPING: You'll find some campgrounds listed for each Virginia location, but two very helpful publications are available if you're planning to come via camper or trailer. Write for "Virginia State Parks General Information" brochure, and the "Cabin/Campsite Information and Reservation Form," from the Division of Parks, 1201 Washington Bldg., Capitol Square, Richmond, VA 23219, and "Camping in Virginia" from the Virginia State Travel Service, 202 N. 9th St., Suite 500, Richmond, VA 23219.

VIRGINIA RESTAURANTS: One thing you can always do—and always do well—in Virginia is eat! From the strictly southern cured (or "Virginia") ham, fried chicken, and blackeyed peas to seafood you can count on to be deliciously fresh, you'll be fed well in restaurants that rival New York or San Francisco establishments, colonial taverns that have been serving food for centuries, plenty of medium-priced modern restaurants staffed by chefs steeped in regional cooking, or sometimes—if you're lucky—in very small, plain, restaurants of the oldtime, small-town-cafe home-cooking tradition. A reassuring thing to know is that compared to big-city prices, those in most restaurants in Virginia are modest.

As for alcoholic beverages, if you're over 19 you can buy beer in state stores and licensed restaurants and food stores, but you'll have to wait for 21 to be served wine or mixed drinks. The licensing of restaurants and lounges to serve alcohol by the drink is on a local-option basis; you may run into a "dry" locality, but don't get upset—in most you can buy mixers and bring your own.

CLIMATE: As you can see, temperatures in Virginia are pretty much in the moderate range, falling slightly lower in fall and winter at Alexandria in the northern part of the state and Roanoke in the west than along the coast.

	High	Low
Alexandria	87	29
Norfolk	88	32
Roanoke	88	29

2. Traveling to Virginia

BY AIR: Most of the larger domestic airlines (including Republic) and several international carriers fly into Washington National Airport and Dulles International, both of which are in Virginia and close to Alexandria. Piedmont, USAir, and Peoples Express also go to Norfolk and Richmond.

BY TRAIN: Amtrak has stops in Alexandria, Fredericksburg, Richmond, Manassas, Charlottesville, Williamsburg, Newport News, Petersburg, Farmville, and Lynchburg. Bear in mind that Amtrak excursion and special discount fares are considerably lower than regular coach fares. Also, your nearest Amtrak tour desk can furnish details on such bargains as "Wonderful Williamsburg" and "Virginia Beach" package tours.

BY BUS: Greyhound and Trailways will take you to almost any destination in the Old Dominion. As with Amtrak, check specials in effect when you plan your trip.

BY CAR: Several Interstate highways cross Virginia: I-64 runs east and west; I-77, north and south in the southwestern corner of the state; I-81, north and south the entire length of the western part of the state; I-95, north and south in the eastern part of the state. **Virginia Information Stations,** in attractive, colonial-style buildings, are located within a mile or two of major entry points.

3. Traveling Within Virginia

BY AIR: Within the state, USAir, United, and Piedmont have service between Washington, D.C.'s two airports (both in Virginia), Richmond, and Norfolk. There are also airports at Newport News, Lynchburg, and Roanoke.

BY TRAIN: You *can* travel around the state via Amtrak, although be forewarned that it takes some doing, with a good deal of planning for connections between major and spur lines, and it will almost certainly involve considerable waits. Nevertheless, Amtrak has stops at Alexandria, Fredericksburg, Richmond, Williamsburg, Newport News, and Petersburg (with a bus connection to Norfolk and Portsmouth) in the east. In other parts of the state, it's possible to go by train to Culpepper, Charlottesville, Monroe, Lynchburg, Danville, Staunton, Clifton Forge, Crewe, Farmville, Bedford, Roanoke, Christiansburg, and Narrows.

BY BUS: Greyhound and Trailways will take you almost anywhere!

BY CAR: Virginia has more than 50,000 miles of paved roads, so driving is a pleasure. My best advice is not to leave home without the official state highway map, issued free by the Department of Highways and Transportation, 1401 E. Broad St., Richmond, VA 23219. A letter will bring it to you, and besides road information, it's loaded with sightseeing information. It's also available at Welcome Centers at all major entry points.

All major car rental firms have offices in key cities, and there are Thrifty offices in Alexandria, Bristol, Fredericksburg, Newport News, Norfolk, Richmond, Roanoke and Springfield.

Chapter III

ALONG THE VIRGINIA COAST

1. Alexandria
2. Williamsburg
3. Tidewater Virginia and the Eastern Shore

FOR SHEER DENSITY of tourist attractions and excursions into Virginia's history, its east coast takes top honors. It was here, after all, that the earliest arrivals set up shop at sites which provided port access for those all-important ships that linked them to England and which would later serve as jumping-off points for the push westward.

1. Alexandria

Alexandria is one of Virginia's 40 independent cities; that is, it is not a part of any county, but a separate entity. A sister city to Georgetown, just across the Potomac River, it was literally put on the map by George Washington, who helped lay out the streets and drew its first map as a 17-year-old surveyor's apprentice in the 1750s. As a matter of fact, our first president had many close ties to the town: he drilled his first troops in Market Square in 1754, held a pew at Christ Episcopal Church, and in later years quite often came up to Alexandria to transact business as well as to find diversion in its busy social life. A little later, Robert E. Lee spent much of his childhood and prepared for West Point in Alexandria.

GETTING THERE: If you're driving, Alexandria can be reached on I-95 from the north and west, I-495 on the south, U.S. 1 from north or south, and Va. 7 from the west. Washington National Airport is just ten minutes north on the George Washington Memorial Parkway, and Dulles International is 30 minutes to the northwest. Both the Greyhound bus terminal and the Southern Railroad train station are just minutes from the historic area of Old Town.

A FIRST STOP: A fantastic restoration and preservation of more than a thousand 18th- and 19th-century buildings in **Old Town** makes it easy for today's visitor to see how this historic port city went about its business in those far-off days. It is even easier if that visitor heads for the historic Ramsay House that dates from 1724 and now houses the **Alexandria Tourist Council** at 221 King St. (tel. 703/549-0205). Their services far exceed those of many agencies of this kind; here are just some of the ways in which they'll make your stop in their town most interesting: they will show you a 13-minute color film; give you a free brochure for a self-guided walking tour; make hotel and restaurant reservations; provide foreign-language guides if you give them enough notice (their brochure is also available in more than 18 languages); arm you with more than 40 area attraction brochures, as well as lists of art galleries, specialty shops, antique shops, restaurants, hotels, and special events; and will even pass out free parking passes for out-of-town cars in the metered parking zones! And if you should need anything beyond all this, the friendly, efficient staff will almost certainly be able to help you out.

WHERE TO STAY: **Guest Quarters-Alexandria** (100 S. Reynolds St.; tel. 703/370-9600, or toll-free 800/424-2900) gives you the luxury of one- or two-bedroom suites in a peaceful setting combined with convenience to historic Old Town, shopping, corporate centers and downtown Washington (which is just about ten minutes away). You'll find their usual high standards of decor and service, and the lovely Quarters Court restaurant. Rates are $95 double in a one-bedroom suite and $125 for two bedrooms. There are also some studio apartments at $94 double. Each additional person pays $10, children under 16 stay free, and there are special weekend rates.

For convenience as well as comfort, there is no better place to stay than the **Holiday Inn** in Old Town, 480 King St. (tel. 703/549-6080). The Robert E. Lee home is just a half-mile away, Mt. Vernon an easy eight-mile drive, and Washington's National Airport just three miles (they furnish free transportation to and from). And all of Old Town is just outside the door. The inn's brick exterior even looks like part of the restoration, and that illusion is reinforced when you walk into its lobby furnished with period reproductions. The Independence Restaurant has the same colonial decor and specializes in American dishes, with roast beef high on the list, as is fresh seafood. The Tavern, just down the hall from the restaurant, is all low lights, dark wood, and pewter, and there's entertainment most of the year. An indoor pool provides year-round swimming. Rooms are spacious and comfortable, and far from budget priced ($80 to $95 double; children under 19 stay free in room with parents), but as a close-at-hand refuge after a day of foot-weary touristing, it can't be beat. Weekend package plans offer attractive savings.

On the north side of town, the **Ramada Inn–Old Town,** 901 N. Fairfax St. (tel. 703/683-6000), is an attractive highrise with a pool, restaurant, and entertainment in the lounge. Rooms are a comfortable size and attractively decorated in bright colors. If you're arriving or departing nearby airports, there's free shuttle service. Rates are in the upper brackets (doubles from $70 to $80), but children under 18 stay free in the room with their parents, and there are lower, weekend rates available.

The **Old Colony Inn,** North Washington at 1st St. (tel. 703/548-6300), is a complex of 11 brick buildings laid out in the style of a colonial estate. Located on the George Washington Memorial Parkway (which is Washington Street when it passes through Alexandria), the Olde Colony is only five minutes away from Washington's National Airport (with free airport and Metro shuttle service every half hour) and especially convenient to Washington sightseeing. The desk clerk here is happy to arrange Gray Line tours, which begin and end at the motel. All 223 rooms are attractively furnished, some with canopied double beds and most are furnished in a modified colonial decor. There's a pool, screened from traffic by a serpentine brick wall and landscaping. Also, a restaurant on the premises as well as a cocktail lounge and free HBO in every room, and there are excellent dining facilities within walking distance (the Yenching Palace is just across the street—see "Where to Eat"). At this member of the Best Western chain, small pets are welcomed, children under 16 stay free when sharing the room with parents, and rates are seasonal. Doubles are in the $65 to $75 range, and kitchenette units, double occupancy, run $55 to $63.

Also on North Washington Street (two miles south of National Airport) is the **Towne Motel,** 808 N. Washington St. (tel. 703/548-3500), which has offered comfortable accommodations at budget prices for some 20 years. Rooms are more modest here, but then so are the rates: doubles in the $40 to $56 range, with seasonal variations. There is no pool at this Quality Inn and no dining room, but three good restaurants are within a one-block radius. Small pets are welcomed.

The **Days Inn Alexandria,** 100 S. Bragg St. (tel. 703/354-4950), is just one block off the I-395/Duke Street intersection, with the top-quality accommodations typical of this chain. There's a pool, playground, and restaurant, and bring your pets along if you like (there's a small additional fee). This location is a good one if you plan much Washington sightseeing, since the Metro bus is just one block away. Rates are seasonal, with doubles running $44.88. Children under 18 pay $1.

Camping

If you're traveling the camper route, where you stay will depend on which direction you come from or are headed. Closest camping toward the west and the Blue Ridge Mountains is the **Greenville Farm Family Campground** at Haymarket (14004 Shelter Lane; tel. 703/754-7944), about 40 miles away on Va. 234, eight miles northwest of I-66. Most of the 150 sites have water and electric hookups; there's a recreation building, pool, laundry, store, and LP gas service. Rates are $10 to $13, depending on full or no hookups.

From Williamsburg, the **Yogi Bear's Jellystone Park Camp-Resort,** Rt. 3, Box 545M, Stafford, VA 22554 (tel. 703/659-3447), is about 20 miles south of Alexandria on I-95 (exit at Aquia interchange and follow the signs). There are 121 sites, full hookups, a recreation building, store, pool, laundry, mini-golf, and LP gas. Also, a nearby nature trail. Rates are $12.

WHERE TO EAT: Alexandria is filled with places to eat, most of them offering above-average fare, and part of the fun will be discovering your own favorites. I strongly recommend that you pick up the *Restaurant Guide* put out by the Tourist Council—it gives a very good rundown on the town's restaurants.

For a trip into the past, in both setting and cuisine, don't miss the **Old Club Restaurant,** 555 S. Washington St. (tel. 549-4555). This lovely old colonial home was once a clubhouse and claimed George Washington (who seems to have slept and eaten at an astonishing number of places) as a member. His club room is lovingly preserved. The large, homey dining room has a fireplace, in use when the weather calls for it, and the menu is strictly southern. Try the Virginia cured ham, peanut butter soup, and pecan pie. And since no colonial menu would be complete without fried chicken, seafood, and turkey, you'll find them here at their best. Prices are in the $5 to $6 range for lunch, and at dinner, in the $10-and-up range. The Old Club is closed Monday, open other days 11:30 a.m. to 3 p.m. for lunch, 5 to 9 p.m. for dinner except for Sunday, when dinner is served from noon to 9 p.m. in the southern tradition of midday Sunday dinner. It's closed Monday. You'd be wise to make reservations, for although the dining room is large, the place is a great favorite of both locals and Washingtonians.

In writing about the **Yenching Palace,** 905 N. Washington St. (tel. 836-3200), it's hard to know where to start. You should, of course, know about the food (superb—more about that later), the service (friendly and very efficient), the ambience (lively but low-keyed), and the decor (one of the most tasteful I've seen—in a sort of modified Oriental style). But almost as important is the history of the place. This is a branch of the original Yenching Palace at 3524 Connecticut Ave. NW in Washington, which has seen more contemporary history in the making than seems possible for a restaurant that is, after all, a public eating place and not a government clubhouse. It was at the Yenching in 1962 that President Kennedy's personal intermediary met with Nikita Khrushchev more than once to try to settle the Cuban missile crisis. Their last meeting there produced the terms that ended the threat of war, and the ABC documentary "The Cuban Crisis" was actually filmed at the restaurant. And when U.S. relations with the People's Republic of China began to warm in 1971, diplomats from both countries chose the Yenching for social get-togethers that included Henry Kissinger and top-ranking officials of both the U.S. and Chinese governments. The Alexandria branch now draws many Washington patrons of high official standing, and who knows what historic decisions will be made here in the future?

For all that, you won't find a trace of the self-importance that sometimes intimidates us lesser mortals when entering the "halls of the great." The à la carte menu is large—almost 150 items—and is written in both English and Chinese. Waiters know every dish and are always glad to help with selections. House specialties such as Palace soup ($2.50, and a delicious medley of vegetables), sliced beef with bamboo shoots, mushrooms, and snow peas ($8), and Peking duck for two (which can be ordered without advance notice at $19) are starred on the menu. This is one of the few restaurants I know that has managed to hold its prices down because of large volume (and they expect to do so at least through 1984) without sacrificing quality one iota. They'll even share their recipes with you and have printed copies of those for kung pao chicken and mu shi pork—just ask or write for your free copy. As Mrs. Jane Liu Shaw, manager and co-owner, explained to me, "The idea is to get people to exchange ideas, swap recipes, and compare experiences." And if you're really into cooking, they'll take you on a tour of the huge kitchen to see your dinner being prepared. A rave review? Well, yes. But it's more than merited. Hours are 11:30 a.m. to 11 p.m. Sunday through Thursday, noon to midnight Friday and Saturday. Reservations are optional, but large parties should book ahead.

Kings Landing, 121 S. Union St. (tel. 836-7010), is in a restored ware-house, and the decor is as charming as the food is good. Each of the dining rooms has its own distinctive atmosphere: three colonial, one modern, and one that of a garden. The menu is semi à la carte and basically French, with specialties like crabmeat-filled crêpes and veal served in special sauces. Lunch prices range from $5 (for the crêpes), and dinners begin at $10.50. Hours during the week are 11:30 a.m. to 2:30 p.m. for lunch, 6:30 to 10:15 p.m. for dinner, light fare until 1 a.m. On Saturday and Sunday, lunch is served from noon to 2:45 p.m., and Sunday dinners are from 5:30 to 9 p.m., light fare until 11 p.m. Every day the Kings Loft, with a fireplace, 40-foot red oak bar, and great view of the Potomac, is open until 2 a.m. with entertainment Tuesday to Saturday evenings.

HISTORIC SITES: When you stop by **Ramsay House,** 221 King St., to pick up those helpful brochures from the visitors center, take time to look around the historic old clapboard house and its garden. No one knows exactly when or where it was built, but it was moved from some early northern Virginia location in 1749. For a time it was the home of William Ramsay and his family. Ramsay was a hard-working Scotsman and a successful tradesman. George Washington walked to Ramsay's funeral in 1785. Before its restoration, the house was used as a tavern, grocery store, rooming house, and even a cigar factory. Of particular interest is the garden through which you enter the visitors center. It's an authentic 18th-century garden, with boxwood, cherry, laurel, a paper mulberry tree, tulips, and plantain lilies, all lovingly tended by the Hunting Creek Garden Club of Alexandria. Hours are 9 a.m. to 5 p.m. except major holidays.

The **Carlyle House,** at 121 N. Fairfax St., was built in 1751–53 as the home of John Carlyle, a Scottish emigrant and merchant who served as one of Alexandria's first trustees. It was here that Gen. Edward Braddock and five colonial governors met and suggested that colonists be taxed to pay for Brad-dock's Duquesne expedition against the French. Furnishings in the restored house and kitchen date from the late 17th century to the late 1780s. In a second-floor bedroom, the original construction of plaster, fireplace openings, and floor beams have been exposed. Open Tuesday through Saturday from 10 a.m. to 5 p.m.; Sunday, noon to 5 p.m. Closed Thanksgiving, Christmas, and New Year's Days. There's a $1.50 fee for adults, $1 for senior citizens, 75¢ for children 6 to 17, and special group rates are available.

The **Old Presbyterian Meeting House** at 321 S. Fairfax St. is where George Washington's funeral service was held when his own Christ Church was unreachable because of bad weather and road conditions. There are many Revolutionary soldiers buried in the old churchyard, including an Unknown Soldier of the American Revolution, whose burial records list him simply as "Old Revolutionary Soldier from Kentucky." The Meeting House is open without charge 9 a.m. to 4 p.m., Sunday through Friday; 9 a.m. to 1 p.m. on Saturday.

America's second-oldest apothecary shop, the **Stabler-Leadbeater Apothecary Shop,** 107 S. Fairfax St., was founded in 1792 and run by five generations of the same family until it closed in 1933. Today it is a museum (with medicines, mortars and pestles, and all sorts of medical equipment) of an early-day drugstore and an antique shop as well. It's open Monday through

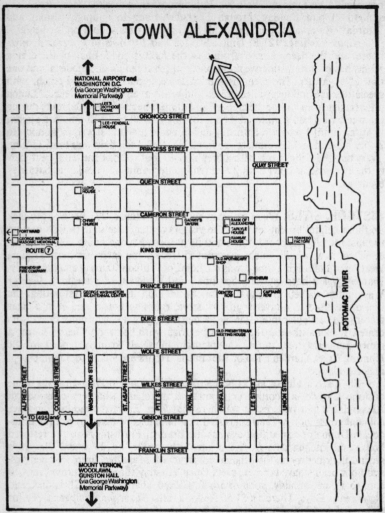

OLD TOWN ALEXANDRIA

Map courtesy of the Alexandria Tourist Council

Saturday from 10 a.m. to 4:30 p.m. At the time of writing, there's no charge but voluntary contributions are *most* welcome.

The **Robert E. Lee boyhood home,** 607 Oronoco St. (tel. 548-8454), was lived in by the great general intermittently from 1811 to 1825, and he went to school next door. There are some who say it's haunted—piano music has been heard by imaginative visitors, as well as the sound of a small boy running accompanied by the barking of a dog. 'Tain't so, says the curator, so bring your imagination if you want to people the house with ghosts (10 a.m. to 4 p.m. Monday through Saturday, noon to 4 p.m. Sunday). Admission is $1.50 for adults, $1 for senior citizens, 75¢ for children. Closed December 15 to February 1.

Gadsby's Tavern, at 134 N. Royal St., is where George Washington used to twirl his Martha around on the second-floor dance floor, as well as gather with cronies on quieter afternoons and nights. You can eat in the former stagecoach inn if you've a mind to (see "Where to Eat"). Even if you don't go for a meal, plan to visit the museum located in the gaming and assembly rooms of the City Tavern, and bedrooms and ballroom of the City Hotel, added in 1792. It's open Tuesday through Saturday from 10 a.m. to 5 p.m., Sunday from 1 to 5 p.m. (last tour at 4:15 p.m.), and admission is $2 for adults, $1 for children 6 to 17.

Gentry Row (200 block of Prince St.) and **Captain's Row** (100 block of Prince) are blocks of 18th- and early 19th-century homes lining the cobble-stoned street. They're privately owned now, as when they were built for sea captains of the sailing ships that regularly sailed from the port city.

OTHER HISTORIC SITES NEARBY: Mount Vernon (c/o Mount Ver-

non's Ladies Association; tel. 703/780-2000), George Washington's home from 1754 until he died in 1799, is nine miles south of Alexandria on the George Washington Memorial Parkway, and nobody in his or her right mind would want to miss it. If our first president has always seemed cool and aloof, he'll become a living presence as you walk through this home he loved above all and where he spent his happiest years. Stand on the wide, two-story, columned porch and you'll see the same peaceful view, with the long, green lawn sweeping down to the river. And inside, those responsible for restoration of the mansion have been careful to preserve the sense of "home" that warmed Washington's heart. Although only 500 of the 8000 acres that made up the estate in its prime are still intact (outlying farms were willed by the president and his wife to various descendants), they have been maintained just as he planned them, with a small group of service buildings close by the mansion. You can visit about a dozen of these "dependencies" for a vivid picture of plantation life. And both George and Martha lie at rest in the tomb "at the foot of the vineyard enclo-sure," as he directed. Don't plan to hurry around Mount Vernon—allow yourself well over an hour to absorb this lovely memorial to our first president. It's open every day of the year, and it's usually jammed during the summer months, particularly on weekends and holidays. But go, even if you have to join the throngs during those times. Hours are from 9 a.m. to 5 p.m. except for November through February, when the gates close at 4 p.m. Admission is $4 for adults, $3 for those 60 and over, $1.50 for children 6 to 11; and there's a free Open House held the third Monday in February to celebrate Washington's birthday.

The Mount Vernon Inn, located at the gate entrance to the Mount Vernon estate, serves moderate-priced lunches (from $4) and dinners (around $9.50) in a colonial atmosphere, with waiters and waitresses in authentic dress. There's also a gift shop and snackbar.

Three miles west of Mount Vernon is **Woodlawn Plantation,** the home built on property that Washington gave Nellie Custis (Martha's granddaugh-ter) and her husband. Visiting hours are 9:30 a.m. to 4:30 p.m. every day except major holidays, and there's a "Touch and Try" exhibit of embroidering and hoop-rolling that's fun for everyone. Admission is $2.50 for adults, $2 for senior citizens, and $1.25 for students (tel. 703/557-7880).

Still farther south of Alexandria (19 miles on the G. W. Parkway and U.S. 1) is **Gunston Hall** (tel. 703/550-9220), one of the most elegant of the historic homes in this area. Built between 1755 and 1758, the brick home was the residence of George Mason, who was often called the "Pen of the Revolution" for his work on the Fairfax Resolves, the first constitution of Virginia, and the Virginia Declaration of Rights (which formed the basis of the Federal Bill of Rights). Its formal interior is noted for the Palladian drawing room and Chinese Chippendale dining room, and the boxwood-bordered gardens are a delight. It's open 9:30 a.m. to 5 p.m. daily except Christmas; admission is $2 for adults, 50¢ for ages 6 to 15.

The entire town of **Fredericksburg** (49 miles south of Alexandria on I-95 or U.S. 1) could qualify as a historic site, for since 1727 it has been witness to events momentous in the birth and development of the United States. James Monroe, Lafayette, and John Paul Jones all lived or visited here, and the **Rising Sun Tavern** was the scene of fiery political rallies before the Revolution. George Washington grew to manhood here, and it was here he chopped down that famous cherry tree. This is also the site of a major Civil War battle. An afternoon's stroll through the town with its many restored homes and public buildings (pick up self-guided walking tour information at the **Fredericksburg Bicentennial Visitor Center** at 706 Caroline St.; tel. 703/373-1776) will leave you feeling you should climb into a carriage or onto a horse to end it rather than into a 20th-century automobile! Aside from museums and historic buildings, you'll find craft shops, antique shops, and colonial-style restaurants to sustain that other-century atmosphere.

Not all history lies south of Alexandria, however. About 20 miles to the west, near the intersection of U.S. 29, 211, and Va. 234, the **Manassas National Battlefield** was the scene of two major Civil War battles, both won by southern troops. There's an informative Visitors Center on the battlefield, and picnic facilities if you want to make a day of it. For full details on the battles and the park, write the National Park Service, Manassas National Battlefield Park, P.O. Box 1830, Manassas, VA 22110.

WOLF TRAP FARM PARK: Just 20 minutes away from Alexandria, the first national park dedicated to the performing arts, Wolf Trap Farm Park, has exciting ballet, opera, modern dance, jazz, symphony, and popular music concerts in its **Filene Center** from early June through the first part of September. Performances are in a red cedar amphitheater, and seats run $6 to $25 for evening shows. But a real bargain—and a delight in nice weather—are the lawn tickets which cost around $6. Bring a picnic if you like (a lot of Washingtonians and northern Virginians do and make it a lawn-party-type evening), or dine at the buffet that is served at 6:30 p.m. To find out about current schedules and reserve for the buffet, call 703/938-3810. Wolf Trap is at Vienna, just off I-495 (Capital Beltway at exit 10, then 2½ miles west on Va. 7). There's also an intimate year-round theater, The Barns of Wolf Trap, which presents drama, films, and music from jazz to opera. For current schedules, tel. 703/938-2404.

2. Williamsburg

Restoration of historic homes, public buildings, and even villages is not unique in the United States. Up and down the Eastern Seaboard and westward all the way to California, the history of the country has been preserved in buildings where much of it happened. But Colonial Williamsburg is unique— there's nothing quite like it anywhere else. It's almost as if, when you walk down the Duke of Gloucester Street, the doors of the Raleigh Tavern may swing open at any moment and Patrick Henry emerge deep in heated discussion with Thomas Jefferson, so true to its original character has this town been restored. And though the faces under bonnets or above 18th-century shirts bear the stamp of today, the clothes, and even the manners, are those of the past. To visit Williamsburg is not to "do" it in the tourist sense, but to become surrounded by and immersed in a way of life that nurtured men who molded, and still mold by their works that have endured over the years, the future of this country.

Men in knee breeches and women in long-skirted, white-collared dresses walk the streets on their way to and from enterprises that engaged Williamsburg citizens back in 1699, when Virginia's capital was moved from Jamestown (the first settlement) up to the inland Middle Plantation, which was given the new name in honor of the reigning British monarch. Just as the town bustled then with the commerce of bootmaker, printer, wigmaker, and blacksmith, it is populated now with costumed artisans carrying on these same crafts. And even the crowds of visitors are fitting, for in the old days, when the courts were in session or the Assembly met, inns, taverns, and rooming houses swelled with outsiders.

After Williamsburg became the political and social center of the colony (it already had the 1693-chartered College of William and Mary, second in age only to Harvard University), the royal governor and Assembly laid out an orderly plan for its development on either side of mile-long Duke of Gloucester Street. A capitol building was erected at the east end of the street, and midway between it and the college, a magnificent Governor's Palace went up in a setting of formal gardens. Thomas Jefferson came in 1760 to study at the college and later met many of the men who would join him to put the growing spirit of independence into words that would pull together a nation from fragmented, widely separated groups of colonists: George Washington, Patrick Henry, Richard Bland, and others. Patrick Henry led the fight against England's infamous Stamp Act of 1765 right here at the capitol, introducing his eloquent Stamp Act Resolves. And in May of 1776, the Virginia Convention sent a resolution from Williamsburg to the Continental Congress that resulted in the Philadelphia declaration that the colonies were "absolved from all allegiance to the British Crown." George Mason's Virginia Declaration of Rights, which became the foundation of our constitutional Bill of Rights, was adopted here in June of the same year.

It was a vigorous, stimulating, sometimes rowdy town during those years, and remained so until the capital was moved again in 1780, this time to Richmond, still farther inland where it would be closer to the center of population and safer from attack by the British. After that, things settled down and Williamsburg's days of glory seemed ended forever, a feeling that intensified when federal troops occupied the area for over two years during the Civil War.

It wasn't until 1926, when the Rev. W. A. R. Goodwin, rector of Bruton Parish Church, infected John D. Rockefeller, Jr., with his own enthusiasm for restoring the colonial capital, that wheels were set in motion to give the American people this authentic, carefully researched and restored link with their past. Rockefeller hovered over the project right up to his death in 1960, pouring vast sums of money into the restoration of some 88 still-standing buildings and the faithful reconstruction of hundreds of other structures on their original foundations. And today, the nonprofit Colonial Williamsburg Foundation, free from any affiliation with other organizations or governmental agencies, watches over the 173 acres, 320 costumed hostesses and craftsmen, 50 or more gardeners, and 2000 other employees, meeting the nearly $50 million annual operating costs through tourist income, investment returns from the permanent endowment left by Rockefeller, and donations.

What all this meticulous care and expenditure of money means to you and me is the opportunity to wander through this 18th-century "city" and literally feel the heartbeat of our nation when it was new in candlelight concerts at the Governor's Palace, fife and drum corps parades on Market Square Green, and in tavern meals that recall those long-ago menus.

GETTING THERE: Williamsburg can be reached by U.S. 60 and I-64 from the west, I-95 from the north and south. Greyhound and Trailways both have bus service, and Amtrak provides train service from Boston, New York, Philadelphia, Baltimore, and Washington. (Their "Wonderful Williamsburg" package is an especially good buy.) Patrick Henry International Airport is only 15 miles away and has limousine service (tel. 877-0279 or 229-2345 for flight pickup) for USAir scheduled flights.

WHERE TO STAY: Back in its colonial youth, Williamsburg boasted more than 30 inns, taverns, and "ordinaries" to accommodate the men of affairs who rode in from plantations, some several days away by horseback, to attend sessions of the legislature. It has been, from the first, a center of hospitality, and in that respect things haven't changed a bit in the last 200 years. The only difference is, of course, in size—today every road leading into Williamsburg is lined with motels; inside the city limits are scores more; there are some 30 privately owned guest houses; and those who carry their accommodations with them in the increasingly popular campers will find some 16 campgrounds within easy driving distance. Whatever your budget, there's a suitable place to stay in Williamsburg.

In spite of this, I would again caution *don't come without a reservation.* Williamsburg's "season" is a long one—mid-March to early November—and visitors from all over the world throng its streets. An excellent way to be sure you will have a place to lay your head is to write for the directory of accommodations, attractions, camping, and dining facilities published by the Williamsburg–James City County Chamber of Commerce, P.O. Box HQ, Williamsburg, VA 23185 (tel. 804/229-6511), under the title "Visitor's Guide to Virginia's Historic Triangle—Jamestown, Williamsburg and Yorktown." The Williamsburg Hotel and Motel Association (tel. toll free 800/446-9244; in Virginia, 800/582-8977) can also furnish current reservation information. And Colonial Williamsburg has a toll-free number for information and reservations for lodgings, dining, and group tours: 800/446-8956, or 800/582-8976 within Virginia. Or you may write Reservations Manager, Colonial Williamsburg, P.O. Box B, Williamsburg, VA 23187.

The Best

If money is no object and you lean toward quiet elegance, there's just one place to stay, the **Williamsburg Inn,** Francis St. (tel. toll free 800/466-8956; from within Virginia, 800/582-8976). Owned and operated by the Colonial Williamsburg Foundation, the sprawling, whitewashed brick inn, located just one block from the restored area, will surround you with the graciousness of the famous 19th-century spa hotels; and its English Regency decor is a sure antidote to any 20th-century tensions you may have brought along. From the moment you step into the lobby, with a fireplace at each end and French doors across the entire rear wall, you'll begin to experience the relaxation that is the inn's keynote. Walk through those French doors and you're on a brick veranda that overlooks swimming pools, croquet grounds, tennis courts, lawn bowling greens, a putting green, a driving range, and two golf courses. Follow a courteous bellboy to your room and you'll find it spacious, modern in every convenience, furnished in the same Regency style as the public rooms. You might well fancy yourself a pampered guest at a Virginia country estate! Or maybe you'll feel like one of the kings and queens who've stayed here (Queen Elizabeth II and Prince Philip are on the royal heads-of-state guest list). U.S. Presidents Harry S Truman and Dwight Eisenhower and foreign presidents also have enjoyed the inn's hospitality. Winston Churchill came to dinner, then reluctantly—audibly so—traveled on to Richmond.

If you stay in the main building, you'll find that rates for double occupancy start at $95, with a bed-sitting room costing $135 and a suite $180. The most luxurious of the inn's rooms are in the newer (1972) Providence Hall, set in a wooded area just east of the main building. There's a private balcony or patio for each room, and each has a superb view. Double-occupancy tariff starts at $98, with suites ranging from $200 up.

There are several package plans at special rates: inquire about the Williamsburg Tavern Plan, Leisure Season, Colonial Weekends, and Tennis or Golf Plans.

Rates at the Williamsburg Lodge, a short distance away on South England Street, and only a little less elegant (the decor is modern, not Regency), are more modest ($70 to $105).

Very Special

For a truly unique vacation experience, reserve at one of the **Colonial Houses** operated by the Williamsburg Inn, Francis St. (tel. toll free 800/446-8956; in Virginia, 800/582-8976). There are 26 of them; ranging in size from a tiny cottage tucked away in a garden to a 16-room tavern. They're all in the Historic Area, furnished in period manner, and carry with them full guest privileges, at the inn, at rates beginning at $80 for a room and $90 and up for a suite or complete house. For full details and reservations, call the toll-free number.

Motels

The **Motor House** is yet another extension of the Williamsburg Inn, Francis St. (tel. toll free 800/446-8956; in Virginia, 800/582-8976), and it too is operated by the Colonial Williamsburg Foundation. Located near the Information Center, it is thoroughly casual and contemporary in style. There are picture-window views from every room and facilities for swimming, horseshoe pitching, table tennis, badminton, a nine-hole putting green, 18-hole miniature golf course, playground, and shuffleboard, as well as guest privileges at the inn's two golf courses. Three restaurants serve the Motor House: the Cascades, specializing in Chesapeake Bay delicacies; the 420-seat cafeteria; and a self-service grill for quick service. Doubles cost $60 and up, corner studios or suites run $70 and up.

The **Holiday Inn 1776 Resort,** Va. 60 Bypass Rd. (tel. 804/220-1776, or toll free 800/238-8000) has over 200 rooms in a beautiful, 42-acre woodland setting. Both the architecture and decor of all rooms are colonial, and some suites even have fireplaces. There's an Olympic-size pool, an 18-hole golf course, and four all-weather tennis courts. You can dine by candlelight in their restaurant, have drinks in the colonial taproom, or enjoy late-night entertainment in the lounge. Rates run from $70 to $80 for doubles.

The **Gov. Spottswood,** (1508 Richmond Rd. (tel. 804/229-6444) has 16 kitchen units and in-room coffee in the remainder of its 70 rooms. Rates are a moderate $35 to $49, and there's a pool and playground on the wooded premises, coffeeshop and restaurant just across the street. It's one mile from the Historic Area.

In the budget category, the **Rochambeau Motel,** 929 Capitol Landing Rd. (tel 804/229-2851), has been rated "good" by AAA. Rates of $37 to $45 make the one-mile drive from the Information Center worthwhile. Rooms are more than adequate and really quite attractive for the price.

Guest Houses

The guest house route is one of my favorite ways to travel, both for the economy of it and the opportunity to meet interesting people. Williamsburg, like many university towns, is blessed with a number of these hospitable residences and all operate under the watchful eye of the Chamber of Commerce.

The Cedars (616 Jamestown Rd., Williamsburg, VA 23185 (tel. 804/229-3591), is a lovely three-story brick home furnished with antiques and presided over by the personable Mrs. Rose DeB. Harris. There are accommodations for 20 guests in the air-conditioned main house, and all rooms have private baths. Mrs. Harris is especially accommodating in setting up special family-suite arrangements. She is also quite knowledgeable about what's going on in Williamsburg, where to eat, etc., and graciously shares that knowledge with her guests. There's an attractive brick country cottage in back of the house that is suitable for as many as six. It's air-conditioned for summer, has electric baseboard heaters and a Franklin stove to add coziness on a winter day, as well as complete kitchen facilities. The Cedars is just opposite the College of William and Mary campus, within easy walking distance of the Historic Area. Rates are $25 and up double, $30 and up for a room for three, $32 and up for four. The cottage rate is $74.

Another guest house possibility: **Mrs. Arthur Gordon,** P.O. Box 221, 312, Williamsburg, VA 23187 (tel. 804/229-1974), rents three rooms in this quiet residential section. Rates begin at $16 for doubles.

Campgrounds

Located 4½ miles west of Williamsburg on U.S. 60, **Williamsburg Campsites,** RFD 3, Box 274, Williamsburg, VA 23189 (tel. 804/564-3101), has 300 sites and there's no charge for water or electric hookups. The swimming pool is also free and there are hot showers, toilets, a laundromat, grocery, and disposal station; $9.50 minimum for up to four people. Additional persons, $2 each, $1 extra for sewer. Open year round and just across the road from Williamsburg Pottery (Exit 53 off I-64).

The **Jamestown Beach Campsite,** P.O. Box CB, Va. 31-S, Williamsburg, VA 23185 (tel. 804/229-7609 or 229-3300), is set on 200 lovely acres along the James River, just 3½ miles from Williamsburg on Va. 31 South. There are 600 sites, plus amusement equipment, swimming in the pool or river, modern restrooms, showers, miniature golf, groceries, and ice. Rates are $8.50 and up for up to four people, $1 for each additional; trailer hookups are extra.

Ten miles west of Williamsburg, on the Chickahominy River, Rt. 1, Box 184 (tel. 804/229-1453), the **Holiday KOA Trav-L-Park** (Va. 5), Williamsburg, VA 23191 has 330 sites, most of which are wooded and on the water. The youth center, motor-boat rentals, pool, and playground make this an especially attractive family center. Modern restrooms, showers, laundry, store, and gift shop provide the conveniences. Rates are $9 to $11 for two, $1 for each additional person.

WHERE TO EAT: "This is the place to come if you really like good food," a Williamsburg native told me—and he's right! Good eating has been a tradition here since the early days, and you can find almost any cuisine your appetite fancies, in settings as varied as a colonial tavern and a New York deli.

True Elegance

The **Williamsburg Inn** ranks first again, with its handsome **Regency Room** highlighted by bronze and crystal chandeliers, hand-painted Chinese wall paintings, tranquil green walls, and curved windows. There's dancing, and gentlemen are, of course, required to wear a jacket and tie at dinner. Breakfast in this elegant setting can be a simple repast for about $5, or you can go all the way with a champagne breakfast for two for $25. And somehow, a champagne breakfast seems appropriate! Lunch consists of sandwiches, salads, fresh fish or meat and vegetable plates ($5 and up).

But it's at dinner that the Regency Room outdoes itself—both cuisine and wine list are internationally respected. You might start with bouquet of shrimps supreme or Virginia ham on Boston lettuce with condiments, move on to lobster bisque Chantilly, then select from a dazzling array of seafoods—perhaps the croustade of lobster au whiskey—or French lamb chops with minted pears from the grill. The salads are true creations, and rolls and breads are all fresh baked and of the melt-in-your-mouth variety. Desserts (if you're still hanging in there) include an extraordinary list of homemade pies, cakes, pastries, and such exotic ice creams (also homemade and *very* rich) as black walnut and rum (made with the real thing, of course). Entrees will run from $13 to $18 on the à la carte menu. All in all, it's a rare epicurean experience. Reservations required (tel. 229-1000).

The **Bay Room** at the **Williamsburg Lodge** also serves breakfast, lunch, and dinner, and features fresh seafood. On Friday and Saturday evenings, its renowned Chesapeake Bay Feast draws hosts of regulars, as well it should. The overflowing buffet has a full array of appetizers—seafood soups and chowders, oysters and clams on the half shell, etc.—and there are as many seafood main dishes as the imagination can conjure up, plus sugar-cured Virginia ham, prime ribs of beef, and fried chicken, with side dishes like Polynesian rice and European-blend vegetables. Each trip to the buffet will doubtless bring on an agony of indecision, and my advice is to keep your helpings small and try to sample some of each. The cost is $17 for adults, $11 for children, and beverages and desserts are extra (there's a very complete list of both alcoholic and nonalcoholic drinks, and try to save room for one of the yummy desserts.) The Feast is served from 6 to 9:15 p.m. Call 229-1600 for reservations.

The **Cascades Restaurant's** Hunt Breakfast Buffet (Information Center Drive) is as sumptuous as the Chesapeake Bay Feast, only here it's early-morning fare. As one Williamsburg devotee advised, "You really should starve the day before so you can appreciate it fully!" Served Monday through Saturday from 7:30 to 10 a.m., the buffet is a modern-day version of the old plantation breakfast, with eggs, sausage, bacon, fritters, ham, fried chicken, grits, beef stew, cherry cobbler, etc., etc., etc. Again there's no limit to the times you can visit the table, and the $6 ($5 for children) charge includes beverage. They also have an equally good Sunday brunch from 8:30 a.m. to 3 p.m. Call 229-1000 for reservations.

The Taverns

Part of the fun of a Williamsburg visit is eating in one of the three restored taverns that specialize in 18th-century food served by waiters in knee breeches and gaiters. You can eat in the garden at two, and have dinner by candlelight at all three. Prices are surprisingly moderate. Dinner reservations are required and can be made at all three taverns by calling 229-2141.

Josiah Chowning's Tavern (adjacent to Market Square; tel. 229-2141) serves lunch and dinner in the garden when weather permits. The Brunswick stew that is traditional here is $5.50 at lunch, $8 at dinner. Welsh rabbit ($5) is also a specialty, but prime ribs, ham, and barbecued pork ribs are all very, very good. Breads and desserts come from the same bake shop that serves the inn (true of all three taverns). But the best part of your meal at Chowning's might well be after it's over, when the "Gambols" begin at 9. You can sit back, order up a clay pipe exactly as Patrick Henry or Thomas Jefferson did, and enjoy the "diversions"—balladeers and games (backgammon, if you like). In fact, even if you dine elsewhere, you can amble over for the Gambols, only don't amble late—seating is on a strictly first-come, first-served basis. Lunch is from 11:30 a.m. to 3:30 p.m., till 4:30 p.m. in the summer in the garden with self-service. The three dinner sittings are at 5, 6:45, and 8:30 p.m.

Christiana Campbell's Tavern, Waller St. (tel. 229-2141), was one of George Washington's favorites. Brunch (from 10 a.m. to 2:30 p.m.) includes such plantation fare as pecan waffles, country sausage, specialty omelets, and chicken dishes, costing from $5 to $7. Ale, beer, lemonade, cider, and iced tea are served, and dinner (with strolling musicians) begins at 5:30 p.m. Spoonbread, muffins, and homemade fig ice cream add just the right exclamation point.

READER'S SELECTION: "Christiana Campbell's Tavern gives out their recipe for sweet potato muffins—in fact, they're already printed and readily available. We found 9 o'clock Sunday morning the loveliest time to visit areas of restored Williamsburg, before the crowds and while waiting to have that nice brunch at Christiana's" (G. Salassi, Baton Rouge, La.).

At the **King's Arms Tavern,** on Duke of Gloucester Street across from the Raleigh Tavern (tel. 229-2141), your costumed waiter will likely be a college student—it's a tradition that dates from the beginning of the restoration. Lunch (it might be Yorkshire meat pie or Virginia ham) is from 11:30 a.m. to 2:30 p.m., with light fare and beverages in the garden from 11:30 a.m. to 4:30 p.m. Dinner begins at 5:30 p.m. and is also served in the garden in summer. The evening menu includes Cornish game hen, filet mignon stuffed with oysters, and colonial game pie (venison, duck, and rabbit), with prices ranging from $10 to $17.

Other Choices

The **Old Chickahominy House,** 1211 Jamestown Rd. (tel. 229-4689), used to be in an old house on the river of that name, but the new location has every bit as much charm as the original. Dale and Maxine Henderson serve breakfast and lunch from 8:30 a.m. to 3 p.m. in a country setting of 18th-century antiques, many of which you can buy and take home if you've a mind. Besides the things for sale in the dining room, there's a large adjoining shop full of unusual items. Service is family-style at large tables which seat from six to ten people (I found it a neat way to meet interesting people) and reservations are not necessary. You can breakfast simply on Miss Melinda's pancakes ($2.50) or fill up on the grits, hot biscuits, and coffee or tea ($4.50). My own lunch favorite is Miss Melinda's special, which starts with a fruit salad, followed by a cup of Brunswick stew, smoked Virginia ham on hot biscuits, homemade pie (try the buttermilk pie for something different), and a beverage. Price? Just $6. They'll sell you Brunswick stew to take home or smoked Virginia ham, cured bacon and sausage, and water-ground corn meal. It's hard to say whether the charm of this place or the food comes out on top!

Beethoven's Inn, 467 Merrimac Trail, in the Be-Lo Center of Va. 143 (tel. 229-7069), is that New York deli I mentioned, and during its short life it has attained a place in the hearts of locals that is just short of beloved. About four years ago, Jim Wesson decided he'd had it with the business world in Washington, D.C., and moved his family here for a pressure-free lifestyle. True to his "quality of life" philosophy, Jim will tell you, "this is the most personality-oriented place you'll run into." He serves the deli food he loves himself, plays only his favorite classical records (most of them works of the great Ludwig, naturally), and even has a modest library of books for sale, but only those by authors of his personal choice. In the pleasant, red-carpeted dining room whose walls are hung with signed photos of performing artists and writers on one side and oil portraits of you-know-who, Mark Twain, Edgar Allan Poe, and the like on the other, you're likely to see students, college faculty, and local residents all munching happily on thick sandwiches of pastrami, liverwurst, and knockwurst with sauerkraut ($2.25 to $3), or smiling over the superb onion soup that is a house specialty ($2). There is even New York cream cheesecake ($1.95) that rivals my Manhattan favorite. And, like its "up nawth" counterparts, it has a take-out service. Reservations aren't necessary—come any time from 11 a.m. to 9:30 p.m., until midnight Friday and Saturday.

A longtime favorite with William and Mary faculty members is the **Green Leafe Cafe,** 765 Scotland St. (tel. 220-3405). The rustic oak interior is an indoor garden (true to its name), accented by stained-glass windows from old Richmond homes that have yielded to the wrecker's ball. The cuisine is continental, featuring excellent Greek dishes. Seafood Michelle, a combination of seafoods in a special sauce topped with melted feta cheese and served with rice, is superb. Prices are in the $9-and-up range. Hours are 11 a.m. to 10 p.m., Monday through Saturday; noon to 10 p.m. on Sunday. They do stay open until 2 a.m. for light snacks and cocktails every day except Tuesday, Thursday, and Sunday.

Budget Eating

You may not know that the two William and Mary cafeterias, **The Commons** and **The Wigwam,** are open to the general public, and they can't be beat for plain food at rock-bottom prices. Ask any student (just stop one on the street) for directions.

WHAT TO SEE: The **Colonial Williamsburg Information Center,** Colonial Parkway and Va. 312 (tel. 229-1000)—just follow the signs posted all over town—is the place to start. A 35-minute color film, titled *Williamsburg—The Story of a Patriot,* is shown continuously until 6 p.m. each day, and do take time to see it. This is the best possible introduction and shouldn't be missed.

Prices quoted here are subject to change without notice, but under the present admissions policy, a ticket to visit ten shops or exhibitions is $10, for 18 exhibitions, $15. Entry for children six to 12 is half price, and under six, free with adults. With a general admission ticket, the Governor's Palace is $3 for adults, $1.50 for children; without the general admission ticket, prices are

$8 and $4. Prices at Bassett Hall are $3 and $1.50 with general admission ticket, $6 and $3 without; and Carter's Grove, $3 and $1.50 with, $8 and $4 without. The Foundation operates a special bus within the Historic Area and your admission ticket allows you to catch it at any of the designated stops and ride as far as you like.

In fact, going the full circle is a good way to begin, after which you can get off at the first of the 15 stops, spend as much time as you like, then reboard to ride to the next one. There are also horse-drawn carriages and wagon rides for just $2 and $1.50 with your general admission ticket. Occasionally, there are oxcart rides, too. For the children, ask about the Tricorn Hat Tour and Craftsman's Apprentice Program at the Information Center—especially designed for the seven-and-up crowd during summer months.

Here follow some highlights:

The **Raleigh Tavern** was the scene of heated political debates, rollicking nighttime gaiety, and grand balls (in the Apollo Room).

The **Capitol** is one of the reconstructed buildings, but is faithful in detail to the original modified Renaissance style. This is where so much pre-Revolution political activity took place.

The **Governor's Palace** was home to seven royal governors and both Patrick Henry and Thomas Jefferson when they served as governor of the new state. What you see is a reconstruction of the original, which was destroyed by fire in 1781; Jefferson's detailed floor plan of 1779 was followed to ensure accuracy in the reconstruction.

The craft shops scattered throughout the Historic Area are functioning work museums, where costumed artisans use hand tools and colonial-vintage methods. There's an apothecary, basketmaker, miller, weaver, musical instrument maker, harnessmaker, and a long list of others.

And don't leave out the beautiful old walled campus of the **College of William and Mary**—look especially for the **Christopher Wren Building**, oldest academic building in America (1695) still in use.

Colonial Williamsburg is open year round, but if you can get there during the quiet months of January and February you'll not only avoid the crowds, you'll have the benefit of many reduced rates and special programs.

SIGHTS AND SITES NEARBY: **Jamestown** and **Jamestown Festival Park** (write: Superintendent, Colonial National Historical Park, P.O. Box 210, Yorktown, VA 23690; tel. 804/898-3400) are six miles away on Va. 31 (the Jamestown Road in Williamsburg) just off the Colonial Parkway. Admission to the island is $2 per car, and the entrance gate is open 8:30 a.m. to 4:30 p.m. Jamestown was the first permanent English settlement in America (May 1607), capital of the Virginia colony from 1607 to 1699, and the place where Capt. John Smith became acquainted with the young Pocahontas through her father, Powhatan. Stop at the visitor center for a film, tour information, and exhibits, all free, before setting out to see the old Church Tower (1639) and other historic sites in the old village. The **Festival Park** is a year-round exhibit that includes replicas of the *Susan Constant* (you can go on board and poke around), the *Godspeed,* and *Discovery,* the three tiny sailing ships in which Jamestown's colonists crossed the Atlantic. There's also a replica of the 1607 Jamestown fort and an Indian lodge. Open 9 a.m. to 5 p.m. every day. Admission is $3.50 per person, children under 6, free.

When Cornwallis surrendered at **Yorktown** in 1781, the fight for American independence was finally over. The free National Park Service visitors center (open 8:30 a.m. to 6 p.m. Summer months, closes at 5:30 p.m. Labor

Day through March) has guided bus and walking tours of the battlefield daily, as well as a film and a lot of interesting exhibits. The Yorktown Victory Center puts on an absolutely smashing Sound and Light show to dramatize the military goings-on here, for which there is a small charge.

Just for fun, visit Europe on this side of the Atlantic at **Busch Gardens,** P.O. Drawer FC, Williamsburg, VA 23187 (tel. 804/253-3350), "The Old Country," located just three miles east of Williamsburg. It's a European-theme amusement park that recreates 17th-century villages of England, France, Italy, and Germany, and throws in shows, restaurants, and rides like the infamous Loch Ness Monster. Billed as the tallest, fastest, fiercest roller coaster in the world, the Loch Ness Monster has double interlocking loops and a 114-foot drop where speed reaches 65 m.p.h. New shows are presented each year (in 1983 there was a tribute to Hollywood musicals, a German Festhaust band with dancers, and a celebrity concert series. Open weekends from April 2 to May 8 and September 10 to October 30, daily from May 14 to September 5. One-day tickets (age 3 years and up) are $13.50; two days cost $16.95; and there's a reduced rate after 5 p.m.

Carter's Grove, a 1755 restored plantation house that has been called "the most beautiful house in America," overlooks the James River just six miles to the southeast on U.S. 60. It's open daily March through December; $4 for adults, $2 for children six to 12.

The **James River** between Williamsburg and Richmond might well be called "plantation row," since both Va. 5 and 10, on its north and south sides, are dotted with restored homes, many of which you can visit for a small fee. Highway markers are posted all along the way, giving directions for turning off the main road to reach them. Two of the more interesting ones are Shirley Plantation and Barkeley Plantation.

Richmond, the state capital since 1780, is 49 miles northwest of Williamsburg on I-64 and is well worth a day. It is rich in history—in 1865, for instance, after four years of almost constant attack by federal troops, it was evacuated and burned by its own citizens! The **Visitors Center** at 1700 Robin Hood Rd., Exit 14 at intersection of I-95 and I-64 (tel. 804/358-5511), will point you in the direction of those sights that interest you, but the following are highlights: the **Capitol Building** (designed by Thomas Jefferson in 1785) at Capitol Square; the **Edgar Allan Poe Museum,** 1914 E. Main St. (he lived in Richmond for many years); the **Museum of the Confederacy,** 12th and Clay (it was Jefferson Davis's Confederate White House); the Virginia Museum of Fine Arts; and the Science Museum of Virginia.

Richmond is one of the few cities in this country whose Chamber of Commerce offers guided tours, and this is one of the best ways to see the city, especially if time is limited. For groups of 30 or more, there's a charge of $1.50 per person, or they'll take individuals for a three-hour tour of the city at varying prices, depending on who furnishes the car. Foreign-language guides and tours of nearby destinations such as Williamsburg can be arranged with advance notice. For detailed information before you come, contact the Richmond Convention and Visitors Bureau, P.O. Box 12324, Richmond, VA 23241 (tel. 804/648-1234).

READER'S SUGGESTION: "For travelers who want to stay over in Richmond, meet someone local, and enjoy a home atmosphere, I can heartily recommend the guesthouse reservation service of Lyn Benson, who can book you into a private home, guest cottages, or apartments in Richmond. She has a variety of accommodations and neighborhoods and is very nice about trying to find just what you're looking for, and almost all her listings include a continental breakfast. Rates are comparable to or lower than motels.

Her address is Lyn M. Benson, Bensonhouse of Richmond, P.O. Box 15131, Richmond, Virginia 23227 (tel. 804/321-6277 or 804/649-4601)" (S. Caliri, Wayne, NJ).

Due south on I-95 at exit 3 is **Petersburg,** yet another Virginia town involved in the early history of this country. It's worth a visit to see the beautiful Victorian Centre Hill Mansion, 400 E. Washington St., and old Blandford Church, 321 S. Crater Rd., with its fifteen Tiffany glass windows. You can wander through the Siege Museum, 15 W. Bank St., which depicts the ten-month siege of the city during the Civil War, the National Battlefield Park, off Va. 36, the U.S. Army Quartermaster Museum, at nearby Fort Lee on Va. 36, and the old Farmers Bank. The museums are free—but they *do* cheerfully accept voluntary donations. Hours at all are 9 a.m. to 5 p.m., Monday through Saturday, 12:30 to 5 p.m. on Sunday, and they're closed only on Christmas and New Year's Day. You can write ahead for maps and brochures to the Petersburg Tourist Information Services, P.O. Box 2107 (FP), Petersburg, VA 23804 (tel. 804/861-8080), drop by the Information Center at the Farmers Bank, 19 Bollingbrook St. (tel. 861-1590).

3. Tidewater Virginia and the Eastern Shore

To Virginians, the term "Tidewater" means that whole area around the mouth of the great Chesapeake Bay, which stretches all the way up to Delaware. It encompasses Norfolk, an important port and U.S. naval base; Portsmouth, with its huge shipyard; Hampton and historic old Fort Monroe; Newport News, home of the world's largest shipbuilding company; and Virginia Beach, one of the most popular beach resorts in the Southeast. The 14-mile-long stretch where the Elizabeth, York, James, and Nansemond Rivers come together into the bay is known as Hampton Roads and is one of the best natural harbors in the world.

The Eastern Shore, across the bay from Tidewater (accessible only by ferry until the 17.6-mile-long Chesapeake Bay Bridge-Tunnel opened in 1964 to connect Cape Charles with Norfolk), has superb surf fishing, and charter boats go out in fleets for the albacore, channel bass, white marlin, bluefish, and other fish that populate waters offshore around uninhabited barrier islands. Pre-Revolution towns, wild ponies near Chincoteague, fishing villages, large strawberry farms, and some of the best oysters and clams to be found on the coast combine to make it a fascinating area to visit.

Virginia Beach makes an ideal base from which to explore both these interesting areas and has the added benefit of an ocean dip at the beginning or end of any sightseeing foray, even in the fall (you can swim comfortably until late September or early October). Driving is also easier from the beach, away from Norfolk's traffic congestion, and all points of interest can be reached on easy day trips.

GETTING THERE: Two excellent highways (U.S. 58 and U.S. 60) plus the Virginia Beach Expressway (Va. 44) lead to the beach from Norfolk. Piedmont and People Express fly into Norfolk from New York, and Amtrak reaches Newport News from Boston, New York, Philadelphia, and Washington, and offers an excellent Virginia Beach package tour with rental car. Both Greyhound and Trailways serve most of the Tidewater area.

WHERE TO STAY IN VIRGINIA BEACH: New luxury hotels, older ones that wear their age with dignity and comfort, full-size apartments, efficiencies, hospitable guest houses—directly on the beach or a little bit away from it at

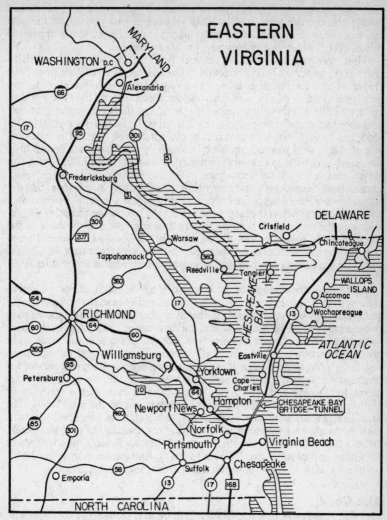

EASTERN VIRGINIA

lower prices—you'll find them all at Virginia Beach. For a complete list, including rates, write the Virginia Beach Visitors Bureau, P.O. Box 89, Virginia Beach, VA 23458 (tel. 804/425-7511), for their free accommodations directory.

The Best

"The hotel that made Virginia Beach famous." That's how **The Cavalier** bills itself. But these days, it's the new Cavalier, directly on the oceanfront at 42nd St. (tel. 804/425-8555). In the days of my Virginia youth, it was the "old" Cavalier, a majestic structure situated across the highway from the ocean on a rise that put it literally head and shoulders above everything else at the beach. The dashing, swashbuckling Cavalier dominated the landscape and the social scene, drawing patrons in the upper brackets from the entire Eastern Seaboard.

Over the years, however, its "swash" "buckled" somewhat and, while not exactly shabby, the grand old building relinquished its prestige to the new building across the road, an 11-story highrise with 270 superbly appointed rooms, each with an ocean view and private balcony.

But now the more-then-50-year-old hotel on the hill is stirring with renewed life under the loving direction of Gene Dixon, whose father owned the property for years. Pouring vast sums into its renovation, he searched out the best in furnishings, fabrics, and other appointments from all over the world to bring back the old Cavalier's former elegance. For those who value graciousness above an oceanfront location, this is a "must." (To reserve, call 804/425-8555, and be *sure* to specify that it's the older hotel you want.) The spaciousness of guest rooms was accomplished by knocking out the walls to double their size, leaving all bath and closet facilities intact—that means *two* full baths and closets in each. Closets are cedar-lined, baths have retained their huge porcelain fixtures from the old days, and many beds are of the king-size variety. Smaller rooms for single occupancy are cozy, not tiny, and just as beautifully decorated with period furniture as the larger ones. Some are interesting, irregular shapes, following the contours of the building. Full dining service is available in the basement Hunt Room with its mammoth fireplace. The 20-acre wooded property has tennis courts and shuffleboard, and the oceanfront isn't all *that* far away. Golf privileges are available at nearby courses. Rates for doubles begin at $74.

Of course, if you come to the beach to *be* at the beach, the new Cavalier is for you. This is elegance in the modern style, and I found the staff as friendly and gracious as you might expect in the older establishment. Most rooms have two double beds (some king-size) and children under 12 stay free in the same room with parents. There's platform tennis, deck shuffleboard, volleyball, archery, a game room, and a children's playground. The list of "extras" is impressive: baby cribs at no charge, irons and ironing boards, a copying service for businessmen, valet and laundry service, airport limousine, and special arrangements for fishing, golf, and water sports. They'll even plan a birthday or anniversary celebration. The Cavalier Lounge is just off the main lobby. The Sand Dollar Restaurant, also off the lobby, serves all three meals and cocktails, with outdoor dining in season at The Breeze overlooking the pool and beach. Orion's Roof (Top of the Cavalier) is one of Virginia Beach's "special" places for dining and dancing (see "Where to Eat"). Rates are seasonal: for double occupancy May 15 through September 15, $95, lower other months.

Also Good

The **Holiday Inn on the Ocean,** 39th St. and Oceanfront (tel. 804/428-1711), is in the exclusive north section of the beach, nor far from the Cavalier. There are two gleaming white and bronze highrise buildings, separated by a pool, patio, and ocean terrace. The south building is devoted to one-bedroom efficiency apartments, a better-than-average restaurant and cocktail lounge (with entertainment) on the top floor, while the north highrise offers spacious rooms, bridal suites, and the glass-walled lobby. On the ground level of the south building, overlooking the pool, there's a moderate-priced restaurant for breakfast, brunch, and lunch and an oceanfront piano lounge. All rooms and apartments have private balconies, and all are beautifully decorated. Double rates from mid-May to mid-September start at $95 ($110 for two-room apartments with full kitchens) and drop during other months.

The **Avamere,** 26th St. and Oceanfront (tel. 804/428-2112), has been operated by Clarence Smith's family for nearly half a century, and he maintains the same atmosphere of easy informality that has made it a favorite on the beach. There are connecting rooms for families, an exceptionally fine dining room, and oceanfront verandas. Rates from mid-May to mid-September begin at $88 for modified American plan (includes breakfast and dinner), lower other seasons.

On a more moderate scale, the **Idlewhyle,** 27th and Oceanfront (tel. 804/428-9341), has a friendly, relaxed atmosphere that brings people back year after year. All rooms are attractively decorated and have two double beds. There's a heated pool on the oceanfront, golf and tennis are within walking distance, and fishing is nearby. They also have a babysitting service, and restaurants are also within walking distance. Rates begin at $60 for doubles during the high season, less other months, and efficiencies run $10 more per day.

The **Traymore Sea Colony,** 9th St. and Oceanfront (tel. 804/428-7033), has been around a long time, but for beachfront rooms at moderate prices, it's still good. This pink, white, and brown hotel also has a motor lodge across the street for drive-to-door convenience, and there are some large family rooms, suites, and efficiencies. There's a pool, recreation room, TV lounge (TV in rooms as well), Ping-Pong, and shuffleboard. The cafeteria and snackbar are open in season. Double-occupancy rates are $50 and up mid-May to mid-September, and lower at other times. Closed September 20 to April 8.

Motel Apartments

This is one of the most economical, relaxed ways to spend a beach vacation, especially for families. There are many motel apartments along the beach, but the two listed here, one right on the ocean and the other across the street, are among the best, in my opinion.

Ocean Lake Motel Apartments 616 Atlantic Ave. (tel. 804/428-1841), is an attractive 80-unit apartment complex located just across the street from the ocean at 7th Street. Catering to families, the Ocean Lake has a pool, fenced play areas, and a social director. Once a week, there's a free hot dog roast and watermelon feast. Nearby are restaurants, grocery stores, gift shops, an amusement park, and fishing pier. Best of all, for the price of a motel room you can have a four- or five-room apartment that will accommodate six to eight people. Apartments consist of living room, separate dining area, one or two bedrooms, kitchen (fully equipped), and bath, and each has its own front lawn. There's central air conditioning, the decor is bright and cheerful, and the units are spotlessly clean. It's such a delightful vacation home that about 70% of their business is repeat and summer reservations begin coming in about the middle of January. Rates for a one-bedroom apartment (accommodates four, more with cots, which are available) are $60 per day, $325 per week, May 19 to June 20; $65 per day, $395 per week June 21 through Labor Day; and less all other times. And, yes, they welcome pets.

Guest House

Conveniently located in the heart of Virginia Beach, just one block from the ocean, **Angie's Guest Cottage,** 302 24th St. (tel. 804/428-4690), has six nice bedrooms (one with private bath—the others convenient to two central baths) and two apartments. All have air conditioning, and some rooms have small refrigerators. Children and small pets are welcomed here, and there's a sundeck, barbecue pit, and picnic tables. All in all, this is a friendly family-type place to stay, just across the street from the Greyhound bus station, and you won't believe the low rates—$25 to $47 per night from Memorial Day to Labor

Day, $15 to $36 other times. And even lower weekly rates are available—just ask Barbara Yates, the proprietress, about them. Backpackers and bikers will find dormitory bunks for only $9.

Campgrounds

The closest campground to the Virginia Beach oceanfront is **Holiday Trav-L-Park,** 1½ miles south of Rudee Inlet Bridge (1075 Gen. Booth Blvd., Virginia Beach, VA 23452; tel. 804/425-0249). It has 1000 sites, full hookups, a recreation building, store, pool, laundry, and LP gas. Prices are $15 to $17 for two persons, $1.50 for each additional.

Also very near the beach (less than five minutes), the **Virginia Beach KOA,** 1240 Gen. Booth Blvd., Virginia Beach, VA 23451 (tel 804/428-1444), has 750 sites, full hookups, two swimming pools, playgrounds, minigolf, a store, and a dump station. They also furnish free bus service to the beach. Prices start at $12.

WHERE TO EAT IN VIRGINIA BEACH: Virginia Beach has restaurants of all persuasions. Space will permit only a very subjective listing, but write the Virginia Beach Visitors Bureau, P.O. Box 89, Virginia Beach, VA 23458 (tel. 804/425-7511), for their *Restaurant Guide* (free), a full roster of pancake houses, coffeeshops, and restaurants serving Chinese, American, French, Greek, Mexican, Italian, Jewish, and, not surprisingly, seafood cuisines.

Fancy and Very Special

Orion's Roof at the new **Cavalier,** 42nd and Oceanfront (tel. 425-8555), is *the* place for a splendiferous evening of gourmet dining and dancing. The rooftop setting, with glass walls that look out on breathtaking ocean and city views, is enhanced by the elegant decor in soft tones of beige and brown. Entering via mosaic-tiled stepping stones over reflecting pools with splashing fountains, you may choose to sit a while in the pleasant, dimly lit lounge and just enjoy the view. It's a nice prelude to candlelight dining in the large dining room, where an orchestra plays for dancing on one side of the room. Most important, both the menu selections and the preparation of the food live up to the surroundings. Seafood dishes are a treat. I liked the scampi Savoy—butterfly shrimp in a special wine sauce served over seasoned rice; others in my party raved about the crabmeat and shrimp Norfolk. Beef dishes range from Chateaubriand for two to beef brochette, and continental specialties include duckling à l'orange. Salads are fresh and crisp, there's a very good wine list, and rolls came to the table piping hot on a covered plate. It all adds up to a marvelous evening of good food in sophisticated surroundings—not always easy to come by at a beach resort. Hours are 6 p.m. to 1 a.m., and dinner from the à la carte menu can run from $15 to $40.

Not So Fancy, But Very Good

Down at the very end of Virginia Beach, at Rudee Inlet, **The Lighthouse** (tel. 428-9851) began many years ago in a small wooden building with one dining room that held about 20 people, plus a screened-in porch overlooking the water. Shrimp, crab, and beer about covered the menu. It's a different story today, however. Robert Herman, who has owned the place for more than 20 years, used to love visiting the place with his wife, saw its potential, and never seems to be quite finished with improvements, additions, and innovations such as an outside patio, upstairs room overlooking the water, and a very nice lounge. Decor is, of course, nautical, but that doesn't begin to describe the interior. Divided into eight separate rooms to prevent a "barny" feeling in the large building, it has grown from that tiny wooden shack to such proportions that they can, and often do, feed 600 at once! There's an almost whimsical touch in the way standing brass ship compasses, mounted blue marlin and other fish (most are caught by Robert or members of the staff), a free-standing aquarium, ship lanterns, etc., are scattered around the place. One of the newer rooms, The Deck, has a heavenly view through bowed skylights. Every table has a sea view. It's simply impossible to summarize the long menu, much less to pick a personal favorite. But to list a few: deluxe lump crabmeat or shrimp sauteed in parsley butter (with soup, salad, baked potato, and coffee or tea), whole fresh flounder broiled or fried, or stuffed with crabmeat (both with all the accompaniments listed above); and a whopping fried seafood platter (fresh flounder, scallops, oysters, shrimp, crab cake, and fried clams). Lunch can run from $4 to $8, dinner from $10 to $23. There's also a full range of sandwiches, beef, salads, and even hot pastrami. Locals have loved this place from its screened-porch days. Open from 10:30 a.m. to 11 p.m., or "whenever the last customer is through eating."

The **Three Ships Inn**, 3800 Shore Dr. (tel. 460-0055), resembles a weathered old inn, with an early English decor and candlelit tables. There's gourmet eating here, with such delicacies as chicken Kiev, quail, roast duckling, frogs legs, Maine lobster, and fresh rainbow trout stuffed with backfin crabmeat, all at reasonable (which means moderate) prices. Flounder and sea trout are caught fresh daily in their own nets. Open for dinner from 5 to 10 p.m. daily.

NIGHTLIFE: Both at Virginia Beach and nearby Norfolk, nightlife is found mostly in restaurants and motel or hotel lounges. Prime examples are **Orion's Roof** at the top of the **New Cavalier**, 42nd and Oceanfront (tel. 425-8555), The **Ramada Inn**, 6360 New Town Rd. (tel. 461-1081), and **Alexander's** in the **Omni International Hotel**, 777 Waterfront Drive at St. Paul's Blvd. (tel. 622-6664). The **Tidewater Dinner Theater**, 6270 Northhampton Blvd. (tel. 461-2933) is in the **Quality Inn;** reservations are necessary and shows change frequently.

THINGS TO SEE AND DO: When I was growing up in Norfolk, the whole Tidewater and Eastern Shore seemed like one big playground to me. The beaches came first, of course; my father liked to fish, both surf casting and deep sea; there were the amusement parks at Virginia Beach and Ocean View; I played tennis on the courts at City Park; and there was always the excitement of living in a navy town, where new friends passed in and out of our lives regularly. It wasn't until my teen years that I began to appreciate the deeper, more meaningful attractions that lay around my hometown. History is all around, of course, but now there's space technology and industrial developments to add a new dimension to the area, and artistic and cultural events are housed in sparkling new edifices. The only way to get a handle on the widespread panorama of things to see and do is to break them up into localities:

At Virginia Beach

The beach itself, complete with boardwalk, amusement park, fishing piers, bowling, tennis, miniature golf, waterskiing, and surf-riding, makes this the complete resort, especially when you add the seafood that's out of this world (in my case, I can't get enough of those Lynnhaven oysters, whether they're on the half shell, fried, or in a creamy stew). And I've always fantasized about the *Norwegian Lady* statue that stands at the very center of town on the ocean-front, a memorial to a sea captain's wife who was rescued by townspeople when his ship broke up during a storm. The **Information Center** is located at 20th St. and Pacific Ave. (tel. 804/425-7511) and will furnish specifics about restaurants, amusements, etc.

For sightseeing, there's the **Cape Henry Lighthouse** in the Fort Story Military Reservation a little north of Virginia Beach on the shore drive. It was the first government-built lighthouse in the U.S. (1791). And close by is the plain cross which marks the landing spot of the colonists who settled at Jamestown in 1607.

The **Adam Thoroughgood House,** thought to be over 300 years old and restored to its original design, is at 1636 Parrish Rd., eight miles northeast via Va. 166 and U.S. 13 on Lynnhaven Bay. It's a lovely old brick cottage-type house with a high-pitched roof, surrounded by ancient trees and boxwood. It's open Tuesday through Saturday from 10 a.m. to 5 p.m., Sunday from noon to 5 p.m. April 1 to November 30; Tuesday through Sunday from noon to 5 p.m. December 1 to March 31. Admission is $2 for adults, $1 for children 6 to 12, under 6 free.

Craft demonstrations are given at **Lynnhaven House,** another 17th-century house, eight miles north off U.S. 225 on Wishart Road. Open Wednesday through Sunday, 10 a.m. to 5 p.m.; admission $2 for adults, $1 for students and children under 12, under 6, free.

Norfolk

Norfolk is first, last, and always a seaport; from its earliest days (which is pretty early—the site was purchased for 10,000 pounds of tobacco in 1682), ships have come and gone from one of the best natural harbors in the world. Commercial ships still make up a great deal of water traffic, but in addition, the town, together with Portsmouth, is the site of one of the oldest U.S. Navy facilities in the country. The Naval Station and Naval Air Station, combined with Portsmouth's Naval Shipyard, comprise one of the largest naval facilities of any nation in the world, and the city's streets are filled at any given time with naval uniforms, both U.S. and foreign. It has been, in its time, a rough, rather rowdy liberty town for sailors (I remember seeing signs on lawns warning "Sailors and Dogs Keep Off the Grass"), but when World War II brought respectability to servicemen, all that changed and there's little left of the seamier sections that used to be the only place enlisted men found a welcome.

Downtown Norfolk has undergone quite a change in recent years with the transformation of historic **Granby Street**'s main shopping area into a beautiful mall lined with trees and shrubs, fountains, and benches for resting weary feet. There are some very good shops within the mall, and sometimes there's street music and other entertainment. The **Scope complex,** a huge domed structure supported by 24 sculptured concrete buttresses, houses concerts, Broadway plays, the Norfolk Symphony Orchestra, and home games of the Tidewater Sharks hockey team.

All in all, it's quite a different town from the one I knew, but it has a lot to see and do, and it's well worth a day or two of exploration. Look for blue and gold signs pointing the way to historic sites.

Before setting out, however, by all means stop by the **Norfolk Convention and Visitors Bureau** on the first floor of the Monticello Arcade, 208 E. Plume St., downtown (tel. 804/441-5266). Or, even better, write before you come:

Monticello Arcade, Norfolk, VA 23510. They do a terrific job in supplying details on the entire Tidewater area.

One of my favorite spots is the lovely **Norfolk Botanical Gardens,** which I knew in my youth as the Azalea Gardens. These botanical gardens are eight miles east of the city, adjacent to the airport, on Azalea Garden Road near the junction of I-64 and Military Highway. Don't miss the 4,000-plant, award-winning Rose Garden or the 300-Flowering-Tree Arboretum. A special feature is the Fragrance Garden for the blind, and there are narrated boat rides and train tours (each $1.50) from mid-March to October. (Prices are expected to rise in the near future.)

There's a 1½-hour narrated cruise of the Norfolk-Portsmouth harbor aboard the **Carrie B,** a replica of a 19th-century Mississippi riverboat. It leaves from the foot of West Main Street (at Boush Street), and fare is $7, with children under 12 paying $3.50. From Portsmouth, you can tour Hampton Roads by boat, leaving from the foot of High Street for the same fares. Write **Harbor Tours,** End of Bay St., Portsmouth, VA 23704 (tel 804/393-4735).

You can tour by bus the gigantic **Naval Station** and the **Naval Air Station,** Hampton and Admiral Taussig Blvds., and even go aboard one or more naval vessels on Saturday and Sunday from 1 to 4:30 p.m. Tours leave from the Naval Base Tour and Information Center at 9809 Hampton Blvd. in Norfolk, and you should call 444-7955 or 623-3222 for exact times, since they change according to the time of year. There's a $3 charge for adults ($1.50 for ages 12 and under) for the naval base tour. Ship visits are free.

The **Myers House** (1792) is at 323 E. Freemason St. (at Bank St.) and is a beautiful old Georgian home filled with over 75% of the original furnishings. From April through November, hours are 10 a.m. to 5 p.m. (noon to 5 p.m. on Sunday) every day except Monday. The rest of the year, it opens at noon. Cost is $2 for adults, $1 ages 6 through 18, under 6, free.

In a restored old courthouse, the **General Douglas MacArthur Memorial,** City Hall Ave. and Bank St., known as MacArthur Square, (tel. 441-2965), holds the general's tomb and memorabilia of his life and military career. There's an interesting film biography. It's free and open 10 a.m. to 5 p.m. Monday through Saturday, from 11 a.m. on Sunday.

The **Chrysler Museum,** Olney Rd. at Mowbray Arch, has been acclaimed as "one of the 20 top museums in the country" by the *Wall Street Journal.* Art from nearly every important culture, civilization, and historical period of the last 5000 years is included in the collection. The museum also houses a 10,000-piece glass collection, considered one of the foremost worldwide; the only museum photography gallery in the state; and a fine collection of Worcester porcelain. Family programs, films, lectures, and concerts are offered in the museum theater on a regular basis. Admission: free. Hours: 10:00 a.m. to 4:00 p.m. Tuesday through Friday, 1:00 to 5:00 p.m. on Sunday. Call 804/622-1211 for further information.

Newport News

During World Wars I and II, Newport News's docks were the jumping-off point for men and supplies headed into battle; they also served as a huge repair shop for naval vessels that had been damaged. Then, as now, it was dominated by the **Newport News Shipbuilding Company,** the world's largest, which has constructed some of our most famous ships—the *United States,* the *Enterprise,* and the *Kennedy* among them. The proud **Victory Arch,** at 25th St. and West Ave., stands as a memorial to American men and women who have served in all the wars of our history. Like Norfolk, Newport News directs you to points of interest with distinctive blue-and-gold markers. Incidentally, the "News" in its name was of the arrival back in the early 1600s of one Capt. Christopher Newport with supplies and settlers from England to join the tiny Jamestown colony. For all kinds of sightseeing assistance, contact: **Newport News Department of Recreation, Parks and Public Relations,** City Hall, Newport News, VA 23607 (tel. 804/838-4182 or 4184).

Mariners Museum (tel. 595-0368), three miles off I-64, exit 62-A, has a marvelous collection of seafaring items and ship models in an 880-acre park with a fishing lake and picnic facilities. The museum is open 9 a.m. to 5 p.m. Monday through Saturday (from noon on Sunday) and costs $1.50 for adults, 75¢ ages 6 to 16.

In **Deer Park,** the **Peninsula Nature and Science Center,** 524 J. Clyde Morris Blvd., has live animal rooms, an aquarium, an observatory, natural science exhibits, nature trails, and a planetarium. Their special "Curiosity Corner," featuring "hands-on" exhibits, is a wow. Open from 9 a.m. to 5 p.m. Monday through Saturday, 1 to 5 p.m. on Sunday; Thursday evening 7 to 9 p.m. Admission is $1.25 for museum, $1.25 for planetarium, $2 for a combination ticket; children under 4, free.

Fort Eustis is located on **Mulberry Island** at the northwest end of the city and is headquarters of the U.S. Transportation Center. Both the fort and the **Army Transportation Museum** (which traces the development of the transportation from the wheel to the flying saucer) are free, and the museum will give you directions for a self-guided auto tour of the grounds.

If you're a frustrated sailor (as I sometimes suspect of myself) and prefer doing your sightseeing by water, contact the Cruise Director, **Harbor Cruise,** 530 12th St. (tel. 804/245-1533), for schedules of their seven-days-a-week sailings. Fares for the daily two-hour Harbor Cruises (April through October) are $8 for adults, $4 for children under 12; for the Sunday-through-Thursday Harbor Lights Cruise (7 to 10 p.m.) mid-June through mid-August, $10 for adults, $5 for those under 12; and for the all-day Intracoastal Waterway Cruises, mid-May to mid-June and September through mid-October (Thursday through Sunday), $27.50 for adults, $20 for children under 12.

Hampton

Your first order of business in Hampton (or even before you come) should be to go by (or write) the **Hampton Information Center,** 413 W. Mercury Blvd., Hampton, VA 23666 (tel. 804/727-6108).

You can tour **Fort Monroe,** three miles southeast of Hampton (it's clearly marked from almost any point in town), free, and it makes for a fascinating day for the whole family. The first battle between the *Monitor* and the *Merrimac* was fought just off the fort in Hampton Roads on March 9, 1862, ending in a draw between the first two ironclads. The fort was held by Union troops throughout the Civil War—Abraham Lincoln plotted strategy against Norfolk here in May of 1862—and Jefferson Davis was imprisoned here following the downfall of the Confederacy. Ironically, Robert E. Lee, as a young engineer in the U.S. Army, helped with the construction of Fort Monroe, but was never able to effect its capture when he commanded Confederate forces. The **Casement Museum** (free) depicts these and many other stories in a panoramic painting, and there are all sorts of intriguing documents, pictures, and models on display. Kids will love the fact that the old fort was encircled by a moat.

The famous **Hampton Institute,** at the east end of Queen Street (exit 5 off I-64), was established in 1868 by the Freedman's Bureau to teach former slaves how to read and write. Today it specializes in science, the liberal arts, business, teaching, nursing, architecture, and graduate studies. Don't miss the **Museum** (free) in the Academy Building—it has an outstanding collection of Indian and African artifacts.

Also free are the film and special exhibits at the **NASA Langley Research Center**, three miles north on Va. 134 (tel. 827-2855), where you can see moon rocks, space suits, and an Apollo command module. Open Monday through Saturday 8:30 a.m. to 4:30 p.m., from noon on Sunday. Closed on major holidays. If you're space-minded, go by the **Hampton Information Center,** 413 W. Mercury Blvd., and see their impressive display of jet aircraft, rockets, missiles, and satellites.

The Eastern Shore

The old Cape Charles ferry used to take almost three hours to cross Chesapeake Bay. Today, you can "Follow the Gulls" (a neat blue-and-white sign with a white silhouetted seagull that points you to the 17.6-mile-long Chesapeake Bay Bridge-Tunnel from almost anywhere in the Tidewater area) and make the crossing in 23 minutes! And the trip is unforgettable—miles and miles of causeway, one rather high bridge, and two mile-long tunnels. This remarkable engineering feat was completed in 1964 and takes you from Norfolk to **Cape Charles.** Cross another causeway and bridge, and you'll reach **Assateague Island National Seashore,** one of the newest of our national parks. U.S. 13 runs through the long peninsula that has come to be known as **Delmarva** because it holds tiny portions of Delaware, Maryland, and Virginia. The toll is $9 each way, including passengers.

As an aside, let me point out that when you spend your day—and it will take a whole one—on the Eastern Shore, there's a very good restaurant at **America House** at the Cape Charles end of the bridge-tunnel which serves all three meals at reasonable prices. However, you're likely to find interesting places to eat also at **Chincoteague** (the town, not the island) or perhaps in other villages along the shore. I personally couldn't eat anything but the oysters, clams, and crabs that are such a specialty out here, and there are several small seafood restaurants scattered around. But the America House is a sure thing, so keep it in mind. If you're an island person or just plain intrigued by this coastal country, you may want to plan more than just one day, in which case see "Where to Stay," below.

If you want to fish on the Eastern Shore, the pier at Cape Charles can furnish bait and tackle. You don't need a license, and there's no limit on the catch. For charter-boat fishing, go on to **Wachapreague** or Chincoteague and look for the charter signs.

Now, back to that National Seashore—it's Va. 175 (from U.S. 13) that will lead you the ten miles to **Chincoteague Island** and on to Assateague. There are two very special times of year to arrive on the islands: the first Wednesday in May is set aside for the Eastern Shore Annual Seafood Festival, which has gained such popularity since it began in 1969 that reservations start coming in as soon as tickets go on sale in October for the next year's festival. If you're early enough, you can (ticket in hand) wander from booth to booth sampling a seaside feast. But you *must* have that ticket, and be warned: they sometimes sell out the very first day they're offered! For ticket information, contact the Chamber of Commerce, P.O. Box 4, Chincoteague, VA 23831 (tel. 804/336-6161). Then, on the last Wednesday and Thursday in July, comes the "penning" of wild Chincoteague ponies, and it's really something! The shaggy little ponies, larger than a Shetland but smaller than a horse, are descendants of horses that swam ashore from a Spanish galleon that perished in these waters, so the legend goes. Through the centuries, their growth became stunted from the steady diet of marsh grass. All year, they roam wild on Assateague Island, but at the end of July, Chincoteague citizens turn into cowboys, herd them into the water for the swim across the channel and sell the foals for prices that range from $75 to $300 (all proceeds go to the volunteer fire department), then drive the mares and stallions back to Assateague for another year of breeding. It's a fun time to be here, with carnival amusements and general hilarity prevailing.

Those are highlights of the year on the Eastern Shore. But no matter when you come, there's much to fill your days. Across the bridge from Chincoteague, the barrier island of **Assateague** was cut off from the longer extension (which runs from Massachusetts to Florida and includes many in South Carolina and Georgia, which we'll get to later in this book) by a storm in 1933. It's about thirty-seven miles long, and its width varies from one-third of a mile to a little over a mile. Its gently shelving sand beach is just spectacular, and swimming is not perilous because the undertow here is very light. Virginia and Maryland share ownership of Assateague, and you can enter via bridges at either end. The State Park Information Center and Campground Registration Office is located at the north end, and there's a Visitors Center just over the bridge from Chincoteague. If you begin your trip from the north, plan to go over to Assateague from near Ocean City, Md. And you should know that because some 22 miles of roadless beach and marsh lie between the two entrances, you won't be able to drive from one end to the other, but must return to the mainland to reach the other end (about a 1½-hour drive). Assateague State Park and Assateague Island National Seashore are at the northern end, Chincoteague National Wildlife Refuge at the southern.

Up at **North Assateague,** you'll find camping sites (see "Where to Stay," below), bathhouses (in summer), bait and tackle shops, limited food service, and picnic tables. Also in summer, there are lifeguards stationed on those marvelous beaches. One of the two herds of wild ponies roams freely over this part of the island, and they are a thrilling sight running in groups or feeding quietly. Remember, these are *wild* animals—keep a respectable distance (they just may bite or kick if crowded), and *don't try to feed them.*

From Chincoteague, a paved road leads three miles through the **National Wildlife Refuge** before it reaches the beach. What you're likely to see along the way depends on the time of year: snow geese, Canada geese, and whistling swans regularly winter here, and there are always the shorebirds, some of which are seldom found anywhere else but along this stretch of coast. And, of course, there's that other herd of wild ponies (the ones that make the swim to Chincoteague each year).

At both ends of Assateague there is excellent fishing, clamming, and crabbing in addition to swimming. Canoe launch areas and camping are permitted on the Maryland portion (the northern end) of Assateague. The Chincoteague National Wildlife Refuge located on the southern end (the Virginia portion) prohibits the landing of a boat anywhere other than at Fishing Point at the very southern tip of the island. Each year, over 275 species of birds visit the refuge, and nature trails that wind through loblolly pines and fresh water marshes provide excellent opportunities to observe bird life, as well as many different mammals, reptiles and amphibians.

Wildlife-oriented auditorium programs and walks are presented daily during the summer and on weekends during the spring and fall. Island Cruises, a concession operation of the Fish & Wildlife Service, conducts cruises and land safaris at various times during the year. For specific information on tours or programs, write Refuge Manager, Chincoteague National Wildlife Refuge, P.O. Box 62, Chincoteague, VA 23336, or telephone 804/336-6122.

This is old, old country, and if its history interests you, stop at **Accomac** to see the **debtor's prison** (there's another one at **Eastville**). Incidentally, the Eastville **court house,** built in 1730, houses court records which date, unbroken, back to 1632!

WHERE TO STAY: There are motel facilities on the Delmarva Peninsula and in Chincoteague, campsites on both ends of Assateague. But my first recommendation may, at first blush, not belong in a guide to the Southeast. I'm putting it in for two reasons: first of all, many readers will be coming to the Eastern Shore from points north; and second, I've found the inn and its owners so completely charming that I think you should know about them.

The **Mainstay Inn,** 635 Columbia Ave., Cape May, N.J. (tel. 609/884-8690), is convenient to the Cape May ferry, one of the most enjoyable ways to reach the Eastern Shore (fare is $9.25 per car and driver, $2.25 for each passenger over age 6), and a delightful place to begin or end a visit there. A lovely old Victorian mansion built in 1872, the Mainstay was once a "gaming parlor" known as Jackson's Clubhouse, where a sweet little old lady was stationed in a rocking chair on the veranda as a lookout for the law. Since then, it has been a rooming house and a local museum. But Tom and Sue Carroll, an enthusiastic young couple in their 30s, have given it a new, and one hopes a lasting, identity by refurbishing ten rooms with Victoriana and the warmth of patchwork quilts, braided rugs, and potted plants everywhere. The furnishings are impressive, with the ten-foot gilt mirror in the parlor a decided focal point. Some of the rooms have private baths; most share two "down the hall" facilities. In the guest house tradition, Tom and Sue serve a marvelous breakfast (included in the rates) and afternoon tea. Sue is usually the chef and sets a breakfast table that rates raves—strawberry crêpes, cheese soufflé, and fried apples are just some of the items that may appear. I don't really know if I am drawn most to this lovingly restored house or to the Carrolls, but I *do* know that there isn't a better travel buy anywhere in the neighborhood. Rates run from $45 to $75, and that includes both breakfast and afternoon tea. They do ask that you not bring pets, but they'll provide beach tags for the city beaches if you bring your own beach towels.

In Chincoteague, the **Channel Bass Inn,** 100 Church St. (tel. 804/336-6148), is another hostelry loaded with charm and spiced by the enthusiasm of its owners. Jim and Kathleen Hanretta bought the rambling old house back in 1972, leaving careers as a classical and flamenco guitarist (Jim) and schoolteacher (Kathy) to devote themselves to converting the former boarding house into a first-class inn. The 11 rooms (eight with private baths) have all been done over with handsome new furnishings and carpeting, and the Hanrettas have developed a restaurant that utilizes the best of all that fresh seafood on the island to turn out gourmet dinners that smack of both French and Spanish cuisine. And most days, Jim tops off everything by a mini-concert on the guitar. Doubles begin at $65. Weekly rates are available, and all are lower January through March. Just one thing: Don't bring the children under 8, and leave Fido home.

Also in Chincoteague, **The Refuge,** one block west of Assateague Bridge, P.O. Box 37B, Chincoteague, Va 23336 (tel. 804/336-5511), is a two-story, 68-room building that overlooks the wildlife refuge and has rental bicycles as well as picnic tables with hibachis. Doubles here start at $45 in season, lower the rest of the year.

For budget accommodations in Chincoteague, you can't do better than the **Lighthouse Motel,** 224 N. Main St. (tel. 804/336-5091). They have both rooms and efficiency apartments, and there's free coffee in rooms, a pool, cookout area, game room, Jacuzzi spas, and outdoor games. No pets. Doubles run $26 to $32, efficiencies $30 to $40, in season; as low as $20 and $25 in winter.

   America House Motor Inn, P.O. Box 472, Cape Charles, Va. 23310 (tel. 804/331-1776), is located on U.S. 13 not far from the Eastern Shore side of the Chesapeake Bay bridge-tunnel. Situated on 40 acres, with ten of them a private sandy beach, America House has spacious rooms that are modern in furnishings, but colonial in atmosphere due to prints, wall hangings, and other decorative touches that recall the Revolution. There's a high observation tower from which to get the lay of the land, and recreational facilities include sailboats, swimming pool, indoor shuffleboard, putting green, golf driving range, picnic areas, chidren's playground, and a game room with Ping-Pong and a pool table. Their restaurant, also in colonial decor, serves outstanding meals at very reasonable prices. Doubles here start at $50 in season (summer), $40 off-season.

CAMPING: On the northern end of **Assateague** there's a modern campground with hot showers, flush toilets, and 311 spaces for campers (no electric or water hookups) which are open most of the year. Space is usually allocated on a first-come, first-served basis, although some sites in summer may be reserved for a full week by contacting the Superintendent, Assateague State Park, Rt. 2, P.O. Box 293, Berlin, MD 21811 (tel. 301/641-2120).

   Immediately south of the state park, the National Park Service operates smaller, primitive campgrounds (portable toilets and cold water only) year round. These family campgrounds and three back-country, hike-in sites are always available on a first-come, first-served basis. Three bayside canoe-in sites are also available. Contact: Superintendent, Assateague Island National Seashore, Rt. 2, P.O. Box 294, Berlin, MD 21811 (tel. 301/641-1441).

Chapter IV

THE BLUE RIDGE MOUNTAINS

1. The Skyline Drive (Virginia)
2. The Blue Ridge Parkway (Virginia and North Carolina)

THERE'S SOMETHING ABOUT MOUNTAINS! "Majestic" is overworked, but it applies. A sense of timelessness—of patience and endurance. And there's just no better antidote to today's impatient rush toward tomorrow than the nearly 600-mile drive along the ridgecrest of the Blue Ridge Mountains that stretches down the western extremities of Virginia and North Carolina.

Beginning at Front Royal, Virginia, the Skyline Drive leads southward through 105 miles of the Shenandoah National Park to meet the Blue Ridge Parkway at Rockfish Gap, between Charlottesville and Waynesboro. The parkway then goes on for some 470 miles south, still along the crests of ancient mountains, until it reaches the Great Smoky Mountains National Park near the North Carolina–Tennessee border.

It's a drive of incredible beauty, with stunning mountain views and that increasingly rare commodity, a look at nature's face where "civilization" has been smart enough to protect it. All sorts of wild animals live here—bobcats, foxes, white-tailed deer, and black bear, to name a few; streams are clear and forests of birch, poplar, beech, hickory, and oak (some more than 300 years old) are undisturbed. To come in late spring is to see green creeping up the peaks as trees leaf out. In summer, wildflowers blossom to make a carpet of colorful blooms. Fall brings vivid reds and yellows and oranges to give a flame-like hue to every mountainside. And the miracle is that although men and women have made their homes here since that first push westward, it is *nature* that endures. In fact, even the broad, well-paved highway, the carefully planned overlooks, the lodges and cabins and restaurants seem only to enhance what was here to begin with. The rigors of wilderness travel have been eliminated to leave only a natural, unspoiled area that can be traveled in comfort. For most of the year, that is. Fog is a problem at times, and some of the higher sections are closed during icy or snowy weather. It's best to plan this drive between mid-May and mid-November, when conditions are almost consistently good.

You *could*, of course, drive straight down the entire length of this gorgeous roadway. But if you did, you'd miss a wealth of sightseeing. All along the way there are not-to-be-missed historic sites and caverns and bridges that have been sculpted by the centuries just a few miles off the Drive and Parkway on either side. If time is a problem—it's a *long* drive and there are a lot of side trips—it's best to take one section at a time and come back later for the others. Personally, I prefer seeing it in small chunks (if those enormous vistas could be called "small"). So let's look at it that way.

1. The Skyline Drive (Virginia)

I find **Charlottesville**, at the southern end of the Drive, a perfect base. It's a full day's trip up to Front Royal and back, but accommodations are more plentiful and it's so central to sightseeing that I can leave the suitcase unpacked for a few days. An appealing alternative is to begin your journey about 15 miles north of Front Royal on I-81 in the little town of Middletown for no other reason than to stay at a very special inn dating back to Revolutionary days. Also, if you plan far enough in advance, the lodges at Big Meadow and Skyland are lovely—read on.

WHERE TO STAY: Both these lodges are almost at the center of the Drive and both are closed during the winter months. (For full details on these and all other accommodations along the Drive, write: ARA Virginia Sky-Line Co., Inc., P.O. Box 727, Luray, VA 22835.)

Skyland Lodge, P.O. Box 727, Luray, VA 22835 (tel. 703/999-2266), opens from early April until mid-November. It's ten miles south of the Thornton Gap entrance from Va. 211. This is the highest point on the Drive, and the glass-enclosed lobby takes full advantage of the spectacular view, with a fireplace to add just the right note of coziness on cool nights. There are rooms in the main lodge, as well as in separate cottages, and all are comfortable and attractive. Some suites have their own fireplaces. This is a great place for children: a playground, recreation room, lawn games, horses available (with trail maps) for hour-long, half- or full-day rides, and a planned children's program. The cafe serves all three meals and there's entertainment in the bar every night except Sunday. Doubles run $40 and up, with suites for two to six people beginning at $70. Children under seven stay free in same room with parents. Pets are welcome, but must be kept on a leash.

Big Meadow Lodge, P.O. Box 727, Luray, VA 22836, 19 miles south of the Thornton Gap entrance (tel. 703/743-5108), is smaller than Skyland and opens from May to early November. Besides the main lodge, there's an annex and cottages. Rooms are quite nice and many have fireplaces. For children, there's a playground and planned activities, a recreation room, and both horses and bicycles are available. All meals are served in the cafe (no room service) and the bar has entertainment every night except Wednesday. The leash rule applies to pets here, too. Rates are $35 and up for double rooms, $45 and up for suites that will sleep up to six. Children under seven, free.

Campsites

Campers will find tent and trailer sites at **Matthews Arm, Big Meadow, Lewis Mountain,** and **Loft Mountain,** but none have hookups. The rate is $5 per day and there's a 14-day limit. Write Superintendent, Shenandoah National Park, Luray, VA 22835 (tel. 703/999-2266), for full details.

In Middletown, Va.

The **Wayside Inn Since 1797,** 7783 Main St. (tel. 703/869-1797), began life in 1797 as Wilkinson's Tavern, offering bed and board to weary travelers in the Virginia wilderness. With the advent of the Shenandoah Valley Turnpike, some 20 years later, it became a relay station for stagecoach drivers, as well as a welcome stop for their passengers. During the Civil War, Yankees and Rebels both frequented the place, and one of the war's fiercest battles was fought at nearby Cedar Creek. Today's motorcar travelers find the same warm hospitality, comfortable rooms, and outstanding food as did those earlier move-abouts. Rooms are decorated in a mixture of styles: heirlooms from England, lovingly brought over by early settlers; locally made, "Early American" furniture; relics of the Victorian era; and touches of Oriental bric-a-brac brought home by wandering sea captains. There are canopied beds in some rooms, and even fireplaces in a few. Each room has its own personality, and when booking, you might specify if you'd prefer colonial, Chinese, Empire, or Victorian decor (no promise you'll get it, but the friendly owners do all they can to please, so it's worth a try). There are six dining rooms (I can't resist the Slave Quarters, with its crackling fire, high-back chairs, and bare wooden tables) and the Coachyard cocktail lounge, a throwback to the English pub tradition. As for the food, it's famed all through the valley—country-cured ham, peanut soup, pan-fried chicken, hot breads, and even chicken gumbo. And if sitting on the verandah in one of the white rocking chairs is a little too tame for your tastes, you can walk just a few yards to the Wayside Theater, where professional actors perform from June to September. The Wayside has become one of the most famous hostelries in Virginia, and in my book that's a reputation well earned. Doubles range from $45 to $110. No pets.

In Charlottesville, Va.

The **Boar's Head Inn,** P.O. Box 5185, Charlottesville, VA 22903 (tel. 804/296-2181), is one mile west of Va. 250-W Bypass and is one of the finest resort inns in the Commonwealth. An inn has stood here since 1763 when Terrell's Ordinary greeted travelers here, and the present building dates its west wing from 1834. Decor is, as you'd expect, colonial, with a liberal supply of antiques in the attractive public areas. Rooms are beautifully decorated, some with lovely views of the mountains or the lake with its ducks and swans. There are facilities for tennis, squash, paddle tennis, and swimming (in season). Also, exceptional health facilities. The bar features live entertainment, and the dining room is considered one of the best places to eat in these parts (see "Where to Eat"). Doubles start at $70 and suites (some with fireplaces) at $100, and if you want to stay in this exceptionally beautiful place, best reserve at least a month ahead. Children under 12 stay free with parents, but there's a $3 charge for pets.

Most of the large, convenient rooms at **Howard Johnson's,** 1309 W. Main St. (tel. 804/296-8121), have balconies and attractive, modern decor. Directly across from the University of Virginia, the motel has indoor parking, an indoor pool, and a restaurant. Doubles run $32 to $40, and the only time advance reservations are necessary is at graduation time at the university (June).

The **Best Western Cavalier Inn,** P.O. Box 5647, Charlottesville, VA 22903 (tel. 804/296-8111), is also across from the university and has a heated pool, with a wading pool for the small fry, and a restaurant. They can also furnish a list of babysitters. Doubles here start at $42, but go up during special university events.

Rooms at the budget-priced **Econolodge,** 2014 Holiday Dr. (tel. 804/295-3185), are clean and comfortable. It's close to the university and a large shopping center. Advance reservations are advisable during June, July, and August. A double room here costs $37 to $45. Children under 12 stay free.

READER'S SUGGESTION: "For lovely bed and breakfast accommodations in the Charlottesville area, contact the **Guesthouses Bed & Breakfast, Inc.,** people at P.O. Box 5737, Charlottesville, VA 22905 (tel. 804/979-7264 or 979-8327). They do a very good job of booking you into just the type of place you want to stay, and there's always continental breakfast included in the rates, which we found on a par with local motels" (C. Harris, Arlington, Va.).

WHERE TO EAT: On the Skyline Drive itself, you'll find good food at moderate prices at both the lodges listed in the previous section. In addition, you'll be able to eat reasonably well at **Panorama,** or if a picnic seems like a good idea (it is!), you can pick up light lunches and groceries at **Elkwallow, Big Meadow,** and **Loft Mountain Waysides.**

In Charlottesville, Va.

The **Old Mill Room** at the **Boar's Head Inn,** one mile west of Va. 250-W Bypass (tel. 296-2181), is in an 1834 gristmill now incorporated into the inn's west wing, and this is colonial-style dining at its best. Waitresses in colonial dress add to the early-days atmosphere in the candlelit room with its yellow-pine beams, fireplace, and antique furnishings. Escalope of veal Oscar is a favorite with patrons (appetizers, salads, and desserts extra). Dinner prices range from $12 to $20, and reservations are absolutely necessary. Lunch runs $5.50 to $7.50, and breakfast $3.50 to $6. Hours are 7:30 to 10:30 a.m., noon to 2 p.m., and 6 to 9:30 p.m.—and best reserve.

The **Ivy Inn,** 2244 Old Ivy Rd., one mile from the University of Virginia, just off Va. 250 Bus. (tel. 977-1222), is in a 19th-century brick house. It, too, has fireplaces, and there's pleasant background music for candlelight dining. Featured dishes are veal, chicken, seafood, and steaks, and prices are in the $8 to $14 range. Lunch from 11:30 a.m. to 2:30 p.m., dinner begins at 5 p.m., and reservations are a good idea. Closed Sunday.

Steve and Martha Tharp are the owner-operators of **Martha's Cafe,** just across from the university at 11 Elliewood Ave. (tel. 295-3418). This pleasant, homey restaurant attracts an appealing local clientele, many of them students, with its homemade dishes and friendly service. Quiches, muffins, and salads are excellent and vegetables are always fresh. Lunch and dinner prices are surprisingly moderate (about $4 for lunch, $6 for dinner). It's a small, inviting restaurant with only 45 seats and reservations are not accepted, so you may have a bit of a wait (the outdoor patio adds 24 seats in summer); but for a light lunch or dinner, this is the place to go.

As one student told me, **The Mousetrap,** 100 14th St. (tel. 296-6873), is "the best place to see students in their native habitat. It's livelier than Martha's, but not at all rowdy." Older people, professionals, and university faculty love the place at lunch, but youth takes over at night, when there is always a rock or folk group in attendance at the rathskeller-type restaurant. Shish kebab, steaks, seafood, and salads are specialties, at prices of about $2.75 for lunch and $3 to $8 for dinner. Let me hasten to add that although youth predominates overwhelmingly in the evening, you won't be barred at the door simply because you're over 30, and they accept Visa and Master Charge.

The Garret, 100 14th St. (tel. 296-6873), is upstairs from the Mousetrap and has become a favorite spot for the university and professional community. It's rustic, yet not without elegance. Specialties are omelets, crêpes, and quiche, although there is a featured entrée and dessert each evening, all at moderate prices. There's an above-average bar offering seasonal concoctions of their own which add to the general sparkle of the place. Sunday brunch here is quickly becoming a local tradition (served from 10:30 a.m. to 2:30 p.m.), and late-night light snacks are also favored by the locals (served only after the kitchen closes for dinner). The Garrett is open from 4 p.m. to 1 a.m. Tuesday through Saturday and 6 p.m. to 1 a.m. on Sunday. They also accept Visa and Master Charge.

For good food on a budget, the **University Cafeteria** (1517 W. Main St.) wins hands down. Bob Stroh, owner of the 40-year-old establishment, puts out such consistently good dishes as fried chicken, country ham and apples, and southern spoonbread that the place has won recognition by several national publications. The decor is pleasant, with enlarged, sepia-tone photographs of the university grounds hung about the walls, and you'll find a relaxed, friendly mix of students, faculty, and townspeople. Prices run about $4 for lunch, $6 for dinner. It's open seven days a week (except during the Christmas school holiday) from 11:30 a.m. to 2 p.m. and 4:45 to 8 p.m.

For a moderate-priced lunch, there's historic old **Michie Tavern** (see "Things to See"), with a cafe that serves from 11:15 a.m. to 3 p.m.

THINGS TO SEE: If you're based at **Charlottesville,** plan at least one day to explore the historic sites and homes in this beautiful mountain town.

You can't miss the **University of Virginia** at the west end of Main Street, and certainly you *shouldn't* miss the experience of rambling around its campus for an hour or two. There are also free historical tours of the grounds and main points of interest that leave from the Rotunda Monday through Friday during the school term (call 924-1019 for times). Thomas Jefferson founded the school and drew plans for its grounds as well as many of its early buildings. Set in broad lawns with huge old trees and sweeping vistas, the handsome red-brick buildings with their white trim have an impressive, simple dignity. A classic example of Jefferson's architectural genius is the Rotunda, focal point of the oldest part of the campus, and the one-brick-thick serpentine wall and the columned porticoes that front student living quarters. Hostesses at the Rotunda will arrange student-guided tours on weekdays during the school year. The university opened its doors in 1825 with a student body of 68 and eight faculty members. Three of the first five U.S. presidents (Jefferson, Madison, and Monroe) served on its first board of trustees! Smaller today than many American universities, it has an annual enrollment of about 16,000—out of which it awards more graduate degrees than any other institution of higher learning in Virginia.

After you've seen the university, stop by the **Thomas Jefferson Visitors Bureau** in the Western Virginia Visitors Center on Va. 20 South (tel. 804/293-6789) for self-directed automobile and walking tours of the Charlottesville area.

Monticello and Vicinity

Jefferson's beloved home, **Monticello** (pronounced "Mont-i-*chell*-o") is on a mountaintop three miles southeast of Charlottesville on **Va.** 53 (tel. 295-8181). He designed and built the house, using materials made right on the spot, from bricks right down to nails, on land that had come to his father in a land grant. Begun in 1769, it wasn't completed until 1809, although he lived in it from 1772. Jefferson died here on July 4, 1826, exactly 50 years after the signing of the Declaration of Independence, and his tomb is in the family cemetery. Restoration continues throughout the house, which contains many original furnishings. The gardens are extensive and include the newly replanted orchard. Open 8 a.m. to 5 p.m. from March to October, 9 a.m. to 4:30 p.m. the remainder of the year. Admission is $3 for adults, $1 for children 6 to 11.

Just 2½ miles southeast of Monticello (off Va. 53 on County Road 795) is where the fifth U.S. president, James Monroe, lived at **Ash Lawn** ("Highlands"), a modest country house on a 550-acre estate. Thomas Jefferson selected the house site and planted orchards for his neighbor. Now restored by the College of William and Mary, Ash Lawn offers tours of the house with its late 18th- and early 19th-century furnishings, including some of Monroe's furniture, periodic homecraft demonstrations, kitchen gardens, and truly magnificent boxwood hedges. There are peacocks among the boxwood, a Piccirilli statue of Monroe, quiet picnic spots, and great views of the Blue Ridge foothills. Special events include summer festivals of music and drama, and Christmas madrigals. Open daily from 9 a.m. to 6 p.m. March through October, from 10 a.m. to 5 p.m. November through February (closed Thanksgiving, Christmas, and New Year's Day). Admission is $2.50 for adults, 75¢ for ages 6 to 11, with special rates for groups of 15 or more.

Located high on a mountainside near Monticello, on Va. 53 (tel. 977-1234), the old **Michie Tavern** is thought to have been built (at least the main portion) by Patrick Henry's father in 1735. A little later it wound up in the hands of one John Michie, who enlarged the house and made it into an inn for travelers. Later on, Michie opened the tavern and attracted about as distinguished a group of patrons as you can imagine: Jefferson, Madison, Monroe, and even Lafayette were among those who ate and drank there. Today, it's operated as a museum, and the ballroom, keeping hall, ladies' parlor-bedroom, and tap bar all contain original furnishings of that period. There are several outbuildings, the Meadow Run Grist Mill and General Store built in 1797 (the General Store sells Virginia handcrafts and antiques), and a 200-year-old converted slave house, "the Ordinary," which serves colonial fried chicken, homemade corn bread, and other southern dishes at quite reasonable prices from 11:30 a.m. to 3 p.m. The museum is open daily from 9 a.m. to 5 p.m., and admission is $2.50 for adults, 75¢ for children six to 12.

George Rogers Clark, famous Revolutionary soldier and frontiersman, older brother of William Clark who opened up the Northwest when he and Meriwether Lewis explored the Louisiana Purchase, was a native son of Charlottesville and a **museum** to his memory is maintained in a rustic cabin that has been restored and moved to his birthsite, two miles northeast of town on Va. 20. There are many period furnishings and Clark memorabilia. It's closed from November to March, open 10 a.m. to 5 p.m. daily other months; $2 for adults, children under 12 free. There's also an impressive **Lewis and Clark Monument** in Midway Park at Ridge and Main Streets.

On and Near the Skyline Drive

There's a $2 charge per car to enter the Drive (for detailed information and pamphlets, contact: Superintendent, Shenandoah National Park, Luray, VA 22835; tel. 703/999-2266), and an *enforced* 35-mile-per-hour speed limit (you won't want to speed through, anyway). The southernmost entrance at Rockfish Gap is 20 miles west of Charlottesville on U.S. 250. Other entries are at Swift Run Gap, between Stanardsville and Elkton on U.S. 33; Thornton Gap, on U.S. 211 between Luray and Sperryville; and at Front Royal (U.S. 340), its northernmost end.

At Big Meadows (Mile 51), the **Harry F. Byrd, Sr., Visitor Center** features a movie exploring man's relationship to the mountains and a historical and cultural museum. It's open every day but only part-time during January and February. From April to November, the **Dickey Ridge Visitor Center** near Front Royal also opens daily. **Shenandoah National Park headquarters** is five miles east of Luray on U.S. 211, and they'll send informative pamphlets if you write: Superintendent, Shenandoah National Park, Luray, VA 22835.

There are free **picnic grounds** with fireplaces, water, tables, and restrooms at Dickey Ridge, Elkwallow, Pinnacles, Big Meadows, Lewis Mountain, South River, and Loft Mountain.

You can **trout fish** in some of the park streams from April to October 15, but you'll need a five-day state license (get them at park concession units).

If you bring Fido along, be *sure* to keep him on a leash—this is one regulation that's rigidly enforced.

You'll need at least one day—another if you plan to take in all the attractions just off the Drive—to drive to Front Royal and back. The views are breathtaking all along the way—across the Shenandoah Valley on your left lie the Massanutten Mountains, and beyond, the Alleghenies. There are parking overlooks at the most spectacular ones, and I defy you to drive right on by without making at least one stop! When you reach the north entrance to **Skyland,** you'll be at the highest point on the Drive, 3680 feet above sea level. And not far from Thornton Gap, you'll pass through a 700-foot tunnel at **Mary's Rock.**

At Thornton Gap, you can turn west on U.S. 211 for a ten-minute drive to the **Luray Caverns.** Its gigantic underground rooms—there's one that measures 300 feet wide, 500 feet long, and 140 feet high—are connected by natural corridors, and one features stereophonic music produced on an organ that uses reverberating stalactites instead of pipes! Be sure to bring that camera, for the lighting system makes color photos possible, and the staggering array of stalactites and stalagmites will arouse the photographer in you. About every 20 minutes or so, guided tours leave from the entrance, beginning at 9 a.m., with the last tour leaving at 6 p.m. all months except November through March, when they stop at 4 p.m. Adults pay $7 to explore this underworld magical kingdom, children seven through 13 pay $3, and those under seven are free when with parents. There's no charge for the 45-minute carillon concerts played every Tuesday, Thursday, Saturday, and Sunday by a world-famous carillonneur at the Luray Singing Tower, whose largest bell weighs 7640 pounds and the smallest, 12½.

Back on the Drive, ride on up to **Front Royal** (which got its name, incidentally, from the order of an out-of-patience drill sergeant to ill-trained

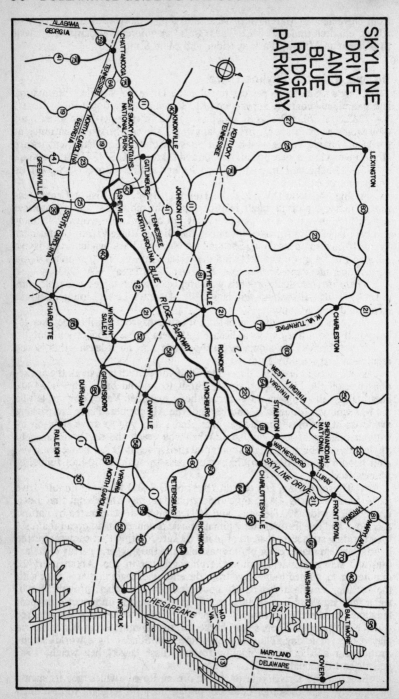

local militia to "front to the royal oak," meaning the "royal" tree of England, when they had trouble following his regulation military command). The excellent **Thunderbird Museum and Archeological Park** (tel. 635-7337) is six miles south on U.S. 340, then half a mile west (you'll see the entrance signs), and here, for a fee of $2 (children eight to 12, $1.50), you can watch archeologists at work during summer months. The museum displays some of their finds and explains exhibits, which show that early man was living here thousands of years before the Roman Empire.

The **Skyline Caverns,** P.O. Box 193, Front Royal, VA 22630 (tel. 635-4545), just one mile south of Front Royal on U.S. 340, have beautiful calcite formations known as "anthodites," which look like flowers, and whose estimated growth is only one inch every 7,000 years. The caverns are well lighted, there's a 37-foot waterfall, and you'll enjoy their Sound and Light show. Topside, a miniature train chugs around the wooded grounds ($1), and there are picnic grounds. Admission to the caverns is $6 (ages 7 to 13, $3), and they're open from 8 a.m. to 6 p.m. or 9 a.m. to 4:15 p.m., depending on the time of year.

On the return trip to Charlottesville, leave the Skyline Drive and take I-81 south to **Staunton** (forget about how it's spelled, pronounce it "Stanton"), one of the oldest cities west of the Blue Ridge Mountains. President Woodrow Wilson was born here, and his birthplace, a three-story, Greek Revival mansion (tel. 885-0891), has many of its original furnishings, plus many mementos of our 28th chief executive. There's an interesting 20-minute film, *Spokesman for Tomorrow.* The house, at 24 N. Coalter St., on U.S. 11, is open every day from 9 a.m. to 5 p.m. (closed on Sunday December through February). Cost to enter is $2 for adults, $1 for children 6 to 16.

One of nature's greatest curiosities is at picturesque **Mt. Solon,** 11 miles north of Staunton on U.S. 11, then west on Va. 646 to Va. 747. "Natural Chimneys" are seven huge limestone columns, rising to a height of 120 feet, which have been carved out of solid rock by the Shenandoah River over millions of years. From some vantage points, they do indeed look like chimneys, but my fancy turns to the turrets and towers of a medieval castle. And I'm certainly not alone in that fancy, for back in 1821, people hereabouts started an annual jousting tournament, in which "knights" with long lances attempt to spear a small, suspended ring while on horseback. Each knight gets three "tilts" and the winner is king of the tournament. If you're in these parts on the third Saturday in August, it's a fun day.

2. The Blue Ridge Parkway
(Virginia and North Carolina)

From Charlottesville south, the Blue Ridge Parkway (write for maps and detailed information to: Superintendent, Blue Ridge Parkway, 700 Northwestern Bank Bldg., Asheville, NC 28801) takes up where the Skyline Drive leaves off, winding and twisting along the mountain crests right on through most of western North Carolina. You'll drive at elevations ranging from 649 to 6053 feet above sea level. There's no toll on the Parkway, and there are rather frequent exits to nearby towns.

There are six visitor centers; nine campgrounds (open May through October only, except for limited winter camping at Otter Creek, Roanoke Mountain, Price Park, and Linville Falls) with drinking water and comfort stations, but no shower or utility hookups (on a first-come, first-served basis—no reservations); restaurants and gas stations; and three lodges plus one location featuring rustic cabins for overnight accommodations (reservations are recommended).

At many overlooks, you'll see a squirrel-rifle-and-powder-horn symbol and the word "trail," which means that there are marked walking trails through the woods. Some take only ten or 20 minutes and provide a delightful, leg-stretching break from the confines of the car. Others are longer and steeper and may take an hour or more if you go the entire way.

There are a few simple rules laid down by the National Park Service, which administers the Parkway: no commercial vehicles are permitted; no swimming in lakes and ponds; no hunting; pets must be kept on leash; and, above all else, *no fire except in campground or picnic area fireplaces.* A good rule of your own to follow is to keep your gas tank half-filled at all times—it's no place to be stranded! The higher sections of the Parkway, west of Asheville, are usually closed from mid-November to mid-April because of the danger of ice and snow, and should dangerous conditions exist at any other time of the year, sections affected are quickly closed to traffic. Oh, yes, the speed limit is 45 miles an hour—and they're quite serious about that.

Although Roanoke is just 113 miles south of Charlottesville, it probably should be your first overnight stop in order to spend at least one day at nearby Lexington and the Natural Bridge. From Roanoke to Asheville, North Carolina (the next city of any size), is too long to attempt in one day unless you're in a rush. And if you're in a rush, stay off the Parkway—first of all, there's that 45-mile speed limit; and second, if you don't have time to amble and drink in the beauty through which you're passing, wait and come back when you do. By breaking the drive at Boone, North Carolina (about ten miles off the Parkway), you'll have time to sightsee along the way and perhaps catch a performance of the outdoor drama *Horn in the West.* The final two legs of the trip—from Boone to Asheville and from there to Fontana Village—are easily accomplished in a day's drive.

FROM CHARLOTTESVILLE TO ROANOKE, VA.: There are two lodges
on the Parkway in Virginia. **Peaks of Otter** (for details and rates, which vary, write Virginia Peaks of Otter Co., P.O. Box 489, Bedford, VA 24523; tel. 703/586-1081), some 86 miles from the northern end of the Parkway; and **Rocky Knob Cabins** (write National Park Concessions, Inc., Meadows of Dan, VA 24120), closer to the North Carolina border and south of Roanoke.

A Very Special Detour
For a taste of that celebrated antebellum life, leave the Parkway at its intersection with I-64 and drive west to Covington, then north on U.S. 220, a total distance of about 60 miles, to the grand old resort hotel, **The Homestead**, at Hot Springs (U.S. 220, Hot Springs, VA 24445; tel. 703/839-5500). This classic, magnificent château holds over 600 rooms, and the tone is set from the minute you enter the Great Hall, with its 16 pillars, 14 chandeliers, log-burning fireplaces, and (during afternoon tea) string orchestra. There are lobbies galore, many lounges, and a shopping arcade, all on a very grand scale, indeed. And in keeping with its grand manner, the Homestead enforces dress rules that eliminate blue jeans and T-shirts (not that you'd *want* to wear them in such elegant surroundings). As for the rooms, there are spacious suites with parlors and big screened porches that overlook the gardens, 11 white clapboard cottages, and penthouse duplexes in the newer South Wing, whose bedroom balconies are reached by spiral staircases (I *told* you this was a very special place). And there's a variety of recreational activities that is just simply outstanding: mineral baths or saunas, which were the original attractions; 16,000

acres of mountain forests and streams and meadows; horseback riding, hiking, buckboard rides; an indoor and outdoor pool; tennis courts (20); and three superb golf courses. Dining here is an experience. Both the cuisine and the service are legendary, and both more than live up to the elegance of the place. And that service doesn't flag even if you opt for room service in a room so beautifully furnished you just can't leave it. All in all, if a splurge is on your agenda or if posh is your natural style of travel, the Homestead is sure to fill the bill: it's been doing that since 1892. What you pay for such pampering is: $100 to $125 (add $50 to $65 for those parlor suites) for doubles; $90 per person for cottages. There are some spa package plans and family rates available—but don't expect huge reductions; it isn't that kind of place.

Where to Stay in Roanoke

Roanoke was just a tiny village (population about 500) until it became a railroad center in the 1880s. One of the remnants of the prosperous times that followed is the **Roanoke Hotel**, 19 N. Jefferson St., P.O. Box 12508, Roanoke, VA 24026 (tel. 703/343-6992), two blocks north off U.S. 220, U.S. 11, and I-581 (look for Downtown exit). The large old "railroad hotel" is in the style of an English inn, albeit an elegant one. And both accommodations and service live up to that elegance. You'll really get the feeling of an era now passed when you settle into the groove of being a much-catered-to guest. There are three dining rooms (you can eat from 7 a.m. to midnight), bars, a heated indoor pool with poolside food service, babysitting service, and golf privileges at nearby courses. Doubles run from $55 up.

There's a **Holiday Inn**, Orange Ave. at Williamson Rd. (tel. 703/342-8961), in downtown Roanoke, with the usual large rooms and modern furnishings. Prices in the dining room (which is open for breakfast, lunch, and dinner) are moderate, and the Torch Club Lounge features entertainment nightly except Sunday. Double-occupancy rooms are $42 and up.

The **Roanoke TraveLodge**, 320 Kimball Ave. NE (tel. 703/344-0981), has a heated pool and 24-hour food service. Doubles are $37 and up.

The always-reliable **Days Inn**, Orange Ave. NE, P.O. Box 12325, Roanoke, VA 24024) tel. 703/342-4551), also has a pool and restaurant at budget prices. Doubles are $29.88 here.

Where to Eat Along the Parkway

Restaurants, cafes, and picnic grounds are all in abundant supply at fairly convenient locations. If you decide on a picnic, however, stock up either before you go or at the first supply store you see—they aren't that plentiful once you're on the Parkway.

Where to Eat in Roanoke

The **Hotel Roanoke's Regency Room** (tel. 343-6992) is far and away the best place to eat in this area. It's an elegant atmosphere (jacket and tie required at dinner), with entertainment and dancing. And there's delightful terrace dining when weather permits. Specialties include spoon bread (they do their own baking, so all breads are delicious), tournedos béarnaise, and steak Diane, and the tab will come to somewhere between $12 and $20 on the semi à la carte menu.

For less expensive meals, try the dining rooms at the motels listed in the "Where to Stay" section.

THINGS TO SEE AND DO: Before setting off down the Parkway, there's a side trip you may want to take for half a day or so, especially if you're a fan of TV's Walton family. Some 30 miles south of Charlottesville, just off Va. 6 on a secondary road (800), the little town of Schuyler is where Earl Hamner grew up and the setting for "The Waltons" series. Aside from the absolutely gorgeous Blue Ridge Mountains scenery, you'll see the "Walton Home" and "Mr. Godsey's store" (Jim Bob's son will be behind the counter to sell you postcards or a snack). Or you can walk around the mill, now a soapstone factory. Don't expect guided tours or admission fees—just an easy, informal atmosphere and conversation with very friendly natives.

Now, back to the Parkway. About five miles from its northern end you'll come to **Humpback Rocks** and a reconstructed mountain farm. There's also a hiking trail a little farther along that leads three-quarters of a mile to the rocks. **At Yankee Horse,** look for an oldtime logging railroad spur, or take a short walk through the woods to see **Wigwam Falls.**

Lexington

Take the U.S. 60 exit west from I-81 to Lexington, home and burial place of two famous Confederate generals, Robert E. Lee and "Stonewall" Jackson. The **Lexington Visitor Center,** 107 E. Washington St. (tel. 463-3777), will provide three self-guided walking tours of historic sites. It's open 9 a.m. to 5 p.m. daily except Thanksgiving, Christmas, and New Year's Day.

Robert E. Lee came to Lexington following the Civil War to assume the presidency of the college which is today Washington and Lee University. The Lee family crypt and General Lee's office, preserved as he left it, are located within the Lee Chapel on the university campus. The chapel is open mid-April to mid-October, Monday through Saturday, 9 a.m. to 5 p.m.; to 4 p.m. the rest of the year; and Sunday from 2 to 5 p.m. except for major holidays.

Jackson's residence, the **Stonewall Jackson House,** 8 E. Washington St. (tel. 463-3777), was the only home he ever owned, and has been faithfully restored to tell the story of "the man behind the beard," who was a professor at VMI prior to the Civil War. The house is just as it was when he and his second wife lived there from 1859 to 1861. It is open year round, Monday through Saturday, 9 a.m. to 4:30 p.m.; Sunday 1 to 4:30 p.m.; and there's an admission charge of $1.50 for adults, 75¢ for children. Closed Easter, Thanksgiving, Christmas, New Year's Day, and Sundays during January and February.

The **Virginia Military Institute,** on U.S. 11 (tel. 463-6207), has been sending graduates to war since the Mexican War of 1846. During the school year (September to May) you can see the colorful Guard Mount every day at 12:30 p.m. in nice weather and the dress parade on Friday at 4:15 p.m. The VMI Museum, one of the finest college museums in the nation, with displays on the history of this unique institution, is free and open daily. During school sessions, guided tours by cadets are available. Gen. George C. Marshall's personal, military, and diplomatic papers are housed in the Marshall Research Foundation's Library at the west end of the Parade Grounds, and there's an electric map that traces World War II developments. It's free and open daily from 9 a.m. to 4 or 5 p.m., depending on the time of year.

Natural Bridge

South of Lexington on U.S. 11, you'll find one of the Seven Natural Wonders of the World, Natural Bridge. The 215-foot-high arch was an object of worship by Indians, and when Thomas Jefferson bought it for "20 shillings of good and lawful money" from King George III of England, he built a small cabin for visitors and hired a caretaker. His guests included such colonial greats as George Washington (who carved his initials in the limestone), Patrick Henry, James Monroe, and John Marshall. You reach the bridge by natural steps that wind down to Cedar Creek, past arborvitae trees estimated to be ten centuries old, or via the bus (round trip is $1). It's open 8 a.m. to 10 p.m. from April 1 to September 30, closing at 9 p.m. other months. There is a $3 charge for either day or night visits ($1.50 for ages six to 12), and a combination ticket (day *and* night) costs $4 ($2 for children six to 12). A music and light show, "The Drama of Creation," is presented every night at 9 p.m. and 10 p.m. in summer months, 7 p.m. and 8 p.m. other months.

You can rejoin the Parkway from Natural Bridge and follow it on to Roanoke.

In and Around Roanoke

First thing on your agenda should be a visit to the **Roanoke Valley Chamber of Commerce**, 14 W. Kirk Ave., Roanoke, VA 24011 (tel. 703/344-5188), for all sorts of helpful literature.

Across the Walnut Avenue Bridge, off Va. 220, the **Mill Mountain city park** has a marvelous panoramic view of the city and its surroundings. There's also a children's zoo and a miniature train. Even if you don't visit the park, you'll be aware of it, for every night a 100-foot-high electric star is visible for miles around.

At the **Transportation Museum**, 802 Wiley Dr. (tel. 342-5670), in **Wasena Park** you can see covered wagons, steam locomotives, antique cars, and a model railroad. It is open daily, May 1 to September 30, from 9 a.m. to 5 p.m., closed on Monday and Tuesday the rest of the year. Admission is $2 for adults, 75¢ for children.

There are two theater groups in Roanoke. The **Mill Mountain Playhouse** performs only from late June through August, Wednesday through Sunday. Call 344-2057 for information about performances and reservations. **Showplace at the Barn Dinner Theatre**, at 6071 Airport Rd., is open year round for in-the-round Broadway musicals, comedies, and dramas with professional casts. Call 362-3333 for reservations.

Booker T. Washington's birthplace is 20 miles southeast of Roanoke. Drive south on Va. 116 to Burnt Chimney, then take Va. 122 north (follow the signs). A Visitor Center has a 17-minute film biography of the black leader's life and accomplishments, as well as other exhibits, and there's a short, self-guiding trail walk past replicas of farm buildings that were on this tobacco farm where he was born as a slave in 1856. The farm is now worked much as it was when he lived here, and you'll see crops and animals similar to those he knew as a boy. The Visitor Center is open 8:30 a.m. to 5 p.m. daily except for major holidays, and for advance information, write: Booker T. Washington National Monument, Rt. 1, Box 195, Hardy, VA 24101 (tel. 703/721-2094).

If you're in Roanoke around July 4th, do take in part of the **Roanoke Valley Horse Show** at the Salem Roanoke Valley Civic Center. It's one of the best in the country, and a fun way to celebrate the holiday.

FROM ROANOKE TO BOONE: Although it's only a 175-mile drive from Roanoke to Boone, you won't want to rush along this scenic route, and a stop at Boone is just about right to give you a full, unhurried day getting there.

Where to Stay in Boone

One of the most exclusive resort lodges in this part of the country is near Boone, and if "deluxe" is your travel style, it will be a mountain visit par excellence if you reserve at **Hound Ears Lodge,** P.O. Box 188, Blowing Rock, NC 28605 (tel. 704/963-4321), which gets its unusual name from a nearby rock formation. It's five miles southwest of Boone on N.C. 105, then three-quarters of a mile south on Country Road 1568 (follow the signs). The setting is gorgeous, the rooms and suites are the ultimate in luxury, and this complete resort, surrounded by beautifully landscaped grounds, has a pool and facilities for golf, tennis, fishing, and skiing (in winter months, of course). Prices are steep—a whopping $130 and up per day for doubles.

Holiday Inn, 710 Blowing Rock Rd. tel. (704/264-2451 or toll-free 800/238-8000), has a pool as well as a restaurant which serves moderately priced meals. Double-occupancy rooms are typical of this chain and range from $44.

Greene's, 536 Blowing Rock Rd. (tel. 704/264-8845), has a heated pool and restaurant. Some of the comfortably furnished rooms (with contemporary decor) have balconies with stunning mountain views. Rates for a double during the skiing season start at $40 (higher on weekends), but are lower the rest of the year.

Where to Eat in Boone

Head straight for the **Dan'l Boone Inn,** 105 Hardin St. (tel. 264-8657), for family-style breakfasts, lunches, or dinners that are really something special—and at prices that won't hurt. Everything is home-cooked, and the fare is definitely southern: country ham and biscuits, fried chicken, and the like. Prices run from $6 for a family-style breakfast to $8 for dinner. Children's plates are $3.

The **Holiday Inn,** 710 Blowing Rock Rd. (tel. 704/264-2451), has an exceptionally nice dining room that specializes in steaks and other beef dishes at moderate prices ($5 to $10 for complete dinners). Like most of this chain's dining rooms, it serves all three meals, with hours from 6 a.m. to 10 p.m.

Things to See and Do

Between Roanoke and the North Carolina border, be sure to stop at **Mabry Mill.** There's a lovely cluster of log cabins, farm buildings, a blacksmith shop, a church, and a water-powered gristmill straight out of pioneer days. The restaurant makes a good lunch stopover, too.

If you're theater-minded, there's a detour off the Parkway onto I-81 that you really should take. In the town of **Abingdon,** something happened back in 1932 that has profoundly influenced the American theater ever since. A young enthusiastic actor, Robert Porterfield, figured out that hungry professional actors all over the country would be happy during those Depression years to exchange their talents for a place to work and food to eat. At the same time, he believed the theater-hungry mountain people (who had food aplenty) would welcome a chance to swap it for live productions. He was right, and the Barter Theatre he established has been a rousing success since those first days when playwrights like Austin Strong, Noel Coward, Thornton Wilder, Robert Sherwood, and Maxwell Anderson accepted hams and other country produce in payment for scripts, and one day's door receipts showed up on the little company's table the next day.

Since 1946, the Barter has been **The State Theatre of Virginia,** supported in part by legislative funds, and admissions nowadays are in the form of coin of the realm (I don't really know what would happen if you showed up with a ham). Many of our theatrical leading lights have had their early training here. Among them: Hume Cronyn, Patricia Neal, Fritz Weaver, Ernest Borgnine, and Gregory Peck. Across the street, the Barter Playhouse has now become a full-fledged member of Actor's Equity and presents established works. The regular season runs from April through October, and people come from several hundred miles around (tourists often make this a primary stop). To find out about schedules and tickets, write the State Theatre of Virginia, Abingdon. VA 24210, or call 703/628-3991.

For an Overnight Stay in Abingdon

It is not inconceivable that the Barter Playhouse or the State Theatre will entice you to stay overnight for a performance. If that happens, run—don't walk—over to the **Martha Washington Inn,** 150 W. Main St. (tel. 703/628-3161). Housed in what was built in 1830 as a private residence and then served nearly 100 years as a college, the inn retains the feeling of graciousness and hospitality native to those long-gone days. Lobbies and sitting rooms are furnished with antique grandfather clocks and glistening chandeliers. An elegant colonial staircase sweeps down into the wide central hall. Upstairs, many rooms have four-poster beds (some with canopies) and fireplaces, and all are beautifully and comfortably furnished. Whether you stay here or not, plan on at least one meal in the dining room, which features country ham and other southern specialties. Doubles are $65 in summer, lower other months, and children under 12 stay free.

Sights In and Around Boone

There's so much to see and do here that it might be a good idea to make this a two- or three-day stop, especially during the summer months. Be sure to check with the **Boone Chamber of Commerce,** 600 Hwy. 105 Extension (tel. 704/264-2225).

The **Boone–Banner Elk–Blowing Rock** area, sometimes called "The High South," has been a summer resort retreat for Southerners since the 1800s. But in recent years, skiers have been attracted to the high slopes during winter months as well. There are now excellent skiing facilities and a wealth of winter accommodations, restaurants, and entertainment spots at **Ski Beech Ski Resort,** P.O. Box 1118, Banner Elk, NC 28604 (tel. 704/387-2011). While I've never been attracted to the sport myself and cannot judge the quality of the snow (there are snowmakers to help out Mother Nature), runs, jumps, etc., friends who head for the hills every winter weekend tell me this is the best skiing in the South and among the best in the country.

Boone itself (named for Daniel, of course—he had a cabin here in the 1760s) draws hunters and fishermen to the abundantly stocked streams and forests. For the nonsportsminded summer visitor, there's a beautifully produced outdoor drama, Kermit Hunter's *Horn in the West,* staged in the **Daniel Boone Theatre,** P.O. Box 295, Boone NC 28607 (tel. 704/264-2120 or 264-9089), every night except Monday from late June through August. It tells a vivid story of pioneer efforts to win the friendship of native Cherokee Indians. Performances begin at 8:30 p.m. and admission is $7 to $8 (12 and under, half price).

In the immediate vicinity, don't miss **Blowing Rock** (two miles southeast of the town of the same name on U.S. 321), where you can stand on The Rock, as it's affectionately called, throw a handkerchief or some other light object off the edge, and have it sent right back up to you by strong updraft winds. And when you're not playing that rather fascinating game, the observation tower, gazebos, and gardens offer really splendid views of the **John's River Gorge** and nearby Blue Ridge peaks. The observation tower is open every day from 9 a.m. to 5 p.m. from late April through October—early November if the weather is good. Adults pay $1.50; from four to 12, $1. Another natural phenomenon at Blowing Rock is **Mystery Hill**, where balls roll and water runs uphill. The **pioneer museum** is interesting and you'll get a kick out of the mock grave marked simply "He Wuz a Revenoor"—a pile of dirt with boots sticking out one end!

Don't think the **Tweetsie Railroad**, (tel. 704/264-9061); halfway between Boone and Blowing Rock, is for the kiddies only; the whole family will enjoy this old narrow-gauge train (I love every toot of the sweet-toned whistle) as it winds through the mountains, suffering mock attacks by "Indians" and "outlaws." Mountain music and other entertainment waits at **Tweetsie Palace** and the Junction and Mining Company are straight out of a history book. The train makes daily runs from 9 a.m. to 6 p.m. from late May through October. Fare is $7 for adults and $6 for ages 4 to 12.

Grandfather Mountain (one mile off the Parkway on U.S. 221 near Linville) is the highest peak in the Blue Ridge. You can see as far as 100 miles from the **Mile High Swinging Bridge,** and the **Environmental Habitat** is home to Mildred the Bear and her black bear friends. This is the place where kilt-clad Scots gather (from Scotland as well as all parts of North America) early in July for the **Annual Highland Games and Gathering of the Clans.** Exciting bagpipe music, dancing, wrestling, and tossing the cabar (a telephone-pole-like shaft) contests—as well as the colorful mix of people bent on two days of fun—make it a spectacle not to be missed.

FROM BOONE TO ASHEVILLE, N.C.: A worthwhile detour from the Parkway at this point is **Burnsville**, where you may even want to stay overnight at the **Nu-Wray Inn**, a real oldtime country inn that makes you feel completely at home. (See "Where to Eat in Asheville" for full details). It is certainly worth a stop for breakfast or dinner if you're heading on to Asheville without another stopover.

Where to Stay in Asheville

Mountain vacationing can be rustic and at the same time luxurious. If you don't believe that, reserve at Asheville's **Grove Park Inn and Country Club,** 290 Macon Ave., Asheville, NC 28804 (tel. 704/252-2711), a favorite of southern gentry since 1913; host over the years to such notables as William Jennings Bryan, F.D.R., Woodrow Wilson, Thomas Edison, and Henry Ford; and listed in the National Register of Historic Places.

Built on the side of Sunset Mountain at an elevation of 3100 feet, the rambling main building is constructed of huge native boulders and its "grand hall" lobby is flanked on each end by 14-foot fireplaces. The dark wood and comfortably padded chairs and sofas create a feeling of coziness despite the 120-foot-long dimensions of the room. On crisp evenings (even in summer nighttime temperatures are often in the 50s and 60s), when fires are lit, a sort of magic takes over to transform travelers from strangers into warm friends.

There is nightly entertainment, and an impromptu jazz concert or old-fashioned singalong has been known to develop spontaneously. Guest rooms are large, comfortable, and attractively furnished in a blend of modern convenience and the historic charm of pieces that date from the inn's beginnings.

Grove Park's food has been famed throughout the region from the start, and its five dining rooms and two cocktail lounges offer everything from full-course meals to snacks, sandwiches, pastries, and your favorite beverages. A special Sunday meal is featured on the Sunset Terrace where you can enjoy the pleasant mountain air while you eat.

Dinners on the Sunset Terrace feature American and European cuisine with such delectable dishes as sauteed mountain trout almandienne, roast ribs of beef, Surf and Turf, and southern-fried chicken. Most dinners cost from $15 to $25. There's music for dining and dancing on the Terrace.

Besides golf, recreational activities include swimming, tennis, and (my favorite) just plain relaxing on the wide front porch in rocking chairs graciously provided. A social hostess arranges tours, sightseeing, and children's activities for those so inclined. For all this, you'll pay rates that are, for sure, more deluxe than rustic—beginning at $65 double, with a choice of European Plan (room only, at that price), American Plan (three meals at an additional charge per person per day), or Modified American Plan (breakfast and dinner, at a slightly lower charge per person per day). Registered guests have full privileges at the Country Club (which dates back to 1893), including use of the Health Club facilities.

The inn is open from mid-April through October, and the Country Club (which has 21 guest rooms) is open year around. Reservations should be made at least three weeks in advance, longer if possible.

If the budget calls for moderate rather than deluxe, head for Loyd and Leone Kirk's **Forest Manor Motor Lodge**, U.S. 25 South, Asheville, NC 28803 (tel. 704/274-3531), 3½ miles from the city center. In a scenic, wooded setting, the bungalow-style rooms are pine paneled and attractively furnished, and each has an inviting front porch entrance bordered by well-tended flower beds. And the Kirks so pride themselves on cleanliness that if you find any evidence of dirt, there's no charge! The sounds of song birds and gentle breezes sighing through pine trees predominate over highway noises, which are reduced to a faint hum by the set-back location. It's a relaxed, very friendly place to stay, open year round at affordable prices ($40 to $58 April through October, $34 to $45 the rest of the year). There are kitchenettes available for a minimum of one week and rollaway beds or cribs are furnished at a small additional charge.

Asheville has a **Days Inn**, I-40 and U.S. 70 East (tel. 704/298-5140), situated on a hillside with mountain views that are especially spectacular when autumn foliage begins to turn. There's a pool, kiddie playground, and Tasty World Restaurant. Only five miles from Biltmore House. Doubles go for $29.88.

Camping from Boone to Asheville

There are four campgrounds operated by the National Park Service on the Blue Ridge Parkway between Boone and Asheville. None has showers, and other facilities are limited, varying from one location to another. Rates are $6 per site and availability is on a first-come, first-served basis. For full details, you can contact each at these addresses:

Open year round: Linville Falls Campground, Rt. 1, Box 798, Spruce Pine, NC 28777 (tel. 704/765-7818); Julian Price Memorial Campground, Blowing Rock, NC 28605 (tel. 704/295-9031).

Open May through October: Doughton Park Campground, Rt. 1, P.O. Box 50, Laurel Springs, NC 28644 (tel. 919/372-8877); Crabtree Meadows Campground, RFD 1, Spruce Pine, NC 28777 (tel. 704/765-5444).

Where to Eat in Asheville

The best eating in Asheville is to be found at the **Grove Park Inn.** Or, if classic French cuisine is as appealing to you as it is to me, you won't want to miss **Jared's,** 60 Haywood St. (tel. 252-8276). Located just half a block from the Civic Center, Jared's warm atmosphere comes from a pleasant combination of contemporary and antique furnishings, fine art, and lots of greenery. The friendly, personal service enhances truly marvelous food (prepared by French-born chef François Peter, who was trained in Lyon). Specialties like canard à l'orange (dramatically flamed at your table), faisan aux champignons (pheasant with wild mushrooms), and boeuf Wellington (for two) are outstanding, but almost anything you order here (there's a wide selection of dinner crêpes) could qualify as gourmet. They even do all their own baking and turn out incredible desserts. Prices are, as you might expect, in the "expensive" category (entrée prices from $10 to $22 at dinner on the à la carte menu; crêpes are in the $6 to $10 range), but you won't regret one penny, since "value for money" takes on real meaning here. Open for lunch from 11:30 a.m. to 3 p.m. ($4 to $8), dinner (reservations are *strongly* advised) from 6 to 11 p.m. There's entertainment in the evenings, adding another nice touch.

Outside of Asheville proper, 37 miles away on U.S. 19E, the **Nu-Wray Inn** (tel. 704/682-2329) on the town square in **Burnsville** serves up a unique dining experience with a distinct southern flavor. Established in 1833, the three-story inn, white with green shutters, was purchased by the Wray family at the close of the Civil War, and Betty Wray Saunders, the present manager, represents the fourth generation of family ownership. From the time you step onto its long, columned front porch lined with rocking chairs, you'll feel at home. That "down home" feeling grows when you sit down to eat at a large table where meals are served family style, with dishes being passed around the table so you can take as much as you please. I guarantee you won't pass up the hickory smoked ham or southern fried chicken! On weekdays, breakfast (the hearty kind, $4.50) is at 8:30 a.m. and dinner ($8.50) at 6:30 p.m. On Sunday, dinner is served midday in the southern tradition from noon to 2:30 p.m. ($9). It's worth the trip just to see the inn itself with its drawing room furnished with antiques, as are the 35 bedrooms (32 with private bath). And if you're on your way to or from Boone, you can stop overnight here at rates that are economical, to say the least: $28 to $35 for doubles. As a guest, you'd also pay slightly less for meals. There are craft shops nearby that provide more than enough browsing to make a stop worthwhile. If you opt for an extended visit after a first look-around, the Nu-Wray has special weekly rates. Closed December to April.

Things to See and Do in the Asheville Area

For detailed information on Asheville's many attractions, write or visit: **Asheville Area Chamber of Commerce** 151 Haywood St., P.O. Box 1011, Asheville, NC 28802 (tel. 704/258-5200).

I've fantasized as long as I can remember about the life of the really rich and what it would be like to have unlimited money. Well, while my chances of ever knowing that lifestyle firsthand are nil (not *practically* nil, all-the-way nil)—the fantasies get a shot in the arm every time I go to see the overwhelmingly magnificent **Biltmore Estate,** P.O. Box 6854, Asheville, NC 28806) in

Asheville (on U.S. 25, two blocks north off I-40). The French Renaissance château built by George W. Vanderbilt has 250 rooms! And talk about the "grand manner"—it fills every nook and cranny of this house and its gardens. There just isn't an ordinary spot in the place, not even the kitchen. Vanderbilt, a man who lived out *my* fantasies, gathered furnishings and art treasures from all over the world for this palace (for instance, Napoleon's chess set and table from St. Helena are here) and then went further to plant one of the most lavish formal gardens you'll ever see. There are more than 200 varieties of azaleas alone, plus thousands of other plants and shrubs. Admission to the house and gardens is $12 for adults, $9 for children six to 12 (under 12, free). You should allow a minimum of two hours for the self-guided tour. If you plan to make a day of it, there's a charming restaurant in a renovated barn.

There's no charge to visit a pet project of Mrs. Vanderbilt's, the **Biltmore Homespun Shops,** two miles north of town on Macon Street via Charlotte Street, on the grounds of the Grove Park Inn (tel. 253-7651). Mrs. Vanderbilt wanted to preserve the ancient wool-manufacturing skills of the mountains and help the weavers turn those skills into a paying industry, so she set up the cluster of old-world-style buildings, found local orders for the beautiful hand-woven fabrics, and eventually a mail-order business evolved which still thrives. You can visit the buildings, now covered with ivy to add to their charm, and see the whole wool-making process, from dyeing and carding to spinning to weaving on homemade oak looms to the final washing and sun-drying. There's an **Antique Automobile Museum,** also free, which holds cars dating back to 1905.

Thomas Wolfe grew up in Asheville and immortalized the town and its citizens (much to their dismay) in his *Look Homeward, Angel.* The boarding house, "Dixieland," that figures so prominently in the book, is at 48 Spruce St., and is maintained as a literary shrine, open Tuesday through Saturday from 9 a.m. to 5 p.m., Sunday from 1 to 5 p.m. Adults pay $1; children through high school, 50¢. Both he and William Sydney Porter (O. Henry) are buried in **Riverside Cemetery** (entrance on Birch Street off Pearson Drive).

Chimney Rock Park is 25 miles southeast of Asheville on U.S. 74 at the junction of U.S. 64 and N.C. 9. The huge granite monolith rises to a height of 315 feet, and you can reach its top by a stairway, a trail, or (as in my own case) by an elevator. There's an observation lounge open every day from March 1 through November, and the charge is $5 for adults, $3 for children 6 to 11. Trails lead to Needle's Eye, Moonshiner's Cave, Devil's Head, and Hickory Nut Falls, twice the height of Niagara. Food service is available as are picnic facilities. For full details, contact: Chimney Rock Co., Box 39, Chimney Rock, NC 29720 (tel. 704/625-9611).

Stately **Mount Mitchell** is in the **state park** that bears its name some 33 miles northeast on the Parkway, then five miles north on N.C. 128. There are a museum, a tower, and an observation lodge at Mount Mitchell; camping and picnicking facilities are available in the park.

About 30 miles southeast of Asheville on U.S. 25 is the little town of **Flat Rock,** home to the **North Carolina State Theater's Flat Rock Playhouse,** which stages performances from late June through August. It is better known, however, as the last home of two-time Pulitzer Prize-winning writer, poet, historian Carl Sandburg, who lived at **Connemara Farm** (on Little River Road, just west of U.S. 25) for some 22 years, longer than he'd ever lived in one place before. His home and the farm are preserved just as they were in his lifetime—the typewriter still sitting on an orange crate in his top-floor hideaway and his guitar propped against a chair in the living room—and there's no charge to visit and stroll around the grounds.

There are things to do in Asheville other than sightsee, however. For instance, if you land here the first week of August, don't miss the **Annual Mountain Dance and Folk Festival** held at the **Asheville Civic Center** on Haywood Street. It begins at sundown and goes on until the last fiddler, banjo picker, ballad singer, dulcimer player, and clog dancer has called it quits and there's nobody interested in one more square-dancing set. This is the oldest such festival in the country, everybody is invited, and you're encouraged to join in even if you don't know a "do-si-do" from a "swing-your-partner."

And if you miss the Festival, every Saturday night from early July through August there's something called a **Shindig-on-the-Green** at the **City County Plaza,** where you'll find many of those same mountain musicians and dancers having an old-fashioned wingding. It's free, lots of fun, and again, you're invited to join in the fun. If sitting on the ground isn't your thing, take along a blanket or chair.

And in **Brevard,** 27 miles southeast of Asheville, there's a **Music Festival** held throughout the summer months (late June through mid-August) at the **Brevard Music Center,** during which you can hear nationally and internationally famous artists perform in symphony, chamber music, band, recitals, choral works, musical comedy, and opera every night. Tickets run $3.50 to $8.50, $2 to $5 for those under 16, and you can write P.O. Box 592, Brevard, NC 28712, or call 704/884-2019, for schedules and reservations.

FROM ASHEVILLE TO FONTANA DAM: The Blue Ridge Parkway comes to an end at **Cherokee,** the largest organized Indian reservation in the East (see below). Just west of the reservation, on N.C. 28, is **Fontana Village,** Fontana Dam, NC 28733 (tel. 704/498-2238), a mountain resort that makes a perfect ending for your Parkway trip. Built near a 30-mile-long lake formed by the construction of Fontana Dam, the resort has an 94-room inn, a 30-room lodge, and 257 cottages with one to three bedrooms. Sportsminded people will be in their element here, with stocked trout ponds, tennis courts, riding horses, and miniature golf (plus a par-three course) right at hand. In addition, there are all sorts of crafts workshops with a charge for materials only and square dances from June through August. It really has something for almost anyone who loves the outdoors and an oldtime atmosphere. During the summer (June 1 through October 31), rates begin at $55 in the inn, $45 for a one-bedroom cottage (which will accommodate up to three if you use the living-room studio couch as a bed). The rest of the year, rates drop considerably, with every seventh day free, making it one of the best fall vacation spots I know of.

As for dining facilities, if you don't cook your own meals in the fully equipped cottage kitchens, there is a cafeteria and the Pioneer Dining Room, where the whole family can eat reasonably.

Things to See and Do

A little south of Asheville on the Parkway, a turn east at Wagon Road Gap will take you down a steep, winding road to the first **forestry school** in the U.S. There's an interesting museum for visitors. Along the way, you go past **Sliding Rock,** where children often delight in sliding down the glass-slick surface, and **Looking Glass Falls.**

Nearer the end of the Parkway, at Maggie Valley on U.S. 19, the **Ghost Town in the Sky,** P.O. Box 790, Maggie Valley, NC 28715 (tel. 704/926-0256), entertainment center is great fun. Separate western, mining, and mountaineer towns have been recreated on different levels of the mountaintop and there's something going on in each one all the time. Shows are staged in the saloons, there are street gunfights, and all sorts of western and mountaineer types wander about. You reach the park, 3364 feet up, by means of twin inclined railways or a chairlift. Kids will enjoy the rides. It opens every day beginning in May at 9 a.m., closing at 6 p.m. until mid-June, when it stays open until 8 p.m. until Labor Day, then back to the earlier closing until the end of October, when it closes for the winter. Admission is $8.95 for adults, $7.95 for ages 5 to 12 (under four, free).

From the middle of December until snow disappears in the spring, there's very good skiing at the **Cataloochee Ranch** at **Maggie Valley.** For full information, write P.O. Box 500, Rt. 1, Maggie Valley, NC 28751, or call 704/926-1401 in summer, 704/926-0285 in winter.

As mentioned, the Blue Ridge Parkway comes to an end at Cherokee, right at the entrance to the **Cherokee Indian Reservation,** where Indian life has moved into the 20th century with all kinds of modern inventions and conveniences, but has held on to age-old traditions. You can see competitions in archery and blowguns, for example, or watch a game of Indian stickball, one of the roughest games anywhere. If you're there at the right time, you'll also see dances that have been handed down from generation to generation. The some 8000 Cherokee who live on the reservation are descendants of a proud tribe, many of whom hid out in the Great Smokies in 1838 to escape that blot on American history, the removal of all eastern tribes to the West. A government Indian agent, one William H. Thomas (part Indian himself), bought part of the land that is now reservation and gave it to the Cherokee who'd managed to stay, and later a total of 50,000 acres was handed over to the tribe by the U.S. government.

A powerful drama, *Unto These Hills,* now tells the moving story of those tragic days when so many Indians traveled the "Trail of Tears." It is presented at the outdoor **Mountainside Theater,** off U.S. 441; P.O. Box 398, Cherokee, NC 28719 (tel. 704/497-2111), from mid-June through late August at 8:45 p.m., Monday through Saturday—and many of the actors are portraying their own ancestors. Tickets are $4 to $8.

The **Museum of the Cherokee Indian,** on U.S. 441 at Drama Road (tel. 704/497-3481), tells the story of the Cherokee through exhibits of such items as spear points several centuries old and multimedia theater shows. It's open daily year round for $3 (children six to 12, $1.50).

But to really see Indian life among the Cherokee 250 years ago, you have to visit **Oconaluftee Indian Village,** off U.S. 441 (Cherokee, NC 28719; tel. 704/497-2111). It's an authentic Cherokee community whose residents wear the tribal dress (most wear conventional clothes in the town of Cherokee and throughout the reservation) and practice the same crafts as their ancestors. You'll see dart guns being made or a log canoe being shaped by fire, and beautiful beadwork taking shape under skilled fingers. And the seven-sided Council House conjures up images of the leaders of seven tribes gathered to thrash out problems or to worship their gods together. It's a kind of living museum of a way of life and a period of our country's history that is all too often distorted by fiction writers and Hollywood scenarios. You can visit the village any day from mid-May through late October for $4.50, $2.50 for children six to 12.

Early-settler life is recreated, sort of, at **Frontierland,** 1¼ miles east of Cherokee on U.S. 19 (P.O. Box 337, Cherokee, NC 28719; tel. 704/497-4311 or 926-1922). There's a western town and frontier fort, with gunfights, Indian dances, and live shows. But there are amusement rides as well, making it more entertaining than educational. Part of the fun is getting there by the old-fashioned train. Admission, which includes all rides, shows, and petting zoo, is $8.95 for adults, $7.95 for children (children under four, free). Open daily Memorial Day through Labor Day, and weekends in May, September, and October.

Youngsters will find Christmas alive and well even in the summer at **Santa's Land Park and Zoo,** 2½ miles east of Cherokee on U.S. 19. Santa and his helpers are busy getting ready for December 25 in a charming Christmas village, and there's a zoo with (what else?) reindeer and other domestic and exotic animals. And just for fun, there are some amusement rides. It's open for visitors late May through October; and adults pay $5.95 (children two through 12, $4.95).

A Sidetrip for Rubies

Gem-quality blood-red rubies are found in only two places in the world—the Magok Valley in Burma and the **Cowee Valley** north of Franklin, N.C. While these ruby and sapphire mines are played out for commercial purposes, rockhounds are still finding many thousands of dollars in gem-quality stones every year. For an admission charge of about $5 a day (8 a.m. to 5 p.m. seven days a week, April to October) and about 25¢ a gallon, you can sort through the gem-bearing gravel—and keep anything you find. Two of the most reliable are the **Holbrook Ruby Mine** (tel. 704/524-3540), one of the original mines in the area, and the **Shuler Ruby Mine** (tel. 704/524-3551), both of which have only native stones and provide assistance to novice gem-seekers. Then stop in at **Ruth and Bud's Cowee Gem Shop** (tel. 704/369-8233), where Bud Schmidt, a former hobbyist rockhound himself, will examine your finds and offer expert faceting and mounting services. If you want to stay for more than a day, bunk in at **Miner's Rest** (within walking distance of the mines), where Ruth and Bud Schmidt provide three completely furnished efficiency apartments, each fully heated and air-conditioned, at $30 a day for three and $35 for four people (weekly and monthly rates available). For reservations, call 704/369-8233 (days) or 704/524-3902 (evenings), or write to Miner's Rest, Rt. 4, Box 474, Franklin, NC 28734.

To get to the mining area, take U.S. 23 from Asheville or U.S. 441 from Cherokee to Franklin, then N.C. Route 28 north for about six miles. After passing the Cowee Baptist Church, turn right into the Cowee Valley and drive about four more miles.

Chapter V

INTRODUCTION TO NORTH CAROLINA

1. By Way of Background
2. Traveling to North Carolina
3. Traveling Within North Carolina

"WE FELT SO SORRY FOR HER," the lady from California told me, "that we came all the way across the country to cheer her up." She was speaking of her daughter, a brand-new lieutenant in the air force who had joined up primarily for the travel benefits. "North Carolina was not exactly what she had in mind," my new-found friend related. The whole family had been disappointed when news came of her assignment to Pope Field, close by Fort Bragg in the center of the state. "But since we've been here, it's a different story," the mother went on with a beaming face, "this state has *everything!* It's been a whole new experience for us, and well worth the trip just to get to know it."

This reaction by first-time visitors to the state that bills itself as the "Variety Vacationland" is not unusual. Although Southerners have long known and enjoyed North Carolina's resorts, "Yankees," Midwesterners, and those from the Far West have, for the most part, tended to think of it merely as a place to pass through on the way to points farther south. Yet within its borders lie tourist and vacation attractions numerous enough and varied enough to offer an appeal to almost any traveler, regardless of his or her special interests.

1. By Way of Background

FROM SIR WALTER RALEIGH TO THE WRIGHT BROTHERS: There's history aplenty, for it was here, on tiny Roanoke Island, that Sir Walter Raleigh's colony of 150 English settlers was "lost" in 1587, a full 20 years before Englishmen arrived further north in Virginia's Jamestown. What happened to them (including Virginia Dare, the first child born of English parents in the New World) remains a mystery, since the only clue—if that's what it is—to their fate was the word "Croatan" (the name of a tribe of friendly Indians) carved on a tree.

Along the coast are stately old plantation homes, some with formal gardens still lovingly tended and open to visitors, which housed the planters who came and stayed to plow prosperity from the rich soil. And further inland, at Winston-Salem, an entire village—Old Salem—has been restored to depict the lifestyle of Moravians who arrived in 1753 and created a community that has lived through the centuries.

To the west in the mountains (the Blue Ridge, Great Smokies, Nantahalas, and others that form the southern Appalachians), history lives in the form of the Cherokee reservation—teeming with residents whose ancestors were here eons before a white face appeared—and towns like Boone (named for you-know-who) and Banner Elk (see Chapter IV for details on all these) that speak of the persevering frontiersmen whose restless western wanderings cleared the way for those who followed to settle down, bringing "civilization" with them.

In more recent times, man literally took off into the Age of Flight right here in North Carolina when Wilbur and Orville Wright made the first powered flight in 1903 at Kitty Hawk.

WITH A VIEW TO THE PRESENT: But if history isn't your thing, the Old North State has an ample supply of other attractions in its grab bag.

Its beaches, from Nags Head to Ocean Isle, are a delight, with broad stretches of white sand, waving sea oats, waves big enough to challenge the most skillful surfer, and seaside resorts located on outer banks, peninsulas, or offshore islands that face sounds and rivers as well as the Atlantic. Fishing, boating, waterskiing, sand-skiing, and even hang-gliding from gigantic dunes are all part of the fun up and down the coastline. (And if you're a "sea nut," enamored of its mystery and many moods, you'll *love* the tales of Blackbeard, that fierce pirate who sailed these waters and met his end here, and looking for relics of the more than 2000 shipwrecks claimed by the "Graveyard of the Atlantic.")

Tennis and golf lovers will find a home in the state, too. Indeed, which of us doesn't equate the very word "golf" with Pinehurst? And no one would deny that the sport is at its best there, but neither should the fact be overlooked that the whole state has excellent courses and courts from one end to the other.

Equestrians will find some of the country's finest horses in North Carolina, along with miles and miles of riding trails. You'll see horses on the beaches, on sandy paths shaded by softly sighing long-leaf pines, and following ancient Indian routes through mountain passes.

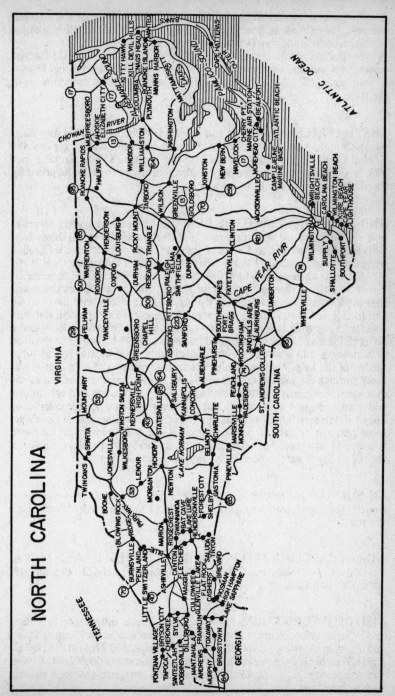

NORTH CAROLINA

And the mountains beckon hikers, climbers, skiers (the snow kind), and campers, then throw in Fontana, where square dancing and other oldtime recreations still hold sway (see, again, Chapter IV).

Naturalists and others who'd rather bed down in a tent than the fanciest resort hotel will find an embarrassment of riches in the four national forests, 25 state parks, 60 public and more than 300 privately owned campgrounds in the state.

THREE STATES IN ONE: As you may have gathered from the foregoing, North Carolina's geographical makeup divides into three distinct regions: the Coastal Plain, the Piedmont Plateau, and the Mountains. You can take your pick or sample all three: either way you're almost certain to be surprised by the sheer number of things to see and do.

AND THEN THERE ARE THE PEOPLE: One of your biggest surprises may well be the people who live here—"Tar Heels" they like to call themselves. (It is said that Gen. Robert E. Lee originated the name when North Carolina troops stuck so tenaciously in the front lines of battle during the Civil War.)

While all three regions have produced certain "personality" characteristics in the natives, there are some traits that all North Carolinians share, and they are a definite bonus to anyone visiting the state. Along with the courtesy and friendliness found among most southern people, those in North Carolina possess an engaging lack of pretense—you'll find few "phonies" here—and a delightful sense of humor. Basic good manners make them helpful at the drop of a question, and a sort of native sophistication may surprise you with the quality of the help. A resourcefulness and determination of high degree has, down through the years, been responsible for North Carolina's position as one of the most progressive Southern states in industry, education, and agriculture; and even in remote areas, you'll find the latest methods being employed by knowledgeable, well-informed citizens. Whether it's a fisherman at Ocracoke, a businessman in Raleigh, or a craftsman in the mountains at Brevard who winds up being a special friend during your visit (and you're bound to find one), the friendship is sure to be a lively, enjoyable, and lasting one.

TO SUM UP: North Carolina, then, does have a little bit of everything— something for everyone—and, as my friend from California said, it's well worth the trip.

NORTH CAROLINA TELEPHONE AREA CODES: Raleigh, 919; Winston-Salem, 919; Nags Head, 919; Wilmington (Wrightsville Beach), 919; Asheville, 704; Charlotte, 704.

VISITOR INFORMATION: For a packet of specific information brochures and bulletins before coming to North Carolina, contact: North Carolina Travel and Tourism Division, 430 N. Salisbury St., Raleigh, NC 27611 (tel. 919/733-4171). Whether it's sightseeing, golf, fishing, or almost any other facet of travel you're interested in, you're likely to receive very complete, thorough answers to your questions.

NORTH CAROLINA HOTELS: You can find just about any-priced hotel accommodation in North Carolina, from the expensive Hyatt House in Winston-Salem to the budget Days Inn chain detailed in the introduction to this book. Aside from price, there is also a wide choice of *type* of accommodation: there are country inns, mountain lodges, tourist homes, and motels and hotels with a distinctive regional flavor.

A Word of Warning

Just because *you* may not have thought of North Carolina as a prime tourist area, don't be deceived into believing that you can come without reserving ahead. 'Taint so, and I can attest to that fact on the basis of my own experience when I arrived "out of season" at the coast, only to find that the nearest room to be had was 40 miles inland because of the 23rd Annual Mullet Fishing Tournament! So, no matter when you plan to travel in the state, do yourself a favor and be sure your accommodations will be waiting.

DINING OUT IN NORTH CAROLINA: North Carolina's food is just as varied as its vacation attractions. And restaurants range all the way from fancy establishments that would rival the best in New York in decor to plain, road-house-looking cafes such as the one I found at Cartaret. At either end of the spectrum, you're likely to find well-prepared, tasty North Carolina specialties —barbecued pork (the spicy, minced-up kind that's unique to this state—in particular, look for the Parker's chain, which serves some of the best barbecue on earth at very moderate prices), country ham, fresh seafood served with hush puppies (cornmeal batter-fried in deep fat), and always, grits served with breakfast (don't knock them until you've tried them served with globs of melting butter). I've tried to point out my own personal finds, but in this state especially, you stand a very good chance of running into a "special" place if you ask about local favorites.

You must be 21 to order anything stronger than beer or wine, which can be bought at age 18.

NORTH CAROLINA CLIMATE: North Carolina's climate is generally moderate, as can be seen from the following yearly highs and lows for various locations in the state:

	High	Low
Cape Hatteras	84	40
Raleigh	88	31
Winston-Salem	88	32
Asheville	85	30

2. Traveling to North Carolina

The best way for *you* to get to North Carolina depends, of course, on where you start, how much you can spend on transportation, and just how much time you have. These are the options that will let you find the mode of travel that best fits your circumstances.

BY AIR: Eastern, United, and Delta have direct flights into Raleigh/Durham, Charlotte, and Greensboro from major cities in the U.S. Piedmont, which flies direct to Asheville, is an airline I especially like for its pleasant, efficient service, and it has the largest number of North Carolina destinations from out of state, though not all are direct: Raleigh, Wilmington, Jacksonville, New Bern, Kinston, Fayetteville, Greensboro, Winston-Salem, Hickory, Charlotte, and Asheville. Inquire about their "Hopscotch" discount fares, some of which connect with other airlines.

BY TRAIN: North Carolina is on Amtrak's several New York/Miami runs, with stops in Raleigh, Hamlet, Rocky Mount, Wilson, and Fayetteville. Southern Railway's Washington/New Orleans *Southern Crescent* stops in Greensboro, Salisbury, and Charlotte. Be sure to check for excursion fares or seasonal specials.

BY BUS: Greyhound and Trailways have good direct service to major cities in North Carolina from out of state, with connections to almost any destination within the state.

BY CAR: From Virginia and South Carolina, you can enter North Carolina on either I-95 or I-85, and I-27 and I-77 also lead in from South Carolina. The main Tennessee entry is I-40. All major border points have attractive, helpful Welcome Centers, some with cookout facilities and playground equipment in a parklike setting.

3. Traveling Within North Carolina

BY AIR: Piedmont, as noted above, has a number of in-state destinations, with connecting flights possible between most. Delta, Eastern, and Commuter all have limited flights within the state.

BY BUS: There are few places you can't reach by either Greyhound or Trailways. In limited locations, Seashore Transportation and Ingram Bus Lines service is available.

BY CAR: Driving is a pleasure on North Carolina's 76,000 miles of toll-free, well-maintained highways. Most Interstate and U.S. highways and some state roads have periodic rest areas with picnic tables and outdoor cooking facilities. For a map that is one of the easiest to use I've come across, as well as a fount of tourist information on the state, write to Public Affairs Office, Dept. of Transportation, P.O. Box 25201, Raleigh, NC 27611, for the **Official Highway Map and Guide to Points of Interest.**

Special Note: North Carolina law is quite specific on *all* traffic coming to a standstill when a school bus is stopped on a highway, and this is stringently enforced. So, if you see a bright-yellow school bus stopped—whether or not you see children getting on or off—save yourself a stiff fine and stop, and that applies whether you're meeting it or following behind.

You will find Thrifty Rent-a-Car locations in Charlotte, Greensboro, and Raleigh.

BY FERRY: I'd go out of my way just to travel on one of this state's most enjoyable transportation facilities, the system of toll-free auto ferries that ply the sounds and rivers of the coastal area. You can cross Currituck Sound from Currituck to Knotts Island, Hatteras Inlet, Pamlico River at Bayview, and Neuse River at Minnesott Beach. All schedules are printed on that wonderfully complete Official North Carolina Highway Map. For an up-to-date printed ferry schedule before you leave home, write: Director, Ferry Division, Room 116, Maritime Bldg., 113 Arendell St., Morehead City, NC 28557 (tel. 919/726-6446 or 726-6413).

Chapter VI

NORTH CAROLINA'S COASTAL PLAIN

1. Nags Head and the Outer Banks
2. Morehead City and Atlantic Beach
3. Wilmington and Wrightsville Beach

THE BEACHES ALONG NORTH CAROLINA'S Atlantic coastline
are, to say the least, unusual. Most of them, in fact, lie technically offshore on
the long string of narrow islands that make up the Outer Banks. And what
beaches they are! The strand is wide, dunes are breathtakingly high, and
interspersed with resort centers that have slowly developed over nearly 200
years, are long stretches of natural beach where you can walk and swim and
surfcast far from the madding crowd. But to begin at the beginning:

1. Nags Head and the Outer Banks
In 1899, when Nathaniel Gould emigrated from Cape Cod to Roanoke
Island, he advised arriving guests at his newly opened Hotel Roanoke to take
"any one of the Merchant and Miners Transportation Company's or the Old
Dominion Steamship Company's boats, both lines stopping at Norfolk, Vir-
ginia, which connects with trains of the Norfolk & Southern Railroad to
Elizabeth City, which connects with Steamer to Roanoke Island. In coming
from the south, take Steamer from New Bern, N.C. Carriages will be in waiting

at the steamboat wharf on the arrival of every boat, taking guests direct to the Hotel."

It's a much simpler matter today to reach the Outer Banks, thanks to a superb network of highways, bridges, and toll-free ferries. U.S. 158 eliminates the need for steamships from the north, and U.S. 64 provides easy access to visitors from the south.

NAGS HEAD: This largest resort in the Outer Banks area is ideal as a place to headquarter during your visit. Its odd name, according to local legend, comes from the practice of canny land pirates who in the old days would hang lanterns from the necks of ponies, parade them along the dunes at night, and lure unsuspecting ships onto shoals where they were grounded and their cargoes promptly stripped by the waiting robbers. Another theory holds that it was named for the highest point of Scilly Island, the last sight English colonists had of their homeland.

However it got its name, Nags Head has been one of the most popular beach resorts in North Carolina for over a century. The town itself is a collection of the usual beach houses, motels, and a few modern luxury hotels, and it has one of the finest beaches to be found in the state. **Jockey's Ridge,** highest sand dune on the East Coast, is located here also. Its 138-foot-high smooth, sandy slopes are popular with the sand-skiing and hang-gliding crowd, and since it is now a state park, it is open to all. And at **Kill Devil Hills** (named for a particularly potent rum once shipped from here), the Wright Brothers made that historic first flight back in 1903.

Roanoke Island is where Sir Walter Raleigh's colony of more than 100 men, women, and children settled when they landed here in 1587 in what was to be England's first permanent foothold in the New World. Virginia Dare, granddaughter of the little band's governor, John White, was born that year, the first child of English parents to be born in America. When White sailed back to England on the ships that had brought the settlers, it was his intention to secure additional provisions and perhaps more colonists, then return within the year. Instead, he found England so threatened by the Spanish Armada that Queen Elizabeth I refused to allow any large ships to leave. It wasn't until 1590 that White was able to get back to Roanoke, and what he found there was a mystery—one that remains to this day. The rude houses he had helped build were all dismantled and the entire area enclosed by a high palisade he later described as "very fort-like." At the entrance of the enclosure, crude letters spelled out the word "CROATAN" on a post from which the bark had been peeled.

Since their prearranged distress signal, a cross, was not there and no evidence suggested violence, his conclusion was that those he'd left on Roanoke Island must have joined the friendly Croatan Indian tribe. An unhappy chain of circumstances, however, forced him to set sail for England before a search could be made. Despite all sorts of theories about their fate, no link was ever established between the "lost" colonists and the Indians, nor was there ever any clue unearthed to reveal exactly what did happen. It would be 1607, at Jamestown, Virginia, before England could claim that permanently established settlement.

The **Fort Raleigh National Historic Site** was named in 1941, and its visitor center tells the story in exhibits and film. Paul Green's symphonic drama *The Lost Colony* brings it to life in the amphitheater that has been constructed at the edge of Roanoke Sound.

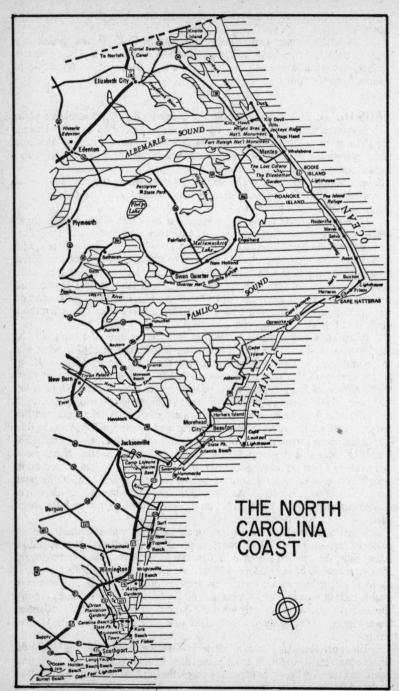

Map courtesy of the Greater Wilmington Chamber of Commerce

From **Whalebone Junction** at south Nags Head, the **Cape Hatteras National Seashore** stretches 70 miles down the Outer Banks barrier islands. The drive along N.C. 12 takes you through a wildlife refuge, pleasant little villages, long stretches of dunes with designated parking areas and ramps leading over to sand beaches that can only be called gorgeous, and on to **Buxton** and the **Cape Hatteras Lighthouse,** tallest on the American coast. It has stood since 1870 as a beacon for ships passing through these treacherous waters that have earned the title "Graveyard of the Atlantic," claiming more than 1500 victims of foul weather, strong rip currents, and shifting shoals. This is where the iron-clad Union gunboat *Monitor* went down in a storm in December of 1862.

At the little village of **Hatteras,** a free auto ferry makes the 40-minute crossing to **Ocracoke Island,** where more than 5000 acres, including 16 miles of beach, are preserved by the National Park Service for recreation. It's also where the pirate Edward Teach (Blackbeard) met his end. From the southern end of the island, a toll auto ferry takes you on a two-hour-and-ten-minute voyage across **Pamlico Sound** to **Cedar Island.**

With no stops, it's about a 4½-hour drive—but by rights, it's an all-day trip or several half-day trips from a Nags Head base. Otherwise, you'll miss those beaches for swimming, fishing, or just walking along the sand, the breathtaking view from the top of Cape Hatteras Lighthouse. Most of all, you'd miss the chance to stop for lunch or a respite or to shop, all of which are perfect excuses to get to know the marvelous people who call this necklace of sand "home." They're hardy "Bankers" who've lived with winds and storms and high seas, and who can—and will, to friendly souls—recount tales of heroism at sea, the ghostly light that bobs over Teach's Hole, and wild ponies that have roamed Ocracoke Island for at least 400 years, all in the soft accent that some say harks back to Devon, home of shipwrecked sailors who came ashore here and stayed to become ancestors of those you'll meet today. If you miss the *people* of the Outer Banks, you'll miss the character of these islands. Take the day!

WHERE TO STAY: The choice of beach accommodations is wide, but one thing should be borne in mind: while the beaches are lined with cottage rentals, many of them are spoken for on a year-to-year basis, and it is absolutely essential to make your reservations well in advance. We'll list a few in the hotel/motel category, but if you'd like to settle down for a week or more, your best bet is to write the **Outer Banks Chamber of Commerce,** P.O. Box 90-D, Kitty Hawk, NC 27949 (tel. 919/261-2626 or 261-3801), which can put you in touch with cottage and apartment owners.

The **Armada** is at the south end of Nags Head where U.S. 158 and U.S. 64 meet, Milepost 17, P.O. Box 307, Nags Head, NC 27959 (tel. 919/441-6315). Children 18 and under stay here *free,* and rates for double occupancy, oceanside, start at $80 Memorial Day through Labor Day, with much lower rates other seasons. Bayside rooms are a better buy at considerably lower rates. All rooms in the seven-story, modern hotel are attractively decorated in a modern manner and oceanfronts have private balconies. The oceanside restaurant is especially pleasant, with above-average food. The Escadrille Lounge, also on the ocean, features top entertainment and dancing during the summer months. They'll pack you a box lunch for day trips, or you stay put on their private beach or the two oceanside pools, where there's a lifeguard on duty during June, July, and August. There's a playground for children, tennis courts for their parents, and a babysitter service to make night prowling possible.

At the other end of the beach—in price as well as distance—is the **Quality Inn John Yancey,** P.O. Box 422, Kill Devil Hills, NC 27948 (tel. 919/441-7727 or toll-free 800/228-5151). Considerably fewer frills, but the moderate price range is a joy, as are the efficiencies, which come completely equipped, right down to the coffee pot. There's no charge for children under 12 if they share a room with parents, and the double-occupancy rates for a room (oceanfront) are from $55 in season all the way down to $35 off-season. Efficiencies cost from $62 to $37, depending on the time of year. Their Pancake House, serving good food at very reasonable prices, which you can eat in or take out, is just across the highway. A swimming pool provides swimming for those too fainthearted to brave the surf. Management here is especially friendly and helpful, the rooms are cheerful, and it represents one of the best moderately priced hotels we found on any of the beaches.

The **Quality Inn Sea Ranch** P.O. Box 325, Kill Devil Hills, NC 27948 (tel. 919/441-7126), at Milepost 7, has a posh oceanfront tower, with glass-enclosed balconies and rooms decorated with real flair. Each has two double beds, and there are 12 efficiencies (with mini-kitchens—not really meant for cooking full dinners). In the main building, you can choose rooms which come with one double and one single bed, or with sitting room area, mini-refrigerator, and two double beds. There's an enclosed pool with a sliding-glass roof and an indoor tennis club. Golf is just minutes away on two 18-hole, championship courses. The window-walled Top of the Dune dining room serves all three meals (dinner is by candlelight), and there's dancing and entertainment in the cocktail lounge. Doubles start at $62 from mid-June to early September and drop by stages to around $32 from late October through mid-March.

At Milepost 11, the **Beacon Motor Lodge,** P.O. Box 729, Nags Head, NC 27959 (tel. 919/441-5501), is a low, rambling complex offering rooms, efficiencies, and apartments. There are two swimming pools and tennis and golf privileges at nearby facilities. Rooms are comfortably furnished and decorated in cool blues and greens. No restaurant on the premises, but several are close by. Doubles start at $45 from late May to early September, less during other months. Apartments are in the $400 to $475 per week range (for up to four persons). Closed from October to March.

WHERE TO EAT: Dining out is no problem anywhere along North Carolina's coast, and Nags Head has plenty of small, good seafood restaurants. I'm listing only four, recognizing that the day's activities influence beach eating more strongly perhaps than in other locations.

The **Seafare,** in Old Nags Head (just about the center of town between mileposts 13 and 14; tel. 441-5555), rivals, in my opinion, some of the finest New York restaurants in cuisine, atmosphere, and service. Apparently, Nags Head regulars share my high opinion of the place, for they've been patronizing it since 1960, when descendants of Nathaniel Gould (the one who gave such explicit steamship instructions to his hotel guests) opened the Seafare after years of operating hotels whose dining rooms had become noted all up and down the coast. It's a large place, with five rooms decorated tastefully in nautical or colonial themes, and the night I was there, the famous Seafare Smorgasbord was being served—a truly groaning board heaped with fresh seafoods, roast beef, fresh salads and vegetables, and a room full of happy patrons returning again and again for refills, all for the shockingly low price of $9. Children eat their fill for only $5. The menu for table service is surprisingly extensive, featuring everything from several seafood combination platters to a Surf and Turf plate of beef tenderloin (8 oz.) and a 6-oz. rock lobster tail to a chateaubriand for two. Dinner, on the semi-à la carte menu, can run from $6 to $22. But it's the food, not the price, that's the attraction here—it's *all* good!

The Seafare doesn't take reservations, and dress is casual, even though most nights during the season there's music for dancing. Incidentally, don't bother asking for the recipe of their famous she-crab soup—that's the one recipe they won't give out. Their selection of 62 fine wines and 22 international beers (manager Michael Kelly's pride and joy) is outstanding. They're open from 6 to 10 p.m. seven days a week.

Just back of the Seafare, with an entrance from U.S. 158 Bypass, is **The Seachest**, serving seafood, steak, and a daily special for lunch and dinner. Or you can take food out—a good idea for a special beach picnic or relaxing dinner back in your room.

A little farther south, next door to the Sea Oatel near the junction of U.S. 158 and U.S. 64, is another longtime Nags Head favorite, the **Dareolina Cove Restaurant** (tel. 441-7477). There are three dining rooms, but the one I especially like has wide windows opening to the Atlantic. It's a pleasant place during the day and downright romantic at night. Open from 7 a.m. to 10 p.m., the Dareolina serves all three meals and will fix box lunches for picnics or fishing trips. The menu is a long one and prices are moderate. As you might expect, fresh seafood is featured, along with prime steaks and home-baked pies and breads. My personal choice is the Nags Head crab (served on avocado halves). Dinner prices are in the $7 to $22 range. Like the Seafare, no reservations are required (at either place, you'll wait no more than 15 to 20 minutes). Closed mid-November to mid-March.

Dinner at **A Restaurant by George**, Milepost 11, Nags Head, NC 27959 (tel. 441-4821), is a real treat. In an elegant East Indian setting, gourmet dishes are brought to table by attentive, well-trained waiters. Prices are surprisingly moderate in light of both food and service, ranging from $9 to $20 (there's a children's menu with lower prices). Open only from mid-March through October, hours are 5:30 to 9:30 p.m. Monday to Wednesday, 5:30 to 10 p.m. Thursday to Saturday, and 5:30 to 9 p.m. on Sunday.

There's a very good restaurant over at **Wanchese** (that's the south end of Roanoke Island), serving the freshest seafood, steaks, and chicken at moderate prices, and overlooking the harbor. **Fisherman's Wharf** (tel. 473-5205) also has a connected retail seafood market. Hours here are 11 a.m. to 3 p.m. for lunch, 5 to 9 p.m. for dinner, and it's closed Sunday.

At Hatteras

The **Channel Bass**, on N.C. 12 at Hatteras (tel. 986-2250), has a clam chowder that will have you calling for seconds. In fact, all their seafood is fresh and cooked to perfection. The menu is semi à la carte, and dinner can run as low as $6 or as high as $15. It's closed from December 1 through March 10, open 5 to 10 p.m. the rest of the year (5 to 9 p.m. on Sunday).

At Ocracoke

The **Island Inn**, P.O. Box 7, Ocracoke Island, NC 27960 (tel. 919/928-4351), has been a part of the island since 1901, when it was built as an Odd Fellow's Lodge and housed the first public school on its ground floor. Over the years, it has been moved across the street, served as a private home, been converted to a small inn, played host to naval officers during World War II as their Officers' Club, had wings added to accommodate more travelers, and wound up under the capable management of one native and another confirmed island lover. Larry Williams (he's the native) and his partner Foy Shaw have refurbished the rooms with plain but comfortable furnishings, and opened a restaurant that's earned an enviable reputation all along the Outer Banks. During the summer, it's open from 7 a.m. to 9 p.m., serving all three meals at moderate prices. Breakfast runs from $1.65 to $2.50 (and it's an islander's breakfast—hearty); lunch (mostly salads and sandwiches) from $1.65 to $5; and dinner—where almost anything that comes from the sea is served up, with sauteed crabmeat, clam chowder, and an enormous seafood platter sharing honors—from $3.75 to $8. This is fishhouse eating as it should be, and if you find a soul response to the little fishing village, you can stay over here for $28 to $50.

THINGS TO SEE AND DO: The Nags Head area has more than its share of things to keep you occupied when not on the beach, and the Outer Banks hold their own special appeal. For sightseeing particulars, contact the **Outer Banks Chamber of Commerce,** P.O. Box 90-D, Kitty Hawk, NC 27949 (tel. 919/261-2626).

In and Near Nags Head

A little to the north, on U.S. 158 Bypass, at **Kill Devil Hills,** the **Wright Brothers National Memorial** is open to the public at no charge. Both the hangar and Orville and Wilbur's living quarters have been restored, and the visitor center holds a replica of that first airplane, as well as exhibits that tell the story of the two brothers who came here on vacations from their Dayton, Ohio, bicycle business to turn their dream into reality. It's an inspiration to see where they worked while you listen to the drone of modern airliners as they fly over this place where it all began.

From Whalebone Junction, U.S. 64-264 leads to **Roanoke Island** and the village of **Manteo.** Four miles west, you'll reach **Fort Raleigh National Historic Site,** where the old fort has been excavated and reconstructed just as it stood in 1585. The **visitor center** (tel. 919/261-2626) is a fascinating first stop, and they'll arrange guided tours by appointment. It's open from 8 a.m. to 8 p.m. from mid-June to September 1, closing at 4:30 p.m. the rest of the year.

It is here, where it all happened, that Joe Layton's production of Paul Green's moving drama, *The Lost Colony,* is presented in the **Waterside Theater,** Fort Raleigh National Historic Site, Manteo NC 27954, Monday through Saturday at 8:30 p.m. from mid-June to late August. It's been running since 1973 (this country's first outdoor drama), and leaves you with a very real sense of what life was like for that courageous little band. The **Elizabethan Gardens** nearby, as well as the Tudor style of auxiliary buildings, remind all of us that this was the first connection between Elizabethan England and what was to become the United States of America. All seats for the outdoor drama are reserved (P.O. Box 40, Manteo, NC 27954; tel. 919/473-2127) and cost $6 for adults, $3 for those under 12). There's a $1.50 charge to enter the gardens (tel. 473-3234), and children under 12 go in for free.

About an hour and a half away from Nags Head (take U.S. 64, turn right at N.C. 37, then left when you reach N.C. 32), a later phase of this country's history is preserved at **Edenton,** a lovely old town whose streets are lined with homes built by the planters and merchants who settled along the Albemarle Sound. The women of Edenton held their own Tea Party in 1774, the first recorded instance of American women taking a purely political action. Stop by the **Barker House** on South Broad Street (signs are posted throughout the town) for walking-tour directions at the visitor center and museum. They also issue a guidebook that tells the story of the buildings open to the public as well as many of the private homes that are of historical significance.

Along the Outer Banks

The Outer Banks Chamber of Commerce has a **visitor center** both at **Kitty Hawk** and at **Bodie Island Lighthouse** (eight miles south of the intersection of U.S. 158 and U.S. 64), where you can pick up pamphlets and nature trail walking-tour directions, and do look for the "Cape Hatteras Visible Shipwrecks" booklet that tells you where to look for the remains of wrecked ships along the beaches (they appear and disappear with shifting tides and sands).

Turn left off N.C. 12 about eight miles south of U.S. 158 to reach **Coquina Beach,** where there are bath shelters, lifeguards (from mid-June to Labor Day), picnic shelters, and beach walks guided by National Park Service naturalists.

Farther south, across **Oregon Inlet** (there's a bridge), the **Pea Island Wildlife Refuge** attracts birdwatchers from all over the country to see the snow geese which winter here and wading shore and upland birds in the summer months. There's a parking area and overlook.

All along N.C. 12, you'll see places to pull off and park to reach the beaches, which are hidden from view by huge protective sand dunes. A word of warning: *Don't* try to park anywhere else—the sands are very soft and it's easy to get stuck!

There are also **campgrounds** at various spots, but you should know in advance that they're flat, sandy areas with no shade and that you'll need tent stakes longer than you'd normally use. And no hookups are provided. Sites are on a first-come, first-served basis, and the maximum stay is 14 days from May 25 through September 10. Fees are $6 a night except at Ocracoke, where it's $3.

For private campgrounds in the area, which do have hookups, call the Chamber of Commerce at 919/261-2626 and they will supply full information.

Whether you're camping or just stopping at the beaches where there are no lifeguards, you should always keep in mind that tides and currents along the Outer Banks are *very* strong and ocean swimming can be dangerous at times.

When you get to **Buxton,** turn left off N.C. 12 to see the **Cape Hatteras Lighthouse**—and if you're the hardy type, climb those 268 steps for a really smashing view of the coastline. Its rotating duplex beacon has a 1000-watt lamp in each side, and the 250,000 candlepower is visible 20 miles.

The little village of **Hatteras** exists now, as it has from the 1700s, as a fishing center, and there are large commercial and sport fleets that operate from its docks and marinas. In the spring and fall, the boats bring in catches of sea trout, king and Spanish mackerel, bluefish, red drum, and striped bass, and in summer most of the action is offshore, where blue marlin and other billfish are in plentiful supply. Even if you're not fishing yourself, it's fun to watch the boats come in between 4 and 6 p.m. And if you'd rather be one of those coming in than a bystander, the **Outer Banks Chamber of Commerce,** P.O. Box 90-D, Kitty Hawk, NC 27949 (tel. 919/261-2626), can supply a list of charter boats available and fishing information.

From Hatteras, a free auto ferry crosses the inlet to **Ocracoke** in 40 minutes. Especially during the summer peak tourist season, however, be prepared to wait in line to board the ferry.

Ocracoke has shown up on maps as far back as the late 1500s, when Sir Walter Raleigh's Roanoke Island party made a landfall here. It is rumored to have been Blackbeard's sailing headquarters and it was definitely his downfall. That wily pirate—who would braid pieces of hemp dipped in tallow into his long black beard and set them afire as he sailed into battle against merchant ships—made his peace with the Crown in 1712, receiving a full pardon from the king. Then, pretending to settle down to a peaceful life in the little town of Bath, he worked hand in glove with Gov. Charles Eden and Tobias Knight, the secretary of the colony, to go right on preying on ships from the Caribbean to the Virginia Capes. That fearsome head ended up, however, in 1718 adorning the prow of a sloop commanded by Lt. Richard Maynard, of the British Royal Navy, after he had engaged the pirate in a bloody duel in Ocracoke Inlet and captured his ship and crew. Maynard then sailed back to Virginia displaying his trophy to let ships along the coast know that the sea lanes were safe once more. Tales persist to this day of treasure stashed away or buried along the coast of North Carolina, but none has ever been found, and it's far more likely that Blackbeard sold his spoils quickly and squandered the proceeds.

When Ocracoke Island was isolated from the mainland and few visitors came by boat, as many as a thousand wild ponies roamed its dunes. Where they came from is uncertain, whether from shipwrecks, early Spanish explorers, or from original English settlers. At any rate, as more and more people traveled to and from the island, more and more ponies were rounded up, shipped to the mainland, and sold. The remnants of the herd—about a dozen—now live on a range seven miles north of Ocracoke village, where the National Park Service looks after them.

In a quiet little corner of Ocracoke Island, there's a bit of England, the **British Graveyard** that holds four British navy seamen whose bodies washed ashore when H.M.S. *Bedfordshire* was torpedoed offshore by a German submarine in 1942. It is leased by the British government, but lovingly tended by townspeople.

Ocracoke village has seen some changes since World War II, when the U.S. Navy dredged out Silver Lake harbor (still called "Cockle Creek" by many natives) and built a base here. They also brought the first public telephones and paved roads. In spite of the invasion of 20th-century mainland improvements, Ocracoke is essentially what it has always been—a fishing village whose manners and speech reflect 17th-century ancestors. It is by far the most picturesque spot on the Outer Banks.

To reach North Carolina's more southerly beaches, there's a ferry from Ocracoke to **Cedar Island.** Not only is there a toll; you have to make a reservation for the two-hour-and-ten-minute trip! If you're leaving from Ocracoke, you must call within 30 days of departure (919/928-3841) and reserve space on one of the scheduled sailings; coming from Cedar Island, call 919/225-3551. The fare is $10 per car and occupants, $2 for bicycle and rider, and $1 for pedestrians. It's a wonderful, semiocean voyage on boats with names like *Pamlico, Silver Lake,* and *Sea Level,* manned by natives of the region whose creed is friendliness.

2. Morehead City and Atlantic Beach

From the Cedar Island ferry landing—where, incidentally, the **Pirate's Den Restaurant** at the **Driftwood Motel** serves very good food at moderate prices, if you hit at eating time—it's almost a two-hour drive south to Morehead City and Atlantic Beach. Not that the distance is that long, it's just that the two-lane highway winds and curves through historic old fishing towns like

Atlantic and Sealevel, under huge old water oaks hung with Spanish moss, emerging at intervals for long, straight patches of marshy savannahs of sea grass: it altogether discourages hurrying along.

Atlantic Beach is the oldest of the resorts on a 24-mile stretch of **Bogue Banks,** and most North Carolinians use the name Atlantic Beach to include the newer vacation centers of Pine Knoll Shores, Indian Beach, Emerald Isle, and Salter Path. The long, thin island began to develop back in 1927 when the first bridge was built across Bogue Sound to Morehead City, and it is now one of the state's most popular coastal areas, with fishing festivals and tournaments in the early spring and late fall making it virtually a year-round resort.

Morehead City, which has been an important port for oceangoing vessels since 1857, is the world's largest tobacco export terminal. Just across the sound, **Beaufort** (pronounced "BO-fort") is a quaint old seaport that seems frozen in time, with narrow streets lined by white frame houses built when the town was young (it goes all the way back to 1709) in a distinctive, almost West Indian, style. It was once, believe it or not, a whaling center.

Less than 50 miles inland, **New Bern** was the provincial capital for several years. Swiss colonists gave it its name, perhaps in a fit of homesickness. When William Tyron was royal governor, he built a splendid "palace" here, considered at the time the "most beautiful building in the New World." Both the palace and the gardens around it have been restored to their former splendor.

But overshadowing everything else, the ocean is the focal point in the area. There is an almost complete preoccupation with fishing and water sports, with historic sites sort of thrown in as a bonus for the tourist, who will have come, the natives have no doubt, to enjoy the sea.

WHERE TO STAY: There are excellent motels spread up and down Bogue Banks, and like the natives, I'll use "Atlantic Beach" as a catch-all name.

The **Islander Motor Inn** at Emerald Isle, P.O. Box 1035, Swansboro, NC 28584 (tel. 919/354-3464), has 80 rooms directly on the ocean and has become one of the most popular motels on the island. Its swimming pool sits right at the edge of a broad sand beach, and there's a sundeck with comfortable lounging chairs. The rooms, some with kitchenettes, are easily accessible to pool, beach, and restaurant. Maynard Hicks and his son Steve (owners and managers) will help arrange charter fishing or golf at the Star Hill Golf and Country Club. There's a lounge with entertainment and dancing on weekends. Oils and watercolors by local artists are on sale at Islander Arts, Ltd., a gallery owned and operated by the Hicks family. The restaurant here has gained a well-earned reputation as one of the better places to eat in eastern North Carolina, and their Sunday buffet has a large local patronage (see "Where to Eat"). From April 1 through Labor Day, doubles start at $47, dropping after Labor Day.

At Atlantic Beach proper, and also directly on the ocean, the **Oceanana Resort Motel,** P.O. Box 250, Atlantic Beach, NC 28512 (tel. 919/726-4111), completely won me over as the perfect family vacation "home." There are so many extras here that it's hard to know where to start listing them. For starters, there's a free fishing pier for guests. Then, to make it easy for fishermen to turn the day's catch into the evening meal, there's a huge bin out by the pool that holds charcoal, grills, firestarter, and even ketchup and mustard (not for fish—they're for the hot dog/hamburger crowd). And there's never a charge for any of them. Picnic tables are right there also to make outdoor eating a pleasure. For the small fry, there's a playground with an attractive assortment of play equipment (like the pirate's lookout tower, swinging bridge, and pioneer wagon). For all ages, the semiweekly watermelon party out by the pool is a festive occasion, and you just have to see the free tropical breakfast spread under an open poolside pavilion to believe it—more than 15 fresh fruits! It's served every morning from 8 to 10 a.m. While the motel has no restaurant of its own, there is a grill for fast-order foods out by the fishing pier, and guests have charge privileges at the **Man-Chun House** just across the highway (which, by the way, serves the best Chinese food this side of New York, as well as a wide selection of American dishes). Every room has a refrigerator, some stoves. And, oh, yes, I forgot to mention that those portable grills may be brought to the lawn area in front of your room (but not on upper-floor decks) to cook dinner right at your front door. Doubles start at $45 from May 20 to Labor Day, then drop.

A.B. Cooper, the owner-manager, tells me that reservations are necessary at least a month in advance—people keep coming back each year and the place stays pretty well booked. And that's been going on so long, over 40 years, that he keeps a "growing scale" posted to measure the height of children who come each year. It really is a super vacation spot, even if the only "family" you bring along is yourself.

Facing 1000 feet of broad ocean beach, the **John Yancey Motor Hotel,** P.O. Box 790, Atlantic Beach, NC 28512 (tel. 919/726-5188), has more than 95 rooms, a pool, and nearby golf and tennis privileges. I find this chain's rooms much more spacious than most, and the rates modest. Doubles during the peak season are $60. From Labor Day to April 15, they drop considerably.

For a very comprehensive listing of motels, restaurants, and attractions, write the **Carteret County Chamber of Commerce,** P.O. Box 1198, Morehead City, NC 28557 (tel. 919/726-6831), and ask for their free "Accommodations Directory."

Campgrounds

The **Salter Path Campground** on Salter Path Road, P.O. Box 721, Morehead City, NC 28557 (tel. 919/247-3525), overlooks the ocean on one side, Bogue Sound on the other. There are full hookups, boat ramps, bathhouses, a playground, and sailboat rentals. Rates are $9 and up.

Also on Salter Path Road, the **Arrowhead** has showers, a store, pier fishing, a playground, drive-through waterfront sites, and golf nearby. Mail address: Rt. 1, Box 792, Morehead City, NC 28557 (tel. 919/726-7974). Rates begin at $9.

WHERE TO EAT: The **Islander Motor Inn's** restaurant at Emerald Isle, P.O. Box 1035, Swansboro, NC 28584 (tel. 326-5121), has become such a favorite of North Carolinians who summer at Atlantic Beach that it's not unusual to find a fall Sunday dinner buffet crowd made up largely of people who live inland but who have made it the focal point of a day's outing. And I must say that the spread justifies the drive—seven or eight meats (including seafood, of course), just as many fresh vegetables, several soups, a full salad bar, and a dessert selection that outdoes itself. It's served every Sunday during the summer from noon to 8 p.m. and costs about $10, less for children. There's a Sunday breakfast buffet from 7 to 11 a.m. Other days, there's continuous service from 7 a.m. to 10 p.m. Seafood is a specialty, but there are such old-time southern favorites as country fried chicken, ham steak, and pork chops with applesauce. You can buy their homemade chicken and rice or vegetable soup by the quart to take out.

The oldest restaurant on the strand, called simply **A & Frances** (it's up the beach at Salter Path; tel. 247-3666), started when "A" (that's all he's ever called) Guthrie and his wife, Frances, began cooking early meals for fishermen who came here before the place began to develop as a resort. They owned one of the few service stations and sold live bait on the side. Frances did the cooking, but if early risers were up and about before she was, they simply came in the door (left open for their convenience), turned on the grill, cooked their own breakfast, and left the money for food and bait in an old cigar box on the counter. When business grew, they filled in the grease pit and built a diner. From that simple beginning, the A & Frances has expanded to five dining rooms that will accommodate 300 people—and during peak season, reservations are absolutely necessary between 6 and 9:30 p.m. Travelers have carried word of the good eating as far as Hawaii and Alaska, and vacationers are constantly dropping in from all over the country to try dishes they've been told about.

Frances is disabled now, and there are some eight cooks, including Lillian and Gail, who've been with them since those first growing years. It's not a fancy place, but has a plain, no-nonsense look that somehow denotes a good seafood house. There's an oyster bar and a take-out service. "A" closes the place down for the month of December, but it is open 6:30 a.m. to 9:30 p.m. the rest of the year. Prices are in the $4 to $8 range for most dishes (and those I sampled certainly deserved their excellent reputation), with combination plates running as high as $9.95.

In **Morehead City**, Mrs. Russell Willis has been serving the public since 1952 at **Mrs. Willis Restaurant** on N.C. 70A, P.O. Box 1646, Morehead City, NC 28557 (tel. 726-3741). There's seafood, as you'd expect in this fishing center, but in addition, you'll find pit barbecue and choice charcoal steaks on the semi à la carte menu, at prices that start at $3.50 and go up to $14. It's a cozy place, with a fireplace, background music, and very friendly service. Open from 11:30 a.m. to 10 p.m.

Less than 20 miles south of Morehead, there are two eating places worth looking up. The **T & W Oyster Bar and Restaurant**, Hwy. 58, Star Rt., Box 74-A, Swansboro, NC 28584 (tel. 326-5101), looks like a country roadhouse from the outside, but inside, the sloping, beamed ceiling and two large dining rooms, each with a fireplace, have a simplicity bordering on sophistication. Seafood is featured, reservations aren't necessary, and dress is casual. Prices for a regular dinner are $5 to $5.50, seafood combination plates run $6 to $8 depending on the assortment you wish to order. The oyster bar is very popular here, with a half-dozen on the half shell costing only $1.50 (a fact that made me cringe when I remembered New York prices). And they sell steamed oysters and clams by the half-*peck* ($4.50). It isn't hard to find. Just take N.C. 24 south from Morehead City, turn right on N.C. 58, and T & W is about five miles down the road. It opens at 5 p.m. and closes around 10 p.m. Monday through Saturday; on Sunday it's open from noon to 10 p.m.

THINGS TO SEE AND DO: Beach activities, naturally, are the top attraction along the coast. And fishing is especially good here—the Gulf Stream brings in blue marlin, tarpon, and other prizes in addition to inshore fish. There are some 80 miles of surf in this area and 400 miles of protected waterways. If you're a boat owner, there's an excellent marina on **Harkers Island**, Calico Jack's Marina (tel. 919/728-3575). And if you don't have your own boat, there's a ferry that leaves from Calico Jack's Marina for Cape Lookout (a 35-minute trip) between April and December for a day of surf fishing or beachcombing (for details, write: Superintendent, Cape Lookout National Seashore, P.O. Box 690, Beaufort, NC 28516). The fee is modest, and once at the cape, you can use the jitney service that roams up and down the sands to move fishermen from one spot to another. Bring a picnic and your own water supply. I love the "get-away-from-it-all" island atmosphere, and it's perfect for anyone who likes sailboats, lots of sun, and miles and miles of sand beach. Incidentally, the unique diamond-patterned lighthouse has stood here since 1859.

If you want to charter a boat or join a charter group to get at some of that Gulf Stream fishing, contact the **Charter Boat Booking Service,** P.O. Box 397, Atlantic Beach, NC 28512 (tel. 919/726-3550).

When you begin to feel a bit waterlogged, plenty of sightseeing is within easy reach. For instance, down at the very tip of **Bogue Island** (you're on it if you stay at Atlantic Beach) sits old **Fort Macon,** a Civil War landmark now restored and open to the public at no charge. The jetties (designed by Robert E. Lee), moats, gun emplacements, and dungeons make up terrific exploring territory. The museum is quite good, though small, and the public beach has bath houses, a snackbar, and lifeguards.

A trip to **Beaufort** is—that overworked phrase—really a "trip back in time." North Carolina's third-oldest town, it dates back to 1713 and still reflects its early history. There are two 200-year-old houses and more than a hundred that are over 100 years old along the narrow streets. The old graveyard (still called the "Burying Ground") positions its occupants facing east so they will be facing the rising sun on "Judgment Morn"; and it holds the remains of a British officer who wanted to be buried with his boots on, so was lowered into the grave in a standing-up position. The earliest markers that are still legible are dated 1756, and the **Beaufort Historical Association** in the 1825 Josiah Bell House, 138 Turner St. (tel. 728-5225) will furnish a map of the cemetery. The last weekend in June, Beaufort holds an **Old Homes Tour** and a reenactment of the Pirate Invasion of 1747. Any time, you can stop by the Historical Association for self-guiding tour maps to **Beaufort Restoration,** a recreated waterfront village with an apothecary shop, doctor's office, old jail, and the headquarters of the association. And don't miss the **Hampton Mariners Museum,** at 120 Turner St. It's state-owned and free.

New Bern, a little inland on U.S. Bus. 70 and U.S. 17, was once the capital of North Carolina when it was a royal colony. The 48-room **Tryon Palace,** 613 Pollock St., built as both the capitol and residence for the royal governor, has been authentically restored and beautifully furnished. It's easy to see, walking through the elegant rooms, why this mansion was once called the most beautiful in America. It was built in 1767–1770; then the main building burned in 1798. After that, it lay in ruins until the restoration in 1952–1959. The handsome grounds and gardens surrounding Tryon Palace are designed in 18th-century style. Two other exhibition landmarks in the 13-acre Tryon Palace complex are the **John Wright Stanly House** (1780), a sophisticated late-Georgian-style mansion, with town house gardens, and the **Stevenson House** (1805), built by a sea captain and noted for its rare Federal antiques. Costumed hostesses guide tours Tuesday through Saturday from 9:30 a.m. to 4 p.m. (from 1:30 to 4 p.m. on Sunday). Closed on Monday (except Easter Monday, Memorial Day, Labor Day) and Thanksgiving Day, December 24 to 26, and New Year's Day. General Admission (good for all tours, the landmarks, and the gardens) is $6 for adults, $2 for children through high school (tickets for individual attractions and gardens only are available). Historical dramas supplement the regular hostess interpretation during the summer months. Special events, including candlelight tours of the complex, are held at Christmas and other seasons.

The **New Bern Firemen's Museum,** 420 Broad St. (tel. 637-3105), is 2½ blocks from the Tryon Palace Restoration and Gardens Complex. Firefighting equipment dating back to the early 19th century, memorabilia from the mother city of Bern, Switzerland, and Civil War artifacts make this a memorable, small museum. Admission is 75¢ for adults, 25¢ for children. Open Tuesday through Saturday from 9:30 a.m. to 5 p.m. (on Sunday from 1 to 5 p.m.).

Historic **Christ Episcopal Church, First Presbyterian Church,** and **National Cemetery** are among the many sites that may be visited in old New Bern. There are over 150 18th- and 19th-century structures in New Bern listed on the National Register of Historic Places. For full details and self-guided walking tours, contact the Chamber of Commerce, 211 Broad St., P.O. Drawer C, New Bern, NC 28560 (tel. 919/637-3111).

3. Wilmington and Wrightsville Beach

Down near the southern end of North Carolina's coast is Wilmington, a city that has figured prominently in the state's history since 1732. Known first as New Carthage, then New Liverpool, New Town, and Newton, in 1739 it was given its present name in honor of the Earl of Wilmington. Technically, it isn't even on the coast—it's inland a bit at the junction of the Cape Fear River's northeast and northwest branches. And given the treacherous shoals that guarded the mouth of the Cape Fear when explorers first arrived in 1524, it's a wonder upriver Wilmington ever developed into an important port. But its protected riverfront site gave access to a valuable waterway for the movement of goods to and from Europe during colonial days, and since then the town has grown steadily as a commercial shipping center.

The first English settlers, from the Massachusetts Bay Colony, actually landed on the west bank of the river in 1662, and they were followed shortly by another group from Barbados. But they suffered mightily from Indian conflicts and from virtual abandonment by England. Pirates roamed the river freely and there wasn't much of a settlement until Brunswick Town was founded about 16 miles south of Wilmington in 1725 and a fort built to guard the passageway up Cape Fear. Soon surrounded by large, thriving plantations (some of them still intact today), Brunswick prospered until the British tried to destroy it by fire in 1776. It never really recovered, and it ceased to exist as a town about 1830, becoming a part of the landholdings of Orton Plantation until it was named a State Historic Site in this century.

Wilmington, too, played a part in the Revolution. In 1765, eight years before the Boston Tea Party, patriots here refused to allow the unloading of stamps to implement the infamous Stamp Act and forced the resignation of the stamp master. But in 1780, the city fell to Lord Cornwallis and he headquartered in a house (still standing) all that winter before leaving for Yorktown and ultimate defeat.

This was one of the principal ports of the Confederacy during the Civil War, and many blockade runners, who eluded both northern ships that patrolled the coastline and the Cape Fear shoals to bring in supplies to the South, found a home berth here. So important was Wilmington that Fort Fisher, on the eastern shore of the river, sustained one of the heaviest bombardments of the war, falling just 90 days before the Confederacy met defeat.

During both World Wars, Wilmington was a major port for the exportation of naval stores. Today, the river is busier than ever with industrial shipping, and the town has become an important rail center as well.

The city holds on to its history in the visible remnants that are lovingly restored and maintained. All those exciting events from the past seem very close to the present when you walk through the old residential section of town (now an official "Historic Area"), around the grounds of Orton Plantation, among the excavated foundations of Brunswick Town houses, or examine blockade runner relics at Fort Fisher. And just a hop, skip, and a jump away over on the coast, Wrightsville Beach (a family-oriented resort for generations) is the perfect place from which to explore the whole region—in between swimming, beachcombing, fishing, sailing, or just plain loafing, that is.

WHERE TO STAY: The **Greater Wilmington Chamber of Commerce,** 514 Market St., P.O. Box 330, Wilmington, NC 28402 (tel. 919/762-2611), will do more than just send you their "Accommodations Guide." If you're in the market for an apartment or cottage for a week or more (a dollar-saving method of vacationing that's hard to beat), and will write them far enough in advance describing just what you have in mind, they'll circulate your requirements in a bulletin that goes to owners and managers in the area who will then contact you directly.

At the **Holiday Inn,** 1706 North Lumina Ave., Wrightsville Beach, NC 28480 (tel. 919/256-2231), all rooms have an ocean view, all have balconies or patios, and all are attractively furnished. Those which actually face the ocean are especially nice, with glass sliding doors opening directly to the beach on the first floor and individual balconies on upper levels. A large, oceanside pool has shade areas and a refreshment bar, and there's a wading pool for young children. The Port O'Call Lounge offers entertainment and dancing year round. Dinners in the charming dining room are good and moderately priced. Guests enjoy golf privileges at a nearby private course, and would-be sailors will find sailboat rentals available. The hotel will also arrange golf package weekends and charter-boat fishing trips. In fact, I found the staff here exceptionally friendly and helpful in all respects during my stay. Seasonal rates for doubles are $58 and up late March through June, lower other months. They've also instituted that very nice practice of giving a 10% discount to senior citizens.

About a mile down the beach, the seven-story **Blockade Runner Motor Hotel,** P.O. Box 555, Wrightsville Beach, NC 28480 (tel. 919/256-2251), has luxury rooms, oceanside pool, nightly entertainment during the summer, a playground for children, and sailboats for rent. The bright, cheerful dining room serves southern cuisine at moderate prices. Double rooms are $60 and up mid-May to mid-September, lower the rest of the year.

The **Waterway Motor Lodge,** as its name implies, is on the Intracoastal Waterway rather than the ocean. It's right at the bridge, about three-quarters of a mile from the beach (P.O. Box 545, Wrightsville Beach, NC 28480; tel. 919/256-3771). There's a pool, a playground, and a babysitter list. A moderately priced restaurant is three short blocks away, and the motel furnishes free morning coffee. Rates are $37 to $50 for doubles during peak season, somewhat lower during fall and winter.

Campgrounds

The **Wilmington Sarfari Campground,** 7415 Market St., Wilmington, NC 28405 (tel. 919/686-7705 on toll-free, 800/558-2954), sits on 43 wooded acres on U.S. 17. There's a pool, recreation room, playground, laundry, grocery store, and propane gas. Rates start at $8.50.

WHERE TO EAT: As is true of so many coastal towns, Wilmington's best dining spots are at the beaches or on its fringes, and you'll find more seafood spots (most of them excellent) than you'll have time to sample.

The one in-town exception listed here, **Tuesday's,** was the first in what has become a chain of unusual, fun places to eat (see the Winston-Salem listing, Piedmont section, for another), started a few years ago by Buddy Gerald when he expanded a very successful string of pizza parlors into restaurants with full meals in settings that are showcases for his collection of antiques. When you see a stagecoach in front of 4106 Oleander Dr. (tel. 791-4955), for example, you'll know you're at Tuesday's. And the inside is chock-full of such items as the old trolley car that used to run from Wilmington to Wrightsville Beach and, as is true in most of the restaurants, an old jail. My first reaction when I saw the Winston-Salem location was that the food probably wouldn't measure up in a place that puts so much emphasis on decor. Well, I was wrong! Everything from hamburgers to steaks is delicious, and each place has a salad bar that includes every ingredient you can imagine, and then some. Prices are moderate ($3 to $12) and the menu is extremely varied. Mr. Gerald obviously enjoys both his collection and his restaurants, and you will, too.

The **King Neptune** is right in the center of Wrightsville Beach at 11 North Lumina St. (tel. 256-2525), and is a very informal, very nautical place with two large dining rooms and a gift shop to one side. Fishnets, shells, reproductions of old pendulum clocks (which can be bought in the gift shop), and a mural of King Neptune riding a sea horse adorn the paneled walls. The menu announces that "It's fun to eat at the King Neptune," and indeed it is, for sometimes it seems that about half the permanent residents and almost all the tourists in town congregate here. The atmosphere is lively and the food is superb. You can probably guess what gets star billing, but there is also a good selection of beef and even a long list of pizza choices. Lunch prices can run anywhere from $2.50 (for a small pizza) to $13 (for a choice T-bone steak). Most dinner entrées on the à la carte menu are in the $5.95 to $12.95 range. Service is continuous from 11:30 a.m. to 11:30 p.m., and they don't accept reservations (except for large parties in the private room).

Right at the Wilmington edge of the Wrightsville Beach–Wilmington drawbridge (on your left if you're coming from the beach), is **The Bridge Tender,** Airlie Road on the Sound (tel. 256-4519). I found it the best possible way: someone told me about it! "It's reasonable," she told me, "yet has an elegant feeling, and it's relaxing to watch the boats go past and the bridge when it's raised." I found the Bridge Tender all of that, and in addition the food was just superb. Manager David Nye told me that Jim Wright, the young owner, purposely keeps the menu limited in order to serve top-quality meats and seafoods cooked by expert chefs. And it *is* limited in the number of items, but certainly not in imaginative preparation. There's an excellent Polynesian chicken, tender filets of chicken breast marinated in a special teriyaki sauce and broiled just right, and tender Alaskan King crab legs served on long-grain and wild rice with drawn butter. Dinner prices run $7 to $14, lower at lunch. And there's a very good salad bar (you serve yourself there with every dinner or lunch entrée). The walnut layer cake brought back fond memories of those my grandmother used to make; it's a very southern dessert and I've rarely run into it in northern climes. They're open seven days a week for lunch (11:30 a.m. to 2 p.m.) and dinner (5:30 to 11 p.m.). It's a good idea to reserve for dinner.

Everybody in the area knows and loves **The Raw Bar,** at 13 E. Salisbury St. at the beach, right where U.S. 74 meets the ocean. This highly informal and very often crowded restaurant serves oysters and clams, both on the half-shell and steamed, as well as delicious seafood platters, either broiled or fried. Prices range from downright inexpensive to moderate. This "drop-in" place is open from 5 to 10 p.m.

Sooner or later, you're bound to hear the name **Calabash** in connection with food. Well, that's a town about 35 miles south of Wilmington (almost to the South Carolina border, in fact) on U.S. 17 that's so small it wasn't even shown on state maps for years. What literally put it on the map is the cluster of about 20 seafood restaurants that vie with each other to serve the biggest and best platter of seafood at the lowest price. The 150 residents of this small village use family recipes handed down from generation to generation and last year they served 1½ *million* people, serving 668,000 pounds of flounder and 378,000 pounds of shrimp, to say nothing of tons and tons of oysters, scallops, and other fish. That's an impressive record, and although I found the Wrightsville Beach area more than adequate when it comes to food, a Calabash trip is an experience. Recommendations for specific restaurants? I wouldn't even try! And you won't need them—according to locals, you can't miss, no matter which one you choose.

THINGS TO SEE AND DO: If you've always yearned to skim over the water in a sailboat but never had the chance, Capt. Bill Baggett (officially, he's **Wrightsville Sound Sailing, Inc.,** Waynick Blvd.; tel. 256-3145) is just the man to make your vacation include a dream come true. He skippers the 30-foot ocean-cruising catamaran *Warrior,* and he'll take you on a two-hour ocean trip that includes several island calls or teach you to handle her yourself. Look for his office and dock directly across from the Blockade Runner Motor Inn at the south end of the beach.

And if the kids get a little tired of all that swimming, take a spin down N.C. 132 to **Carolina Beach** and the **Seashore Amusement Park,** where a ferris wheel, merry-go-round, moon rocket, bumper cars, kiddie boats, and other rides will give them a change of pace.

Before you begin any sort of sightseeing tour, I strongly suggest that you stop by the **Greater Wilmington Chamber of Commerce,** 514 Market St. (tel. 726-2611), to pick up their free brochures on the many attractions of Cape Fear County. There's a self-guided walking tour of historic Wilmington in great detail, giving background information on everything you'll want to see, including the **Cotton Exchange.** That's an in-town shopping center of malls, arcades, and courtyards in the old cotton exchange with its two-foot-thick brick walls and hurricane rods. The small shops and restaurants are a delight, and the wrought-iron lanterns and benches add to the charm of their setting. It's right on the riverfront, just across from the Hilton Inn, and there's an ample parking deck adjacent.

If you'd rather have a guide for that walking tour, they're available at **Thalian Hall** (Historic Wilmington Tours, 3rd and Princess Sts.; tel. 763-9328). Tickets are $5 for adults, $1 for students; children under six are free. Those prices cover an audiovisual orientation and admission to all buildings, as well as your guide.

In the **Historic Wilmington** old residential area, bounded roughly by Nun, Princess, Front, and 4th Streets, the **Burgwin-Wright House,** 224 Market St., was built in 1771 and used by Lord Cornwallis as his headquarters in 1781. It's a perfect, beautifully restored example of a colonial gentleman's town house. You can tour the interior from Tuesday through Saturday. Adults pay $2; children, 50¢.

Also at 3rd and Market is **St. James Episcopal Church,** a beautiful building erected in 1839 to replace the 1751 church which had been used by the British as a stable during the Revolution. The Spanish painting *Ecce Homo* which hangs inside was taken from a captured pirate ship in 1748 and has been estimated to be between 400 and 600 years old.

The **Governor Dudley Mansion** (tel. 762-2511) on the southwest corner of Front and Nun Streets is an imposing Georgian home built for North Carolina's first elected governor in 1825. It serves as headquarters for the Historic Wilmington Foundation these days, and you can tour the interior on Tuesday through Saturday, 10 a.m. to 5 p.m. Adults pay $1.50; children, 25¢.

These are only highlights—just walking the old tree-shaded streets is an exercise in imagination.

Outside Wilmington, take U.S. 76 toward the beach and watch for **Airlie Gardens.** Once the plantation home of a wealthy rice planter, Airlie is surrounded by huge lawns, serene lakes, and natural, wooded gardens that hold just about every kind of azalea in existence. Admission is $4 per person, $1.50 for children, and the gardens are open during daylight hours from early March until late fall. The blooms are at their height in the early spring, but even when they've faded, this is a lovely spot that will set you dreaming of Old South life.

Poplar Grove Plantation, a restored Greek Revival manor house and estate, is 18 miles northeast of town on U.S. 17 (tel. 686-0172). Outbuildings include a smokehouse and slave quarters, and there's a country store and tearoom. Guided tours are conducted (adults pay $2; under 12, 75¢) daily from 9 a.m. to 5 p.m., except for the month of February, when it's closed.

Greenfield Gardens, just off U.S. 421 South, is Wilmington's largest municipal park justly famous for its scenic millpond, a sunken garden of native North Carolina flowers, and the Venus fly trap, which is native to no other place in the world except this state. In the spring and summer, camellias, azaleas, and roses bloom in profusion, and the five-mile drive around Greenfield Lake is beautiful any time of the year.

Follow U.S. 421 South from the park and you'll reach **Fort Fisher,** which finally fell to Union forces during the Civil War after the heaviest bombardment of the war and the largest American land-sea battle prior to World War I. The museum holds relics of that era, as well as blockade runner mementos. The Visitor Center and Museum are open Tuesday through Saturday from 9 a.m. to 5 p.m., opening at 1 p.m. on Sunday; there's no charge.

Not far from Fort Fisher, a toll ($1.50 for car and passengers) ferry makes the half-hour crossing of the Cape Fear River and deposits you at the quaint little village of Southport. Turning north on N.C. 87, then left at N.C. 133, you'll reach **Old Brunswick Town Historic Site.** The excavated home foundations have been left as archeological exhibits, but there are displays that recreate colonial life here, and the walls of St. Phillip's Anglican Church are still partially standing. The visitor center is open from 9 a.m. to 5 p.m. Tuesday through Saturday, from 1 to 5 p.m. on Sunday, and there's no admission charge.

Orton Plantation, between Southport and Wilmington on N.C. 133, Winnabow, NC 28476 (tel. 371-6851), is a private residence and the mansion is not open to the public. But the magnificent gardens, bordered by long avenues of live oaks and planted with camellias, azaleas, and thousands of other ornamental plants, can be seen March through November (8 a.m. to 5 p.m.) for an admission of $4 ($1 for children six to 12).

Back at Wilmington, you'll see signs on U.S. 74 (it's also U.S. 17 and U.S. 76 at this point) leading to the **U.S.S. North Carolina Battleship Memorial** (tel. 762-1829). The ship, which was commissioned in 1941, is permanently berthed here as a memorial to the state's World War II dead. You can tour most of the ship, and the museum presents a pictorial history of the *North Carolina*'s Pacific campaigns. It opens daily from 8 a.m. to sunset, and costs

$2.50 for adults, $1 for children six to 11. From early June through Labor Day, there's a 70-minute Sound and Light show, "The Immortal Showboat," at 9 p.m. every night, at a cost of $2 for adults, $1 for children.

North Carolina's first battle of the Revolution took place 20 miles northwest of Wilmington (via U.S. 421 and N.C. 210) at **Moores Creek.** The battlefield is now a National Military Park, as well it might be, since the victory of local patriots squelched a Tory scheme to invade and seize all the southern colonies. The earthworks and bridge have been reconstructed, and there's a visitor center and museum.

Chapter VII

PIEDMONT NORTH CAROLINA

1. Raleigh, Durham, Chapel Hill
2. Winston-Salem
3. Pinehurst
4. Charlotte

PERHAPS NOWHERE IN THE SOUTH do the old and the new come together quite so dramatically as in that section of North Carolina that lies between the coastal plains and the mountains. The Piedmont, as this region is called, holds mementos of American history that predate the Revolution (it was in 1771 that some 2000 farmers of Alamance County organized to protest British taxation and were savagely subdued by a royal governor at the Battle of Alamance near Burlington) as well as the first nuclear reactor building in the country devoted exclusively to the peaceful use of the atom (on the North Carolina State University campus in Raleigh).

The contrast is especially marked in cities such as Winston-Salem, where the mammoth tobacco industry is represented by R. J. Reynolds Tobacco Company, manufacturers of several major cigarette brands and pipe blends, and the Joseph Schlitz Brewing Company produces over four million barrels of beer each year in one of the largest such plants under a single roof; while in another part of town the streets and buildings of Old Salem are perfectly restored to reflect the life of Moravians who planned the community in 1766.

The land itself is as varied in this region as the industry, agriculture, and recreation that utilize it. From the red clay hills around Raleigh and Greensboro, to the flat fields of tobacco, peanuts, and vegetables in the midlands, to the rolling sand dunes alive with long-leaf pines and peach orchards in the Sandhills farther south, there is a pleasant, ever-changing character to the landscape. Some of my most cherished childhood memories were formed against the background of wind softly sighing through those pines, and the white blossoms of dogwood growing wild in wooded stretches along the highways always reminded me of snowdrifts sprinkled among other just-greening trees in early spring. Azaleas, camellias, and a host of summer-blooming flowers add to the visual beauty of this part of the state.

Higher forms of education are also an important part of the Piedmont character, where the "Research Triangle" you'll run across so often in conversation and directions refers to Duke University in Durham, the University of North Carolina in Chapel Hill, and North Carolina State in Raleigh. Wake Forest University, founded in 1834 in the town of that name near Raleigh and relocated to the western edge of Winston-Salem in the 1950s, is another leading educational institution. And literally scores of small private colleges and junior colleges are located throughout the region.

For the visitor, the Piedmont has sophisticated entertainment in its cities, the simplicity of rustic, outdoor life in fishing camps along the Catawba, Cape Fear, and Neuse Rivers, the excitement of intramural collegiate sports competitions, and the challenge of some of the world's greatest championship golf courses. Throw in sightseeing trips that will delight any history buff, and you have in this one, 21,000-square-mile region much of the "variety" of that "Variety Vacationland" slogan.

1. Raleigh, Durham, Chapel Hill

RALEIGH: State government has been the principal business conducted in Raleigh since 1792, when it became the state's capital. A five-acre square that holds the State Capitol is the focal point for a cluster of state office buildings in the heart of the city. From it radiate wide boulevards and lovely residential streets shaded by trees that frame some of the older homes. Downtown Raleigh has been transformed by a brand-new, $2-million mall, where trees and fountains and statuary create a parklike shopping oasis from the Capitol to the Civic Center. No fewer than six college campuses dot the city streets with wide lawns and impressive brick buildings. The oldest, St. Mary's College, was founded in 1842, and the "youngest," North Carolina State University, in 1887. New suburbs and gigantic shopping centers dominate the outskirts, but they somehow escape the "little boxes" image of so much suburban construction, with nicely designed homes blending into a landscape that retains much of its original wooded character.

Raleigh has, of course, witnessed much of the state's history: it was the setting for fiery legislative debate just prior to the Civil War that led at last to North Carolina's secession from the Union in 1861 (the last southern state to pull out): it endured Union occupation by General Sherman in 1865; and it saw the west wing of its imposing Grecian Doric capitol building turned into a rowdy barroom by "carpetbagger" and "scalawag" legislators during Reconstruction days, its steps permanently nicked from whiskey barrels rolling in and out of the building. It was the stage on which Gov. Charles Aycock launched his campaign for education revival in the early 1900s, and from its state buildings has come strong support for industrial development that makes North Carolina one of the most progressive of the southern states.

All of this, plus the abundance of good accommodations, makes Raleigh the ideal base from which to explore the Triangle area—which is what we'll do here. Both Chapel Hill and Durham are within easy reach for day trips, and after a day of sightseeing, the capital city becomes an entertainment center for anything from smart, supperclub shows and dancing to Broadway theater to cultural events.

Where to Stay

If you're going first class or feel the need to splurge for a night or two and want a truly "southern" ambience, your best bet is the **Plantation Inn,** P.O. Box 11333 Raleigh, NC 27604 (tel. 919/876-1411), located in a restful, pine-wooded setting on U.S. 1 North, some five miles out of town. The main building, a colonial, white-columned structure, evokes visions of the Old South. And that legendary southern hospitality is embodied in a coffee bar which dispenses free cups 24 hours a day in the gracious lobby (sporting portraits of Robert E. Lee and Stonewall Jackson), which opens onto a terrazzo terrace overlooking the lake and wooded lawn. Rates for the large, handsomely furnished rooms begin at $45 for a double; and the tastefully appointed restaurant serves everything from a hamburger to a superb buffet at lunch or dinner featuring roast prime ribs of beef au jus at $15. There's live organ music during dinner hours, and the Carriage Club Lounge on the lake level of the main building is a pleasant before- or after-dinner retreat. This is a favorite of international business travelers, and you may well encounter an Arab executive in native dress or a Japanese technician and his family quartered here while looking for a permanent home. Because it is popular, it's advisable to reserve rooms at least three weeks in advance.

More centrally located, and a great local favorite, is the **Velvet Cloak Inn,** 1505 Hillsborough St. (tel. 919/828-0333), within a few blocks of both downtown and the North Carolina State University campus. A pseudo-New Orleans motif is carried out with wrought-iron balconies and in the room decor. There is an indoor swimming pool, and the Charter Room Restaurant is on the premises. Rates here range from $65 upward for doubles.

The **Holiday Inn North,** on U.S. 1 North, 2815 North Blvd. (tel. 919/872-7666), is an exceptionally nice member of this chain, having just added a new tower, renovated all older guest rooms, built a Holidome that encloses an indoor pool, Jacuzzi, mini-golf, and assorted games, all surrounded by an abundance of plants and trees and fountains. The new Syd's Holidome Restaurant serves all three meals, and there's dancing in Syd's Lounge every night except Sunday. Doubles here start at $55.

Raleigh has a **Days Inn,** 6329 Glenwood Ave. (tel. 919/781-7904), with this chain's usual spacious, well-appointed rooms. There's a pool, 24-hour restaurant, and cribs and cots are furnished at no charge. Doubles here are $30.88.

At the Raleigh-Durham Airport (2½ miles west of U.S. 70), the **Triangle,** P.O. Box 10951 Raleigh, NC 27605 (tel. 919/787-8121) has well-decorated rooms in a moderate price range. Beds here are extra-long, and a special feature is a wheelchair ramp for the disabled. There's a pool, and a 24-hour cafe is just a block away. Doubles start at $40.

The **Econo-Travel Motel,** 5110 Holly Ridge Dr. (tel. 919/782-3201) is right next door to a large shopping center. Rooms are especially nice for the budget price, and while there's no restaurant on the premises, there are an even dozen within a half-mile. Doubles run from $30 up.

Where to Eat

For dinner in an elegant setting (French provincial furnishings, gold-framed mirrors, candlelight and silk flowers on each table), do reserve at the **Scotch Bonnets Restaurant** in the Marriott Hotel, 4500 Marriott Drive (tel. 781-7000). The menu is continental, with emphasis on fresh seafood dishes such as stir-fried crab, scallops and shrimp with seasonal vegetables, or salmon poached or sautéed to perfection and served with a bearnaise sauce. For meat-eaters, there are steak, veal, and chicken offerings, as well, and each night there's a Chef's Special of the Day. Table d'hôte prices range from $10 to $19, and the freshly baked dessert soufflé comes compliments of the chef. To top off your dinner with an elegance that matches its setting, however, you really should order one of their luscious flambéed desserts (bananas Foster or baked Alaska, at about $7) and finish with one of the exotic coffees, prepared at your table from a tray of condiments such as chocolate bits, brown sugar, lemon rind, cinammon sticks, etc. There's a selection of five to choose from (cafe Amaretto, Irish coffee, cafe l'orange, etc.) at a cost of $3.50—and the presentation is as special as the final product, which is very good, indeed. Hours are 6 to 10:30 p.m. every night except Sunday.

For "country" rather than "elegant," there's **Allies**, 4600 Marriott Dr. (tel. 781-7000). With a comfortable and homey atmosphere (red-checked table-cloths, dim lights, etc.) and patrons dressed in casual attire, this is a place to relax and enjoy down-home specialties such as barbecued ribs at dinner, or sausage 'n biscuits at breakfast. All three meals are served, and prices are in the $4 to $6 price for breakfast, $4.50 to $8 for lunch, and $8 to $15 for dinner. Hours are 7 to 11 a.m., 11 a.m. to 2:30 p.m., and 5 to 11 p.m. every day of the week.

Edwina Shaw (who teaches French cooking, as well) is the moving force behind **Edwina's Cuisine** (with **O'Henry's Bar**) at 2929 Essex Circle (tel. 787-8660). O'Henry's is an old-fashioned room, dimly lit, with a piano player on Friday and Saturday nights. Edwina's Cuisine, however, has linen table cloths with silver place settings, brass chandeliers, and the look of a quiet little French restaurant. Burgers, quiche, and other light meals are served in the bar at moderate prices, but in the dining room, it's French cooking all the way, with specialties like shrimp served with freshly made angel-hair pasta and a champagne sauce or sautéed chicken in calvados. For $25, you can order the very special six-course French dinner, otherwise, dinner prices will run from $9 to $19 on the table d'hôte menu. Hours are 6:30 to 10:30 p.m. for the restaurant, 5 to 11 p.m. for the bar ('til 1 a.m. on Friday and Saturday).

The best description of the **Irregardless Cafe**, 901 W. Morgan St. (tel. 833-9920), is "earthy." No table cloths, a blackboard menu, posters on the walls, jazzy background music—and emphasis on health foods, with a marvelous selection of salads and yogurt made on the premises daily. You'll see all age groups here, from young children to retirees. Prices are in the $4.50 to $7 range, with some offerings as low as $2.50. Lunch is served Monday to Friday from 11:30 a.m. to 2 p.m., dinner Monday to Saturday from 6 to 10 p.m., and there's a 12:30 p.m. Sunday brunch. And there's entertainment nightly.

For the younger crowd (of any age), it's **Darryl's 1849 Restaurant**, N.C. 70 West (tel. 782-1849), **Darryl's 1906 Restaurant and Tavern** at 1906 Hillsborough St. (tel. 833-1906), or **Darryl's 1840 Restaurant** at 4309 Old Wake Forest Rd. (tel. 872-1840). All are rustic in atmosphere and feature first-rate

Italian dinners, a wide variety of sandwiches, beef ribs, and pizza. Beer comes by the mug or pitcher, cocktails are served, and prices are moderate. This is a popular chain, with branches in Durham, Greensboro, Greenville, Charlotte, and Winston-Salem.

About 12½ miles northwest on U.S. 70 West, you'll find the **Angus Barn** (tel. 787-3505), one of the best charcoal-broiled steak or choice ribs of beef places in these parts. The setting is rustic (it's a restored 19th-century barn), but you'll not feel like one of the "overalls" set here. Fireplaces add a grace note and the food is superior. Semi à la carte prices range from $9 to $20, with beer, wine, and cocktails available. It's open from 5:30 to 11:30 p.m. every day (closes at 10 p.m. on Sunday) and is well worth the drive. Better reserve.

Special Note: I've eaten barbecued pork in a lot of places, but nowhere on earth does it taste quite like that of Piedmont North Carolina. Slow-cooked in an open pit over hickory chips and basted all the while with a highly seasoned sauce, then finely chopped (no slabs of pork slathered with sauce, such as you get in New York, for instance), it is truly a food fit for kings. But you really have to know your cook, even in North Carolina, and almost every locality has a favorite. In Rocky Mount, it's **Bob Melton's;** in Wilson, it's **Parkers,** etc. Well, the word in Raleigh is that **Cooper's Barbecue,** 109 E. Davie St., is *the* place. My best advice is GO! Even if you're a fan of that Texas stuff, you'll leave Cooper's a convert. Prices are reasonable and portions are generous. One final word: Don't expect anything elegant by way of decor—part of the mystique of North Carolina barbecue is that it's always served in plain surroundings, with lots of hushpuppies and cole slaw. And that's what you'll find here.

For good food at truly budget prices, look for the **K & W Cafeteria** in the North Hills Shopping Center, about five miles out the U.S. 1/64 Bypass (tel. 782-0353), where lunch will run about $4, dinner no more than $5. Hours are 10:45 a.m. to 8 p.m.

There's nighttime entertainment and dancing at the **Hilton Inn,** 1707 Hillsborough St. (tel. 828-0811), every night except Sunday. Dancing every night except Sunday, also, at the Holiday Inn North, 2815 North Blvd. (tel. 872-7666). And the **Velvet Cloak Inn** has both entertainment and dancing except Sunday (1505 Hillsborough St.; tel. 828-0333). Check local newspapers for the current disco scene, which tends to change too frequently to report in this book.

The **Raleigh Little Theatre,** one of the best community playhouses in the country, presents Broadway productions (check local newspapers for current shows and prices), and during fall and winter months the **North Carolina Symphony** is heard at **Memorial Auditorium.** Nationally and internationally known concert artists also appear at the Auditorium during the season, and while most seats are sold on a subscription basis, it is sometimes possible to obtain single tickets.

Things to See and Do

For sightseeing brochures, maps, etc., write or go by the **Raleigh Chamber of Commerce,** 335 S. Salisbury St., Raleigh, NC 27602 (tel. 919/833-3005).

Besides sightseeing, which we'll get to in a minute, there are several recreational possibilities in the Triangle area. **William B. Umstead State Park,** N.C. 8, P.O. Box 130, Raleigh, NC 27612, halfway between Raleigh and Durham on U.S. 70, has camping (on a first-come, first-served basis) and picnicking facilities (for details call 787-3033). You can fish or just enjoy boating at the municipally owned and operated **Lake Wheeler,** five miles southwest of Raleigh on Rhamkatte Road, from 10 a.m. until sundown every day except Monday for a modest fee (phone 772-1173 for details).

Now, for the best possible tour of the capital city, your first stop should be the **Capital Area Visitor Center.** It's in a 1918 mansion called the Andrews-London House at 301 N. Blount St. (tel. 733-3456). It's open from 8 a.m. to 5 p.m. Monday through Saturday, 1 to 5 p.m. on Sunday, and they'll start you off with an orientation film, arm you with brochures and loads of background information, and coordinate walking or driving tours of the area.

The **State Capitol,** a stately Greek Revival structure (constructed 1833-1840), has been named a National Historic Landmark and is currently being refurnished to its 1840-1865 appearance. All state business was conducted here until 1888. The building now contains the offices of the governor and secretary of state as well as restored legislative chambers. Beneath the awe-inspiring 97½-foot copper dome, there's a duplicate of Antonio Canova's marble statute of George Washington, dressed as a Roman general. The Capitol, on Capitol Square, is open from 8 a.m. to 5 p.m. Monday through Saturday, 1 to 5 p.m. on Sunday, is free, and takes about 30 to 45 minutes to tour.

Across from the Capitol, on Bicentennial Plaza, the **Museum of Natural History** is so full of fascinating displays of the state's gems, gold nuggets, Indian artifacts, animals, and plants that you'll need at least an hour to explore its contents. There's even a bird hall and live snake collection. One of my favorites here is the whale fossil found near the center of North Carolina, evidence of a long-ago coastline quite different from that of today. There's no charge here, and it's open from 9 a.m. to 5 p.m. Monday through Saturday, 1 to 6 p.m. on Sunday.

The **Legislative Building,** on Jones Street between Wilmington and Salisbury Streets, is a striking contemporary building designed by Edward Durrell Stone, the same architect who drew plans for the Kennedy Center for the Performing Arts in Washington, D.C. Allow about 45 minutes to go through it, longer if you happen to hit there when the legislature is in session, since you'll be able to watch the proceedings. It's free and open from 8 a.m. to 5 p.m. Monday through Friday, 9 a.m. to 5 p.m. on Saturday, and 1 to 5 p.m. on Sunday.

Be sure and save a half hour or so to see the **Governor's Mansion** at 200 N. Blount St. You'll have to make an appointment through the visitor center, but the grand old Victorian home shouldn't be missed. It's built of North Carolina brick and wood, and although it was begun in 1883, the first occupant didn't move in until 1891. There's no charge for a look around.

At 109 E. Jones St., the state's history is pictured in relics of colonial, Revolutionary, and Civil War eras at the **North Carolina Museum of History,** which is also free to visitors. It closes on Monday, and opens 9 a.m. to 5 p.m. Tuesday through Saturday, 1 to 6 p.m. on Sunday, and you'll want to plan about an hour and a half here.

The **North Carolina Museum of Art,** which reopened in a spacious new building at 2110 Blue Ridge Blvd. in 1983, houses an important collection of European painting and sculpture. Among its works are Italian Renaissance and baroque paintings from the Samuel H. Kress collection. There are also American, 20th-century, ancient, African, Oceanic, and New World collections. Hours are 10 a.m. to 5 p.m., Tuesday through Saturday, 1 to 5 p.m. Sunday, and there's no admission charge.

One of North Carolina's three native sons who became president, Andrew Johnson, was born in a small cabin about a block from the capitol building. The 17th president's birthplace has been moved to **Mordecai Place** and is open to visitors.

And speaking of Mordecai Place, be sure to see the 1785 restored **Mordecai House** (it's at 1 Mimosa St. off Wake Forest Road). Five generations of one of North Carolina's oldest families lived here (until 1964, in fact), and the original furnishings give it a "lived in" look. There's no admission charge, although donations are accepted. A guide will show you around from 11 a.m. to 2 p.m. Tuesday through Thursday and 2 to 4 p.m. on Sunday.

Christ Episcopal Church, at 120 E. Edenton St., is a lovely Gothic Revival building which dates back to the 1840s. When Sherman's troops left town after occupying Raleigh and the state capitol building during the 1860s, they had so stripped the town that it was said the weathercock on this church's steeple was the only chicken left in town.

By contrast to all that history, the "age of the atom" is very much a part of the Raleigh scene, and you can visit the first college-owned reactor in the country on the North Carolina State University campus. Emphasis here is on *peaceful* utilization of atom-splitting. The university is on Hillsborough Street, and you can't miss it. Once on campus, ask for directions to the nuclear reactor building.

One final note about Raleigh: If you get there in mid-October, you're in luck, for the **North Carolina State Fair** is a real oldtime event that draws crowds from all over and is fun from one end of the fairgrounds to the other (they're located five miles west of town on U.S. 1). For exact dates the year you plan to come, contact: NC State Fair, 1025 Blue Ridge Blvd., Raleigh, NC 27607 (tel. 919/733-2145).

RESEARCH TRIANGLE PARK: By the time you leave Raleigh for Durham or Chapel Hill, you'll have seen highway signs pointing to the Research Triangle Park, which is located on 5200 acres in the center of a rough triangle formed by the three cities. While it doesn't qualify as a true "sightseeing" destination, it's worthwhile to turn off the highway and drive around, for this is one of the most unique research centers in the country. Some of our brightest scientific minds work here in an atmosphere that carries the "think tank" concept a step further to application of research principles to industry, environment, and government.

Some 26 institutions (including the Environmental Protection Agency, the National Institute for Environmental Health Sciences, the Burroughs-Wellcome Foundation, and IBM Corporation) represent a total investment of more than $250 million in projects underway, completed, or projected. The payroll (to more than 12,000 staffers) exceeds $170 million annually.

To reach the park, turn off the East-West Expressway from Raleigh to Durham onto N.C. 54—actually, you don't have to bother with highway numbers, the markers are that numerous and prominent.

DURHAM: A real-life "American dream" success story was played out in Durham back in the late 1880s, when Washington Duke walked 137 miles back to his farm after being mustered out of the Confederate forces at the end of the Civil War and took up life again as a tobacco farmer. That first year, he started grinding and packaging the crop to sell in small packets. Then, in 1880, Duke decided there was a future in the novelty "cigarettes" and set to work with his three sons to manufacture them on a small scale. By 1890, business had grown so that they formed the American Tobacco Company, and a legendary American manufacturing empire was underway. Durham, which was a small village when Duke came home from war, blossomed into an industrial city, taking its commercial life from the "golden weed." And it still does. From September until the end of December, tobacco warehouses ring with the chants of auctioneers moving from one batch of the cured tobacco to the next, followed by buyers who indicate their bids with nods or hand signals (remember that "Sold American" commercial back in the heyday of radio?). And there's a constant traffic all year of bright leaf tobacco coming into the city and cigarettes and pipe tobacco leaving it.

Even Duke University, the cultural heart of Durham, owes its life's breath to tobacco, for it was little noticed as Trinity College until national and international prominence came with a Duke family endowment of $40 million in 1924. Along with a change in name, the university gained a new West Campus, complete with massive Gothic structures of native stone, flagstone walks, and box hedges that would do justice to Oxford or Cambridge. Its Medical Center has become one of the most highly respected in the world.

Where to Eat in Durham

You'll find **Claire's Cafe and Bar,** 2701 Chapel Hill Rd. (tel. 493-5721), in a 1909 house that has been renovated to accommodate three dining rooms, with outdoor dining in the planning process. There's a nice selection of appetizers (try the fried eggplant sticks or mushrooms, both coated in beer batter), cheese and spinach pastries, salads, omelettes (including a creole shrimp creation)—all at *very* moderate prices—in the $4 to $6 range. Hours are 11:30 a.m. to 10 p.m. (with a 9 p.m. closing on Sunday and a late-night bar opening until 1 a.m. Thursday to Saturday, and food service until 1 a.m. on weekends).

Things to See and Do in Durham

Stop by the **Greater Durham Chamber of Commerce,** 201 N. Roxboro St, Northwestern Bank Bldg., Durham, NC 27701 (tel. 919/682-2133) for detailed sightseeing information.

Washington Duke's homestead, where it all began, has been named a State Historic Site and National Historic Landmark and you can visit the home, the original factory building, and farm. There's a visitor center and it's open at no charge from 1 to 5 p.m. Tuesday through Sunday. It's located on (what else!) Duke Homestead Road, half a mile north of I-85 and the Guess Road exit. While there, take time to go through the **Tobacco Museum,** which traces the history of tobacco from Indian days to the present.

To see today's counterpart of those early cigarette factories, take a 45-minute guided tour (it's free) through the **American Tobacco Company,** at 201 W. Pettigrew St. (tel. 682-2101 at least one day in advance). You'll see Tareytons, Pall Malls, Silva Thins, Icebergs, Carlton Filters, and Carlton Menthols being made and come away with a profound respect for Mr. Duke and his 1800s vision. Tours run by appointment only Monday through Friday.

The East and West Campuses of **Duke University** cover more than 1000 acres on the west side of the city, and it's a good idea to keep the car handy to drive from one "walking tour" to another. The **East Campus,** which was the old Trinity College, features Georgian architecture, and its red-brick and limestone buildings border a half-mile-long grassy mall. There's an excellent **Art Museum** on this campus, just off West Main Street, that's free (open 9 a.m. to 5 p.m. Tuesday through Friday, from 10 a.m. to 1 p.m. on Saturday and 2 to 5 p.m. on Sunday) and holds marvelous collections of classical art, Navajo rugs, and pre-Columbian, African, medieval, and Oriental art, and coins.

It's the **West Campus** (a short drive away on winding, wooded Campus Drive), however, that really steals the university show. Its Gothic-style buildings and beautifully landscaped grounds are nothing short of breathtaking. And the showplace of this showplace is **Duke Chapel,** which brings back memories of England's Canterbury Cathedral. James B. Duke felt strongly that religion should play a prominent part in university life, and the splendor of this chapel assures a religious emphasis at Duke. The bell tower of the majestic cruciform chapel rises 210 feet and houses a 50-bell carillon that rings out at the end of each work day and on Sunday. There's a half-million-dollar Flentrop organ with more than 5000 pipes (said to be one of the finest in the Western Hemisphere) in a special oak gallery, its case 40 feet high. Renowned organists perform at the console in public recitals on the first Sunday of each month.

It's impossible to describe the sheer beauty of the chapel's interior: 77 stained-glass windows light the long nave with soft shades of reds, blues, greens, and yellows, and highlight an ornate screen and carved oak choir stalls. Visiting hours are 8:30 a.m. to 5 p.m. daily, and there are interdenominational services every Sunday at 11 a.m.

The university's **Botany Department Greenhouses** (some 13 rooms of plants, both native and rare) are open to the public from 10 a.m. to 4:30 p.m. every day of the week and hold the most diverse collection of plants in the Carolinas.

The West Campus is also the setting of Duke's **Medical Center,** which has gained worldwide fame for its extensive treatment facilities and varied research programs.

To find out more about Duke, call the Special Events Office, 403 Union Tower (tel. 684-3710). They'll be glad to arrange special guided tours, and one I especially recommend is the **Sarah P. Duke Memorial Gardens,** a 55-acre garden on the West Campus that draws more than 100,000 visitors each year. This beauty spot lies in a valley bordered by a pine forest and features a lily pond, stone terraces, and a wisteria-draped pergola, with seasonal plantings that provide an ever-changing color scheme. It's open every day from 8 a.m. to 5 p.m. and is a good place to end a day of campus sightseeing.

Durham's **Museum of Life and Science,** 433 Murray Ave., is especially planned for children, but no matter what your age, I'll wager you'll be intrigued by the lifesize models of dinosaurs, live animals, and the three NASA spacecraft that trace an "evolutionary trail," highlighted by a large diorama of the Apollo 15 lunar landing site and a sample of moon rock from that site. The 78 acres also hold a wildlife sanctuary and a mile-long, narrow-gauge railroad. From Tuesday through Saturday hours are 10 a.m. to 5 p.m., from 1 p.m. on Sunday. Adults pay $2, for ages six to 12 it's $1, under-sixes and handicapped go in free.

CHAPEL HILL: The third point of the Triangle area is Chapel Hill, a small city that has managed to hold on to its "village" atmosphere in spite of a university that annually enrolls almost 20,000 students. Chapel Hill *is* the University of North Carolina, and it has been universally loved by graduates since 1795, when it was the first state university in the country. The 2000-acre campus holds 125 buildings, ranging from Old East, the oldest state university building in the country (its cornerstone was laid in 1793), to Morehead Planetarium, which was an astronaut-training center in the early days of manned space flights. And its history is as varied as its buildings. When the Civil War erupted, the student body was second only to Yale in size—until the fighting started and most of the undergraduates and faculty left for battlefields. Reconstruction finished its destruction and it closed down from 1868 to 1875.

Since its reopening, however, it has consistently been a leader in American education and a center of liberal intellectualism (rather surprising, since North Carolina is a generally conservative state). So strong is the attachment and affection of those connected with the university that more than once it and Chapel Hill have been described as "the southern part of heaven."

Chapel Hill's appearance may be village-like but its spirit is lively. Those ivy-covered brick buildings have nurtured such mavericks of the literary world as Thomas Wolfe and Paul Green (who wrote the first outdoor drama produced in the country). And the quiet, tree-lined streets lined with homes set in flower-bordered lawns have been "home" to some of the most innovative intellectuals America has produced.

Where to Eat in Chapel Hill

Restaurant La Residence, 220 W. Rosemary St. (tel. 967-2506), is in a 50-year-old residence surrounded by gardens. Each of the small dining rooms has its own decor, and the menu changes daily in order to utilize the freshest available ingredients (they get fresh mountain trout weekly, and if that's your weakness, call to see which day they expect it). The menu, while limited, is composed of exquisite—and delicious—creations which the chef boasts is "the most innovative food in the whole Triangle area." You might, for instance, order the chicken stuffed (under the skin) with spinach; or from July through September, North Carolina duck with blackberry sauce. As for desserts, don't pass up their homemade ice creams and sorbets, unless, that is, you yield to the temptation of white chocolate charlotte with raspberry sauce, or the cappuccino cheesecake. Dinner hours are 6 to 9:30 p.m., and it's best to reserve. As you might expect, there's an exceptionally fine (but limited) wine list. Prices for the table d'hôte dinner will run anywhere from $12 to $20.

Elegance in the modern vein best describes dining at the **Hotel Europa,** Europa Drive (tel. 968-4900 or 493-1414). In a setting of off-white, grays, pinks, beiges, and tan, the atmosphere is one of lighthearted luxury, with a distinctly French accent. An unusual feature of the hotel is its stained-glass elevator! Tea is served in the lounge/lobby every day from 3:30 to 5:30 p.m. and features the delicious homemade pastries for which they are locally famous. At lunch, there are light luncheon selections (like the lobster quiche) at moderate prices, as well as more substantial fare such as veal, beef, or seafood, most prepared in the French style (like the red snapper and oysters poached in chablis). The dinner menu is quite extensive, with specialties such as lobster and veal sautéed in a sherry sauce, a marvelous, herb-seasoned rack of lamb, or the roasted pheasant flamed in apple brandy. Prices are in the $10 to $20 range at dinner, lower for lunch, and if you just want a touch of elegance, drop in for breakfast, which will run $7 to $8. Hours are 6:30 a.m. to 10 a.m., 11:30 a.m. to 2:30 p.m., and 6:30 to 10:30 p.m. There's a Sunday brunch from 11 a.m. to 2:30 p.m.

The decor is Victorian at **Pyewacket's,** in The Courtyard, West Franklin St. (tel. 929-0297). The cozy lounge has comfortable couches and is dimly lit; there are two high-ceilinged rooms done in rust and brown, and the greenhouse dining room is windowed all around, filled with plants (no smokers allowed in this area). There's a nice selection of sandwiches, omelettes, salads, and desserts at lunch with prices that run from $2.50 to $6, and at dinner seafood and vegetable entrees are featured at prices of $4.50 to $12. A wide variety of coffees features espresso made in their own espresso machine. Hours are 11:30 a.m. to 1 a.m., Monday through Saturday.

"Natural" best describes the **Looking Glass Cafe,** University Square (tel. 929-0296)—in decor, food, and the people who run this bright and cheerful place. All walls but one are windowed, there's a slanted sun roof of white glass, and ferns hang from the windows. The menu is a light one, consisting of sandwiches (made from lovely fresh breads—including pumpernickle, rye, and sunflower!) burgers, pastas, and salads. Hours? 24! And breakfast is served through the night, from 11 p.m. to 11 a.m. Carrot cake is delicious and a local favorite, the house wine is Pricipato, and there are several brands of beer. On hand Thursday through Saturday nights is a local singer, who entertains from 11 p.m. to 2 a.m. Prices are amazingly low—$1.50 to $4.50—and there's a take-out service.

For something a little different, try the **Mariakakis Restaurant,** on U.S. 15–501 Bypass, across from the Holiday Inn (tel. 942-1453). The menu is not confined to foods from Greece, but includes those of Italy, Russia, France, Germany, Poland, Ireland, India, and the Middle East. Prices are moderate, and the restaurant's open for lunch and dinner. Hours are 11 a.m. to 11:30 p.m., Monday to Saturday, 4 to 8:30 p.m. on Sundays.

READER'S SUGGESTION: "In Chapel Hill, one of the best restaurants, food and dollarwise, is the **Hunan Restaurant** (Chinese), 132 W. Franklin St. (tel. 967-6133). This very reasonably priced place serves a tasty and quick lunch, including soup, main course, and fried or plain rice on lo-mein noodles for $2.75. Service is fast, so don't worry if it looks crowded. Dinner is also reasonable and good, and it is open every day of the week" (M. Newhouse, Chapel Hill, N.C.).

Things to See and Do in Chapel Hill

To best arm yourself for sightseeing, contact the **Chapel Hill Chamber of Commerce,** 104 South Estes Dr., P.O. Box 2897, Chapel Hill, NC 27514 (tel. 919/967-7075).

Your best introduction to the **university** community is a free, one-hour campus tour that leaves from Morehead Planetarium (the west entrance) on East Franklin Street at 2:15 p.m. daily.

With the tour or on your own, look for the **Old Well,** once the only source of drinking water for Chapel Hill. It stands in the center of the campus on Cameron Avenue, in a small, temple-like enclosure with a dome supported by classic columns. Just east of it is **Old East,** begun in 1793 and the country's oldest state university building. Across the way stands the "newcomer," **Old West,** built in 1824. **South Main Building** is nearby, a structure that was begun in 1798 and not finished until 1814—students lived inside the empty shell in rude huts during that time. And look for the **Coker Arboretum** at Cameron Avenue and Raleigh Street, where five acres are planted in a wide variety of temperate-zone plants. As you walk the campus you'll hear popular tunes coming from the 167-foot **Morehead-Patterson Bell Tower,** whose Italian Renaissance campanile rings throughout the day. And just back of the bell tower is **Kenan Stadium,** in a wooded natural bowl setting, with a 44,000-seat capacity.

And, of course, you won't want to miss **Morehead Planetarium.** It was a 1947 gift of John Motley Morehead and houses the first Carl Zeiss instrument located on a U.S. college campus (there are only 12 in the whole country) in a 68-foot doomed theater. The "star" of its permanent scientific exhibits is a large orrery showing the simultaneous action of planets revolving around the sun, moons revolving around planets, and planets rotating on their axes. There are shows Monday through Sunday at 8 p.m., on Saturday at 11 a.m., 1 and 3 p.m., and on Sunday at 2, 3, and 8 p.m. Admission is $2.75 for adults, $2 for students, and $1.35 for children under 12. Oh, yes, the planetarium is on East Franklin Street (Bus. 501). Telephone 962-1248 for detailed information.

Try to catch a **Playmakers** Repertory Company production at the **Playmakers Theatre,** (tel. 962-1121), a Greek Revival structure whose Corinthian columns are adorned with corn and wheat designs instead of the traditional acanthus leaves. You could see classical or contemporary drama—they're professional in both areas and sometimes perform in the modern Paul Green Theatre.

Off campus, the **North Carolina Botanical Garden,** on Laurel Hill Rd. and U.S. 15–501 Bypass (tel. 967-2246), is open from 8 a.m. to 5 p.m. weekdays, and its three miles of easily followed nature trails are lined with native plants of this region. It's free, and a botanical education with herb gardens, and carnivorous plants and native plants in habitat settings.

2. Winston-Salem

Before 1913, the twin communities of Winston and Salem coexisted in perfect harmony, and their incorporation that year into a single city has proved a happy, productive union. Winston, founded in 1849, contributed an industry-based economy, while Salem added the crafts, educational emphasis, and sense of order that its Moravian settlers brought from Pennsylvania in 1766.

Actually, Salem (the name comes from the Hebrew word *shalom,* meaning peace) was the last of three settlements by Moravian clergy and laymen who came to the Piedmont looking for townsites in the early 1750s—the little towns of Bethabara and Bethania came first. But Salem proved to be the main establishment, and the hard-working newcomers laid out a pleasant community with their traditional Single Brothers and Single Sisters houses as focal points for unmarried members of the congregation. Once married, the couples often set up shop right in their own homes. They were hardy, devout, Germanic people who had fled persecution in Europe and brought to the New World their artisans' skills, a deep love of music and education, and absolute rejection of violence in any form.

As "progress" began to encroach on the boundaries of the beautiful, orderly old congregational town, an organized effort was begun in 1949 to restore those homes and shops which were in a state of deterioration and to reconstruct others which had disappeared. Today, there are more than 30 buildings restored with meticulous attention to authenticity and still others in the process of renovation. Devout the Moravians were, glum they were not; and the bright, cheerful reds and blues and soft greens and yellows in the restored interiors (exteriors as well) are duplicates of the colors with which they surrounded themselves in those early days. They also loved good food, and that, too, has been lovingly preserved in Old Salem: today's tourist can sit down to lunch or dinner in the Tavern Dining Rooms (see below) to a lunch or dinner of *schmorhuhn* (smothered chicken), braised ham in tarragon cream, ragoût of pork and chestnuts, or trout poached in white wine prepared by recipes that are as authentically Old Salem as the surroundings.

Flowing around the center island of Old Salem, the vigorous new city goes about its business of commerce and industry in a manner that somehow escapes the environmental blight that marks other manufacturing centers. Maybe that's due in part to the fact that it is not too large (latest population figures are 143,000), or maybe it's because its citizens have retained a sense of aesthetic values handed down from those early arrivals. At any rate, although this is the home base for such giants as R. J. Reynolds Industries, the South's largest bank

(Wachovia National), and Piedmont Airlines, there is a genteel air about the place that almost convinces you progress doesn't *have* to be abrasive.

For the traveler, there are points of interest outside Winston-Salem itself, making Winston-Salem a perfect base for day trips to Greensboro, High Point, and the pottery center at Seagrove which dates back 200 years.

WHERE TO STAY: It's not in town, but the **Tanglewood Park, Lodge and Manor House,** Clemmons, NC 27012 (tel. 919/766-6461), is an experience not to be missed. It's about 12 miles west of Winston-Salem, just off I-40 (the exit is marked). Once upon a time, Indians roamed this lush, wooded section of the Yadkin River Valley. When the Moravians arrived in 1753 and settled the Wachovia tract, one square mile of land was deeded by Lord Linville to the Ellis family, who leased it briefly for "five shillings lawful money of Great Britain in hand and a yearly rent of one peppercorn payment at the Feast of Saint Michael, the archangel." In 1757, the Johnson family acquired it and held on to it until 1921, when William N. Reynolds, the tobacco tycoon, decided it was just the place to build his country home. Never a man to do things on a small scale, "Mr. Will" kept adding acres of contiguous land until the total stood at 1100. The lovely old Johnson homeplace, built in 1859, sprouted wings on either side and became a true manor house. The Reynoldses named the estate Tanglewood.

Well, five shillings and a peppercorn won't get you far at Tanglewood these days, but the Manor House *can* be your country home, if only for a day—since 1951, Tanglewood (officially, it's the William and Kate B. Reynolds Memorial Park) has been open to the public, operated as a department of county government. For remarkably reasonable rates, you can sleep in a spacious master bedroom complete with fireplace and canopied double beds, dine in an elegant colonial-style dining room (there are five, one with a mammoth stone fireplace) on gourmet fare, roam the well-kept terraces and lawns, and play the country squire to your heart's content. The cost of this plush living runs from $32 to $43.

There are only 11 bedrooms in the Manor House, so there's no mob scene to detract from your fantasy of "lord of the manor," and the nearby Motor Lodge has just 18 units and an apartment, with rates from $35 to $45. If your idea of country living runs along more rustic lines, there are five vacation cottages in a secluded wooded area overlooking Mallard Lake. The two- and three-bedroom cottages, completely furnished and fully equipped kitchens, rent for $175 to $225 per week for five or fewer people. More rugged types can reserve one of the 100 family campground sites in one corner of the vast estate. Most have electric and water hookups, all have picnic tables and campfire space, and there are two large bathhouses and a dumping station: $10 a day for those with hookups ($57 per week) and $9 without.

If you think "country" equates with "boredom," 'taint so, at least not here. At Tanglewood, you can play tennis on one of nine courts, swim in a large pool, go paddleboating or canoeing or trail riding. And, of course, there's golf, on an excellent course right on the grounds. There's even steeplechase racing the third Saturday of every April, the last meet of the year on the Carolina circuit; but don't expect to stay at Tanglewood then—all rooms and cottages are held for racing participants. As for other times of the year, better reserve three or four weeks ahead, because the place is a year-round favorite with regulars.

In Winston-Salem

Right in the heart of town (300 W. 5th St.; tel. toll free 800/228-9000, or 919/723-9111), is the **Hyatt Winston-Salem,** and it's a winner for travelers going the deluxe route. The nine-story open lobby has the look of an indoor park, and its glass-bubble elevators overlook reflecting pools, fountains, hanging gardens, and a 30-foot waterfall that splashes into the second-story-level swimming pool. For all its modern luxury, the place can lay claim to a southern heritage, since for more than half a century this was the site of the Robert E. Lee Hotel, and a portrait of the general hangs in the lobby, on loan from the local chapter of the United Daughters of the Confederacy (who even imported Robert E. Lee IV for their presentation ceremonies). The Salem Tavern, which hosted George Washington in 1791, is preserved in spirit in Hugo's Rotisserie, with an excellent menu and warm, comfortable atmosphere. A specialty is the very popular roasted Long Island duckling (dinner prices range from $9.95 to $19.95), and desserts that range from fresh strawberry tart to chocolate fondue with fruits. A testament to the restaurant's excellence is its popularity with the local gentry. The adjoining Fox's Lair Lounge is a great place to relax and unwind, with live entertainment and dancing. The Greenhouse Restaurant, overlooking the lobby, offers everything from a hearty country breakfast to sandwiches to steaks, and is open from 7 a.m. until 11 p.m.

As for the rooms, each of the 305 has either a balcony view of the lobby or an outside view of the city, but if you're ready for some very special pampering, ask for a room on the ninth-floor Regency Club level. You begin the day there in a graciously appointed drawing room with a continental breakfast buffet and end it with sherry and cheese. Rates on this level range from $80 to $95 and include the services of a concierge, who will do everything from making travel, rental car, or dinner reservations to finding a babysitter. The *Wall Street Journal* and other out-of-town newspapers appear at your door every morning—just state your preference. Less elegant rooms (although all are first class) run from $70 to $90.

In a more moderate price category, the **Holiday Inn North,** North Cherry-Marshall Expressway (tel. 919/723-2911), is a good bet. Just across from the center of all major sports events in this area (you guessed it—the Coliseum), it also affords easy access to most sightseeing spots. For example, Old Salem is a straight shot through the city center on the expressway (clearly marked) and R. J. Reynolds World and Reynolda House and Gardens are close by. Rooms are large and decor is modern (doubles are $49 and up) and local telephone calls are free, as is transportation to and from the airport. There's piano music in the Southern Squire Dining Room, where "Miss Lib" Bennett's southern fried chicken has brought travelers and local residents back for more over the years. Pets are welcomed here if they stay in the kennel.

Special Note: Right across the expressway is one of those treasures travelers dream about—an inexpensive place to eat with food that's *really* good! At **The Biscuit House,** Charles Munday serves a menu that's limited but southern to the core, at prices you won't believe. For $1.50, you can buy two pieces of fried chicken and a large, light, yummy buttered biscuit (as one who grew up with the world's best biscuit-cooking mother, I *know* my biscuits and can speak with authority!). You can have a full dinner with two pieces, and if you're really a chicken lover, the four-piece dinner. Mr. Munday also serves biscuits with ham, sausage, and steak for under $2. The chicken is as good as the biscuits, and that says it all—and there's a new addition to the menu, a chicken filet. For just pennies, a bowl of delicious, home-cooked pinto beans accents any of the above. Don't miss this one, even if money is no object. Incidentally, since

I first discovered Mr. Munday and his biscuits, he's opened four more locations (Thruway Shopping Center, 801 Waughton St., Ogburn Shopping Center, and a store in Kannapolis, N.C.) and they're all open 6 a.m. to 9 p.m. Monday through Saturday, 7 a.m. to 2 p.m. on Sunday.

Back to accommodations. The **Ramada Inn** (nine miles west on I-40 at the Clemmons exit; tel. 919/766-9121) has lovely, comfortable rooms in a scenic setting, a heated pool with poolside food service, a restaurant that's open from 6 a.m. to 10 p.m., plus a taproom that serves wine, beer, and setups, and has entertainment and dancing Monday through Saturday. There are also golf privileges at a nearby course. Two rooms are specially equipped for paraplegics. Double rooms here begin at $40.

The **Winston-Salem Hilton**, Marshall and High Sts. (tel. 919/723-7911), also has dancing in its sophisticated lounge, and the rooms are Hilton quality. Food service is available at poolside, there's a babysitter list, and family rates are available. A double room here costs about $57.

In Nearby Greensboro

There's an elegant **Guest Quarters** at 5929 W. Friendly Ave., Greensboro, NC 27410 (tel. 919/292-9821), with one- and two-bedroom suites and all the exceptional service features of this fine chain (see Chapter I). This location has tennis courts and jogging trails, as well as a lovely swimming pool with deck area. Convenient to the airport and the city's corporate centers, Guest Quarters rates here are $74 double for the one-bedroom suites and $80 double for two bedrooms.

WHERE TO EAT: Far and away the most atmospheric place to eat is the **Old Salem Tavern**, 736 S. Main St. in Old Salem (tel. 748-8585). Here, as everywhere else in the restored village, authenticity is the keynote. The dining rooms were built in 1816 as an annex to the 1784 Tavern next door, and the simply furnished rooms and colonial-costumed waiters and waitresses provide an appropriate, early 18th-century ambience for your lunch (11 a.m. to 2 p.m.) or après-sightseeing dinner (6 to 8:30 p.m.). During summer months, you can eat in the outdoor arbor, which, like the indoor rooms, is candlelit at night. Always available are the usual southern favorites: Tavern chicken pie (at lunch) and Blue Ridge rainbow trout (dinner only). The pumpkin and raisin muffins are a specialty. Reservations are preferred for parties of four or more; otherwise, just drop in. Lunch runs $5 to $10; dinner, $9 to $16.

You can have a meal behind bars at **Tuesday's 1865 Eating Establishment** (tel. 768-2132), in the sprawling Hanes Mall just off I-40 (look for the Silas Creek Parkway exit)—after which you're free to leave. Nostalgia is the theme, and good food at reasonable prices in a fun atmosphere is the name of the game at this new-old restaurant. The rustic old barn doors open to stained glass, carved woodwork, gaslights, ceiling fans, and a collection of memorabilia that is a delight. As for the authentic old jail, complete with massive barred doors, it has been moved intact to the balcony; and if that doesn't suit your fancy, you can choose to sit beneath the painted hobby horses that prance across the ceiling or in sight of the early-vintage Shell gas pump and advertising sign for Clabber Girl Baking Powder. Every item is a genuine antique, many salvaged from old homes and junkyards in North Carolina and Virginia. (For the story of how this all came about, see the writeup of Tuesday's in the Wilmington section of Chapter VI.)

As for the food, it's both good and, as mentioned, affordable. The self-service salad wagon is an especially good buy—it's the most extensive selection I've encountered in a long time, with all the usual fare, plus such unexpected treats as herring, apple rings, and a large variety of fresh fruits. You go for refills as many times as your appetite dictates. Deviled mushrooms are a personal lunchtime favorite, but heartier meals like the ranch hand rib eye loin, wrangler's sirloin (that's N.Y. strip steak), or stuffed flounder come with salad from the salad wagon, a choice of baked or french-fried potatoes, or corn on the cob, and homemade bread at moderate prices. The large antique bar serves beer and wines (quite a good selection). If you've ever longed for "the good old days," turn off I-40 and find Tuesday's. It's large and reservations are not necessary.

For other good eating spots, try the Hyatt House and Holiday Inn eateries, and *don't* overlook those marvelous **Biscuit House** restaurants (see "Where to Stay," above).

THINGS TO DO AND SEE: For detailed sightseeing information, contact the **Winston-Salem Chamber of Commerce,** P.O. Box 1408, Winston-Salem, NC 27102 (tel. 919/725-2361).

Near the very center of the city (just off U.S. 52 on Old Salem Road), Old Salem has *got* to be the place you head for first in Winston-Salem. The **Reception Center,** on Old Salem Road, will start you off with exhibits which trace the Moravians' journey from Europe to America and finally to North Carolina. And they'll sell you combination tickets to the nine restored buildings that are open Monday through Saturday from 9:30 a.m. to 4:30 p.m. (1:30 to 4:30 p.m. on Sunday)—$6 for adults, $3 for students. Of course, if you want to include the **Museum of Early Southern Decoration,** the price goes up—$7 and $3.50. Individual admission to each building is $1. Costumed hosts and hostesses will show you around, and you'll also see craftsmen in colonial dress practicing the trades of the original settlement.

And speaking of crafts, when Moravian boys reached the age of 14, they moved into the **Single Brothers House,** the first, half-timbered section of which was built in 1769 and the newer, brick wing in 1786, where they began an apprenticeship to a master artisan for seven years. Academic studies went on as they learned to be gunsmiths, tailors, potters, shoemakers, or whatever. Adolescent girls, too, left home, to live in the **Single Sisters House,** diagonally across the town square, and learn the domestic arts they would need when marrying time arrived. Single girls *still* live in this building—it's a dormitory for Salem College—although their present-day education differs considerably.

Be sure to go into the **Tavern.** The one you see was built in 1784 to replace an earlier one which burned, and once inside you'll understand why travelers often came out of their way to stop here and enjoy its hospitality. George Washington spent two nights here in 1791 and commented in his diary on the industriousness of the Moravians. The dining rooms, sleeping rooms, barns, and grounds are not much different now than when he stopped by, and those cooking utensils you see in the stone-floored kitchen with its twin fireplaces are the real thing.

The **Wachovia Museum** (this whole area was named Wachovia by the original settlers after a district in Saxony that had offered refuge to the sect) was once the boys' school. There are tape recordings of music being played on the old musical instruments you see displayed here and a host of other historical items. You can also visit the **Market-Firehouse** and the **Winkler Bakery.** Bread and cookies are still baked in the big wood-burning ovens at the bakery.

Many of the homes have distinctive signs hanging outside to identify the shops inside, and one of my favorites is the tobacco shop of Matthew Miksch, a sunny-yellow weather-boarded log cottage with a miniature man hanging at the door clutching tobacco leaves and a snuff box.

Like the Historic District of Williamsburg, Virginia, Old Salem still functions as a living community, and many of the homes you see restored on the outside are private residences, as modern inside as a contemporary ranch-style. And the young people you see walking the old streets with such familiarity are no doubt students at Salem College, living a 20th-century campus life in an 18th-century setting.

On the square, the **Home Moravian Church,** which dates from 1800, is the center of the denomination in the South. Visitors are always welcomed to the services, and hundreds show up for the Easter Sunrise Service (held continuously in Old Salem for over 200 years), the Christmas Lovefeasts (on December 24), and the New Year's Eve Watch Night Service. One block north of the square, the graveyard named "God's Acre" is a visual reminder that death is the great equalizer, since the more than 4000 graves are marked with almost identical stones—prince and pauper are shown the same respect.

Three miles northwest of Winston-Salem, near Cherry Marshall and University Highways (just follow the signs), is historic **Bethabara Park,** site of the first Moravian settlement in North Carolina. There are two restored 18th-century buildings, an early 19th-century Brewer's House, and the excavated foundations of the town of Bethabara, begun in 1753, along with a rebuilt fort in its original trench. The guided tour is free (9:30 a.m. to 4:30 p.m. Monday through Friday; 1:30 to 4:30 p.m. Saturday, Sunday, and holidays) and there are nature trails and picnic grounds. Open Easter to November 30.

A prominent citizen of Winston lived at **Reynolda House** (just off Reynolda Road near Wake Forest University): R. J. Reynolds, the tobacco tycoon, built the mansion, which now holds an excellent collection of furnishings and American art, as well as a 1905–1950 ladies' costume display. The gardens are especially lovely in late March or early April, when they're abloom with Japanese cherry trees. The house is open Tuesday through Saturday from 9:30 a.m. to 4:30 p.m. (Sunday from 1:30 p.m.) and costs $3 for adults, $1 for students and children. The gardens are free and open every day from 7:30 a.m. to 5 p.m.

No matter where you choose to stay in Winston-Salem, include **Tanglewood** in your sightseeing (see "Where to Stay," above). The beautiful recreation area is ten miles southwest of town on U.S. 158, and the exit is marked.

Both the **Joseph Schlitz Brewing Company,** 5½ miles south on U.S. 52 (tel. 788-6710, ext. 252) and the **R. J. Reynolds Tobacco Company,** off Cherry St. on 33rd St. (tel. 773-5718), will show you through their plants.

O. Henry's hometown, Greensboro, is less than 30 miles away. Of course, the short story writer was known as William Sidney Porter in these parts, and you can see an exhibit illustrating his life and work at the **Greensboro Historical Museum,** 130 Summit Ave. Greensboro was also the birthplace of Dolley Madison. This museum houses a fine collection from her life as North Carolina's only first lady. Other exhibits include Indian relics, early modes of transportation, furnishings, pottery, textiles, and military artifacts. There is no admission charge. Hours are 10 a.m. to 5 p.m. Tuesday through Saturday, and 2 to 5 p.m. on Sunday. (Tel. 919/373-2043)

Six miles northwest of Greensboro on U.S. 220, a 220-acre park—**Guilford Courthouse National Military Park,** P.O. Box 9806, Greensboro, NC 27408 (tel. 288-1776)—marks one of the closing battles of the Revolution, the Battle of Guilford Courthouse on March 15, 1781. Gen. Nathanael Greene (Greensboro was named for him) led a group of inexperienced troops against Lord Cornwallis, and although he was defeated, he inflicted severe losses on the British. Cornwallis hotfooted it out of this part of the country and headed for Yorktown, Virginia, where he surrendered his depleted forces just seven months later, on October 19. The Visitor Center is open from 8:30 a.m. to 6 p.m. (it closes at 5 p.m. during the fall and winter), and has films, brochures, and displays about the historic battle. There are also wayside exhibits along the two-mile, self-guided walking trail that leads to some of the many monuments. No charge.

Six miles southwest of nearby Burlington, on N.C. 62, is where those upstart farmers marched against Royal Governor Tryon in 1771 to protest British taxes. Ill-trained and poorly equipped, they were soundly defeated—the battle lasted only two hours—but the stouthearted "Regulators" were among the first southern colonists to demonstrate their objection to royal rule. The **Alamance Battleground State Historic Site** has a Visitor Center (with audiovisual presentations) that's open Tuesday through Saturday from 9 a.m. to 5 p.m., Sunday from 1 p.m.

Just south of Greensboro, **High Point** is one of the leading furniture-manufacturing centers in the U.S. High Point (which got its name because it was the highest point along the 1853 North Carolina and Midland Railroad from Salem to Fayetteville) has a very good **museum** at 1805 E. Lexington Ave. (at McGuinn Ave.), with displays of Indian artifacts and Quaker history exhibits. Right next door, there's a restored 1786 Flemish bond-pattern-brick stage-coach stop, the **John Haley House,** a Quaker home with a still-functioning blacksmith shop.

3. Pinehurst

The Sandhills' porous, sandy soil is a reminder that in prehistoric times Atlantic Ocean waves rolled over the land. It also provides an ideal drainage situation that is a big factor in the area's "Golf Capital, U.S.A." standing, for no matter what the rainfall, no puddles accumulate on the rolling green golf courses (there are 26 within a 15-mile radius). And with temperatures that range between 78° and 44°, the games go on year round.

But golf hasn't always been king here. In fact, when Boston philanthropist James Walker Tufts bought up 5000 acres of land in 1895 at $1 per, his main thought was to build the little resort village of Pinehurst as a retreat from harsher climes for wealthy Northerners. Recreation for guests back then consisted mainly of croquet on the grassy lawns, outdoor concerts, hayrides, or just quiet walks through the pines. The story goes that his attention first turned to golf, which had only recently arrived in the U.S. from Great Britain, when one of his dairy employees complained that guests were "hitting the cows with a little white ball." By 1900, Tufts had enlisted Donald Ross (whose skill had been gained at Scotland's St. Andrews) to come to Pinehurst and introduce golf. In time (he remained in the Sandhills the rest of his life), Ross designed courses here that drew some of the most distinguished golfers in the world: Ben Hogan, Walter Travis, Bobby Jones, Walter Hagen, Patty Berg, Sam Snead, Arnold Palmer, Gary Player, Jack Nicklaus—and that's only a partial list!

For years, golf on the superb courses, beginning and ending at the Pinehurst Country Club's clubhouse, was by invitation only, and the list of invitees was so exclusive that Walter Hagen is reported to have said (after finally receiving the treasured summons) on returning from his first game, "The place is so exclusive that, hell, the Duke of Windsor would have trouble getting in!" Today, however, although the golf world's top players no doubt consider

Pinehurst their own turf, you don't have to wait for an invitation, nor do you have to be a millionaire to play. Prices are certainly high enough at the Pinehurst Hotel, but they're not exorbitant by comparison with other luxury hotels around the country. And there is a profusion of other hotels and motels, something in almost any price range; and, expert or duffer, guests can always play the courses.

In 1973, the first World Open Championship was played in Pinehurst, replaced in 1977 by the Colgate-Hall of Fame Classic. In September of 1974, President Gerald Ford presided at the opening of the World Golf Hall of Fame, overlooking Ross's famous Number Two Course (one of the top ten in the country), with all the living inductees there for the ceremonies.

Through all the hullabaloo over celebrity golf matches, Pinehurst has retained its New England village air, built in by Frederick Law Olmsted (the architect-landscaper who also planned New York's Central Park), with a Village Green and shaded residential streets, many paved only by a carpet of pine needles. It hasn't changed, but continues to carry out the Tufts concept of a retreat here in the Sandhills. Year-round greenery is provided by pines (some with needles 15 inches long), stately magnolias, and hollies. Moderate temperatures account for color through all seasons—camellias, azaleas, wisteria, peach trees, dogwoods, and summer-blooming yard flowers. And the village is a private business, owned and operated since 1971 by the Diamondhead Corporation. Shops, restaurants, hotels, and other business enterprises make it a complete, self-sufficient community, yet none intrude in an abrasive way, all adhering to the original style and preserving a leisurely graciousness that is as refreshing to the spirit as to the eye.

For those whose idea of a good time is *not* chasing around after that elusive little white ball (you can count me in that esteemed company), there are plenty of other things to do. There's a tennis club, any number of excellent courts, over 200 miles of riding trails and stables with good mounts for hire, boating on a 200-acre lake, trap and skeet ranges, archery, over 9000 acres of woods to explore via meandering pathways, and shopping in the little boutiques that is out of this world.

Pinehurst's sister town (it's a *real* town, not corporation owned), **Southern Pines**, is a delight, too. The short drive on Midland Road (N.C. 2), a double-lane highway divided by a strip of pines and bordered by lovely homes and lavish gardens, goes right past **Midland Crafters.** You'll see it on your right, and take my word for it, stop. The rambling white building is a virtual gallery of American crafts, ranging from beanbags to paintings to furniture, to candles, to pottery, to glassware, to . . . well, almost any handcraft you can think of.

Stop, too, at the Chamber of Commerce, on the corner of Pennsylvania Ave. and SE Broad St., 125 South East Broad St. (tel. 692-3926)—it's right in the middle of town, you can't miss it, to pick up information on the area and meet the friendly, helpful staff. And park your car—this is as pretty a walking town as you'll find anywhere. It will take you longer than you imagine just to wander up and down the five or six blocks of Broad Street, Pennsylvania Avenue, and Bennett Street. Like those in Pinehurst, shops here are small, charming, and filled with interesting, often exquisite items. Outstanding among the offbeat shops is **Something Special,** on Pennsylvania Avenue. Inside are collectors' dolls and dollhouses, miniature grandfather clocks that keep time, all kinds of materials to make your own dollhouse, and items so unique (like the miniature dentures I saw there) that people are coming here from all over the Southeast to have a look. The handsome Georgian house on East Connecticut Avenue, once the Campbell family residence, is a cultural and visitor center, with a small golf museum and an equestrian room filled with trophies, racing silks, and prints of hunts and races. That's not surprising, since there are so many fine horse farms in the Sandhills. Steeplechasers trained here show up regularly at tracks in New York, Florida, Kentucky, and Maryland. Trotters and pacers are also trained around here, and Del Cameron, one of only two living three-time winners of the Hambletonian, has kept a winter training stable in this area for more than 30 years.

All this will give you some idea of what to expect when you come to this part of North Carolina's Piedmont, but I strongly recommend that you write ahead for detailed information on Pinehurst (Pinehurst Hotel and Country Club, Pinehurst, NC 28374) and the entire Sandhills (Sandhills Area Chamber of Commerce, P.O. Box 458, Southern Pines, NC 28387).

WHERE TO STAY: Although the **Pinehurst Hotel and Country Club**, P.O. Box 4000 Pinehurst, NC 28374 (tel. 919/295-6811 or toll free 800/334-9560) is still *the* place to stay in Pinehurst, as it has been from the beginning, there are several other hotels in the village that offer luxury on a smaller scale and graciousness on the same level at somewhat more moderate prices. And, of course, Southern Pines is close by, with numerous motels catering to Pinehurst visitors.

About that grand old Pinehurst Hotel: Until the Diamondhead Corporation took over in 1971 and put some $10 million into a general facelift (much of it into the hotel itself), it had slipped into an almost shabby state. Now, however, it proudly rears its head with all the splendid aristocracy of the past enhanced by the most modern improvements (for example, in the old days, the only air conditioning came from open windows or fans). The white, four-story, 300-room building, with wings on each side sporting broad, columned porches lined with comfortable rocking chairs, was called The Carolina for years, and you'll still hear residents refer to it by that name. Whatever you call it, when you drive up to the columned portico and walk through its huge lobby furnished with a pleasing mixture of antique and contemporary fittings, you'll know this is a place where the art of gracious living is still practiced. Public rooms and guest rooms have undergone extensive renovation, and while bright, cheerful colors predominate in the spacious accommodations, there's an air of subdued elegance that newer establishments never seem quite able to achieve. And besides the main building, there are over 300 one-, two-, and three-bedroom condominiums called the Golf Course Villas, and 48 golf and tennis lodges right on the course or at the tennis courts.

The tennis complex, with some 24 courts (18 are clay), is presided over by a highly professional staff. Clinics and individual instruction are available to all guests.

For equestrians, saddle horses are available, and there are miles of riding trails, supervised and unsupervised riding, instruction, and, if you bring your own mount, boarding. The stables also offer carriage rides, a particularly charming way to see the village. Archery is available, and there are nine trap and skeet fields (two of which are lighted). Children are anything but neglected in the Pinehurst scheme of things, with an all-day recreation and activities program and babysitters on hand for gallivanting parents.

But, of course, the major attraction is those six 18-hole golf courses, especially the world-famous Number Two. Five begin and end at the clubhouse (and that, alone, is worth the trip, even if you're the world's worst duffer—it is everything a clubhouse should be and more, with the same elegant air and attention to service as the hotel). Greens fees for all except Number Two are $20. Number Two fees are higher, and you must have a caddy.

To all this add bicycles, pedicycles, a huge L-shaped pool and deck area, a game room, health spa, and fishing, boating, and swimming at Lake Pinehurst (200 acres worth), and you have a resort with facilities second to none. As for food and sophisticated dinner dancing and entertainment, the hotel draws a large crowd of North Carolinians who sometimes travel quite a distance, as well as guests who seldom venture elsewhere for nighttime activities.

There are three seasons in Pinehurst: March to June and September to December are high season; February to March and June to September, midseason; and December to January, off-season. During high season, rates for the main building begin at $145; Golf Course Condominium Villas, $100; golf and tennis lodges, $90. They are considerably lower the rest of the year. There are a number of attractive golf and tennis package plans offered by the hotel, as well as American and Modified American plans.

Another resort with extensive facilities is the **Mid Pines Club** on Midland Road out from Southern Pines (tel. 919/692-2114). It's a graceful, colonial-style building with wings stretching out on either side of the main entrance. That main entrance leads to a lobby rotunda that is strikingly beautiful, with green carpet, green and white wallpaper, and twin white staircases. There are 63 rooms in the three-storied hotel, and all are decorated with style. And if cottage living suits you best, there are several on the premises, some with fireplaces, accommodating up to 14. There's an 18-hole golf course, a putting green, a landscaped pool (set off by a charming split-rail fence), four tennis courts which are lighted at night, and a recreation room. Both the lovely formal dining room and the more informal Terrace (overlooking the fairways of the championship golf course) serve excellent meals—I especially liked the buffet lunch on the Terrace—at moderate to expensive prices. Double room rates (full American plan) run $120 to $144 in season, lower other months, and cottages are $72 to $90 per person.

The **Pine Crest Inn,** right in the heart of the Village on Dogwood Road (919/295-6121), was described by an English visitor as having "all the flavor and courtesies of our countryside inns," but for me, it is the southern counterpart of New York's Algonquin Hotel—the same informal, semielegance and friendly, makes-you-feel-at-home feeling, the same small, intimate sort of place that draws people back year after year. In fact, Bob Barrett (proprietor since 1961) tells me some 80% of his guests are returnees. And small wonder, for the two-storied, white-columned building radiates warmth from the moment you enter the lobby with its comfortable armchairs, fireplace, and informal dining room and bar to one side; and guest rooms reflect the same inviting "stay a while" atmosphere. Meals in the three dining rooms (with fireplaces and pretty, flowered wallpaper) are of such quality that they draw people from Raleigh and Charlotte as well as the immediate vicinity (see "Dining in and Around Pinehurst," below). Golf privileges, it goes without saying, are extended to guests here, and Mr. Barrett will even arrange starting times. Serious golfers can practice putting and then see their swings, slices, or whatever on a giant, seven-foot television screen. Tennis and horseback riding can be arranged at nearby facilities. Modified American plan (breakfast and dinner) rates per person, double occupancy, run from $30 to $47, depending on the season. Golf and "all sports" packages are available.

The **Sheraton Motor Inn,** on U.S. 1 at Morgantown Road in Southern Pines (tel. 919/692-8585) has oversize beds in its cheerful, modern rooms. Two lounges provide entertainment and dancing, and there are tennis courts and a jogging trail. And, of course, golf privileges. Doubles here range from $47 to $55 in season, lower other months.

Campgrounds

The **Heritage Farm Campground,** N.C. 3, Whispering Pines, NC 28327 (tel. 919/949-3433), is one of the most peaceful, relaxing sites you can imagine. With a spring-fed, 14-acre lake (for swimming, pedal boats, fishing), a playground, Ping-Pong, a putting green, nature trails, and horseback riding, there's no lack of things to do, but it's the beautiful wooded setting that gives this place special appeal. There are 50 sites (22 with full hookups), flush toilets, hot showers, sewage disposal, laundry, ice, picnic tables, and firewood. Rates start at $10.

DINING IN AND AROUND PINEHURST: Almost all the inns, hotels, and motels in the Pinehurst area have very good dining rooms. Noteworthy are the **Pine Needles dining room,** as well as those at **Whispering Pines** and **Foxfire,** which overlook lakes and golf courses. For good measure, I'm listing a small, very good luncheon spot in Southern Pines, a delightful midday stop when you're browsing through the shops that line Broad Street.

The **Carolina Room** at the **Pinehurst Hotel** (tel. 295-6811) is a formal dining room that serves dinner from 6:30 to 11 p.m. in candelit elegance. The menu is extensive and a five-course meal will average $20. Needless to say, the service is impeccable. During the season, there's often top-flight entertainment and dinner dancing.

Although small, the **Pine Crest Inn** (tel. 295-6121) has made such a name for itself in the food field that reservations are made from towns all over the state. Their prime beef, homemade pastries, and insistence on the freshest of vegetables are the reasons for that reputation. And as good as the food is, I'm firmly convinced people come back, too, for the warm hospitality that pervades this place. There's dancing in Mr. B's Lounge. Dinner prices range from $7.50 to $14.50 complete, and you really must reserve ahead here.

Another very popular place with locals is the **Manor Hotel,** on Magnolia Road (tel. 295-6176). The all-you-can-eat country breakfast is a special favorite, as is the Sunday buffet brunch which comes with complimentary champagne. The main dining room serves excellent lunches and dinners—at *affordable* prices—especially the Friday night Seafood Extravaganza. This is, as locals have discovered, one of the best moderate-priced dining spots in the area.

About that lunch spot in Southern Pines: it's called the **Quarter,** 130 S.W. Broad St., and is open for lunch only. Joann Duffield, the owner, has converted almost all of the first floor of her gift and women's sportswear shop into a very special sort of tearoom. The ladderback chairs, paisley print cloths, and bamboo accents in furniture and accessories create a light, airy feeling that is complemented by a limited menu of soups and sandwiches and pastries, all homemade. The chicken gumbo is a treat, and tomato aspic here has a tangy flavor that I found unique. For dessert, try a "tassy," a small tart about the size of a fifty-cent piece—I don't know what's in it, but it's very, very good, and Joann tells me it is one of their most popular items. The oil paintings you see are for sale, and the dress shop stock is especially tasteful. Lunch hours are noon to 3 p.m., and an average tab is about $2.50.

THINGS TO SEE AND DO: For advance sightseeing information, you can contact **Pinehurst, Inc.,** P.O. Box 4000, Pinehurst, NC 28374 (tel. 919/295-6811), and/or the Chamber of Commerce, Southern Pines, NC 28387 (tel. 919/692-3926).

Golf, golf, and more golf—that's really why most people come to Pinehurst. And if there's a hotel or motel that doesn't arrange play for its guests, I didn't find it. Most can also set you up for tennis, cycling, or boat rentals on one of the many lakes around.

Horseback riders can arrange for mounts by calling the **Pinehurst Stables** (tel. 295-6625), where expert instruction is available for novices; Mrs. Harold Sadler at **The Heritage** (tel. 949-3433); or the **Full Cry Farm** (tel. 692-2838), which specializes in instruction.

Aside from recreation facilities, the Pinehurst area also offers the **World Golf Hall of Fame,** and even nongolfers will be impressed by the white-columned porticoes and sparkling fountains of the Entrance Pavilion, which overlooks Pinehurst Country Club's Number Two course. The Entrance Pavilion is centered by a pool and another fountain and leads to the main lobby of the museum. Even before you enter the lobby, you'll see a ten-foot statue of Bobby Jones through the glass doors. The north and south wings of the museum tell the story of the development of golf and people associated with it like Henry VIII's first wife, Katherine, who loved it as much as Scotland's three Kings James (II, III, and IV) hated it. And hundreds of golf items from the past are displayed (there are balls used from 1750 to 1850 made of tanned animal hides stuffed with feathers). The theater is the only one in the world devoted exclusively to golf, and it features films of major tournaments as well as instructional pictures. Behind the museum is the actual Hall of Fame, a shrine completely surrounded by water, approached by a covered walkway. It is open from 9 a.m. to 5 p.m. every day of the year except Christmas, and admission is $2 for adults, and free for those under 16.

On the Fort Bragg—Aberdeen Road, 1½ miles southeast of Southern Pines, you'll come to **Weymouth Woods-Sandhills Nature Preserve,** a beautiful nature spot with foot and bridle paths and some 600 acres of pine-covered "sandridges." There's also a natural history museum, free, that's open Monday through Saturday from 9 a.m. to 6 p.m.; Sunday, noon to 5 p.m.

In late August, the annual PGA tournament, the Hall of Fame Golf Classic, is held here as part of Pinehurst's **Grand Week of Golf,** with net proceeds from the $250,000 Classic going to the nonprofit World Golf Hall of Fame Foundation.

The **Mid-South Horse Show Association** holds schooling shows every Sunday afternoon from January to April; in early March there's the **Moore County Hounds Hunter Trials** at Scotts Corner, Southern Pines, with reserved parking spaces overlooking the course for spectators; and the **Stoneybrook Steeplechase Races** are held on a Saturday in early April on a farm near Southern Pines where race horses are bred and trained the rest of the year by Michael G. Walsh, owner, an Irishman from County Cork. The Sandhills Area Chamber of Commerce, P.O. Box 458, Southern Pines, NC 28387, can furnish exact dates and full details on all these events.

About halfway between Southern Pines and Pinehurst, on Midland Road, you'll find one of those craft shops mentioned in Chapter 1. It's the **Midland Crafters,** run by Vesta and Bob Stearn. Inside, you'll find all sorts of North American craft items—pottery, woodwork, jewelry, etc.—as well as paintings and a million other things which will tempt you to part with your money. Not all are locally made, but all are good quality, and there's a good price spread so you can "pick up that little something" or perhaps discover a lasting treasure. *Note to the ladies:* Right next door is Papillon, a marvelous shop filled with fine sportswear, formal wear, and accessories.

About an hour's drive to the northwest is the little town of **Seagrove** (it's on U.S. 220), which has been turning out pottery for over 200 years. The red and gray clays of this section of the Piedmont were first used by settlers from Staffordshire, England, and the very first items they produced were jugs for transporting whiskey. The art is practiced today just as it was then: clays are ground and mixed by machines turned by mules, simple designs are fashioned on kick wheels, and glazing is still done in wood-burning kilns. Many of the potters work in or behind their homes, with only a small sign outside to identify their trade, so if you have difficulty finding them, stop and ask—everybody does, so don't be shy. There are some sales rooms in the town, but the real fun is seeing the pottery actually being made. And while you're asking, inquire about Jugtown, a group of rustic, log-hewn buildings in a grove of pines where potters demonstrate their art with pride Monday through Saturday. On Sunday there's no one there, only a sign that proclaims "'Tis the Sabbath."

A little north of Seagrove (still on U.S. 220), you'll come to **Asheboro,** where you should turn on to U.S. 64, going southeast, to reach the **North Carolina Zoological Park,** (c/o N.C. Zoological Society, P.O. Box Zoo, Asheboro, NC 27203 (tel. 919/692-2144). On 1371 acres, exotic African animals live in barless, cageless natural habitats. Zebras, ostriches, giraffes, lions, chimpanzees, elephants, rhinoceroses, baboons, and a host of birds are on hand. Open daily, 9 a.m. to 5 p.m., at $3 for adults, $1 for ages two to 15.

4. Charlotte

The largest city in the Piedmont—in both North and South Carolina, as a matter of fact—is Charlotte. It was named for King George III's wife, Queen Charlotte, but evidently its residents didn't take their royal affiliation too seriously, for when Lord Cornwallis occupied the town briefly in 1780, he was so annoyed by patriot activities that he called the town a "hornet's nest," a name that stuck and now proudly adorns the city seal. He should have known what to expect, because more than a year before the Declaration of Independence was signed in Philadelphia, the Mecklenburg document declaring independence from Britain was signed in Charlotte—on May 20, 1775, to be exact. Present-day citizens will tell you that Thomas Jefferson used *their* declaration as a model for the one he wrote. Charlotte was prominent in national history again in 1865, when Jefferson Davis convened his last full cabinet meeting here that year.

After the Confederacy fell and the local boys came home from war, the city set out on a course that would free it of dependence on slave labor and that would eventually lead it to a position of industrial leadership in the South. The Catawba River furnished a rich supply of water power for industrialization, and development of manufacturing plants and textile mills was rather rapid. There are now more than 600 textile plants within a 100-mile radius.

Charlotte is also the center of a region that was for years the major gold producer for the United States. In fact, a U.S. mint was located here from 1836 to 1913, although it was inoperative from 1861 to 1867 because of the Civil War. Material from that old building has been used to create a replica that is an important art museum and performing arts center.

In the last decade or so, Charlotte has sprouted skyscrapers at an amazing rate, and one of the most interesting punctuation points of its skyline is the 40-story, trapezoid steel-and-glass tower of the North Carolina National Bank Plaza. Suburban areas, too, have mushroomed, with landscaped housing developments and enormous shopping malls springing up in every direction. This is one of the Southeast's most graphic examples of the "new" South building squarely on the foundation of that fabled Old South.

WHERE TO STAY: The **Radisson Plaza Hotel,** 2 NCNB Plaza (tel. 704/377-0400), is of trapezoid shape to blend harmoniously with the North Carolina National Bank Plaza of which it is a part. It is connected by a covered walkway above the street to Charlotte's new Convention Center. The 381 rooms are the ultimate in comfort and contemporary design, and there are two restaurants and a coffeeshop on the premises. Double accommodations here begin at $79, and it is one of the most convenient locations in town, at the center of Trade and Tryon Streets.

At the **Executive Inn,** 631 N. Tryon St. (tel. 704/332-3121), cribs are free. There's food service at poolside, a restaurant, and a taproom. Rooms are comfortable, and doubles run from $32 to $40.

The dependable **Days Inn** people have three motels in Charlotte, and I especially like the one at 122 W. Woodlawn Rd. (tel. 704/527-1620), which is convenient to the airport and Carowinds. I've never yet run across a Days Inn with disappointing accommodations, and this was no exception. Rooms are always adequate in size, comfortable, and the decor pleasing. This one has a pool, a restaurant, and one unit especially fitted for the handicapped. Doubles are $36.88

The **Charlotte Econo Lodge,** 2222 E. Independence Blvd. (tel. 704/372-6250), is on U.S. 74, just two miles from downtown, and convenient to the Coliseum. There's a pool, and cribs are provided free. No pets. Doubles are in the $28 to $35 range.

WHERE TO EAT: For broiled live lobster, steak, or prime ribs, you probably can't do better in the Charlotte area than the **Epicurean,** 1324 East Blvd. (tel. 377-4529). This is a chef-owned establishment, which probably accounts for the excellence of its food and its popularity locally. The semi à la carte prices range from $6.95 to $18.95, but there are children's plates for $5. It's advisable to call ahead to reserve for dinner, which is served from 6 to 10 p.m. Closed Sunday and the first two weeks in July.

Staley's Charcoal Steak House, 2401 Wilkinson Blvd. (tel. 376-3626), is another good steak and prime ribs place. In fact, you can watch the cooking at their open-hearth grill. Dinner is especially nice here, with an organist providing background music. It opens for lunch weekdays from 11:30 a.m. to 2:30 p.m., and for dinner from 5 to 11 p.m. It's dinner only on Saturday and Sunday. Lunch prices are $4 to $6; dinner, $6 to $12. It's a good idea to reserve for dinner.

You can also get all three meals at **Le Steak Cafe,** 631 N. Tryon St., at 10th St. (tel. 332-3121), in the **Executive Inn.** They do their own baking and there's background music in this pleasant restaurant. Breakfast is served from 7 a.m. to 11 a.m. (about $3); lunch from 11:30 a.m. to 2 p.m. ($4 buffet style); and dinner from 5:30 to 10 p.m. ($6.50 to $15). Reservations are not generally necessary.

There's an **S & W Cafeteria** in Charlotte, a good bet for good food at budget prices in attractive surroundings. You can breakfast for a little over $1, lunch for about $2.10, and dinner seldom runs over $3.50. They do their own baking; if you're in doubt as you move down the line, go for the roast beef or one of their salad plates, both very good. It's open from 11 a.m. to 2:15 p.m.

and 5 to 7:30 p.m. and is at 1601 Woodlawn Rd. at the Park Road Shopping Center (tel. 523-2866).

THINGS TO DO AND SEE: For sightseeing in detail, contact: **Visitors Bureau,** P.O. Box 32785, Charlotte, NC 28232 (tel. 704/377-6911).

The **Mint Museum of Art,** 501 Hempstead Pl., adjacent to Eastover Park, is free and holds an art school and center for the performing arts, as well as sculpture gardens and impressive collections of Renaissance, pre-Columbian, Western, and European and American art. It's closed Monday, open 10 a.m. to 5 p.m. other weekdays, 2 to 5 p.m. on weekends.

If you're in Charlotte during April and May, drive north on N.C. 49 to the **University of North Carolina at Charlotte** campus to see their rhododendron garden—spectacular! And if you're on campus at either 7:50 a.m. or 5:15 p.m., you'll get in on the carillon concerts (on Sunday, it's 3:30 p.m.).

Take the children to the **Charlotte Nature Museum and Planetarium** at 1658 Sterling Rd. (enter via East Blvd.)—exhibits are especially planned for developing an awareness and appreciation of nature through exhibits and programs designed especially for young children. There's also a planetarium, a puppet theater, and a nature trail. Admission to the museum is free, and hours are 9 a.m. to 5 p.m. Monday through Saturday, 2 to 5 p.m. on Sunday. Planetarium shows are at 3 and 4 p.m. Saturday and Sunday and cost $1 for adults and 75¢ for students. Special children's show at 1:30 and 2:30 p.m. Saturday, 2:30 p.m. Sunday, costs 75¢ for all ages.

Joining with the Nature Museum to form the combined Science Museums of Charlotte, Inc. is the **Discovery Place Science and Technology Center** at 301 N. Tryon St. in uptown Charlotte (enter via Trade St.). Also geared to young children, Discovery Place takes them through eight major exhibit areas, including a tropical rain forest, an aquarium, and a life center, and stresses a "hands-on" approach to learning. There's a $2.50 admission for adults, $1.50 for students, and hours are 9 a.m. to 5 p.m. Monday through Friday, 'til 6 p.m. on Saturday, and 1 to 6 p.m. on Sunday.

The 11th president of the United States, James K. Polk, was born at **Pineville,** just 12 miles south of Charlotte on U.S. 521. His log cabin and the outbuildings have been reconstructed and there's a Visitor Center which shows an interesting film. It's free and open from 9 a.m. to 5 p.m. Tuesday through Saturday, from 1 p.m. on Sunday.

The **Charlotte Motor Speedway,** 12 miles northeast of Charlotte on U.S. 29 (or just off I-85), is host in late May of each year to the **World 600 Stock Car Race,** longest and richest such race in the U.S., which draws upward of 80,000 enthusiastic fans. If you're a devotee of the daredevil sport, you may want to plan your trip then or in mid-October, when the **National 500 Stock Car Race** is run. You can get exact dates and full details of both events by writing P.O. Box 600, Harrisburg, NC 28075, or calling 704/455-2121.

If you're taking children along on your Charlotte trip, you undoubtedly already know about **Carowinds Theme Park,** P.O. Box 240516, Charlotte, NC 28224 (tel. 704/588-2606). But even without the kids, it's worth a day, just for fun. The $40-million park straddles the North and South Carolina state line, and has eight theme areas reflecting facets of the two states' past and present. The rides are entertaining and inventive, especially the flume and mine train rides, although I must confess my romantic favorite is the sternwheeler that set me thinking of slower days. For the more adventurous, the "Thunder Road" and "White Lightnin'" roller coasters may beckon. On the sightseeing side of things, look for a re-creation of the Old Charleston waterfront, Pirate Island, wood crafts and leather shop, and bird show in the Troubadour's Roost Theater; and the shops and crafts (from the days of British rule) at Queen's Colony; and bluegrass music in Harmony Hall. One cautionary word: They won't let you bring pets in; however, there is a kennel for stashing them. Admission, which includes all rides and most entertainments, is $12 per person, with those under four free, and there's a $2 parking fee. The park is open every day except Friday, 10 a.m. to 8 p.m. June through August; closes at 8 p.m. on Saturday and Sunday in April, May, and September, and is closed from October through March.

Chapter VIII

INTRODUCTION TO SOUTH CAROLINA

1. By Way of Background
2. Traveling to South Carolina
3. Traveling Within South Carolina

THERE ARE REALLY TWO South Carolinas, with differences between the coastal "low country" and the "up country" (including the rolling midlands) so distinct I sometimes feel there should be a state line between the two. South Carolinians, however, seem able to hold on to those divisions and at the same time take great pride in presenting a united front to the rest of the world.

1. By Way of Background

1526 TO 1984: It isn't only the topography of the state that makes for the distinctiveness of each section, although like most states along the Atlantic, South Carolina has its coastal plain, piedmont, and mountains. The differences really spring from a history of settlement and development that saw aristocratic rice and indigo planters build one lifestyle along the coast and German, Scottish-Irish, and Welsh immigrants gravitate further inland to build another. The first attempts to settle along the coast were as early as 1526 and 1562, but nothing came of them. It wasn't until Charles II of England granted both the

Carolinas to eight noblemen, the lords proprietors, that colonists arrived to stay. Charles Towne was established at Albemarle Point in 1670, then moved ten years later to the peninsula formed by the Ashley and Cooper Rivers.

That low, marshy country proved ideal for large rice and indigo plantations, and Charles Towne's harbor was perfect for shipping these crops around the world. Successful planters maintained huge homes on outlying farms, and most built sumptuous mansions in town as well. A life of formal ease and graciousness developed that has never entirely disappeared, even though the low country has seen great fortunes come and go with the changes of time.

Away from the coast, those hardy frontiersmen—who set up small farms, built up a brisk trade in pelts, and fought off Indians, often with no help from their British landlords—had little time or inclination for the social goings-on in Charles Towne. And a sore point was the issue of taxation—but with a local twist: in spite of the fact that everyone paid taxes, only the low country had any say in how things were run. And that remained the case until 1770, even though there had been popular representation in the colonial government as early as 1693. The rift between the two groups would be a long time healing, and even during the Revolution (although the first decisive American victory was won here at Fort Moultrie in June 1776), South Carolina suffered about equally from British troops and local loyalists, mostly from the low country.

When Charles Towne was finally occupied by the British in 1780, it was supposed to be the jumping-off point for a spearhead drive to join forces in the north which would crush Washington's troops. But thanks to the efforts of Continental troops under Gen. Nathanael Greene and South Carolina natives who followed "the Swamp Fox" (Frances Marion) and "the Game-cock" (Thomas Sumter) in a very effective sort of guerrilla warfare, the royal soldiers were more or less confined to Charles Towne (renamed Charleston in 1783). There are some historians who contend that the battles of Kings Mountain (in 1780) and Cowpens (1781) were *the* decisive encounters of the Revolution. When independence was finally achieved, South Carolina was the eighth state to ratify the Federal Constitution, in 1788.

By 1790, those cantankerous up-country citizens made such a fuss about the state's capital remaining in low-country Charleston, when four-fifths of the white population lived inland, that the state government was moved to neutral ground, centrally located Columbia. Not to be outdone, the low-country population (which controlled four-fifths of the *wealth*) continued to maintain state offices, and the Supreme Court actually met in both cities to hear appeals until 1865.

When tensions between the North and South reached the breaking point in 1860, fiery John C. Calhoun led the state legislature to pass an Ordinance of Secession in December that made South Carolina the first state to secede from the Union. And in *that* step, citizens seemed united. In fact, their first military action was to take Fort Sumter from the federal troops garrisoned there, and they continued to hold it until 1865. Altogether, the state lost 22% of its population in the bitter Civil War; and General Sherman, in his "march to the sea," saw to it that just about the entire state was left in shambles.

If there's one thing *all* South Carolinians—low or up country—have in abundance, it's pride. And that pride suffered greatly, along with the economy, as carpetbaggers and scalawags moved in during Reconstruction. I always feel, when traveling in this state, that "Yankee" and "Rebel" distinctions are more alive here today than in any other single place in the South. That's not really surprising, however, when you remember that not until *World War II* did South Carolina begin to get back on its feet economically. Ironically, it was "Yankee" industry, moving to a location of enormous waterpowered energy supply and a ready labor market, that led the state's booming industrialization. And just in the last ten or 20 years, the Civil War scars have faded more quickly than before.

As a place to visit, the state is a tourist's goldmine—more than 280 miles of seashore, with lovely white sand beaches shaded by palms, resort islands like Hilton Head that are a world apart, and Charleston's gracious Old South charm still intact. The area around Columbia reflects both the "New South" of vitality and some of the Old in the university campus which has served, with its great old oaks and early 1800s buildings, as the background for several movies about antebellum life. Sportsmen, drawn to coastal and inland fishing, also come here for the unusually long hunting season (Thanksgiving, more or less, to March 1) for such game as deer, wild turkey, quail, fox, and many more. Equestrians come for horse shows, polo, the Carolina Cup Steeplechase (in early April) and Colonial Cup Steeplechase (in mid-November) at Camden, and harness racing and other horse events in Aiken (beginning about the middle of March). And the Darlington Raceway features the "Rebel 500" (in mid-April) and "Southern 500" (Labor Day) late-model stock-car races. History buffs, of course, can retrace all those colonial, Revolution, and Civil War events to their hearts' content.

SOUTH CAROLINA TELEPHONE AREA CODE: All areas are in the 803 area code zone.

ABOUT SOUTH CAROLINA'S HOTELS: You'll find just about every imaginable type of accommodation in South Carolina, although there's not always a wide range of choice in a specific location. Coastal resorts offer everything from posh luxury hotels to modest, inexpensive motels. And Charleston has one six-room "hotel" that offers southern hospitality of the Old South style which simply cannot be equaled. In between, almost every town and city has representatives of the major chains and independently owned modern motels which more than adequately meet the traveler's needs. As everywhere else, it pays to reserve ahead. If you should get here *without* a reservation, there are Welcome Centers at nine major entry points whose hostesses operate a free reservations service. But that's risky, especially if you come during spring or summer—rooms can even be scarce as late as October along the coast.

An alternative to hotel/motel vacationing—and one that works particularly well for families, I think—is the rental of a cottage or apartment. South Carolina's resort areas have literally hundreds available on a weekly basis, and it's a fairly simple matter to engage one *if you plan far enough in advance.*

There are also cabin accommodations available all year in 13 of South Carolina's state parks. All are heated and air-conditioned and fully equipped, including cooking utensils, tableware, and linens. Rentals range from $90 to $300 per week, and the cabins accommodate anywhere from four to 12 persons. Here again, however, advance planning is absolutely necessary for summer reservations. For full details on these cabins, how to file an application, rates, and accommodations at the 31 other state parks, write: **South Carolina State Parks,** 1205 Pendleton St., Columbia, SC 29201 (tel. 803/758-3622).

AS FOR FOOD: South Carolina menus vary across the state in a reflection of its population mix. Low-country seafood ragoûts and Charleston's famous she-crab soup dominate coastal cooking, while country ham and grits served up with "red eye" gravy are prominent on inland tables. The best meals are

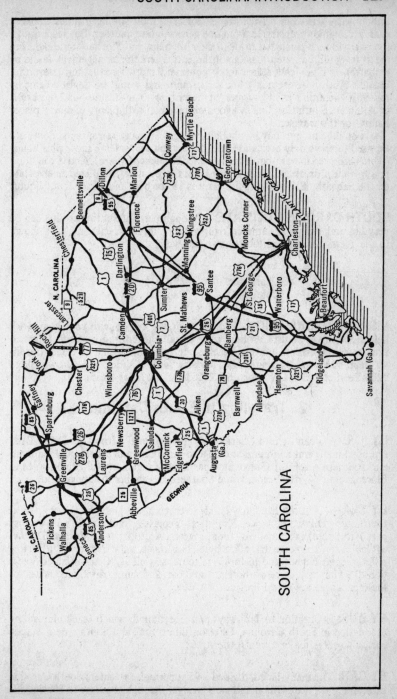

SOUTH CAROLINA

undoubtedly served in private homes, for as in most southern states, cooking is an art lovingly transferred from one generation to another. But restaurants, too, seem to take particular pride in their kitchens, and I've had some exquisite meals in small, unpretentious establishments where the management would be embarrassed if you called their food "gourmet," but where that term nevertheless fits. And there are many fine restaurants that would no doubt be embarrassed if you *didn't* use "gourmet" in describing their cuisine—and most of it is. All in all, South Carolina is a good place to eat, with plenty of dining places handy for the traveler.

You'll be able to buy alcoholic beverages in many restaurants. Some are licensed to serve only beer and wine, but a great many serve those plus liquor (which is served in mini-bottles to be added to cocktail mixes). And if you think you'll want a drink on Sunday, stock up: there's no alcohol sold in the state on the Sabbath. The drinking age limit is 18 for beer and wine, 21 for liquor.

SOUTH CAROLINA CLIMATE: Although parts of South Carolina can be very hot and steamy in summer, temperatures never are extreme, as is shown in the average highs and lows shown below.

	High	*Low*
Charleston	88	44
Columbia	93	35

VISITOR INFORMATION: In order to do a good job with your homework before coming to South Carolina, write or call ahead for any specific information on sports (fishing, hunting, beaches, etc.) and sightseeing to: **South Carolina Dept. of Parks, Recreation & Tourism**, Suite 113, Edgar A. Brown Bldg., 1205 Pendleton St., Columbia, SC 29201 (tel. 803/758-8735).

2. Traveling to South Carolina

BY AIR: You can fly into Charleston's International Airport on Delta, Eastern, Piedmont, and Southern, and all also serve Columbia. Eastern, Piedmont, and Southern reach the Greenville-Spartanburg region, and Piedmont goes to Florence and Myrtle Beach, while Southern has flights to Greenwood.

BY TRAIN: Amtrak has fairly good coverage of the state, with terminals at Charleston, Dillon, Florence, Kingstree, Yemassee, and Columbia. Also, as part of its "Southeast Sojourns" tour program, Amtrak has a four-day "Discover Charleston" package that offers hotel, breakfasts, self-drive car with 100 free miles, theater tickets, and historic site tours, as well as "Coastal Island Vacations," which include resort hotels, rental car, and dinner discounts. Rates for these packages are a real bargain.

BY BUS: In addition to Trailways and Greyhound, which reach almost any destination in South Carolina, Jefferson Lines, Inc., and Southeastern Stages, Inc., also serve major cities in the state.

BY CAR: The many-laned, divided I-95 superhighway enters South Carolina from the north near Dillon and runs straight through the state to Hardeeville on the Georgia border. From Georgia, U.S. 301 also crosses the entire state to North Carolina. The major east-west highway artery is I-26, from Charleston northwest through Columbia and on up to Hendersonville, North Carolina. Along the coast, U.S. 17 stretches from Georgia to North Carolina. In the western region, I-85 crosses from Georgia to North Carolina. The state does a beautiful job of furnishing travel information to motorists, and there are well-equipped, efficiently staffed Visitor Welcome Centers at the northern entrances of U.S. 17, I-95, I-85, and I-26, as well as the southern ends of I-85, I-20, and U.S. 301.

3. Traveling Within South Carolina

BY AIR: Southern, Delta, Piedmont, and Commuter airlines all have connecting flights to South Carolina airports, although schedules are sometimes awkward for connections.

BY TRAIN: Amtrak stops at Spartanburg, Greenville, Clemson, Cheraw, Camden, Columbia, Dillard, Florence, Kingstree, Charleston, and Yemassee.

BY BUS: Greyhound, Trailways, and Southeastern States, Inc., operate intrastate routes, as does Jefferson Lines, Inc.

BY CAR: Those marvelous Interstate and U.S. highways listed in the above section give South Carolina a network of exceptionally good roadways. However, even when you leave the highways for the state-maintained byways, driving is easy on well-maintained roads. South Carolina used to be one of those notorious "speedtrap" states for visitors, and while the setups and rigged stoplights have been gone for a while now, it *does* pay to watch the speed limits: they still keep an eye on out-of-state drivers (and in-state, as well, I suspect).

You will find **Thrifty Rent-a-Car** locations in Charleston, Columbia, Greenville-Spartanburg, and Hilton Head, with their usual good service and rates.

Chapter IX

"LOW COUNTRY" SOUTH CAROLINA

1. The Grand Strand
2. Charleston
3. Hilton Head Island

ALL THE ROMANCE, BEAUTY, and graciousness of the Old South manage to survive in South Carolina's low country. Well, maybe it isn't all that evident visually along the Grand Strand up around Myrtle Beach, which looks pretty much like most other beach resort areas—although even this section exudes southern charm in its slow-paced vacation outlook and the warm hospitality of the locals. A little farther south, however, at Georgetown, then Charleston, and all the way to Beaufort at the bottom of the state's coastline, automobiles, and modern dress seem almost out of place when you drive through old, cobblestone streets under trees draped with the mysterious Spanish moss and past antebellum homes built in the early days of this country. Oh, they've been outfitted with all the conveniences of today, but I often think they could revert easily to their original state and keep occupants comfortable even in the face of an oil crisis that forced the return of wood-burning fireplaces and kerosene lamps or candles. As for the people who live in them, you'll find they possess for the most part an appreciation of up-to-date, sophisticated lifestyles (very few, if any, rednecks in *this* part of the South!), as well as an active memory of things as they once were—a happy mixture, indeed.

Physically, the low country is almost breathtakingly beautiful. Its broad, white-sand beaches are warmed by the Gulf Stream just a few miles offshore and fringed with palm trees and rolling dunes. Palms mingle with live oaks, dogwood, and pines all along the coast, and everywhere you'll see the silver-gray something called Spanish moss that drapes airily from tree branches, lending a dreamlike softness to the landscape. I call it "something" because even scientists can't quite figure out what it is—it isn't *really* a moss, because that grows on the ground; it isn't a parasite, because it doesn't feed on sap from the trees; and it has no roots, seeming to extract nourishment somehow from the air. They call it an epiphyte (air plant), but as yet they aren't sure—even after exhaustive tests—just how it manages to keep alive and grow. My favorite quotation about Spanish moss is the answer given northern tourists by a South Carolina publication to all those questions about the lovely mystery: "Yes, it does grow on trees; no, it isn't a parasite; no, they *don't* take it in at night and put it out in the morning."

Speaking of native plants: whatever you do, don't pull the graceful sea oats that grow on sand-dune stretches along the beaches—it's against the law and an infraction carries a stiff fine. The hardy plant (it grows from Cape Charles, Virginia, to the Gulf Coast of Mexico and is officially named *Uniola paniculato*) not only acts as a natural anchor for the dunes, but also serves as a plentiful food supply for shore birds. Actually, it is also instrumental in the forming of new or higher dunes, since it catches and holds blowing sands. So look, enjoy their spare beauty, but don't touch.

As I've said, low-country South Carolina is full of memories, but it's also a place to *make* memories—whether of the recreation, sightseeing, or just plain relaxing genre. The subtropical climate, where spring arrives early and summer lingers until late October, permits golf (there are over 55 courses on the coast, 30 of them on the Grand Strand alone), tennis (271 coastal tennis courts), fishing (13 public piers, at Cherry Grove Beach, Tilghman Beach, Crescent Beach, Windy Hill, Myrtle Beach, Isle of Palms, and Folly Beach; and charter boats for deep-sea fishing), sightseeing in that grand old lady of the low country, Charleston, or sitting on an uncrowded beach (as I did once for an entire October week at Hilton Head). There are islands that don't even require a boat for a visit (South Carolina has provided marvelous double-laned causeways), like Pawleys, Seabrook, Edisto, and Hilton Island.

1. The Grand Strand

Myrtle Beach, with a permanent population of about 15,000, is at the center of the Grand Strand, a 55-mile string of beaches that includes Little River, Cherry Grove, Crescent Beach, Ocean Drive, Atlantic Beach, Surfside Beach, Garden City, Murrells Inlet, Litchfield Beach, and Pawleys Island. And besides the beaches, there are amusement parks, stock-car races, nightspots with top entertainment, an internationally known sculpture garden, some of the best seafood restaurants on the Atlantic coast, and all those golf courses. Named for all the myrtle trees in this area, Myrtle Beach itself is an ideal base for a Grand Strand vacation. Maybe I should say here that my personal feeling about this resort is that if you're looking for a wild, swinging kind of beach resort, this isn't it—there's plenty to do, of course, and it certainly isn't dull, but the whole tone is that of a *family* resort, with almost as much attention paid at the various hotels and motels to children's needs as to those of adults. Many provide activity programs and playgrounds with supervision, and nearly all have babysitter lists for parents who like a little nightlife. It's a nice sort of place and one that looks out for all members of the family.

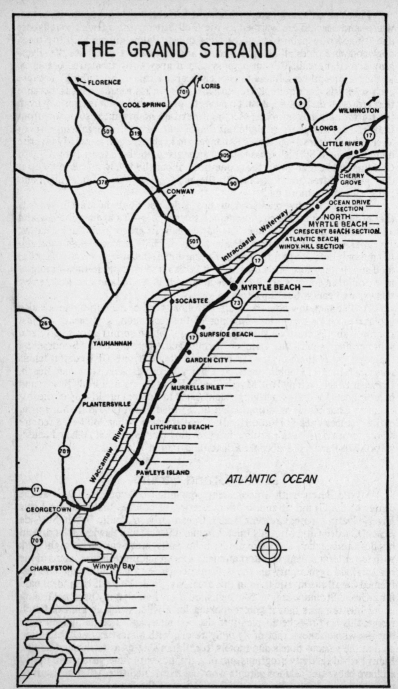

THE GRAND STRAND

Map courtesy of the Greater Myrtle Beach Chamber of Commerce

WHERE TO STAY: The Grand Strand is literally lined with hotels, motels, condominiums, and cottages. The **Myrtle Beach Area Chamber of Commerce,** P.O. Box 2115, Myrtle Beach, SC 29578 (tel. 803/626-7444), publishes two directories which will be a great help in making a selection and both are free. Because of its central location, Myrtle Beach itself is my personal choice—attractions north or south of it are within easy reach—and with only one exception (included because of its special character) all the listings that follow are either in Myrtle Beach or just a short distance north of the city limits. "In season" means June 15 through Labor Day, and rates quoted are for double occupancy. And, once again, I would remind you that the prices quoted are *as of the time of writing* and (like everything else in these inflationary times) subject to change.

Deluxe

The **Beachcomber,** 1705 S. Ocean Blvd. (tel. 803/448-4345), offers deluxe rooms (with refrigerators) and one- or two-bedroom, fully equipped efficiencies. Oceanfront units have private balconies, and connecting units are available. There are two pools (one for children), and there's a washerette on the premises. Both golf and tennis privileges are available at nearby facilities. Shopping and amusement centers, as well as restaurants, are close at hand. In-season rates for oceanfront rooms start at $65. After Labor Day, the same accommodations drop considerably. Open all year.

Moderate

The **Jamaican,** 3006 N. Ocean Blvd. (tel. 803/448-4321), is an inviting, five-story motel at the edge of Myrtle Beach's north-end residential section. Its rooms, efficiencies, and suites are bright and airy, each with a private balcony and ocean view, and I found the staff here exceptionally pleasant and helpful. The beach is less crowded here, and right next door is one of the area's top restaurants, the Sea Captain's House (see "Where to Eat," below). The boardwalk, Pavilion, and amusement area are 20 rather short blocks to the south—a very long stroll or a short drive away. There's an oceanfront pool (a kiddie pool is also on the ocean), and both golf and tennis facilities are close by. This is, in my opinion, one of the best motels on the beach in the moderate price range. In season, rooms begin at $59, efficiencies at $60, with varying lower rates the rest of the year. Weekly rates are available.

The **Carolinian,** 2506 N. Ocean Blvd. (tel. 803/448-6861), is a pretty, oceanfront motel that caters to families ("family" means children, but no pets, please). In a setting of palm trees, the building is designed to provide maximum privacy on the redwood-railed balconies that front each room and the sunbathing patios. Rooms are spacious and the efficiencies have fully equipped electric kitchens. You can relax about the children, since lifeguards are on duty at pool and beach. Mamas and papas enjoy golf privileges at nearby courses. Restaurants are a short walk away. In-season rates run from $50 up. Closed November 1 to March 1.

Not just a motel, but a complete resort, **The Sea Mist,** 1200 S. Ocean Blvd. (tel. 803/448-1551, or toll free 800/845-0669), has six pools (two are enclosed for year-round use), three tennis courts, supervised children's programs, playgrounds, a recreation room, ice cream parlor, gift cove, and guest privileges at 23 golf courses. The 367 units consist of large rooms, apartments, suites, and even a penthouse. There are special package plans for honeymooners, tennis players, and golfers. The elegant dining room, softly lit by candles, has old-world charm, and the Prime Rib Room features entertainment most of the year, along with prime beef and fresh seafood. Rates during the season range from $40 to $77, but there's a special low rate between September and May (and don't forget that swimming is good here until late October).

For luxury rooms, efficiencies, and suites at moderate prices, the **St. John's Inn**, 6801 N. Ocean Blvd. (tel. 803/449-5251), is one of the best. All rooms have balconies and an ocean view. Children are kept entertained with planned activities, the swimming pool is heated on cool days, and golf and tennis packages are available. There's a restaurant and coffeeshop. Rates are in the $62 to $75 range in season, lower other times. Open year round.

The **Dunes Village**, 5200 N. Ocean Blvd. (tel. 803/449-5275), is another exceptionally nice motel in the moderate range, with a heated pool, a wading pool for the kiddies, tennis, shuffleboard, picnic tables, and grills. Most of the well-appointed rooms have an ocean view, and some are oceanfront. Doubles rent for $55 to $60 in season (kitchen apartments for up to four people, $135), but drop in other months.

The **Jade Tree**, 5308 N. Ocean Blvd. (tel. 803/449-5221), is just up the beach from the Dunes Village and has rooms with a contemporary decor, a babysitter list, heated pool, playground, and a restaurant that's open every day except Monday in season. Doubles are $40 to $60 in season, and many have refrigerators.

Budget

The **Sea Horse Court**, 2505 N. Court, 2505 N. Ocean Blvd. (tel. 803/448-3959), is across the street from the beach. Efficiencies and apartments are available, a shopping mall and restaurants within walking distance. Recreation facilities include a heated pool, kiddie pool, shuffleboard, and golf privileges. Rooms are above average for this price range. Rates during the season range from $32 up and later drop to under $20.

Campgrounds

There are more than 12,000 campsites along the Grand Strand, many on the oceanfront. Rates at the 15 privately operated campgrounds drop considerably after Labor Day. Most will accept families only—no singles. The following are all located about halfway between Myrtle Beach and North Myrtle Beach, and all are on the ocean.

Lake Arrowhead Family Campground, 9750 Kings Rd. (tel. 803/449-5816), has 1300 spacious (50 × 50 feet) sites on 140 wooded acres, with two freshwater lakes, rental units, and free swimming pool on the premises. There is city water, electricity, sewer hookups, shade shelters at oceanfront sites, dump stations, tiled showers and baths (including one equipped for the handicapped), a trading post, bottled-gas service, a laundromat, fishing, carpet golf, lighted tennis courts, shuffleboard, horseshoe pitching, paddle boats, a playground, and golf privileges. Rates are $10 to $17, a $20 deposit is required, and it's a good idea to reserve at least a month in advance during the summer. It's open all year.

There are 760 sites at the **Apache Family Campground**, Star Rt. 2 (tel. 803/449-7323). Here the amenities include a free swimming pool and recreation pavilion, water, electricity, shade shelters, modern bathhouses with hot water, sewer hookups, carpet golf, a laundromat, trading post, playground, public telephones, ice, beach umbrellas, floats for rent, and golf privileges. You can reserve here year round except for the week of July 4th. Rates are $9 to $15.

READERS' SUGGESTIONS: "About fifteen miles northeast of Myrtle Beach, halfway between there and Wilmington, N.C., we found beautiful oceanfront accommodations at **The Winds of Ocean Isle,** P.O. Box 503, Ocean Isle Beach, NC 28459 (tel. 919/579-6275). They have motel units, studio efficiencies, suites, and villa units at rates we thought were very reasonable for this quiet, get-away-from-it-all bit of beach paradise. Daily rates aren't always available for all types of accommodations, but we can't imagine not wanting to spend a week" (S. Ramsauer, Orangeburg, S.C.).

"Our family loves to spend our beach time in a cottage of our own, and this year we found a lovely little beach with a wide selection of rental properties at **Ocean Isle Beach,** N.C. We rented through Sloane Realty (tel. 919/579-6216 or 579-6217) and were quite happy both with the cottage and the price. We can certainly recommend that anyone interested in this kind of freedom and privacy contact Mr. Tripp Sloane. The beach is quiet, but there's every kind of service and sports facility you could possibly want right close by" (J. Dailey, Venice, Fl).

WHERE TO EAT: You may be tempted to eat more than three meals a day just to sample the many restaurants along the Grand Strand. My own weakness for fresh seafood well prepared always produces a noticeable expansion of the waistline during my stay. And price should by no means be a measure of quality, for prices are unexpectedly moderate at even the best of the lot.

Not to Be Missed

Treat yourself to at least one dinner at **The Rice Planter's,** 6707 Kings Hwy. North, which is another name for Highway 17 (tel. 449-3456). The present large, old-brick building replaces the original which burned in 1975, resulting in a loss of irreplaceable artifacts and antiques from rice plantations in the area. Not lost, however, was the charm of the place, which is as much alive in the new as it was in the old. The high-ceilinged main dining room, warmed by a fire in the brick hearth on cool nights, is overlooked by an open balcony reached by a graceful stairway and divided into alcoves for individual parties of six or eight. Exposed brick walls, copper kettles at the fireplace, dark-stained woodwork and beams, old-fashioned ceiling fans and frosted glass chandeliers, red-checked tablecloths, and candlelight add up to a perfect setting for dining that can only be described as sumptuous. And the personable manager, David Spangler, seems to be everywhere at once with a warm welcome and a watchful eye on the service, which matches the food in excellence. Seafood is featured, and a favorite is the Rice Planter's Dinner, which begins with shrimp or oyster cocktail, followed by clam chowder, fried shrimp, filet of fish, oysters, baked crabmeat, shrimp creole, and deep-sea scallops. It comes with a crisp salad of greens, potato, cole slaw, tartar sauce, and home-baked bread. And—would you believe it?—the price is just $15.95. If you're not a seafood lover, try one of their low-country specialties: Carolina country ham steak or southern fried chicken, both served with a fresh vegetable, rice and gravy, salad, and that same good home-baked bread. It's open for dinner only, from 5 to 10 p.m., with prices ranging from $7 to $16.

Over on the beach, Bob Chapman presides over the **Sea Captain's House,** 3002 N. Ocean Blvd. (tel. 448-8082), in an old beach home. The restaurant has been family-run since 1963 and is known and loved by a host of South Carolinians, as well as "outsider" regulars who vacation at Myrtle Beach year after year. There's a fireplace in the paneled inner dining room and its glow adds to the informal, friendly atmosphere on cool nights. A many-windowed porch room affords a superb ocean view. She-crab soup is on the menu; the seafood platter includes five different fish, served with slaw, potatoes, and hushpuppies; and there's a selection of flame-broiled steaks, lamb chops, and country ham steak at prices from $6 to $17. Lunch is served from 11:30 a.m. to 2:30 p.m., and dinner from 5 p.m. to 10 p.m. seven days a week during June, July, and August. It closes on Monday the rest of the year.

Two Motel Dining Rooms

The **Safari Room** at the **Breakers,** Oceanfront at 21st Ave. (tel. 448-2474), serves such delicacies as flounder stuffed with crabmeat, sauteed shrimp, and beef tips with mushrooms, peppers, and onions with an extensive salad bar, vegetables, potato, and rolls or hushpuppies included for prices averaging $10. Its Friday night seafood buffet (all you can eat for $10.95) is so popular that reservations must be made ahead as early as Monday night!

At the **Ocean Dunes,** 74th Ave. North (tel. 449-7441), there's dancing and entertainment year round in the **Brass Anchor** lounge and restaurant. Particularly noteworthy is the seafood buffet on Tuesday and Friday, one of the best in the area ($13.50). Wednesday and Sunday, prime ribs (served buffet style, all you can eat) are featured at $12.75. All prices are for complete dinners and include a trip to the very good salad bar. Dinner hours are from 6 to 10 p.m., but the lounge is active from 4 p.m. to 1:30 a.m.

Right next door to the Ocean Dunes, the **Sand Dunes** (same management) (tel. 449-3313) also has dancing and live entertainment. The unique decor of the dining room and lounge carries out an aviation theme—very attractive—and both food and entertainment are tops. Breakfast, lunch, and dinner are served in the dining room; lounge hours are 4 p.m. to 1:30 a.m.

Family Dining at Budget Prices

It is possible to eat quite well without spending a fortune at Myrtle Beach, and here's a quick rundown on just a few of the budget restaurants in town.

There are two locations for **Western Sizzlin Steak House,** 2300 S. Kings Hwy. and 2900 N. Kings Hwy., and both serve steak and a variety of other dishes at extremely moderate prices. They're open 11 a.m. to 11 p.m. seven days a week.

North on the Strand

Little River, a fishing village on the Intracoastal Waterway at the northern tip of the Grand Strand, has several good restaurants that feature just-caught fish. The best known is **Captain Juel's Hurricane** (tel. 249-2211), which began back in 1945 as a tiny waterfront restaurant nestled in a grove of 300-year-old, moss-draped live oaks and has grown to become one of the largest seafood restaurants in the area. Pana Robertson and Helen Kaltsunis, the present owners, see to it, however, that the small-restaurant atmosphere is maintained. There are six separate rooms, each with an individual character (my favorite is the glass-enclosed porch where you can watch boats traveling past) and there's music most nights. Prices are moderate, salad bar (each dinner includes as many trips as you wish) is really spectacular, and the seafood platter a real bargain.

To the South

Way back when, low-country families used to entertain and dine on the wide porches that ran between the main house and the summer kitchen out back. One of the finest restaurants along the Strand takes its name from that custom, and it's a "must" for good eating in a garden atmosphere that recreates the graciousness of the old days. **The Back Porch** at Murrell's Inlet, U.S. 17S and Wachesaw Road (tel. 651-5263 and 651-5544), is in an old farmhouse built before the turn of the century, and photos hanging just inside the entrance show it as it used to be. The new interior is bright and cheerful, done in garden colors accented by lots of white—white chairs, white latticework partitions, etc. You can dine on enclosed porches that run down each side, but my favorite is the main room with its cathedral ceiling and fireplace at one end. The Spring House lounge is all done up in keeping with the rest of the house and features frozen cocktails that have become legendary. Since it's operated by the Rice Planter's people, I don't have to tell you that the food is superb (and similarly priced), but I *should* tell you about the Back Porch Inlet Dinner, a seafood feast that goes on and on and on. Hours here are 5 to 10 p.m.

You might easily pass by **Red Tyner's Sea Breeze Restaurant,** U.S. 17, just at the Murrell Inlet cutoff. It's set back from the highway and has the look of a roadside cafe. But a stop at the small, bright restaurant will be rewarded with home-cooked meals and a genuinely friendly welcome from the owners. Mr. Tyner presides in the kitchen and the Mrs. handles your order, and take my word for it, you won't find better food anywhere. It's not a fancy cuisine, just plain, country cooking, like country ham, fried chicken, and a fresh floun-der dinner. Breakfast is served any time of the day (try one of Mr. Tyner's excellent omelets accompanied by hash browns), and there's a variety of sand-wiches. Prices may be budget, but the food here ranks with the best of its type.

NIGHTLIFE: Most of the nightlife along the Grand Strand is centered in hotel or motel lounges, some in leading restaurants. Music may vary from country and western to jazz to nostalgia to rock and roll to disco. Among the better places (where there's usually dancing as well as entertainment), are:

The **Brass Anchor** lounge in the Ocean Dunes, 74th Ave. North (tel. 449-7441)—see "Where to Eat," above—has top vocal groups and entertainers.

At the **Sheraton,** there's the lovely rooftop **Pinnacle Supper Club,** 7100 N. Ocean Blvd. (tel. 449-4411), that really shouldn't be missed by nightlifers.

The **Top of the Green Lounge** at **The Breakers,** Oceanfront at 21st Ave. North (tel. 448-2474), has dancing and entertainment from 5 p.m. until 2 a.m. Monday through Friday, 5 p.m. until midnight on Saturday.

And if you've a yen for the "oldies" in music, drop by the **Santa Maria,** 6900 N. Ocean Blvd., adjacent to the Caravelle Hotel.

THINGS TO SEE AND DO: There are two publications just filled with specific information on what, where, when, and how much along the Grand Strand, and either or both will be helpful in planning your vacation here. *Coast* is distributed free by most hotels and motels and is also on counters in many retail establishments and restaurants. The Myrtle Beach Area Chamber of Commerce puts out *See & Do,* and they'll send you a copy if you write them at P.O. Box 2115, Myrtle Beach, SC 29578 (tel. 803/626-7444), or drop by their 1301 N. Kings Hwy. office.

Of course, the *big* attraction is the **beach**—and sunbathing, swimming, boating, and all the other water sports rank first among things to do. **Fishing** is right up there with them, and whether you cast your line from the surf, a public pier, or a charter boat, you'll probably wind up with a pretty good catch. Surf fishing is permitted all along the beach, and there are fishing piers at

Garden City, Surfside, Second Avenue, State Park, Windy Hill, Kits, Crescent Beach, Tilghman Beach, Cherry Grove, and Springmaid.

Charter boats (if you want to sound like a native, call them "head boats") are available at marinas up and down the Strand. In Little River, Capt. Joe Elliott has the *New Rascal,* which sails at 8 a.m., returning at 4 p.m. (tel. 249-2527); Capt. Evertte Ayers operates half-day trips aboard the *New Inlet Princess* from Capt. Dick's Marina at Murrells Inlet (tel. 236-2125); *The Flying Fisher* will take you out for six hours (from the Anchor Marina at Murrells Inlet; tel. 236-5700); and Capt. Frank Juel's *Hurricane* is available for charter at Little River (tel. 249-1711 or 249-1860). These are just a few, but they're typical, and even at the height of the season you'll be able to book a trip without much difficulty. Depending on the season, your catch may include croaker, bluefish, flounder, spot, pompano, black seabass, or whiting.

If you're not swimming or fishing, chances are you'll be out on the links swinging a **golf** club. Most, if not all, of the motels and hotels hold memberships in more than one club and will issue guest cards (which entitle you to reduced greens fees). Fees may run anywhere from $10 to $20, depending on the club and the time of the year. It really doesn't matter much *which* course you play—they're all well laid out and maintained. As for the time of year, the "season" is virtually year round, extending from February through November. Play is heaviest, however, from early February until late April. A golfer friend tells me that if you're planning to spend much time on the Grand Strand courses, you should practice your long shots from the sand; not being a devotee of the game, I'm not quite sure what that means, but it probably has something to do with the sandy roughs I hear mentioned in golfing conversations. At any rate, for what it's worth, I pass it along.

Your **tennis** racquet will get a workout if you bring it along, for there are scores of public and private courts open, with a total of over 200 planned in the next year. A typical tennis facility is the **Dunes Golf and Beach Club** in the Dunes section of Myrtle Beach (tel. 449-5914), which has asphalt courts and charges $4.50 per person per hour for singles.

And when you get tired of all that sports activity, there's the **Pavilion and Amusement Park** on the ocean at 9th Ave. North (open every day from late May through September; closed October until late March; open weekends only from then until May). It's a fairly large park and has some 24 rides, a large arcade with games, souvenir shops, and fast foods, a grandstand act in front of the Pavilion, and dancing to two live bands in the "Magic Attic" every night except Sunday. It will be a sure hit for the kids, and there are few mamas and papas who don't rediscover a little kid inside themselves when they make the obligatory trip—in fact, I must confess that I've made a trip or two on my own without a kid in sight as my excuse!

Myrtle Beach is a good touring center when you tire of the beach, and if you'd rather leave the driving to someone else, **Leisure Time Unlimited** has an excellent schedule of historic tours, both north and south of the Grand Strand. They use a 15-passenger touring van, furnish lunch, and visit such places as Georgetown, Charleston, Orton Plantation, and Historic Wilmington (N.C.), and low-country, privately owned plantations. Fees range from $15 for a special Saturday children's tour to $30 for the Charleston and Wilmington trips. For current schedules and reservations, call them at 448-9483.

If you'd rather do it yourself, **Georgetown** is a short drive south on U.S. 17, but an incredibly long step back in time. The pre-Revolutionary houses, churches, and public buildings are best seen on a train tour that runs daily at 10 and 11 a.m. and 1, 2, and 3 p.m. with an excellent commentary. For reservations and fare information, contact the **Chamber of Commerce,** Front

Street (tel. 546-8436). They will also set you out on self-guided tours armed with maps and brochures.

On your way to or from Georgetown, you'll pass **Pawley's Island,** which has been a resort for over 200 years and is a great place to shop for handcrafts, like the famous Pawley's Island rope hammock. In fact, look for the **Hammock Shop,** which is in a sort of village of handcraft shops called **Plantation Stores,** where you'll find wicker, pewter, miniature doll furniture, brass, china, and all sorts of goodies.

Halfway between Myrtle Beach and Georgetown on U.S. 17 (near Litch-field Beach) is a unique sculpture garden and wildlife park on the grounds of a colonial rice plantation. **Brookgreen Gardens** (tel. 803/237-4218) was begun in 1930 as a setting for representative American garden sculpture from the mid-19th century to the present. Archer Milton and Anna Hyatt Huntington, who planned the garden, constructed a winding, open-work brick wall around it, then designed garden walks in the shape of a butterfly with outspread wings, all leading back to the central space which was the site of the plantation house. On opposite sides of this space are the Small Sculpture Gallery and the original plantation kitchen. In the wildlife park, an outstanding feature is the Cypress Bird Sanctuary, a 90-foot-tall aviary housing species of wading birds within half an acre of cypress swamp. The gardens are open daily from 9:30 a.m. to 4:45 p.m., and admission is $2 for adults, 50¢ for children six to 12, free to those under 6.

READER'S SUGGESTION: "We found **golf on Kiawah Island** (not far from Myrtle Beach) to be absolutely superb, and the place itself is an ecological wonderland. The peace and quiet and chance to see so much of nature left unspoiled were a real treat—this is one place man has managed to make room for his own pleasures without displacing the natural inhabitants" (T. Gleason, Bogota, N.J.).

2. Charleston

If the Old South still lives all through South Carolina's low country, it positively thrives in Charleston. And that's just as it should be, for all our romantic notions of antebellum days—stately homes, courtly manners, gracious hospitality, and, above all, gentle dignity—are facts of everyday life in the old city. Oh, it's kept pace with the times, all right—in fact, many "firsts" in its history mark it as a *leader* in changing trends. Just a few examples: The first indigo crop in the U.S. was grown here in 1690 and proved the basis, along with rice, for many a Charleston family fortune; America's first fire insurance company, "The Friendly Society for the Mutual Insurance of Houses Against Fire," was established in 1736 in Charleston (but was wiped out financially when a disastrous fire in 1740 burned down half the city); the first "weather man" in America, Dr. John Lening, began recording daily temperatures in 1738 to study the effect of weather on the human body; the first shipment of American cotton abroad (seven bags exported to England, at a value of about $873) was from Charleston in 1748; its Chamber of Commerce, organized in 1773, was the first in America; a British flag was pulled down in Charleston and replaced by the Stars and Stripes in 1775, the first time it happened in the colonies; the country's first "fireproof" building was constructed here in 1826, designed by Robert Mills (designer of the Washington Monument, among other landmarks); the first steam locomotive hauling passengers in America ran from Charleston to Hamberg, S.C., in 1831, as one newspaper reported, "on the wings of the wind, annihilating space and leaving all the world behind at the fantastic speed of 15 m.p.h."; the first shot in the "War for Southern Independence" was fired here in 1861; and, more recently, Charleston was the first port in the world to approve the transport of atomic material. From this impressive *partial* list of leadership, you can see that this "grand old southern belle" has always been—and still is—quite a dame!

Her history clearly shows Charleston to have been a spirited lady right from the start. It all began when King Charles of England magnanimously gave eight of his royal friends a strip of land that included the area between the 29th and 36th parallels of latitude and westward to the Pacific (somehow overlooking the fact that France and Spain already claimed much of that land). Anyway, the lords proprietors sent out colonists who first settled at Albemarle Point, then moved to the peninsula as a location more easily defensible against surprise attack. By the mid-1770s, Charleston (originally named Charles Towne) was an important seaport. As the mood for independence grew, Charlestonians threw out the last royal governor, built a palmetto-log and sand fort on Sullivan's Island (that was Fort Moultrie, and it stayed a working fort right on through World War II), repulsed a British fleet on June 28, 1776, then sent couriers to Philadelphia to tell of the victory just in time to convince the Continental Congress that it could be done. The British returned, however, in 1780 with a large land force and took the city, holding it (with the support of loyal Tories) until December of 1782, when it took more than 300 ships to move them out—soldiers, Tories, slaves, and tons of loot.

Then, in 1797, Charleston's spirit reared its head again when a native son, Charles Cotesworth Pinkney, then minister to the French Republic, spoke the supremely American words, "Millions for defense, but not one damned penny for tribute!"—and very nearly got us into war with France.

That first Ordinance of Secession, passed in Columbia in 1860, was actually signed here in Charleston when an epidemic caused the legislature to move, and that fateful shot from Fort Johnson against the Union-held Fort Sumter set the Civil War off and running. The city remained a Confederate stronghold until February of 1865, although it was attacked again and again during the war.

During all those tumultuous years, Charleston was essentially a center of gentility and culture, of wealthy rice and indigo planters who pleasured themselves with imported luxuries, built magnificent town houses (to which they regularly repaired for the summer on May 10 of each year to escape backcountry mosquitoes and malaria), supported the first theater in America, held glittering "socials," originated the "Planters Punch" drink, and ran the state government with an iron hand (in the classic silk glove, of course) until upcountry people forced a new capital in 1790.

Many of those families still own and live in the homes their planter ancestors built, and they still take pride in beautiful, walled gardens, a cultured lifestyle, and a gracious welcome to visitors. Despite the ups and downs of family fortunes, Charlestonians manage to maintain a way of life that, in many respects, has little to do with wealth. I lived here a while during World War II, when there wasn't much socializing, yet the simplest encounter with Charleston natives—even in such ordinary activities as grocery shopping—seemed invested with a "social" air, as though I were a valued guest to be pleased. And I've met with that same treatment on each return trip. Now I've met those who feel a certain snobbishness in Charlestonians, and in truth, I think you'd have to live here a few hundred years to be considered an "insider" —but I'll settle for this kind of "outsider" (I prefer to think it's really "guest") acceptance any time!

Walk along the palmetto-lined Battery or through narrow, crooked streets (some are called "alleys"—but they're not your usual ashcan alleys), or down Cabbage Row (which you will know as Catfish Row of *Porgy and Bess* fame), or drive out to the famous Middleton or Magnolia plantation gardens, and by all means get to know Charlestonians in restaurants or simply on the street, and you'll leave the city as much a "Charleston lover" as everyone else who visits here.

WHERE TO STAY: Charleston's hotels and motels are priced in direct ratio to their proximity to the 789-acre historic district, but if the tariffs close in are too high for your budget, it's really no great problem to drive in from "west of the Ashley," where rates are lower.

Unique

This gracious old city boasts one "hotel" that isn't a hotel at all; rather, a lovely 18th-century home with just five rooms for rent, rooms which combine all the modern conveniences with a special Old Charleston charm. At the **Sword Gate Inn,** 111 Tradd St. (tel. 803/723-8518), you'll be treated like a private house guest: fresh fruit and flowers in every room, bicycles furnished at no charge, and every morning begins with a real Charleston breakfast that includes coffee cakes which come to the table piping hot, nutty Charleston grits, and plenty of butter and jam. You'll be served by your hosts, David and Suzanne Redd, and like any house guest, you can help yourself to coffee or tea from the tiny dining room whenever you like. The rooms themselves are homelike, furnished with antiques (but with a very modern color TV, telephone, private bath, and air conditioning) and made cozy by floral sheets, pillowcases, dust ruffles, and quilts like those handmade in the old days. Each of the four downstairs rooms opens directly onto the cobbled brick courtyard, surrounded by magnolia and holly trees, camellias, azaleas, and gardenias. The one room on the third floor overlooks the city's rooftops, and guests here sleep in a canopied bed.

The second floor of the house (which may or may not have a resident ghost) has a magnificent ballroom that will set you dreaming of southern belles in hoop skirts and Rhett Butlers in frock coats. The floor-to-ceiling mirror at one end reflects polished tables, antique sofas, and a mammoth marble fireplace at the opposite end of the room.

The Sword Gate is the perfect place to come "home" to after strolling the narrow streets "south of Broad Street" (and in Charleston you'll find yourself slowing to a stroll—it's not a place to hurry around) or exploring the old market area. If you plan to treat yourself to this Old South brand of coddling, reserve at least two months in advance and be prepared to pay the cost: $55 single, $68 double (rates include the hearty breakfast, the bikes, and a newspaper at your door in the morning). For my money, it's the best possible way to visit Charleston, no matter what the cost.

The Best of the Rest

Not in the historic district, but only five minutes away, the red and white **Charleston Inn,** 35 Lockwood Blvd. (tel. 803/723-7461), is on the banks of the Ashley River right at U.S. 17. The 116 units are well kept and attractive, there's a pool (the largest in Charleston) and children's playground, and Richard Lynch, the accommodating general manager, can arrange deep-sea fishing charters. Facilities include a lounge and an excellent restaurant. I especially liked the spacious lobby and the fact that special rates are provided prospective patients at the huge hospital across the way as well as families visiting patients there—says something very nice about the management, I think. There are also

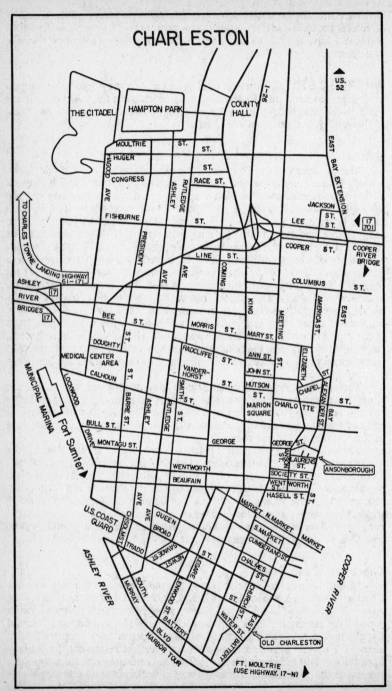

Map courtesy of the Charleston Trident Chamber of Commerce

discounts for AARP, NRTA, APA, and ACT members. Rates are under $40 for doubles, and children 14 and under are accommodated free in the same room with parents.

Across the Ashley River Bridge on U.S. 17S (1501 Savannah Hwy.; tel. 803/766-1611), the 49-unit **Lord Ashley** is a well-run, pleasant place to stay. Golf privileges are extended and babysitters can be arranged. There is a pool, though no dining room (restaurants are not far away). Rates are in the $30 to $35 range.

The **Best Western King Charles Inn**, 237 Meeting St. (tel. 803/723-7451), has bright, comfortable rooms, a pool with poolside food service, a restaurant that serves all three meals, and a lounge with entertainment and dancing. They'll also let you keep Fido in your room. Doubles here start at $52.

Situated across the road from a shopping center, the **Sheraton Motor Inn**, 5981 Rivers Blvd., nine miles west at the junction of Aviation Blvd. and I-26 (tel. 803/744-2501), has the well-furnished rooms you'd expect from this chain and a host of fringe benefits: a dining room open from 6 a.m. to 10 p.m., a lounge with entertainment and dancing six nights a week, free cribs, some oversize beds, and free airport bus service. Doubles are in the $47 to $52 range.

The circular, 13-story **Holiday Inn-Riverview**, U.S. 17 at Ashley River (tel. 803/556-7100), overlooks the river and the city on the opposite bank. It's just two miles from the center of town, not at all inconvenient. Rooms have balconies; there's a pool, a dining room that serves all meals, and a lounge that features entertainment and dancing. Two rooms have been fitted for the handicapped. Doubles begin at $48.

If Charleston's famous gardens are on your "must see" lists, the **Econo-Lodge**, 2237 Savannah Hwy. (tel. 803/571-1880), offers budget prices combined with convenience. Both Magnolia and Middleton Gardens are close by, as is Charlestowne Landing. Several golf courses are also in the vicinity. As is true of all members of this chain, there is no pool and no restaurant (Perkins Pancake House is just down the road, however). Rooms are more than adequate, and the price of a double is only $25 to $32.

Guest Houses

Just a few minutes from the Ashley River Bridge, on the Savannah Highway (that's U.S. 17S), there is a two-block stretch of guest homes, any one of which you'll find comfortable and well run. My personal choice is **Stocker Manor**, 97 Savannah Hwy. (tel. 803/766-1706), which has eight rooms, all with private baths and all with kitchenettes (the only one to offer this added convenience). Mrs. Elizabeth Schaal charges $15 and up, depending on whether the room has tub and shower or just a shower. She stays pretty well booked, so call in advance, but if she's full, she will very graciously help you find accommodations in one of the other guest houses on the street.

READERS' SELECTIONS: "In Charleston, we made a special find. We stayed at the **Battery Carriage House**, 20 South Battery (tel. 803/723-9881), a ten-room carriage house which had just been restored to a guest house (we were there the first month). The rooms were most attractive, the owners pleasant and helpful, and the service elegant (a butler served a continental breakfast on a silver tray). [*Author's Note:* 1983 rates here were $58 to $85.] Also in Charleston, we had a delicious meal at the lovely **Mills Hyatt House Hotel**" (J. Prince, Pottstown, Penna.).

"Not enough recommendations can be given Charleston's **Sweet Grass Inn**, 23 Vendue Range. It is superbly managed by a minister and his charming wife. What a find! Full southern breakfast is included, either in a quaint and tastefully decorated dining room, in your own room, or on the roof terrace with its views of the river and the city.

The room, which was quite large, was beautifully furnished with antiques" (M. Ryan, NY, NY).

Campgrounds

The **Charleston KOA** (write Ladson, SC 29456; tel. 803/797-1045) is about 15 miles northwest on U.S. 78, one mile west of its junction with I-26. There are shaded (and some open), level sites, a disposal station, laundry, store, propane gas, pool, recreation room, and playground. You'll need to send a deposit to hold your reservation. Rates are $11 and up.

DINING IN CHARLESTON: There's good eating everywhere you turn in Charleston, so I've made the arbitrary decision to list a very personal selection of restaurants, most of them in the historic old market area—the character of the city is most reflected here, I think. There are three exceptions to this geographic rule, one place which also has a distinctive Charleston atmosphere and the other choices based on economic considerations.

In or Near the Market

Robert Dickson, owner, chef, and star attraction of **Robert's of Charleston**, 42 N. Market St. in the Rainbow Market (tel. 577-7565), asked me to explain to readers that because the elegant but small restaurant seats only 38, reservations for weekend evenings must be made two months or more in advance. Since the place has received rave reviews in popular publications, this young man has had to disappoint hundreds of travelers who simply don't understand the space limitations. Well, now that you're forewarned, I'll tell you what you're likely to miss unless you can plan to come during the week. Robert and his wife, Pam, are displaced Yankees now firmly entrenched in the South who serve a six-course, prix-fixe dinner, with one sitting at 8 p.m. every night except Sunday and Monday. The entrée is confined to a single item each evening, and is always a masterpiece of perfection, as are the appetizer, salad, fish course, fresh fruit, fresh vegetables, and dessert. Robert introduces each course with song, either show music or opera, in a rich bass baritone, and dinner becomes an event. The cost is a whopping $50—and cheap at the price (includes dinner, wine, and gratuities). As I said, it's very hard for those on the road to be a participant, but call to be put on the waiting list.

Henry's, 48–54 Market St., is a Charleston institution, having been in the same location and run by the same family since the 1930s. There are three dining rooms, one dominated by a carved mahogany bar. Prices run from $5.50 for a half-dozen oysters to $10 for baked stuffed flounder à la Gherardi, beautifully seasoned and moistened with sherry. You don't need reservations, just come in any time from noon to 10 p.m. Closed Sunday.

Another Charleston institution, **Perditas**, 10 Exchange St. (tel. 577-4364), radiates charm in an old-world elegance style. Opened back in 1951, it is set in a seashell tabby building of mid-1700s vintage, and in its time has been a cotton exchange and a sailor's tavern, both a far cry from this beautiful restaurant. Although relatively small (it seats a total of 116 diners), space is divided into separate rooms, each with its own character. Brick arches and red-leather latticed-back chairs grace the main dining room; a tiny balustraded room has chairs adorned with carved cameos; velvet flocked walls and antique paintings are featured in another. And service, from waiters with 15 to 20 years of Perditas training, is knowledgeable and polished—you're pampered from the time you're seated until it's time to leave. As for food, Michael Bennett, son of the founder, carries on a tradition of serving dishes that are perfection. This is, in fact, one of only five restaurants in the United States to have been awarded the prestigious Council of Paris Medal of Honor. You'll know why when you sample any one of their famous seafoods (she-crab soup or shrimp and lobster en papillotte) or beef specialties like tenderloin tips in a luscious mushroom sauce. Dinner here is a bit pricey—in the $10.50 to $16 range—and reservations are strongly recommended. Those prices are semi à la carte, which means that entrées come with German potatoes, salad, and beverages. The wine list, incidentally, is superb. Dinner hours are 6 to 9 p.m. every day but Sunday and major holidays, and Monday from Labor Day through February.

Just a few blocks away on the waterfront, the **Colony House,** 35 Prioleau St.—look for the sign on East Bay St. (tel. 723-3424), occupies a historic old warehouse, but there's nothing in its present appearance that even remotely suggests that lowly past. "Elegant" is the only word for the sparkling white exterior with black shutters framing windows adorned inside with rich draperies. The Garden Room features murals of Charleston's famous Cypress, Middleton, and Magnolia gardens, and offers seafood such as a shellfish platter or Meeting Street crab; while the Wine Cellar—a charming room you really have to see to appreciate—offers delicacies like escallope de veau aux chanterelles and is open for dinner only. The charming **Sam Prioleau's Tavern** serves creative drinks. Prices are expensive by Charleston standards ($3 to $10 at lunch, $7 to $18 at dinner), but both food and atmosphere are memorable. Lunch is 11:30 a.m. to 3 p.m., dinner 5:30 to 10:30 p.m., and reservations are advisable.

The Best for the Budget

In an unpainted wooden house on stilts right at the edge of the Ashley River, next to the Municipal Marina, the **Variety Store** (tel. 723-6325) is a good place to feed an entire family on appetizing dishes without serious injury to the pocketbook. The restaurant occupies one side of a store that sells fishing supplies and souvenirs. You can enjoy okra soup (I'll bet you've never tasted it—do, it's delicious!) or chili, a variety of sandwiches, or fried fish dinners, all at budget prices. Breakfast is served anytime: two eggs, bacon or sausage, toast, and, of course, grits, cost $2.50. Picture windows frame the comings and goings of all sorts of boats—I even saw a Chinese junk sail past. Orders are placed at the counter and waitresses bring the food to comfortable booths. There's a relaxed atmosphere that I, for one, thoroughly enjoyed. Mike Altine, Jr., manager and son of the owner, tells me that the store has been in its present building a little over a year, but that it used to be next door and has been serving locals and boat owners who put in to the adjacent dock for some 25 years. It's open 7 a.m. to 7 p.m. Sunday to Tuesday, until 10 p.m. Wednesday to Saturday.

THINGS TO SEE AND DO: The **Visitor Information Center** at 85 Calhoun St. (across from the Municipal Auditorium) should be your first destination. They have brochures, self-guided walking and driving tours, up-to-the-minute information on cultural events, and a staff that exemplifies Charleston charm. You might want to write ahead, in fact, for their vacation guide (P.O. Box 975, Charleston SC 29402; tel. 803/722-8338). The center stays open from 8:30 a.m. to 5 p.m. every day of the week from March to October, 10 a.m. to 3 p.m. other months.

A Charlestonian once told me that in 1860 "South Carolina seceded from the Union, Charleston seceded from South Carolina, and South of Broad Street seceded from Charleston." Well, I don't know about *that,* but I *do* know that "south of Broad Street" is the heart of Old Charleston and the place to walk or cycle back to another world.

I always head for the **Battery** (if you want to be official about it, the **White Point Gardens**) to get back into the feel of this city. It's right on the end of the peninsula, facing the Cooper River and the harbor. There's a lovely park, shaded by palmettos and live oaks and filled with walkways past old monuments, cannon, and other war relics, and that view of the harbor looks out to Fort Sumter. I like to walk along the sea wall on East Battery and Murray Boulevard (where a blue marlin or some such large ocean fish entertained me with acrobatics one afternoon for nearly an hour) and sink slowly into the history of Charleston. Turning your back to the water, you'll face a row of large, graceful houses that line South Battery, so that when you walk away from the park, it's as though you're going through a sort of gateway into the rest of the town.

Once off South Battery, almost every home is of historic or architectural interest, and I'd need an entire book to tell you about them all. But some you really shouldn't miss are: the **Edmondston-Alston House,** 21 East Battery, built in 1828 by a wealthy merchant and wharf owner and later bought by a Colonel Alston, whose son redid it in the Greek Revival style. Guided tours run from 10 a.m. to 5 p.m., Monday through Saturday; 2 to 5 p.m. on Sunday and holidays; and cost $2.50. You can purchase combination tickets that include this and the Russell House for $4. The **Russell House,** 51 Meeting St., was built before 1809 and has a lovely, unusual, free-flying staircase. Hours and prices are the same as above. The 1803 **Joseph Manigault House,** 350 Meeting St., is an Adams-style structure and also has a notable staircase. It's open every day from 10 a.m. to 5 p.m.; adults pay $2.50; children 6 to 18, $1. The **Heyward-Washington House,** 87 Church St., was built in 1770, and a signer of the Declaration of Independence lived here. Open every day 10 a.m. to 4:30 p.m.; admission is $2.50.

And don't miss the **Dock Street Theatre,** at the corner of Church and Queen Streets. When it opened in 1736, it was the first building in the colonies planned just for theater. The first building burned, and in the early 1800s the Planters Hotel, a very popular local drinking spot, was built around its ruins (that's where "Planters Punch" came from, they say). The theater's back now (since 1936), remodeled and still doing business, with plays, ballet performances, concerts, and other events (it's the longtime home of The Footlight Players, Charleston's resident theater company). The Chamber of Commerce can give you a current "Schedule of Events," but even if nothing is going on at the moment, you can visit the theater Monday through Friday from 10 a.m. to 1 p.m. and 2 to 5 p.m.

Charleston has been a church town from the start, and there are several worth a visit: **St. Michael's Episcopal Church,** Meeting at Broad, is the oldest in the city, dating back to 1761. Its eight bells (imported in 1764) are historic and well traveled: they were taken as a British prize of war in the Revolution and sent back to England, then burned during the Civil War, having to cross the Atlantic again for recasting. The chandelier, installed in 1803, has been lighted by candles, gas, and electricity. Washington worshipped here during his 1791 southern tour.

At 136 Church St., the present **French Huguenot Church** (1844–1845) is the fourth version on this site, the first being built in 1687. In the early days, so many of the congregation came downriver by boat that services were planned so they could arrive on the ebb tide and go home on the flood. It is the only French Huguenot church in the U.S. which still uses the French liturgy.

Congregation Beth Elohim, 90 Hassel St., is the oldest synagogue in continuous use in the U.S., and the second oldest in the country, dating from 1840. This is a replacement for the original, built in 1794, which burned in 1838, and its Greek Revival architecture is considered one of America's finest examples of that style.

The Mother Church of the Roman Catholic dioceses of South Carolina, North Carolina, and Georgia is **St. Mary's,** at 89 Hasell St. It's another replacement (in 1839) for an earlier church (1789) which burned in 1838.

Now, about **Catfish Row**—its real name is **Cabbage Row** (because of the vegetables that used to be sold on the sidewalk) and it's a row of connected buildings from 89 to 91 Church St. that surround a courtyard. DuBose Heyward changed its name in his novel *Porgy,* and when he and George Gershwin collaborated on the *Porgy and Bess* opera, its fame spread all over the world.

The **Old City Market,** at East Bay and Market Streets, still functions, its open stalls under brick sheds with tiled roofs that stretch for roughly three blocks. All sorts of things are sold at the stalls, one of the most interesting being Sea Island vegetables brought in daily by owners of small outlying farms. On either side of the open sheds, old market buildings have been leased to small boutiques filled with marvelous linens, cookware, clothing, gifts, etc. Some of the best restaurants (and some of the oldest) are here also (see "Dining in Charleston," above). A few blocks away from the market, at the corner of Meeting and Broad Streets, look for the **"Flower Ladies"** who sell colorful bunches of blooms from the nearby islands.

The **Citadel,** Moultrie St. and Elmwood Ave., was established in 1842. In 1922 it was moved to its present location, the site of a fortress originally built as an arsenal to suppress slave uprising (and as a refuge for whites if it came to that). The campus of this military school, with its buildings of Moorish design, including crenelated battlements and sentry towers, is especially interesting when the college is in session; and the public is invited to a precision drill parade on the quadrangle at 3:45 p.m. every Friday. To book free guided tours, call 792-5006. There's also an interesting World War II photomural of Europe, with narration, among the Gen. Mark Clark archives (he was president of the college from 1954 to 1965) at the **Citadel Memorial Archives Museum** (free; open Monday through Friday from 2 to 5 p.m., Saturday from 9 a.m., Sunday from 10 a.m.).

I sometimes get the feeling that the whole city is a museum, but then I remember its several outstanding museums of the "standard" sort. For instance, there's the **Charleston Museum,** founded in 1773, making it the oldest in the country. It's in a new, $6-million complex at the corner of Meeting and John Streets (360 Meeting St.; tel. 722-2996). There are more than a million items on display, including early crafts of the area, period rooms, natural history relics, historical dioramas, and anthropological exhibits. It's open 9 a.m. to 5 p.m. every day (adults pay $2; children, 50¢).

The **Old Slave Museum,** 6 Chalmers St., on the National Register of Historic Places, is the oldest museum in the country (1938) devoted exclusively to the contributions of blacks to American culture. It is poetic justice, indeed, that this building, once used to auction slaves, now exhibits African arts and crafts as well as those of American blacks both before and after the days of slavery. Open Monday through Saturday from 10 a.m. to 4:30 p.m. Adults pay $1.50; children, 50¢.

Kids will love the aircraft carrier U.S.S. *Yorktown* at Patriot's Point (on the Mt. Pleasant side of the Cooper River Bridge), and I suspect all navy veterans will, too. The World War II, Korea, and Vietnam exploits of "the Fighting Lady" are, as you'd expect, well documented, and in addition naval history is illustrated through models of ships, planes, and weapons. You can wander through the bridge, wheelhouse, flight and hangar decks, chapel, sick bay, and several other areas. It's open to the public daily from 9 a.m. to 6 p.m.; adults pay $4.50; ages 6 to 11, $2.75.

Charles Towne Landing, on the site of that first 1670 settlement, is a 663-acre park on S.C. 171 at 1500 Old Town Rd., between U.S. 17 and I-126 (tel. 556-4450). An open-air, rather modernistic Interpretive Center has underground exhibits that show the colony's history, and there's a re-creation of a small village, a full-scale replica of a 17th-century trading ship, and a tram tour for 75¢ (or you can rent a bike for $1 an hour). Best of all, there's no flashy "theme park" atmosphere: what you see as you walk under huge old oaks, past freshwater lagoons, and through the Animal Forest (which has animals of the same species that lived here in 1670) is what those early settlers saw. The park is open every day, all year, from 9 a.m. to 5 p.m. Adults pay $3; children 6 to 14, $1, senior citizens and the handicapped, $1.50.

A lot of people come to Charleston just for the "gardens"—and they are lovely. Of course, there are gardens everywhere you look in the city, but when natives use the word, they're referring to Middleton Place, Magnolia Plantation, Cypress Gardens, Charles Towne Landing's 85-acre English Park Garden, and Boone Hall Plantation.

The formal Gardens at **Middleton Place** (14 miles northwest on S.C. 61) is America's oldest, laid out in 1741 and requiring ten years to complete its terraces, ornamental lakes, and plantings of camellias, azaleas, magnolias, and crêpe myrtles. Its creator, Henry Middleton, was the president of the first Continental Congress. The house was built in 1755 (all but the south flank was ransacked and burned by Union troops in 1865) and was restored in the 1870s as a family residence. It now holds period portraits, silver, and antiques. The whole estate is breathtakingly beautiful, but children will probably want to head straight for the stableyards, which are maintained as if for a working low-country plantation, with animals, artifacts, and craft exhibits. There's a cozy restaurant that serves plantation fare like okra gumbo, she-crab soup, plantation chicken, and ham biscuits. Lunch costs less than $7. Hours are 10 a.m. to 4 p.m. for the house (it's closed in late winter), 9 a.m. to 5 p.m. for gardens and stableyard. Admission is $6.50 for adults, $3 for children four to 12 ($3 extra to tour the house).

Ten generations of the Drayton family have lived continuously at **Magnolia Plantation** since the 1670s (ten miles northwest on S.C. 61; tel. 571-1266). They haven't had much luck keeping a roof over their heads: the first mansion burned just after the Revolution and its replacement was burned by Sherman. But you can't call *its* replacement "modern"—a simple, pre-Revolutionary house was barged down from Summerville and set on the basement foundations of its unfortunate predecessors. The magnificent gardens of camellias and azaleas, however, have been among the most beautiful in America down through the years. They reach their height of bloom in March and April, but the gardens are colorful year round. You can tour the house, the gardens (which include a herb garden, horticultural maze, and Biblical garden), and a petting zoo, ride canoes through a 125-acre waterfowl refuge, or walk or cycle through wildlife trails. It's open daily from 8 a.m. to dusk, and costs $5 for adults, $3 for ages 13 to 21, $2 for four to 12 (under four, free). Prices go up $1 in March and April.

There are footpaths and boats to take you through flower-filled **Cypress Gardens,** 23 miles from Charleston on S.C. 52 (look for turnoff signs). The swamp garden was used as a freshwater reserve for Dean Hall, a huge Cooper River rice plantation, and was given to the city in 1963. Hours are 8 a.m. to

5 p.m. daily from February 15 through May 1, and admission is $5 for adults,
$2 for children 13 to 20 and for servicemen and their families. Boat rides are
$1 extra.

Boone Hall, six miles north on U.S. 17 (tel. 884-4371), is approached by
a famous "Avenue of Oaks," huge old moss-draped trees planted in 1743 by
one Capt. Thomas Boone. The first floor of the beautiful plantation house is
elegantly furnished and open to the public. Hours are 8:30 a.m. to 6:30 p.m.
Monday through Saturday, 1 to 6:30 p.m. on Sunday, March 15 through Labor
Day; 9 a.m. to 5 p.m. and 1 to 5 p.m. other times. The guided tour is $4 for
adults, 50¢ for ages six to 12.

Twelve miles from Charleston, on the Ashley River Road (S.C. 61), **Drayton Hall** is one of the oldest surviving plantations (built in 1738 and owned by
the Drayton family until 1974). Framed by majestic live oaks, the lovely old
Georgian-Palladian house is now a property of the National Trust for Historic
Preservation (and if you're a member of the Trust, you get in free with membership card). It's open from 10 a.m. to 4 p.m. daily, with tours on the hour (last
one at 3 p.m.). Rates are seasonal: $4 and $2 mid-March through October, $3
and $2 other months. Closed Thanksgiving, Christmas, and New Year's Day.

Tours

There are several very good tours of Charleston and the area, among them:
the **Gray Line Harbor Tour,** City Mariner, Lockwood Blvd. (tel. 722-1112 or
723-5858), a two-hour lecture tour, covering 70 points of interest within 25
miles ($6 for adults, $3 for ages two to 11). **Charleston Carriage Company,** 96
N. Market St. (tel. 577-0042), horse-drawn carriage tours (narrated) depart
from "The Buggy Whip," 96 N. Market St. on the hour from 9 a.m. until dusk
at $7 for adults, $4 ages two to 12 (call to reserve); narrated carriage tours from
the Battery, **Palmetto Carriage Works, Ltd.,** 8 Guignard St. (tel. 723-8145),
$7 for adults, $4, ages three to 12; cassette walking or driving tours from
Charles Towne Tours, P.O. Box 243, Charleston, SC 29402 (tel. 803/722-2988
or 723-6993), available at the Mills Hyatt House gift shop, the Golden Eagle
Motel, and Downtown Holiday Inn, which cost $6; **Gray Line Bus Tours**
(leave from Frances Marion Hotel; tel. 722-4444), two-hour lecture tours.

Both **Fort Moultrie,** on Sullivan's Island, West Middle St., ten miles east
of the city (tel. 833-3123), and **Fort Sumter** (in the harbor) are open to visitors.
There's no charge at Fort Moultrie, which opens 9 a.m. to 6 p.m. in summer
and 9 a.m. to 5 p.m. in winter, and there's a visitor center. To reach Fort
Sumter, the U.S. Coast Guard supervises sightseeing yachts operated by **Fort
Sumter Tours,** write to them at Box 59, Charleston, SC 29402 (located in the
Municipal Marina at the foot of Calhoun St. on Lockwood Drive; tel. 722-
1691). The 2½-hour tours are scheduled at hours that vary seasonally. Fare
is $5.50; $3 for those under 12. Besides visiting the fort, on the swing around
the harbor you'll see the **U.S. Coast Guard Base** (on the site of an old rice mill),
Fort Johnson (the one that fired on Sumter to start "the war"), Fort Moultrie
(from the water), the **Cooper River Bridges** (two of the largest in the world),
and several other harbor sights, all the subject of an interesting commentary
as you pass by.

One last "thing to do": In May of 1977, Charleston inaugurated an annual
Spoleto Festival U.S.A., a 12-day culture explosion that brought 600 performers and over 100 events (opera, theater, ballet, jazz, symphony, choral concerts,
and art and film shows) directed by Gian Carlo Menotti, who orchestrates the
Spoleto, Italy, festival each summer. The first festival was a rousing success,
fun for everybody, and it gets better every year. Write Spoleto U.S.A., P.O. Box

509, Charleston, SC 29402 (tel. 803/722-2764) for future dates if you're interested.

3. Hilton Head Island

Colonization efforts and squabbling over ownership of Hilton Head—the largest sea island between New Jersey and Florida—went on among Spain, France, and England from the early 1600s until the mid-1700s. Native Indians, *certain* of their claim to the land, harassed them all. But by the end of the 18th century, things had quieted down enough for large plantations to flourish, and a leisurely island lifestyle evolved. Today's "plantations" (most resort areas define their boundaries by the term) hold on to that leisure—indeed, offer it to all comers—and modern "crops" come in the form of tourism instead of rice. Some 450,000 to 500,000 resort guests visit the island annually, and that's some "harvest" for a permanent population of about 7500 (most of whom are engaged in attracting or servicing the visitors).

Although only 42 square miles in area (12 miles long and five miles at its widest), Hilton Head has a feeling of spaciousness, due to judicious planning from the start of its development in 1952. The only "city" (of sorts) is Harbour Town at Sea Pines Plantation. The broad beaches on its ocean side, beautiful sea marshes over on the sound, natural wooded areas of live and water oak, pine, bay, and palmetto trees have all been carefully preserved amid the commercial enterprise that has created over 1500 hotel rooms (mostly oceanfront) and some 4000 vacation villas, condominiums, and retirement homes. It's an environmental paradise that regularly attracts artists, writers, musicians (jazz, classical, and even rock), theater groups, and craftsmen.

Recreation, Hilton Head's economic base, goes on year round in a subtropical climate that ranges from the low 50s in winter to mid-80s in summer. There are 16 golf courses (11 are championship caliber—the Heritage Golf Classic and Women's International Professional are annual events), over 175 tennis courts (which are settings for the World Invitational Tennis Classic, Avon Futures Tennis Championship, and the Family Circle Cup), six marinas that can dock yachts up to 100 feet long, a sailing club, all sorts of rental boats, charter fishing boats for hire (there's an annual billfishing tournament), miles and miles of beach (some up to 600 feet wide at low tide), rental bicycles and 14 miles of rambling bike paths, three riding stables (with boarding facilities for those who bring their own mounts), 15 shopping centers (with exquisite craft shops and elegant resort-apparel boutiques), 90 restaurants, and . . . well, you name it and it's probably here. Nightlife is found chiefly in hotel or shopping-center lounges, which can be quiet, intimate rendezvous spots or lively entertainment centers with sophisticated bands for dancing and top performers doing their thing.

GETTING THERE: Even though Hilton Head is an island, you get there over a bridge (about 40 miles east of I-95, 30 miles north of Savannah, Georgia). Delta and Eastern Airlines fly into Savannah and there's limousine service. Of course, if you fly your own, you'll land directly at the island's airport, a 3700-foot paved runway that can handle most nonjet private planes. For boat owners, getting there is simple, since it's directly on the Intracoastal Waterway. Amtrak, Greyhound, and Trailways take train and bus riders to Savannah.

Incidentally, the **Hilton Head Island Chamber of Commerce, P.O. Box 5647, Hilton Head Island, SC 29938 (tel. 803/785-3673)**, is especially helpful in planning a visit, either before or after your arrival.

WHERE TO STAY: There is really no such thing as "budget" on Hilton Head Island. However, it *is* possible these days to spend time here for a *reasonable* cost. Of course, the older resort establishments (called plantations) are the very embodiment of luxury, with prices to match.

There is, however, a central reservation service which can book you into various rooms and villas almost anywhere on the island. Write or call: Hilton Head Central Reservation Service, P.O. Box 5312, Hilton Head Island, SC 29938 (tel. 803/785-9050 or toll free 800/845-7018).

Another suggestion is the rental of private cottages, and for up-to-date availability, rates, and bookings, you can contact: Island Rentals and Real Estate Inc., P.O. Box 5915, Hilton Head Island, SC 29938 (tel. 803/785-3813 or toll free 800/845-6134).

The Luxury Level

Sea Pines Plantation (write Sea Pines Resort, Hilton Head Island, SC 29938; tel. toll free 800/845-6131, in South Carolina 800/922-7042) was Hilton Head's first resort and has a faithful following who would not stay anywhere else. Spread over more than 4500 acres, it has four miles of ocean beach, 14 miles of bike trails, three championship golf courses, 72 tennis courts, an outstanding children's summer recreation program, and over a dozen restaurants and entertainment spots within its boundaries. You can eat, shop, or enjoy nightlife without being a Sea Pines guest, but there's a small fee to enter the grounds if you're not. Double rooms at the oceanfront Hilton Head Inn rent for $100 and up per night in season (late March to December), and there are over 1000 rental villas, completely furnished, which rent for $80 to $225 per day and range from one to four bedrooms. Prices vary by season, location, view, and number of bedrooms. There are package plans for golf, tennis, families, and honeymooners, and the best way to get full details is to write for their free "Sea Pines Vacation Guide" and package brochure.

The **Hyatt on Hilton Head Island,** P.O. Box 6167, Hilton Head, SC 29938 (tel. 803/785-1234), is a 372-room deluxe oceanfront hotel, and here, too, there are complete resort facilities. There's a pool, a wading pool, a children's program during the summer months, an excellent restaurant, a snackbar, three bars with entertainment and dancing, two 18-hole golf courses, 25 tennis courts, and sailboats. Rooms have private balconies. Rates start at $97 and go up to $140.

The "Reasonable" Level

The **Sea Crest Motel,** P.O. Box 5818, Hilton Head, SC 29938 (tel. 803/785-2121), has 92 rooms, all of which overlook either pool or ocean. The exceptionally large and attractive rooms all have two double beds ($67 oceanfront, $57 poolside) and there are two-bedroom apartments ($600 and $540 weekly) and rooms with kitchenettes ($480 and $420 weekly) available. These are seasonal rates—March 1 to November 1—and they drop considerably at other times. Golf and tennis plans can be arranged here. This is, I think, the prettiest of the reasonably priced motels, and it's the site of two fine restaurants. The gourmet dining room, the Captain's Table, is unquestionably the island's finest (see "Dining on the Island," below).

Accommodations are also either poolside or oceanfront at the **Adventure Inn Resort,** P.O. Box 5646, Hilton Head, SC 29938 (tel. 803/785-5151). The light, airy rooms are a little larger than average. There's a restaurant, and the lounge offers entertainment nightly. Guest privileges are extended at nearby golf courses and tennis courts. Rates at the inn run from $62 to $77, double occupancy.

Campgrounds

Those with recreational vehicles will find over 400 paved lots, full hookups, tennis courts, a pool, recreation area, and health club at the **Outdoor Resorts of America.** For current rates and bookings, contact them at: P.O. Box 5405, Hilton Head Island, SC 29938 (tel. 803/785-7699).

DINING ON THE ISLAND: I counted over 90 eating spots on Hilton Head —and I may have missed a few. So, whatever else you have in mind, rest assured that a restaurant—and a good one—will never be far away during your stay. Needless to say, every one of the hotels offers food, and most of the dining rooms are pretty good. I am listing only one such here, and that only because it is superior to anything else on the island; but mostly, I want to tell you about those places *other* than hotels where you'll find good food and/or atmosphere.

The Oldest and the Best

There's no printed menu at **The Captain's Table,** in the **Sea Crest Motel,** Avocet St., on the ocean just north of Coligny Circle (tel. 785-4950), and dinner is by reservation only. Gourmet dinners are supervised by Franz Auer, an Austrian who came to Hilton Head by way of Paris, Montréal, and New York. His partner, Klaus Jackel, began life in Berlin, was maitre d' at New York's Rainbow Room for a spell, and met Franz in Montréal. Sharing an entrance with the Treasure Cove Restaurant (see below), the Captain's Table is a romantic, candlelit room with a nautical decor (what else!) and serves only 50 at one sitting. The à la carte continental menu at the Captain's Table features beef, veal, seafood, or whatever else Franz has on for the evening. Ingredients are always the very best and the freshest, and preparation is absolutely perfection. This is dining at its very best in an atmosphere of intimate elegance. And, as is fitting, jackets and ties are required. Dinner is from 6 to 10 p.m. and entrées run $10 to $20—and remember, it's by reservation only (a day or two in advance, if possible, or you may be disappointed).

Also Very Good

The Treasure Cove, also run by the abovementioned Klaus and Franz, is one of the prettiest restaurants around. The high, sloping ceiling has baskets of greenery hanging from exposed beams, and nautical artifacts are tastefully displayed around the room. "I'm Chris," my friendly and efficient waitress introduced herself, "and if you want anything, please let me know." Well, I never had to take her up on that, for my dinner companion and I were served every course at exactly the right time; it turned out to be a leisurely meal, without either a sense of hurry or those gaps that sometimes leave you wondering what comes next—or when. Our filet of flounder (the "Catch of the Day") was beautifully broiled, moist, and tender, and same-day fresh. Home-baked bread arrived hot and wrapped to keep it that way. There were other seafood selections on the menu, including a local-recipe low-country seafood ragoût (oysters, shrimp, and chicken in a white wine sauce) and several beef dishes, all served with fresh salad (we chose Franz's cheese dressing, which I would classify as "gourmet" in itself), parsley potatoes, and a delicately seasoned medley of peas, carrots, and cauliflower. Reservations are not necessary for breakfast (7 to 10 a.m.), lunch (noon to 2:30 p.m.), or dinner (6 to 10 p.m.) and dress is casual. Entrees begin at $5.50.

Hudson's Seafood House on the Docks, on the water between Intracoastal Waterway markers 13 and 14 (tel. 785-2772), was built as a seafood processing factory in 1912 and still processes fish, clams, and oysters for local distribution —so there's no need to mention freshness. Service is on a first-come, first-served basis, and if you're seated in the north dining room, you'll be eating in the original oyster factory. A few "drydock" courses show up on the menu (a 12-oz. rib eye steak, for example), but I strongly recommend that you opt for seafood, such as stuffed prawns or "Cha-Sha" (jumbo shrimp tempura with sweet-and-sour sauce). Everything is cooked to order and very, very good. Before and after dinner (5 to 10 p.m. except Sunday, when it's closed), you're welcome to stroll on the docks past shrimp boats and enjoy the view of the mainland and nearby Parris Island. Sunsets here are always spectacular, and are accompanied by live entertainment.

Over at Harbour Town, a former artist's studio has been turned into a delightful restaurant and lounge that serves lunch from 11:30 a.m. to 3 p.m. and dinner from 6:30 to 10 p.m. Monday through Saturday. The glassed-in porch area at **CQ's,** Area 4, Lighthouse Rd., Harbour Town, Sea Pines Plantation (tel. 671-2779), is shaded by huge oaks and pines, and the decor is reminiscent of a New York pub. Quiches, crêpes, seafood, and beef specialties are excellent—as well as quite moderate in price. The staff here is one of the friendliest and most helpful anywhere, which helps account for CQ's popularity (you may have a short wait to be seated, but *do* stay).

The attractive, energetic young owners of CQ's, Dick Werth and Orrie Scarminach, have recently opened another restaurant located in Palmetto Dunes Resort. **Alexander's,** Area 2, Queen's Folly Rd., Palmetto Dunes Resort (tel. 785-4999), features high ceilings, lots of glass, and is on a picturesque lagoon close to the Hyatt Hotel. Lunch is served from noon to 3 p.m., dinner from 6:30 to 10 p.m., Monday through Saturday (dinner only on Sunday).

READER'S SUGGESTION: "Some of the best eating we found on Hilton Head was at **Fulvio's Restaurant.** It's at Area 2, Highway 278 and New Orleans Rd., and you can telephone them at 785-5008. I suggest that no visitor miss having at least one dinner there—they don't serve lunch, and they're closed Sunday, but their continental dishes are really superb, and we considered it truly fine dining" (S. Barr, Atlanta, Ga.).

THINGS TO SEE AND DO: Golf and tennis compete with beach activities for first place on the "what to do" list. Facilities for all three come with your hotel reservation. Greens fees will run $12 to $15. Court fees are in the $5- to $10-per-hour range. Instruction is available in both sports.

Sailing devotees can join a three-hour cruise aboard the 41-foot *Ocean House* (which carries up to six) by contacting the **Harbour Town Marine** (671-4534). For old-hand sailors, both sail and motor boats can be rented through **Island Boat Rentals,** Palmetto Bay Village Marina, 164 Palmetto Bay Rd. (tel. 785-6004).

For fishing information and reservations, call Harbour Town Fishing Office (tel. 671-4534).

In Hilton Head Plantation, **Seabrook Farm Stables** can furnish horses and guides for beach and trail rides, Monday through Saturday. Call 785-5415.

Cyclists can rent bikes from **Sea Pines Bicycle Rentals** (tel. 671-5899).

Ann Parker's Island Tour, 1 Dune Lane (tel. 785-7373), costs $17 for two hours of narrated sightseeing around Hilton Head, Monday through Friday. The tour includes a half-hour browsing time in Harbour Town, and Ann can extend it to include lunch, shopping, art gallery visits, or boat cruises, with appropriate price adjustments.

Exploring South Carolina's low country off the island is fun, and **Travel Ventures** (tel. 785-5237) will arrange a four-hour tour of Historic Savannah, an eight-hour visit to Charleston and Middleton Gardens, or a four-hour tour of Beaufort, Parris Island (to visit the museum at the U.S. Marine Corps base there), and various rice, indigo, and cotton plantation sites, all in air-conditioned motorcoaches with knowledgeable guides.

An interesting do-it-yourself tour is a half-day drive to **Beaufort** (low-country pronunciation is BEW-fort), the picturesque old seaport just a few miles away on S.C. 170. "Quaint" is the only way to describe its narrow streets shaded by huge old live oaks and homes that have survived from the 1700s (the oldest was built in 1717 and is at Port Republic and New Streets). This was the second area in North America discovered by the Spanish (1520), the site of the first fort (1525) and of the first attempted settlement (1562), and several forts have been excavated which date from 1566 and 1577. The **Chamber of Commerce** on Freedom Mall, 1006 Bay St., P.O. Box 910, Beaufort, SC 29902 (tel. 803/524-3163) has self-guided tours and lots of other information about the historic town. And if your trip plans are for mid-March, write the **Historic Beaufort Foundation**, P.O. Box 11, Beaufort, SC 29902 (tel. 803/524-6334), for specific dates and detailed information on their three days of antebellum plantations and gardens tours.

READERS' SUGGESTION: "It's terrific to stay in a real antebellum home in Beaufort, like the **Bay Street Inn** at 601 Bay St. (tel. 803/524-7720). All five of their third-floor rooms have marvelous river views and a fireplace. Also, private baths. Breakfast can be either in your room or the garden, and they furnish bicycles for touring" (M. Lee, Savannah, Ga.).

"There's a neat bed-and-breakfast place in Beaufort, run by **Ellie and Norman MacPherson.** It's really nice, with great views from the bedrooms, which are located over their antique shop at 1106 Carteret St. (tel. 803/524-4678). Two really fine restaurants are the **Anchorage**, on Bay St., and the **White Hall Inn**, across the river from Beaufort" (P. Brown, New York, N.Y.).

Chapter X

SOUTH CAROLINA: THE MIDLANDS AND "UP COUNTRY"

1. Columbia
2. Around Columbia

THE "NEW SOUTH" IS REFLECTED all across this part of South Carolina. Industries such as textiles, chemicals, precision-tool making, and metalworks, making full use of the abundant waterpower, thrive happily alongside large dairy farms and others that produce tobacco, soybeans, peaches, wheat, and cotton as money crops, and still others with large stands of pine trees for an ever-growing paper industry. There's a vitality which springs no doubt from those early settlers who scorned the leisurely "low-country" pace from the start—yet there's certainly no lack of warmth and hospitality throughout the region. Traditional southern customs are very much alive and well, but they mingle without friction with those of the modern world.

1. Columbia

Columbia, unlike many of our older cities, has the orderly look of a planned community, with streets laid out in an almost unbroken checkerboard pattern, and broad boulevards giving it a particularly graceful beauty. All of that is not surprising, since it was, in fact, created back in 1786 as a compromise capital to satisfy both "low-" and "up"-country factions. It is just three miles from the exact geographical center of the state, and no point in South Carolina is more than two hours' drive from the capital city. Washington paid a visit to Columbia in 1791, just one year after the first General Assembly convened in the brand-new city.

It was here that things came to a head in the North/South dispute that eventually became the Civil War. The trouble that had been brewing for years erupted in a convention held in the First Baptist Church here which passed the first Ordinance of Secession in the southern states on December 17, 1860. (Because of a local smallpox epidemic, however, it was actually signed in Charleston.) The city itself was little touched by battle until General Sherman arrived with his Union troops on February 17, 1865, and virtually wiped out the town by fire: an 84-block area and some 1386 buildings were left in ashes, although the new State House (still under construction), the university, and the home of the French consul on Main Street were spared.

Although recovery during Reconstruction was slow, the city that emerged from almost complete devastation is one of stately homes and public buildings, with government and education (there are seven colleges located here) playing leading roles in its economy, followed closely by a wide diversity of industry. Fort Jackson, a U.S. Army basic training post on the southeast edge of town, with its more than 25,000 troops, adds another element to the economic mix.

WHERE TO STAY: The **Carolina Inn,** 937 Assembly St. (tel. 803/799-8200), is a 14-story highrise, with some 240 rooms, located within walking distance of the State House, the University of South Carolina, the Coliseum, the Columbia Museum of Art, and downtown shopping, theaters, and restaurants. Spacious rooms are tastefully furnished in a traditional decor, and many have oversized beds. There's an Olympic-size pool, and Beau's Lounge, which features "no cover, no minimum" popular, beach and dance music. Beau's Dining Room on the first floor is a great favorite of local business people and politicians and opens for breakfast and lunch from 7 a.m. to 2:30 p.m., dinner from 6 to 11 p.m. (prices in the $10 to $18 range). Doubles start at $50.

Another centrally located, very popular motel is the **Carolina Town House,** 1615 Gervais St., at Henderson St. (tel. 803/771-8711). Maybe it was that convenient location that led General Sherman to pick the site as his headquarters in February of 1865—but you won't find any evidence there today of that gentleman's brief encampment on the spot. The motel is heavily patronized by government personnel (both the F.B.I. and state legislators get special room rates), and local industrial firms often quarter important visitors here. The rather elegant decor extends from the lobby to the Chandelier Room (see "Where to Eat") to guest rooms (which are larger than most and decorated with deep shag carpeting, velvet-flocked draperies, and coordinated bedspreads). There's a pool, steam baths, and the really lovely Tiffany Lounge. Also, the staff here is especially friendly and helpful. How much you pay for a double room depends on where your room is situated (there's not that much difference in the quality among the rooms themselves): those in the newer section (facing Gervais St.) start at $50, a little less farther back in an older part, and still less in the oldest building. There's no charge for children up to 18 in the same room with parents.

In Cayce (that's really Columbia, and just a mile from the State Capitol), the **Tremont Motor Inn,** 111 Knox Abbott Dr., Cayce, SC 29033 (tel. 803/796-

6240), is set back from the road in wooded, landscaped grounds. Not only is the staff at the Tremont extremely helpful and friendly, the list of extras is also impressive. To begin with, beds are oversize in the cheerfully decorated rooms. Then, there are irons and ironing boards available, a swimming pool, coin laundry, valet service, room service (unusual in a motel), babysitting service, children's playground, and complimentary coffee in the lobby. There's a 24-hour restaurant and a lounge that's open until the wee hours. Rates for doubles range from $32 to $40.

At the Broad River Road exit on I-20, the **Quality Inn,** 1029 Briargate Circle (tel. 803/772-0270), is also out of the downtown area, a convenient location for getting to the lovely Riverbanks Park. Rooms are large (some have kitchens), there's a heated pool, they'll let you bring Fido along, and the office keeps an up-to-date babysitter list—all of which makes this a good family vacation headquarters. The dining room is open from 6:30 a.m. to 2 p.m. and 5 to 10 p.m., the bar from 5 p.m. to 1 a.m. They also arrange golf privileges at one of Columbia's private golf courses. Double rooms start at $45; those with kitchens cost an additional $5.

The **Holiday Inn-Northwest,** P.O. Box 258, West Columbia, SC 29169 (tel. 303/794-9440), is five miles from downtown at the intersection of U.S. 1 and I-26. Some of the attractive rooms have king-size beds, and all are large and comfortable. In addition to the pool, there's a children's playground and a kennel for pets. The dining room serves all meals and there's entertainment in the lounge every night except Sunday and Monday. Double rooms are in the $45 to $50 range and they can arrange family-plan rates.

Economy-minded travelers will find the **Days Inn,** 7128 Parklane Rd.—2 blocks off I-20 (tel. 803/736-0000), a comfortable, budget-priced place to stay, with a Tasty World restaurant on the premises. Double rooms here cost a mere $33.88.

WHERE TO EAT: The Market, 1205 Assembly St., at Gervais (tel. 779-5010), is a popular dining spot for locals, and it's small wonder, what with seafood specialties like lobster and red snapper, and baking done in their own kitchen. Background music here, too, is no intrusion on conversation, just a nice accompaniment. Lunch prices run $4.50 and up, and at dinner you can expect prices in the $6.50 to $15 range. Lunch hours are 11:30 a.m. to 2:30 p.m., dinner from 5 to 11 p.m.

Over on the university campus in a tall dormitory building with a circular top, between Green and Pendleton Streets on Barnwell, there's a lovely restaurant, the **Top of Carolina** (tel. 777-8198). It isn't allowed to advertise because it is a part of the university, but it's a favored lunch place for everyone in the know in Columbia. It's a circular, revolving dining room (the motor came from the New York World's Fair) that makes a complete rotation every 59 minutes —that's pretty fast, and you can detect the movement as well as enjoy the changing view of Columbia. They feature a very good buffet at prices that can only be called budget, especially in such surroundings, and it's so popular that reservations are a good idea (many of the city's leading business people are regulars). Lunch is 11:45 a.m. to 2 p.m. Monday through Friday, and 11:30 a.m. to 2 p.m. on Sunday.

Columbia has one of those homey, pleasant eateries serving good, plain food in an unpretentious setting at reasonable (correction: budget) prices that always delight me—they're usually known only to residents, and I always seem to find them almost by accident. The **Winner's Circle Restaurant,** 1111 Green St. (tel. 799-5242), has a loyal following among university students and faculty and the local white-collar crowd, none of whom seem to mind its grill-like, plastic-booth decor. My daughter (who lives in Columbia and loves this place) classifies the food as "pretty good southern to very good southern," and I have to go along with her. Turnip greens, cornbread, and blackeyed peas just don't show up on too many menus, and when they do, they all too often don't have that home-cooked flavor; here, they do! But that's not all they serve: there's a wide variety of sandwiches, ranging from $1.50 to $3; a nice selection of salads (including Greek), from $1.50 to $3; a supper special of half a fried chicken or an eight-ounce steak, with baked potato or french fries, tossed salad, and french bread for $4; and a buffet that features fried chicken, knockwurst, fish, roast beef, ham, and country-fried steak, two vegetables, bread, and beverage for an unbelievable $4! Breakfast, which is served from 7 to 10:45 a.m., costs about $2 (that's for two eggs, ham, bacon, or sausage, grits, toast and jelly, and coffee). On weekdays, lunch and dinner are served nonstop from 11 a.m. to 8 p.m., and on Sunday it's 11 a.m. to 3 p.m.

THINGS TO SEE AND DO: Before you do anything else in Columbia, go by the **Chamber of Commerce** at 1308 Laurel St. Columbia, SC 29202 (tel. 779-5350). They have an excellent Visitor Center there and can be invaluable in helping you plan sightseeing in the Greater Columbia area.

The **State House,** Main and Gervais Sts., was begun in 1855 and only half-finished when General Sherman bombarded Columbia in 1865. The west and south walls are marked with bronze stars where shells struck. In the fire that wiped out so much of the city, the State House escaped destruction, but the architect's plans were burned, with the result that the dome is not the one originally envisioned. Despite that, the building, with its Corinthian granite columns, is considered one of the most beautiful state capitols in the country. It is always interesting to visit—the landscaped grounds hold memorial tablets and monuments and inside are portraits and statues of South Carolina greats— but especially so when the legislature is in session from mid-January through April. The building is open every weekday from 9 a.m. to 5 p.m.

The **Governor's Mansion,** 800 Richland St. at Gadsden St., was originally built as officers' quarters for Arsenal Academy. When Sherman swept through the town, this was the only building on the Academy grounds left standing. South Carolina governors have lived here since 1868. For a free, 30-minute-guided tour (Tuesday through Thursday), call 758-3452 for an appointment.

There's no charge to visit the **Columbia Museums of Art and Science** (except for the planetarium shows which cost 75¢ for adults, 50¢ for students, military personnel, and children six though 11). There's an outstanding collection of Renaissance paintings and sculpture (including two Tintorettos and a Botticelli from the Samuel H. Kress collection), as well as a host of South Carolina historical silver, pottery, and furniture. Each month, several temporary collections go on exhibit. Check to see if musical concerts or historical lectures are scheduled during your stay—some of them are quite good. Changing temporary shows, a nature garden, and physical science and aquatic displays are featured in the science section. Films on subject matter ranging from history to astronomy to art are shown Sunday at 3 p.m. The planetarium shows are at 2 and 4 p.m. on Saturday and Sunday, and children under six are treated to a special show at 3 p.m. on Saturday and Sunday (they aren't admitted to the regularly scheduled ones).

The 218-acre **University of South Carolina campus** is bounded by Gregg, Pendleton, and Main Streets. The grounds are really lovely—so beautiful, in fact, that Hollywood has several times filmed antebellum story background shots on the Horseshoe, lined with buildings dating from the early 1800s (the university was founded in 1801) and filled with ancient oaks and magnolias. While you're there, it's worth half an hour or so to go by the McKissick Museums which are housed in the fine old McKissick Library Building, located at the head of the historic Horseshoe on the corner of Pendleton and Sumter Streets. Remodeled in 1976 to serve as a center for the university's museums, art gallery, and archives, the museums are open from 9 a.m. to 4 p.m. Monday through Friday, and during the school year on Sunday from 1 to 5 p.m. There is no admission charge.

You can buy a ticket for **Woodrow Wilson's boyhood home** at 1705 Hampton St., the restored 1820 **Hampton-Preston House** at 1615 Blanding St., or the **Robert Mills Historic House and Park** at 1616 Blanding St. for $4 (students pay $2). Separately, they cost $2 for the Mills House, $1.50 for each of the other two (half-price for students). Woodrow Wilson you know; Wade Hampton was a South Carolina hero from a family of state leaders; and Robert Mills served seven presidents as our first federal architect, designing such landmarks as the Washington Monument, the U.S. Treasury Building, and the Old Patent Office in Washington. All three houses are furnished with originals, and the Mills House has some outstanding mantels and chandeliers of the Regency period. They're open from 10 a.m. to 4 p.m. Tuesday through Saturday, 2 to 5 p.m. on Sunday; closed the last two weeks in December.

If you're a lover of church architecture, be sure to visit **Trinity Church** on Sumter Street between Senate and Gervaise. It's an exquisite example of English Gothic, modeled after York Cathedral in England. It's open Monday through Friday from 9 a.m. to 4 p.m., on Saturday from 9 a.m. to noon.

Whatever else you plan to do in Columbia, save time to drive out to the **Riverbanks Zoological Gardens** at the intersection of Greystone Blvd. and I-126 (tel. 779-8717 or 779-8730). In a relatively small space, something of a miracle has been accomplished in establishing a refuge for many endangered species (such as the American bald eagle). The animals and birds (more than 700!) here are the healthiest, liveliest I've ever seen in a zoo—for instance, rather than simply standing around, two young elephants I saw were playing as naturally and delightfully as if they were in their native habitat. Penguins are kept happy in an environmental duplicate of the bacteria-free Antarctic ice shelf. Botanically significant trees and plants are labeled throughout the park. It's open seven days a week from 9 a.m. to 5 p.m., with a $3 charge for adults, $1.25 for children six to 12 (parking costs 50¢). The last tickets are sold one hour before closing.

I don't know if the back of a commercial building can really be called a "sightseeing" item, but there's one in Columbia that I found absolutely intriguing. The **Farm Credit Bank,** on Marion Street where it intersects with Hampton Street, has turned its parking lot into a sort of "event" by commissioning a local artist with the interesting name of Blue Sky to paint a 50x75-foot mural on the back of the bank building. Now, outdoor paintings aren't that unusual, but this one, to quote a local publication, could literally drive you "up a wall." Named *Tunnelvision,* it pictures a highway tunnel opening onto a mountain sunrise so realistically that it looks as if you drive right into it! And, indeed, you *can* drive through the lot and up to the wall itself, which is even spookier if you park at the "tunnel's" entrance. If you're in this part of town, even at night (when it's floodlit), swing by and take a look—it's really something.

2. Around Columbia

Within an hour or two of Columbia, there are several places worth the drive. For example, on I-85 just across the border from North Carolina the **Kings Mountain National Military Park** marks the site of a Revolutionary battle that some historians label crucial to the eventual American victory. The southern Appalachians had been almost totally undisturbed by the war until 1780, when British Maj. Patrick Ferguson, who had threatened to "lay the country waste with fire and sword," set up camp here with a large Loyalist force. Well, local backwoodsmen recruited Whigs from Virginia and North Carolina to form a largely untrained, but very determined, army to throw the invaders out. The colonists were not only ill-trained, they were outnumbered, but they converged on Kings Mountain and simply kept on advancing on Ferguson's men—in spite of wave after wave of bayonet charges—until they took the summit. Ferguson himself was killed in the battle, and the Appalachians were once more under colonial control. You can see the battle re-created in a diorama at the Visitor Center, along with other relics. It's open every day of the year except Christmas, from 9 a.m. to 5 p.m., and it's free.

In the same general area (11 miles northwest of Gaffney at the junction of S.C. 11 and 110), another decisive colonial victory was won at **The Cowpens** in January of 1781. Gen. Nathanael Greene, who headed the American forces in the South, sent one Daniel Morgan to divert Cornwallis (who was still in South Carolina with a large British force) from his reorganization of colonial troops. When General Morgan threatened the British fort at Ninety-Six, Cornwallis dispatched a large number of infantry and dragoons to repulse the backwoods army, and the two forces met at The Cowpens (named for a nearby winter cattle enclosure). Morgan was brilliant in his use of guerilla tactics and when the British were at last defeated, they had suffered 110 men killed, 200 wounded, and another 550 captured—while Morgan lost 12 men and counted 60 wounded! This defeat of a corps of professional British Regulars was not only important militarily; it also spurred some patriots into action who had previously doubted an American victory and probably swung over a good many wavering loyalists.

If you take I-85 south from Gaffney through Spartanburg, you'll find a really superb example of a colonial plantation house—although it won't fit most people's image of that term: it's simply a large farmhouse typical of landowners' homes in this region, not the stately, columned sort found in the low country. **Walnut Grove Plantation** (tel. 803/576-6546) is 9½ miles south of I-85 on I-26, just one mile from its intersection with U.S. 221. It was built in 1765 on a land grant from King George III when this was the western frontier. The house itself is fascinating, with its authentic furnishings (I loved the separate kitchen filled with early vintage gadgets), and the outbuildings include a barn which holds a Conestoga-type wagon. Walnut Grove is open from April to October, from 11 a.m. to 5 p.m. Tuesday through Saturday, and on Sunday from 2 to 5 p.m. all year, closed on major holidays. Adults pay $2.50 for a tour; students, $1.50.

Incidentally, while you're poking around this area, keep an eye out for "fish camp" signs—very often you'll run across terrific fish dinners (all you can eat for practically nothing!) in rustic cafes down unpaved side roads. If that whets your appetite, stop at a gas station or some other local establishment and ask—everybody has a favorite, and believe me, it's worth an exploratory detour to find the hospitable fish camp eateries, if you like that sort of thing. (I've also picked up some classic fish stories in these surroundings.)

The **Pendleton Historic District**, 15 miles north of Anderson off U.S. 76, has free self-guided tours, a 2½-hour guided tour ($3) and auto tape tours ($4) of some 45 historic homes and town buildings. Stop by the **Historical and Recreational Commission** at 125 E. Queen St. in Pendleton (tel. 646-3782) for tour information and to see their museum, research library, and arts and crafts shop.

West and south of Anderson via U.S. 29 or S.C. 24, the **Hartwell Dam** and lake has 962 miles of shoreline and all sorts of water sports facilities (swimming, fishing, waterskiing, etc.), as well as free primitive campsites and developed campsites which rent (from the U.S. Army Corps of Engineers) on a first-come, first-served basis (tel. 404/376-4788).

Members of the "horsey set" can use Columbia as a base from which to run down to **Aiken** (south on U.S. 1) for all sorts of horse events from January through April. For instance, there are polo games at Whitney Field every Sunday afternoon (starting at 3:30 p.m.) during that period. And harness racing at Aiken Mile Track (Triple Crown harness races are held the last three weekends in May); steeplechase at Steeplechase Field; trials at Aiken Training Track; horse shows in mid-March; and . . . well, check the Columbia newspaper sports pages to see what's going on in Aiken.

To visit beautiful **Edisto Gardens,** drive southeast from Columbia to **Orangeburg.** The 110-acre city park located on U.S. 301, along the banks of the North Edisto River, is a wonderland of moss-draped oaks, camellias, and azaleas (which bloom from mid-March to mid-April), flowering crabapple, day lilies, dogwoods, and over 9500 roses which bloom from the middle of April until early October. It's one of the loveliest truly "southern" gardens anywhere. There are also tennis courts and picnic areas, and it's free (open every day).

Incidentally, just across from the Edisto Gardens entrance, there's a marvelous restaurant you're likely to ride right by because of its rather misleading name. It's the **House of Pizza,** 910 Calhoun Dr., Orangeburg, SC (tel. 531-4000). Well, they *do* serve pizza, all right—16 versions, in fact—as well as sandwiches and salads. But the real specialties in this superb eatery are the Greek dishes like moussaka, or biftekia, or the Greek-style stuffed peppers and tomatoes, or—my own weakness—the honey-sweet baklava. Their Greek salad is nothing short of spectacular. And there's beer and wine to accompany whatever you choose. Surprising to find this cuisine in a South Carolina setting, but it seems that the Dimopoulos brothers, after leaving Greece for several years in Massachusetts, tired of the climate in the North and simply headed south with their families. Orangeburg is where they settled, and their House of Pizza quickly became a favorite with locals, as well as travelers. Prices are budget to moderate; the place has a bright, cheerful atmosphere, with Greek music playing softly in the background, and they have a take-out service if you should want to picnic in the Gardens. Hours are 11 a.m. to 10:30 p.m. Monday to Thursday, 11 a.m. to 11:30 p.m. Friday and Saturday, and 4 to 10:30 p.m. on Sunday. I strongly suggest you stop, whether your tastes run to pizza or the Greek specialties.

READER'S DINING SELECTION: "We found a gem of a restaurant in Orangeburg, S.C., called **Berry's on the Hill.** They have an excellent buffet lunch. For under $5, you get soup, salad bar, fried chicken or a choice of three other meats, and all the vegetables (mashed potatoes, yams, greens, wax beans, cole slaw, and many more). This includes biscuits, corn sticks, sweet rolls, and beverage. For an extra 50¢, you may have a second meat dish also. The owner won the 1977 Restaurant Award for South Carolina" (G. Resnick, Baltimore, Md.).

Chapter XI

INTRODUCTION TO GEORGIA

1. By Way of Background
2. Traveling to Georgia
3. Traveling Within Georgia

GEORGIA IS NOT ONLY the largest state east of the Mississippi—it is also one of the most varied and complex. Its public image is all too often an antebellum one, full of Tara-like plantations, a slow-moving social life, and a warm southern climate that encourages drowsiness. Well, all of that is there, but from the beginning there has been an energetic bustle about Georgia's commerce that marked even those early planters and was the very basis of much interior settlement. Savannah, surrounded by cotton and rice plantations, was always an enterprising seaport, with its plantation owners as much involved in shipping and the course of trade as in overseeing their large land holdings. Atlanta began as a railroad terminal; and Columbus came into being because of the waterpower of the Chattahoochee and its nine-foot-deep channel (navigable all the way to the Gulf of Mexico) that provided easy access to the world's markets for industrial products. Unlike many other southern states, industry and agriculture, social graciousness, and business activity have not been sharply defined by either the state's geography or its citizens' interests—all those elements have been intertwined into a Georgia that very often comes as a surprise to a first-time visitor.

1. By Way of Background

FROM HERNANDO DE SOTO TO JIMMY CARTER: As is always the case, Georgia's present (and most probably her future) is explained by and built solidly on her past. That past reaches back to 1540 and Hernando de Soto's first European exploration of Creek and Cherokee lands along the coast. Spanish missions had settled in by 1566 (but not to stay, as it turned out), and by 1733 the English had arrived in the person of Gen. James Oglethorpe and his small band of settlers (whose personal motives for colonization were several degrees loftier than those of King George II, who was keeping a wary eye on the Spanish in Florida and along the Georgia coast). But it was not until a back-and-forth, four-year struggle called the War of Jenkins Ear (1739–1743) was settled by Oglethorpe's decisive victory at the Battle of Bloody Marsh that the future course of the colony could be determined. From 1745, when Oglethorpe and his trustees surrendered their charter to the king, until 1788, when Georgia became the fourth of the original 13 states, the region was a royal province.

As news of Georgia's wealth of natural resources spread, it drew new settlers from the north and from all over Europe; Germans, Scottish Highlanders, Swiss, Welsh, French, and Irish all arrived with varying dreams and aspirations, but perhaps most important, with a driving industriousness. They followed the rivers inland, explored and settled the rolling piedmont, and pushed on into the western mountains. As the Revolution approached, those from the north spread their burning zeal for freedom from the British and were in bitter conflict with the entrenched loyalists along the coast—until they managed to convince most of the 50,000 residents that the troubles of the northern colonies were the troubles of all colonies and Georgia unanimously joined in the fight for independence.

There was division and conflict among Georgians again just prior to the Civil War over the issue of slavery, a conflict that was finally settled when the state seceded from the Union in 1861 and joined the Confederacy. The war was a complete disaster for the state. Its manufacturing plants lay in ruins, plantations and small farms alike were burned over, and most of the young men were either killed or suffered lifelong wounds. It remained for the older leaders to rebuild a shattered economy, and they did it (with the help of youngsters not old enough to go off to war) in a surprisingly short span. What had been large plantations, useless without slave labor, became small, privately owned farms. Out of the ashes of Atlanta rose an even greater metropolis, still based on transportation (railroads then, airlines today); manufacturing plants sprouted all over the state; the textile industry became important as a means of converting one of the state's most important crops into finished products; Jimmy Carter went from peanut farming to the governor's chair, then on to the U.S. presidency; and all the native industriousness and emotional intensity Georgians had inherited from their forebears led them to create present-day Georgia, a state that cherishes its past, but does not dwell on it, looking instead to the future.

The same diversity that characterizes Georgia in everything else extends to recreation and sightseeing. The beaches and creature comforts of the Golden Isles would probably claim first place on my own list of where to go and what to do. But that's most likely because Brunswick and Savannah, with history enough to fill any vacation, aren't that far away. And then, the big-city excitement of Atlanta has its own special lure. If you're looking for that antebellum Old South, Thomasville's plantation country is perfect (and the Chamber of

Commerce there aids and abets any such quest with lots of maps and information). Outdoorsmen can fish and hunt, white-water enthusiasts will have no trouble finding canoe trails down the state's rushing rivers, golfers bump into excellent courses all over the state (or can simply gape at the world's finest players in the Masters Golf Tournament in April every year at Augusta), and—well, I just can't think of any vacation activity you *won't* find in Georgia. Which accounts, I suppose, for the fact that tourism is high among its principal industries, with close to $2 billion a year coming into the state in the form of tourist dollars.

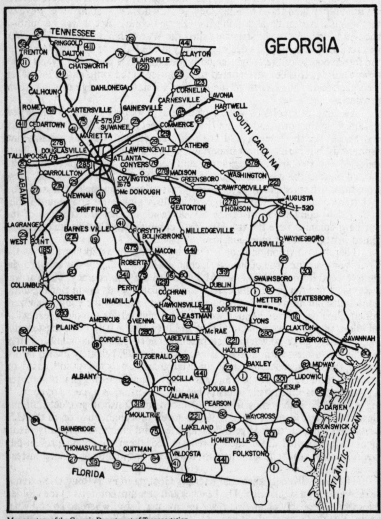

Map courtesy of the Georgia Department of Transportation

GEORGIA AREA CODES: Savannah, 912; Brunswick and the Golden Isles, 912; Atlanta, 404; Columbus and Pine Mountain, 404.

GEORGIA'S HOTELS: These range from the beachfront luxury of the Cloisters on Sea Island to the skyscraper luxury of Atlanta's soaring Peachtree Plaza to a multitude of Holiday Inns and other moderate-priced motels to one of the best budget-priced chains in the country, Days Inn (with headquarters in Atlanta and a good distribution of locations. As always, advance reservations will spare you a lot of grief.

CAMPING IN GEORGIA: There are 41 state parks in Georgia, which welcome campers (on a first-come, first-served basis for sites that rent for $5.50 to $6.50 per night). In addition, 24 parks have vacation cottages which rent for $28, $36, and $42 daily, $196, $252, and $294 weekly. For detailed park information contact: Department of Natural Resources, Office of Information, 270 Washington St. SW, Atlanta, GA 30334 (tel. 404/656-3530).

GEORGIA'S RESTAURANTS: Eating out in Georgia can mean having southern-style meals in a rustic setting; spicy, low-country cuisine in Savannah's elegant and historic restaurants; or sophisticated continental dishes in Atlanta's cosmopolitan dining rooms. As for price, except for a few "ultra-elegant" restaurants in Atlanta, even the costliest meals are in the lower register of "expensive." And all across the state, you'll find quite good food at surprisingly modest prices.

As for alcoholic beverages, you can buy them at retail package stores between 8 a.m. and 11:45 p.m. (except on Sunday, election days, Thanksgiving, and Christmas); and whether or not you'll be able to buy mixed drinks in lounges and restaurants depends on which county you're in—that's a local option, although beer and wines are available everywhere. Of course, you have to be 19 to indulge.

GEORGIA CLIMATE: The average high and low temperatures at coastal Savannah and central Atlanta show that "low-country" locations are somewhat warmer year round than those further inland.

	High	*Low*
Savannah	91	40
Atlanta	88	36
Columbus	92	37

VISITOR INFORMATION: For advance reading and planning before you come to Georgia contact: **Division of Tourism,** Georgia Dept. of Industry & Trade, P.O. Box 1776, Atlanta GA 30301 (tel. 404/646-3545). Be sure to ask for information on specific interests such as fishing, golfing, beach resorts, etc., but inquire as well about the comprehensive booklet "Georgia, This Way to Fun," which gives details on all regions within the state. Also, at least until the end of February 1984 (and there are plans to extend it), there is a marvelous discount program in effect called "Nobody Treats You Better Than Georgia." The discount card will entitle travelers within the state to substantial discounts at a wide variety of sightseeing, shopping, accommodation, and restaurant spots, and there's a booklet which lists all participants. Ask them, as well, for a calendar of events—some pretty special things happen around the state during the year.

2. Traveling to Georgia

BY AIR: Atlanta's busy airport is reached by no less than 16 major airlines. Republic, alone, has some 357 flights a week into the city! From Atlanta, there are connecting flights into Augusta, Savannah, Albany, Brunswick, and (on commuter lines) into several smaller cities around the state. Travel agents or any of the leading airlines can furnish specific information about possibilities through Atlanta's airport, which is one of the busiest in the country.

BY TRAIN: Amtrak has stops in Atlanta, Savannah, Waycross, Valdosta, and Thomasville. Amtrak frequently has real bargain fares in effect for limited periods, and you should always check for the most economical way to schedule your trip. As we go to press, attractive Amtrak tours are available to Atlanta and Savannah at bargain prices.

BY BUS: Both Greyhound and Trailways reach not only the major points in Georgia, but also go into almost any smaller town you might want to visit in the state. As with Amtrak, the bus lines run periodic special rates that are real money-savers, so check.

BY CAR: I can remember driving in Georgia over unpaved red-clay roads which turned into slippery obstacle courses that not infrequently slid you right into a roadside ditch. But that was a long time ago, and today the state's highways are a real pleasure to travel. Several Interstate highways crisscross the state, giving easy access to major points: from west to east, I-16 goes through Macon, Dublin, and Savannah; and I-20 reaches Atlanta, Decatur, Conyers, Madison, Thomson, and Augusta. From north to south, I-75 runs from Dalton to Calhoun to Marietta to Atlanta to Macon to Perry to Cordele to Tifton to Valdosta; I-85 reaches Lavonia, Atlanta, La Grange, and West Point; and I-95 goes to Savannah, Brunswick, and Kingsland. There are state-run **Welcome Centers** at all major points of entry, staffed with knowledgeable, helpful Georgians who can often give you local tips as to timesaving routes.

You will find Thrifty Rent-a-Car offices in Atlanta, Augusta, Brunswick, and Savannah.

3. Traveling Within Georgia

BY AIR: Piedmont, Southern, Delta, Eastern, and Commuter airlines all have connecting service within the state. (For other possibilities from Atlanta, see "Traveling to Georgia" above.)

BY TRAIN: Amtrak stops in Atlanta, Savannah, Waycross, Valdosta, and Thomasville; and Georgia Railroad operates between Atlanta and Augusta.

BY BUS: Besides Trailways and Greyhound, Southeastern Motor Lines, Inc., operates to intrastate cities and smaller towns.

BY CAR: In addition to the Interstates that make it easy to get around the state, U.S. 84 crosses from the Alabama state line southeast to Macon and

Valdosta and on south to Florida; and U.S. 441 runs from the North Carolina border south to Athens, Dublin, and the Florida state line.

Chapter XII

GEORGIA'S COAST

1. Savannah
2. Brunswick and the Golden Isles
3. Cumberland Island

NO MORE THAN 150 miles long, Georgia's coastline is everything you'd imagine a semitropical, wildly romantic, richly historic stretch of waterfront to be. There are moss-draped live oaks and palmettos (some of the prettiest driving in the South is along Georgia's portion of U.S. 17), broad beaches, creeks and rivers, the remains of early-day plantations, offshore islands with resort accommodations that make you feel like an instant member of the "millionaires' club" that first developed them, that ladylike queen of Atlantic seaports, Savannah, and the newest National Seashore, still under development. Since 1540 (when Hernando de Soto became the first European to set foot on what would one day be Georgia), it has sheltered Indians, Spanish missionaries, British colonists, pirates, cotton growers and shippers, English troops, an infamous (to the southern way of thinking; "ruthless" to Northerners) Union general during the Civil War, wealthy Yankees seeking an unspoiled retreat, and most recently, a former president of the United States.

Spanish missions had gained a foothold on St. Simons and Jekyll Islands as early as 1566, but civilization came to stay on this part of the Atlantic coast with Gen. James Oglethorpe and a tiny band of settlers in 1733, who looked to the New World for a new beginning that would win respectability for former inmates of England's debtor prisons and Protestants (both groups held in the same contempt back home). The Revolution brought bitter conflict between prosperous, "status quo" Loyalists and those who sympathized with the cause of American independence, with Savannah changing hands with the tide of battle.

The Civil War brought almost complete devastation to the area, since Sherman ended his "march to the sea" here in Savannah (which, however, escaped almost unscathed). But a Yankee invasion of another sort has since blossomed into the prosperity of tourism, and today's visitor will find the coast a real delight, from Savannah all the way down to Brunswick and those offshore "golden isles."

1. Savannah

When Gen. James Oglethorpe landed at Yamacraw Bluff on February 12, 1733, with his 125 English settlers, his idealism went beyond a new future for those unfortunates he'd brought with him, and extended to a town plan that would assure spaciousness, beauty, and comfort for every resident of the colony. A sketch in Robert Castell's *Village of the Ancients* inspired him to lay out a settlement of houses, each with its own garden plot, town squares (there were 24 in the original plan), and an orderly mercantile section. Thus, Savannah was America's very first "planned city," and it is still studied by modern urban planners.

The natural deep-water harbor very soon attracted Spanish, Portuguese, German, Scottish, and Irish immigrants, and as wharves sprang up along the bustling waterfront, a lively sea trade brought seafarers from all over the world—along with hordes of pirates who put into the port from time to time. The town never lost its atmosphere of gentility, but rowdyism was rampant along the docks and in seamen's inns and taverns.

When Savannah got word of the colonial victory at Lexington, there was jubilation, a "liberty pole," and a hastily formed patriot battalion, all of which led the royal governor to ship out for Nova Scotia. He came back, however, in December of 1778 and stayed until 1782, when "Mad Anthony" Wayne was finally sucessful in recapturing the city. There had been an unsuccessful attempt by American and French troops to take the city in the fall of 1779, with disastrous defeat for "our" side—some 800 men were lost, including the Polish hero, Count Casimir Pulaski. Savannah, which had been named the state capital following the 1776 Declaration of Independence, remained so until 1807, when proslavers managed to have it moved to Milledgeville.

The years between the Revolutionary and Civil Wars were a period of great prosperity for Savannah, and many of the Classic Revival, Regency, and Georgian colonial homes you'll see restored today were built at that time. It was the day of "King Cotton" and great tobacco farms. Cotton "factors" (brokers) kept track of huge fortunes along River Street on what came to be known as Factors' Row. And always, builders, merchants, and shippers kept to Oglethorpe's master plan for the city, preserving the parks and squares in the midst of all that commercial hubbub.

When secession rumblings reached fever pitch in 1861, Georgia's Governor Brown ordered state troops to seize Fort Pulaski, 15 miles east of Savannah, even though the state did not withdraw from the Union until 16 days later. So in a sense, the Civil War could be said to have begun here. And it certainly ended for Georgia in Savannah, when Sherman marched in more quietly than was his usual custom, since Confederate General Hardee had evacuated his troops to prevent the destruction Sherman had left in his wake all across the state. In spite of Reconstruction difficulties, Savannah's port was soon humming again, with cotton once more ruling the economy, closely followed by a

developing lumber and resin trade based on its surrounding pine forests. Manufacturing began to take hold, and by the early 1900s there were infant industries
that would grow to a total of 200 by the outbreak of World War II. Shipbuilding was a natural here and led the list during both World Wars.

Today, the economy and much of city life still revolve around port activity.
But for the visitor, it's Old Savannah, in a beautifully restored and maintained
Historic Area, that draws the most attention. And for that we can thank seven
Savannah ladies who literally snatched the first restoration from the wrecker's
ball in 1954. They had watched mansion after mansion go down in the name
of "progress" and managed to raise funds to buy the Isaiah Davenport house
(which had deteriorated into a virtual slum) just hours before it was slated for
demolition to make way for a funeral parlor's parking lot. What has grown
from that first determined effort to preserve Savannah's history is an inspiration
to other American cities, which seem headed more and more toward the
facelessness of "no-character" glass and steel. They banded together as the
Historic Savannah Foundation, then went to work buying up architecturally
valuable buildings and (herein lies the sheer genius of their plan) reselling them
to private owners *who would promise to restore them.* As a result of the foresight and dedication of those ladies and others who joined them, more than 800
of the 1100 historic buildings of Old Savannah have been restored (they're even
painted in the original colors of the town, after volunteers chipped away layers
of paint to disclose the pinks and reds and blues and greens first used). The
"living museum" they've created is now the largest urban National Historic
Landmark District in the country—some 2½ square miles, including 20 one-
acre squares that still survive from Oglethorpe's dream of a gracious city.

An entire book could be written about this charming and lively city—I'll
do my best to tell you about it in our limited space.

WHERE TO STAY: There are several major motel chains represented in
Savannah, all pretty standard for their chain. I am listing them here (because
reservations are sometimes hard to come by in Savannah and you may not be
able to book your first choice) after those local hostelries which provide a very
special, regional atmosphere.

In the Old South Tradition

Back in the 1920s, a group of Savannah's wealthiest citizens banded
together to build an elegant and exclusive resort hotel of the country club
variety just outside the city on Wilmington Island. Their efforts and investment
were such that today when you drive up to the **Sheraton Savannah Resort and
Country Club,** 612 Wilmington Island Rd. (tel. 912/897-1612), there's a sense
of driving back in time to an era when such establishments were of a classic
and enduring nature. Just across the Wilmington River Bridge, a short drive
from town, the resort is set in more than 200 lush coastal acres, with a championship golf course on the premises (this is the scene of the annual Michelob
Georgia Open), as well as facilities for tennis, fishing, sailing, boating, jogging
(along scenic trails), horseback riding, bicycling, and sunning on a manmade
beach (there's an Olympic-size pool for swimming).

Accommodations here have always been posh, but there is now underway
a renovation program to the tune of some $4.1 million which will see every
guest room in the beautiful main building, as well as the Country Club Villas,
refurbished, although the same elegant style will prevail, with fine period
reproductions (and most have either two double or king-size beds). The splen-

did public rooms are graciously furnished, with the warm glow of carved wood reflecting in the shimmer of crystal chandeliers. All three eateries are also undergoing the same careful renovation: the Clubhouse Grille, an ideal place for casual breakfasting and lunching; the 19th Hold Lounge, which serves cocktails from 11 a.m. until 7 p.m. (after which H.P.'s Lounge takes over and adds entertainment until 1 a.m.); and H.P.'s Restaurant, which overlooks the water, serves some of the best seafood dishes around (as well as beef, chicken, and veal entrées), and throws in spectacular sunset views. Miraculously, renovations have been so carefully planned that there has been no disruption for current guests, and by the time you read this, most will have been completed (sometime in early 1984).

Double-room rates at this very special place begin at $95, with the villas starting at $190. They offer many attractive golf packages, as well as a very good honeymoon special (and I, personally, cannot think of a better place in which to begin married life!).

Deluxe in the Historic District

Located on the site of the historic DeSoto Hotel (gone many years now), the **DeSoto Hilton**, 15 E. Liberty St., P.O. Box 8207, Savannah, GA 31412 (tel. 912/232-9000), is in the very heart of downtown Savannah, within easy walking distance of the riverfront, almost all major historical attractions, shopping, and some of the finest restaurants in town. There's a tour service located right in the lobby, as well as some airline reservation services. Rooms are definitely in the deluxe class, and the dining room is elegant. An outdoor pool is on the premises, and the lounge offers entertainment nightly. Rates vary according to location within the hotel, and run from $74 up, with no charge for children staying in the same room with parents.

Also in the Historic District and right on the riverfront is the spectacular **Hyatt Regency Savannah**, 2 W. Bay St., P.O. Box 1467 (tel. 912/238-1234). Its style is strikingly contemporary, yet blends surprisingly into Riverfront Plaza restorations. There's a seven-story, open-atrium lobby (complete with concierge to give personalized attention to guests) which features a cocktail lounge named, appropriately, The Landing; a delightful, casual Patrick's Porch restaurant which serves all three meals at moderate prices (from 6:30 a.m. to 11 p.m., midnight on Friday and Saturday); the elegant Windows restaurant for lunch and dinner, overlooking the river and specializing in superb seafood dishes (11:30 a.m. to 2 p.m. and 6 to 11 p.m., dinner prices in the $8.95 to $19 range) and Sunday brunch from 10:30 a.m. to 3 p.m.; and M.D.'s Lounge for cocktails and live entertainment. Guest rooms are lovely, definitely in the luxury class, and there's a rooftop Jacuzzi and sundeck. Doubles range from $80 up.

Lovely, Historic Small Inns

If you want to experience Savannah graciousness firsthand, then by all means book into one of the small inns springing up in the Historic District, most in lovely old homes which have been brought up to date with the most modern conveniences, while retaining every bit of their original charm. One of my personal favorites is the **Ballastone Inn**, 14 E. Oglethorpe Ave., Savannah, GA 31401 (tel. 912/236-1484). It's right next door to the Juliette Gordon Low Girl Scout shrine, and convenient to everything in the Historic District. The 19 rooms are all superbly decorated with antiques or authentic reproductions, ceiling fans (air conditioning is also provided), and Scalamandré wallpapers,

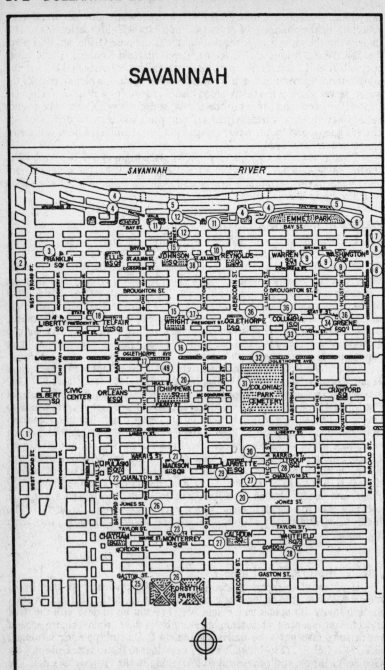

SAVANNAH

GUIDE TO THE NUMBERED REFERENCES ON THE "SAVANNAH" MAP: 1. Savannah Visitors Center and Chamber of Commerce; 2. Scarbrough House; 3. First African Baptist Church; 4. Factors Walk; 5. River Street; 6. Emmet Park; 7. Ft. Wayne; 8. Trustees' Garden; 9. Washington Square Area; 10. Reynolds Square; 11. Cotton and Naval Stores Exchange, and the City Exchange Bell; 12. U.S. Customs House and Washington Guns; 13. City Hall and Oglethorpe Bench; 14. Johnson Square; 15. Wright Square; 16. Juliette Gordon Low Birthplace; 17. Oglethorpe Avenue; 18. Telfair Academy of Arts and Sciences; 19. Independent Presbyterian Church; 20. Chippewa Square; 21. Madison Square; 22. Pulaski Square; 23. Monterrey Square; 24. Forsyth Park; 25. Gaston Street; 26. Jones Street; 27. Wesley Monumental Methodist Church; 28. Whitefield, Troup, and Lafayette Squares; 29. Colonial Dames House; 30. Cathedral of St. John the Baptist; 31. Colonial Park Cemetery; 32. Oglethorpe Avenue; 33. Columbia Square; 34. Green Square; 35. Davenport House; 36. Owens-Thomas House; 37. Lutheran Church of the Ascension; 38. Christ Episcopal Church.

---

and each has a distinctive decorative theme. Many regulars have become attached to "their" particular room, and the friendly staff here do their best to cater to such personal tastes. Incidentally, if your tastes happen to run to low-ceilinged coziness rather than the more formal elegance of 14-foot ceilings, ask for one of the garden-level rooms, which are in the original servants' quarters and have a more rustic appearance, with brick walls, exposed beams, and more casual furnishings. Even more gracious than furnishings at the Balla-stone is the pampering each guest receives—that friendly staff has seen to it that fresh fruit and flowers are in your room on arrival, shoes left outside the door will be polished overnight, and that your bed is turned down, with mint on pillow and a brandy on the bedside table when it's time to retire. A continental breakfast is included in the rate, and you can have it in the privacy of your room or in the lovely little courtyard with other guests. A feature I especially enjoy is the inviting parlor, where there is always coffee or tea available, as well as almost any liquid refreshment you could wish for, from fresh fruit juice to a cocktail. It's especially pleasant to end the day here (by an open fire on cool evenings) in the company of other guests. Rates begin at $75 for most rooms, $155 for Master Rooms, which are especially large and have a separate dressing room and wet bar. Incidentally, it's a good idea to book well in advance.

Laurie and Jim Widman have restored the historic **Eliza Thompson House**, 5 W. Jones St., Savannah, GA 31401 (tel. 912/236-3620), which dates from 1847. They've added a new courtyard wing, and all 26 guest rooms have private baths and are furnished with low country antiques. Lovely suites are available on the garden level. Doubles here run from $80 except in July, August, November, and December, when lower, off-season rates apply. If you happen to be planning a wedding in the near future, ask about their attractive honeymoon package, which includes iced champagne and many other extras.

Unlike the two inns above, the **Mulberry Inn**, 601 E. Bay St., Savannah, GA 31401 (tel. 912/238-1200), is located in what was a warehouse back in the 1860s. It then became the area's first Coca-Cola bottling factory, and when it began life as a small inn, in the fall of 1982, its size had been doubled with new construction designed to blend nicely with the original structure. The plain, cream-colored exterior, with its mulberry-striped awnings, gives little hint of the elegance inside. The Regency entranceway opens to a three-story open area, from which you can see the dining room (more about that later), the registration desk, and the gift shop. Some guest rooms open onto a covered walkway alongside that interior courtyard (which is landscapped with native shrubs and a fountain), and some suites overlook the river. All furnishings are either antiques or authentic reproductions from the Victorian, American Federal, and Regency periods, and Savannah colors of burgundy, aqua, and peach have been used throughout. So outstanding are the paintings, furnishings, and fabrics used in decorating the inn, that they have taken the unusual step of compiling a written guide for guests and visitors to use on a walking tour of the interior!

The dining room specializes in low country fare, with fresh seafood, delicate sauces, and fresh fruits and vegetables. It is furnished with formal, Regency furniture and features a fireplace and a lovely custommade china. An especially nice function is the formal afternoon tea served in this gracious room, although any meal is a special occasion here.

Rates for double rooms (which are all luxuriously furnished) begin at $75, and those riverfront suites (sitting room, bedroom, and service area with sink and refrigerator) begin at $95.

Charming Guest Houses

For an even more personal touch of Savannah hospitality, let me suggest from my heart that you book for your stay by dialing 912/BEDROOM (233-7666) between the hours of 9 a.m. and 9 p.m. any day of the week. That's a reservation service which can put you into private homes in the Historic District or nearby in either a bed-and-breakfast room or self-contained suite that will probably include a continental breakfast in its rate. In every case, you'll be hosted by a prime example of Savannah charm, and in many, you'll be surrounded by antique furnishings, brass beds and the like, fireplaces which actually work, and enough intimate knowledge of the city and what it holds for the visitor to make you want to double the length of your stay. Rates can range from $35 to $90, depending on what you want.

Mary Lee's Guest Accommodations, 117 E. Jones St., P.O. Box 607, Savannah, GA 31402 (tel. 912/236-7101 or 232-0891), was the first Savannah hostess to open her home to guests in this manner, and in terms of friendliness and genuine helpfulness, she set a high standard, indeed. The carriage house of her over-120-year-old home in the Historic District has been converted into three lovely apartments, complete with full kitchen, living room, bedroom, and bath, as well as your own telephone. There's another, with the same facilities, on the ground floor of her own home. A continental breakfast of melt-in-your-mouth pastries, fresh juice, and the makings for coffee and tea comes daily; and as for Mary Lee herself, perhaps the story of how she once befriended two young English students stranded in Savannah when there was not a room to be had, put them up in her daughter's room, and then steered them to youth-oriented places of interest, will tell you something of her character.

Just down the street, at the **Remshart Inn,** 112 W. Jones St., Savannah, GA 31402 (tel. 912/232-4337), Mrs. Martha Brooks has only one unit on the ground floor. Her guests are invited to use the courtyard, and Mrs. Brooks, like Ms. Lee, is a knowledgeable and hospitable hostess. The apartment consists of a living room, bedroom, kitchen, and bath, with a working fireplace in both living and bedroom. There's a library of books about Savannah, some family heirloom furniture (including the pencil-poster bed), and interesting artwork, mostly Savannah scenes painted by Savannah artists. Here, also, a continental breakfast of pastries, fruit juice, and coffee or tea, is included in the rate.

If you'd just as soon not stay right in the heart of all the sightseeing attractions (and there can be advantages, such as parking and the like), then you couldn't ask for a nicer place than the apartment which **Betty Palmer,** 519

E. 45th St. (tel. 912/233-2969 or 236-1396), keeps for paying guests. A short (about five minutes) drive will take you into the heart of the city from this pretty, quiet residential section known as Ardsley Park, and Betty, a native, is quick to help with sightseeing, dining, or entertainment suggestions. The apartment consists of a wood-paneled living room with brick fireplace, exceptionally pretty bedroom with a king-size bed, and walk-in closet, and although there's no kitchen, a continental breakfast is served each morning. There is a separate entrance, but from the moment you arrive, you'll be treated as a family guest, and Betty's home is a virtual art gallery, with works of some of Savannah's best artists.

Local Motels

Savannah, or rather Tybee Island, saw the beginning of that dependable budget motel chain, Days Inn, because its founder, the late George Day, spent so many summers there in his younger days. Well, now there's a Days Inn that deserves special mention, and it's smack in the middle of the Historic District. When a new building was constructed here for the **Days Inn** at 201 W. Bay St., Savannah, GA 31401 (tel. 912/236-4440), in 1981, it was cited by the Historical Savannah Foundation "For their sensitive design of a new hotel within Savannah's historic Market District," and indeed you would be forgiven for taking the new structure for one of the area's original warehouses that had been lovingly restored. The 196 rooms are all up to the usual Days Inn high standards, there's a 24-hour restaurant right on the premises, parking facilities, and a game room, as well as a tour service. Rates for doubles run from $35 to $40. Adjacent to the new building, there is a Days Lodge that would justify another award for its renovation of a building that really is a part of the city's history. Much care has been taken in creating some 57 new suites (each with a kitchen complete right down to a dishwasher, living room, bedroom, and bath and views of either the river, one block away, or the historic city center) not to violate the exterior, but to keep the four-storied brick building's façade much as it was when it was a part of the active market district. Holding to its usual budget rate structure, Days Inn will charge rates of $45 to $65 for these choice accommodations in a choice location during 1984, with an expected slight increase in 1985.

For the budget-minded who don't mind being on the outskirts of town, **Tedder's Motel**, 4009 Ogeechee Rd., which is U.S. 17S (tel. 912/236-6378), is a small, pleasant, well-kept stopping place. Rooms are more than adequate, there is a pool, and best of all, rates for double occupancy are a modest $26.50.

Chain Motels

In the expensive category, Ramada Inn, 231 W. Boundary St. (tel. 912/232-1262), charges $48 and up for doubles. **Holiday Inn,** 121 W. Boundary St. (tel. 912/236-1355), has doubles for $50 and up; **Howard Johnson's–Downtown,** near the Historic Area, 224 W. Boundary St. (tel. 912/232-4371), charges $57; and **Best Western,** 1 Gateway Blvd. (tel. 912/925-2420), $42 to $50.

Two budget-priced chains are: **Quality Inn,** 300 W. Bay St. (tel. 912/236-6321), $35; and another **Days Inn,** 114 Mall Blvd. (tel. 912/352-4455), $34.88.

Campground

The **Safari Bellaire Woods Campground,** Ga. 204, 2½ miles west of I-95, 4½ miles west of U.S. 17—write Rt. 4, Box 451-B, Savannah, GA 31405 (tel.

912/748-4000), is 12 miles from Savannah on the banks of the Ogeechee River. There are full hookups, LP gas service, a store, self-service gas and diesel fuel, dump station, hot showers, laundry, swimming pool, and recreation hall. Golf, tennis, and boat rentals with a boat ramp are also available. Rates start at $10 and reservations are accepted with a $10 deposit.

THAT GOOD SAVANNAH EATING: Savannah cuisine is a happy combination of coastal and low-country cooking with a special dash of its own added to hearty okra and vegetable soups. If you're asked "One or two?" when soup comes to the tables in a steaming tureen, your host is inquiring how many little green hot peppers you want mashed in the plate before soup is poured. Your answer should depend, of course, on your personal taste, but even if you have a cast-iron stomach, don't fail to remove the pepper itself, for as one native puts it, "a touch of the pepper is purgatory undiluted!"

A Savannah Institution

Remember the days of the boarding houses, when everybody sat together and food was served in big dishes placed in the center of the table? Well, **Mrs. Sema Wilkes** has been serving locals and travelers in just that manner since the 1940s, and for some of the region's best home cooking, practice up that "boarding house reach" and head for 107 W. Jones St. between 11:30 a.m. and 3 p.m. any weekday. You won't find a sign ("it would look so commercial, not at all like home," according to Mrs. Wilkes), but what you're likely to find is a long line of people patiently waiting for a seat at one of the six tables in the basement dining room of an 1870 gray brick house with curving steps and cast-iron trim. If you take your place and wait it out (as Kate Smith, Richard Chamberlain, and scores of other celebrities have in the past), you'll be rewarded by a tasty, well-balanced lunch cooked to perfection with whatever fresh foods are available. Mrs. Wilkes believes in freshness and plans her daily menu around the seasons. She also believes in people getting enough to eat, and $6.50 buys all you can put down. Rest assured your food will be a true reflection of the cuisine Savannah residents have enjoyed for generations.

The Best of the Rest

I heard about the **Boar's Head**, 1 N. Lincoln St. (tel. 232-3196), in Atlanta, New Orleans, and Miami, and truthfully, I was inclined to doubt that it could live up to all the accolades. Well, it can, and I can now be counted a loyal member of its widespread fan club. Situated on the waterfront (Lincoln Street is one of those that dead-ends into River Street) in a 200-year-old warehouse, the Boar's Head has a sophistication in atmosphere and service and an excellence in cuisine that would make it outstanding in any setting. First of all, there's that marvelous river view, and every table is placed to take advantage of it. Then, fresh flowers on every table, hanging baskets of greenery, and soft candlelight make for a cozy, intimate atmosphere that creates just the right mood for the professionalism that comes from the kitchen. Most of this is directly due to Heinz Lindeman, the owner-manager, but credit must also go to the staff he has assembled. From Edwin, the handsome host, to Tony, my waiter who began things by introducing himself, there was no snag in providing a memorable meal. The menu is continental and American, with superb seafood, veal, and steaks. My selection was a bouillabaisse that turned out to be perfect, but others in my party sampled dishes such as a seafood casserole au gratin and pepper steak. All were excellent with prices of $9 to $15. It's open daily for lunch from noon to 2:30 p.m. and dinner from 6 to 10:30 p.m., and reservations are strongly suggested, since it's been a favorite with locals for years, as well as with tourists.

The **Pirates' House,** 20 E. Broad St. (tel. 233-5757), holds a restaurant, a rain forest bar, gift shop, and museum. The 1754 inn was a rendezvous for pirates and rough-and-tumble sailors who put into the port of Savannah way back when. There are legends galore associated with the place, and Robert Louis Stevenson used it as part of the setting of *Treasure Island.* It's listed as an authentic house museum by the American Museum Society, and you'll want to set aside time to explore every one of the 23 fascinating dining rooms. There are seafood specialties, of course, like oysters Savannah or sherry-flavored shrimp and crabmeat Newburg, as well as chicken cordon bleu, duck à l'orange, and a variety of flaming entrées and some 36 desserts. If you come during summer months without a reservation, you're likely to have a wait. But that's not all that bad—if there isn't room at the bar, a cocktail waitress will come down the line and take your order (but do try for the rain forest bar—it's entertaining and lively). And bring the children: the friendly staff here will give them special attention, and they'll each leave with a pirate's mask as a souvenir. The food here is very good, and more than that, it's a fun place to dine. Prices range from $8.75 to $15.95 at dinner, $4.75 to $9.95 at lunch. This winner of the National Restaurant Association's Great Menu Award is open seven days a week from 11:30 a.m. to 2:30 p.m. and 5 to 9:45 p.m.

Decor at the **Shrimp Factory,** 313 River St. (tel. 236-4229), reflects the whimsical mind of Janie Harris, a lively lady who (with her husband, Frank) is determined to set a table truly representative of this region. In a setting of exposed old brick, wooden plank walls, and a marvelous salad bar resting in a miniature shrimp boat, the Harrises serve the freshest seafoods from local waters (their Savannah shrimp creole is without peer), salads that are real creations, and steak and chicken dishes for those who can pass up seafood. Prices at dinner range from $7.95 to $12.95 and include salad bar and after-dinner cordial. Now, while seafood may be a bit old hat along the coast, you aren't likely to find pine bark stew many places other than the Shrimp Factory. It's a terrific seafood stew, served in a little iron pot with a bottle of sherry on the side, that's been simmered with a delicate herb seasoning and comes with french bread and a whipped cheese spread. You won't have to ask how it came by its peculiar name—the legend is printed right on the menu. At lunch, there's a soup, sandwich, and salad bar combination for just $4. Janie is almost always on hand. The large bar is a popular hangout for Savannahians both before and after dinner and there's live music in the bar most nights. Hours are 11 a.m. to 10 p.m. Monday through Thursday, to 11 p.m. on Friday and Saturday. Oh, be sure to ask about their Chatham Artillery Punch, and if you dare, try one—$4.95 and delicious (also, potent).

The **Olde Pink House Restaurant and Planters' Tavern,** 23 Abercorn St. (tel. 232-4286), is another dining spot that will send you spinning back in time. Built in 1771, the old house has been a private residence, a bank, headquarters for one of Sherman's generals, and a tearoom. Now restored and containing an antique shop as well as the restaurant, it's an ideal spot for lunch Monday through Friday from 11:30 a.m. to 2:30 p.m. in a lovely colonial room or in front of the Planters' Tavern's large open fireplaces. Lunch prices run $4.95 to $6.50. Dinner is by candlelight and quite elegant (Monday through Saturday, 6 to 11 p.m.). Prices start at $14.50 for complete dinners which include such dishes as riverfront gumbo, black turtle bean soup, baby flounder stuffed with crab, Old Savannah trifle, and the like, all delicious!

The **Crystal Beer Parlor**, 301 W. Jones St. (tel. 232-1153), has been a favorite of just about everybody in Savannah since it opened its doors in the Depression days of 1933 and sold huge sandwiches for a dime. Prices may have gone up since then, but the affection for this plain, unpretentious place has diminished not one whit. So popular is it that my best advice is to try to go earlier or later than peak lunch or dinner hours (if you get there at noon, you'll be in for a lengthy wait). Inside, things haven't changed all that much since its opening; Budweiser beer is still served in the old-style bottles, or you can order draft beer in a frosted mug. Owner Conrad Thompson still serves up great fried oyster and shrimp salad sandwiches, crab stew and chili, but you really shouldn't miss the seafood gumbo, one of the best in the Southeast, in my personal opinion. Hours are 11:30 a.m. to 10 p.m., prices are in the modest range (no item on the menu runs over $4!), and there's ample parking in the lot off Jones Street. This is a "don't miss" for me.

There's been a **Frank Paris Seafood Restaurant** in Savannah since the present owner's father first opened his doors downtown in 1923. He moved out to the old Tybee Road in 1930, and when the new Thunderbolt Bridge was built, Frank Paris, Jr., simply moved the restaurant back to accommodate the wider highway. What you'll find these days on Highway 80 (just past the Thunderbolt Bridge at 3521 Macceo Drive, Savannah, GA 31410; tel. 897-2155) is a relaxed, friendly atmosphere, attentive service, and seafood that is outstanding. Everything, from crab stew, shrimp Creole, Alaskan king crab legs, and crab au gratin to the special shore dinner and combination seafood platters, is prepared to perfection. And if seafood isn't your particular passion, there are Italian dishes like rigatoni, spaghetti, and spaghetti Genovesa, as well as steaks, hamburgers, and sandwiches. Prices are moderate, to say the least, in the $6.50 to $10 range for dinner, with a lunch buffet every day except Monday for just $5. Hours are 11 a.m. to 3 p.m. for lunch, 6 to 10:30 p.m. for dinner (to 11:30 p.m. on weekends).

Also, **Pablo's Mexican Food** (tel. 355-2484), on Posey Street between Abercorn and White Bluff, serves good homemade Mexican specialties in an attractive setting at budget prices from 11 a.m. to 9 p.m. every day except Monday. Imported Mexican beer and margaritas are specialties, also. The **Exchange Tavern**, 201 E. River St. (tel. 234-9311), has a great selection of sandwiches, an interesting clock collection, and is open from 10:30 a.m. to 2 a.m., on Sunday from noon to 6 p.m. Beer and cocktails are served in this tavern that really *looks* like a tavern, and it proved to be one of my favorite "drop in" places, for food, atmosphere, and relaxation.

READERS' SUGGESTIONS: "I would highly recommend **Tassey's Pier**, in nearby Thunderbolt, as a great seafood restaurant, and a good value" (Mrs. M. Jackson, Columbus, Ga. Author's note: It's on River Rd., about five miles out of town [P.O. Box 3812; tel. 354-2973].)

"Even if you don't take in **Capt. Sam's** river cruises, you shouldn't miss the excellent food on his riverboat moored at River St. The best barbecued ribs we found in the South, along with sandwiches and salads at lunch and complete dinners in the evening. There's even live music from time to time. For more elegant eating, we loved **Elizabeth's Restaurant and Dessert Cafe** at 105 E. 37th, on the corner of Drayton and 37th" (D. Jones, New York, N.Y.).

A WORD ABOUT NIGHTLIFE: As is true in so many southern cities, Savannah's nightlife is largely to be found in motel or hotel lounges or restaurants that offer dinner dancing. But for my money, hotel lounges are hotel lounges the world over, and the nighttime Savannah *I* like best is in the taverns over on the waterfront. **Spanky's Pizza Galley & Saloon**, 317 E. River

St. (tel. 236-3009), is a fun place, where the food is both good and inexpensive. Right next door, and under the same management, there's country folk music (live) at **Molly McGuire's,** 401 E. River St., from 9 p.m. to 2 a.m. Wednesday through Saturday, as well as a lively crowd on hand every night. **Kevin Barry's,** 117 W. River St. (tel. 233-9626), is a typical Irish pub, open seven days a week from 11:30 a.m. to 3 a.m., with both food and music (the music is live Thursday through Saturday). The **Night Flight,** 113 E. River St. (tel. 236-7309), has live entertainment (jazz, blues, bluegrass, folk, rock, or country music, depending on the current resident musician) nightly (very popular) from 4 p.m. (noon on Saturday) to 2:45 a.m. (closed Sunday). There's entertainment Monday through Saturday at the **Long Branch Saloon,** 215 E. River St. (tel. 236-9350), along with soups, salads, and sandwiches. **Shucker's,** 225 W. River St. (tel. 236-1427), is always a lively place after dark. I'm sure you'll find your own favorites—just walk along River Street and join the other nightlifers who've discovered this strip of Old Savannah that invites tavern hopping.

More sedate dance music can be found out at the Savannah Resort's H.P.'s Lounge, in Johnny Harris's popular restaurant on Victory Drive, and at Tassey's Pier, in Thunderbolt.

SHOPPING: There's great shopping all along River Street and on Factors Walk. Don't miss **The Home Maiden,** 124 E. Upper Factors Walk (tel. 234-6895), where Bill and Faye Tompkins have local handcrafts. Bill will engrave any glassware you purchase (three initials or first name, free, and there's a large assortment of designs from which to choose). At **The Ship's Wheel,** 123 E. River St. (tel. 232-1625), you'll find almost anything you can imagine (and a few things you couldn't) in the nautical line. Ships wheels, clocks, flags, brass items, lamps, and even hatchcover furniture. For clothing of a nautical nature, as well as intriguing giftware, try **Washed Ashore,** 101 River St. (tel. 234-6100). And inside the lobby of the Hyatt Regency, 2 W. Bay St. (tel. 236-5556), there's a nice selection of classic fashions at the **Carolina Closet.**

SAVANNAH SIGHTS: Savannah's **Visitor Center** (which also houses the Savannah Area Chamber of Commerce and the Convention and Visitors Bureau) *is* one of the city's sights. It's in the restored Central of Georgia Railroad passenger station dating from the late 1850s, part of a 35-acre railroad-yard complex that once bustled with train traffic. The Mid-Victorian building is decorated with "Savannah colors" (the Factor's Red, Tabby White, and Geechee Teal, among others, unearthed by all those determined, chisel-wielding citizens who chipped away at building exteriors until they revealed original 18th- and 19th-century paints), and the train shed out back houses two old steam locomotives. The extremely friendly and efficient staff can tell you anything you want to know about Georgia's "mother city," give you a free orientation slide show, help you join an organized tour (several originate here), or send you off on self-guided walking, driving, or bike (very popular) tours with excellent maps, cassette tapes, and brochures. From I-16, you reach the center by taking the "Downtown" exit and turning left at the first traffic light. The route is well marked, and there's plenty of free parking. (The address is 301 W. Broad St. Savannah, GA 31499 (tel. 912/233-3067; and it's open 9 a.m. to 5 p.m. every day except Christmas.)

You may want to pick up a copy of *Sojourn in Savannah,* which was approved before it went to press by both the Chamber of Commerce and the Historic Savannah Foundation. It is such an interesting, informative guide to this city and the surrounding area that I think it may be underpriced at $3.50. It's on sale at the center, or you can order by writing *Sojourn in Savannah,* 134 E. 45th St., Savannah GA 31405. It's a beautifully printed book and a lasting souvenir of your visit.

There's so much to see in Savannah that it's really hard to say where to start. Personally, I like a stroll along the **waterfront**—it's unlike any you'll find elsewhere. Like the rest of the city's restored and preserved historical district, the old buildings that line Factors' Row are in actual use, not set aside as sterile museums. It's as lively a commercial center today as it was in its rowdier days, the only difference being that now there are charming boutiques, restaurants, and taverns in what used to be brokers' offices and warehouses. Strung along the river's edge alongside a high bluff, the brick buildings rise three (sometimes more) stories above River Street and date from the early 1800s. Each level has its own street—River Street, Lower Factors' Walk, Upper Factors' Walk—and there are bridgeways connecting each level to streets along the bluff. The entrance ramps, from Bay Street down to River Street are paved with cobblestones that crossed the Atlantic as ballast in sailing ships. It's a fascinating, fun sort of place that (perhaps even more than those lovely homes that border Savannah's wide streets) gives you a feeling of the *continuing* history of this town. And if you happen to be there on the first Saturday of any month, you'll be swept up in a River Street festival, with live entertainment, street vendors, and sidewalk artists and craftsmen, that is something special.

Incidentally, that statue at the foot of the East Broad Street ramp of a young girl waving toward the harbor is in memory of Florence Martus, who (so they say) fell in love with a sailor, promised to greet every ship until he returned to marry her, and henceforth for 44 years waved a white cloth by day and a lantern by night to every ship entering the harbor past the Elba Island Light, where she lived with her brother who tended the light. She was greatly loved by seamen and was looked for eagerly, never missing a ship (she said she could "feel" one approaching) and assisting in at least one heroic rescue of sailors from a sinking ship. Sadly, her own sailor never returned for the wedding. Her story is the subject of a ballet, *The Legend of the Waving Girl,* choreographed by the Savannah Ballet's artistic director, Bojan Spassoff, presented for the first time in January of 1977.

Then there's **Bull Street**, stretching south from the river and marking the division between east and west on streets which cross it. It was named for Col. William Bull, an aide to General Oglethorpe, and it holds five of those lovely squares, coming at last to Forsyth Park. Revolutionary War Hero Nathanael Greene is buried in **Johnson Square,** the first of the five, between Bay and Congress Streets. **Wright Square**, between York and State, holds a large boulder honoring Tomochi-chi, the Yamacraw Indian chief without whose friendship the Oglethorpe settlement might have perished. A bronze figure of Oglethorpe himself stands in **Chippewa Square** (between Perry and Hull); and **Madison Square** (between Harris and Charlton) and **Monterey Square** (between Taylor and Gordon) each have monuments and statues commemorating people important to Savannah's history. The people of Savannah love their squares, and they are wonderfully relaxed "people-watching" stations.

Forsyth Park's white, cast-iron fountain is one focal point for Savannah residents, who sit on its railing, feed pigeons, listen to strolling musicians, and generally take a break from the rigors of modern-day life. But aside from the squares and parks, just strolling the streets is an escape from today into yesterday. **Gordon Row,** for example, has town houses with graceful curving stair rails made from ornate ironwork, and **Marshall Row's** handsome brick homes face a broad avenue with grass and trees down its center. Indeed, to my way of thinking, sightseeing in Savannah should either begin or end with a day of walking—along the waterfront, through the squares, and along the streets—in order to get an overall picture of what the city is all about.

Old Savannah

To see where those seven determined ladies started the whole restoration thing, see the **Davenport House** at 324 E. State St. (on Columbia Square), built between 1815 and 1820 by master builder Isaiah Davenport. It is one of the truly great Federal-style houses in this country, and has lovely, delicate ironwork and a handsome elliptical stairway. The furnishings have been gathered mostly from the Savannah area and accurately reflect its period. The house is open Monday to Saturday from 10 a.m. to 4:30 p.m., on Sunday from 1:30 to 4:30 p.m. (it closes Thanksgiving, Christmas, and New Year's Days), and admission is $2 for adults, 75¢ for ages 6 to 10.

The Gothic-style **Green–Meldrim Home,** 14 W. Macon St., is where General Sherman headquartered when his troops occupied Savannah in 1864. In fact, it was from this house that the general sent his famous (in Savannah, at least) telegram to President Lincoln offering him the city as a Christmas gift. The house now belongs to St. John's Church, which uses the former kitchen, servants' quarters, and stable as its rectory. The rest of the premises is open to visitors on Tuesday, Thursday, Friday, and Saturday from 10 a.m. to 4 p.m. (adults pay $2; students, $1; under 6, free).

Girl Scouts will be especially interested in **Juliette Gordon Low's birthplace** at 142 Bull and Oglethorpe Ave. (as will non-Girl Scouts). The founder of Girl Scouting lived in a Regency-style house that is maintained both as a memorial to her and as a national program center. The Victorian additions to the 1818 house were made in 1886, just before Juliette (called "Daisy" by her family) married William Mackay Low. It is open daily, except Wednesday, from 10 a.m. to 4 p.m., Sunday from 11 a.m. to 4:30 p.m. (closed Sunday in January and December). Admission is $2.25 for adults, $1.25 for students (Girl Scout leaders pay $1.50; Girl Scouts under 18, $1).

After her marriage, Juliette lived at what is now the **Andrew Low House** (built in 1848) at 329 Abercorn St., facing Lafayette Square, and it was here that she actually founded the Girl Scouts. She died here in 1927. The classic mid-19th-century house is of stucco over brick with elaborate ironwork outside, jalousied porches, carved woodwork, and crystal chandeliers. William Makepeace Thackeray visited here twice (the desk at which he worked is in one bedroom), as did Robert E. Lee, in 1870, who was entertained at a gala reception in the double parlors. The carriage house is now headquarters for the local Girl Scout council. Visiting hours are 10:30 a.m. to 4:30 p.m., with a donation of $2 for adults, $1 for students, and 75¢ for Girl Scouts and those under 12 (prices are subject to change).

The National Endowment for Humanities underwrites an exhibition in the **William Scarbrough House,** 41 W. Broad St., of Savannah-made items, as well as some imports, dating from 1820 to 1860, a period of rapid growth for the town from a small center of some 7500 to an important cotton port of more than 22,000. The house is now a National Historic Landmark, a museum, and headquarters for the Historic Savannah Foundation. It's open to the public Monday to Saturday from 10 a.m. to 4 p.m. (closed holidays and Saturdays December and January) for a donation of $1.50 from adults, 75¢ from children.

Museums

Tidal-river (that's what the Savannah River is) reptiles and amphibians can be seen at the **Savannah Science Museum,** 4405 Paulsen St., along with native plants, saltwater aquariums, and science, industry, and Indian exhibits. There's a $1 charge (children, 50¢), and it's open Tuesday through Saturday from 10 a.m. to 5 p.m., 2 to 5 p.m. on Sunday. There is also a planetarium lecture every Sunday at 3 p.m. And a reptile and amphibian "hands on" lecture at 3 p.m. every Saturday.

When you're on the riverfront, do go in to the **Museum of Antique Cars,** 313 W. River St. (tel. 233-3525). Located in one of the old cotton warehouses, the museum holds a fine private collection of rare automobiles that includes a 1930 Rolls Royce Golfclub Coupe, 1919 Maxwell, and even some turn-of-the-century vehicles. There are old gas pumps and carriage lamps, as well as a collection of clothing worn during early motoring years. It's closed on Monday, open 9 a.m. to 5 p.m. other days, except Sunday, when hours are 10 a.m. to 6 p.m.

Not exactly a museum, but a historical presentation the whole family will enjoy, is the **Magical History Tour of Savannah,** 1 E. River St. (tel. 233-7275), a narrated history of Savannah using Disney-like, audio-animated, life-size figures. Filled with little-known anecdotes and even some beloved songs from the past, the tour is a delight. Open every day from 10 a.m. to 5 p.m., with adults paying $2.50, children $1.50.

Tours

The river has always been a focal point for Savannah, and one of the best ways to see the city is from the water, aboard the *Harbor Queen* or *Waving Girl,* under the able hand of Capt. Sam Stevens. Cap'n Sam has been on the river for most of his lifetime and shares with his passengers a knowledge that comes from long (nearly 60 years) association with Savannah's growth. Tours leave seven days a week at noon from a dock on River St. at the foot of Bull St., behind City Hall. The two-hour trip includes a tour of historic Fort Jackson. There's also a twilight cocktail cruise from May through September, as well as moonlight supper cruises. The two-hour harbor cruise costs $6.50 for adults, $3.25 for children under 12. Call 234-7248 for information (reservations not usually necessary).

Another delightful way to see Savannah (and save your feet) is by **horse-drawn carriage.** Authentic antique carriages, painstakingly restored, carry you over cobblestone streets as the coachman spins a tale of the town's history. The one-hour tours cover 15 of the 20 squares, and originate at 10 W. Liberty St., just west of the DeSoto Hilton Hotel, from Tuesday through Saturday. Reservations are required—contact: Savannah Carriage Co., DeSoto Hilton Hotel, Liberty and Bull Sts. (tel. 236-6756) to reserve and for departure times.

Landmark Tours, Inc., 216 E. 53rd St. (tel. 236-9604), and **Historic Savannah Foundation Tours** (tel. 233-7787) have narrated bus tours of museums, squares, parks, and homes, with a price of $8.50 for adults, $3.50 for children. Reservations must be made for all tours, and most have starting points at the Visitor Center and pickup points at various hotels and motels.

There are tours on tape for self-guided driving, walking, or bike excursions available at costs ranging from $6 to $12 (including a tape player and maps) from **Tours on Tape,** 17 Price St. Telephone 234-9992 for information on locations where tapes may be rented.

In late March or early April, the **Homes and Gardens Tour** shows off more than 30 homes, gardens, and museums in four days of daylight and candlelight tours. For specific dates, hours, and charges, write Savannah Tour of Homes and Gardens, 18 Abercorn St., Savannah, GA 31401 (tel. 912/234-8054).

Outside the City

About 2½ miles from downtown Savannah, via U.S. 80, there's a fort with a nine-foot-deep tidal moat around its brick walls. It's **Fort Jackson,** which was built by the U.S. Corps of Engineers between 1809 and 1879 at a strategic point on the Savannah River. This is the fort that Georgia troops occupied before the outbreak of the Civil War and held until Sherman arrived in 1864. Its arched rooms (designed to support the weight of heavy cannon mounted above, which commanded the harbor entrance) hold 13 exhibit areas. Hours are Tuesday through Sunday from 9 a.m. to 5 p.m., and admission is $1.50 for adults, $1 for students, military personnel and senior citizens; call 232-3945 if you need additional information.

Fort McAllister is ten miles east of U.S. 17 at Richmond Hill, on the banks of the Great Ogeechee River, and was a Confederate earthenwork fortification. There's a visitor center with historic exhibits, and there's a $1 fee for adults, 50¢ for children. Open Tuesday to Saturday, 9 a.m. to 5 p.m.; Sunday, 2 to 5:30 p.m.

Fort Pulaski, a National Monument, is 15 miles east of Savannah off U.S. 80 on Cockspur and McQueens Islands at the very mouth of the Savannah River. It took 18 years to complete the massive, pentagonally shaped fort, with its casemate galleries and drawbridges crossing the moat. It was captured by Union troops in 1862 after a 30-hour bombardment, and you can still see shells from that battle embedded in the walls. There are exhibits on the fort's history in the visitor center, which is open every day except Christmas from 8:30 a.m. to 5:30 p.m. (7 p.m. in summer), and admission is $1 per car. (For complete information, write: Superintendent, Fort Pulaski, P.O. Box 98, Savannah, GA 31328.)

There's a quiet little beach over on **Tybee Island,** a short drive from Savannah on U.S. 80. Oglethorpe built a lighthouse here in 1736, which was destroyed by a storm and replaced in 1773 with a structure you can visit and even climb. Pirates sought haven on Tybee Island, and it was a favorite place for duels between Savannah gentlemen—but today it's a relaxing memorial park playground, with a fishing pier, boat-launching ramp, marina, and a museum featuring historical dioramas, documents, relics, and artwork. For details, contact the Chamber of Commerce, P.O. Box 491, Tybee Island, GA 31328 (tel. 912/786-4077).

If you opt for a few days at this friendly, very casual beach settlement, the very first **Days Inn,** 1402 Butler Ave., P.O. Box 696, Tybee Island, GA 31328 (tel. 912/786-4576), is still here—it was built in 1970, and is a plain, two-story building just off the oceanfront. Rates are seasonal, with doubles running from $25.88 to $44.88. Directly behind it, on the waterfront, the pleasant Veranda Restaurant serves everything from snacks to full meals (homecooked and delicious) at very moderate prices.

Some Very Special Events

On the third Sunday of June every year, shrimp boats in and around Savannah gather at Thunderbolt (just over the bridge) for the annual **Blessing of the Fleet.** But if you'd like to see this traditional ceremony and the colorful religious pageant that accompanies it, by all means plan to get there at least three days in advance. There are all sorts of gala activities before the big day itself, and the dances, street fairs, art exhibits, and a general air of celebration create a sort of carnival atmosphere.

They say in New York that "there's a little of Irish in every New Yorker on St. Paddy's Day." Well, in Savannah the same thing goes—their **St. Patrick's Day Parade** on March 17 is second in size only to New York's, and everybody gets into the act, even the Savannah River, which they tell me is dyed green for the day (can't really vouch for *that*, but I *can* tell you it's a great time to be in the city.

No matter what your ethnic background, you'll fit right in at the annual **Night in Old Savannah,** which celebrates *all* this country's cultural groups. Blocks are set aside for what amounts to a massive street fair. The date is usually in late April, and the whole thing is sponsored by the local Girl Scout council. You can write or call them for specific dates and details: Girl Scouts of Savannah, P.O. Box 9389, Savannah, GA 31412 (tel. 912/236-1571).

Christmas in Savannah is a time of warm sociability, and if you plan to be there during that season, be sure to book for the **Christmas Tour of Homes** sponsored by the Downtown Neighborhood Association. Seven homes are shown on one day of the weekend event, with another seven the next, and there's a candlelight tour included in your ticket. Carriage rides, complete with hand-bell ringers and carolers, are a part of the experience, too. For dates, prices, and reservations, contact: Tickets, P.O. Box 9416, Savannah, GA 31412 (tel. 912/234-0225, 232-6494, or 232-0891).

2. Brunswick and the Golden Isles

Brunswick is just 81 miles south of Savannah (I-95 is quicker, U.S. 17 more beautiful, although a little longer in mileage). A stopover at **Midway,** some 30 miles south of Savannah, is worthwhile if only to see the **Midway Church,** which dates back to 1792 (an earlier one burned—this is the "new" church), with its large slave gallery, high pulpit, and colonial-era headstones in the tiny graveyard.

The Colonial Council of the Royal Province of Georgia laid out Brunswick's streets back in 1771, making it another of early Georgia's planned cities. It has always been an important port, with a natural harbor that can handle oceangoing ships. Over the years, it has also developed into quite a manufacturing and food-processing center (principally seafood), but there are still several vestiges of its colonial past. It is also a very pretty town, with palms, flowering shrubs, and moss-draped live oaks all over the place. And watching the large fleet of shrimp boats (Brunswick calls itself "Shrimp Capital of the World") put in on a sunny afternoon is a favorite pastime for both locals and visitors.

In addition, Brunswick is the gateway to Georgia's "Golden Isles" (a local appellation), the three best known of that string of lush, semitropical islands that runs the length of the state's coastline. Sea Island and St. Simons are just across the Torras Causeway (which passes over the famous "Marshes of Glynn" immortalized by poet Sidney Lanier, who came from these parts), and Jekyll Island is south of town across the Lanier Bridge, then south on Ga. 50 (don't bother looking for highway numbers, though—large signs point the way). Together, they form one of the loveliest resort areas along the entire Atlantic coast.

The island haven't always been dedicated to fun in the sun, however. The Spanish had missions on them as early as 1566, and there were peaceful Creek Indians fishing, hunting, and farming here from 2500 B.C., say anthropologists who've studied the evidence. And St. Simons was the scene of the small but important "Battle of Bloody Marsh" in 1742 that probably determined once and for all that the southern part of the country would remain under British, not Spanish, domination. General Oglethorpe had built Fort Frederica on the west side of St. Simons and a smaller battery, Fort St. Simon, on the south end as a defense against the Spanish, who were entrenched in nearby Florida and had a greedy eye on the lands to their north. He didn't have nearly enough troops to repulse any serious Spanish attack, but after the British victory at Bloody Marsh, and some brillant strategy that included parading the same seven horsemen up and down a faraway beach during one whole day of negotiations to give the illusion of a full complement of cavalry, the Spanish finally were convinced that his position was much stronger than it really was and withdrew from the territory for good.

After the Revolution, the islands were world famous for their Sea Island cotton, grown on huge plantations supported mainly by slave labor. So important was slavery to their economy, in fact, that the last slaver, the *Wanderer,* landed its cargo of Africans on Jekyll Island as late as 1858, with the world looking on: the importing of slaves was by that time illegal, and its crew was promptly arrested. After the Civil War, without their large labor force, the plantations languished and finally disappeared. There was a brief period of prosperity based on a lumber mill on St. Simons (from the 1870s to 1903), and the first daily postal service began in 1876.

It was in the late 1880s, however, that the Golden Isles got into the resort business, when a group of Yankee millionaires "discovered" Jekyll Island and decided it was the ideal retreat from shivery northern weather during January, February, and March. They bought the island for $125,000 and built "cottages" with anywhere from 15 to 25 rooms (remember, these were men with names like J.P. Morgan, P. Lorillard, Vanderbilt, Goodyear, etc.) and a Club House large enough to accommodate up to 100 members. From then until 1947, when second-generation members of the Jekyll Island Club found the island life less glamorous than other "jet set" resorts and sold Jekyll to the state of Georgia for $675,000, the "Millionaires' Village" was so exclusive that no uninvited guest *ever* set foot on the place and even invited guests were limited to visits of no more than two weeks if they stayed in the Club House. Many of those cottages are open to visitors today, and all the attractions that drew those men of wealth and their families are public property, with plenty of accommodations to take care of us "ordinary" folk. One of the not-so-ordinary people to look for relaxation on St. Simons is former President Jimmy Carter, who headed straight there following his election.

As for Sea Island, it was purchased back in 1927 by Howard Coffin (he already owned another "golden isle," Sapelo Island), who built a causeway from St. Simons to reach the five-mile-long barrier island, then set about developing what has become a world-famous resort, The Cloister, which opened in October 1928.

Incidentally, no matter how you approach Brunswick, I strongly recommend a trip to the **Brunswick–Golden Isles Information Center,** P.O. Box 250, Brunswick, GA 31520 (tel. 912/265-0620), about ten miles north of town on I-95. The attractive center rivals any state welcome center I've ever seen. The friendly staff, headed by charming, efficient manager Vickie Leverette, can give you any kind of area information you want (and some you may not have even known you wanted); and if you should happen to land here without reservations (God forbid!), they have an electronic reservations board for more than 20 hotels and motels with up-to-the-minute vacancy data and can book a room for you right there.

WHERE TO STAY: Where you stay will probably depend on how you plan to visit the islands. If this is only a way station for you, with just a quick look around, then your best bet is to stop at one of the motels clustered at the U.S. 341/I-95 interchange, where restaurants, service stations, stores, gift shops, and easy access to the islands causeway add up to real convenience. It's a different story, of course, if a few days' escape from the cares of civilization in an island setting is what you're after.

Stopover Only

At the "Brunswick, U.S.A." complex (mailing address: U.S. 341/I-95, Brunswick GA 31520), the most expensive accommodations are at the **Holiday Inn** (tel. 912/264-4033; $49 and up for a double), where the Gazebo Restaurant has a buffet lunch and features a salad bar with dinner. **Howard Johnson's** (tel. 912/264-4720) dining room has a delicious clam chowder and those famous 28 flavors of ice cream. Doubles run $45 and up. **Ramada Inn** (tel. 912/264-3621; $45 and up for doubles) has the Pier 17 Restaurant serving fresh local seafood. For economy, it's the **Days Inn** (tel. 912/264-4330; $33.88 for a double), with a Tasty World Restaurant that serves breakfast, lunch, and dinner (seafood, steaks, and low-country dishes) at quite reasonable prices. Rooms are all pretty much "motel chain standard," and quite frankly, I couldn't see much difference in rooms despite the price range.

Sea Island

Sea Island (northernmost of the Golden Isles) *means* the world-famous **Cloister Hotel**, Sea Island, GA 31561 (tel. toll free 800/841-3223, in Georgia, 800/342-6874). Operating on full American plan (which means three superb meals a day are included). The Cloister, a Spanish-Moorish-style complex roofed with red tile, has 264 rooms in the main building and adjacent low-rise hotel structures (separately sited, with garden-like surroundings), all complete with the ultimate in luxury, convenience, and comfort. Hotel guests and occupants of some 350 privately owned homes (often available for rental) enjoy the Seal Island Beach Club, with a diving pool, heated swimming pool, wading pool, sundecks for acquiring that island tan, luxurious dining rooms right at the ocean's edge, and the particularly charming Spanish Lounge, with three cloister windows, high wooden ceilings, wood-burning fireplaces, and oversize armchairs. Facilities also include golf (54 holes), tennis (18 all-weather courts), riding stables, skeet and trap shooting, fishing and boating docks, bicycles (the best way of all to get around, in my humble opinion), and lawn sports like croquet, shuffleboard, and chip and putt. There's dancing every night and special events feature plantation suppers, cookouts, musical happenings, and alfresco dinner dances. This elegant place has been family owned since it opened in 1928, and with a staff ratio of three employees to every two guests, you'll begin to get that pampered feeling the minute you register. Rates change with the seasons and vary according to room type and location. From March 15 to May 31, doubles run from $240 up, but drop drastically other months. And remember, *rates include all meals.* Golf, tennis, and honeymoon (and what a perfect honeymoon spot!) package plans are available.

St. Simons

The **King and Prince Beach Hotel**, Arnold Road (tel. 912/638-3631), is more an experience than just a hotel. The 95-room inn is directly on the ocean, and from the moment you step into the elegant lobby, it's relaxation time.

"Handsome" is the only word for room decor here, and long verandas and patios, shaded by ancient oaks and lots and lots of palm trees, are an open invitation to sit and unwind. The food is legendary and includes a chicken with wine sauce and a "Mile High Pie" that is out of this world. When you're tired of sitting, there's a pool (and the beach, of course), tennis, golf, fishing, sailing, horseback riding, and bikes for exploring the island. Oceanfront doubles start at $85, with rates descending for ocean view, courtyard view (charming), and studio rooms. Cabana suites are $95.) Children under ten stay free in same room with parents.

The less expensive **Sea Gate Inn,** 1014 Ocean Blvd. (tel. 912/638-8661), has 49 rooms. All are bright and colorful and some have kitchens, private patios, or balconies. There's free coffee for all, and although there is no dining room, restaurants are only three blocks away. Rates range from $35 to $45, kitchen units from $48 to $57, and suites start at $58.

Queen's Court Motel, 437 Kings Way (tel. 912/638-8459), is a complex of two-story buildings surrounding a shaded, grassy lawn. Rooms come with one double bed or two single beds, and there are suites with two double beds and a large sitting room, as well as kitchenette units. Rates for doubles range from $32 to $45, depending on the type of accommodation. No pets allowed.

At the far end of the island, just next door to the East Beach Coast Guard Station and right on the ocean, **Craft's Ocean Court,** 1568 Wood Ave. (tel. 912/638-3676), has large, nicely decorated rooms, some kitchenette units, and family units, with rates which range from $36 to $46.

Private cottages are available for weekly or monthly rental on St. Simon's, and you can get an illustrated brochure with rates and availability information from: Parker-Kaufman Realtors, 1699 Frederica Rd., St. Simon's Island, GA 31522 (tel. 912/638-3368).

Jekyll Island

The **Buccaneer,** 85 Beachview Dr. (tel. toll free 800/841-6266 or 912/635-2261), is a 214-room beach resort in a setting of lush foliage. Rooms all have a private balcony or terrace and border on the luxurious. For families, there are kitchenettes available and the children's playground comes in handy. Golfers and tennis buffs will find a home here, and there's a pool in addition to that gorgeous beach. The ocean-view restaurant features very good regional cooking. Rates (with children under 16 free) April through Labor Day are $46 to $60 for double rooms, $55 and up for kitchenettes, with lower rates the rest of the year.

Villa-by-the-Sea, 1175 N. Beachview Dr. (tel. toll free 800/841-6262, or 912/635-2521), has 160 villas for an oceanside home away from home. They furnish free island and airport transportation, and other amenities include daily maid service, laundromats, babysitting, and planned activities for adults and children. Golf, tennis, and pool or ocean swimming come along with the sumptuous apartments. An excellent restaurant specializes in fresh seafood, and there's a lounge with entertainment. Double-occupancy rates range from $62 to $125.

Jekyll Island Hilton Inn, 975 N. Beachview Dr. (tel. 912/635-2531), on the northern end of Jekyll Island, is a cluster of town-house accommodations and 272 spacious rooms. All are beautifully appointed and offer a wide selection of location and view. All town houses are fully equipped with kitchens. There's a Youth Activity Center catering to the little folk while their parents play, explore, or relax. The restaurant features coastal seafood specialties, and there's a lounge and disco that commands a spectacular view of the Atlantic Ocean.

Rates: June 16 to September 15, $70 and up; lower other months. Very good golf packages are offered.

Jekyll Island cottage rental rates and availability can be obtained through Parker-Kaufman Realtors, Beachview Dr., P.O. Box 3126, Jekyll Island, GA 31520 (tel. 912/635-2512).

Camping

Jekyll Island has a family campground with per night or weekly rates. The **Cherokee Campground** (tel. 912/635-2592) charges $10 per night or $52 per week for sites with electric and/or sewer hookup, $7.50 and $39 without. Facilities include bathhouses, automatic laundry equipment, pure tapwater, garbage pickup (as well as an emptying station for self-contained units), LP gas service, and bike rentals. Some tent sites are also available at lower rates.

EATING ON THE ISLANDS: Gourmet dining reigns supreme at most of the hotels listed for all three islands, but be sure to reserve for dinner at places like **The Cloister** (use the telephone numbers shown for the hotels, above). However, excellent dining at less expensive prices is also available on St. Simons.

Blanche's Courtyard, 440 Kings Way (tel. 638-3030), serves mostly seafood in a Victorian atmosphere, with lots of old brickwork, antiques, and a private patio. On Friday and Saturday, there's entertainment (dress is casual). Dinner hours are 6 to 10 p.m., and prices range from $9 to $15.

Altogether different is the rustic decor of **The Crab Trap,** 1209 Ocean Blvd. (tel. 638-3552). No fancy trappings, but the seafood is superb. Fresh local shrimp, oysters, and scallops come with cole slaw and hushpuppies, at prices that range from $6 to $12. Dinner is served, Monday through Saturday, from 5 to 10 p.m.

Emmeline and Hessie (at the Golden Isles Marina; tel. 638-9084) was named after two ferries that once plied the waters between Brunswick and St. Simons, a fitting appellation for this unique restaurant overlooking the Intracoastal Waterway and St. Simon's Bay. So well does it fit into its setting that raccoons come right up to the picture windows, begging to be fed. Inside, its ship decor is cozied up by plants and more plants. As you'd expect, seafood tops the menu here, with a live lobster tank, specialty shrimp dishes, and an excellent oyster bar. They do their own baking and dish up homemade soup and sauces. Hours are 11:30 a.m. to midnight daily, and dinner prices are in the $7 to $18 range (with children's plates from $4 to $5). The men in your party should wear jackets.

A warm, rustic interior with lots of exposed beams greets you at **Frederica House,** 3611 Frederica Rd. (tel. 638-6789). It's right in the center of St. Simons, and serves regional seafood specialties, as well as beef dishes, at lunch and dinner. Hours are 11:30 a.m. to 2:30 p.m. and 6 to 10 p.m., and reservations are definitely in order (casual dress is also in order).

At **Poor Stephen's,** on Frederica Rd. (tel. 638-7316), they serve burgers, chowder, salads, and *great* sandwiches from noon until ? (that usually means about 11 p.m., but they refuse to post a quitting time). There's a lounge, very popular with islanders, that stays open from noon until 2 a.m. Prices run from under a dollar to about $5, dress is casual, and this place is a real find.

On Jekyll Island, look for the small, rustic cafe at the end of the pier at the Marina, where fresh-caught seafood is sold at remarkably low prices.

READERS' SUGGESTIONS: "A nice stop for us at St. Simons was **Dana's,** near the St. Simon's pier—good chili and other snacks, very reasonable, in a woody, barnlike building" (M. Ryan, New York, N.Y.) . . . "We had breakfast twice at a funny little place in St. Simon's called **Higdon's**. All the locals eat there and have their own coffee cups hanging on the wall. It has an atmosphere all its own—very small town—try it" (G. Resnick, Baltimore, Md.).

ISLAND ACTIVITIES: Well, there are the beaches—and they're absolutely gorgeous on all three islands. Sunning or splashing, you'll find the fine-sand strand and the gentle-surfed ocean ideal. There are beachfront bathhouses on Jekyll's east shore.

Golfers can pretend they're Jekyll Island millionaires and play the Ocean-side Nine holes those gentlemen patterned after the "olde" course at St. An-drews, Scotland. Or the three 18-hole courses on the island, **Oleander, Pine Lakes,** and **Indian Mound.** Fees are $8 a day for nine holes, $10 for 18.

Also on Jekyll Island are eight outdoor tennis courts ($5 to $7 fees) and one indoor (same rates), bicycle rentals ($1.50 an hour, $6 per day) and bike paths, pier fishing (at no charge), and charter boats for offshore and inlet fishing. No license is required for saltwater fishing; freshwater licenses cost $6 for five days and can be obtained at most hardware or sporting goods stores or at the **Howard Coffin Recreational Park** in Brunswick (freshwater fish around here include bream, red breast, crappie or white perch, shad, bass, and trout). Deep-sea fishing can be arranged by calling the **Troupe Creek Marina** (it's on Yacht Road, east of U.S. 17N) at 264-3862.

The **Aquarama,** on Beachview Drive and Parkway, is a modernistic struc-ture with a circular ballroom for dancing and a glass-walled indoor swimming pool overlooking the ocean. Check when you get there about dancing times and charges.

You can see Jekyll Island's **Millionaires' Village "cottages"** (translate "mansions") via an open-air tram with an interpretive guide. The tour orginates at the Macy Cottage Reception Center, 375 Riverview Dr. (tel. 635-2762 or 635-2727). Highlights of the tour include a stained-glass window that Louis Comfort Tiffany personally installed in Faith Chapel in 1904 and four of the buildings themselves (all others may only be seen from the outside). Adults pay $4, students 6 to 18 years, $3, and children under 6, $1).

Jekyll is also the site of Georgia's first **brewery** (on the northwest end of the island), started by General Oglethorpe, who evidently knew how to "put first things first" for his settlers. Very near the brewery stand the ruins of a home built in 1738 by William Horton, one of Oglethorpe's captains. It was constructed of "tabby," a mortar made of lime, sand, oyster shells, and water, and much used in coastal areas during colonial times.

St. Simons Island is real sightseeing territory. No sightseer worthy of the name would miss **Fort Frederica National Monument** on the northwest end of the island. About all that's left of the original construction is a small portion of the King's Magazine and the barracks tower, but archeological excavations have unearthed many foundations, and the visitor center has a film on the history of the fort and the town, which once had a population of 1000. There's no charge, and it's open every day from 8 a.m. to 5 p.m., later during the summer.

I guess my personal favorite on St. Simons is the **Museum of Coastal History,** in the restored lighthouse keeper's house next to the St. Simons Light (600 Beachview Dr.). There are four rooms of artifacts, books, letters, photos, and a Victorian parlor that sets my romantic mind dreaming. I also like the "folk culture" room, where the museum staff demonstrates some of the spin-ning wheels which still function. No charge, and hours are 10 a.m. to 5 p.m.

every day except Sunday, when it opens at 1:30 p.m., and Monday, when it is closed.

Then there's the **Island Art Center,** on Demere Road near the airport, where local and "traveling" art and craft exhibits are displayed, and there are lectures, classes, and demonstrations. It opens from 11 a.m. to 5 p.m. weekdays September through May; 10 a.m. to 5 p.m. June, July, and August; on Sunday from 1 to 5 p.m.

Scattered from end to end of St. Simons are ruins of the plantation era: **Hampton Plantation** (where Aaron Burr spent a month after his duel with Alexander Hamilton), and **Cannon's Point** on the north; **West Point, Pines Bluff,** and **Hamilton Plantations** on the west along the Frederica River; **Harrington Hall** and **Mulberry Grove** in the interior; **Lawrence, St. Clair, Black Banks, The Village,** and **Kelvyn Grove** on the east; and **Retreat Plantation** on the south end. Ruins are about all you'll see today, but there's a restored chapel on the West Point Plantation (made of tabby, the mortar turned pink because of an unusual lichen; natives say it reflected blood on the hands of Dr. Thomas Hazzard, who killed a neighbor in a land dispute and built the chapel after being so ostracized by island society that he would not attend Christ Church), and tabby slave cabins which have been restored and put to use (one is an activity center of the Methodist-run Epworth-by-the-Sea, another is home of the Island Garden Club on Gascoigne Bluff).

Christ Church (on Frederica Road at the north end of the island) was built first in 1820, on ground where John and Charles Wesley had preached under the oaks in 1736. It was virtually destroyed when Union troops camped here during the Civil War, burning pews for firewood and butchering cattle in the chapel. Then, in 1884, Anson Phelps Green Dodge, Jr., restored it as a memorial to his first wife, who had died on their honeymoon. It's a serene, white wooden building nestled under huge old oaks and looks exactly as an island church should. The doors are open every day from 2 to 5 p.m. during Daylight Savings Time months, 1 to 4 p.m. other times, and there is, of course, no charge to go inside.

NIGHTLIFE: After dark, social life centers around motel lounges, like the Buccaneer's **Leeward Lounge** or the Wanderer's **Pirates Cove,** with more elegant entertainment at **The Cloister.** There's entertainment also at **Misty's Lounge** in the Hilton Inn. Check with the Information Center on Jekyll Island to see what's going on when you're there.

EXCURSIONS FROM THE GOLDEN ISLES: There are several day and half-day trips from the islands. **Brunswick,** for example, has some sights to see: the **James Oglethorpe Monument** (a statue of Georgia's founder) in Queens Square on the east side of Newcastle Street; the **Lover's Oak,** a giant, 900-year-old oak at Albany and Prince Streets; **Lanier's Oak** (honoring the poet) half a mile south of town on U.S. 17; and **Bay Street** (between Third and Gloucester), lined with seafood-processing plants, where you can watch the shrimp boats dock beginning about 3 p.m., a lively, interesting spectacle.

A longer trip is the one inland to Waycross to visit the **Okefenokee Swamp.** This is the largest freshwater swamp still preserved in the U.S., some 700 square miles, and it really presents a picture of nature in the raw. The best entrance is about eight miles south of Waycross on U.S. 1, U.S. 23, and Ga. 177, where there are cypress boardwalks out over the swamp, an observation tower, serpentarium, picnic area, and interpretive centers. The admission charge ($5 for adults, $3 for children under 12) includes a two-mile boat trip along waterways lined with thickly tangled growth and alive with snakes, alligators, and lovely white blossoms of water plants. The swamp is a fantastic "other world," but it may not be for you if you're squeamish when it comes to reptiles, spiders (they come in giant sizes), and the like. If you're squeamish but still interested, a better place to visit is the **Okefenokee Heritage Center,** two miles west of Waycross on U.S. 82, where there are a restored 1912 steam locomotive and depot, an "operating" 1890 print shop, and general exhibits on local history, the arts, sciences, and special studies. There is a $1 admission charge for adults, 50¢ for students under 18; and children under four are admitted free. Hours are 10 a.m. to 5 p.m. Tuesday through Saturday, and 2 to 4 p.m. on Sunday.

3. Cumberland Island

If the semisophistication and wide variety of things to do at the above islands are what you're looking for on Georgia's coast, you're not likely to want to come to Cumberland Island. If, on the other hand, total peace, unspoiled natural surroundings, and a sense of what these islands were like from the beginning of time until man started "developing" them, have special meaning for you, then Cumberland will draw you like a magnet! Nowhere else on the East Coast are those island qualities so perfectly preserved.

On this little bit of offshore land (just 16 miles long and 3 miles across at its widest point), man has been in residence as long as 4000 years ago, but rather than "develop" the resources here, he has lived in harmony with all manner of wildlife and spectacular tree and plant life, using only those necessary for survival and moving in rhythm with nature's patterns. True, timber was harvested here at one time to supply shipbuilders. True, also, that cotton was once cultivated on the island as a commercial crop. But neither was undertaken on a destructive, industrial basis, and nothing was done to upset the balance struck by natural forces as they piled up sand and marshes to create this little bit of paradise that one writer describes as existing "somewhere between Atlantis, Bali Hai, and the Garden of Eden."

To step onto Cumberland Island is to step into a wilderness of maritime forest (with tunnel-like roads canopied by live oaks, cabbage palms, magnolia, holly, red cedar, and pine), salt marshes alive with waving grasses, sand dunes arranged by wind and tide into a double line of defense against destruction by those very forces, and gleaming sand beaches that measure a few hundred yards at low tide. It is to enter a breathtaking world of animal life, where alligators wallow in marshes, whitetailed deer bound through the trees or graze peacefully at dusk, wild pigs snuffle the undergrowth for food, armadillos move their armored-tank shapes about freely, wild turkeys roam unmolested, over 300 species of birds wheel overhead, and wild horses canter in herds or pick their way peacefully to watering holes.

It's enchanted, this island.

WHERE TO STAY: There's only one place *to* stay on Cumberland, and it's no less enchanted than the island, itself. The only commercial building (if you can call it that), **Greyfield Inn** (Drawer B, Fernandina Beach, FL 32034; tel. 904/261-6408) is a three-story plantation mansion with a wide, inviting verandah, set in a grove of live oaks. Built shortly after the turn of the century as a summer retreat by Thomas Carnegie (Andrew's brother and partner), Greyfield has remained family property ever since. Guests today are treated very much like family visitors in years past—the extensive and very valuable library is open for your perusal; furnishings are those the family has always used; the bar is an open one, operated on an honor system (you simply pour your own and note it on a pad); meals are served buffet style from a mahogany sideboard —you dine at the long family table, adorned with heirloom silver candlesticks; and you're at liberty to browse through old family photo albums, scrapbooks, and other memorabilia scattered about the large, paneled living room (if the weather is cool, there'll be a fire in the oversize fireplace). Soft chimes announce meals (dinnertime means "dress"—informal dresses and jackets, no shorts or jeans). And what meals! Seafood is likely to have been caught that very morning, and cooked to perfection. It's roast beef on Saturday night, and a fun-for-all oyster roast every Sunday night. Breakfasts are also sumptuous, and if beachcombing or exploring is what you have in mind for the day, the inn will pack a picnic lunch to carry along. As for the upstairs rooms, they vary in size from the large suite once used by Lucy Carnegie Ferguson (Thomas's granddaughter and the present owner) to less spacious ones. Bathrooms are shared and still hold the original, old-fashioned massive fittings.

In short, you will, as I said before, feel exactly like a family guest at Greyfield. Best of all, the friendly staff will *treat* you like family. The inn is staffed by Mrs. Ferguson's grandchildren. They're all on a first-name basis with guests and full of knowledge about Cumberland and how to enjoy it.

Rates, which include all three meals, are $75 a day (10% discount for children under ten)—and at Greyfield, that's a bargain! Since there are accommodations for only 17 guests, reservations must be made well in advance. A 50% deposit is required, and a 15% gratuity will be added to your bill, as well as a 5% tax.

How to Get There

There's an airstrip near the inn, and air taxi arrangements can be made from Jacksonville or St. Simons Island (call the inn for details). But the best way to reach Greyfield is by its own ferry, the *Robert W. Ferguson,* which maintains a regular schedule to Fernandina Beach, Florida (a few miles east of I-95 on Ga. 40). Reservations are necessary on the *R. W.,* as it is affectionately known, and must be made through the inn. Roundtrip for passengers is $15. For cars, there's a $35 one-way fare. I strongly urge that you take your car or a bicycle, since there's no transportation on the island. If you don't wish to do so, however, you can leave your car with complete safety in the Fernandina Beach parking lot (across from the police station) until you return.

THINGS TO SEE AND DO: Don't look for a swimming pool, tennis courts, or a golf course—Cumberland's attractions are a different sort. The inn is just a short walk from those high sand dunes and a wild, undeveloped beach that had me looking for Long John Silver's longboat coming through the swells. Beachcombing, swimming, shelling, and fishing are high on the list of activities, but exploring the island and drinking in its long history offer stiff competition.

There are no signs left of the Indians who lived here some 4000 years ago, unless you count the base of shells that underlies almost all roadways on the island. Nor can you find traces of Franciscan missionaries who came to convert the Indians during the 1500s. No ruins exist of the forts built at each end by Gen. James Oglethorpe in the 1700s as protection against Spanish invaders. The only thing that remains of Oglethorpe's hunting lodge is its name, Dungeness, a name that has clung to Gen. Nathanael Greene's post-Revolutionary mansion built of tabby (which burned to the ground after the Civil War) and its successor, a massive Carnegie mansion built on the same site.

What you *can* find as you poke around this fascinating place are: the ruins of Carnegie's Dungeness (which burned in 1959) and the still-standing recreation building which housed spacious guest rooms, an indoor swimming pool, squash court, gymnasium, and billiard room; the Greene-Miller (Phineas Miller was Mrs. Greene's second husband) cemetery that first held the remains of Henry "Lighthorse Harry" Lee before they were removed to Virginia and still evokes ghosts of its inhabitants from Revolutionary times right through the Civil War era; Stafford plantation house and, down the lane a bit, "the chimneys," a melancholy ruin of post-Civil War drama (ask at the inn for the full story); Plum Orchard, a magnificent Carnegie mansion, fully furnished but unoccupied and now the property of the National Park Service; and most of all, the hushed solemnity of island roads, pathways, and fields being reclaimed by native plants and wildlife. In a very real sense, the past lives vividly in today's unchanged island environment.

SPECIAL NOTE: Since 1972, most of Cumberland Island has been a National Seashore administered by the National Park Service. Ferry service is available from St. Mary's, Ga., by reservation (write: Superintendent, P.O. Box 806, St. Marys, GA 31558; tel. 912/882-4335). There are two trips in each direction daily except Tuesday and Wednesday, although schedules and fares are subject to change.

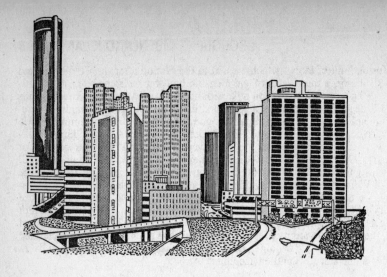

Chapter XIII

CENTRAL AND WESTERN GEORGIA

1. Atlanta
2. Pine Mountain
3. Plains and Other Area Attractions

THIS INLAND SECTION of Georgia is the land of Scarlett O'Hara, Martin Luther King, Jr., Coca-Cola, peach orchards, pecan groves, and of course, Jimmy Carter. It is also a land of giant textile mills, pulp and paper plants, and manufacturing centers for automobiles, metal, chemicals, and furniture that bear the definite stamp of the New South. Which is not to say that Georgia, which suffered mightily under the heel of General Sherman during the Civil War, does not retain and value its Old South heritage. It does, and there are symbols of it everywhere. But primarily, this part of the state looks forward, not backward.

Atlanta, the state's capital since 1868, typifies the economic vigor of inland Georgia, having recovered from almost total destruction to become the leading manufacturing and commercial center in the entire South. Agriculture, which has always been important, is now practiced on a grand scale, with tobacco, watermelons, sugarcane, okra, and pimiento peppers following close behind peaches, pecans, and peanuts in importance. And the region is rich in commercial clays and limestone, marble, granite, bauxite, talc, and feldspar, all of which are mined profitably.

1. Atlanta

Georgia's capital is literally a railroad city. In fact, for a long time it had no name except "The Terminus," since it was the southern end of a Western and Atlantic Railroad spur linking the state with Tennessee and points west. A civil engineer who had surveyed the rail route is said to have predicted that it would "be a good location for one tavern, a blacksmith shop, a grocery store and nothing else." That was back in 1837 (the first run on the line didn't come until 1842), and the little settlement of dirt-floored shacks and wide-open bars kept its "work camp" atmosphere through two name changes (first to Marthasville, then Atlanta—a female form of the "Atlantic" in the railroad's name) and a municipal charter in 1847 that made it a legitimate town.

But as more and more rail lines met at the junction, life became more civilized and businessmen arrived to attend to the warehousing, distributing, and wholesaling of freight coming in by rail. When the Confederacy came into being, Atlanta was an important supply and arms center, a role for which it paid dearly when Gen. William T. Sherman fought a long, bitter battle to win the city for the Union, kept it under harsh military rule from September to November of 1864 (most civilians were evacuated during this period), then burned all but 400 of its 3600 homes and destroyed its railroads before setting out on his "march to the sea."

Only four years later, however, Atlanta had recovered to the point that it could be named the state capital (partly because of its location and the accessibility through rebuilt railroads to all parts of the state). The collapse of a slavery-based plantation economy proved a boon to this trade-oriented city and its growth hasn't faltered since those Reconstruction recovery days. It has enlarged its rail transportation system, brought in six Interstate highways (the trucking industry is now an important part of the local scene), and acquired an airport second only to Chicago's O'Hare in traffic. Its standing in the business world is such that 450 of the "Fortune 500" national corporations have offices here, and many have moved their home offices to the city.

The effect on Atlantans of all this commerce with the outside world has been to breed a cosmopolitanism and sort of acquired sophistication that keeps them constantly working to bring culture (whether it be in the form of the classical arts or entertainment of the "popular" genre) to their city. Although it never has been one of those legendary "sleepy southern towns," Atlanta today almost wiggles visibly with cultural activity. There are concerts and cabarets, ballets and bar-lounges, art galleries and avant-garde "happenings"— and the influx of European-cuisine restaurants has made it harder and harder to find fried chicken, country ham, hot biscuits, and grits. Today's Atlantans will tell you that their town is the "New York of the South"—and then proceed to take you by the hand and prove it.

GETTING AROUND ATLANTA: I'd like to give one vital bit of advice to any Atlanta visitor—if a native *does* offer to show you around, by all means go! Either that, or park your car and use taxis ($2 for the first mile and $1 for each mile thereafter) or the city's excellent bus and rail system. MARTA (the Metropolitan Atlanta Rapid Transit Authority) has 140 different bus routes in operation, and a "last word" east-west monorail line. There are no tokens for the 60¢ fare, and you must have exact change. Senior citizens ride for 30¢ after 9 a.m. You can call 522-4711 for all bus routes and schedules to get from where you are to where you want to go. *A word of warning, however:* this number will almost *always* be busy on your first few attempts, so either keep at it, or stop by one of the rail stations or bus supervisor's booths downtown and pick up

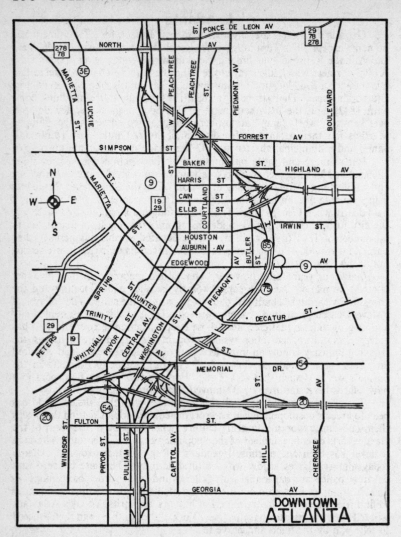

DOWNTOWN
ATLANTA

bus and rail maps and timetables.

I can tell you from a long history of turning around and going back that Atlanta is one of the hardest cities on the face of the earth to get around if you weren't born and raised in its street "system," which isn't a system at all, just a perplexing maze of streets (at least to a stranger) that seem to have no particular plan. I don't think I've ever been in the city behind a wheel without being lost at least once. On the other hand, the buses or the monorail go everywhere, taxis are plentiful although you usually have to get them at a hotel stand or by telephoning (Yellow Cab, tel. 521-0200; Checker Cab, tel. 525-5466), and even if you get lost while driving, some helpful local will set you straight with a friendly smile.

Having said all that, for what it's worth here are a few tips about Atlanta's streets. In the center of the downtown area, Peachtree, Marietta, Decatur, Edgewood, and Whitehall Streets come together at **Five Points Intersection;** and all those NE, NW, SE, and SW addresses stem from this point. Peachtree runs north and south through the city, North Avenue and Ponce de Leon run east and west, and I-75 (Northwest and South Expressways) and I-85 (Northeast Expressway) circle downtown. I-20 (the East and West Expressways) runs through the city center. And don't be misled by "Expressway": at rush hours, they're as clogged as city streets, so plan accordingly. Another thing to remember is that "Peachtree" doesn't always mean Peachtree *Street* (which is the *real* main street in Atlanta): there are 26 "Peachtrees"—if it's followed by Drive, View, Circle, Avenue, or anything else, it isn't *the* Peachtree Street!

ATLANTA CAR RENTALS: If you arrive in Atlanta via public transportation, but feel the need for wheels during your stay, there are two firms you should know about to save considerably over rates at major rental firms. **Nearly New Rent-a-Car,** 2448 Cheshire Bridge Rd. NE—right off I-85 (tel. 404/633-6006), rents two- and three-year-old models, with unlimited mileage (must not be taken beyond a 40-mile radius of the city) for about *half* the cost of new-car rentals. **Rent-a-Bug,** 1377 Virginia Ave., East Point, Atlanta, GA 30344—that's near the airport (tel. 404/763-2313) has, as you may have guessed, VWs. However, they also rent Toyotas, Ford Escorts and a few other makes. There are 200 free miles for daily rentals, 1000 on a weekly basis. Rates are a little above Nearly New, but still far below others. You pay for gas with both and you should give as much advance notice as possible, since both are extremely popular.

WHERE TO STAY: Two of Atlanta's newest—and splashiest—hotels are in large complexes. The Peachtree Plaza is surrounded by a forest of shops, and the Omni International Hotel is neighbor to shops, movie theaters, discos, restaurants, an ice-skating rink, and a three-block-long convention center. Both are in the heart of town, and both are terribly expensive. But luxury hotels are nothing new to Atlanta, and although I have tried throughout this book to stress moderate-priced accommodations (and will do so here, as well), there are hotels which fall into the expensive category that simply cannot be omitted in any discussion of this city.

Expensive

The **Westin Peachtree Plaza,** (210 Peachtree St. NE; tel. 404/659-1400 or toll-free 800/228-3000), is that circular tower you'll notice soaring over Atlanta's skyline. It's 73 stories high, the world's tallest hotel, designed by Atlanta architect John Portman, who helped set the trend to atrium-lobby hotels with the Hyatt Regency a few years back. There's a half-acre lake in this eight-story atrium (with "cocktail islands" scattered about), a waterfall, hanging vines, and lots of escalators to boutiques on the various levels. A glass elevator climbs all the way to the top on the outside of the building. Rooms are plush, to say the least, with vibrant, modern furnishings. Needless to say, nothing has been overlooked in the way of guest facilities: there's a heated pool with poolside food and beverage service, several cafes and restaurants, a health club and sauna, a revolving rooftop bar and Sun Dial Restaurant (which also has a stationary level just in case you don't *want* to revolve), entertainment in the Inner Circle Lounge, and barber and beauty shop service. If BIG, innovative, and opulent is your thing, this is certainly the place to find it! Double rooms start at $85 and go up—and if you're really a big spender, you can get a two-floor "super-suite" for $1000!

The **Omni International,** 1 Omni International (tel. 404/659-0000) is in a giant glass-and-steel "megastructure" that is a sort of inner-city "city," with just about everything you can think of for shopping, entertainment, and dining right at your fingertips. The extravagant lobby and posh rooms are not quite as breathtaking, perhaps, as those at the Peachtree Plaza, but definitely "luxury." Doubles are in the $90 to $130 range, and some of the rooms have views of the shopping malls and skating rink.

The **Hyatt Regency,** 265 Peachtree St. NE (tel. 404/577-1234), was the first of Atlanta's "super hotels," and I confess to preferring it over most of the others. Its 23-story atrium lobby is somewhat more subdued, although it definitely is striking, with a gold and silver aluminum and stainless-steel sculpture that extends from the second level to the 12th, much greenery, and glass elevators that go all the way to the blue-domed, revolving restaurant and cocktail lounge. This hotel, with a newly completed tower, is now the largest luxury hotel in the Southeast, with over 1300 rooms and suites, all of which are elegant. There's a pool, several lounges, and five restaurants (including a supper club with two shows a night). Doubles run $95 to $150, with deluxe suites (some with fireplaces) ranging from $235 to $375.

The **Atlanta Hilton,** 255 Courtland St. at Harris St. (tel. 404/659-2000), is built around a five-story atrium and also has glass-enclosed exterior elevators. It rises 29 stories in three wings, is just a block off Peachtree, and has stores, lounges, and restaurants on the premises. There's a pool, of course, and tennis, as well as a health club and sauna. The rooms are stylishly decorated and everything has that Hilton shine. Double rooms cost from $88 to $116.

All-Suites

There are two Guest Quarters locations in Atlanta, one slightly lower in rates than the other, both superbly equipped with all the deluxe features that distinguish this chain (see Chapter 1). There is one addition in both hotels, however, which is definitely worth a mention—it's the wittily written "Best of Atlanta" guide furnished each guest, which details the top dining, entertainment, shopping, and "pertinent and impertinent" spots in the city. Compiled with a great deal of care, and even more personality, it provides good reading as well as useful information.

The **Guest Quarters-Perimeter Center,** 111 Perimeter Center W., Atlanta, GA 30346 (tel. 404/396-6800 or toll free 800/424-2900), is just off I-285, and furnishes courtesy transportation for nearby tennis and golf facilities. There are some 242 suites, surrounded by landscaped grounds, and the Perimeter Mall Shopping Center is just across the highway. Double occupancy rates here are $121 for a one-bedroom suite, $172 for two bedrooms.

The garden-type **Guest Quarters-Roswell Road,** 7000 Roswell Rd., Atlanta, GA 30328 (tel. 404/394-6300 or toll free 800/424-2900), also provides tennis, golf, and health club privileges, and many of the suites have private patios. Rates begin at $89 for one bedroom, $93 for two, and $97 for three—all for double occupancy. Single occupancy rates are slightly lower.

Moderate

With two exceptions most of the moderate-priced motels in the Atlanta area are members of national chains.

One exception is the **Hotel York,** 683 Peachtree St. N.E., Atlanta, GA 30308 (tel. 404/874-9200). Atlantans will remember it as the old Cox-Carlton Hotel which was converted to apartments for single businessmen when this was the business center of the city. Then, in the forties, business began to move away from this midtown location, and the hotel fell on hard times. Now it is being upgraded to standards that are probably the highest in its history. Location for the traveler is ideal, since it is just across the street from the Fox Theater and less than five minutes' ride from the World Congress Convention Center and many sightseeing attractions. There's a MARTA subway station less than a block away, and bus service at the corner, which simplifies moving around the city considerably.

As for the hotel, its lobby has a distinctly European flavor, with antique-reproduction furnishings, large square columns, and an almost-ceiling-high lacquered folding screen of black and gold, depicting two seasons on one side, two on the other (need I say it is turned with the seasons?). The clientele, too, is composed of a liberal sprinkling of Europeans. All guestrooms have not, as we go to press, been completely renovated, but all are comfortably and attractively furnished, and such details as all-porcelain bathroom fixtures will delight those who are somewhat tired of more splashy present-day fittings. There's an elegant and excellent 24-hour restaurant, the Palms, which serves on the outside terrace in good weather, as well as in the beautifully appointed main dining room. Downstairs, the Plush Room is an intimate, dimly lit lounge with entertainment that, in its short life, has featured such outstanding talent as Eartha Kitt. The staff is friendly and helpful, rounding out a list of attributes that make the Hotel York a good choice, indeed. Double occupancy rates range from $59 to $65, with suites that accommodate up to four going for $108—moderate rates, indeed, for such centrally located accommodations in Atlanta.

The second exception is the **Habersham Hotel,** 330 Peachtree St. NE (tel. collect 404/577-1980, or toll free 800/241-4288), a small, well-run hotel in downtown Atlanta which wears a semi-European air. For example, there's a concierge staff at your beck and call to arrange theater or cultural events tickets, dinner reservations, or what-have-you. The complimentary continental breakfast of fresh-squeezed juice, pastry, fresh fruit, coffee, and tea is set out each morning on an English sideboard, and in the evenings that same handsome piece holds cocktails and hors d'oeuvres. There are executive-size rooms, king-size beds, and in some rooms a wet bar with refrigerator. Doubles start at $65, and there are family plans and weekend packages available.

There is little to distinguish the chains from one another except location, although facilities do vary slightly. Those listed here can be assumed to have the standard, motel-quality rooms and decor, and I've added some of the nicer locally owned hostelries.

The **Holiday Inn–Downtown,** 175 Piedmont Ave. NE (tel. 404/659-2727), is within walking distance of Peachtree Street, the Civic Center, and several shopping plazas. The 470 rooms, most with two double beds, are available at a reasonable average rate of $65, and children under 18 stay free with parents. An outdoor swimming pool, dining room (open from 6 a.m. to 10 p.m.), and two lounges, one with live entertainment, offer a choice of relaxed or active atmosphere. It's very much the same out at the **Holiday Inn–Airport,** 1380 Virginia Ave. (tel. 404/762-8411), which is about seven miles from the city center. There's free shuttle-bus service to and from the airport, lighted tennis courts, sauna, pool, disco, and live entertainment in the lounges, and two restaurants. Doubles start at $65, and children under 18 stay free in room with parents.

Howard Johnson's Stadium, 759 Washington St. SW (tel. 404/688-8665), is two blocks from the Atlanta Stadium, which means it's about two miles south (about a five-minute drive) of the center of town. Rooms have patios or balconies, and a few are fitted for the handicapped. There is tennis, a pool, sauna, and a playground for kids. Doubles run $42 and up.

The **Atlanta Central TraveLodge,** 311 Courtland St. NE (tel. 404/659-4545), furnishes free coffee (there's a 24-hour restaurant just half a block away), allows pets, has a heated pool, queen-size beds in many rooms, and furnishes irons and ironing boards on request. Doubles start at $48.

The **Ramada Inn–Central,** I-85 at Monroe Drive, 480 Plasters Ave. (tel. 404/873-4661), has a pool, restaurant, and lounge with entertainment. Double rooms, which are very attractively decorated, are in the $47 to $57 range, with no charge for children under 17 in same room with parents.

Stone Mountain Inn, P.O. Box 775, Stone Mountain, GA 30086 (tel. 404/469-3311), is 16 miles east of the city, but there's public transportation on city buses from Stone Mountain Park, and it's a good location for avoiding city traffic. Rooms are especially comfortable and nicely decorated, there's a heated pool (with a wading section for the kids and beverage service for the grownups), basketball, volleyball, and Ping-Pong. Rates are seasonal, $46 to $55 for double rooms from June 1 through Labor Day, a little lower other months.

Budget

Atlanta is headquarters for my favorite budget chain, **Days Inn,** and they have 11 locations in the metropolitan area, five of them called **Days Lodges,** with three-room apartment suites nicely furnished with all-electric kitchens, dishwashers, and disposals. Rates start at about $30.88 for doubles or $32.88 for suites depending on the Days Inn location. All have pools and most have Tasty World Restaurants. As I've commented before in this book, I have yet to be disappointed in rooms at this chain's motels; they are, without exception, spacious, clean, comfortable, and much more attractive than you'd expect in their price range. For a nation-wide Days Inn directory, contact: Days Inns of America, Inc., 2751 Buford Hwy N.E., Atlanta, GA 30324.

The best news for budget travelers is that Days Inn has now opened a hotel right in the heart of downtown, with all the care and attention to detail so evident in their other properties. Directly across from the Atlanta Merchandise Mart, and only four blocks from the World Congress Center, a mile from the State Capitol and a half-mile from the Civic Center, the **Days Inn Downtown Atlanta,** Spring St. at Baker St., Atlanta, GA 30303 (tel. 404/523-1144), offers doubles for $46.88, and there's a restaurant and a pool. If convenience matters, this is the one to book—otherwise, the following offer lower rates.

Lodges Northeast of the city: 2461 Old Stone Mountain Rd. (Buford Hwy.), in Chamblee (tel. 404/458-9323); off I-85, 2782 Shallowford Rd. (tel. 404/458-8821); 4815 Buford Hwy., in Chamblee (tel. 404/458-8011).

Lodges South of Atlanta: Off I-75, 4888 I-75 Access Road (exit at Forest Parkway from the north and at Frontage Road from the south; tel. 404/363-0800); and on I-285 and U.S. 41S, at 4552 Old Dixie Hwy. (tel. 404/363-4250).

Inn Locations: 2910 Clairmont Rd. (tel. 404/633-8411); 2768 Chamblee Tucker Rd. (tel. 404/458-8711); 2867 Northeast Expressway (tel. 404/633-8451); 4120 Fulton Industrial Blvd. (tel. 404/696-4690); 2788 Forest Hills Dr. (tel. 404/768-7750); and 4200 Wesley Chapel Dr. (tel. 404/288-7110).

Bed and Breakfast

B&Bs have arrived in Atlanta in grand style—host homes range from modest, middle-class houses to some of the city's finest residences. And they're located in the downtown area, suburban neighborhoods, and even in Stone Mountain. So, if this is your favorite way to get to know an area, you're sure to find one convenient to your personal interests. As a bonus, you'll probably effect even greater savings as local hosts clue you in to shopping bargains, entertainment, etc. As far in advance as possible, contact **Bed & Breakfast Atlanta,** 1221 Fairview Rd. NE, Atlanta, GA 30306 (tel. 404/378-6026). They carefully screen all host homes and will place you as nearly as possible to the section of the city you prefer. Rates, as we go to press, are $24 to $40, with some exceptional lodgings in the $40 to $60 range. And that includes a continental breakfast.

Campgrounds

To the east of the city, about 16 miles, the **Stone Mountain Campground** has 500 sites, full hookups, LP gas, showers, a laundry, supply store, restaurant, mini-golf, swimming, boating, and fishing. Rates begin at $7. To reach it, take I-285 to the Stone Mountain exit, then drive 7½ miles east on Hwy. 78 to Stone Mountain Park and then follow the signs. For full details, write Stone Mountain Campground, P.O. Box 778, Stone Mountain, GA 30086 (tel. 404/469-9831).

ATLANTA'S RESTAURANTS: It's a point of pride with Atlantans that their town has more fine restaurants than any other major southern city (excluding, of course, New Orleans and Miami, each in a class by itself). Well, it *is* true that you'll find restaurant after restaurant here with lavish decor and elegant service (that can border on the pretentious). But one food critic recently observed, "The main problem with the city's better restaurants is inconsistency and a tendency to use flash instead of culinary finesse," and I'm afraid I have to go along with that. I have paid expensive prices in Atlanta for mediocre food, although at other times the same restaurant presents the same dishes perfectly prepared, and I have had some truly fine meals in much less fine surroundings.

Another point that should be made is that *real* southern cooking is hard to come by in Atlanta's restaurants. What there is tends to be overdone, soggy, and far from the cuisine of southern homes (if you can wangle a dinner invitation "at home," you'll taste the real thing). There are two establishments that do a good job in this department, however, and because I've tried to emphasize regional cuisine throughout this book, these top my list of places to eat, even though neither is expensive or flashy—the important thing is that both are "southern."

Now I don't mean to imply that it's difficult to get a good meal in Atlanta —far from it, as you will see in the writeups that follow. It is simply that, in their haste to live up to the city's new-found reputation for urbanity, Atlanta's restaurateurs tend to take on airs. Sophistication is a patina that develops naturally—and it will most certainly happen in Atlanta, as elsewhere, over time.

To "Eat Southern"

Atlanta's best southern restaurant isn't in Atlanta at all, but in nearby Smyrna. I remember fondly the delicious meals and entertaining evenings I had at **Aunt Fanny's Cabin,** 2155 Campbell Rd., Smyrna (tel. 436-5218), when my home was in this area—but it's more than nostalgia: Aunt Fanny's is always the same when I return. Be forewarned, however, that the restaurant, in a former slave cabin, has a decided "plantation days" atmosphere both in the cuisine and its presentation. There really was an "Aunt Fanny" Williams, and this was her home (and some of the employees have worked here over 30 years). It is over 130 years old and Aunt Fanny was in her 70s when she first began serving meals to the public in 1941. She bustled around the kitchen as long as she was able, then took to a rocking chair to personally greet guests. The fireplaces, the antique furniture, the old copper cookware hanging about, and the soft glow of candlelight in an essentially rustic setting all combine to recreate the world in which Aunt Fanny grew up (she died in 1949); and people from 59 countries have dined here over the years, including foreign ministers, cabinet members, state governors, senators, and countless entertainment personalities.

In all, it's a thoroughly delightful, very friendly place, and the food, too, is straight out of the Old South (in fact, many of the recipes were Aunt Fanny's). The menu is limited—fried chicken, Smithfield ham, charcoal-broiled steak, and fresh rainbow trout—and all entrées except fried chicken ($9.95) and steak ($13.45) are $10.45. Vegetables are fresh, with a true home-cooked flavor—their baked squash belongs in a culinary hall of fame, as far as I'm concerned! All dishes are served family style, coming to the table in large dishes: and if there's chicken, for instance, left on the platter at the end of a meal, brown bags appear for you to take the remains home. Both beer and wine are served, and there's a bar that serves mint juleps along with other cocktails. Aunt Fanny's is open from 11:30 a.m. to 2 p.m. and 6 to 10 p.m. Monday through Friday, 6 until 10:30 p.m. on Saturday, and from 1 to 10 p.m. on Sunday, and it's worth the drive for the experience.

On the northern edge of the midtown section, **Mary Mac's Tea Room,** 224 Ponce de Leon (tel. 875-4337), advertises "southern hospitality with damyan-kee efficiency." With some 2000 people served daily, they *have* to be efficient, but that doesn't seem to diminish either the hospitality or the quality of food. Fried chicken and country ham are really good here, and they—like Aunt Fanny's—do an especially good job with fresh vegetables and hot breads. Mary Mac's is open from 11:15 a.m. to 2 p.m. for lunch, 5 to 8 p.m. for dinner, and prices are very moderate: most dinners (meat, four vegetables, bread, and beverage) run $6 to $9.

Expensive

The **Abbey,** 163 Ponce de Leon (tel. 261-8831), has won the *Holiday* Award for excellence in dining eight years running. Located in a renovated (I almost said converted) church, the restaurant is lovely with lots of stained glass, waiters in monks' robes, and candlelight giving a soft glow to the whole scene. Prices are high here, but entrées are usually good and there's a luxury atmosphere that comes with them. Specialties are noisettes of venison served with chanterelles in a light cream green-pepper sauce, salad Capri, and pheasant roasted in Madeira sauce with pâté de foie gras and truffles. Dinner hours are 6 to 11 p.m. Monday through Saturday, 6 to 10 p.m. on Sunday, and reservations are strongly suggested. Entrées run from $12.75 to $25. Oh, yes, they have an outstanding wine cellar.

The **Coach and Six,** 1776 Peachtree St. (tel. 872-6666), has been a local favorite since 1962, and it, too, is in the award-winning category. The decor features antique brick, fine oil paintings, and candlelight. It's renowned for prime steaks, triple-cut loin lamb chops, two-pound Maine lobsters, veal specialties, and fresh (not frozen) fish. Their home-baked breads are exceptional, too. Lunch is served Monday through Friday from 11:30 a.m. to 2:30 p.m. (prices start at $5.50), dinner from 6 to midnight ($11.50 and up).

Moderate

Bugatti, in the **Omni International Hotel** at the corner of Techwood and Marietta Sts., lobby level (tel. 659-0000), is one of the best northern Italian restaurants in town. The decor is contemporary, to fit its surroundings, and there is an adjoining lounge. It's hard to spotlight a specialty—they're all good—but I like their spaghetti pescatore, with tiny shrimps, mussels, and scallops. Prices are in the $8 to $12 range. Lunch is served Monday through Saturday from noon to 2 p.m., dinner every night from 6:30 to 10:30 p.m., and there's a super Sunday brunch 11 a.m. to 3 p.m. at $12.50 (high, but it's the only meal you'll want for the day) for adults, $6.95 for children. Valet parking is free, and reservations are in order.

Two blocks south of Atlanta's famous Fox Theater, the **Pleasant Peasant,** 555 Peachtree St. (tel. 874-3223), is in what used to be a Victorian ice-cream parlor, which, although renovated, retains much of that old style. Live plants and antiques scattered about give it an almost intimate atmosphere. They don't accept reservations, and it's always crowded, but the service is consistently good. There is a daily special (might be veal paprikash, a specialty), and other menu items include scallops parisienne and pork piquant at prices ranging from $6.50 to $15.50. There is full bar service and a respectable wine list. Dinner hours are 5:30 p.m. to midnight every day except Friday and Saturday, when they serve until 1 a.m. A nice touch here is the special burger menu for the last hour every evening.

Just a few minutes away from downtown, yet light-years away from it in atmosphere, **The Mansion,** 179 Ponce de Leon (tel. 876-0727), is in a wooded setting that occupies the whole block. As its name implies, the house is a Victorian-style mansion, built in 1885, and the spiral staircases, period furniture, window-enclosed dining rooms, and candlelit tables with linen cloths create a relaxing dining atmosphere right in the middle of bustling city streets. You can lunch on sandwiches, salads, egg dishes, and daily specials (11:30 a.m. to 2:30 p.m.) for $3.50 to $6.50, and the dinner menu includes such selections as filet mignon Aïda ($14.95) and red snapper à la careme ($10.95). It's best to reserve for dinner, 6 to 11 p.m., Monday through Saturday, and there's brunch from 10:30 a.m. to 4 p.m. Saturday and Sunday.

A bit out of town, **Sidney's Just South,** 4225 Roswell Rd. (tel. 256-2339), is one of those special places well worth the drive. It's one block (toward Buckhead) from the intersection of Roswell and W. Wieuca Rds., on the left, and is housed in a restored cottage. A romantic atmosphere pervades the main dining room, as well as three smaller rooms (one of which has a fireplace), with lots of flowers and plants, candlelight, and soft classical background music. Four main attraction gourmet specialties change daily (if Basque beef is listed don't miss it—choice tenderloin with a sauce of wine, scallions, mushrooms, and tomatoes) as well as specials of plainer fare, many in the "nouvelle cuisine" style. Prices run from $12 to $16, (including soup or salad, vegetable, and sweet noodle pudding); hours are 6 to 11 p.m. daily. The wine list is excellent and extensive. Sidney's calls itself country-French-Jewish-American, and that about says it. Oh, yes, the cheesecake (homemade) can hold its own with New York's finest.

Good seafood specialties at moderate prices ($4.50 to $20) can be found at **O'Henry's Steak House & Seafood Restaurant,** 230 Peachtree St. NE (tel. 524-5175), open from 11:30 a.m. to 10:30 p.m..

Those of us who find Greek food irresistible, will want to return again and again to **Niko's Greek Restaurant,** 1803 Cheshire Bridge Rd. (tel. 872-1254). Nikos Letsos, his wife, Anna, and their three daughters run this marvelous place in northeast Atlanta, creating an atmosphere which is both relaxing and zestful at the same time, something that seems to come naturally to Greeks. To begin with, specialties like the saganaki appetizer which is flamed at your table with accompanying shouts of "Opa" from waiters and other diners. And the Zorba Special—a combination plate of moussaka, pastitsio, and dolmades served with Greek beans and Greek salad—will bring you to your feet with "Opas" of your own. Then, there are those luscious Greek desserts like baklava and rizogalo. All to the accompaniment of Greek music. Makes me hungry just remembering my last feast at this friendly and lively place! Prices are extremely moderate, in the $5.75 to $8.95 range, and there's a "Menu for Little Greeks." Hours are 11 a.m. to 11 p.m. Monday through Friday, noon to 11 p.m. on Saturday, and 5 to 10:30 p.m. on Sunday.

Houlihan's Old Place, 3393 Peachtree *Road* NE, in Lenox Square (tel. 261-5323), has a distinctive, imaginative decor accented by antiques, stained glass, posters, colorful fabrics, and lots of greenery. You can order anything from steak and duck to escargots, crêpes, and omelets at prices that start as low as $4.50. Food service is continuous from 11 a.m. to midnight Monday to Thursday, until 1 a.m. Friday and Saturday. On Sunday, there's a special brunch from 10 a.m. to 3 p.m., and dinner is served until 11 p.m.

Budget

"Budget" doesn't have to mean "fast-food" in Atlanta. Consider the following. Breakfast and lunch bargains can be found at **Goodfriends Restaurant,** 798 Peachtree St. NE (tel. 876-4663), with a great breakfast, chili, quiche, homemade soups, and buttermilk pie at $1 to $4 prices (open 7:30 a.m. to 2:30 p.m. Monday through Friday). At **Katz's Delicatessen,** 2205 Cheshire Bridge Rd. NE (tel. 321-7444), you'll find pastrami, corned beef, pastries, homemade soups, and homebaked bread from 8 a.m. to 10 p.m. every day except Friday and Saturday, when it's open until midnight (closed Tuesday), at prices of $2 to $6. Or **Aunt Charley's,** 3107 Peachtree Rd. NE (tel. 231-8503), where a satisfying meal of homemade soups, outstanding salads, and sandwiches will cost no more than $2 to $5 (open from 11:30 a.m. to 2 a.m. every day). **Jilly's The Place for Ribs,** 4420 Roswell Rd. NE (tel. 256-2803), serves ribs southern style in a warm, casual atmosphere from 11 a.m. to 4 a.m. daily at $3 to $8, and throws in entertainment, as well.

If you're a born shopper and plan to spend a lot of time in Atlanta's fabulous malls, eating won't break the budget. At Lenox Square Shopping Center, there are simply too many to name—just look around when your feet begin to hurt, and you're sure to spot one. In the Cherokee Plaza Shopping Center, lunch of homemade soup, quiche (or other entree), salad, and pastry will cost no more than $5 at **Maison Robert,** 3867 Peachtree Rd. NE (tel. 237-3675), Monday through Friday from 11:30 a.m. to 2:30 p.m.

There are 11 locations of the **Old Hickory House** around Atlanta, all serving barbecued pork, beef, chicken, and ribs at prices that range from budget to moderate. If southern barbecue is a weakness, keep an eye out for their sign—I've had better in the South, but the Hickory House brand is above average. All locations feature a rustic decor and prices that range from $3.50

to $6.50. Hours vary, but most are open 11 a.m. to 10:30 p.m., some until 11 p.m.

There are two good cafeterias in Atlanta: **Morrison's,** opposite the Atlanta Airport, 1025 Virginia Ave., Hapeville, is open from 11 a.m. to 8 p.m., and lunch entrées run about $3; dinner, $5; and **Davis Brothers,** at Forest Parkway and I-75 in the Georgia State Farmers' Market, is open 24 hours a day, with breakfast costing about $2.50; lunch, $3.50; and dinner, $3.75 to $4.50.

Just a couple of blocks from the Georgia Tech campus (alongside I-75 and I-85 where North Avenue crosses over the highway) is an Atlanta institution—the **Varsity Drive-In.** Now maybe a drive-in doesn't qualify as a "restaurant," but for budget eating, you just can't beat the Varsity, and some 16,000 people a day agree with me. The food is good, service (both carside and inside, where they have seats and stand-up eating counters) is excellent and very fast, and prices are definitely budget for the hot dog, hamburger, french fries fare. They're open from 7 a.m. until midnight.

Virginia Highlands

In the past few years, a lively, interesting resurrection has been taking place out at the intersection of Virginia and Highland Avenues, an area which had become more or less rundown until its discovery by an energetic, youngish crowd. Now there has sprung up a cluster of restaurants and shops that are well worth a visit. Perhaps the most intriguing of its new restaurants (and certainly the most expensive) is **Walter Mitty's,** 816 N. Highland Ave. NE (tel. 876-7115). It's in an elegantly restored building, and outstanding beef and seafood dishes are featured at prices of $7 to $15. Jazz groups entertain in a downstairs room. Hours are 6 to 11 p.m. (to midnight on Friday and Saturday), jazz hours are 9 p.m. to 2 a.m. seven days a week, and it's best to reserve. Less pricey, but equally good in the food department, is **Capo's Cafe,** 992 Virginia Ave. NE (tel. 876-6655). A small, homey (and very popular) place, it specializes in scallops, beef, chicken, and a fettuccini Alfredo that's out of this world. Prices are $5.25 to $7.95, and hours are 5:30 to 10:45 p.m. Here, too, it's a good idea to call for reservations. For your sweet tooth, **The Dessert Place,** 1000 Virginia Ave. NE (tel. 892-8912), has yummy pastries, cakes, cookies, and a long list of special coffees. Take them out, or have a seat in the garden-type back room. Open from 11:30 a.m. to 8 p.m.

For Cheese Lovers

It's hard to know just *where* to list **Dante's Down the Hatch,** 3380 Peachtree *Road,* across the street from Lenox Square (tel. 266-1600). Because its menu is made up largely of cheese trays, cheese and beef fondues, and four complete fondue dinners, I'm not sure it qualifies as a restaurant. On the other hand, if you are a dedicated cheese lover, as I am, Dante's should top all other eating spots on your Atlanta list. Never mind the unique setting, service by people who know and care about cheeses, and superb entertainment (more about that in the nightlife section)—it's the *cheeses* under discussion here. As every cheeselover knows, ordering Brie in a restaurant is chancey, to say the least. It has to be the most temperamental of them all, and I've nibbled at underripe, "green" Brie, spooned up runny, overripe Brie, and just walked away from Brie impossible to eat for whatever mysterious reason. Not so at Dante's. The cheese board that arrived at my table held a Brie worthy of a poetic hymn of praise, and I have it on good authority (Atlanta friends who are regulars here, backed up by Jerry Margolus, longtime manager here) that this was no accident—when the unpredictable delicacy *doesn't* measure up, it comes off the menu. For my money, that speaks volumes for this place. Fondues are prepared with imported cheeses and loving care, and if you're in the mood for meat, the quality of beef is just as good as that Brie. Restaurant, nightspot, or whatnot, Dante's Down the Hatch is a cheeselover's haven. It's open seven days a week from 1 p.m. to 2 a.m., and prices are in the $6 to $12 range. Reservations are a good idea.

READER'S DINING SELECTION: "We had the most outstanding meal on our trip at **Pano's and Paul's,** 1232 W. Paces Ferry Rd. (tel. 261-4739). It's not cheap but if you stay away from the wine and the Coffee Diablo, I would guess a couple could dine sumptuously for under $30. This is a top drawer place" (G. Reeves, Philadelphia, Pa.).

ATLANTA NIGHTLIFE: If there is one thing Atlanta is rich in, it's nightlife —of all kinds! There is dinner theater, symphony, ballet, nightclub, lounge music (country and western, jazz, and rock and roll), cabaret, and almost any other kind of nocturnal entertainment you could name. Most hotels and motels distribute free the publications *Where, Key—This Week in Atlanta,* or *After Hours,* all good guides for where to find what. And for a complete rundown on what's going on while you're there, pick up the Saturday edition of the *Atlanta Constitution* (the local morning newspaper) with its "Weekend" amusement section. Depending on the time of year, you'll see listed performances by the Atlanta Symphony Orchestra and Chamber Chorus, the Atlanta Ballet (the country's oldest regional company), the Southern Ballet of Atlanta, the Ruth Mitchell Dance Company, the Academy Theatre, Alliance Theatre, and scores of other concerts or other cultural events. And no matter when you come to town, you'll find entertainment at the following:

Nightclubs, Cabarets, Lounges, Etc.

My own longtime favorite after-dark has been **Dante's Down the Hatch** across the street from Lenox Square (3380 Peachtree *Road;* tel. 266-1600), with entertainment, and those cheeses I carried on so about earlier. Let me tell you about that decor: Dante has created the illusion of a pirate ship tied up to an old Mediterranean wharf, and the result is an engaging spot that combines fun with sophistication. In the "wharf" section, there is folk singing during the week, classical and flamenco guitar on Sunday. The Paul Mitchell Trio is on hand in the "ship" section. Paul is a jazz pianist who ranks with the greats, and his sidemen match his brilliant artistry. As for the "crew," most have been aboard for a long time, and all really make you feel cared for. Then, of course, there are those cheeses, fondues, special drinks, and an excellent wine list. Add to this the fact that Dante, himself, is always on hand to see that you have a good time, and you have a truly outstanding place to spend an evening. It's so popular that reservations are really a "must," and there's an entertainment charge of $1 per person after 7 p.m. on the ship, 50¢ on the wharf.

The **Plush Room** in the midtown Hotel York, 683 Peachtree (tel. 874-9200), is an intimate, sophisticated room that has hosted such talents as Eartha Kitt, Maxene Andrews, Sharon McNight, etc. It also showcases outstanding local talent, and because of its location just across from the Fox Theater, its audiences frequently include cast members from productions playing there who drop in after their own working hours.

Most of the leading hotels and motels have entertainment and dancing in their lounges (see "Where to Stay," above), and among the most sophisticated are: **Another World,** on top of the **Atlanta Hilton,** Courtland and Harris Sts.

NE (tel. 659-2000), with its breathtaking view of the city, exotic decor, and music artistically blended from every era; **Club Atlantis**, in the **Hyatt Regency** at 265 Peachtree St. NE (tel. 577-1234), the dramatic lounge that slowly revolves 300 feet above the city; and the **Inner Circle Lounge**, in the **Peachtree Plaza Hotel**, Peachtree at International Blvd. NW (tel. 659-1400).

Elsewhere around town, you'll find jazz at **Clarence Foster's**, 1915 Peachtree Rd. NE (tel. 351-0002), after 9 p.m. (the restaurant opens for lunch and dinner, but entertainment is the big drawing card) and on until 2 a.m. daily; jazz at **Walter Mitty's Jazz Club**, 616 N. Highland Ave. NE (tel. 876-7115), where reservations are usually necessary; and big-band music à la the '30s and '40s at **Johnny's Hideaway**, 3771 Roswell Rd. NW (tel. 233-8026).

ATLANTA SHOPPING: There's no doubt about it, Atlanta is probably the best shopping city in the Southeast, with regional shopping centers on or near every one of the metropolitan freeways. Downtown Atlanta is far from being a depressed shopping area drained off by these outlying malls, however, and there are two outstanding places to spend your money right at its heart.

In the **Omni International** Megastructure, 1 Omni International Blvd., you'll find what is locally termed "luxury row"—a group of shops carrying names like Lanvin, Hermès, Givenchy, and Pucci. Not far away is **Rich's Downtown**, home store for the national chain of Federated Stores.

In **Peachtree Center**, there are such nationally known names as **Davison's** (it's a branch of New York's Macy's).

Buckhead, a little north of the downtown area, has **Lenox Square**, with more than 130 stores in its enclosed mall, and **Phipps Plaza**, diagonally across the intersection, with branches of New York stores such as Saks Fifth Avenue, Lord & Taylor, and Tiffany.

SPORTS: When I lived near Atlanta (almost two decades ago), the city was as sports-happy as it is today. The only difference is that then it was concerned primarily with collegiate events, and now (while college competitions *still* keep alumni glued to TV sets and the bookies busy) it has added professional teams that elicit the same sort of loyalty.

Depending on which season finds you in Atlanta, call the following numbers for sports information: Braves baseball, 522-7630; Falcons football, 588-1111; Hawks basketball, 681-3600; International Raceway (auto), 946-4411.

SIGHTSEEING IN ATLANTA: Before you start out sightseeing, contact the **Visitors Bureau**, Harris Tower, Suite 200, 233 Peachtree St. NE, Atlanta, GA 30343 (tel. 404/659-4270), or go by the Welcome Center at Peachtree Center Mall or Lenox Square Mall.

If you come looking for Margaret Mitchell's *Gone with the Wind* antebellum Atlanta, you won't find it, thanks to General Sherman, who burned it all down in 1864. However, it's worth the time and effort to drive northwest of the city's business district (five miles or so out Peachtree Street) to Peachtree Battle Avenue, then left to Habersham Drive, Northside Drive, West Paces Ferry Road (that's the **Governor's Mansion** at no. 391, by the way, and it's open 10 to 11:45 a.m. Tuesday through Thursday at no charge), to Tuxedo Road. It's in a residential area that can, despite its more recent vintage, rival any antebellum section, with dogwoods, azaleas, magnolias, and some of the most beautiful private residences you could find anywhere in the country. Not far from the Governor's Mansion, the Atlanta Historical Society maintains the

Swan House (3101 Andrews Dr. N.W.), an opulent 1920s Palladian-style mansion, and the **Tullie Smith House** (same address), an 1840s southern farmhouse and opened them to the public (with a combined admission of $3, children under six free, from 10:30 a.m. to 4:30 p.m. Tuesday through Saturday, 2 to 4:30 p.m. on Sunday). Atlanta's history and its present affluence are perhaps epitomized in this section of town.

A short drive to the little community of **Roswell,** just north of Atlanta, will also take you back to pre-Civil War days. There are a number of homes of that vintage which have either been preserved through continuous residency or restored by enthusiastic and appreciative new owners. The childhood home of President Theodore Roosevelt's mother, Bulloch Hall, is in Roswell.

Right in the center of town, a four-block tract of Atlanta's history lies beneath newer city streets. Called **Underground Atlanta,** this was an empty catacomb that lay deserted and gathering dust for the better part of a century when railroad viaducts were built over its rococo buildings in post-Civil War days. Then a group of far-sighted and determined Atlanta businessmen decided to restore the crumbling area, and the result was an authentic, completely charming picture of Atlanta in the 1800s. Then, over the years, the historic "city beneath a city" became a little shabby, so much so that in 1977 a new renovation effort was mounted. For a time after that, the Underground fairly sparkled with specialty shops, restaurants, and bars—even street entertainment. Now, it seems, another decline has set in and as this is written, the Underground is closed for what looks like a fairly long time. Various plans have been advanced for its restoration, the most promising of which involves converting the old railroad depot into a deluxe shopping and restaurant area. If this goes through, it will be an interesting, exciting tourist center—the 1869 depot is the oldest building in downtown Atlanta (rebuilt after that disastrous visit by Sherman) and will be rebuilt to its original design. Since this is literally the point at which Atlanta was born, with the planting of Zero Milepost in 1837, it is to be hoped that the city fathers and interested developers will not deprive visitors of a valuable bit of the past. Check on its status when you're there.

At the **Ebenezer Baptist Church,** 413 Auburn Ave. NE, you'll find the simple marble tomb of Dr. Martin Luther King, Jr., who preached here (his father still does; his mother lost her life to a shotgun assassin during a Sunday morning service here a few years ago) until his assassination in 1968. Eventually, there will be an Institute of Nonviolent Social Change on the empty land you see around the tomb and church. Dr. King was born a block west, at 501 Auburn.

Much of your Atlanta sightseeing will be concentrated in **Grant Park,** at Cherokee Avenue and Boulevard SE. There are miles and miles of walkways and roads through the park, some of them along the breastwork built for the city's defense in 1864. The **zoo** is here, and it's a good one, with a special children's zoo and a miniature railroad. Admission is $2.50 for adults, $1.25 for ages four to 11, three and under are free but not admitted without an adult. You can also see in the park a restored Confederate battery, **Fort Walker** (no charge), with guns and ammunition wagons in their original positions for the Battle of Atlanta. But if you really want to *see* that milestone battle, go by the marble building that houses the **Cyclorama,** 800 Cherokee Ave. in Grant Park (tel. 624-1671), a 50-foot-high, 400-foot-circumference painting with a three-dimensional effect and special lighting and sound effects. When you see this monumental work, you'll know why Sherman made his famous "War is hell" remark. Open 9 a.m. to 3:45 p.m. daily. Adults pay $3; ages seven to 12, $1.50.

The **State Capitol,** built in 1884, is on Capitol Square, and the gold-topped dome stands 237 feet above the city. Besides a **Hall of Fame** (with busts of famous Georgians) and a **Hall of Flags** (with U.S., state, and Confederate battle flags), it houses the **Georgia State Museum,** which is free and open from 8 a.m. to 5:30 p.m. Monday through Friday. In the museum, you'll find collections of Georgia minerals and Indian artifacts, dioramas of famous places in the state, and fish and wildlife exhibits.

Remember the "Uncle Remus" stories? Well, Joel Chandler Harris, who created the lovable character and his stories, lived at 1050 Gordon St. SW. **Wren's Nest,** his home, has the original furnishings and his books and photographs, and is open from Monday through Saturday from 9:30 a.m. to 5 p.m. (Sunday from 2 p.m.) at a charge of $2.50 for adults, $1.25 for teenagers, and 75¢ for ages 4 to 12.

About ten miles west of downtown, just off I-20 West, the **Six Flags Over Georgia** theme park, 7561 Six Flags Rd., is one of the best in the country. There are more than 100 rides (including the giant "Great American Scream Machine" roller coaster), a multitude of shows, riverboat and locomotive trips, and several restaurants. The $12 admission charge covers all rides and shows. It's open from late May through Labor Day, from 10 a.m. to 11 p.m., seven days a week (until midnight on Friday and Saturday); weekends only other times (call toll free 800/282-0456 for specific information). The park is dedicated to Georgia's history under the flags of England, France, Spain, the Confederacy, Georgia, and the U.S., with each section of the park depicting one era. Hours and prices are subject to change, so call 948-9290 to check.

Sixteen miles east, on U.S. 78, **Stone Mountain Park,** P.O. Box 776, Stone Mountain, GA 30086 (tel. 469-9831), has been built around a gigantic granite outcropping which juts 825 feet above the surrounding plain. It took three sculptors nearly 20 years to complete the deep-relief carvings of Robert E. Lee, "Stonewall" Jackson, and Jefferson Davis on the face of the monolith. At the top of the mountain, which you can reach by foot or by cable car ($2.50 for adults, $1.50 for children under 12), there's a reflecting pool and observation tower (the view is spellbinding!), museum, and snackbar. In the park around the base of Stone Mountain, there is a 19-building complex that reconstructs an antebellum plantation, with period furnishings, cookhouse, slave quarters, and the traditional outbuildings. Admission is $2.25 for adults, $1.25 for children. A full-size replica of a Civil War train makes the five-mile trip around the base of the mountain (attacked by "Indians" along the way) for $3 adult fare, $1.50 for children (June 15 through Labor Day). And the steamboat *Henry Grady* makes scenic voyages around the 363-acre lake ($1.50 for adults, 75¢ for children). A host of other attractions includes a golf course ($8 weekdays, $9.50 weekends, for 18 holes), a public beach with bathhouse and snackbar ($1.75; children $1.25), and an "Industries of the Old South" area (free) with restored gristmill, sorghum mill, and cider press.

Tours

Gray Line, 3745 Zip Industrial Blvd. (tel. 404/767-0594), has a "Grand Circle" tour that can run from $12 to $18, depending on how "grand" you want your "circle" to be. They also have a *great* "Gone with the Wind" tour that lasts about 4½ hours and visits old plantations around Atlanta. Call for specific dates and times (it doesn't run every day).

2. Pine Mountain

Over on Georgia's western edge, almost at the Alabama line, there's a resort that comes close to qualifying as a philanthropic enterprise and makes an ideal headquarters for exploring points west and south of Atlanta.

Callaway Gardens, on U.S. 27 at Pine Mountain, were begun back in the '30s, and—like Colonial Williamsburg—every cent of profit generated by the resort is plowed back into development. In other words, the Callaway family, which built this beautiful place, derives no private gain at all from its operation, with all monies administered by a nonprofit, state-chartered foundation.

The gardens themselves are a fantastically complete collection of native plants and flowers, to which experimental gardening adds an exotic note. Recreational facilities include swimming and boating, 63 holes of golf on courses that serve as the site of the PGA National Junior Championships and the PGA Club Professional Championships, 19 tennis courts, fishing, biking, horseback trail riding, quail hunting, and skeet and trap shooting. And all this on 2500 acres of what used to be abandoned, worn-out farmland.

This lovely resort is the result of one man's dedicated efforts to restore the natural beauty of the region and create a restful, scenic recreational environment for Georgia residents. Cason Callaway, head of one of Georgia's most prosperous textile mills, once said, "What I'm trying to do here is hang the picture a little higher on the wall for the people of this region. Every child ought to see something beautiful before he's six years old. . . . all I've done is try to fix it so that anybody who came here would see something beautiful wherever he might look." So well did he succeed that people from all over the world visit Callaway Gardens each year.

By rebuilding the soil, nurturing the plant life already there and importing more, building a sand beach that is the largest man-made inland beach in the world, providing inn and cottage accommodations, and opening it all to people of modest means, Cason Callaway did indeed "hang his picture a little higher"; and by the time of his death in 1961 thousands were walking the nature trails and making full use of the facilities he'd provided in a breathtaking scenic setting. And it would have gladdened his heart to see the busloads of school children that roll into the gardens each academic year for free horticultural, botanical, and nature study educational programs sponsored by the Foundation.

WHERE TO STAY: The best possible place to stay is at the gardens themselves. However, because of their popularity, reservations must be made as far in advance as possible—at least a month, longer if you can.

There are 365 rooms in the **Callaway Gardens Inn,** Pine Mountain, GA 31822 (tel. 404/663-2281), all spacious with a brightly colored, homey decor that seems just right for this setting. Two pools and a wading pool, nature programs, bicycles, fishing, and access to beach facilities are part of the package when you stay at Callaway Gardens. There are fees, however, for fishing, tennis, horseback riding, hunting, and skeet and trap (see "Things to See and Do," below).

Rates are seasonal, with doubles ranging from $90 to $150.

In addition to the inn, there are 175 cottages, fully equipped with all cooking utensils and dishes, linens, televisions, and outdoor grills. The one-bedroom size will accommodate four adults, or a family of up to six (or eight if you squeeze a little). These are beautifully situated on wooded sites and make a great stopover on an extended trip or an ideal "home away from home" on a "stay put" vacation in this area. The same free family facilities apply to the cottages as at the inn. Cottages are available on a per-day basis any time except the summer months when they are reserved for families only, on a weekly basis. For cottage rates and reservations you should write well in advance to Central Reservations, Dept. R., Callaway Gardens, Pine Mountain, GA 31822, or call 404/663-2281.

Note: Both the inn and the cottages have golf and tennis package deals, and both offer courtesy cars for transportation throughout the gardens.

Other Choices in the Area

Very close to Callaway Gardens, the **Davis Inn,** Pine Mountain (tel. 404/663-2522), is on Ga. 354, just a quarter-mile east of its junction with U.S. 27. It's small (just 22 units), but very high in quality, with some kitchenettes among the modern, colorfully decorated rooms. Rates are in the $27 to $42 range, depending on the season, and they include admission to the gardens for all guests. Neither the Davis Inn nor the **White Columns Motel** (tel. 404/663-2312) has a pool or restaurant, but both are comfortable, convenient locations, with the beach entrance to Callaway Gardens just a hop, skip, and a jump away. Rates at the White Columns vary from $30 up, seasonally.

And at the little town of Hamilton, just five miles away, the **Valley Motel** (tel. 404/628-4454) is also a small, well-run motel with accommodations that are sort of "motel standard," plus a pool and restaurant. Rates (which include admission to the gardens) range from $30 up over the course of the year.

If you run into trouble booking a room in the immediate area (which sometimes happens in peak summer months), there's a quite nice **Holiday Inn** over the state line (Lanette, Alabama; tel. 205/644-2181) just 15 miles away. It has a pool, kennel, restaurant, and some queen-size beds in rooms that are like those you'd see in most Holiday Inns. Double rooms are in the $45 and up range year round.

DINING AT THE GARDENS: There are three places to eat in the gardens themselves, all very good. The **Plantation Room,** in the inn itself, is tastefully decorated in a country-dining-room style, with flowered wallpaper, deep carpets, and comfortable oak chairs. There's an à la carte menu and children's plates (with baked ham, fried chicken, roast beef, and the like), but it really outdoes itself in the three buffets each day. For breakfast ($6.27) there's an array of bacon, sausage, ham (all homemade), eggs, french toast, their own speckled heart grits, fresh berries and fruits (according to season), the beverage of your choice, and almost anything you can imagine—really a feast, and one of the best meals of the day at the inn. The lunch buffet ($6.27) and the one at dinner ($11.50) not only offer the meats mentioned above, but sometimes throw in continental dishes like crêpes and quiche. And on Friday, the evening Captain's Galley seafood buffet ($14.13) can only be called sumptuous. As for vegetables, well, they're the freshest, especially during the summer, when they come to the table just one or two hours after being picked in Mr. Cason's Vegetable Garden—and I've always found the seasonings excellent, with the taste of "southern" but without the overcooking that so often goes with it. If you've never eaten corn just pulled from the stalk, for example, you'll find out here that it's quite different from the "store-bought" kind pulled days before.

The English Tudor-style **Gardens Restaurant** also has a country air, and it overlooks Mountain Creek Lake and the Lake View Golf Course. No breakfast here, but lunch (from 11:30 a.m. to 2 p.m.) is sometimes a soup and salad buffet (salads are a real specialty in this room, with ingredients coming from the Vegetable Garden in the summer), and there's always a good variety of hot dishes. Prices are in the moderate ($7 to $9) range. At dinner (6:30 to 9:30 p.m.), the star of the menu, I think, is the French onion soup—delicious! Entrées usually include baked ham, chicken in one form or another, and one or two other meats (veal, lamb, etc.).

Up in the country store, the **Country Kitchen** has a cozy, old-fashioned atmosphere and serves breakfast and lunch only (hours are 8:30 a.m. to 5 p.m., and they'll fix breakfast any time of the day). The ham, bacon, and sausage are homemade and the speckled heart grits are a trademark of the gardens and the Country Kitchen. Also, don't miss trying the many varieties of muscadine sauces, jams, and jellies that you'll find on your table. These are grown and manufactured right in the gardens. The luncheon menu features generous salads, hamburgers (big, juicy, and good), and the prices are slightly higher than, say, Burger King (only to be expected, since "hamburger" here means much more than meat on a bun).

Golf and tennis pro shops both have snackshops, with hot dogs, hamburgers, soft drinks, etc., at budget prices.

THINGS TO SEE AND DO: Callaway Gardens—which includes floral and hiking trails, a greenhouse complex, Pioneer Log Cabin, the Ida Cason Callaway Memorial Chapel (a lovely native-fieldstone and log structure by a waterfall on a small lake), Mr. Cason's Vegetable Garden, and acres of picnic grounds—has an admission price of $3 for adults and $1 for children six to 11 (children under six, free). Of course, if you're a guest at the inn or the cottages, there's no charge.

The best place to start any exploration of the gardens is the **Information Center,** where an eight-minute slide show lets you get your bearings as to what is here, as well as giving you the fascinating history of this place. Spring is especially lovely, with more than 600 varieties of azaleas, but it doesn't matter what season it is outside when you step inside the **Greenhouse Conservatory Complex.** The **Vegetable Garden** comprises 7½ acres planted with fruits and vegetables, and the 160-year-old **Pioneer Log Cabin,** with authentic furnishings, paints a vivid picture of early settler life. The nondenominational **Ida Cason Callaway Memorial Chapel** (named for Cason Callaway's mother) is simplicity itself, yet quite elegant, with stained-glass windows depicting the seasons at the gardens. Organ concerts are scheduled throughout the year, marriages take place within its walls with comparative frequency, and it's open for a moment of quiet meditation at all times.

One of my favorite spots in the gardens is the **Country Store** (actually, it isn't in the gardens, but close by the entrance). In fact, for several years following my trek north, I ordered three-pound slabs of their marvelous country-cured bacon sent to me in New York each month, where my family pronounced it "real" bacon, as opposed to the thin-sliced, "chip" bacon available in supermarkets. The bacon and cured ham, preserves, grits, waterground corn meal, and hundreds of other items, both locally made and imported, keep me window-shopping long after I've met the upper limits of my shopping budget.

As for recreation, if you're a day visitor in the summer, the charge is $6.50 for adults, $4 for ages six to 11, no charge for those under six, for admission to the **Robin Lake Beach.** That one price entitles you to swim (the sand beach is a man-made creation that rivals the things nature does herself), ride bikes (at no rental fee), play miniature golf, use paddleboats for the deep water, and ride a riverboat, train, or canoe; as well as enjoy a Water Ski Spectacular and a "Flying High Circus," performed by members of the Florida State University troupe. These facilities, like the gardens, are free to guests at the inn or cottages.

Golfers will find three 18-hole courses as well as one 9-hole executive (par 31) course, with two pro shops and fees that run as follows: $16 to $18 for daily greens fees, $17 for power cart for 18 holes. A three-day greens-fee card can be purchased for $48. Tennis courts (including eight rubico and 11 all-weather) cost $10 and $8, respectively, per hour.

Fishing (with artificial lures only) is available at $6 per person for a half-day (includes boat with electric trolling motor), $10 for two people, and $1.50 for children 11 and under who fish with adults. You can rent fishing gear, in case you didn't come prepared, at nominal rates.

For equestrians, there are 45-minute guided trail rides for $8; a 2½-hour mountain ride (available June, July, and August) is $14.

Hunters can go for quail on a large preserve that's open from October 1 to March 31 for $100 for a half-day (which includes guides and dogs) if they have the required Georgia hunting license—and there's skeet and trap shooting every day at the hunting preserve for $3 per round, plus shells (no charge for guns). The ranges are lighted for night shooting.

3. Plains and Other Area Attractions

This corner of Georgia has had special significance for two U.S. presidents. Franklin D. Roosevelt retreated to his "Little White House" at Warm Springs for spiritual and physical refreshment, and Jimmy Carter was born in Plains, a little town that often didn't even appear on state maps. Both are within easy sightseeing distance from Callaway Gardens, which I recommend as the overnight base. In addition, Columbus is just 30 miles away, with antebellum and Victorian homes, plus an opera house dating from the Civil War that was rescued from decay and destruction by city citizens. There's an infamous Civil War prison camp, Andersonville, just a day trip away, a restored 1850s village, Westville, and in between, driving is made a pleasure by scenery that varies from mountains to rolling plains, from wooded areas to prosperous farms.

WARM SPRINGS: Just 17 miles from Callaway Gardens (take Ga. 190 and follow the signs) is the simple white wooden house that was FDR's **"Little White House."** He had discovered Warm Springs as far back as 1924, shortly after he contracted polio, when he went there for the beneficial effect of swimming in the warm spring water; then in 1926 he bought the springs, hotel, and some cottages and began developing facilities to help paralytic patients from all over the country through the Georgia Warm Springs Foundation, which he founded. Later, when he became president, this was the retreat he loved most, and the house you visit today is much as he left it when he suffered a massive cerebral hemorrhage in 1945 and died while sitting for a portrait in the Warm Springs cottage. The unfinished portrait (by artist Elizabeth Shoumatoff), his wheelchair, Fala's dog chain, ship models, sea paintings, and gifts from citizens of which he was particularly fond are preserved as he last saw them.

Next door, the **Franklin D. Roosevelt Museum** holds more memorabilia and shows a 12-minute movie depicting his life when in Warm Springs. It is open daily from 9 a.m. to 5 p.m. (6 p.m. in summer on weekends), and costs $3 for adults, $1.50 for ages 6 to 12.

PLAINS: Jimmy Carter, 39th president of the U.S., was born 80 miles southeast of the Gardens (U.S. 27 south to Columbus, then Ga. 280 east). You'll know Plains by the little green-and-white train depot, the water tower brightly painted with the stars and stripes. Despite the fame of its most outstanding citizens, there is still a small-town charm that clings to both the town and the people. The early 1900s buildings are much like they were before the Depression of the '30s forced their closing (most were used as warehouses until Jimmy Carter's campaign got underway and brought business back to town). Turner's Hardware and Walters Grocery Store are longtime establishments. The depot (built in 1888) now houses a gift and book shop, but its looks haven't changed a great deal. All in all, Plains can be proud of the common sense that has recognized the importance of preserving the surroundings from which a rural peanut grower went out and became president of the U.S.

Of course, you can almost stand in the middle of "downtown" and see the whole town, but for do-it-yourself walking or driving tours, go by the **Plains Visitor Center,** east of Plains on U.S. 280, where Sibyl McGlaun and her very friendly staff will furnish maps and brochures. If you'd like advance information, write them at P.O. Box 69, Plains, GA 31780. Two publications I particularly liked (and have had fun reading even after coming home) are "Plains, Carter Country U.S.A." ($2.50) and "Armchair Tour of Jimmy Carter Country" ($2.25), both of which I picked up at the depot.

The one-story, ranch-style brick house that is **home** to our former Chief Executive is on Woodland Drive, and there are Secret Service booths at both this entrance and the one on Paschal Street (you can get a pretty good look at it by walking or driving west on Church Street). Then there's the **Plains Methodist Church,** at the corner of Church and Thomas, where Jimmy asked Rosalynn for their first date, and the **Plains Baptist Church,** where the president taught Sunday School and is still a regular attendant when home from traveling. If you want to see an even *more* rural, now-historic site, take a 2½-mile drive out to **Archery,** where Jimmy Carter lived as a child when his father operated a country store. It is west of town on U.S. 280 (it's really *off* U.S. 280, but anybody in town can give you explicit directions).

In nearby Americus, on the grounds of Georgia Southwestern College, Wheatly & Glessner Sts., Americas, GA (tel. 912/928-1273), the James Earl Carter Library holds a permanent display of memorabilia of the Carter family, with the focus on the former president and his first lady.

ANDERSONVILLE: Twenty miles northeast of Plains (U.S. 280 to Americus, then Ga. 49 north) is a National Historic Site that marks the most infamous of Confederate prison camps. Conditions at Andersonville were unspeakably horrible, with severe overcrowding (it was built to hold 10,000, but had at one time a prisoner population of over 32,000), polluted water (from a creek), and starvation rations which led to nearly 15,000 deaths. The commander, Capt. Henry Wirtz, although powerless to prevent the fatalities and an absolute victim of circumstances he had no way of controlling, was tried and hung after the Civil War on charges of having conspired to murder Union prisoners of war. Today you can visit a small museum, see slide shows on the sad camp's history, see the remains of wells and escape tunnels, and see Providence Springs, which legend says gushed up in answer to prayers of prisoners during the drought of 1864. The site is open daily, and there's no admission charge.

WESTVILLE: An intriguing day trip from Callaway Gardens is the 50-mile drive south on U.S. 27 to Lumpkin and the little village of Westville, a restored 1850s town with unpaved streets, 19th-century buildings and homes, and craftsmen who demonstrate such oldtime skills as syrup-making, cotton-ginning, and blacksmithing. It is open every day except major holidays from 10 a.m. to 5 p.m. during the week, 1 to 5 p.m. on Sunday; and admission is $3 for adults, $1.50 for students, no charge for preschoolers.

COLUMBUS: This was the last frontier town of the original 13 colonies, and its wide streets (99 to 164 feet), shaded by marvelous old trees in grass plots, still reveal much of the original city plan of 1828. Situated on the Chattahoochee River at the foot of a series of falls, Columbus early utilized its water supply to become an important manufacturing center, supplying swords, pistols, cannon, gunboats, and other articles of war to the Confederate Army during the Civil War (it fell to Union forces in April of 1865 in one of the last battles of the war). Today there's a lovely riverside walkway, the **Columbus Chattahoochee Promenade,** with gazebos and historical displays, stretching from the Columbus Iron Works Trade and Convention Center to Oglethorpe Bridge, which is open from 10 a.m. to 5 p.m. Tuesday through Friday, 1 to 5 p.m. on Saturday and Sunday. The **Chamber of Commerce,** 412 Broadway (tel. 322-1613), and the **Georgia Welcome Center,** Victory Dr. and 10th Ave. (tel. 571-7455) have very good self-guided tour maps of the city. And **Heritage Tours** leave (from the Welcome Center) Wednesday through Saturday at 10 a.m. for two-hour guided tours that visit the **Springer Opera House** (a restored 1871 theater in which Edwin Booth and other distinguished actors performed, and which was refurbished by Columbians to become a cultural center once again) and several other historic houses. The tour fee is $5 for adults, $2.50 for ages six through 12 and for military personnel in uniform.

Fort Benning is five miles south of the city on U.S. 27, and there is an interesting **National Infantry Museum** reflecting the history of the footsoldier from Revolutionary days up to the present. It's free, and open weekdays except Monday from 10 a.m. to 4:30 p.m., from 12:30 p.m. Saturday and Sunday.

Chapter XIV

INTRODUCTION TO FLORIDA

1. By Way of Background
2. Traveling to Florida
3. Traveling Within Florida

FLORIDA. The word has a magic ring. To some 29 million visitors every year it means two weeks or more in the sun. To almost 9 million more it is home in a year-round tropical climate. To countless others it is the promised land of retirement at the end of a lifetime's work, in less friendly climes. To those who till its soil, it is the source of over $1.99 *billion* in agricultural products every year. To commercial fishermen, it is a happy hunting ground for more than 200 million pounds of fish and shellfish annually. To entertainers it's what the Palace once was to vaudeville stars. To kids, it's Disney World. To golfers it's more than 400 courses, many of championship caliber. To the sportsman it's the dogs at Tampa-St. Pete, the horses at Hialeah, jai-alai, and deep-sea fishing almost anywhere off its 8426-mile shoreline. To mapmakers, it's that 447-mile-long peninsula at the eastern bottom of the U.S., little more than 150 miles wide at any point. To weathermen, it is very often the warmest spot on the weather map. To the aerospace world, it's the jumping-off point to the unknown. To historians, it is the site of this country's first permanent European settlement. To the U.S. Navy, it's Pensacola or Jacksonville. To the Seminole Indians it's the Everglades. To artists and writers it's Key West or Sarasota. In short, Florida is. . .well, it's *Florida!*

1. By Way of Background

FROM THE FOUNTAIN OF YOUTH TO DISNEY WORLD: There has always been a "promised land" aura about Florida, with riches of one sort or another the goal of even its earliest tourists. Ponce de Leon came in April of 1513, after hearing tales from Puerto Rican Indians of a land of much gold and a miraculous, health-restoring fountain of youth. He landed near what would become St. Augustine, named the disappointingly poor land "La Florida," then left after only six days. Later, Panfilo de Narvaez would land near Tampa Bay; Hernando de Soto would pass through in 1539 on his explorations which would end in death on the Mississippi; and the Spanish, under various leaders, would rule Florida until 1763, in spite of a brief, unsuccessful attempt by the French to establish a foothold in 1564. Spain traded it to the eager British in 1763 for repossession of Havana. By 1783, Spain had recaptured West Florida and the Bahamas, and the Treaty of Paris gave them back the rest of the state. In 1812, a group of Americans (70 Georgians and nine Floridians) raised a "patriot flag" and declared it an independent republic, and in 1819, the U.S. paid Spain $5 million and formally took title.

By then, Florida had seen the flags of Spain, France, Great Britain, the State of Muskogee (unfurled by one William Augustus Bowles, who got himself elected "Director General of the State of Muskogee" by a congress of Seminoles and Creeks in 1799 and claimed the state for almost four years), the patriots, and even Mexico (for three months in 1817) fly in its sunlit skies. Small wonder then that in 1845 when it was admitted to the Union its first state flag declared in bold letters, LET US ALONE!

Well, although the slogan disappeared from the flag in short order, people pretty much did leave Florida alone until Henry Plant built his Atlantic Coast railroad system through central Florida to Tampa in 1881, joining east and west coasts. Then Henry Flagler, a Standard Oil associate of the Rockefellers, began his Florida East Coast Line in 1883, and the two millionaires embarked on a luxury-hotel-resort-building battle that started an influx of tourists that has just kept growing ever since. It reached frenzy proportions in the 1920s when land values soared and more than $100 million was spent in Miami on new buildings in one year. Then came the crash in 1929, which really only slowed tourism down, and by the '40s the state was back on its feet. World War II brought prosperity in the form of military installations, and the '50s saw many ex-servicemen returning to the scene to vacation or to set up residence. Since then, prosperity hasn't even slowed down—and I expect instant execution would be the fate of any present-day Floridian who dared utter that old slogan "Let Us Alone."

When Plant and Flagler began their promotion of the state, they touted its warm winters, and for many years that's when the crowds came. However, soon after World War II, people from all over the country began to capitalize on the lower summer rates and to pour in during the months the kids were out of school. Nowadays, more people come in summer than in winter, and "the season" has less and less meaning. Of course, the wealthier still favor winter months—they stay longer and spend more money—and Miami and Palm Beach fairly reek of money from December through May. But when they depart, families not only take their place in the "off-season" half-priced luxury

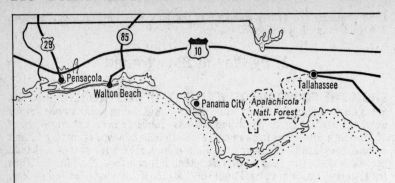

GULF OF MEXICO

FLORIDA

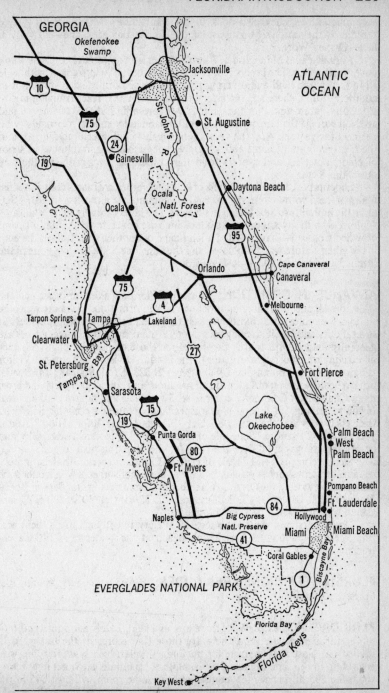

accommodations, they also flock to the Panhandle's Miracle Strip (where summer *is* the season), St. Augustine, the Tampa Bay area, and—all year, in fact—Disney World.

Actually, that old dream of Florida riches isn't so farfetched if you think in vacation terms. The beaches, of course, are a sort of "white gold," with wide strands of white sand and differing Atlantic and Gulf of Mexico surfs. But in addition to that, there are 166 rivers, more than 30,000 lakes (ranging in size from tiny "mud holes" to the giant 700-square-mile Lake Okeechobee), and artesian springs that are crystal clear and inhabited by ersatz "mermaids" who perform for visitors. And the vegetation is lush—cool, green pines up around the Georgia border, palms and sea grape, bougainvillea and hibiscus in a riot of color, sawgrass and cypress from the mysterious Everglades all the way down the Keys.

Superimposed on all these gifts of Mother Nature are man's contributions, many of them with no purpose except to accommodate a tourism industry that annually amounts to $8.8 billion in revenue. The hotels, motels, and restaurants —along with flashy amusement centers, highrise concrete condominiums, and crowded freeways—have created a landscape of another sort. But, in the end, it's Mother Nature who dominates, and the Sunshine State has lost none of the lure it held back in Ponce de Leon's day.

ADVANCE INFORMATION: Tourism is Florida's chief business, and the state goes all out to be sure no tourist will lack information. There are welcome stations for motorists at most major entrances and state-run visitor centers at several outstanding sightseeing attractions around the state. Travel agents are generally loaded with tourist brochures for those coming by plane or other nondriving transportation. A letter to the Florida **Division of Tourism,** Visitor Inquiry, 126 Van Buren St., Tallahassee, FL 32301 (tel. 904/487-1462), will bring a healthy packet of statewide information, and almost every city and town has a Chamber of Commerce eager to send you facts and figures on their area. If you're driving, it's a good idea to specifically request a copy of the official state road map and the handy booklet "Florida Driver Information." And if you ask, they'll send a "Schedule of Events," which is issued seasonally and covers the goings-on all over the state for the time you plan to go.

Senior citizens get a break in central Florida at certain hotels, motels, restaurants, and shops. You can get a list of the establishments which offer such discounts by writing the Orlando Chamber of Commerce, Senior Season (specify *year*), 5200 Diplomat Circle, Orlando, FL 32810 (tel. 305/629-5669), and asking for the "Senior Season" brochure.

Boaters arriving via the Intracoastal Waterway will find an excellent Marine Welcome Station at Fernandina Beach at the Waterway's Florida entrance.

FLORIDA TELEPHONE AREA CODES: St. Augustine, 904; Miami, 305; St. Petersburg, 813.

FLORIDA'S HOTELS: Well, there are, as I said, hotels and motels *ad infinitum* throughout the state. There are those that represent the last word in luxury and those that compete for the budget dollar. Nearly *all* vary in price according to the time of year. For example, a Miami deluxe hotel may rent a room for $95 during winter months and the same room will cost $45 in the summer. Farther north, in St. Augustine, the reverse is true. Generally speaking, the best accommodation buys in South Florida are in October and November, when warm weather is a contrast to colder northern states and the winter rates are not yet in effect (they usually go up about December 15). In the upper part of the state, you'll get reductions after Labor Day until spring. Many hotels, in all price brackets, offer special weekend, golf, or tennis package plans which are real money-savers.

READER'S ACCOMMODATION SELECTION: This motel recommendation, in an area not covered by the text, is passed along in case you should be in Pompano Beach. "The **Palm Aire Motel**, 1990 N. Federal Hwy., Pompano Beach (tel. 305/946-2550), is a tremendous place to stay. It is run by Mr. and Mrs. Art Boice. They are charming and helpful people who really care about their guests. Most of all, their rates are very reasonable. The location is great, too—directly across the street from the large, enclosed Pompano Fashion Square Shopping Mall and surrounded by restaurants, both large and small. It is also two blocks from the Intracoastal Waterway and a harbor cruise restaurant. The Palm Aire has color TVs and a swimming pool, and is very clean. Even though it is on the highway, the rooms are behind the office and are quiet. Truly a nice place to stay, in and out of season" (S. Higgins, Laurence Harbor, N.J.).

CAMPING IN FLORIDA: It seems that every major commercial campground chain has camps in Florida—you'll see them all along the way. In addition, the state has 40 state parks with camping facilities; sites cost $6 plus tax (more in the Keys) per night (electricity is $2 per night), with a two-week limit for your stay at any one park. Half these may be reserved in advance by telephone. There are also vacation cabins available in parks. For a complete list of state parks, regulations, and telephone numbers to reserve, write: **Florida Department of Natural Resources**, Bureau of Education and Information, 3900 Commonwealth Blvd., Tallahassee, FL 32303, and ask for *Florida State Parks Guide*.

FLORIDA'S RESTAURANTS: All those restaurants in Florida include lavishly decorated gourmet rooms with exorbitantly priced menus and dockside seafood bars where you can eat well for a pittance—and often they're right across the dock from each other. Except in the notoriously high-priced establishments (mostly in Palm Beach and Miami), I find prices more reasonable than expensive, at least as measured by those in other resort areas of the country. And there is very good eating in motel and hotel dining rooms, which usually are in the moderate range. Also, most of the major fast-food and budget-food chains (McDonald's, International House of Pancakes, etc.) have branches scattered all over the state, where prices and quality are pretty dependable.

Most restaurants of any size or reputation sell alcoholic beverages by the drink, and wine and beer show up on the most unexpected menus. You can buy your own at retail liquor stores (Sunday sales, however, are subject to local option). Legal drinking age is 19.

READER'S RESTAURANT SELECTION: "We found the **Red Lobster restaurant chain** in Florida to be a reliable source for good seafood at very reasonable prices, and they are located in almost every town in Florida" (A. Nunez, Lodi, N.J.).

FLORIDA CLIMATE: The Gulf Stream in the Atlantic and the tropical currents of the Gulf of Mexico keep the state warmer than most of the rest of the continental United States in winter and can make temperatures as high as 95 in the summer. However, in Miami, summer temperatures average between

80 and 85 and winter temperatures are generally in the mid-70s. The most *comfortable* time to visit southern Florida, if you can't come in winter, is late April through May, before really hot weather sets in and before summer showers, which are an almost daily occurrence (although they're quite brief), begin. In the upper part of the state, you can count on things being about ten degrees cooler in every season. Some representative averages around the state are:

	High	Low
St. Augustine	89	47
Miami	90	58
Tampa–St. Petersburg	90	51

Humidity can be a problem, making temperatures feel much higher than they are, so if you're going in midsummer, take along cool, airy clothes. Insects, however, which were once such a nuisance in the tropical climate, have been reduced considerably due to an effective pest-control program in most sections of the state.

2. Traveling to Florida

BY AIR: Florida has five international airports, with every major airline (and some not so major) reaching the state from almost anywhere in the United States and major overseas departure points. There are nearly always special promotional fares being offered to Florida, so be *sure* to shop around.

Serving Jacksonville: Delta, Eastern, Pan Am, Southern, and Florida Airlines.

Serving Fort Lauderdale (including Hollywood, Pompano Beach, South Palm Beach, and North Dade County): United, Delta, Eastern, Northwest Orient, Southern, Makay International, Florida Airlines, and Air South.

Serving Orlando: Delta, Eastern, Pan Am, Southern, and Air Florida.

Serving Miami: American, Pan Am, TWA, Delta, Eastern, United, Continental, Southern, Northwest Orient, Air Panama, Cayman Airways, Lacsa, Iberia, Air Canada, Aeroperu, Lan Chile, Air France, British Airways, KLM-Royal Dutch Airlines, Air Jamaica, B.W.I.A., Dominicana, TACA International S.A., Viasa, Mexicana, Aerolineas Argentinas, and Transportes Aeros Nacionales.

Serving Tampa-St. Petersburg: Northwest Orient, Delta, Eastern, TWA, Pan Am, United, and Air Canada.

Package Deals

Many of the major airlines offer packages to Miami and Orlando (Disney World) which can represent real savings. Your travel agent or local airline office can fill you in on current offerings and prices, but a sample package at the time of writing is this one by Republic for eight days and seven nights in Miami: airfare plus $127 includes hotel room and compact car for entire stay with unlimited mileage.

BY TRAIN: Amtrak has service to Florida from all across the country—direct routes down the Eastern Seaboard and from the Midwest, connecting schedules from the West Coast. For example, to come from Los Angeles to Miami, you would travel first to Chicago, then to Florida after a change of trains. Check Amtrak's excellent special rates, which change from time to time, but which are real dollar-stretchers. So, be sure to check out current specials when planning your trip by train. There are also many attractive Amtrak package tours to Florida's most popular spots.

Also, check on the status of that planned auto/train package from just south of Washington, D.C., to a central Florida destination (see Chapter 1).

BY BUS: Both Greyhound and Trailways have rather direct express routes to major Florida cities from most points in the country. Both offer much lower excursion rates from time to time, and you should be sure to look into these carefully.

BY CAR: Both I-95 and I-75 are major arteries entering Florida from Georgia. I-95 runs all the way south to Miami and is by far the quickest way to get there. U.S. 1 also enters from the northeast and runs along Florida's east coast, but this is a frustrating, stoplight-infested way to go, and a better choice (albeit a little slower) is the scenic A1A, which hugs the shoreline, often affording beautiful sea vistas, and leisurely zigzags through coastal resort towns. I-75 goes through north central Florida, then swings west to Tampa–St. Petersburg.

From Alabama, I-10 runs across northern Florida to Jacksonville; U.S. 98 follows the Panhandle coastline to U.S. 19, which goes down the Gulf Coast to Tampa–St. Petersburg and joins U.S. 41 (the Tamiami Trail), which in turn follows the west coast down to Naples, where it turns across the state, skirting the Everglades, to terminate in Miami.

3. Traveling Within Florida

BY AIR: Within the state, Eastern, Pan Am/National, Delta, Southern, Commuter, Air Florida, and Air South fly to Daytona Beach, Eglin Air Force Base, Fort Lauderdale, Fort Myers, Gainesville, Lakeland, Melbourne, Ocala, Pensacola, Punta Gorda, Titusville, and Vero Beach.

BY TRAIN: Amtrak stops within the state are at: Jacksonville, Palm Beach, Delray Beach, Fort Lauderdale, Miami, Orlando, Kissimmee, Lakeland, Sebring, Tampa, Clearwater, St. Petersburg, Gainesville, Ocala, Wildwood, Palatka, Sanford, and Winter Park. A new service in 1983 connects Miami Beach and Tampa, with a link to Walt Disney World.

BY BUS: Gulf Coast Motor Lines has intrastate service, and, of course, Greyhound and Trailways both have connecting service to most points within the state.

Bus Tours

Gray Lines offer excellent one- and two-day tours from most major cities to sightseeing attractions such as Disney World and Key West. And for those who truly want to "leave the driving" to someone else, **Tauck Tours** has an excellent seven-day Florida Triangle Tour departing from Tampa. Travel is on comfortable, air-conditioned motor coaches, with seating shifted twice each day. During the seven days, there is a total of 15 hours' riding time, with hotel accommodations and meals included in the tour price. Arrangements for both tours can be made through travel agents all over the country.

BY CAR: Florida is crisscrossed by an excellent network of highways. Major Interstates run through or close to the following towns:

I-75, traveling north to south, goes through Jennings, Jasper, Lake City, Gainesville, Ocala, Bushnell, Dade City, Tampa, and terminates at St. Petersburg.

I-95, on the east coast, runs north to south through Yulee, Jacksonville, St. Augustine and St. Augustine Beach, Marineland, Daytona Beach, Cocoa Beach, Melbourne, Vero Beach, Port St. Lucie, Fort Pierce, Stuart, Palm Beach and West Palm Beach, Lake Worth, Delray Beach, Boca Raton, Pompano Beach, Fort Lauderdale, Hollywood, Hallandale, Surfside, Hialeah, Miami and Miami Beach, and Coral Gables.

From west to east, I-10 goes to Pensacola, Crestview, Tallahassee, Lake City, and Jacksonville.

In the center of the state, also west to east, I-4 begins at St. Petersburg and runs through Tampa, Lakeland, Winter Haven, Haines City, Kissimmee (Disney World), Lake Buena Vista, Winter Garden, Orlando, Winter Park, Sanford, Deland, and Daytona Beach.

Thrifty Rent-a-Car locations are scattered throughout the state, at: Daytona Beach, Delray Beach, Fort Lauderdale, Fort Myers, Gainesville, Hollywood, Jacksonville, Miami, Ocala, Orlando, Panama City, Pensacola, Pompano Beach, Sarasota, St. Petersburg, Stuart, Tallahassee, Tampa, and West Palm Beach.

BY BOAT: There are 349 miles of the Intracoastal Waterway from Jacksonville to Miami, with many canals connecting it to the ocean. If you're planning to float to Florida, an excellent, informative booklet, "Florida Boating," is available from the Department of Natural Resources, 3900 Commonwealth Blvd., Tallahassee, FL 32303.

Chapter XV

FLORIDA: DOWN THE EAST COAST

1. St. Augustine
2. Daytona Beach
3. Disney World and Epcot Center
4. Palm Beach

FLORIDA'S EAST COAST from St. Augustine to Palm Beach is a varied, fascinating world unto itself. It encompasses this country's oldest city, St. Augustine, and the point from which we launched our nation into the Space Age, Cape Canaveral. It holds a fantasyland of the imagination, Disney World, and a fantasyland of untold wealth and its attendant lifestyle, Palm Beach. And by the time you get from one end of this world to another, even the "season" will have changed—around St. Augustine, the "season" is the summer; at Palm Beach, winter is the favored time of year.

1. St. Augustine

It would take a separate book to do justice to the rich history of the United States' oldest city. And dates like 1513 and 1565 make the "lost" colonists of North Carolina and the Massachusetts Pilgrims sound like Johnny-come-latelies. With such an early start, Spain might have changed the course of world history by extending her colonization and holding on to her New World territories, with the result that a lot more people might very well have surnames and accents reflecting Spanish rather than English and northern European culture. But she didn't, and most of our Spanish heritage today comes from the Caribbean, via a roundabout course from the homeland.

Ponce de Leon was the first Spaniard to land here, in 1513, vainly looking for eternal youth. He didn't find it, of course, but he did plant Spain's flag and claim possession. Pedro Menendez de Aviles arrived in 1565 to establish St. Augustine, the first permanent European settlement in the U.S. It was a strategic location, but also very vulnerable, and twice the city was sacked by pirates, once in the 16th century and again in the 17th. By the time the English started looking south at Spain's foothold on the continent, St. Augustine had been the seat of government for some 30 missions along the coast, as well as all other Spanish possessions in Florida and Georgia. As the English threat grew, the Spanish began construction of the Castillo de San Marcos in 1672, at a cost of some $30 million.

What the British couldn't win by battle, they took by treaty, and St. Augustine was ceded to them in 1763. It was an important point of refuge for loyalists during the Revolution, and the Castillo was used to imprison patriots who had chosen the "wrong" side from the British point of view.

In 1783, Florida went back to Spain, again by treaty, and the Spanish were lavish with land grants, moving hundreds of Americans into lands vacated by former British owners. The United States gained possession of the state in 1821, and St. Augustine was peaceful until the 1830s, when the Seminole Wars broke out and it once again played a military role (now the Castillo held Indian prisoners).

Of the American influences that have marked St. Augustine, that of Henry W. Flagler is probably the most important. In his zest to develop the whole state, he built two extravagant hotels to lure the North's wealthy to St. Augustine and made it the headquarters for his Florida East Coast Railroad.

Today, you'll find traces of every phase of its history written across St. Augustine's face, and there has been a concerted effort in recent years to restore the old Spanish city for visitors. The heart of the restoration area is narrow, quaint St. George Street, which starts at the City Gate and runs to Plaza de la Constitucion, with more than 50 houses along the way, either on St. George Street or those that branch off it. And for beach-oriented vacationers, there are miles and miles of beach across the Bridge of Lions at St. Augustine Beach.

WHERE TO STAY: Whether you stay in the city itself, at Vilano Beach (A1A North), or St. Augustine Beach (A1A South) will depend largely on whether you're sightseeing or beach oriented. Their proximity makes any one convenient to the other. Because I, personally, love the history of the place, the city is my preference, but there are good choices in all three locations.

In St. Augustine

The **Marion Motor Lodge,** 120 Avenida de Menendez (tel. 904/829-2261), is a sparkling-white motel, accented by wrought-iron balconies and hanging baskets of greenery, almost directly across from the Municipal Yacht Pier. A Marion has been on this site for 45 years, the present structure replacing a luxury hotel that was torn down a few years ago. Rooms are bright and colorful (they all face the bay), and there's a pool and sundeck. Two fine restaurants are within 200 feet of the motel, and it's an easy walk to the Historic Restoration Area. The friendly management will arrange all sorts of sightseeing tours and can fix you up with charter-boat fishing. Rates for double occupancy are $38 to $45.

Also close to the Historic Restoration Area, **Whetstone's Motor Inn,** 138 Avenida de Menendez (tel. 904/829-5598), has large rooms, a swimming pool, and a beautiful view of Matanzas Bay. Architecture is Spanish, and the atmosphere relaxing. No restaurant, but several are within walking distance. Doubles run from $30 to $45.

Across the Bridge of Lions from the heart of town, six blocks south on A1A, **Ponce's By the Sea Resort,** 57 Comares Ave. (tel. 904/829-8646), is in a quiet, secluded, palm-shaded area right on the water. There's a fishing pier, boat slips, sailboat rentals, private patios, picnic tables, a pool, and a private beach. There's also an attractive lounge and restaurant. Rooms are quite nice, but vary in size, and doubles go for $40 to $48. There are some efficiencies, with rates of $48 up to $125 for "champagne suites."

The large (200 rooms) **Ponce de Leon,** Ponce de Leon Blvd. (tel. 904/824-2821), is a short three miles north of the center of town on U.S. 1, and its spacious grounds hold a rather complete resort. In addition to the huge, clover-leaf pool, there's a golf course, lighted tennis courts, a lovely restaurant, dancing, and entertainment. The rooms are all large, done up in bright, resort colors, and some have extra basins in the dressing area. Private patios and balconies abound. Doubles here are in the $45 to $54 range.

At the edge of town, but very convenient to sightseeing attractions, the **Keystone Court,** 290 San Marco Ave. (tel. 904/829-3850), has rooms—a little on the small side, but clean and comfortable—in quiet and cozy cottages set back from the street on a circular drive. No pool or restaurant at this budget-priced motel, but there are TV and some refrigerators. Rates for doubles start at $18.

Vilano Beach (A1A North)

There is a very good family-style motel at this quiet, uncrowded beach just across the Intracoastal Waterway from St. Augustine. Viva and John Moxley and their son, Brad, operate the **Town and Country Motel,** 110 Vilano Beach Rd. (tel. 904/824-5078). The neat white and blue motel has 24 units, all with completely furnished kitchens, and it has a coin-operated laundry on the premises. Furnishings in all units are modern and comfortable. The beach is a short walk away, and there's a grocery, neighborhood pub, two good restaurants (seafood and Italian), and boat rentals, all close by. St. Augustine sightseeing attractions are about a ten-minute drive across the bridge. Rates begin at $30, double occupancy, in the winter, somewhat higher in the summer.

St. Augustine Beach (Anastasia Isle—A1A South)

The **Sheraton Anastasia Inn,** A1A at Pope Rd. (tel. 904/471-2575) offers deluxe beach accommodations directly on the ocean at slightly more than moderate prices. There are kitchenettes among the 144 units, a pool, a restaurant, and a lounge with entertainment and dancing. In-season (summer) rates are $50 to $64 for large rooms furnished in a modern decor; off-season rates are lower.

Budget prices that begin at $18 prevail at the **Sea Shore Motel,** A1A at 12th St. (tel. 904/471-3101), which is also on the ocean side of the highway. Many units here have kitchenettes and all are exceptionally well furnished for the price. Restaurants, a grocery store, and laundry are nearby. Weekly rates are also available (location and time of year determine the rates, but all are budget).

Campgrounds

This is an especially good camping base, with Jacksonville to the north and A1A's long stretches of undeveloped beach south to Flagler Beach. There are eight commercial campgrounds in the area, and the St. Augustine Chamber of Commerce can furnish a complete list. The one I most liked was the **Bryn Mawr Camp Resort** (Rt. 5, A1A, Box 18P, St. Augustine Beach FL 32084; tel. toll free 800/327-1552, or 904/829-6725), eight miles south on A1A in a quiet, clean oceanfront setting. The 240 sites have electric, water, and sewer hookups, there's a dumping station, laundry facilities, pool, tennis court, shuffleboard, game room, and adult lounge. Rates begin at $13 and some credit cards are accepted.

WHERE TO EAT: Good eating doesn't come high in St. Augustine. Most restaurants are quite moderate in price, and there are some very good places to dine.

"This is my trade—I love to cater to people," Claude Sinatsches, Swiss-trained chef at **Le Pavillon**, 45 San Marco Ave. (tel. 824-6202), will tell you, and cater to them he does. In fact, part of the pleasure in eating here comes from the warmth and graciousness of Claude, his wife Gisele, and her brother Fritz Dold. The German-Swiss family group has turned an 85-year-old St. Augustine home into an utterly charming European restaurant with specialties such as wienerschnitzel Viennese style, sauerbraten and spätzle, and red snapper in papillote, all accompanied by the special house salad, German home-fried potatoes, red cabbage, and hot rolls. If you happen to be a crêpe lover (which I confess to be), there's an amazing variety of fillings, and the crêpes themselves are perfection. The low $4 tab includes three crêpes, tossed greens or fresh fruit salad, and parmesan sticks. Whether you eat on the candlelit, screened-in front porch or in one of the inner rooms, best reserve ahead for dinner, when there's live entertainment and always a large contingent of local folks. Open for lunch from 11 a.m. to 3 p.m., dinner from 5 to 11 p.m. at prices of about $8.

The **Caravan Restaurant,** in the **Quality Inn,** 2500 Ponce de Leon Blvd. (tel. 824-3123), serves all three meals (breakfast and lunch from 7 a.m. to 2:30 p.m., dinner from 5 to 10 p.m.). Roast prime rib of beef and Alaskan king crab legs are both specialties, and there's a salad bar with over 40 items. Florida seafood is also featured, there are lunch and dinner specials, and prices are moderate. It's a lively, friendly place that draws a lot of locals as well as travelers.

You could go to the **Chimes Restaurant,** 12 Avenida de Menendez (tel. 829-8141), just for the view—it overlooks Matanzas Bay and the Castillo de San Marcos—but it's reassuring to know that the food is *almost* as good as the view. James Kalivas, the owner-chef, makes all the pastries and puts out breakfast waffles that are as much a treat as the seafood and steaks he serves at lunch and dinner. The restaurant is open seven days a week from 7 a.m. to 9 p.m., and I found the prices very low for the high-quality meals. Breakfast is in the $2 to $3.75 range, lunch is $3 to $6, and dinner runs $6 to $15.

There's a little corner of France right where picturesque Charlotte Street and Artillery Lane come together in the heart of the restored area. The **Guy Denoel French Pastry Shop,** like its European counterparts, sells fresh-baked, melt-in-your-mouth pastries (75¢ to $1.50 each) that you can take out or eat (with coffee if you like) at one of the small tables in this bistro-like setting. It's an ideal sit-down break in the day's sightseeing; and Guy and Christine Denoel, who've been at this location for the last 16 years, will send you away refreshed, with a definite "hang the calories" attitude. The pleasant shop is closed Monday and Tuesday, open 10 a.m. to 6 p.m. other days.

NIGHTLIFE: You'll find most after-dark activity centered in St. Augustine's hotel and motel cocktail lounges, some simply "bend an elbow" spots, others with live entertainment and dancing.

The **Sheraton Anastasia**, out on St. Augustine Beach, has entertainment until 1 a.m. every night in the lounge (which opens at 4 p.m.). Casual, beach-type dress in order (tel. 471-2575).

On Ocean Trace Rd. at St. Augustine Beach, the **Holiday Inn by the Sea** has live entertainment and dancing in its **Ship Ahoy Lounge** until 1 a.m.

On Cuna St. (across from the Old Fort), the **White Lion Tavern** has an old English pub atmosphere, Ladies Night on Monday, and entertainment every night until 1 a.m.

THINGS TO SEE AND DO: Stop by the **Visitor Information Center** at 10 Castillo Dr., St Augustine, FL 32084 (it's near the City Gate) to see a free orientation movie (shown twice every hour) that will make any subsequent sightseeing more meaningful. They can also furnish complete guided tour information and brochures to help do-it-yourselfers.

In my opinion, there's no better way to sightsee St. Augustine's historic area than aboard the delightful motorized **tour trains**, 3 Cordova St. (tel. 829-6545). The open cars have rain curtains; the guides give a lively, informative spiel as you move from place to place; and your $4 ticket ($2 for ages six through 12) is good for 24 hours—you can stop off and spend as much time as you want at various destinations and, since the trains run on 15- to 20-minute schedules, there's no long wait to hop on the next one to move on. Besides, given the city's narrow streets, sometimes heavy traffic, parking problems, etc., it's *so* much easier! There are also horse-drawn carriage tours run by the **St. Augustine Transfer Company** (tel. 829-2818) for $4, $2 for ages four to 12, and free for under-fours. Phone for exact times and pickup points.

The **Old City Gate**, not far from the Visitor Information Center, was once the only entrance to the town through the wall that surrounded it. A moat ran eastward from the San Sebastian River to the Castillo, and a drawbridge at this gate was raised each evening and lowered at daybreak. St. George Street, which begins here and runs south, was once known as "The Street that goes to the Land Gate." Close by, you'll see the **Old World Shop** (it's the main office of the sightseeing trains), which has complete tourist information, all sorts of souvenirs, and light snacks.

You might also want to visit the **City Gate Craft Shops,** where there's a carpenter, candle shop, "Kitchen Korner" cookware shop, toys, quilts, a broommaker, several other craftsmen, and the Mill Top Restaurant. They're clustered around the **Oldest Wooden Schoolhouse,** which was constructed sometime during the first Spanish period (1565–1763) and served both as a private home and a schoolhouse prior to "the war" (Civil, that is). It is open every day from 9 a.m. to 5 p.m. June through August, to 5 p.m. September through May; admission is $2 for adults, 75¢ for ages 6 through 11.

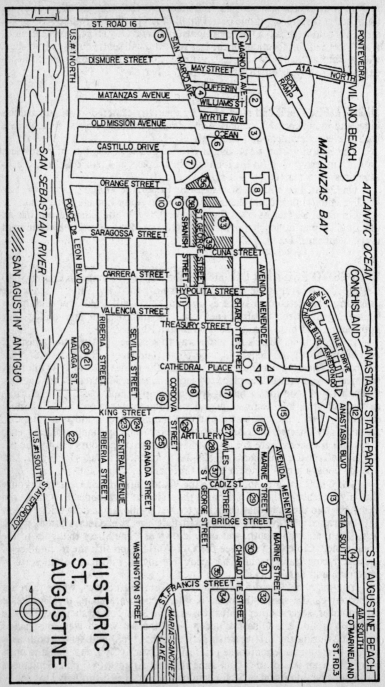

**GUIDE TO THE NUMBERED REFERENCES ON THE "HISTORIC ST. AUGUSTINE"
MAP:** 1. Florida School for the Deaf & Blind; 2. Fountain of Youth; 3. Mission of
Nombre de Dios; 4. Authentic Old Jail; 5. Old Sugar Mill; 6. Ripley Museum; 7.
Visitors Information Center; 8. Castillo De San Marcos; 9. Old World Shop; 10. The
Old Drugstore and the Spanish Cemetery; 11. Museum; 12. Lighthouse Park &
Fishing Pier; 13. St. Augustine Alligator Farm; 14. Cross & Sword Amphitheater; 15.
Marina and Sightseeing Boat Cruise; 16. Potter's Wax Museum; 17. Old Market; 18.
Government House; 19. Flagler College; 20. Trailways Bus Station; 21. Greyhound
Bus Station; 22. Shrimp Boat Docks; 23. U.S. Post Office; 24. Zorayda Castle; 25.
Lightner Municipal Expo.; 26. County Building; 27. Spanish Hospital; 28. Old Store
Museum; 29. Art Center; 30. Historical Society Library; 31. Oldest House; 32. State
Arsenal; 33. Indian Museum; 34. Llambias House; 35. St. Francis Inn; 36. City
Gates; 37. Ximenes-Fatio House; 38. Old School House; 39. San Augustin Antiguo
Museum Houses.

The **Castillo de San Marcos,** 1 Castillo Dr., is one of the most impressive
things you'll see in St. Augustine. Begun in 1672 by the Spanish, it is the oldest
masonry fortification in the U.S. (it replaced an earlier wooden one which had
rotted away). It's built of coquina, a shellrock formation quarried on Anastasia
Island, and it withstood two English sieges—in fact, it was never captured by
an enemy. General Oglethorpe, from his Georgia base, once vowed to take the
Castillo or leave his bones before its walls, but as it turned out, he did neither.
Over the years, it has held "rebels" during the Revolution, Seminole leaders,
both Confederate and Union troops during the Civil War, and American
deserters during the Spanish-American War. Rangers are on duty for interpretive talks, and during the summer months weapon-firing demonstrations are
presented on weekends. Admission costs 50¢ (children 15 and under are free
when accompanied by an adult), and it's open from 8:30 a.m. to 5:15 p.m. from
the last Sunday in October to the last Saturday in April, and 9:00 a.m. to 5:45
p.m. from the last Sunday in April to the last Saturday in October. The park
is open daily except Christmas Day.

Across from the Castillo is a restored 18th-century Spanish colonial village—**San Augustin Antiguo** on St. George Street. You pay a general admission
$2.50 ($1.25 for students six to 18) which admits you to several houses inside
that have individual fees. There are authentically furnished homes (some with
lifesize wax figures), craft demonstrations (a blacksmith, leather worker, pottery, print shop, and Spanish bakery), and the Pan American Center, with
Latin American artwork and cultural exhibits.

That elaborate complex of buildings you see on King Street was once the
most flamboyant resort hotel built by railroad tycoon Henry Flagler, the Ponce
de Leon. It took three years to complete, 1885 to 1888, and became a mecca
for wealthy Northerners at the turn of the century. It remained a hotel until
1967, when **Flagler College,** a four-year liberal arts school, moved in.

Across the street, the **Lightner Museum** was another Flagler hostelry, the
Alcazar Hotel, built in 1888. It lasted as a hotel only until 1930, and remained
vacant until 1947, when Otto C. Lightner, of Chicago, bought it, moved in his
substantial personal collection of artworks, then donated it to the city. The
museum's atmosphere is essentially that of the Gay '90s, with a "Victorian
Village," Tiffany glass, and such, but it also holds such treasures as Napoleon's
desk, doll collections, a natural science wing with an Egyptian mummy, and
a quilt made by Abraham Lincoln's wife. The building and gardens cover three
city blocks, and St. Augustine's City Hall is on the grounds. The museum is

open daily from 9 a.m. to 5 p.m. and costs $2 for adults, 75¢ for ages 12 through 18.

The **Oldest House,** 14 St. Francis St., was built soon after St. Augustine was burned in the siege of 1702, but the site has been used for a residence since the early 1600s. It is built of coquina, with tabby (a mixture of limestone, sand, and seashells) floors, and it is furnished with authentic antiques. Both the house and the adjacent museum (the **Tovar House,** an interpretive museum of the city's history) are maintained by the St. Augustine Historic Society. Both are open from 9 a.m. to 5:30 p.m. every day and your $1.50 admission (50¢ for ages 10 through 18) covers both.

That mythical **Fountain of Youth** (which I sometimes think we're still searching for in Florida) supposedly flows from the stone fountain at 155 Magnolia Ave. What the heck, you might as well take a drink! The park is a memorial to Juan Ponce de Leon and his landing in this area in 1513, and the grounds also hold a planetarium and space globe, as well as a museum and swan pool. It's open 9 a.m. to 5 p.m. every day and costs $3 for adults, $1.50 for children.

There's a real "castle" in St. Augustine, the **Zorayda Castle** at 83 King St. Built in 1883, it's a one-tenth scale replica of one wing of Spain's Alhambra, and inside you get a vivid picture of how the Moorish kings lived and entertained. We don't have many castles in this country, and this one is fun to visit—certainly the kids will love it! Hours are 9 a.m. to 5:30 p.m. and admission is $2 for adults, $1 for military personnel in uniform and ages six through 12.

Another place that's fun for kids as well as their parents is **Potter's Wax Museum,** 1 King St. There are wax museums and there are wax museums, but this one is spectacular, with beautifully done lifelike figures (more than 240) and costumes and settings that are outstanding. Lecture tours give each exhibit's historical background. Admission is $3.50 for adults, $2 for ages six through 11, free under six.

Cross and Sword, the official state play of Florida, an excellent outdoor musical drama, is performed nightly (except Sunday) by a cast of 70 singers, dancers, and actors from mid-June through August in the St. Augustine Amphitheater (south of the city on A1A). It tells the story of the city's founding and early days, and tickets are $5 and $4 for reserved seats, $3 for general admission (under 12, general admission is $2).

Also, if you happen to be in St. Augustine in mid-August, check with the Visitor Information Center for exact dates of the annual **"Days in Spain,"** a three-day festival held in St. George Street near the City Gate. Sword fighting, parades, fireworks, nightly entertainment, and general merriment in the streets celebrate St. Augustine's founding, and the whole affair is climaxed by the cutting of a birthday cake.

Special Day Trips

Fourteen miles south of St. Augustine on what is now A1A, the Matanzas Inlet has been the entrance to a waterway navigable all the way to St. Augustine, providing an open back door to that city. Therefore, in 1569, the Spanish built successive wooden watchtowers to watch the inlet. In 1740, the Spanish felt the need to erect a strong masonry fort there to prevent enemy use of the Matanzas Inlet and River into St. Augustine, and to keep an alternate avenue of communication open if St. Augustine Inlet were to be blocked. In 1742, **Fort Matanzas** was completed, and became an integral part of the defenses of St. Augustine. The fort was occupied by both the Spanish and the British; however, in 1821, when the United States gained the Territory of Florida, its military use was ended.

Visitors are provided with free passenger ferry service from the visitor center area to Rattlesnake Island, the site of Fort Matanzas. The ferry operates from 9 a.m. to 4:45 p.m. seven days a week between Memorial Day and Labor Day (Thursday through Monday the rest of the year.) The ferry schedule may change so for correct and updated information, call 904/471-1006.

There is no admission charge at Fort Matanzas National Monument. Rangers are on duty to provide additional historical information. The park is open daily, except Christmas Day, from 9 a.m. to 6 p.m. from the last Sunday in April to the last Saturday in October, and 8:30 a.m. to 5:30 p.m. from the last Sunday in October to the last Saturday in April.

Still farther south on A1A, about 18 miles from the city, **Marineland of Florida** presents six daily programs that are a real delight. There are performing porpoises, penguins in Whitney Park, marine exhibits, and a truly unique, multidimensional film presentation in the new Aquarius Theatre. The all-inclusive admission is $8 for adults, $4 for ages six through 11.

2. Daytona Beach

The beach at Daytona, a little over 23 miles long and some 500 feet wide at low tide, made it one of Florida's first popular resorts, back in the 1870s. It was the automobile, however, that brought it into its own. The hard-packed sand on the strand was a natural speedway, and records were being set here as early as 1903, when Alexander Winton hit the phenomenal speed of 68 miles per hour—the fastest in the world at that time. In subsequent years, Sir Malcolm Campbell and other auto-racing stars have come here to set faster and faster world records. Nowadays, races are held at the Daytona International Speedway, about 2½ miles west of the beach on U.S. 92.

You can still drive along the water's edge, however, all the way from Ormond Beach to Ponce de Leon Inlet—but no racing. The speed limit is 10 miles per hour, and it's strictly enforced. If you're going for a beach drive, do it at low tide or when the tide is going out, and *never* drive into the water or in the soft areas, which are well marked. There's unlimited parking on the beach during daylight, but overnight parking and camping are illegal.

Besides all that marvelous beach and almost year-round swimming temperatures, Daytona Beach has an amusement area near the fishing pier with a sightseeing tower and sky ride, as well as numerous other games, shops, and food stands. A wide promenade runs through it right along the oceanfront, making strolling a real pleasure.

WHERE TO STAY: Like so many of Florida's resort areas, Daytona Beach is lined with highrise hotels and motels. Almost every major chain is represented, and I suggest that you write the **Daytona Beach Chamber of Commerce,** P.O. Box 2775, Daytona Beach, FL 32015 (tel. 305/255-0981), for their free directory. A word of warning: Rates at most of the larger hotels and motels go up $5 to $10 when racing events are scheduled, so be *sure* you get a confirmed quotation before you come. And note that among the range of prices quoted here, the higher prices apply to ocean-front location, lower prices to rooms not directly facing the ocean, although almost all have an ocean view of some sort.

The **Holiday Inn's Surfside Resort,** 2700 N. Atlantic Ave. (tel. 904/672-3770), has a lounge and supperclub, car rentals right at the resort, planned children's activities, and a convenient location adjacent to a shopping center with some 63 stores, a service station, bowling alley, and movie theater. They also run daily bus trips to Disney World (about 70 miles inland). Under their family plan, children 19 and under stay free in same room with parents. Rooms are a step above those usually found in this chain, with colorful, resort-type furnishings, balconies, and some king-size beds. Doubles run $65 and up in season (June through Labor Day), somewhat lower other months.

The **Castaway Beach Motel**, 2075 S. Atlantic Ave. (tel. 904/255-6461), is only slightly smaller, and about half the units here have kitchenettes. There are two large pools, a wading pool and playgrounds for the small fry, shuffleboard, basketball, volleyball, Ping-Pong, an exercise room and sauna, a lounge with entertainment and dancing, and a moderately priced dining room. Rooms here are every bit as nice as those at the Holiday Inn, with a "beachy" decor. Rates in season are $42 and up for doubles ($49 and up for kitchen units).

The **Talisman Lodge**, 3411 S. Atlantic Ave. (tel. 904/761-0511), also has some kitchen units among its typically "beach-style" rooms, some of which have balconies. There are picnic tables and a grill on the grounds, a heated pool, shuffleboard, and a recreation room with pool tables. The dining room is open for breakfast and lunch only at this writing. Doubles are $27 to $45 during the season, lower other months, and kitchen units run $35 to $48.

The **Daytona Sands Beach**, 2523 S. Atlantic Ave. (tel. 904/767-2551), comes close to being in the budget range, as prices go at Daytona Beach. Yet its rooms certainly don't have a "budget" look—they are bright and colorful, with modern decor, and some have private patios or balconies. There's the obligatory heated pool and ironing boards are standard equipment in the rooms (you can request an iron from the office). They also have free morning coffee; no dining room, but there's a restaurant across the highway. Doubles run $28 to $37 in season, and there are some kitchenettes, which cost $35 and up. *Note:* If you don't mind crossing the highway to get to the beach, the Daytona Sands has ten lower-priced rooms on that side.

WHERE TO EAT: I admit to a clear preference among the restaurants in this area—the **Anchor Inn**, 608 W. Dunlawton Ave. in Port Orange, just across the bridge from Daytona Beach (tel. 767-0845), which has been well known to locals for over 30 years, but hard for outsiders to find. "Just ask anybody at the Port Orange Shopping Center," a friend told me in St. Augustine (see above). "Otherwise you'll never find it." Skeptically, I did as he said, asked the first person I saw there—and received instant directions, given with a smile and a "you'll really love it." The Port Orange Shopping Center will be right in front of you if you follow A1A from Daytona Beach to its junction with U.S. 1. Turn right at the junction (there's a stoplight), go a very short block to the next stoplight, and take a left—that's Dunlawton Avenue, and you follow it all the way to its end, over a railroad track and a short stretch more, where you'll find a low, yellow stucco building on your left, nestled under huge old oaks, palms, and pines. There's a parking lot across the road and another behind the restaurant, and you may have trouble finding a space. This place is so popular locally that people come prepared to wait as much as an hour to be seated if they come without reservations. Fortunately, I arrived on a Sunday afternoon about 3 p.m. (after the church crowd and before dinner), and there was practically no line.

The mostly seafood menu here covers just about every kind of fish, and when I tasted the fried scallops, it was clear to me why it wouldn't be a chore to wait on line; they were so fresh you could taste the sea, with a deep-brown crispness surrounding tender, flaky meat. Delicious! Jim Fisher and his wife Joyce brought years of expertise to the Anchor when they bought it a few years back. In fact, Jim (a chef well known in the area) had quite a following of his own to add to the Anchor's faithful. Hours are 4 to 9:30 p.m. Tuesday through Saturday, noon to 3:30 p.m. and 4 to 8:30 p.m. on Sunday. Prices are unbelievably moderate, ranging from $5.95 to $12.95. There are children's plates and a small selection of nonseafood offerings (chicken, hamburger, steak, etc.). One more thing—if you have trouble finding it, just stop at the shopping center and ask anybody!

A few blocks west of A1A, **Chez Bruchez** 304 Seabreeze Blvd. (tel. 252-6656) serves a French-American menu in a charming French Provincial atmosphere—with background music that's a pleasure, not an intrusion. There are specialties like frog legs provençale, but I particularly liked the rich, creamy mousse au chocolat. Lunch hours are 11:30 a.m. to 2 p.m. ($5 to $8), dinner from 5 to 9 p.m. ($7.50 to $16), and reservations are definitely in order. Closed Sunday.

In a Spanish setting, the **King's Cellar,** in the Best Western Americano, 1260 N. Atlantic Ave. (tel. 255-3014), purveys Italian dishes, along with seafood and prime ribs. The lovely atmosphere is enhanced by dinner music and dancing, and there's a bar. Prices, which are semi à la carte, are $5.50 and up (children's menu $5), and dinner is served from 5 p.m. to 2 a.m.

Morrison's, 200 N. Ridgewood (tel. 258-6396), has one of its good, inexpensive cafeterias here, and like most in this excellent chain, they do their own baking. It's standard cafeteria fare, of course, but consistently good (and I think their apple dumplings are super). Lunch will set you back about $4, dinner only a little more. Hours are 11 a.m. to 8 p.m., and they also have a take-out service.

NIGHTLIFE: Most of the after-dark activity is found in hotel and motel lounges, and while the "names" that play here aren't such big ones (not to be compared with Miami Beach, for example), there's often quite good entertainment around. It's a good place to lounge-hop until you find the entertainer who suits you best.

Musical events that range from light classical to pop take place in the bandshell at the north end of the promenade in the amusement area (in **Oceanfront Park**) almost every night in season. Concert times vary, and sometimes nonmusical acts appear. Whatever's going on, however, is free, and sitting under the stars with the ocean in the background is enjoyable.

The **Daytona Playhouse** (100 Jessamine Blvd.) presents light musical productions and plays year round at prices that run $6 and under. You can phone 255-2431 for current schedules.

THINGS TO SEE AND DO: Say "Daytona" to most people, and you're saying "racing"! And although the **Daytona International Speedway,** 1801 Speedway Blvd., west on U.S. 92 (tel. 253-6711), is *sometimes* empty, there are races scheduled all during the year. The Daytona "500" is in February, the Firecracker "400" stock-car race is July 4, AMA motorcycle races are early in March, and if you want to know what's doing when you'll be there, write P.O. Box S, Daytona Beach, FL 32015, for a schedule.

There is racing other than the motor kind at Daytona Beach: the greyhounds run at the **Kennel Club** (west on U.S. 92) from early May to mid-September every night except Sunday, but you can't take the kids along—no minors allowed. Post time is 8 p.m., with 1:30 p.m. races on Monday, Wednesday, and Saturday. Admission is 50¢; clubhouse, $1.25 (for reservations, call 252-6484), and yes, there *is* pari-mutuel betting.

Imagine a Florida sightseeing attraction that's *free!* One of the few in the state is **Sugar Mill Gardens** (follow U.S. 1 to Port Orange, then turn west one mile on Herbert St. (tel. 736-2700), which, besides the machinery and boiling kettles of the old 1763 sugarmill, offers dinosaur figures in a jungle-like setting. It opens from 9 a.m. to 5 p.m. every day.

Golfers will find 36 holes at **Daytona Beach Golf and Country Club,** 600 Wilder Blvd. (tel. 255-4517), open every day, with greens fees of $8.50. There's also the **Par-3 Golf Club and Driving Range** four miles west on U.S. 92, 2500 Volusia Ave. (tel. 252-3983), charging $6 for 18 holes, $3 for nine.

You can wager on jai-alai at the **Daytona Beach Jai-Alai Fronton,** just east of I-4 and I-95 on U.S. 92 (P.O. Box 2630 Daytona Beach, FL 32015 (tel. 255-0222), from February through mid-July, every night except Sunday and Tuesday. Posttime is 7:15 p.m., Saturday at 7 p.m. Matinees are Tuesday and Saturday at noon. Admissions are $1 and up, and sorry, no minors.

3. Disney World and Epcot Center

Back in the '60s, I drove across Florida's midlands on the way to visit my parents on the west coast. It wasn't a particularly scenic or interesting trip, with miles and miles of flatland covered with palmetto and a kind of scrub under-growth, and from time to time outcroppings of palms and pines. Snake country, I thought, and wondered how many of the cattle that seemed to be the major "crop" along the way (I remember my surprise at seeing Florida cowboys) fell victim to snakebite. Winter Haven was there, of course, with the Cypress Gardens and their spectacular water show, and I could have detoured south to Lake Wales and the beautiful Bok Singing Tower—but aside from those bright spots, not much else besides a landscape with an almost desolate kind of beauty.

Well, that drive from Orlando to Tampa is a completely different story today. And the difference is due almost entirely to the late Walt Disney's choice of some 43 square miles on this route for his gigantic Disney World resort area. Besides the Magic Kingdom and Epcot Center, there are hotels, golf courses, riding paths, lakes, campgrounds, and all the conveniences—and luxuries—that tourists expect at a Disney-run resort. The cows are still there, and Kissim-mee (it takes some practice, but pronounce it "kis-SEM-mee") is a rather important livestock market. But I am quite sure that some of those cowboys I saw more than a decade ago (as well as others who would have grown up to that profession) are now happily herding tourists around Disney World or otherwise engaged in seeing that they are housed, fed, and sent away happy, clutching souvenirs of every description. I don't know precisely what Disney World has meant to this area's economy in terms of dollars and cents, but the figure must be astronomical. On just one December day in 1982, over 120,000 people passed through the gates; and since the resort opened in 1971, more than 100 million have been drawn here, among them three U.S. presidents (Nixon, Ford, and Carter). It's staggering, and both Kissimmee and Lake Buena Vista are modern-day boom towns, with nearby Orlando (20 miles east) coming in for its share of the prosperity, as well.

As for the Magic Kingdom, that's exactly what it is—magic. And Epcot Center is a sort of magical glimpse into the future. I must confess that I first approached the whole thing with some cynicism. "Bring money" was my first thought, and I rather expected a glorified kind of ripoff. Not so. First of all, not only is everything well managed (*nothing* has been overlooked in planning

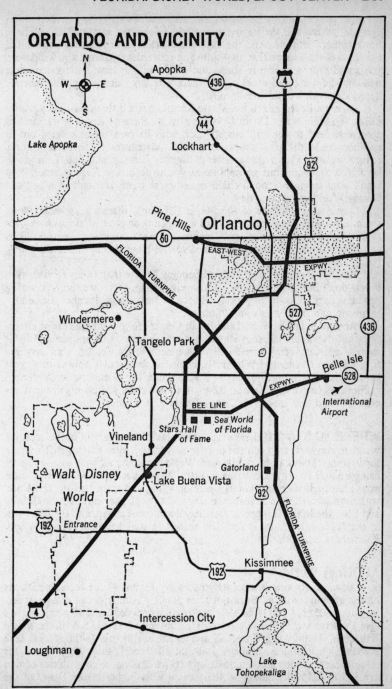

ORLANDO AND VICINITY

Apopka

Lake Apopka

Lockhart

Pine Hills Orlando

FLORIDA TURNPIKE

EAST-WEST EXPWY.

Windermere

Tangelo Park

Belle Isle

BEE LINE EXPWY.

International Airport

Stars Hall of Fame Sea World of Florida

Vineland

Gatorland

Walt Disney World

Lake Buena Vista

Entrance

FLORIDA TURNPIKE

Kissimmee

Intercession City

Loughman

Lake Tohopekaliga

for such crowds), but my lasting impression is one of a staff enjoying their duties every bit as much as the paying guests and a delightful kind of "let's all have fun together" attitude. And the cost was another surprise. After your initial ticket purchase, I found that, depending on your sales resistance and willpower, you could drop a bundle in shops and restaurants or have a marvelous time window shopping and snacking. If there was any "hustle" in this relaxed, happy carnival, I didn't run into it.

Even your entrance to the Magic Kingdom is a little magical—by monorail to the Main Street Depot (you can also get there by ferry), whose arched entryways lead to the six "lands," each with its own theme carried out in architecture, landscaping, shops, music, and "adventures": Main Street U.S.A., Adventureland, Frontierland, Liberty Square, Fantasyland, and Tomorrowland. Another monorail journey takes you to futuristic Epcot Center. You won't want to rush through either once you're there, so don't plan to "do" Disney World in just one day.

Outside the confines of the Magic Kingdom, there's horseback riding; swimming, sailing, motorboating, and waterskiing on clear lakes that have over four miles of sandy beaches; golf, tennis, steamboat excursions, nature hikes, and delightful picnic spots—all linked to the Kingdom by monorail trains, buses, launches, or ferryboats.

At Lake Buena Vista, there's a Shopping Village that's a joy to visit, even if you don't buy a single item. In a lovely setting, there are shops featuring products from all over the world, all sorts of restaurants, lounges with entertainment, and pedal boats and "flote botes."

And while Disney World and Epcot Center are certainly the major attractions in this whole area, they should not eclipse others that are just a little bit away. Cape Canaveral, with NASA's Kennedy Space Center, is an easy day trip; Cypress Gardens at Winter Haven are as spectacular now as they were before Disney's competition arrived; Kissimmee has Gatorland for a glimpse of Florida's native wildlife; and there are several other sightseeing destinations close at hand that make the Disney World area an ideal base.

WHERE TO STAY: If there's one thing you'll find plenty of in the area, it's places to stay, and they run the price gamut from luxury to budget. There are three resort hotels right on Disney World grounds, as well as a 600-acre campground. Nearby Lake Buena Vista (four miles and about ten minutes away) has highrise resort hotels, vacation villas, and town houses. These are, without doubt, the choice places to stay and they all provide transportation to and from the Magic Kingdom. But they don't come cheap, and the other end of that large price range is found in motels clustered around Disney World, Kissimmee, and Orlando.

At Disney World

Advance booking is absolutely necessary for any of the accommodations on the grounds (with as much notice as possible), and you can reserve at any by calling 305/824-8000 (the best time to call is between 5 and 11 p.m.). There's also a reservation service in the City Hall on Main Street U.S.A. in the Magic Kingdom, should you go for a day and decide to stay over (although you take a chance on finding a vacancy). Rates at all three Disney World hotels for double rooms (which accommodate up to three children along with two adults) are $95 to $115, depending on the view, a little higher in the Tower at the Contemporary Resort. Under-18s stay free in the same room with parents.

The **Polynesian Village's** architecture and setting will make you start shopping for a grass skirt—it's that "South Seas" in atmosphere and decor. Its 636 rooms are in two-story "longhouses" and there's entertainment and dining in the "Great Ceremonial House." The whole complex is set in tropical gardens with winding pathways right on the Seven Seas Lagoon. The South Seas motif extends to the rooms, which are certainly in the luxury class, some with king-size beds and all colorfully decorated. There are two pools (with lifeguards), a sand beach, and the smaller people will find a playground. There's a home for Fido in the kennel, a sauna, beauty and barber shops, and shopping in several boutiques.

The **Contemporary Resort** borders on the futuristic in design and decor, and its huge lobby has a monorail stop. The rooms are as modern as tomorrow, with extra-large beds and two washbasins. There are two pools, a beach, a playground, health club and sauna, and Ping-Pong in the recreation room. Pets are also welcome here in the kennel. Lounges provide entertainment and music for dancing; and there are several dining rooms.

The third Disney resort hotel was built with golfers in mind. Appropriately named the **Golf Resort,** it is right next to the fairways. It's smaller than the other two, but has entertainment in the lounges and excellent dining rooms. Guest rooms are contemporary in decor and very nicely furnished. You don't *have* to play golf, of course—there's tennis (on lighted courts), and a heated pool.

Campers never had it so good as at **Fort Wilderness Campground,** a 600-acre resort for outdoor people. In total, 828 sites (including some for tents) are located in the wooded area. Those for campers have full hookups, a grill, water, and a disposal system. And for those would-be campers among you, Fort Wilderness offers Fleetwood Trailers that will sleep up to six and are fully equipped. There's a restaurant in Pioneer Hall and the Campfire Snackbar, as well. Two trading posts sell camping supplies, groceries, beer, and film. Full campsites are $20 to $26; Fleetwood Trailers, $95.

At Lake Buena Vista

You'll be surrounded by luxury at any one of the four resort hotels in Lake Buena Vista, so if you don't get the booking you prefer, rest assured that you won't be disappointed with a substitute. Space doesn't permit a detailed description of rooms, decor, etc., but all rooms are spacious, well appointed, and tastefully decorated; all four have excellent dining facilities; most have entertainment in lounges; and all look askance at pets except for Howard Johnson's, where they're welcome. There is frequent shuttlebus service to and from the Magic Kingdom from Hotel Plaza (where all are located), but there is a small fee each way. (Mail should be addressed to each hotel, c/o Hotel Plaza, Lake Buena Vista, FL 32830.)

The **Americana Dutch Resort Hotel** (tel. 305/828-4444) has double rooms that will accommodate two adults and up to three children for $75 and up. The **TraveLodge Tower's** (tel. 305/828-2424) rates begin at $85. **Howard Johnson's** (tel. 305/846-3500) charges $85 and up, and the **Hotel Royal Plaza's** (tel. 305/828-2828) rates range from $85 up.

For really plush accommodations, Lake Buena Vista has provided 133 **Vistana Vacation Villas,** P.O. Box 22051, Lake Buena Vista, FL 32830 (tel. 305/846-1200), town houses, all luxuriously furnished and completely equipped for housekeeping. The villas are clustered around Buena Vista Lagoon, with rolling green lawns down to its shores. Town houses start at $130.

Elsewhere in the Area

I don't really know how many motels there are in the Greater Disney World Area, but one of my lasting impressions is of the "mini-cities" made up of nothing but clusters of motels along every major highway. And those highways are important: when you have your confirmed reservation, be *sure* and note the *exact* location of the motel, or you could wind up, as I once did, driving through the maze of highways and Interstates from one member of the chain to another before you reach the right one! For example, Holiday Inn has five motels in this area; I counted eight Howard Johnson's (not including the one at Lake Buena Vista); and Days Inn has some 16(!) within easy driving distance. So, if there's a highway exit number given, mark it in red on your map and look carefully to save yourself a lot of time and aggravation.

It is seldom that I feel "a motel is a motel is a motel," but I must confess that I saw little to distinguish one from the other here, except in the case of one or two luxury, resort-type motels (such as the **Orlando Hyatt Hotel,** 6375 W. Spacecoast Parkway; tel. 305/396-1234), and since their rates are only a little lower than those inside Disney World and at Lake Buena Vista, I'd opt any time for the latter. For that reason, I'll skip detailed descriptions of the ones below unless there's something really distinctive about a particular one, and you may assume that a Holiday Inn is a Holiday Inn is a Holiday Inn. From my own experience, I'd say that price and location (i.e., convenience to Disney World) should be the guiding factors in making a choice, and none of these listed is more than 30 minutes away. When reserving, be sure to ask about bus transportation to and from Disney World—many motels furnish it for guests. Keep in mind that I-4 runs southwest from Orlando right past Disney World, whose main entrance is on U.S. 192 not far west of its intersection with I-4; the Florida Turnpike is north of the main entrance, but its intersection with I-4 is within convenient driving distance; and an address of "Turnpike Exit 65" will be *east* of Kissimmee, further away from Disney World than the other two intersections.

In the moderate price range, these are all good, dependable motels with standard accommodations:

The **Holiday Inn East,** 5678 Spacecoast Parkway (tel. 305/846-4488)—on U.S. 192 just east of I-4—has 512 rooms, the Gingerbread House restaurant for children, two swimming pools, and a lounge with entertainment and dancing. Double room rates are seasonal, ranging from $40 to $70.

Larson's Lodge–Kissimmee, 2009 W. Vine St., Kissimmee (tel. 305/846-2713)—on U.S. 192 seven miles east of I-4—has entertainment and dancing in the lounge; doubles start at $42.

The **Holiday Inn,** Haines City (tel. 813/424-2211)—at the junction of I-4 and U.S. 27, about a 15-minute drive to Disney World—has family-type entertainment and soft drinks for the kids in its Circus Lounge. There's also bus transportation (for a small fee) to and from Disney World. Doubles start at $40.

The **Days Lodge–Disney East,** 5820 Spacecoast Parkway (tel. toll free 305/396-7969—on U.S. 192, 3 miles east of Disney World—is an apartment motel with one-bedroom housekeeping apartments, all completely equipped (there's a small utensil deposit), which sleep six comfortably for the modest price of $42.88.

The **Terrace Rodeway Inn,** 5245 Spacecoast Parkway (tel. 305/396-7700) —on U.S. 192 one mile east of I-4—has double rooms for $40 and up.

In the *budget* range, the **Colonial Motor Lodge,** 1815 W. Vine St., Kissimmee (tel. 305/847-6121)—on U.S. 192 east of I-4—has some kitchen units, two pools, and double room rates of $32 to $40 (kitchens cost $40 to $56).

The **Days Inn** at the intersection of I-4 and Fla. 528A, 7200 Sandlake Rd. (tel. 305/351-1900), has lake fishing from the shore, golf privileges, restaurant, pools, and playgrounds. Double rooms are $34.88 to $39.88.

A very conveniently located **Days Inn** is at 7980 Spacecoast Parkway (tel. 305/396-1000), on U.S. 192 five miles west of I-4. Here double room rates are $37.88 and $40.88.

Campers who feel the Fort Wilderness fees are beyond the upper reaches of their budgets will find an inexpensive **campground at Southport Park,** in a secluded wooded area about 20 miles south of Kissimmee on the shores of Lake Tohopekaliga (south from Kissimmee on Fla. 531, 13 miles to Southport Rd., then six miles east). There are full-service sites and some "primitive" ones for those who really like to rough it. There is a store, two comfort stations, a pavilion, picnic shelters, a boat ramp, boat basin, and access channel to the lake. It's a long way from the gloss of the Disney World campground, but then so are the rates: $9 for water, electricity, and sewer hookups; $8.50 for water and electricity only; and $7 for undeveloped sites. For reservations, contact the Park Manager, Southport Park, 2001 Southport Rd., Kissimmee, FL 32741 (tel. 305/348-5822).

DINING AT DISNEY WORLD: Go elegant or go casual—you'll find the right place to eat either way at Disney World or Lake Buena Vista. Whether it's pancakes and eggs as you start your exploration of the Magic Kingdom or a champagne brunch you need to get your day off on the right foot, the Disney folks have anticipated your needs and provided for them.

Casual Dining

To begin with, Main Street U.S.A. can furnish breakfast, lunch, or dinner at the **Town Square Cafe,** a Victorian-style restaurant with prices in the $3 to $7 range (lunch and dinner), or at the garden-style **Crystal Palace Restaurant** (same price range). Or you can stop anytime for pastries and coffee at the **Main Street Bakery,** for ice cream cones at **Borden's Ice Cream Parlor,** for hamburgers and hot dogs at the **Plaza Pavilion** or **Refreshment Center,** for snacks and soft drinks at the **Station Break** directly below the railroad station.

Adventureland serves Polynesian entrées (as well as hamburgers and hot sandwiches) at the **Adventureland Veranda,** tropical punch and snacks at the **Veranda Juice Bar** and **Sunshine Tree Terrace,** and hot dogs and beverages at **El Pirata Y El Perico.**

Aunt Polly's serves sandwiches, snacks, and beverages on a porch overlooking the water on Tom Sawyer Island in Frontierland (and there's also a **Mile Long Bar** and **Pecos Bill's Cafe** in this "land").

Liberty Square has one of my favorite eating places in Disney World, the **Liberty Tree Tavern,** a colonial-style eatery with lunches and dinners that run from $5 to $8 and that feature Patriot's Pot Roast. For seafood and fried chicken, it's the **Columbia Harbour House,** also in Liberty Square, which has the **Fife and Drum** and **Sleepy Hollow Refreshments** for snacks.

In Fantasyland, **King Stefan's Banquet Hall** (in Cinderella Castle) has beef, chicken, seafood, and salads (in that same moderate price range) at lunch and dinner, and you can snack at **Lancer's Inn, The Round Table, Troubador Tavern,** and **Pinocchio Village Haus.**

Tomorrowland has a great natural-foods specialty shop, the **Lunching Pad,** that serves yogurt, sandwiches, salads, snacks, and juices. Hot dogs, hamburgers, and sandwiches are featured at the **Tomorrowland Terrace** and the **Space Bar.**

At Epcot Center, you'll find casual eating at every one of the international pavilions in the World Showcase area around the lagoon. Depending on your ethnic preference at the moment, you can sample the wares at Mexico's Cantina de San Angel, Germany's huge Biergarten or France's Au Petit Cafe, all at snack-food prices.

I sampled the wares of several of these and found all to be of high quality and hot dinners and lunches quite tasty, so I don't hesitate to say that it is quite possible to eat every meal in the Magic Kingdom and go away well fed and not much poorer. Especially compared to prices in other resort areas, these are surprisingly low.

The same applies at Walt Disney World Village and Lake Buena Vista, where the **Lite Bite** and **Heidelberger's Deli** have sandwiches and other snacks; **Cap'n Jack's Oyster Bar** has seafood (of course); the **Village Verandah** serves all three meals; and the **Village Restaurant,** although casual, has gourmet dinners and hot sandwiches, seafood, and salads for lunch.

Dining in Style

For more elegant eating, there are the resort hotels in Disney World and Lake Buena Vista, and just because you've bought an all-day ticket, you aren't precluded from slipping out for lunch or dinner and then returning without an additional fee—just be sure to have your hand stamped as you leave, and you'll be waved right through when you get back.

That champagne brunch I mentioned earlier takes place every Sunday from 9 a.m. to 2:30 p.m. at the **Contemporary Resort Hotel** in the 15th floor **Top of the World.** It costs $10.50 for adults, $8.50 for children (under 12, $6). There's also a pretty good breakfast buffet here on other mornings that goes for $5 and $3, and a luncheon buffet from noon to 2 p.m. for $7 and $3.50. The lovely, gracious **Gulf Coast Room** on the second floor serves dinner from 6:30 to 10 p.m. and provides entertainment as well. Men must wear jackets, and reservations are a must (tel. 824-1000). Dinners are in the $11 to $16 range.

The **Papeete Bay Verandah** in the **Polynesian Village Resort Hotel's Great Ceremonial House** is probably the most exotic setting in the whole complex for breakfast, lunch, or dinner. Breakfast is buffet-style from 8 to 10:30 a.m., at $5 for adults, $3.50 for under-12s. The luncheon buffet (with yummy Polynesian entrées) is served from 11:30 a.m. to 2:30 p.m., with a tab of $7 for adults, $4.50 for children. There's entertainment in the evening, with seating on the half-hour from 5:30 to 10 p.m.; prices start at $9. Best reserve (tel. 824-2000).

Over in Walt Disney World Village at Lake Buena Vista, the finest gourmet fare comes to table in the **Empress Room** on the Promenade Deck of *The Empress Lilly Riverboat,* a replica of an authentic 1800s sternwheeler anchored in the lagoon. The decor is elegant Louis XV, cuisine and service are very French, and prices run from $13 to $35. You must reserve here (tel. 828-3900), and coats and ties are required. Also on the Promenade Deck is the **Empress Lounge,** a lovely setting for after-dinner coffee flambé or liqueur.

AFTER DARK: There's something going on all over Disney World when the sun goes down.

There's **Captain Cook's Hideaway Lounge** in the **Great Ceremonial House** (on the lobby level, open from 6:30 p.m. to 1:30 a.m. (last call for drinks, 1 a.m.).

The **Top of the World,** in the **Contemporary Resort Hotel** (on the 15th floor), has dinner-dancing shows with big-name entertainment (in season). There's an entertainment charge of $7.50 for adults, $3.75 for children (seating for dinner is at 6:30 p.m. for the 8:15 p.m. show, 9:45 for the 11:30 p.m. performance). To reserve, phone 824-8000.

Entertainment in a relaxed atmosphere prevails at the **Golf Resort Hotel's Trophy Room.**

In Lake Buena Vista Village, the **Baton Rouge Lounge** on the main deck of the *Empress Lilly* is a Dixieland jazz spot every night; and the **Village Lounge** has some of the top jazz musicians from all over the country every night except Sunday. No cover, no minimum in Baton Rouge Lounge, $5 minimum at The Village Lounge.

THINGS TO SEE AND DO: There's a right way and a wrong way to plan a Disney World visit. The *wrong* way is to allow only half a day, with no regard for the scope of the place and the time you'll spend moving around. The following tips from my own experience will, I hope, help you plan to "do" this enchanting world the right way.

First of all, before you leave your motel, *dress comfortably.* You'll be doing a lot of walking, so be sure your shoes are old friends, even if they don't look quite as spiffy as those new ones. And while shorts are certainly acceptable (and you'll see a lot of them), remember the intensity of that Florida sun and protect shoulders and other vulnerable parts of your anatomy (it's a good idea to take along a small bottle of suntan lotion). And whatever you do, don't forget sunglasses—the glare is sometimes brilliant.

Arrival time can be important for a hassle-free visit. Even though the park doesn't open until 9 a.m., the 12,000-car parking lot will be open by 8:30 a.m., trams will be running to the main entrance (ticket windows also open early), and the Main Street U.S.A. stores are open then. Breakfast on Main Street while you're waiting for the attractions and rides to open, and before the crowds descend, is a relaxed way to begin the day. One very important note: Be *sure* you note (write it down, if need be) the name of your parking lot section (they're named for the seven dwarfs, Goofy, Doc, etc.)—it's a *big* lot! Parking, incidentally, costs $1. And because the heat can turn your car into an oven during the day, leave the windows down just a little—not all the way, because Florida rains come up very suddenly.

Among the things that impressed me most about the meticulous planning that has gone into Disney World were the facilities for handicapped visitors. For example, there's a special parking lot for guests in wheelchairs (it's adjacent to the Ticket Center; inquire at the Auto Plaza when you drive in). Wheelchairs can also be rented for $1.50 a day at the Stroller Shop just inside the entrance (or you can bring your own, of course), and there are ramps for wheelchairs at each street corner in the Main Street U.S.A. section. A first-aid station is located just off Main Street beside the Crystal Palace.

Once inside, it's important not to try to see everything at once and not to walk until you're exhausted. There are plenty of snackbars and refreshment centers handy for a short rest break, and the whole day will be more pleasant if you take advantage of them. Besides, crowd-watching can be a very enjoyable part of your visit, and it's easier to do when you're not mingling.

What will it cost? Well, you can buy a one-day ticket at $15 for adults, $14 for ages 12 to 17, or $12 for ages through 11. But that will entitle you to *either* the Magic Kingdom or Epcot Center—not to both. Unless you're really pressed for time, a much better deal is the three-day World Passport: $35 for adults, $33 for ages 12 to 17, and $28 for ages three to 11 years. An even better bargain (in the same age brackets) is the four-day World Passport: $45, $42, and $36. These give you admission to Epcot Center and Magic Kingdom attractions, plus unlimited use of the transportation facilities throughout the system. If you wish to leave the grounds at any time during the day and return later on, be sure to have your hand stamped at the exit gate for re-entry on the same day.

There's a complete Official Guide to Walt Disney World available at most bookstores, or you can order it by mail: send $4.95 plus $1 for postage and handling to Walt Disney Specialty Products, P.O. Box 4387, Anaheim, CA 92803. If you need any further details, contact: Walt Disney World Co., Dept. GL-N, P.O. Box 40, Lake Buena Vista, FL 32830 (tel. 305/824-4321).

Now, as they say at Disney World, you're ready for your "Magic Kingdom Adventure" and a futuristic adventure at Epcot Center. You'll step off the monorail at the Walt Disney World Railroad Station, with a floral portrait of Mickey Mouse out front, and walk right onto Main Street U.S.A., a two-block stretch that leads to Cinderella Castle. And if the sight of that 18-story medieval castle doesn't get you in the mood for a day of pure fantasy, then you probably should turn around and go home! You may be surprised, too, as I was, to see how the landscaping enhances every part of the park—some of the most beautiful plantings I've encountered in Florida are in the plazas and along the walkways here.

How you plan your day, of course, is a personal thing, but here's some of what you'll find in each "land" in the Magic Kingdom, each radiating from the castle like spokes in a wheel.

READER'S RECOMMENDATION: "To avoid the waiting lines, try going counterclockwise around the park. Most people do not think of it, and you reach the attractions after the first rush. It has worked for us every time, even in the crowded Easter season" (S. Higgins, Laurence Harbor, N.J.).

Main Street U.S.A.

You'll be in turn-of-the-century America here, and along the street is a silent "cinema," penny arcade, and an old-fashioned ice-cream parlor. It is an excellent set-the-mood atmosphere, with horse-drawn trolley and horseless carriages passing by, plus street entertainment and parades of Disney characters from time to time (which is true in every section).

Adventureland

You'll have to look close to see that those gorillas, elephants, hippos, and Tiki birds are "Audio-Animatronics" creations and not the real thing in this jungle setting. The Swiss Family Island Treehouse is here; there's a Jungle Cruise, a Caribbean Arcade with pirate games, and a Spanish fort, where you sail through mysterious grottos, plunge down a waterfall, and land in the midst of a pirate raid.

Frontierland

A Wild West "front street," lined with boardwalks, even has a brass-railed saloon, and there are wooden forts complete with Indian raids, a "Country Bear Jamboree" with a zany troupe of singing bears. And across the river is Tom Sawyer Island with Injun Joe's Cave, the Magnetic Mystery Mine, Big Thunder Mountain Railroad, and old Fort Sam Clemens (you can cross over by log raft or on "explorer canoes").

Liberty Square

This is Colonial America brought to life, and if you don't see anything else, try not to miss the Hall of Presidents, where animated, lifesize figures are so real and the presentation so effective that you truly believe that *is* Abraham Lincoln rising to speak. Not far away is the lively Haunted Mansion, where it's fun to be frightened out of your wits. You can catch the show at the Diamond Horseshoe Revue or take a river cruise on sternwheel steamboats.

Fantasyland

Don't be so sure this one's only for the kids—grownups, too, love the charm of all those Disney characters wandering around. You'll see Dumbo, Snow White (and her Dwarfs, it goes without saying), and scores of other familiar figures. They all perform in concert at the Mickey Mouse Revue, and you can ride on Peter Pan's Flight, Mr. Toad's Wild Ride, or the Cinderella Golden Carousel. "It's a Small World" features doll-like figures in costumes from all over the world, and "20,000 Leagues Under the Sea" takes you aboard a Jules Verne submarine for a journey under the sea.

Tomorrowland

If you've ever wanted to blast off on a rocket trip, Space Mountain is the place to do it. "Mission to Mars" is fun, too, and the "Carousel of Progress" is a liberal education in the contributions electricity has made to our lives.

River Country

A separate ticket is required for this recreated "Ol' Swimming Hole" located west of Pioneer Hall in Fort Wilderness. You get there by boat or coach from the Magic Kingdom (pick up tickets at the main entrance); and if you're camping at Fort Wilderness, the narrow-gauge railroad will take you within walking distance. However you get there, bring a bathing suit. There's a 260-foot water-flume slide, rafts you can pole down winding rapids and under waterfalls, and even rope swings out over the water. Your admission ticket covers all charges, except for snacks and box lunches at "Pop's Place" and beach towel rentals at the bathhouse.

EPCOT CENTER: You can get from the Magic Kingdom to Epcot (whose full name is "Environmental Prototype Community of Tomorrow") by monorail and from some of the Resort hotels by bus. For details on either, call the special information line at 824-4500. Drivers will find an Epcot Center exit on I-4 about halfway between those for Rt. 535 and U.S. 1-92, and parking costs $1.

At Epcot, you'll encounter "worlds" instead of "lands," and if you find some variance from the descriptions in this book, keep in mind Walt Disney's own words when speaking of the concept back in 1966: "It will be a community of tomorrow that will never be completed." Thus, the present Epcot will be constantly changing as new technologies are introduced, old exhibits altered, and every effort made to keep up with our changing world. However, the following will give you some idea of what to expect, and all your surprises are sure to be pleasant ones.

First of all, Epcot Center is nearly twice as large as the Magic Kingdom, so plan on a *lot* of walking. Its shape is something like a huge hourglass, with Future World at the top, World Showcase at the bottom.

Future World

This is where you'll find the huge "geosphere" which has become Epcot's symbol. Known as **Spaceship Earth,** it holds "time machine" rides which take you through some 40,000 years to show the development of communication. From Egyptian hieroglyphics to the Phoenician alphabet to manuscripts laboriously copied in monasteries to Gutenberg's first printing press, to the most modern means of communication, you'll see realistic scenes presented in great detail until you finally arrive at the top of the geosphere and its vast dome sprinkled with tiny sparkling stars.

Your descent from that lofty perch will land you at **Earth Station,** a sort of official "City Hall" of Epcot Center. This is where you can learn how the whole complex operates, locate lost children (or other items), make dinner reservations at one of the restaurants on the grounds, and get an immediate answer to almost any query from the WorldKey Information Service.

Communicore, comprised of two glass-walled arcs on either side of a pleasant plaza, is devoted to last-minute technology, and this is perhaps the area that will see the most changes over the years as every new development is incorporated and old methods discarded. Communicore East is the scene of an entertainment revue named the "Astuter Computer Revue," which will educate you on just how all the mechanics of running Epcot are managed through the use of computers. Of special interest, too, is the Energy Exchange sponsored by Exxon, which explores all sources of energy—past, present, and future. In Communicore West, there's the fascinating Futurecom exhibit devoted to information gathering, with some exciting new methods of display.

That asymmetrical, mirrored pyramid is the home of the **Universe of Energy,** where you ride in solar-powered vehicles through scenes depicting the entire spectrum of energy uses, from prehistoric times to the space age. The **World of Motion** (appropriately enough, housed in a wheel-shaped structure) traces man's efforts to move more swiftly, from the invention of the wheel to spaceships. Some of the most spectacular special effects in all of Epcot are found in the **Journey Into Imagination** show, presented in a truncated glass pyramid. In addition to the show and endless opportunities to turn your own imagination loose, there's a very good 3-D motion picture which presents the world from a child's point of view. And in a huge, six-acre, skylighted pavilion, **The Land** examines the production of food in all its aspects. There's also a short boat ride passing through three distinct environments: a rain forest, prairie, and desert.

World Showcase

Arranged along the shore of the World Showcase Lagoon, pavilions of Canada, China, France, Germany, Italy, Japan, Mexico, and the United Kingdom radiate from the central American Adventure. Designed to present the *essence* of each culture, each will leave you with much the same impressions you would bring home from an actual visit to the country. There are shops, restaurants, films, craft exhibits, and entertainment, as well as larger-than-life World Showcase "dolls" in ethnic costumes strolling the walkways. This is a good place to end your Epcot day, and if you should find yourself at one pavilion with a yen to be at one across the lagoon, there are boats to save you the long walk around.

Other Attractions in the Area

Between Orlando and Walt Disney World, at I-4 and the Bee Line Expressway, is **Sea World of Florida,** 7007 Sea World Dr. (tel. 351-0021, the world's largest marine-life theme park. It takes four to six hours to see the five major shows, which include performances by Shamu, the killer whale, "Charley's Dolphins," seals, sea lions, and otters. There are daily ski shows, too, featuring guest participation, and seal and dolphin feeder pools, where guests also get into the act. Exhibits include a 150,000-gallon re-creation of a coral reef. Antarctic penguins cavort in their home kept at a frosty 30 degrees. Hundreds of exquisitely plumed birds roam freely through the 135-acre park. You can take a rest at the Fountain Fantasy Theatre, where a cheerful medley of fountains, films, and music is woven into a fanciful multimedia show. Pet the deer in the Japanese Village, or shop for a pearl-bearing oyster whose prize can be mounted in nearby gift shops. More than a dozen concessions, ranging from snow cone kiosks to full-service restaurants, serve a variety of foods. Park hours are from 9 a.m. to 7 p.m. (later during summer, Christmas, and Easter), year round. Admission is $10.75 for adults and $9.75 for children four through 12.

Located at I-4 and Fla. 435N in southwest Orlando, the **Mystery Fun House,** 5767 Major Blvd. (tel. 351-3355), has magic floors, laughing doors, fortunetellers, and—well, maybe it would spoil the fun if you knew *everything* to expect. Adults pay $3.95; kids, $2.95.

About a half-hour away on I-4 and U.S. 27, **Circus World,** P.O. Box 800, Orlando, FL 32801 (tel. 305/422-0643), features thrilling live circus performances daily in the Circus Spectacular, circus participation for guests in the "Be-a-Star" Circus, spine-tingling rides in the "Thrill Circus" (including the Center Ring, the Flying Daredevil, and the Roaring Tiger Roller Coaster), the Cinema Circus, the Circus of Skills, the Backstage Circus, the Illusion Circus, the "Be-a-Clown" Circus, the Exotic Animal Circus, plus shops and restaurants. It's open daily 9 a.m. to 6 p.m. Admission (which includes all live shows, attractions, and rides) is $11.50 for adults, $10.50 for ages four to 12. It's a day of both viewing and participating, so if you've ever wanted to run away and join the circus, here's your chance.

Day Trips from Disney World

It will take you about an hour to drive east to Cape Canaveral Air Force Station and the **Kennedy Space Center.** The entrances are well marked off U.S. 1, Fla. 405, 520, 528, and State Road 3. The 140,000-acre space center has a free **Visitor's Center,** where you can get an in-depth look at our space programs through free space science demonstrations, space movies, and special exhibits. You should allow at least two hours—and don't forget your camera. In the Hall of History, there are actual spacecraft used in the Mercury, Gemini, and Apollo programs, as well as the spaceship used in the U.S.-Soviet rendezvous in space. The center also has a Carousel Cafeteria and souvenir gift shop.

Two two-hour guided bus trips leave from the Visitor's Center ($3 for adults, $1.75 for ages 13 to 18, and $1 for ages three to 12 accompanied by adults). The Red Tour of Kennedy Space Center leaves continuously during the day, as does the Blue Tour of the Cape Canaveral Air Force Station, with the first tours departing at 9:15 a.m. The commentary is in English, but foreign-language tapes are available for groups. The Red Tour stops at the Moon Launch and Space Shuttle Launch pads and the 525-foot Vertical Assembly Building. The Space Center is the home of this country's new manned-space program, the space shuttle, and you'll see preparations underway for its launchings. The Blue Tour covers the Cape Canaveral Air Force Station, including the Air Force Space Museum. *Note:* On most Sundays, from 9 a.m. to 3 p.m., drive-through tours in your own automobile are available at the Air Force Station.

It's less than an hour's drive south to Winter Haven and Florida **Cypress Gardens** (just off State Road 540 West), an entertaining day for the entire family. You'll find beautiful walkways through the largest botanical garden in the world, themed to special settings (like Little Mexican Gardens, Oriental, Gazebo, and many others), as well as scenic boat cruises along the Original Gardens and Lake Eloise. Cypress Gardens was the originator of the waterski show, and one of the finest to be found is still presented several times daily, featuring kiteflyers, barefoot skiers, lovely aquamaid ballet, and more. Over 30 attractions have recently been added, including the Living Forest and Southern Crossroads featuring indoor theaters, children's themed areas, and live animal shows. For camera buffs, it's a field day, and you're pretty sure to get good shots, since correct camera settings are announced in a special area. Restaurants, specialty gift shops, and snackbars are open daily from 8 a.m. to 6 p.m. Admission is $8.75 for adults, $5.25 for ages six through 11, and under sixes come in free.

Silver Springs is about 90 minutes away to the northwest, and here you'll encounter the world's largest group of crystal-clear springs, which you can view through glass-bottom boats. There is also a deer park (petting allowed, even encouraged) and on a semitropical island a Reptile Institute (petting not advised). All told, you'll probably need about four hours if you want to take it all in. It is open from 9 a.m. to 5:30 p.m., and one admission covers everything inside, even boat rides (adults pay $7.75, ages three through 11, $5.75).

4. Palm Beach

Back during the Civil War, a northern horticulturist named A. O. Lang made the decision that noninvolvement in the conflict was his own best personal course of action (pacifist or deserter? he's been called both!) and headed for a region as far removed as possible from the battlefields. He landed in Florida in what is now Palm Beach, and although he had no such intention, profoundly influenced the future direction of the area. You see, he became intensely interested in native plant life and experimenting with new plants, and the natives followed his lead. Otherwise, they might never have planted the coconuts that washed ashore when the Spanish barque *Providencia* was shipwrecked offshore in 1878. The palms that grew from those victims of the sea literally transformed a barren ribbon of sand into a tropical setting that led Henry M. Flagler, the railroad magnate who started the winter migration south to Florida, to build a magnificent hotel, institute civic improvements, and begin the formal landscaping that has characterized Palm Beach ever since. The little resort was first named Palm City but was hurriedly renamed (in time to get the change off by a waiting mail boat) when the U.S. Postal Service advised there was already a Florida city by that name and a new one was necessary. (So who's ever heard of Palm City. . . ?)

The rest is history, of course. Encouraged by Flagler, the wealthy came in droves, making Palm Beach the "Newport of the South"; and they brought with them an opulence that still lingers, although a creeping commercialism can be discerned around the edges. Automobiles, for example, were once banned on many streets but now drive freely, although bicycling on paths closed to motorists is still a favorite way of getting around.

Palm Beach is on the northern end of a 14-mile-long island only three-quarters of a mile wide at its widest point. Across Lake Worth, its western water boundary, lies West Palm Beach, which Flagler envisioned as a center for commercial enterprises that would be banned in Palm Beach itself. It has, however, developed into a resort in its own right, connected to Atlantic beaches by bridges and offering Lake Worth boating and other water sports.

Together, the Palm Beaches have a lot of charm to offer today's traveler, whether in that rarified millionaire class or a middle-income tourist with an itch to vacation in an atmosphere of restrained elegance.

WHERE TO STAY: You don't have to be a millionaire to vacation at Palm Beach, but let's face it, money helps. The truly wealthy, of course, stay in those magnificent private "vacation villas" of 20-some and more rooms that line County Road and North Ocean Blvd. But there have always been hotels for those a shade less rich, and some of them rival the mansions in elegance. Recent years have seen more and more highrise rental properties, even motels, go up against the Palm Beach horizon, and while "budget" doesn't really apply to most, "reasonable" (at least, by Palm Beach standards) is possible.

The Oldest, the Most Expensive, and the Best

The hotel scene at Palm Beach has been dominated almost from the start by **The Breakers**, S. County Rd. (tel. 305/655-6611). The stately Renaissance-style Breakers has all the grandeur of a palatial Italian villa, and it is a visual beauty both inside and out. Elegance pervades the entrance. the lobby, and other reception rooms and extends to every one of the 600 guest rooms and suites. The lush tropical gardens, swaying palms, and manicured lawns add to the Mediterranean illusion. This is one of those memorable hotels that has hosted royalty, and the well-trained, gracious staff makes every single guest feel he's (or she's) joined that august company. Tennis, anyone? There are an even dozen courts. Golf? Tee off at one of the two 18-hole golf courses, or try out the putting green. And there's lawn bowling, plus indoor and outdoor swimming pools. As for cuisine, continental dining in the magnificent Florentine Room is the ultimate! Food, wines, and service vie for top billing, and there's dinner music for dancing. Even if you don't stay in the hotel, treat yourself to at least one six-course dinner—they start at $29 and 6 p.m. (jackets and reservations are a must). The intimate Alcazar Lounge, with a marvelous ocean view, has nightly entertainment. The Breakers has been called a "Palace by the Sea," and it takes that compliment very seriously. During "the season" (December 15 to April 1), doubles start at an astronomical $175, dropping from June 1 through September 30.

Newer

The **Palm Beach Ocean Hotel**, 2770 and 2830 S. Ocean Blvd. (tel. 305/582-5381), occupies more than 10 acres of oceanfront property. This is "plush" in the modern vein, and guest rooms are the last word in comfort and eye appeal. Two of the four salt and freshwater pools are heated, while the younger set has its own kiddie pool and playground. There are tennis courts and shuffleboard. Doubles start at $85 from February 1 to April 5, and drop from May 1 to December 15.

The **Heart of Palm Beach Motor Hotel,** 160 Royal Palm Way (tel. 305/655-5600), is not on the ocean, but the lovely, palm-lined street on which it stands is only minutes away. Rooms are beautifully decorated in contemporary fashion, and the Bird in Hand cocktail lounge overlooks a really smashing pool. It is within walking distance of Worth Avenue, the financial district, and several fine restaurants (no dining room in the motel, only a coffeeshop open from 7 a.m. to 10 p.m.). Double room rates descend from $72 seasonally.

Howard Johnson's, 2870 S. County Rd. (tel. 305/582-2581), is one of the best of this chain that I've visited. Rooms border on plush, with tasteful resort decor, balconies, extra washbasins, and many king-size beds; there's a pool, very nice dining room, and a cocktail lounge. Rates for double rooms range from $75 down, depending on the season.

WHERE TO EAT: Palm Beach prides itself on its fine restaurants, as well it might. They do, after all, cater to a moneyed clientele that knows—and demands—good food and service.

Chez Guido, 251 Royal Palm Way (tel. 655-2600), is one of the finest, where you're likely to see Palm Beachers in the know relaxing in the attractive setting of rattan furniture, tropical flowers and beach-scene paintings. The top-notch continental cuisine includes such specialties as grenadin de veau, lobster bisque, steak Diane flambé, and veal Normande. The European chefs know what they're about, as the several *Holiday* Awards displayed here attest. Lunch ($6 to $9) is served from 11:30 a.m. to 2:30 p.m., dinner ($10 to $25) from 6 to 11 p.m., and there's entertainment in the lounge from 7 p.m. It's closed on Sunday between Mother's Day and Thanksgiving, jackets are required at dinner, and reservations are an absolute must.

The **Petite Marmite,** 315 Worth Ave. (tel. 655-0115), has been a recipient of that coveted *Holiday* Award for years, too, and one sample of their French or Italian specialties will explain why. "Gourmet" extends to the wine list, which includes rare vintages. There's service from 11:30 a.m. to 11 p.m., with an à la carte menu prevailing at lunch. Dinner and cocktails in the pretty lounge available from 4 to 11 p.m. Dinner costs about $12 to $25 complete, reservations are required—and, men, don't show up without a jacket.

Palm Beach was the winner when Marcello Capriccio moved his restaurant south from Long Island. **Capriccio's,** on Royal Poinciana Plaza just opposite the Poinciana Playhouse (tel. 659-5955), is quietly elegant, with vine-covered ironwork, chandeliers, and tables set with linen cloths and crystal glasses in a room decorated in browns, golds, and greens. The menu is continental, with a heavy Italian emphasis, and before the move from New York, it had received four stars from the *New York Times's* fussy Craig Claiborne. Lunch is in the $8 to $9 range (11:30 a.m. to 2:30 p.m.), dinner from $12 to $16 (5:30 to 11 p.m.), and there are special pretheater dinners and late suppers when the Playhouse is in production. Best reserve for dinner. Closed Sunday and Saturday for lunch.

Testa's, 221 Royal Poinciana Way (tel. 832-0992), is one of Palm Beach's oldest restaurants, having been run by the same family for over half a century. Italian specialties (like veal, boned chicken cacciatore, etc.) are superb, as you might expect, and sirloin steak, seafood, and (especially) strawberry pie are just as good. Besides serving delicious food, this place is loaded with charm, whether you eat indoors, on the patio, or at the sidewalk cafe. Open from 7 a.m. to 1 a.m., Testa's serves all three meals at moderate prices (breakfast, $3 to $8; lunch, $6 to $14; dinner, $6 to $16).

AFTER DARK: You'll find Palm Beach's nightlife in the cocktail rooms of major hotels, like the elegant **Colony**, 155 Hammon Ave., and **Breakers**, South County Road), and in restaurant lounges such as **Chez Guido**, 251 Royal Palm Way, and **Willoughby's**, 456 Ocean Blvd.

The **Royal Poinciana Playhouse**, 70 Royal Poinciana Plaza (tel. 659-3310), presents first-rate Broadway musicals and dramas, though these are usually scheduled during the January-March "season." There are exceptions, however, so it's worth a call to see if they're in production while you're there.

Check, too, to see what is in production at the **Burt Reynolds Dinner Theater**, 1001 Indiantown Rd., Jupiter (tel. 746-5566). Top stars often appear in musicals and drama.

THINGS TO SEE AND DO: For detailed sightseeing information, contact the **Chamber of Commerce**, 45 Cocoanut Row, Palm Beach, FL 33480 (tel. 305/655-3282).

Back in 1901, Henry M. Flagler, the Standard Oil tycoon and pioneer developer of the Florida east coast, built a magnificent marble palace at Palm Beach for his wife. After it was sold by his heirs in 1925, it was a luxury hotel until Flagler's granddaughter became president of a group that bought the mansion, restored the rooms and furnishings, and opened it to the public as the **Henry Morrison Flagler Museum.** From the 110- by 40-foot columned marble entrance hall, with its painted ceilings and gilt Louis XIV furniture, through a succession of period rooms, the museum reflects the lifestyle of the Flaglers when they were residents here, and many of the pieces you see are the original furnishings. In addition, there are special collections of paintings, porcelain, dolls, and family memorabilia. The Historical Room holds relics of early Florida and of Palm Beach's most lavish period. It's open every day except Monday from 10 a.m. to 5 p.m., with a $3 admission for adults, $1.50 for children (under six free). It's on Whitehall Way (tel. 655-2833).

Lion Country Safari, 15 miles west of West Palm Beach, provides a close-up look at free-roaming prides of lions, antelopes, giraffes, zebras, and many other exotic animals. It's just off of Fla. 80 (from the Florida Turnpike, take exit 36 or 40 and follow the signs; from I-95, take exit 50 west). They don't permit convertibles inside the wildlife preserve (and I, for one, wouldn't really want to explore it with the top down), but there's free parking and you can rent an air-conditioned closed car. And if you bring along a pet, there are very good (and free) accommodations for them while you're visiting the wild animals. Lion Country is open every day of the year from 9:30 a.m. to 4:30 p.m., and there's a $7.95 charge for everyone over three, free under three. That includes the Safari Camp and several rides (like the elephant ride) in the theme park.

On **Hutchinson Island** (five miles east of Stuart, on East Ocean Blvd.), over a scenic drive of causeways and bridges, there's a unique leftover from 1876. A colony of six "houses of refuge" was built here for people shipwrecked off the Florida coast, and the one you'll see is the only one remaining. It was first called "Gilbert's Bar Station" after a 19th-century Spanish pirate who made his headquarters in a local inlet, from which he sallied forth to plague coastal shipping before he was caught and hanged in Boston in 1834. The restored **House of Refuge** is now open every day except Monday and holidays from 1 to 5 p.m., with a charge of 75¢ for adults, 50¢ for children. An interesting look at life along the coast a hundred years ago.

Pier fishing (no charge) is available at the **Lake Worth** and **Juno Beach** piers.

There are more than 70 golf courses in the immediate area, and among those open to the public are: **North Palm Beach Country Club** (U.S. 1, North Palm Beach; tel. 626-4344), greens fee $12 and carts $10 each; the **West Palm Beach Country Club** (Parker Ave. and Forest Hill Blvd. intersection, West Palm Beach; tel. 582-2019), greens fee varies from $10 to $5 over the year, and carts are $10; **Palm Beach Lakes Golf Club** (1100 N. Congress Ave., West Palm Beach; tel. 683-2700), greens fee $6 to $12, carts $8 to $11; the **Forest Hill Golf Club** (3332 Forest Hill Blvd., West Palm Beach, a quarter-mile west of Congress Ave.; tel. 965-2332), greens fee $5 to $10, carts $10.

Tennis courts in the area open to the public include: the **Lake Worth Racquet and Swim Club**, 4090 Coconut Rd., Lake Worth, off Lake Worth Road east of Military Trail (tel. 967-3900), a private club open to visitors if courts are available. There are 15 courts, an Olympic-size pool, dining room, and lounge. Fees are $8 per hour.

There's greyhound racing at the **Palm Beach Kennel Club**, Belvedere and Congress Roads (tel. 683-2222), from late December almost to the end of May, every night except Sunday at 8 p.m., with 1 p.m. matinees on Monday, Wednesday, and Saturday. Admission is $1, and no minors are admitted.

Jai-alai can be viewed at the **Palm Beach Sports Theatre**, 1415 W. 45th St. (tel. 844-2444), from early November through most of March every night except Sunday at 7:30 p.m., and there are noon matinees on Monday, Wednesday, and Saturday. Admissions range from $1 to $5. No one under 18 admitted.

The **Gulfstream Polo Field,** nine miles southwest off the Sunshine State Parkway on Lake Worth Road (tel. 965-2057), has matches at 3 p.m. every Saturday and Sunday from January through April, with a $3 admission charge (12 and under, free).

SHOPPING: Whether just looking or buying, shopping is almost a recreation in Palm Beach because of the concentration of exclusive boutiques, unique specialty shops, and the sheer beauty of the shopping districts. There are branches of world-famous department stores (Saks Fifth Avenue, for instance), Paris couture clothing shops (Courrèges is one), famous American designer clothes (like Lilly Pulitzer), jewelry shops, novelty shops, and . . . well, the list is endless. You can find most of them in one of these shopping areas:

Worth Avenue, a palm-lined, world-famed avenue of shops, galleries, and restaurants, has courtyards and "vias" that give it an old-world flavor.

The **Royal Poinciana Plaza,** on Royal Poinciana Way at Cocoanut Row, is a relatively new addition to the shopping scene, but one which retains the traditional flavor of Palm Beach architecture. There are over 28 shops, restaurants, free parking areas, and the Poinciana Playhouse.

Palm Beach Mall is in the western section, on Palm Beach Lakes Blvd. at I-95 in West Palm Beach, and it's the largest shopping mall in the Palm Beaches, with more than 90 stores, pools, fountains, and scenic bridges.

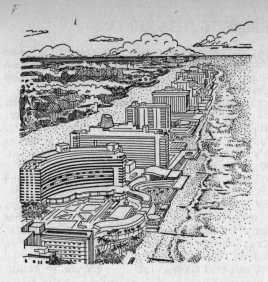

Chapter XVI

MIAMI AND MIAMI BEACH

1. Getting Your Bearings
2. Where to Stay
3. Where to Eat
4. Nightlife
5. Sports
6. Shopping
7. Tours
8. Sightseeing

IF, AS O. HENRY WROTE, New York is "Baghdad on the Hudson," then surely Miami and Miami Beach could be called "Baghdad on Biscayne Bay"! Metropolitan Miami is like nothing so much as one large bazaar from which you can pick and choose the wares that suit you best—glittering hotels so elaborate they assume an unreal air rising against Miami Beach's skyline; rows of less pretentious motels for less affluent travelers; magnificent rococo estates built by "up north" millionaires during the '20s; lush tropical plantings everywhere; streets teeming with throngs of sun worshippers tanned a nutty brown and busy doing everything *but* worshipping the sun; lavish nightclubs and intimate lounges; an entire section that is Old Havana transplanted; patches of arty shops and bohemian artists; other islands of stores so exclusive they're almost intimidating; and an assortment of sightseeing attractions so vast they could make it hard for you to get to that glorious beach, the star attraction that started the whole thing. And some 12 million visitors gravitate to this mecca of golden treasures every year.

It hasn't always been so. In fact, Miami is comparatively young as a resort area, its march toward its present top position having begun only slightly more than 50 years ago. As with much of the rest of Florida, Henry Flagler probably is largely responsible for Miami's development, since his railroad in the late 1800s (built, it is said, after he received a gift of frost-free oranges from Mrs. Julia Tuttle at a time when citrus fruits were frozen as far south as Palm Beach) made it easy to reach. By 1913, there was a wooden bridge leading from Miami to Miami Beach, a swampy mangrove strip of land that John Collins had tried unsuccessfully to use for growing coconuts and avocados as money crops. Collins, however, made the first of Miami Beach's spectacular land deals when he sold 1600 acres—much of it under water—to an Indianapolis industrialist, Carl G. Fisher. Undaunted, Fisher set about dredging up the bay and building a series of small islands, offered a block of oceanfront land to anyone who would put a luxury hotel on it, and built six polo fields as an appeal to wealthy Northerners.

With the 1920s boom came the payoff for Fisher's investment; his holdings were estimated to have a value of over $100 million, and those sun-seeking crowds were pouring in. Across the bay, Miami had been transformed by the railroad from a remote tropical village of weather-beaten shacks into a bustling business center. The future for the metropolitan area wasn't just rosy—it looked positively golden. Then came the 1929 crash, and it hit hard, with fortunes disappearing overnight and land values spiraling downward. But as the national economy began to recover and people once more could turn their attention to leisure-time pursuits, Miami came out of the doldrums and once more transformed its natural resources of tropical temperatures and long stretches of beach into money-making assets. By the end of World War II, it was solidly on its feet again, and in the years immediately after the war, it built more new hotels than any one single area in the world.

In the last few years, Miami Beach south of Lincoln Road has seen a resurgence in what had become a rather seedy, rundown section of the town. Thanks to the interest and efforts of a dedicated group of Art Deco buffs, more and more of the interesting buildings of the late '20s and early '30s are being restored to their original state. Two hotels have been refurbished in the style of that era, and one by one others are being brought back to reflect Miami Beach in its heyday.

While Miami has had more than its share of bad press in recent years with respect to crime and the Cuban refugee flood, most tourists are not touched by either. Normal precautions, of course, are in order (keep valuables locked in hotel safes, etc.), but on the whole the area presents a pleasant, safe atmosphere.

Today's visitors will be welcomed with open arms, and Miami, according to their tastes and income, will be luxurious or gaudy, quiet and restful, or lively and honky-tonk, a sports center for golfing and taking in the races, or a splendid showcase for high fashions to be shown off at celebrity-filled watering spots.

1. Getting Your Bearings

"Miami" to most of us means the entire metropolitan area—Miami itself, Miami Beach, Coral Gables, Coconut Grove, Key Biscayne, Bal Harbour, Golden Beach—and some people even consider Hollywood, Hallandale, and Fort Lauderdale a part of "Miami" (but *not* the people who live there). Actually, I suppose you could lump most of coastal Dade County (Hollywood, Hallandale, and Fort Lauderdale are over the line in Broward) under the "Miami" label for practical purposes.

MIAMI: Biscayne Boulevard (U.S. 1) is Miami's "show" street, with hotels and business buildings lining parts of it (its boast is that you can buy anything from a 55¢ orange drink to a $75,000 yacht along the boulevard); an eight-lane stretch shaded by royal palms (between SE 1st St. and NE 5th St.); 62-acre **Bayfront Park** (where you can pick up tons of information from the **Greater Miami Chamber of Commerce** in the City Auditorium, or stroll down shaded walkways bordered with brilliant flowering plants, or take in an open-air concert at the bandshell); and an access road leading off to **Dodge Island,** the 300-acre seaport from which cruise ships depart for the Bahamas and West Indies.

Once off Biscayne Blvd., however, the street system can be confusing, to say the least—you can cover a lot of ground backtracking when you've reached *North*west 8th St. instead of *South*west 8th. The thing to remember is that the street-numbering system begins at **Miami Avenue and Flagler Street** and is divided into quadrants from that point: northeast, northwest, southeast, and southwest. Streets and terraces run east and west, avenues and places north and south. Sounds simple enough, doesn't it? Well, it *is*—until you hit Coral Gables, for just one example, with its Spanish-named streets, or Hialeah, where a nonsystem of streets and avenues is so perplexing your only salvation will be a map and sheer persistence.

As a matter of fact, your very *first* acquisition if you're driving should be a city map, either from the Chamber of Commerce (234 W. Flagler St. Miami, FL 33130; tel. 579-4694) or a news vendor. If you *still* get lost, my best advice is to ask directions (which can get confusing, too), or park the car and take a cab. A cheaper way of getting around, of course, is the excellent network of **Metropolitan Transit Authority** buses (basic fare is 75¢, but that increases in some zones; and there's an "exact fare" policy). Special fare discounts are available for the elderly, handicapped, and students. The Chamber of Commerce can furnish route maps, or you can call MTA at 638-6700 for specific route information.

Since the advent of Castro, Miami has served as a gateway to the U.S. for Cubans who could not, or did not wish to, live under his regime. So many have come here and settled down, in fact, that the entire city has taken on a Latin flavor, with the native Anglo culture gaining an exuberance and *espirito* which adds a decided fillip to any visit.

In an area of small, two-story homes and sometimes sagging shops around SW 8th St. and West Flagler St., the concentration of Cuban culture is so heavy that a "Little Havana" has come into being. "Calle Ocho" (which is SW 8th St., U.S. 41, or the Tamiami Trail, depending on which map you're reading) is Little Havana's "Main Street"—and a stroll down any part of its 30-block length is like a trip to Old Havana with a slightly anglicized architecture (although Spanish-style street lamps and window signs that read "English spoken here" tend to overshadow building styles). There are shops of all descriptions, factories where cigars are rolled by hand, over 300 restaurants, and lots of sidewalk coffee counters where the strong, aromatic Cuban coffee is an ideal pick-me-up when you're suffering from street fatigue. (For more about "Little Havana," see "Sightseeing.")

Across the Rickenbacker Causeway (toll is 25¢ going over, nothing coming back) lies **Key Biscayne,** but **Virginia Key** comes first as you cross the

Copyright © Pierre Dupeyroux

parklike causeway (there are swimming, boating, and fishing areas all along the sides of the four-lane road). The Seaquarium and Marine Stadium are both on this palm-filled island (see "Sightseeing"), and a bridge connects it to Key Biscayne, a 4½-mile island that holds Crandon Park with its outstanding zoo, elegant private homes and hotels, and Cape Florida State Park at the southern tip (again, see "Sightseeing").

Back on the Miami side of the Rickenbacker Causeway, **Coconut Grove** is a tropical Greenwich Village, with resident and visiting artists, musicians, craftspersons, boutiques with all sorts of artwork for sale, excellent restaurants, and tiny, winding roads and streets with homes of every architectural style set back in wooded plots. The best and most fun way to see Coconut Grove is on a bike, and there are several rental shops where you can get one for an hour, a half-day, or an entire day.

FLORIDA: MIAMI/MIAMI BEACH 257

GUIDE TO THE NUMBERED POINTS OF INTEREST ON THE "GREATER MIAMI" MAP (north to south): 1. Seminole Okalee Indian Village—4 miles north on U.S. 441; 2. Gulfstream Park Race Track; 3. Calder Race Course; 4. Monastery of St. Bernard; 5. Biscayne Kennel Club; 6. Barry College; 7. Hialeah Race Track; 8. Miami Jai-Alai Fronton; 9. Miami Stadium; 10. Miami Dade County Chamber of Commerce; 11. Watson Park: Japanese Gardens, blimp base, seaplane base; 12. Miami Beach Auditorium, Convention Hall & Conservatory, Miami Beach Chamber of Commerce; 13. Lincoln Road Mall; 14. Miami Merchandise Mart; 15. Flagler Kennel Club; 16. Dade County Auditorium; 17. Orange Bowl; 18. Miamarina, Bayfront Park, Bandshell, JFK Torch of Friendship, Library; 19. Miami Beach Kennel Club; 20. Florida International University; 21. Tamiami Trail: Indian villages, airboat rides, Shark Valley Loop Rd. in Everglades National Park; 22. "Little Havana" Cuban district, Latin restaurants; 23. Marine Stadium; 24. Venetian Pool; 25. Museum of Science, Planetarium, Historical Museum; 26. University of Miami; 27. Coconut Grove artists district, Grove House, Dinner Key Auditorium; 28. Historical Lighthouse & Museum; 29. Orchid Jungle; 30. Coral Castle; 31. Redlands Fruit groves & farming; 32. Everglades National Park—entrance 10 miles from Homestead; 33. Art Deco Historic District.

Coral Gables is a different cup of tea—handsome (sometimes elegant) homes set in landscaped grounds, a wide shopping boulevard (Miracle Mile—see "Shopping"), and a street "system" that will drive you wild. Unless you want to just wander, which isn't a bad idea, arm yourself with a Miami city map. Despite the trouble, though, Coral Gables warrants a look-see, for it is a totally planned community, with a strict building code, no billboards, and a confined business district. All in all, it is probably tropical city living as we all envision it and as we seldom see it.

The Orange Bowl Stadium, in the 1500 block of NW 3rd St., is where the Miami Dolphin football team plays its home games and, of course, where the Orange Bowl Festival culminates three weeks of festivities with that all-important Orange Bowl game on January 1.

Hialeah (see "Sports"), with its beautiful race track, is up in the northwest section, and it's a distribution center for many of the city's department stores and appliance manufacturers. Like Coral Gables, it requires a map for any detailed exploration.

MIAMI BEACH:
Miami Beach is connected to the mainland, three miles west across Biscayne Bay, by five causeways. The oldest, **MacArthur Causeway,** leaves the beach at 5th St., arriving at Miami's 12th and 13th Sts. You'll see several small, well-cared-for islands to the north as you drive across, with private homes and docks out front (Al Capone lived on one for a while). The Japanese Tea Garden (see "Sightseeing") is on Watson Island near the Miami side, and this is also where the Goodyear blimp and helicopters offer airborne sightseeing tours (see "Tours"). Dade Blvd., just north of Miami Beach's 17th St., runs into the **Venetian Causeway** (there's a 25¢ toll), which ends at Miami's 15th St. That enormous waterfront building you see on the Miami side is the *Miami Herald* building, one of the most modern newspaper plants in the world, and you can arrange a guided tour by telephone (350-2491). At 41st St. (Miami Beach), the **Julia Tuttle Causeway** is one of the most heavily traveled of the five, since the drive over is quick and it connects with expressways at Miami's 36th St. Then comes the **John F. Kennedy Causeway,** at Miami

Beach's 71st Sts., but if you use that name, you're likely to get very strange, blank looks from the natives—it exits at 79th St. in Miami, and I've never heard it called anything but the **79th St. Causeway** (even addresses of restaurants along its route are listed that way). Farther north, the **Broad Causeway** (96th St. at the beach, 125th St. on the mainland) charges a 15¢ toll.

The long (7½ miles), narrow (one to three miles wide) island that is Miami Beach is considerably easier to get around than its older, larger sister city across the bay. Its main artery is **Collins Avenue,** which runs north and south its entire length, with the Atlantic on one side, Indian Creek on the other. East-west streets are numbered, beginning at the south end of the island. **Lincoln Road** (an eight-block shopping mall sometimes called the Fifth Avenue of the South—see "Shopping") is a major east-west dividing street between 16th and 17th Sts., with the older, less expensive hotels to the south, (some of which, dating from the '30s and '40s, are being restored to their original art-deco beauty), those fabulous new (and expensive) establishments running all the way north to 87th St., through exclusive **Surfside** and **Bal Harbour** to **Haulover Park** at 108th St. Although hotels stand shoulder to shoulder the entire route, the beach is dotted with block-long parks at **23rd, 46th, 65th,** and **71st Sts.** Beyond Haulover Park, which has every sort of resort facility open to the public—beaches, rental boats, inexpensive restaurants, bicycles, tennis courts, etc.—the more moderately priced motels begin at 159th St. and run through the **Sunny Isles** section all the way up to 195th St., giving way there to the quiet residential community of **Golden Beach.**

The beach, which has suffered from erosion in recent years and is being repaired by the U.S. Army Corps of Engineers, is best, in my opinion, both at the Sunny Isles section to the north of Miami Beach proper and at **South Beach,** on the southern tip of the island, although it really is fine all the way up.

One of your lasting impressions of Miami Beach is bound to be of the lush, vibrant tropical trees and plants that line the streets, fill the parks, and create a garden-like setting for the whole place. Well, those gorgeous, flower-filled vistas weren't plunked there by Mother Nature—remember, this was once nothing more than mud and mangroves. The city nursery spends a fortune each year to raise more than a million plants, renewing the elaborate displays with just-blooming flowers as each species fades.

There are two vacation attractions I've never seen advertised for Miami Beach, yet they both are free, fun, and almost unavoidable. The first is people-watching (which can be fascinating here because of the incredible mix of rich and not-so-rich, knowns and unknowns, and the wide variety of ethnic groups), and the other is lobby-hopping (you can *feel* rich just by walking through those gilded portals, and it doesn't cost a cent to look!). Of course, with all that beach and the wealth of sightseeing to be done in the area, you may have to skip the lobbies, but for a spare hour or two, you can't beat it, especially for the price.

2. Where to Stay

The cost of a motel or hotel room in Miami Beach will depend on several factors. First of all, the location makes a *big* difference in price. Miami Beach proper runs from Government Cut (an access channel to Miami's port facilities) north to 88th St. South of Lincoln Road (which is between 16th and 17th Sts.) rates tend to be less and hotels older. The fabulous and very expensive "Hotel Row" extends from Lincoln Road north all the way through Surfside and Bal Harbour to Haulover Park. North of Haulover Park, from 159th to

195th, Sunny Isles is lined with a more moderate-priced "Motel Row." Since that entire stretch is only about 12 miles long, and since the beach itself above and below "Hotel Row" is as good as that of the high-rent district, a visitor looking primarily for sun and surf can save an unbelievable amount just by staying at one end or the other. And even more savings can be effected by the location of the *room*. Often by foregoing an oceanfront room, you can save between $5 and $10 a day. And, of course, the quality of the motel or hotel will help determine your cost. Almost all, however, will have a pool, the beach is either right out front or just across the street, and many of the moderate-priced motels have extras that compare favorably with expensive places in other resorts.

When you go will also have a tremendous bearing on what you pay. The winter months are, as you'd expect, the most expensive, and from December 15 to April 1, "budget" often moves up into the "moderate" range. However, as more and more people discover that Miami Beach is well within their means in the summer, if not the winter, and that year-round attractions are just as appealing in July as in December, the "seasons" are blurring in everything but price, with much the same service, entertainment, and plush-resort atmosphere all year. The prices I've listed with each accommodation indicate the lowest and the highest charged during the year: there are usually several gradations in between. Lowest rates are generally in effect May and June and from September through mid-December, and July and August rates as a rule run lower than December to April. Of course, you may not see as many celebrities on the beaches or "big-name" performers in the clubs during these lesser seasons (Miami Beach doesn't really have an *off*-season anymore); but then, that may not be why you're going!

Unless otherwise noted, the hotels and motels listed below are oceanfront.

If the wealth of accommodations available at Miami Beach seems a little overwhelming, the Miami Beach Resort Hotel Association can make your booking simpler—and probably save you money, as well. They have established a toll-free telephone service (800/641-1111) to provide reservations at major hotels, or if you wish, find a package booking to cover hotel, rental car, nightclub tickets, and sightseeing arrangements. Everything is included except airfare. In 1983, depending on your choice of hotel, you could have just such a package for a seven-night stay for $129 and up. The package deals (and many are available with discount airline fares) may be booked through travel agents as well as directly through the central reservations number.

DELUXE: The **Fontainebleau Hilton,** 4441 Collins Ave. (tel. 305/538-2000), has long been queen of the beach, with her graceful, gleaming white quarter-circle main structure overlooking the newly rebuilt 300-foot-wide white sand beach and the Atlantic on one side, the picturesque Intracoastal Waterway and Collins Avenue on the other. Now, fresh from a $35-million spruce-up and expanded by the acquisition of an adjoining hotel, she almost seems to preen in the Miami Beach sun. The 1224 rooms, including 61 suites, are, indeed, something to preen about—their size, to begin with, and their comfort and luxurious furnishings to finish with. Some have period decor, others contemporary, but all are, simply put, smashing. And then there are the public rooms: a vast lobby edged with live tropical plants, black and white marble columns, and a marble floor partially covered by a bright, tropical green carpet. There are huge standing candelabra, crystal chandeliers, and a baby grand piano over by the circular bar which looks out onto the grounds and the sea beyond. Every service you can imagine is offered to guests, and you can dine whenever and wherever the notion strikes you, from a snack at poolside to elegant continental dishes in The Dining Galleries to early-morning or late-night meals in the garden-style Chez Bon Bon. And there's entertainment aplenty, with the Poo-dle Lounge keeping late hours alive or LaRonde's sophisticated audiences applauding sophisticated performers. On the 18 acres of grounds, there's a gigantic half-acre pool complete with an island and five-story-high "magic mountain" which sports four waterfalls and a 43-foot-long waterslide. There are lighted tennis courts, free golf privileges (with transportation to and from the courses), a putting green, pool tables, shuffleboard, sailing, and windsurfing, and if you can't find what you want on their grounds, there's a unique program that allows you to use the facilities of the Eden Roc, next door, or the Doral-on-the-Ocean, right down the street.

As for prices, well, they are not cheap (doubles start at $120 and suites at $270), but the Fontainebleau offers special packages that are well within the bargain range for this type of accommodation. In 1983, for example, there was a seven-night, six-day package for the extraordinary price of $279. Also, they follow the Hilton policy of not charging for children who share their parents' quarters. Incidentally, the prices quoted here are for high season and drop other months.

The **Doral-on-the-Ocean,** 4833 Collins Ave. (tel. 305/532-3600), is quite a place all by itself, but its guests also enjoy use of the elegant Doral Country Club's facilities over in Miami (five golf courses, 19 tennis courts, lake fishing, etc.). The oceanfront Doral also has tennis, as well as basketball, volleyball, Ping-Pong, a heated pool, and cabanas for beachgoers. Rooms carry out the stunning baroque decor of its lobby and public rooms, and have refrigerators, extra washbasins in separate dressing rooms, and (the height of luxury!) bath-room phones. And there's a lovely rooftop dining room with a view. Cocktail lounges, of course. Doubles start, seasonally, at $95 to $130.

Less flamboyant, the **Eden Roc,** 4525 Collins Ave. (tel. toll free 800/327-8337, or 305/532-2561), is just up the street from the Fontainebleau, with the same atmosphere of pampered luxury. The high-ceilinged lobby with its beige tones, wicker furniture, and abundance of plants, sets a European tone, and rooms are tastefully decorated in low-keyed earth-tones. All have a large bath and dressing room, and oversize walk-in closet. The Porch dining room serves regional American specialties. Two pools (one freshwater, one saltwater) domi-nate the deck area. Double-room rates begin at $95 to $135, seasonally.

ART DECO HOTELS: For a totally different Miami Beach vacation, head down south of Lincoln Road to the Art Deco National Historic District and two hotels that reflect what has come to be called "Tropical Deco." The **Cardozo Hotel,** 1300 Ocean Dr., Miami Beach 33139 (tel. 305/531-1235), and the **Carlyle Hotel** (on the opposite corner—same telephone number) are both on the National Register of Historic Places, and both are owned and operated by a partnership headed by Andrew Capitman, whose mother actually spear-headed the Art Deco revitalization movement. Just across Ocean Drive from Lummus Park and the sea, they have been restored to the era of their birth with loving care.

The Cardozo, built in 1939, was one of the most fashionable resorts on the beach before World War II. You may recognize it as the setting for the Frank Sinatra film, *Hole in the Head,* although since that filming, Andrew and his crew have stripped away all the wallpapers, quasi-luxurious carpeting, and other trappings that hid its original artistry in layers added over the years. There are 70 rooms, smaller than luxury hotels of today, but charmingly furnished in the style of the '30s and guaranteed to give you delusions of having stepped into one of the movies from that period. The Carlyle Hotel, built in 1941, has the same classic Art Deco features as its older sister, and its 76 rooms perfectly complement the wraparound period exterior. Both the Cafe Cardozo and the Cafe Carlyle have become gathering spots to Miami Beach residents and the young artists who are beginning to congregate in droves in this area. Double rates range from $55 to $75, and there are special package deals offered from time to time.

EXPENSIVE: The **Golden Nugget Resort Motel,** 18555 Collins Ave. (tel. 305/932-1445), has an exceptionally nice private beach, three pools (one is just for the small fry), and a children's counselor who heads planned activities. There are efficiencies among the 120 rooms, all of which are brightly decorated, and most rooms face either pool or ocean. There's a very nice dining room, a coffeeshop, and a cocktail lounge. Seasonal rates here range from $40 to $75 for doubles, efficiencies are an additional $9 a day.

The **Aztec Resort Motel,** 15901 Collins Ave. (tel. toll free 800/327-0241, or call collect 305/947-1481), is just that, a resort all by itself. There are 300 rooms, many with kitchenettes, and all with two double beds. The private beach extends some 600 feet, there are four pools, free tennis privileges, shuffleboard courts, a game and rumpus room for teens, and a children's counselor with daily planned activities. The coffeeshop and dining room have quite good menus, moderately priced, for all three meals (in fact, there's a modified American plan here for a slight additional charge). The Tequila cocktail lounge and nightclub offers entertainment and dancing, even off-season. Out at the Patio Bar, look for Fran, one of the friendliest bartenders you'll find in Miami. Guest activities include frequent Bingo and cocktail parties. Rates for doubles vary seasonally from $40 to $58 and the third and fourth persons in the same room stay free—adult or child! This is one of the best buys at the beach, in my opinion, and the casual, informal atmosphere is very much enhanced by an attentive, friendly staff.

Many of the 162 rooms at the **Chateau,** 19115 Collins Ave. (tel. 305/931-8800), have balconies, and some have private patios. Rooms are about average in size, sporting comfortable, contemporary furnishings, and there are some kitchenettes available. Facilities include an oversize heated swimming pool, a wading pool, a playground, free golf privileges, a recreation room, Ping-Pong, and free in-house movies. For nighttime recreation, the bar has entertainment and dancing year-round. Double-room rates run from $35 to $65 seasonally (cots and cribs are free).

Patches of green lawn and plantings of flowers and shrubs give the **Pan American Resort Motel,** 17875 Collins Ave. (tel. 305/932-1100), a pleasing, manicured look, and inside, there's the same well-kept air. Furnishings are modern, with bright resort colors dominating, and rooms (which open to a private terrace or balcony) have refrigerators and two double beds. In addition to the Olympic-size pool, you'll find shuffleboard and a nine-hole putting green. Both the dining room and lounge (which has entertainment at night) have beamed ceilings and lots of light woods around. Double rooms range in season from $80 to $105, lower the rest of the year, and cribs and cots are free.

The air of subdued elegance in the pretty lobby of the **Monaco Luxury Resort Motel,** 17501 Collins Ave. (tel. 305/932-2100), extends to most of the rooms. Colors are cheerful and bright, furnishings modern, and there's a refrigerator in every room. The private beach is some 200 feet long, and there's a heated pool and a kiddie pool. Depending on location of the room and the season, double rooms range from $26 to $64, efficiencies from $29 to $71, and rooms can be arranged to accommodate up to four people.

You can call collect to reserve at the **Suez Resort Motel,** 18215 Collins Ave. (tel. 305/932-0661). Most of the modern-decor rooms have refrigerators, and there are kitchenettes available. Recreation facilities are on a par with those elsewhere—two pools (and a lifeguard), a wading pool, tennis court, children's playground, shuffleboard, volleyball, and a children's counselor. The ocean-front dining terrace is delightful (but you can eat inside if you prefer) and the cocktail lounge has nightly entertainment. Double rooms run from $57 to $67, seasonally; kitchenettes are an extra $10.

MODERATE: From the moment you walk into the light, airy, glass-walled lobby of the **Dunes Motel,** on the ocean at 170th St. (tel. toll free 800/327-1261, or 305/947-7511), decorated in soft yellows, greens, and white, you'll encounter a kind of casual elegance that you'll find also in the beautifully appointed rooms. This is one of the prettiest of the moderate-priced motels, with large, picture-windowed rooms, palm-thatched shade shelters, an Olympic-size pool alongside the smaller one for children, a patio-pool bar, and supervised activities for the younger set. The private beach runs for more than 400 feet out front. It's also within walking distance of shopping and theaters (some restaurants as well, although the one on the premises is excellent). There's entertainment and dancing at night in the cocktail lounge. Double-room rates vary according to location as well as season, and range from $40 to $65, with efficiencies $10 extra.

The huge **Sheraton Beach Resort,** 19400 Collins Ave. (tel. toll free 800/325-3535, or 305/932-1234), is set on 20 well-kept acres at the far northern end of "Motel Row," extending along some 700 feet of oceanfront. The rooms, most opening onto private terraces, are spacious and decorated in a modern style, and of the 498 units, 300 are efficiencies. Two pools, whirlpool, *and* a kiddie pool here, four clay tennis courts, shuffleboard, a children's playground (with organized activities), and a putting green. Doubles run $35 to $70, seasonally; kitchenettes are $10 extra. Children under 17 are free with parents.

Near the northern end of "Motel Row," the **Ocean Roc Resort Motel,** 19505 Collins Ave. (tel. toll free 800/327-0553, or 305/931-7600), used to be a Holiday Inn. It's an unusually well-maintained place, with extra-large rooms (all with two double beds and nicely furnished) which have private balconies. There's a swimming pool with a separate section for kids, a dining room with an ocean view, and a bar. Tennis is free. The location is quieter and more restful than most, yet still convenient to shopping. Rates are in the $45 to $55 range, with efficiencies an additional $6.

Guests enjoy the Sunday wiener roast and pool party at the **Sandy Shores Motel,** 16251 Collins Ave. (tel. 305/947-3581), as well as the nicely maintained, average-size rooms and efficiencies. The pool is saltwater, and there are shuffleboard courts, a coffeeshop, and a cocktail lounge. Rates range from $35 to $48, with kitchenettes $6 extra.

Another former Holiday Inn, the **Pier House Inn,** 17451 Collins Ave. (tel. 305/931-7500), has rather large rooms with modern furnishings in light resort colors. The heated pool is on the second-story rooftop, and through the underwater portholes you can look right into the lobby area. Other recreation facilities include shuffleboard and Ping-Pong. The coffeeshop serves breakfast and lunch only, closing at 4 p.m., but there are many good restaurants nearby. Rates here run $45 to $50, and cribs are furnished free.

Opposite a large shopping center, the **Blue Grass Motel**, 18325 Collins Ave. (tel. 305/931-8300), serves free coffee to guests and has a babysitter list. Rooms are not fancy, but they are quite comfortable and you'll find them more than adequate. The heated pool has a lifeguard, and there are golf privileges, a putting green, shuffleboard, and Ping-Pong, movies, and outdoor wiener roasts for guests. Double rooms go for $35 to $53, with kitchenettes another $8; both cribs and cots are free.

If you prefer to be right in the heart of Miami Beach, in the Lincoln Road area you'll find two recommendable hotels in the moderate to moderate-high range. The **Fairfax Hotel**, Collins Ave. at 18th St. (tel. 305/538-3837), is one of Miami Beach's nicest small hotels (only 87 rooms), and an exception to the usual impersonal hotel service. The Fairfax staff is friendly, as well as efficient and helpful. Rooms are unusually large and nicely done up, and there are apartments just right for families. Although not on the ocean, Fairfax guests have the use of a private pool and beach just across the street. This is a good buy for those facts alone, but bonuses come in the form of Abe and David Sheffman, father-and-son owners, and Mrs. Gertrude Miller, the genial, long-time manager. Seasonally varying rates for doubles range from $24 to $48.

BUDGET: It is true in Miami as elsewhere that budget travelers must give up some of the convenience of location, newness of construction, and room size found in the higher priced accommodations. Sad to say, in Miami there is seldom the compensating charm of the small, pension-type hotels that can be found elsewhere in this country and all over Europe. Although some of the budget hotels below are indeed small, they don't necessarily provide personalized attention. All are, however, clean and well kept, and although facilities are somewhat limited (for Miami Beach), they're either right on the ocean or just across the street. And at all the price is right—off-season they're downright cheap! Here, then, are my favorites:

Up in the Sunny Isles section (north of 159th St.), there are two budget-priced motels that will be particularly appreciated by those who want to get away from the highrise district of central Miami Beach. **Bimini Bay Resort Motel**, 17480 Collins Ave. (tel. 305/931-7242), first of all, is a family-owned and operated place with a "just scrubbed" look about it. It's just across the street from the ocean and has access to the beach; there's a pool on the premises, plus lovely little garden spots, a putting green, shuffleboard, and barbecue facilities. Rooms are tastefully decorated and there are some available with kitchens. No dining room or cocktail lounge, but restaurants and bars are within easy walking distance. Rates start at a low $20 and go as high as $35 during the year.

Located on the Intracoastal Waterway—with a private dock for guests—the **Malibu Motel**, 16100 Collins Ave. (tel. 305/947-4878), is a small motel with an atmosphere of peace and quiet, and here you'll find beautifully furnished rooms and efficiencies. There's access to the ocean beaches (across the street), and you can fish from the dock or tan on the sundeck. There's a coffee shop. Double-room rates begin at $19 and go to $30.

Now, for those of you who prefer the stimulation of street activity to just plain peace and quiet, the following budget hotels in the Lincoln Road area (or just south of it) may have greater appeal—particularly if you like being near unlimited shopping.

Haddon Hall Hotel, 1500 Collins Ave. (tel. 305/531-1251), is a well-run, 123-room hotel across the street from the public beaches. Rooms are nicely furnished and all have TV and cooking facilities. There's an Olympic-size swimming pool. You'll have to eat elsewhere, for the Haddon Hall doesn't have a dining room, but there are several restaurants within a one-block distance. Spanish, French, and Yiddish are spoken by the staff. Rates range from $15 to $40, and there are special monthly rates.

(The Haddon Hall people also operate the **Welworth Apartment Hotel** —7326 Collins Ave.; tel. 305/861-2426—which has fully equipped apartments and some hotel rooms with refrigerators at budget prices from $15 to $40, even lower at special monthly rates.)

CAMPGROUNDS: Holiday Park, 3140 W. Hallandale Beach Blvd., Hallandale (tel. 305/981-4414), and **Holiday Towers,** 3300 Pembroke Rd., Hollywood (tel. 305/962-7400), are just a mile apart, with 350 full-hookup sites each, heated pools, showers, recreation hall, and laundry facilities, all convenient to Metropolitan Miami, dog tracks, race tracks, golf course, jai-alai, etc. Rates start at $11.

3. Where to Eat

When visitors to the Greater Miami area aren't sunning themselves on the beaches or traveling from one sightseeing attraction to another, they're eating —sometimes it seems to me there are almost as many places to eat as there are hotel *rooms!* They range from gourmet restaurants to sandwich shops, from French haute cuisine to seafood to steaks to kosher-deli fare. Prices, too, run the gamut from the top of the bank account to the bottom of the budget register. Each section of this metropolitan and beach area has its own "special" places, and I've listed them for you. And since Latin cuisine is a category all its own, you'll find Spanish and Cuban restaurants listed separately.

MIAMI BEACH: Cafe Chauveron, 9561 E. Bay Harbor Dr., Bay Harbor Islands (tel. 866-8779), was internationally known even before the restaurant moved from New York to Miami Beach. The Provençal cuisine still rates the prestigious Mobil five-star award, and the lovely waterfront setting makes it an even more exciting dining experience. In fact, there's a cocktail terrace right on the water—for those who arrive by boat! Inside, all is subdued elegance, with oil paintings, white linen and hand-blown wine glasses on the table, and perhaps the best, most knowledgeable service in these parts (the wine list is truly a fine one, and the staff can guide the inexperienced through its labels). Menu selections include seafood (in the French manner, of course), beef, veal, lamb (which is superb), and game in season, and prices (they're à la carte) start at $12. The doors open at 5:30 p.m. daily and they take orders until 10:30 p.m., but don't think you can just drop in—reservations are absolutely necessary, and the jacket requirement strictly observed. In my book, this is *the* place for extra-special dining, and even if it scuttles the budget temporarily, one dinner here is worth a week of hamburgers later.

The **Dining Galleries** in the Fontainebleau Hotel, 4441 Collins Ave. (tel. 538-2000), is just about the ultimate in elegance. Luxurious furnishings, rich fabrics, crystal chandeliers, statuary and other works of art, fresh flowers and growing plants in abundance, and a standard of service hard to come by even in the most expensive restaurants. All that, and food which can only be described as gourmet. Veal Romanoff is only one of the continental specialties of this magnificent room, which overlooks the gardens. Breads and pastries are baked in their own kitchen, and there's dancing (entertainment from time to time). Prices are in the $17 to $22 range for entrees on the à la carte dinner menu, and on Sunday there's a table d'hôte brunch, $19 for adults, $9.50 for children. The wine list is excellent, as is the selection of European desserts and coffees, so use these prices as a beginning point. Whatever your final charge, it will be little enough for such elegance.

The Forge, 432 Arthur Godfrey Rd. (tel. 538-8533), just *may* be the most opulent eatery on the Gold Coast of Florida. Several dining "salons," each unique in its own grandeur, are filled with exquisite antiques, art objects, crystal chandeliers, stained-glass Tiffany lamps, and a staggering collection of art nouveau. There is an expensive hush throughout—all noise is absorbed by intricately designed crushed velvet which covers the floors and some of the walls. The Forge's fabulous walk-in wine cellar boasts one of the most extensive collections of classical rare wines in the country, most of which are museum pieces purchased at special auctions. The cellar is also stocked with an enormous selection of French, Italian, American, Spanish, Austrian, and Greek table wines. Cuisine at the Forge is sophisticated American liberally dotted with unusual continental and nouvelle cuisine specialties. À la carte entrées start at $14.95. Steaks and roast rib of beef are prime aged, and there is a great assortment of international appetizers, entrées, and fabulous desserts. The Lounge at the Forge features live musical entertainment for listening and dancing, and the beat goes on from 9:30 p.m. to 5 a.m., seven days a week. The Forge serves from 6 p.m. to 2:30 a.m. and reservations are suggested.

A Miami Beach tradition since 1948, the Embers, 245 22nd St., just off Collins (tel. 538-4345), also serves prime beef, plus ribs, chicken, duck, and pheasant, all of which you can see being broiled over hickory charcoal (through glass windows—no smoke blowing in your eyes or cooking odors). There's also a large selection of seafood, including fresh stone crabs, Icelandic flounder, and Maine lobster stuffed with shrimp. The setting is lavish, with lots of rich red all about and crystal chandeliers, but prices are really in the moderate range, beginning at $7.95. Hours are 5:30 p.m. to midnight every day, and reservations are a good idea.

THREE MIAMI BEACH INSTITUTIONS: Joe's Stone Crab Restaurant, 227 Biscayne St. (tel. 673-0365), takes honors in the institution department— it's been here since 1913 and has been collecting one of those coveted *Holiday* Awards every year since 1961. The large, 350-seat place has a simple decor of tile floors, dark pecky-cypress walls, and high ceilings. Stone crabs are, of course, the star of the extensive menu, and they're costly, but the other seafood items are more reasonably priced and perfectly cooked. Prices run all the way from $3.50 (for fried oysters) to $21. Joe's is open from 5 p.m. to 10 p.m. every day; and in spite of its size, you'll have to wait (it can be as long as two hours)—there are no reservations, and no exceptions.

Gatti Restaurant, 1427 West Ave. (tel. 673-1717), has been operated by the same family for almost sixty years, and is the second oldest restaurant on the Beach. Well-loved by residents and visitors who return each season, it is almost a social center as well as a first-class restaurant—come to dinner on opening day at Hialeah, and you'll find the racing crowd gathering here after they've won or lost at the track. Many celebrities have made this a regular eating place, both because of the cuisine and because they, too, met with a friendly reception, with little fuss or feathers about their presence. As for the food, it's Italian, featuring outstanding pasta, the freshest of seafoods, and classic dishes such as veal Parmigiana or chicken cacciatore. The service is fast and friendly, even when the place gets crowded, as it frequently does. The wine list is good, the pastries are luscious, and entrees on the à la carte menu range from $9.50 to $20. Hours are 5:30 to 10:30 p.m. except for Monday, when it's closed, and I strongly recommend reservations. Closed from Mother's Day to November 1.

There's been a Roney Pub in this area (the first was in Coral Gables) for over 25 years, and if Saul Kaplan has his way, his pub tradition will just go on and on. With the emphasis on dark woods, beamed ceilings, lots of brass, and good food at prices which send you away stuffed for under $6, there seems to be little danger of its disappearing. The long lines are attracted in part by the low prices, in part by the ample portions (everybody leaves the Roney with a doggy bag—it's a Miami Beach tradition), and in large part by the quality of the food. The large menu offers fresh seafood, duck, chicken, beef, and combination platters, and all entrees include a potato (with a choice of baked, stuffed, or fried or a potato pancake) and large salad, as well as freshly baked bread. All for prices that range from $5.95 (for which you can get a half of a baked chicken large enough for two) to $10.95 (only if you have a huge appetite). This is the place to take the family, or just come alone for good eating that won't break the budget. You'll find the **Roney Pub and Restaurant,** 2305 Collins Ave. (tel. 532-3353), and never mind reservations, you'll just have to wait on line, although it moves quickly under the expert guidance of pretty hostess Patricia Connelly. Hours are 11 a.m. to 2:30 p.m., 5 to 11 p.m.

OTHERS: You can also get good seafood in an atmospheric setting (and at moderate prices) at the **Old Key West Fishing Village** up in the Sunny Isles section, 18288 Collins Ave. (tel. 931-8420). Dress is casual, it opens at 5 p.m., and prices begin at $7.95.

Benihana of Tokyo Steak House, 1665 NE 79th St. Causeway (tel. 866-2768), is the place for Japanese cuisine. Its decor is that of a country inn in Japan, and after your order has been taken by one of the traditionally dressed Oriental waitresses, food is prepared right at your table by chefs who are really culinary artists. Hibachi prime steak, shrimp, and chicken are the specialties, at prices that start at $8.95. Open every day from 5 p.m. (Sunday from 4 p.m.).

On the lower level of the Fontainebleau Hotel, 4441 Collins Ave. (tel. 538-2000), the delightful **Chez Bon Bon** stays open from 7 a.m. to 2 a.m.—a cheerful place to begin the day or to end a late evening when hunger pangs attack at bedtime. There's a garden motif to the decor and a casual atmosphere no matter what the hour. Breakfast menus are extensive and range from 95¢ to $6.50; lunch entrees (including a burger selection) are $4.95 to $9.50; and dinner selections, $7 to $14 (except for burgers, which are the same $4.95 as at lunch). There are good offerings of fresh seafood, beef, chicken and pasta.

There are several good, inexpensive places to eat at Miami Beach. Well-known **Wolfie's,** with two locations (195 Lincoln Rd., tel. 538-0326; and 2038 Collins Ave., tel. 538-6626), and **Pumpernik's,** 6700 Collins Ave. (tel. 866-0246), have a complete deli menu, with blintzes, corned beef and pastrami, smoked fish, bagels, etc., overstuffed sandwiches, and very good desserts. A complete dinner at any one of these will run no more than $4.95, and of course, you can put together one of your own for less. They are both open seven days a week.

READER'S DINING SELECTION: "Do not—I repeat, do *not*—miss the fabulous Cuban food and very reasonable prices at the **Puerto Sagua** restaurant, 700 Collins Ave., Miami Beach: *fresh* french-fried potatoes, Cuban batidos, fresh-fruit milkshakes. There's counter or lovely dining room service. A Cuban main dish such as ropa vieja is served with Cuban bread and butter, potatoes or rice, and fried plantain for incredibly low prices. Great tasting and great value" (L. Wolk, Greenfield Park, N.Y.)

MIAMI: The main dining room of **The Depot,** 5830 S. Dixie Hwy., that's U.S. 1 South (tel. 665-6261), is a reproduction of a South Florida, turn-of-the-century railroad station, and this whole place will gladden the heart of any confirmed train lover. There's railroad memorabilia all over the place, but the tables themselves are really the star attraction. Each has a glass top through which you view a miniature N-gauge train traveling through a tiny American countryside. Or if you prefer, you can dine in a reproduction of Henry Flagler's private dining car, complete with opulent 1895 furnishings. With so much attention given to decor, it wouldn't be surprising to find the food less than spectacular, but such is *not* the case at the Depot. They've won the *Holiday* Award every year since 1974, and recently received *Institution* magazine's menu design award. Just one example of the care given to food preparation: The prime ribs are roasted in a rock-salt cast to preserve natural juices. Other specialties include lobster thermidor and veal au chasseur. Entrées start at $18.95, and cocktails, dinner, and a late supper are served from 5 p.m. until 2 a.m. every day except Monday. Don't come without a reservation.

The **Sorrento,** 3059 SW 8th St. (tel. 643-3111), has been owned and operated by the same family for over 30 years. The Amanzio family serves a classic Italian menu in a simple, unpretentious setting, with Florentine statues, paintings, and lovely chandeliers. Located in the "Little Havana" section of Miami, it draws a diversified clientele. Specialites include chicken Florentina, veal Valdostana, and crabmeat cannelloni, and prices are moderate. It's a friendly, relaxing place; and is open from 11:30 a.m. to 11 p.m. weekdays except Tuesday, when it's closed, until midnight on Friday and Saturday, and from 2 to 11 p.m. on Sunday.

Right in the heart of downtown, **Arthur's Eating House,** 1444 Biscayne Blvd. (tel. 371-1444), is a rather grand, modern, moderately priced lunch and dinner spot. The menu runs to steaks, spare ribs, veal cutlets, chops, and fresh seafood, and lunch prices range from $5 to $7, dinner from $9 up to $18. Hours are 11:30 a.m. to 4:30 p.m. and then from 5 p.m. to midnight, Monday through Saturday (open until 1 a.m. on Friday and Saturday), and there's entertainment in the evening.

A delightful lunch spot is in Decorators Row, 35 NE 40th St.—the **Piccadilly Hearth** (tel. 576-1818), in a secluded little plaza surrounded by antique shops, interior decorator shops, and a piano garden with a fountain. Inside, it has the dark-wood look of an English pub, and the lunch menu (priced from $3.75) features quiche, salads, sandwiches, and chili con carne, along with seafoods, burgers, and eggs Benedict. The lounge has "jolly hours" from 4:30 to 7 p.m., with reduced prices, and there's dinner, featuring continental cuisine, fresh seafood, and romantic candlelight (much more expensive than lunch, beginning at $10.95) from 5:30 to 10 p.m. It's open every day except Sunday.

READER'S SEAFOOD RECOMMENDATIONS: "Try the **Lagoon** on 163rd St., and the **Port of Call,** 14441 Biscayne Blvd.), for good seafood, especially the bouillabaisse at the Port of Call. They have early bird dinners, too" (M. Ozer, Philadelphia, Penna.).

LATIN: Miami's "Little Havana" is filled with Cuban- and Spanish-style restaurants, and half the fun is finding your own favorite (see "Sightseeing," below). Latin cuisine shows up, too, in several other restaurants around town.

In the hodgepodge architecture around it, **Vizcaya,** 2436 SW 8th St. (tel. 642-2452), is a spectacular standout. Surrounded by a high wrought-iron fence, the two-story white stucco buiiding with its red tile roof is like a transplanted elegant old Spanish home, with a lovely interior not unlike that of a Basque inn. Murals inside are of jai-alai scenes, which may explain its popularity with the city's fronton players, but more likely they come here for the mouthwatering Spanish and Basque-French food. Paella à la Valencia and seafood à la Basque head the list of specialties (complete dinners start at $7.95, à la carte entrées at $5.25). Service is continuous from noon to 11 p.m. every day, and on Friday and Saturday there's a late-supper menu from 11 p.m. to 2 a.m.

Authentic Spanish dishes are also the specialty of the **Madrid**, 2475 SW 37th Ave. (tel. 446-2250), a longtime Miami favorite. Arroz con pollo, shrimp enchilada, and fried spiced pork are bestsellers, and prices range from $5 to $14, although there are lunch specials as low as $3.50. Incidentally, if you get there during "Happy Hour," 4 to 6 p.m., drinks are only $1.50 and hot Spanish hors d'oeuvres are free. Monday through Thursday, hours are 11 a.m. to 11 p.m.; they're open until midnight Friday and Saturday.

Juanito's Centro Vasco, 2235 SW 8th St. (tel. 643-9606), has a Spanish-Basque tavern air, and the owner-chef is known for his lobster thermidor (my personal favorite, though, were the eggs flamenco—delicious!). The very modest prices (dinners start at $3.95 à la carte, $8.95 for complete dinner) belie the quality of the food here. It's open every day from noon to midnight—a friendly place for good, inexpensive Latin meals.

Just across Palm Avenue from the back entrance and stables of Hialeah Race Track, **El Viajante Segundo,** 2846 Palm Ave. (tel. 888-5465), is a family-run Cuban restaurant that is large, bright (almost to the point of gaudiness, with lots of red Formica, veined mirrors, black iron gratings, and fluorescent lights), moderately priced, with some of the best Latin food in the city. Fried plantains, arroz con pollo, paella, black or white bean soup, and snapper in green sauce are just a few of the dishes they do really well. Prices start at $6.95, but what comes to the table at that price is as tasty as anything you'll find at more expensive restaurants. In fact, both food and service are way above what you'd expect for the cost, and among its regular patrons are many Miamians who can well afford to eat in more elegant surroundings. It's open from noon until 11 p.m. every day.

There are loads more places to try in "Little Havana"—see "Sightseeing," below, for additional suggestions.

4. Nightlife

Nightlife in Miami Beach can be almost anything—spectacular shows and revues with elaborately costumed showgirls, "name" entertainers in supperclub acts, jazz ranging from classical to pop, or "singalong" entertainment in small bars and lounges. You can even pop over to Freeport for a night's gambling. Be forewarned, however, that the splashy shows (mostly in the larger hotels) don't come cheap—depending on your thirst and whether or not you have dinner, you can pay as much as $150 for a table for four! If you're there for the show only, although many of the rooms advertise "no cover, no minimum," there is often a "beverage charge" (translation: "cover") which will probably include only one drink—after that, you pay and pay and pay. The smaller establishments usually have no such charge and your tab will be strictly up to you, although they *do* frown on nursing a single drink through an entire evening's entertainment.

Not all the excitement after dark is at the beach. Miami's Cuban nightspots are as lavish as those across the bay (and a good deal cheaper) and there are jazz places that feature the country's best.

The really *big* names come to Miami Beach after Christmas and stay for the "season"; in fact, some of the hotel rooms close down during the summer and fall, so check on this before you plan your evening out. If the star element is what you want for your money, you'd best plan to come in season, but I must add that the Latin shows I've seen in Miami were terrific, without a "headliner" in sight—and the food was superb, too.

One final word of caution: The after-dark scene is a fast-changing one, and while these listings represent what's going on *at the time of writing,* be sure to call ahead and also check current newspapers and entertainment guides found at most hotels and motels.

MIAMI BEACH: The **Sheraton Bal Harbour,** 9701 Collins Ave. (tel. 865-7511), puts on what many believe to be the most lavish, best-produced show in Miami Beach in its **Bal Masque Room.** This French revue features casts of up to 30 showgirls, Ziegfeld-like sets and costumes, some pretty exciting dancing, and top entertainment stars. Show times are 9 p.m. (dinner served from 7 p.m.) and 11 p.m. (no food). Be sure to reserve—and bring money!

At the Fontainebleau, 4441 Collins Ave. (tel. 538-2000), **Poodles** is the place for a swinging late night; La Ronde for more sophisticated entertainment.

For dinner and dancing in luxurious settings, try the **Starlight Roof** at the **Doral,** 4833 Collins Ave. (tel. 532-3600); or **Henri's** at the **Konover,** 5445 Collins Ave. (tel. 854-1500).

The **New Swinger Lounge, Bird Lounge,** and **Persian Room** in the **Marco Polo Hotel,** 192nd St. and Collins Ave. (tel. 932-2233), offer musical entertainment, often featuring top-name entertainers. No cover or minimum or beverage charge (at least, not at the time of this writing).

The **Athenian Club** in the **Desert Inn,** 172nd St. and Collins Ave. (tel. 944-0312), features bellydancers, international singers, and authentic Greek music. Shows are at 10:30 p.m. and 12:30 a.m., and reservations are a good idea.

MIAMI: Miami's most flamboyant nightclubs are both Latin, both run by the same people, and both (for my money) representative of the best buys in this kind of nightlife. The **Flamenco,** at 991 NE 79th St. (tel. 751-8631) features a Spanish musical group and show orchestra, and entrées that run from $2 to $25. At night, the large room (plush with lots of red velvet and Victorian-style white furniture) is the setting for two different shows, both lavish and both so Spanish you'll think you're in sunny Spain. Show times are 9:30 and 11:30 p.m., and jackets are required. The same is true at **Les Violins,** 1751 Biscayne Blvd. (tel. 371-8668). The quality of both productions is just tops, and there's a sense of fun that reflects their Cuban ownership. Best of all, if you really want to make a night of it, you pay the modest cover charge just once and can stay through both shows, with perhaps dinner in between. Incidentally, the food is as good as the entertainment, with continental and Spanish cuisine featured (for example, there's pork Havana style and coquille violin) on a menu with more than 30 entrées.

MUSIC AND DRAMA: For concert-goers and Broadway show-lovers, Miami periodically provides evening entertainment of the first order. Although not everything listed below will be in production at all times, a phone call to any one of them will let you in on what's current when you're there.

The **Greater Miami Opera Association,** 1200 Coral Way (tel. 854-1643), presents both grand and light opera from January through April in the **Dade County Auditorium,** 2901 W. Flagler St., Miami. There are also productions by the **International Cultural Exchange** at the Auditorium from September through April.

The **Theatre of the Performing Arts,** 1700 Washington Ave., Miami Beach (tel. 673-8300), brings Broadway shows like the long-running *Grease* to town at various times during the year, with top-caliber stars. The **Miami Beach Symphony** also performs here with outstanding soloists.

Broadway musicals and drama can also be seen at the **Coconut Grove Playhouse,** one of the best-equipped in the country (3500 Main Highway; tel. 442-2000).

5. Sports

Sports facilities in the Miami Beach area are practically unlimited, whether you want to participate or just spectate.

FISHING: There's bridge fishing at both the **MacArthur** and **Rickenbacker Causeways;** the Rickenbacker has over 2800 feet of catwalks equipped with benches. And there are piers which allow fishing at **Haulover Park,** north of Bal Harbour on A1A (go straight out Collins Ave. from Miami Beach); the **Sunny Isles Pier,** 167th St. and Collins Ave., and **Pier Park,** Ocean Drive and 1st St., Miami Beach. For deep-sea fishing, there are charter boats available at most of the area marinas, including the **Bayfront Miamarina** in downtown Miami, the **Chamber of Commerce docks** at the east end of MacArthur Causeway, **Crandon Park Marina** on Key Biscayne, **Dinner Key Marina** in Coconut Grove, and **Haulover Park,** on A1A north of Bal Harbour. Charges run about $45 per person for a half-day.

GOLF: The City of Miami **Melreese Municipal Course,** 1802 NW 37th Ave., Miami (tel. 635-6770), has 18 holes, greens fees of $8 in winter, $6 in summer, and a charge of $10 to $12 for carts.

The **Key Biscayne Course** on Crandon Blvd. (tel. 361-9129) charges $10 greens fee weekdays, $12 weekends (hours are 8 a.m. to 4 p.m.). From 4 p.m. until dark, fees are reduced to $5 during the week, $6 on weekends. Carts are $14 for 18 holes, $8 for 9.

The **Doral Country Club,** 4400 NW 87th Ave., Miami (tel. 592-2000), has five courses open to the public after guest reservations have been filled. Greens fees here are $14 to $22; carts, $18.

Haulover Beach Park, 10800 Collins Ave. (tel. 947-3525), charges $4 per nine holes during the day, $4.75 at night.

Your hotel or motel may very well have guest privileges at these or other area courses, so be sure you check before striking off on your own.

TENNIS: **Flamingo Park,** Michigan Ave. at 12th St., Miami Beach (tel. 673-7761), has 17 public courts, 13 of which are lighted for night play. Hours are 9 a.m. to 9 p.m., with a small fee, and lessons can be arranged.

Haulover Beach Park, 10800 Collins Ave., north of Bal Harbour (tel. 947-3525), has six units of public courts with a $1.50-an-hour fee for daytime play, $2 at night.

North Shore Park, 350 73rd St., Miami Beach (tel. 673-7754), has 13 public parks, 11 lighted, with a fee of $5. Lessons are available, and hours are 9 a.m. to 10 p.m.

The four units of public courts at **Calusa Park,** Crandon Blvd. on Key Biscayne (tel. 361-2215), are free, and lessons are available.

HORSE RACING: Hialeah Park, one of the world's most beautiful sites, has been honored and dedicated as a National Historic Place. Located in Hialeah, just north of Miami International Airport (E. 4th Ave. between 21st and 32nd Sts.), the park is open year round, but closed to visitors two weeks prior to racing season. Other times, it is open to the public without charge, and horse-lover or not, you shouldn't miss it, if only for its beautiful colony of some 400 flamingos. A few were imported from Cuba in 1932, and thanks to this wildlife sanctuary, they have proliferated to the present number.

The grounds at Hialeah are a masterpiece of landscaping, with lush tropical palms, pines, and oak shading vibrant flowering plants. There are formal gardens, complete with fountains and statuary, and the stunning French Mediterranean clubhouse and grandstand, with ivy-covered walls and sweeping stone staircases. Here, too, is the Shipwreck Aquarium, the cabin of a sunken clipper ship recreated to house coral reef fish; plus an exhibit of English carriages, stagecoaches, a French walking ring, and of course the paddocks and race-track itself. For a modest charge you can tour by tram, which makes several stops as it circles the grounds. Lunch is available at the sightseeing center snackbar on the clubhouse terrace that overlooks the infield lake (and don't miss the displays of racing silks and memorabilia inside the elegant clubhouse). Hours are 9:30 a.m. to 5 p.m. daily except during the racing season. When the horses are running, admission is $2 to the grandstand, $4 to the clubhouse. (No minors allowed during racing hours). Call 885-8000 for current information.

Calder Broward Race Course, 210th St. and 27th Ave. NW, Miami (tel. 625-1311), has summer (from May 5), fall, and winter (till mid-January) thoroughbred racing (post time, 1 p.m.). Admission is $1 to the grandstand, $2 to the clubhouse. If you want a reserved seat in either location there's an additional $1 charge, and you can reserve by phone. The grandstand has a cafeteria and snackbars, and more elegant dining is available in the clubhouse and Turf Club.

Gulfstream Park Race Track, U.S. 1, Hallandale, has racing from January through early March, with a $2 charge for grandstand admission, $4 for the clubhouse.

Special buses are run to all three tracks by **American Sightseeing** (tel. 871-2370), **Gray Line** (tel. 633-0375), and **MTA** (tel. 638-6117).

GREYHOUND RACING: Dog racing is a year-round Florida attraction, and you can watch and wager on the greyhounds at **Flagler Dog Track,** NW 37th Ave. and 7th St., Miami, **Biscayne Kennel Club,** I-95 at NW 115th St., Miami, or **Hollywood Greyhound Track,** Pembroke Rd., Hollywood. Racing is offered nightly except Sundays, with matinees as scheduled. Check local schedules for the track which is open, hours, and other details.

JAI-ALAI: If you've never seen a jai-alai game and like your sports fast and furious, you're in for a treat. The game originated with 17th-century Basques and came here from Spain. The *pelota,* a virgin-rubber ball covered with goatskin, is kept in play by skillful players using a *cesta,* a curved basket of reed, strapped to the wrist. Play is exciting and dangerous, and jai-alai players are regarded with much respect. The **Jai-Alai Fronton** is at NW 36th St. and 36th

Ave., Miami (tel. 633-9661). Games start at 7:30 p.m., admission is $2, and the season is from mid-December through mid-September. Oh, yes, there's pari-mutuel betting.

6. Shopping

Miami has some of the best shopping areas on the East Coast, and you'll find specialty shops of every description not far from wherever you stay. Here follows just a sampling of what to expect:

The exclusive, very elegant **Bal Harbour Shops** center, at Collins Ave. and 97th St., is a 600-foot-long mall liberally sprinkled with over 100 flowering orange trees, shrubs, and bushes interspersed with splashing fountains. The 31 stores on the mall include such famous names as Neiman-Marcus and Martha (designer fashions), and prices are as high as the names are famous.

Farther south, there's the **Lincoln Road Mall,** where about 180 shops occupy eight blocks of an open-air mall beautifully decorated with walkways lined with greenery, flowering plants, and fountains. Also known as the International Market Place, it's great strolling and browsing territory. Or, if you want to give your feet a break, there's an electric tram to take you from one end of the mall (which is blocked to traffic) to the other. There are some exclusive shops in the Market Place, but there are also many little specialty boutiques with unusual items for sale at moderate prices.

Over on the mainland, the **163rd Street Shopping Center,** NE 163rd St. between 12th and 15th Aves., is also an open-air mall, with more than 75 stores. Prices range all over the scale from one shop to another.

"Miracle Mile" is in Coral Gables, a four-block-long parkway lined with planters, benches, and some 150 beautiful shops and restaurants. More exclusive names here, along with generally higher prices.

Even if you're only window shopping, don't miss the experience of shopping "à la Latino" along **Calle Ocho,** SW 8th St. in Miami. The variety is staggering—delicately carved Spanish guitars, mantillas, bullfight posters, lovely filigree jewelry, oil paintings, sculptures, clothing (the garment industry here is second only to New York's), Spanish versions of Scrabble (a neat way to pick up the language), and even furniture (only lack of space prevented my bringing home a rocker patterned after those Cuban mothers use to lull their babies to sleep). It's a colorful, lively area, with plenty of little Cuban restaurants and sandwich shops for foot-resting stops. Prices are less expensive here, although you shouldn't expect "native" bargains—this *is* Miami, not the real Havana. (See "Sightseeing," below, for some specific shopping stops in "Little Havana.")

And if all this isn't enough, there are more than 500 shops and department stores in downtown Miami.

7. Tours

If you'd like to leave the driving to **American Sightseeing,** 4300 NW 14th St., Miami, a half-day bus tour of Miami Beach and Miami costs $14.50 for adults, $7.50 for children. Call 871-4992 for reservations.

For romantic **boat tours** of Miami Beach's Millionaire's Row, **Nikko Sightseeing Boats** offers a two-hour cruise that also includes Biscayne Bay leaving at 10 a.m. and 2 p.m. at $7 for adults, $3.50 for children. The *Gold Coast Special,* including the Seaquarium and Vizcaya, sails from 10 a.m. to 5:30 p.m., costing $21 for adults, $10.50 for children. Covering Miami Beach and the Seaquarium, another cruise leaves at 10 a.m. and at noon. It costs adults

$14.50; children $7. For reservations, call 945-5461, at the Haulover Park Docks.

For a nautical night out, try an evening cruise of the Miami Beach area aboard the *Viking Sun,* from 7:30 to 11 p.m. at the Haulover Park Marina. The price of $15.95 includes dinner and entertainment. For reservations, call 947-6105.

The *Island Queen* covers the Miami Beach waterfront with two-hour cruises leaving at 10:30 a.m., and 1:30 and 3:30 p.m. Tickets are $5.50 for adults and $4.50 for children. For further information, call 379-5119. The boat leaves from Bicentennial Park in Miami.

For **walking tours** of historically significant art-deco buildings, stop by the office of the **Miami Design Preservation League,** 1300 Ocean Dr. (tel. 672-1836 or 672-2014).

If you're interested in a bus tour of **Jewish points of interest** in Miami Beach, contact **Dr. Sam Brown,** Newport "S," Apt. 4086, Deerfield Beach, FL 33441 (tel. 421-8431). His day-long bus and walking tours cover such diverse sites as the Cuban Hebrew Circle Congregation and a mikveh, a bathhouse for ritual purification. Dr. Brown also offers a separate cultural and artistic tour of the Miami Beach area including Temple Emanuel, the Bass Museum, Garden Center, the Hebrew Academy, and other attractions.

Gray Line, c/o A-1 Bus Lines, 65 NE 27th St., Miami (tel. 573-0550), has bus tours that go as far afield as Disney World and the Florida Keys. Call for times and prices.

8. Sightseeing

Miami sightseeing can be almost anything you want it to be, from strolling down Calle Ocho to visiting an elaborate Renaissance palace, to watching Flipper the dolphin perform, to witnessing the extraction of deadly snake venom for use in antitoxins. For full details of Miami, go by the **Metro-Dade Dept. of Tourism,** 234 W. Flager St. Miami, FL 33130 (tel. 579-4694). In Miami Beach, it's the **Visitor Authority,** 555 17th St. Miami, FL 33139 (tel. 673-7080).

ART DECO HISTORICAL DISTRICT: What has been called a "rebirth" has begun at the south end of Miami Beach, with the restoration of many fine buildings constructed during the '30s in the then fashionable Art Deco style. Spearheaded by the Miami Beach Design Preservation League (in the Cardozo Hotel, 1300 Ocean Dr.; tel. 672-1836 or 672-2014), the move to bring back the colors originally used in these distinctive buildings, as well as the artwork, furnishings, and fixtures of the period, has resulted in a delightfully fresh atmosphere in this area, which had become rundown over the years. There's been an influx of talented young artists, writers, photographers, etc., which lends excitement, as well. All this is not to say that you won't encounter plenty of those retirees who have made this part of the Beach their home for years—it's just that there's a new spirit afoot, and you'll miss an important part of what's going on in Miami Beach if you fail to spend some time south of Lincoln Road.

First of all, stop by the office of the Preservation League to pick up their guide of the district—you'll want to loiter awhile in the Cafe Cardozo to soak up some of the atmosphere, since this hotel has undergone one of the best restorations of all. Armed with the guide, you can then set out on foot to see what has been accomplished in a relatively short time. **Washington Avenue is** a key Art Deco showcase, and one of the most striking buildings is the **Washington Storage Company,** designed as a storage facility for the wealthy who visited Miami Beach only during the season. Then, there's the Post Office with its rotunda sporting a W.P.A. mural depicting Florida historical scenes. Then, there's . . . well, space limitations prevent my listing more, but the guide and the friendly staff of the Preservation League (as well as just about anyone you meet along the streets down here) will fill you in.

READER'S SUGGESTION: "For great atmosphere, go to the **Cardozo Cafe** or the **Carlyle Grill.** It's like stepping back to the light and tropical days of the 1930s. The Carlyle and the whole Art Deco district is the best—absolutely the best—vacation spot in Miami Beach!" (C. Andersen and T. King, Dyersburg, Tenn.).

LITTLE HAVANA: Miami's Cuban quarter covers a wide area, but Calle Ocho (SW 8th St.) spreads out a huge sightseeing feast along a 30-block stretch, with colorful shops, intriguing restaurants, and always the industrious, friendly Cubans and their infectious gaiety. The best way to explore this little bit of Old Havana (and I say this from foot-weary experience) is to ride by car or bus (bus route 5, 28, or 29 will take you there) from 7th Ave. to SW 37th Ave., taking in the scene as you pass by and picking out the areas particularly appealing to you; then make your way back east, parking your car (or getting off the bus) at each one. You'll spot SW 37th Ave. by the beautiful Spanish-style Douglas entrance to Coral Gables.

You may want to stop at the **Versailles Plaza,** at SW 35th Ave., to explore the shopping center containing stores like **Carrousel las Piñatas,** specializing in those candy- and toy-filled papier-mâché figures that Latins take great delight in breaking open at children's parties. If you do, stop in the **Versailles Restaurant** for a Cuban sandwich (more like a complete meal than a sandwich) or a *media noche* (less filling), both stuffed with ham, pork, Swiss cheese, pickles, and mustard. **Bello Plaza,** at SW 25th Ave., is more traditional-Spanish in style, with decorative lampposts and wooden balconies—note the beautiful **Vizcaya Restaurant** (see "Where to Eat," above), with its wrought-iron fence and red-tile roof. Just a block away from this rather elegant restaurant, the inexpensive **Lechonera Restaurant** serves pork dishes with a Cuban flavor. On the block between SW 23rd and SW 22nd Aves., look for the **Madrid Gift Shop,** a veritable treasure trove of Spanish handicrafts, wrought-iron wall lamps, wine bags, woven shawls, even Toledo swords to take home and hang on the wall. Right next door is the narrow **Mini-Gallery,** really just a hallway, hung its whole length with paintings. Look for **El Torreon Restaurant,** on the corner of Calle Ocho and 22nd Ave.—the Cuban creole food is terrific here and prices low. At SW 19th Ave., the **Libros Espanoles** carries only books published in Spain, an interesting place to browse, even if you're not really fluent in the language.

In the block between 18th and 19th Aves., you'll see sidewalk displays (crates, actually, filled to the brim) of tropical fruits set out by the **Amado Fruit Shop** in front of the Monaco Building. The **Tamiami Shopping Center** is here, too, and it and the Monaco Building are filled with specialty shops of all descriptions (there's even a Chinese restaurant in the shopping center). Between 18th and 17th Aves., you'll find the **Hector and Lily Tobacco Company,** where they still hand-roll the Cuban-style cigars, and the **Miguel Company** in the middle of the block sells handmade guitars that are works of art. Right around the corner, on 17th Ave., there's a many-hued outdoor garden where the **Pouparina Florists** feature hanging baskets of flowers and plants.

You'll want to see both sides of Calle Ocho between 15th and 16th Aves. **El Pescador Fish Market and Seafood Restaurant** is a "don't miss" on the north side; across the street, **Badia's Restaurant** has Cuban sandwiches and fruit shakes called *batidos,* at **Ultra Records** you can buy the latest Spanish "top ten," or you can catch a flick in Spanish at the **Tower Theater.** At 13th Ave., you'll come to the **Cuban Memorial Plaza,** with its Bay of Pigs Monument, a place that has deep meaning for the Cubans living here. There's **Fritas Domino** at 12th Ave. (with Cuban hamburgers and skinny french fries served in a bun), **Lisboa Restaurant** a little farther east (another inexpensive Cuban eatery), **La Gran Via Bakery** at 9th Court, and . . . well, it's all territory best explored personally. You're certain to find your own special part of Calle Ocho, and wherever it is, there will be those marvelous little sidewalk coffee counters selling steaming cups of strong Cuban coffee. One thing is sure, when you climb back in the car or on the bus, you'll feel you're returning from a foreign country and should have your passport handy!

KEY BISCAYNE: Do yourself a favor and plan at least one full day to explore Key Biscayne. Actually, it'll take you some time to get there (across Rickenbacker Causeway, with a 50¢ roundtrip toll), because who could drive past **Virginia Key** without stopping? Not only is the island a joy to drive around, with its palm-fringed beaches; it also holds three not-to-be-missed sightseeing attractions. First of all, there's the **Seaquarium** (tel. 361-5703), a 60-acre complex of re-created habitats that make sea mammals, rare birds, and even rare turtles feel right at home. There's the Flipper Show (you remember him— the TV star performing dolphin)—he and his friends do high jumps and other tricks; Salty the sea lion and friends star in IT's Magic Show where the audience joins right in; the Top Deck Show where a family of dolphins compete in athletic games and even walk on their tails. Lots more here too, and the monorail trip gives you a terrific view of Virginia Key, Key Biscayne, and the whole bay area. The Seaquarium is open every day from 9 a.m. to 6:30 p.m. (shows are continuous): adults pay $7; ages six to 12, $3.50.

Right across the highway is **Planet Ocean** (tel. 361-5786), where you can see Florida's only iceberg! You can also climb inside a submarine on a make-believe "voyage to the bottom of the sea," listen in on radio transmissions between ships at sea, examine more than 100 exhibits that explain the importance of the oceans to this planet, and see films on the history of the planet Earth. Admission is $5 for adults, $2.50 for children six to 12 (under six, free); hours are 10 a.m. to 6 p.m., but the box office closes at 4:30 p.m.

Nearby is the $2-million, 6500-seat **Marine Stadium,** a huge concrete structure which serves as a viewing stand for motorboat racing and for evening concerts with the orchestra playing from a barge moored in front. The concerts have been going on since 1965, with consistent full houses. Private boats can pull up and enjoy the music, and boat owners find it's a good way to beat traffic jams going home. When the weather is good (and that's most of the time), concerts are on Friday or Saturday nights. When nothing is scheduled, you can inspect the stadium itself, at no charge, from 8 a.m. to 5:30 p.m.

Over the bridge from Virginia Key is Key Biscayne, and **Crandon Park** (once a coconut plantation), with beautifully landscaped picnic grounds and play areas and a 2½-mile palm-lined beach. For $1, you can ride a narrow-gauge railroad through the park, and $2 (if you're over 12; under that, it's free if you come with an adult, 75¢ by yourself) will get you into the southernmost zoo in the U.S. The more than 1000 animals, birds, and reptiles include everything from baby aardvarks to giraffes and pygmy hippos. There's a children's petting zoo as well, and just outside the zoo, an amusement park with a roller-skating rink and several rides. The zoo (tel. 361-5421) is open every day from 9:30 a.m. to 4:30 p.m.

The center section of Key Biscayne holds its shopping area and luxurious private residences (this is where Richard Nixon had his Florida White House when he was president, in a cul de sac with strategically placed guardhouses to keep away the gawkers and the demonstrators). On down at the very southern tip of the Key is lovely **Cape Florida State Park** (you may hear this called the Bill Baggs Park—it's the same thing): 406 acres of palm, native trees and plants and wildlife, and a museum complex that features the **Cape Florida Lighthouse**, with the keeper's home and office restored to its 1830s condition. In 1836, Seminole Indians attacked this lighthouse and set fire to its interior, trapping the keeper at the top. That wily character, however, threw a barrel of gunpowder down into the flames, killing enough of the Indians to frighten the others away and making enough of a bang to be heard by the navy ship *Motto,* which steamed in to his rescue from 12 miles out at sea. If you can make it up the spiral staircase to the top, your huffing and puffing will be rewarded with a really spectacular view of the whole Biscayne Bay area and an Atlantic seascape that's breathtaking. Tours of the lighthouse are at 9 and 10 a.m. and 1 and 2:30 p.m. It's closed on Tuesday. Admission to the park is 50¢, and there's another 50¢ charge for the museum and lighthouse. Hours for the park are 8 a.m. to sunset, 9 a.m. to 5 p.m. for the lighthouse and museum.

FORT LAUDERDALE: Although Fort Lauderdale is *not* in Metropolitan Miami (as its residents and devotees will be quick to tell you), it is well worth the short drive north on I-95 or U.S. 1 for a few hours of looking around this American "Venice." One-tenth of the city is water surface, and some 165 miles of man-made canals and natural waterways wind within the city limits, bordered by lovely (sometimes lavish) homes, almost all with at least one boat docked out front. Despite its air of leisure and tropical beauty, Fort Lauderdale is also a busy commercial center for marine supplies and citrus products. **Port Everglades**, a deep-water harbor just two miles south, adds both luxury liners and cargo transports to the water traffic.

Incidentally, if you're here during Easter or Christmas vacation periods, you may want to skip this junket—as many as 40,000 college students annually descend on the city then, causing massive traffic jams and disrupting the normally placid tone of life here. On the other hand, their lively hijinks on the beach create a carnival atmosphere that can be fun.

A relaxing way to see the town is via the **Voyager Sightseeing Train,** 600 Seabreeze Ave. at A1A (tel. 463-0401 or 467-3149), that leaves from the Bahia-Mar Yacht Basin for 90-minute narrated tours of old and new Fort Lauderdale every day at 10 a.m., noon, 2, and 4 p.m. Fares are $3.95 for adults, $1.75 for ages 3 through 12. On Tuesday, Thursday, and Saturday, there are also 3½-hour **Safari Tours** (same address and phone) that include a visit to Flamingo Orange Grove and the Kapok Tree ($6.95 for adults, $3.50 for 3- to 12-year-olds).

Where to Eat in Fort Lauderdale

It's worth making your sightseeing trip to Fort Lauderdale an afternoon one just to stay for dinner at the **Mai-Kai,** 3599 N. Federal Hwy (tel. 563-3272), a long-time favorite in this area, which is about as authentically Polynesian as you can get this side of the Pacific. Owner Bob Thornton has run the restaurant complex for more than 26 years with the assistance of his wife, who was born in Tahiti. Under her guidance, they have created what is very nearly a native village, with landscaped gardens set about with carvings and artifacts brought from the South Pacific. The extensive menu has been carefully developed to offer such dishes as Peking duck, Chinese steamed trout, and a delicious chicken curry. One of the things which makes the Mai-Kai special, however, is the nightly entertainment—native dancers are brought over regularly to perform authentic dances which illustrate ancient legends and rituals. It's a first-rate show in its own right, but an education in Polynesian lore, as well. There are two shows nightly: one for the early dinner (5 to 6:30 p.m., with a price range of $9 to $19), and one for the later seating at 7 to 8:30 p.m. (with prices of $11 to $23). You don't have to dine in the show room—there are lovely, smaller rooms that are quieter and more intimate (and it is only in those rooms that the elaborate specials listed above may be ordered), and if you order from the lighter menu in the Molokai Lounge, there's a second-drink-free policy during the early dinner hours. All in all, the Mai-Kai is a treat not to be missed and could provide one of the most memorable evenings of your Florida holiday. Best reserve.

Harrison's On The Water, 3000 NE 32nd Ave. (tel. 566-9667), is right on the water's edge, with marvelous sunset views and docking for those who arrive by boat. There's an outside deck for drinks, and inside the atmosphere is clubby, with red leather booths and chair coverings, dark wood, brass accents, and a decidedly sportsman's atmosphere. That isn't really surprising when you learn that owner George Harrison is an avid golfer and sports fan and that the restaurant's patrons over the years have included Arnold Palmer, Joe Namath, Whitey Ford, Mickey Mantle, and other sports figures. The menu here is seafood oriented, with scampi a specialty, but equally good are the steaks, Canadian baby back ribs, and baked short ribs of beef. Lunch hours are 11:30 a.m. to 3:30 p.m., dinner from 5:30 p.m. to midnight, and reservations are very much in order at this popular spot.

JAPANESE TEAHOUSE AND GARDEN: On **Watson Island,** just east of U.S. 1 on MacArthur Causeway, the Japanese Teahouse and Garden is a memorial to a Tokyo industrialist's admiration for Miami and Miami Beach. When he visited here some years ago, he was so impressed with the place that he started sending gifts back to the city—first several hundred wild orchids, an eight-ton statue of the Japanese god of good fortune, Hotei, an ancient stone lantern, and finally a ceremonial teahouse which was built in Japan, then taken apart and shipped to Miami. Japanese carpenters came with the pieces to see that they were put back together properly. Like "Little Havana," it's like a visit to another country, and it doesn't cost a cent. Open from 9 a.m. to 6 p.m. every day.

VIZCAYA: In 1914, James Deering, the International Harvester tycoon, began construction on what turned out to be a Renaissance palace to hold artworks he'd been collecting abroad for 20 years or more. He named it the Villa Vizcaya, 3251 S. Miami Ave., just off U.S. 1; you can't miss it, signs are prominently posted for several miles, and it's estimated to have cost Deering some $10 million by the time the 70 rooms and elaborate gardens were completed. Small wonder, for he kept more than 1000 craftsmen working for five years, and architects were given ample time to plan rooms around some of his treasures. The formal gardens, with seven separate areas, fountains, statuary, and reflecting pools, cover some 10 acres, and there are another 20 acres of unspoiled "jungle." Inside the mansion, there are splendid frescoed ceilings, a tapestry that belonged to Robert Browning when he lived in Italy, and priceless antiques and paintings in every room. Offshore (from the steps leading down to the bay), a stone version of Cleopatra's barge serves as a breakwater. The estate is open every day except Christmas from 9:30 a.m. to 5 p.m. (last tickets sold 4:30 p.m.), admission is $5 for adults and $3.50 for ages six to 11. You can see just the gardens for $3.50.

MUSEUM OF SCIENCE AND SPACE TRANSIT PLANETARIUM:
Right across the street from Vizcaya is the Museum of Science and the Space Transit Planetarium, 3280 S. Miami Ave. (tel. 854-4242), with free parking and picnic tables on the grounds. The museum is completely refurbished in the exciting mode of the Exploratorium in San Francisco, with over 80 hands-on exhibits in the fields of energy, sound, light, chemistry, biology, physics, and optics, as well as fascinating displays of unusual natural history dioramas of the Everglades and coral reefs, including slides and movies. Also included in the $1.50 and $1 admission price is the Animal Exploratorium where you can tickle tarantulas, hug boas, and handle salt-water animals in their small tanks. Upstairs, the Southern Cross Observatory allows a close look at the heavens on weekend evenings. The Space Transit Planetarium has hourly shows from noon until 8 p.m., with programs in Spanish on Saturday and Sunday at 5:30 p.m. Admission is $3 for adults and $1.50 for children ages 2 to 12.

MIAMI WAX MUSEUM: More than 40 dioramas with lifelike wax figures ranging from Columbus to the astronauts are explained by continuous recorded tours at the Miami Wax Museum, 13899 Biscayne Blvd., at NE 139th St., Miami (tel. 945-3641). They are beautifully done and make this country's history come vividly alive. Well worth the $4 charge for adults ($2 for ages six through 14). Hours are 9:30 a.m. to 9:30 p.m. Monday through Saturday, 10:30 a.m. to 9:30 p.m. on Sunday.

PARROT JUNGLE: The Parrot Jungle, 11000 SW 57th Ave., 11 miles southwest of Miami at the junction of Red Road, which is also SW 57th Ave., and Killian Drive, which is SW 112th St. (tel. 666-7834), is nothing less than paradise for bird lovers. Macaws and rainbow-colored exotic birds fly free; more than 100 flamingos, cranes, and swans cluster around a lake; and chatty mynah birds keep up a steady stream of conversation. For a few cents in a vending machine, you can buy birdseed and perhaps coax one onto your shoulder for a memorable snapshot. There's a 45-minute open-air show in which birds ride tiny bicycles, roller skate, drive a car, and do simple arithmetic tricks. Adults pay $6; ages six to 12, $3.

SERPENTARIUM: If you're into snakes (ugh!) or interested from a strictly scientific point of view, a short drive south from Parrot Jungle will bring you to the Serpentarium, 12655 S. Dixie Hwy., that's U.S. 1 South (tel. 235-5722). Here a snake will educate you in the ways of reptiles, and you'll see the extraction of deadly venom from a live snake to be used by the medical profession. Owner Bill Haast, a world-renowned authority on snakes who has survived more than 140 snakebites, is usually on hand and frequently mingles with

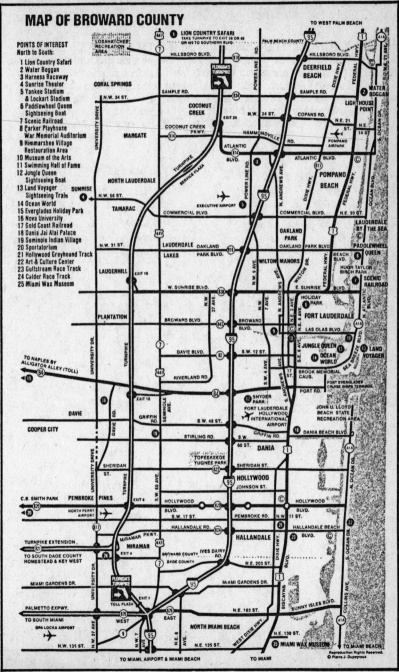

MAP OF BROWARD COUNTY

POINTS OF INTEREST
North to South:

1 Lion Country Safari
2 Water Boggan
3 Harness Raceway
4 Sunrise Theater
5 Yankee Stadium
  & Lockart Stadium
6 Paddlewheel Queen
  Sightseeing Boat
7 Scenic Railroad
8 Parker Playhouse
  War Memorial Auditorium
9 Himmarshee Village
  Restauration Area
10 Museum of the Arts
11 Swimming Hall of Fame
12 Jungle Queen
  Sightseeing Boat
13 Land Voyager
  Sightseeing Train
14 Ocean World
15 Everglades Holiday Park
16 Nova University
17 Gold Coast Railroad
18 Dania Jai Alai Palace
19 Seminole Indian Village
20 Sportatorium
21 Hollywood Greyhound Track
22 Art & Culture Center
23 Gulfstream Race Track
24 Calder Race Track
25 Miami Wax Museum

visitors. Hours are 9 a.m. to 5 p.m., with a $6 admission for adults, $2 for ages six to 13; free for under sixes.

MONKEY JUNGLE: Still farther south, off U.S. 1 at 14805 SW 216th St. (tel. 235-1611), the monkeys at Monkey Jungle must get a big kick out of running free while the humans are caged! In a re-created Amazon rain forest, you'll see foliage from South America and strange-looking monkeys. King and Mitzi, two charming gorillas, live here, and there are shows every hour with monkeys riding toy cars and performing other tricks. It's open from 9:30 a.m. to 5 p.m. every day, and admission is $5 for adults, $2.50 for ages five through 12.

Chapter XVII

THE FLORIDA KEYS AND THE EVERGLADES

1. From Key Largo to Key West
2. Key West
3. The Everglades

THE SOUTHERN END OF FLORIDA is exclusively devoted to nature —wild and unspoiled in the Everglades National Park, civilized and exploited to the hilt by mankind along the Keys. Perhaps "exploited" is not the right word, for although all the natural treasures of that string of 45 islands reaching 100 miles out to sea southwest of the continental United States are utilized for sea-oriented occupations or leisure pursuits, a slowed-down, no-hassle outlook so pervades the Keys that commercialism loses its sharp edge and seems more like convenience than exploitation.

At any rate, Mother Nature outdoes herself from Miami south to Key West and due west across the Everglades to where the state's west coast curves north along the Gulf of Mexico.

1. From Key Largo to Key West

Before you set out on the Overseas Highway (that's U.S. 1, which runs the length of the East Coast from Fort Kent, Maine, to Key West), you should know that almost any kind of vacation amusement you're looking for will be

THE FLORIDA KEYS

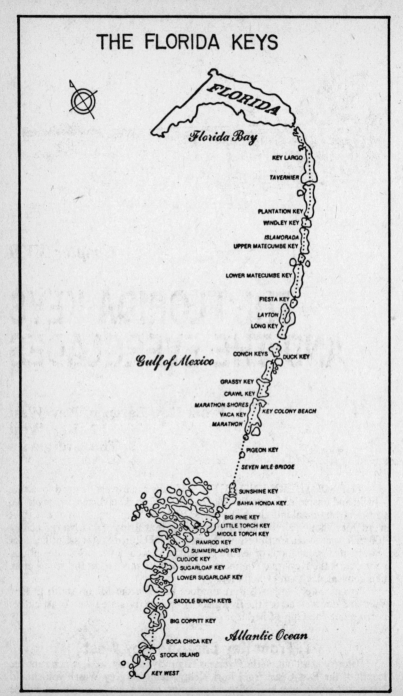

FLORIDA

Florida Bay

KEY LARGO

TAVERNIER

PLANTATION KEY
WINDLEY KEY

ISLAMORADA
UPPER MATECUMBE KEY

LOWER MATECUMBE KEY

FIESTA KEY

LAYTON
LONG KEY

CONCH KEYS
DUCK KEY

Gulf of Mexico

GRASSY KEY
CRAWL KEY
MARATHON SHORES
VACA KEY   KEY COLONY BEACH
MARATHON

PIGEON KEY

SEVEN MILE BRIDGE

SUNSHINE KEY
BAHIA HONDA KEY

BIG PINE KEY
LITTLE TORCH KEY
MIDDLE TORCH KEY
RAMROD KEY
SUMMERLAND KEY
CUDJOE KEY
SUGARLOAF KEY
LOWER SUGARLOAF KEY

SADDLE BUNCH KEYS

BIG COPPITT KEY

BOCA CHICA KEY   Atlantic Ocean

STOCK ISLAND

KEY WEST

somewhere along that drive. Sportsmen will find all the water sports, of course (there are over 600 varieties of fish in these waters, a living coral reef, and underwater shipwrecks to be explored by divers, and pleasure boats for hire), as well as golf, tennis, and horseback riding. For solitude-seekers, there are secluded fishing camps and quiet motels on the smaller keys (with more than 150 motels and some 5000 rooms from which to choose, you can find the right one). For livelier sorts, there are lounges with nightly entertainment and 130 restaurants for eating that can border on the exciting. Sightseers will find performing sea mammals, a state park full of natural wonders, and cruise boats (some with glass bottoms to reveal the reef). It is, if you drive straight through, only a 3½-hour drive, but you'll be missing too much if you do it that way— plan at least half a day; or even better, spend the entire day ambling over the 42 bridges that connect the Florida Keys. Incidentally, 37 of those bridges have been widened, making the drive much easier.

It hasn't always been so easy to reach the Keys. Until 1912, in fact, they lay in tropical, mosquito- and roach-infested isolation (a local legend says that before the advent of radio communication, natives could tell a storm was brewing when the roaches got restless). But then Henry M. Flagler ran his Florida East Coast Railroad all the way to Key West, with a ferry train going on to Havana, and the outside world poured in. After a killer hurricane left the railroad in shambles in 1935, the U.S. government took over the right-of-way and opened up the Overseas Highway in 1938. The mainland connection, however, failed to disturb the West Indies island atmosphere of the Keys, an asset that is probably responsible for most of that large influx of visitors. A trip to the Keys is something like a visit to the Bahamas; and for the best orientation before you "set out to sea in your car," stop by the **Florida Keys Information Center** at the Florida City exit of the Sunshine State Parkway (you'll see it no matter which approach to Key Largo you use).

As you head south on U.S. 1, the easternmost fringes of the Everglades National Park will be on your right, and on both sides of the road are vast vistas of red mangrove, that hardy plant whose twisted roots build up land surfaces and provide a natural shelter for native birds and fish. **Jewfish Creek Bridge** is the first of the 42 you'll cross (those huge mounds of branches on top of power poles are osprey nests, added on to each year by the industrious birds). The 18-inch aluminum pipeline on your left is something of an engineering marvel and a true "lifeline," for it carries fresh drinking water from the mainland to Key West—it is above ground (or water) most of the way.

Key Largo, where buccaneers once put in to fill their water casks, is the first key (key means a low island or coral reef, by the way), and the 21-mile-long, 3½-mile-wide John Pennekamp Coral Reef State Park is here. The only continental underseas park in the country, it was named for an associate editor of the *Miami Herald* who was largely responsible for preserving both this stretch of coast and the Everglades. Divers have a field day exploring the living coral reef, and less venturesome souls can view it by glass-bottomed boat. Key Largo also has a plentiful supply of rental boats and guides for bone fishing, as well as a concentration of air-conditioned, full-service motels and a huge shopping plaza.

You'll notice the milepost markers all along the Overseas Highway: they keep you informed of the mileage from each one to Key West. At MP (milepost) 87, on **Plantation Key,** you'll see the Museum of Sunken Treasure, with relics from shipwrecks in these treacherous waters ranging from Spanish galleons to World War II tankers, wrecks that have been recorded as far back as 1733. Farther south, at MP 84, only a few minutes from **Islamorada,** is the Theatre of the Sea, where you can pet a shark, shake hands with a porpoise, or just watch them go through their acts. Islamorada means "purple isle" in Spanish, and the name was given this key when a Spanish explorer saw mounds of the violet Janthina sea snails on its shores. The town by that name is the third largest in the Keys, and there are good motels, restaurants, and shops here, as well as a memorial monument to those who perished in the 1935 hurricane. On **Long Key,** between MP 69 and 68, the town of **Layton** was a favorite haunt of Zane Grey, the writer of Old West stories, and one of the town's waterways is named for him. Flipper's Sea School, where continuous shows are put on by playful sea mammals, is between MP 60 and 57 on **Grassy Key,** and when you reach MP 56 you'll be in the very heart of the Keys, where the towns of **Key Colony Beach, Marathon Shores,** and **Marathon** have a total population of 8000, the second largest in the islands. At MP 54, there's an interesting stretch of specialty shops, a seafood restaurant, and the Aqua Dome Aquarium (a floating barge with a geodesic dome) on your right, a picturesque, relaxing stopping point. Marathon's municipal airport has scheduled daily flights both south to Key West and north to Miami, Tampa, and Kissimmee (Disney World territory) and charter service to wherever you want to fly. If you plan to spend a few days on the Keys before going on to Key West, Marathon is a good location, since it's midway.

Leaving Marathon, you begin the most famous stretch of the Overseas Highway, the **Seven Mile Bridge** (which is really two-tenths of a mile shorter than seven miles). It's a spectacular drive, with the green waters of the Atlantic and blue Gulf of Mexico coming together directly under your car! Beyond **Sunshine Key,** the southern exit of the Seven Mile Bridge, there's a state park on **Bahia Honda Key** and a still-standing remnant of Flagler's railroad. Next comes **Big Pine Key,** second in size only to Key Largo and the only one on which you'll find Caribbean pines and tiny white-tail key deer (only 38 inches from stem to stern and 26 to 32 inches high), which are so shy they're seldom seen, except in the very early morning or at dusk. Those small islands scattered between MP 16 and 11 are the **Saddlebunch Keys,** many of them unnamed, and a naval air station is on **Boca Chica,** between MP 8 and 6. **Stock Island,** at MP 5, is now a part of the municipality of Key West, and this is where the all-important water desalination plant converts sea water to fresh. Shrimp boats dock here, too, and sometimes luxury yachts as long as 100 feet can be seen moored at the docks. We'll take in all these sights one by one, but first let's find some shelter for the night.

WHERE TO STAY: At MP 82, the Cheeca Lodge, P.O. Box 527, Islamorada, FL 33036 (tel. 305/664-4651 or toll free 800/327-2888), is probably best known as a sportsmen's spot, with emphasis on the excellent fishing. But for dedicated beachcombers like me, it has an appeal hard to equal. Built by A&P millionaires as an exclusive fishing club, the lodge sits right on the edge of the Atlantic, and is approached through landscaped grounds that serve as a buffer from highway noise—you enter another world when you turn into its gates. The main lodge looks serenely out over the water, with a pretty, glassed-in dining room for superbly prepared meals and guest rooms beautifully furnished and designed for the ultimate in comfort. Those on the top floor have balconies. In addition to the lodge, there are "villas," or individual cottages, which may be had with just bedroom and screened porch or with a studio/kitchenette and Bahama beds. There's an executive golf course, four tennis courts, a swimming pool, and a 525-foot fishing pier (they'll cook your catch for your dinner) for more active types. For me, it's quite enough to savor the peace and relaxation at the Cheeca, strolling along the water's edge or perhaps keeping an eye on

Frank, the resident pelican who presides over the fishing pier. The staff, from manager to bell captain, is both friendly and efficient, creating a sort of small-town atmosphere. Double occupancy rates for lodge rooms run from $135 to $150, depending on whether you have an ocean or pool view (the penthouse goes for $155), and villas facing the ocean are $165, others, $155.

The **Key Colony Beach Motel,** Ocean Drive, Marathon Shores (tel. 305/289-0411), is on the northern end of **Marathon Key.** To reach it, turn off U.S. 1 toward the Atlantic Ocean at the blinking light north of Marathon, drive to the end of the main road leading through Key Colony Beach, then turn right—the pretty blue and white motel is just a short half-block down Ocean Drive. The attractive bedrooms, furnished in modern style with cool, clear resort colors, have couches that open to sleep two, a refrigerator, and an oceanfront location or an ocean view. A private white sand ocean beach, a freshwater heated pool, a fishing pier, boat and scuba-diving equipment rentals, and an excellent restaurant and lounge (with entertainment) are all within easy walking distance. Golf is also available in the area. Winter rates start at $49, summer rates are lower. Southeast Airways has daily flights from Marathon to both Miami and Key West, and there is an 8000-foot runway for private planes (the motel offers courtesy-car pickup at both public and private airports).

Campgrounds

Nine miles south of Marathon (on U.S. 1, of course), the **Sunshine Key Campground** has almost 400 sites with full hookups, LP gas service, flush toilets, a laundry, store, snackbar, recreation hall, shuffleboard, tennis, swimming, boating, and fishing. Rates are $17 and up (with monthly rates available), depending on location. For reservations, write Rt. 1, Box 790, Sunshine Key, FL 33043 (tel. 305/872-2217).

The **Pelican Campground,** Fla. 1, Box 528, Marathon, FL 33050, is six miles north of Marathon on U.S. 1 and is open all year. There are full hookups, LP gas service, flush toilets, a laundry, store, shuffleboard, swimming pool, boating, and fishing, at rates that start at $12.

On Big Pine Key, the **Sea Horse Campground,** Box 516, Big Pine Key, FL 33043, has 113 sites (most with full hookups), a dump, flush toilets, laundry, a recreation hall, shuffleboard, swimming, boating, and fishing. Rates start at $10.

WHERE TO EAT: The seafood's great from Key Largo to Key West, and no matter where you stop to eat on the drive down, you're likely to spot a place farther along that you'll be sorry you missed.

But before listing some of the better known spots, let me tell you about **Herbie's,** at MP 51 in Marathon. It is a real "island" sort of place and has become perhaps my own favorite stopping point on any drive along the Keys.

A low, one-story, green-and-white building set back from the highway, it is easy to bypass, but keep an eye out for the tall sign announcing Herbie's Seafood, and you'll be in for a real treat. It's been here since the '40s (was known for years as Maggie's Chowder House) and serves some of the freshest seafood (they get two fresh deliveries a day) you'll find hereabouts at low, low prices and in an atmosphere that's almost convivial. The conch fritters are without doubt the best on the Keys, and there's a full selection of chowders, fish (on plates or sandwiches), and for non-seafood lovers, burgers and chili. The raw bar opens at 2 p.m. Prices are in the low range of $1.25 to $2.75! Best of all, you'll eat with locals in either the screened-in, porch-style bar area or in a slightly larger dining area entered by an oldtime screened door. Hours are 11 a.m. to 10 p.m. Week days, 11:30 a.m. to 10 p.m. on Saturday, and it's closed on Sunday.

Another good place to stop is **Peg Leg's Restaurant** at the Mariner Resort on Big Pine Key. To get there, turn right at MP 31 (driving south) and drive to where the road dead-ends at the Mariner. Peg Leg's is right on the water, in a sprawling wooden building with a decided South Seas look. All walls are lined with windows that look out over the water, ceilings are beamed, and there's lots of brass and tropical furniture and lovely antique pieces. Dining is outside on a covered porch as well as inside, and, as co-owner Joann Kump explained to me, they firmly believe in "fresh" when it comes to food. In fact, they have their own fishing boats to ensure freshness of the seafood they prepare so well. For a sampling, try Peg Leg's seafood platter: it includes shrimp, scallops, crab cake, and half a stuffed local lobster, with a salad, baked potato or Cuban black beans and yellow rice, plus freshly baked bread. There are beef dishes, as well, and a children's menu. Or, if you simply can't choose from the menu, opt for the hot buffet, where you'll find shrimp and fish dishes, roast beef, an amazing array of freshly made salads, every dressing you've ever heard of, and other nightly specials. The buffet is $10.95, a real culinary buy. On Sunday, there's a brunch from 11 a.m. to 3 p.m., served buffet style, that features all those salads, plus pastries of every description, rolls, eggs, hash brown potatoes, sausage, bacon, green beans, blintzes, quiches, and roast beef. The Sunday I dropped in, one of their more affluent diners was arriving by private helicopter, which set down on the lawn outside at the water's edge—one look at the buffet, and I understood why! Peg Leg's serves from 11 a.m. to 10 p.m. with prices ranging from $8.95 to $22.95, except for nightly specials, which can be as low as $5.95 (call 872-2222 or 872-2850 for reservations).

At the Islamorada Yacht Basin (look for the large mermaid signboard), the **Lorelei Restaurant** (664-4657) is built out on the dock, and its decor is a faithful reproduction of early Keys furnishings, with Bahama fans, turn-of-the-century, hand-blown crystal light fixtures, rustic furniture, and trellis-supported greenery used as partitions between tables. Seafood is the specialty here, and a real treat is the Shrimp Lor-e-lie (sauteed in butter with a touch of garlic, mushrooms, and imported cheese, broiled to utter perfection) at $14.95. Even if you come for lunch, it's worth a return evening trip here just to watch the spectacular sunset from such a lovely spot. And if you're a dessert lover, the Key lime pie is so good here that one lady offered to trade her yacht for the recipe! Open daily from 11 a.m. to 2:30 p.m. and 5:30 to 10:30 p.m.

With a more rustic dockside atmosphere, the **Castaway** is at the foot of 15th St. in Marathon. You'll have to look for this one—it's at the water's edge in the heart of a little fishing community, and you'll see its name on a highway sign (on your left driving south) that lists six other establishments. Turn left and go to the end of 15th St., then turn right and you'll see the blue and white Castaway (tel. 743-6247) dead ahead. It's been famous in the area for over 30 years for shrimp steamed in beer, and since the original owner retired Frank Hosek has kept things just as they've always been. You can eat inside in a small, plain room with fishing nets on the walls and red-checked tablecloths, or outside right over the water. The famed specialty comes with french fries and cole slaw; seconds are on the house. There's a whole menu of other seafood dishes, all at moderate prices, and beer and wine are both available.

Up on Islamorada, a fish eater's paradise stretches for about an eighth of a mile, where some six or more excellent restaurants line U.S. 1: **Marker 88, The Chesapeake, The Plantation Yacht Harbor, Ziggies, The Coral Grill, Sid and Roxie's Green Turtle Inn,** and probably another one or two by the time you read this. All have fairly moderate prices, all serve food so fresh you can taste the sea, and none will be a disappointment. So if this is where you are when it's time to eat, close your eyes and pick one.

READERS' DINING SELECTIONS: "The best moderate-priced seafood buffet anywhere is the **Coral Grill**, at Islamorada. It is served 4:30 to 10 p.m. weekdays and noon to 3 p.m. on Sunday. Check it out in the upstairs dining room" (M. Ozer, Philadelphia, Penna.).

A reader wrote in about **Mac's Bar-B-Que**, Box 120-D, Rt. 1, Key Largo, FL (tel. 451-9954), to say that, "it doesn't look like much on the outside, but what food!" Well, it certainly is unpretentious from the outside, and he most certainly is right about the food you'll find inside. Between MP 101 and 102, Mac McGilvary has been dishing up what he calls "Alabama-style" barbecue for the past 20 years, and it has become a favorite of locals, as well as travelers. The tangy, spicy-sweet barbecue comes in the form of pork or beef, ribs, and chicken, and you can have full plates (complete with salad, potato, and garlic bread) or sandwiches. Mac also offers good local seafood and desserts which feature homemade key lime pie. Prices range from $1.50 to $8, and he's open from 11 a.m. to 9 p.m. every day except Wednesday. Beer and wine.

THINGS TO SEE AND DO: First of all, let me say that with all that water, the Keys are not true beach country. There is good swimming at state parks and a few campsites where sand has been pumped up to create beaches, but in general, the water is shallow, without much surf, and even wading isn't such a good idea because of sharp coral rock underwater. So swimmers should probably stick to the more than 120 pools at motels and recreation areas.

The Keys *are*, however, a fisherman's dream come true, and there's never a charter boat far away for deep-sea fishing or smaller rental boats for close-in waters. Divers, also, will find diving shops all along the Keys, many with scheduled boat trips and instructors with maps of particularly interesting diving sites.

The **John Pennekamp Coral Reef State Park** is on the east coast (well, *off* the coast, actually, since it's underwater) of Key Largo and has a fantastic, brilliantly colored array of marine and plant life. Facilities include a Visitors Center, picnic sites, swimming and wading areas, fishing, a marina, boat rentals and launching ramps, a snackbar, and nature trails. But the highlight of a stop here has to be either diving (and many visitors try their hand at underwater photography) or viewing the vivid coral from glass-bottom boats. The 2½-hour boat trip costs $6.50 for adults, half that for ages three through 12, and they leave at 9 a.m., noon, and 3 p.m. There are guides to accompany divers (for reservations and rates, call 451-1621). The park is open from 8 a.m. to sunset, and there's a 50¢-per-person admission charge.

At Islamorada, the **Theater of the Sea** (it's 1½ miles north of town at MP 84) has continuous marine-life performances, with sharks, huge sea turtles, stingrays, jewfish, tarpon, sea lions, and five dolphins. Each 90-minute show costs $5.50 for adults, $3.25 for ages five to 12. Hours are 9 a.m. to 4 p.m.

2. Key West

Key West has been robbed of its major industry three times so far: a lighthouse and an active U.S. Coast Guard did away with the lucrative "wrecker" trade that made Key West the richest community per capita in the country; a thriving cigar-making population was lured to Tampa after a disastrous fire destroyed many of the Key West cottages and factories; and Greek sponge divers arrived, stayed just long enough to put Key West divers out of business with their newer, faster method of collecting sponges, then moved on to Tarpon Springs, taking the sponge business with them. Yet, hardy, not-to-be-defeated

Key Westers have pulled themselves up by the bootstraps once again and today the tourist business is booming so well that it would be no real surprise to see that "richest community" tag someday reappear.

"Individualistic" is the one word that applies to almost every phase of Key West life—it has a positive talent for taking bits and pieces of architecture, culture, business enterprise, and personality from any source that comes along, putting them together, and coming up with something that is uniquely Key West. "Conchs" (it's pronounced "konk" and means a native-born; you're a "freshwater Conch" if you move here and stay for seven years, but you have to be *born* in Key West to drop the "freshwater") have a genealogical background that might be English, Bahamian, Cuban, New England, or U.S. southern—or an interesting combination of several of these. They live and work in buildings that might have been brought over from the Bahamas board by board and reassembled, constructed in the Cuban style by the cigar makers, put together by skilled ship's carpenters, or all three. And what comes out of all this many-ingredient blend is a highly individualistic, survival-oriented Key West personality—realistic yet lighthearted, canny in business dealings yet open-handed with all visitors.

The five-mile long, three-mile-wide island of Key West was discovered by Spanish explorers in the 16th century and named Cayo Hueso, which means "bone island," corrupted over the years to its present name. Its first owner, a Spanish cavalry officer, sold the island in 1821 to John Simonton, an Alabama merchant. After Commodore David Porter rid the area of pirates (by using shallow-draft barges to chase the blackguards into the shallow key coastal waters), a U.S. naval base was established in 1823, and in 1828, Key West incorporated to become a bona fide town. Spongers and fishermen came from the Bahamas, and by 1850 the sponge industry employed 180 ships and did a $750,000 annual trade. But they used long poles to spear sponges from the boat after spotting them through glass-bottomed buckets and refused to adopt the "walk along the bottom" techniques of Greek newcomers, which ultimately brought about their downfall. Salvagers of shipwrecks (which they did nothing to prevent and were accused of encouraging) made fantastic fortunes. There is even one story of a "wrecker" who brought a coffin, complete with corpse, ashore from a wreck, then ransomed it to the grieving family, much to the glee of his fellow Conchs. Then the reefs were marked by lighthouses and that bonanza from the sea disappeared.

Cuban cigar makers, fleeing Spanish rule in their homeland, came over in 1868 and were soon producing as many as 100 million cigars a year. Then fire struck and the Tampa city fathers offered them the world on a silver platter if they'd bring the industry there, which they did. During the Civil War, although there was a substantial Rebel population, the Union managed to hold the port all through the war. Henry Flagler gave the city a new lease on life, the Depression and 1935 hurricane took it away again, and it remained for the freshwater pipeline from the mainland and World War II (which made it a major antisubmarine and training base) to get things going again. Key West now looks to its tourist trade for not only a lasting prosperity this time, but an ever-growing one, and it will go to almost any length to develop it (there was a time when a city administrator ordered all men to wear shorts in order to look "quaint" for the tourists—needless to say, that didn't last long).

GETTING YOUR BEARINGS: The best way to get an overall look at all this rich background is to take the **Conch Tour Train** or Old Town Trolley (see "Tours") 1½-hour trip around the town, with commentary on more than 60 points of interest and how they figure into Key West's checkered history. After that, walking or bike riding (or a moped, if you prefer) is the best means of transportation; some streets are narrow and winding, and driving can be difficult if you don't know your way around.

There are also first-rate city buses on all the main Key West streets that will get you back and forth. You'll recognize them by the legend "Guagua de Cayo Hueso" on their sides—don't worry about how to say it, everybody in Key West calls them the "Wah-Wah," which is more or less how *guagua* sounds.

You might start at **Mallory Square** (it used to be headquarters for the Mallory Steamship Company), with the now-abandoned naval station on one side and the site of that Havana railroad ferry depot on the other. This is where Key Westers and visitors congregate each day to view what has got to be the most gorgeous sunset in the Western Hemisphere and to give a healthy cheer when the sun quite suddenly drops below the horizon. It's also a gathering place for all sorts of street musicians and craftspeople, giving it a carnival air at the end of the day. Facing the water is a cluster of small shops, restaurants, and bars; if you decide to begin looking around Key West here, be sure to allow enough time, it's the best loitering area in town! The **Chamber of Commerce** is on the square, too, with plenty of maps, brochures, and a friendly staff.

However you get around, you can pretty well find the historical points by following **Pelican Path,** a well-marked, carefully planned route through Old Town (we'll head there ourselves later). Incidentally, a big part of Key West's renewed prosperity is due to the foresight back in 1960 of native son Mitchell Wolfson, who bought up the stately old home in which James J. Audubon was a guest when he made his famous folio of birds in this area, then restored it and opened it to the public as the Audubon House. Never slow to recognize a good thing, other Conchs got together to begin a restoration that literally changed the face of the older part of Key West, which was seedy, to say the least. As a result, you can now wander through such landmarks as the Oldest House (built in 1828), Ernest Hemingway's Key West home (he lived here from 1931 to 1961, loved the town because "people don't stare at me here," and here wrote such classics as *To Have and Have Not, Snows of Kilimanjaro,* and *For Whom the Bell Tolls*), the East and West Martello Forts, and some of the most charming little shops you'll find anywhere in restored old buildings along Duval Street (look for **Pirate's Alley** in a pint-sized cul-de-sac with a fountain —it's special).

The other end of Key West is another story. This is modern Key West, separated from the Old Town, as one native told me, "by about three miles and 150 years." Many of the larger motels are here, and shopping centers are very much like those you'd expect to see almost anywhere.

WHERE TO STAY: If you bring the children, chances are you'll prefer to stay on the north end of the key—it's quieter there and motels have more family-geared facilities. If, on the other hand, strolling through Old Town at all hours and participating in the swinging (and sometimes noisy) nightlife is what you have in mind, there are hotels and motels galore clustered at the southern end of town.

Along the Northern Rim

The **Best Western Key Ambassador**, 1000 S. Roosevelt Blvd., Key West, FL 33040 (tel. 305/296-3500 or toll-free 800/528-1234), has been owned by the same family since it opened back in 1952. Since then, it has grown into a complex of buildings housing more than 100 guest rooms with classifications of deluxe, moderate, and standard. Those deluxe rooms are equipped with a king-size bed, queen-size sleeping sofa, and a refrigerator. Others come with two double beds, or with one double and one twin or with one king-size. All are nicely furnished, and all have private balconies, almost all screened. A nice touch here is the complimentary continental breakfast served in a bright breakfast room on the premises. There's also free coffee in the lobby 24 hours a day, and on Friday and Saturday, there's an outdoor barbecue for guests. You can have a light lunch out by the heated swimming pool at the Cheekie Hut, and picnic in facilities right on the grounds. The staff, most with long years of service here, are exceptionally friendly and concerned for your comfort and helpful in assisting your sightseeing (also, the Old Town Trolley makes a stop here, a great convenience). Rates are seasonal, ranging from $50 to $118, and senior citizens receive a 10% discount in low season (April 1 to December 20).

The **Holiday Inn**, 1111 N. Roosevelt Blvd. (tel. 305/294-2571), is an especially handsome member of this chain, in a landscaped setting. There's a large pool, playground, and a private beach on the gulf. Tennis courts are well maintained. The restaurant serves all three meals, and there's a cocktail lounge as well. They will pick up and deliver to the airport if you wish to fly in. Rates are seasonal—beginning at $65 for a double in December and dropping after April.

The **Day's Inn Motel**, 3852 N. Roosevelt Blvd. (tel. 305/294-3742), has 18 suites and 116 rooms, all with modern furnishings and color TV, in a pretty, landscaped setting. There's a pool and children's playground. Transportation is provided to and from the airport. Rates start at $40.88, in the summer, $57.88 in winter. There's also a family priced restaurant and 24-hour gasoline service.

At the Southern Tip of the Island

Back in 1921, the Flagler organization (of railroad fame hereabouts) opened the doors of a grand, 200-room, Spanish Renaissance-style hotel on the triangular property at the foot of Reynolds Street, with more than 1100 feet of prime beachfront, and named it the Casa Marina. It very quickly became the winter playground of wealthy Northerners like the Astors, actors (including Gregory Peck), poets Robert Frost and Wallace Stevens, bandleader Guy Lombardo, and a host of other celebrities. With the demise of the railroad after that disastrous hurricane, the hotel fell on lean times, and over the years has seen service as an officers' club for the army during World War II, a training center for the Peace Corps, and a military command post during the missile crisis at nearby Cuba. Then, in 1962 its doors closed and the once-elegant hotel quietly went to seed. In 1978, the Marriott chain purchased the still-solid building and has poured nearly $10 million into a restoration and renovation that makes **Marriott's Casa Marina Resort**, 1500 Reynolds St., Key West, FL 33040 (tel. 305/296-3535), once more a real showplace.

Determined to keep the building's exterior essentially the same as it was in Flagler's day, Marriott retained the red tile roof and high arched windows of the lobby. Nor did they destroy the massive wooden staircase that circles up from the lobby to the third floor. That lobby sets the tone for the grandeur of the rest of the hotel, and magnificent wooden columns and beams frame some pretty impressive artifacts and furnishings dating back to the '20s and '30s. The Key West Historical Society has recognized the excellence of the restoration with an award. Landscaping on the grounds is so impressive, it has won two awards. And an interesting note on the restoration is the network of cisterns discovered beneath the building which were used to catch rainwater which fed into them from spouts on the roof. Although water is not a problem now, Marriott has opened up the cisterns and plans to use them to store rainwater to be used in landscaping.

All 251 rooms (some in a new wing) are quite large and furnished with wicker and rattan accented by bright tropical colors. There's a freeform, heated, freshwater pool (with a delightful open-air bar and barbecue stand), a 20-foot Jacuzzi, a fishing and boating pier, lighted tennis courts, a game room, exercise room, an elegant restaurant (Henry's) with elegant food and service, and the Calabash Lounge, with top-quality show-band entertainment (much patronized by natives as well as by visitors). A final comment: While the Casa Marina *is* elegant, it is anything but pretentious, and you'll find the same relaxed, laid-back atmosphere that prevails in the rest of Key West. Seasonal rates range from $110 to $185 for doubles in winter, less during summer months.

Over on South Beach (the Atlantic side), the pretty **Santa Maria Motel,** 1401 Simonton St. (tel. 305/296-5678), has rooms, efficiencies, and suites. Furnishings are modern and comfortable. In addition to the pool, there are beach facilities only a few steps away. The West Indies Lounge is lively, with frequent entertainment, and there's a good restaurant. They'll pick up from the airport. Doubles run $55 and up in winter, but drop other months.

On a quiet residential street, just two blocks from the beach and tennis courts, **El Patio Motel & Apartments,** 800 Washington St., Key West, FL 33040 (tel. 305/296-6531), is a charming place to stay. Its Spanish-style main building surrounds an inner courtyard with tropical plantings. The swimming pool has a sundeck, and there's another rooftop deck for sunning. All Old Town attractions and restaurants are within easy walking distance. There are standard motel rooms, efficiencies, and two-room apartments, all nicely furnished. Winter rates begin at $57, summer and spring, $33.

For a room directly on the Atlantic, there's just one place to find it—the **South Beach Oceanfront Motel,** 508 South St. (tel. 305/296-5611). Rooms are attractively furnished, and I found the Olympic-size pool, private fishing pier, and sundeck to be centers of congeniality for guests to chat, share outdoor snacks, and even enjoy impromptu concerts. Rates start at $50 for doubles in summer, $70 in winter (efficiencies, $65).

Budget and Very, Very Good

Although I don't always travel budget, my next stay in Key West will most assuredly be spent at **Key Lime Village,** 727 Truman Ave. (tel. 305/294-6222). This delightful complex of accommodations sits back from the street amid lush tropical planting and consists of cottages, efficiencies, motel rooms, and (truly budget) rooms in the inn. The two-story, yellow and white inn was Key West's first motel located in the heart of Old Town, and if for no other reason, I'd stay there for the friendliness and helpfulness of the staff. However, the rooms themselves are far above average for the price range, and the cottages are self-contained homes away from home, fully equipped, and all are air conditioned. There's a pool and sundeck, with a shaded lounging area (a small, perfect garden centered by an impressive sculpture) just perfect for afternoon or evening cocktails (no service, you bring your own). In addition, the community room holds TV, music, and games. Rates? Unbelievably low. Cottages are $26 in summer, $48 in winter; efficiencies run $28 in summer, $50 in winter; and rooms with private baths cost $24 and $43, without baths (you share the one down the hall), are $18 and $36. There's a rather macabre story centered around a resident in the '40s—if you've a strong stomach, ask Paco about it. All rates are for single or double occupancy.

Guest House Accommodations

Guest houses are beginning to bloom like tropical plants in Key West, and it's an ideal way to travel, so I'll tell you about my own favorite here.

The **Eden House,** 1015 Fleming St., Key West, FL 33040 (tel. 305/296-6868), is in a renovated 1924 Conch house close to almost everything in Old Town. It's a relaxing place, with a cool, white lobby complete with Bermuda fans and wicker furniture. Relaxing, yes; dull, decidedly not. There's a sense of subdued liveliness about the place that is very appealing, and it seems to attract interesting guests. The rooms are simply furnished and comfortable, with ceiling fans instead of air conditioning (there's also a pool to cool you off), and you share a guest television in the hall or lobby. Rooms are available with private bath or shower, with a bath shared by adjoining rooms, and with bath and shower down the hall. A nice feature here is Rich's Restaurant, which serves all three meals at moderate prices (and the food is very good). Seasonal rates are $30 to $47 for private bath; $26 to $39 for adjoining bath; and $22 to $36 without bath.

Campgrounds

Seaside Resort, Inc. is six miles northeast of town on U.S. 1, with 250 sites, most with full hookups. There's LP gas service, flush toilets, a laundry, store, recreation hall, shuffleboard, pool (as well as ocean swimming), boating, and fishing, and rates start at $15. To reserve, write: U.S. 1 and Boca Chica Road, Key West, FL 33040 (tel. 305/294-9515).

A turn left at the city limits on U.S. 1 (MP 5), then three blocks south on Stock Island, will bring you to **Boyd's Key West Campground,** Stock Island, Key West, FL 33040 (tel. 305/294-1465), with 100 sites, most of them full hookups. They have LP gas service, flush toilets, a laundry, recreation room, swimming in pool or ocean, boating, and fishing. Leave dogs at home; most other pets allowed. Rates start at $15.

WHERE TO EAT: Seafood, Cuban dishes, French menus—they're all in Key West and in astounding numbers. These are a few of my favorites:

The **Pier House Restaurant,** 1 Duval St., at Key West Harbor (tel. 294-9541), is sheer luxury, both in setting and cuisine. The glass-walled waterfront room is a delight, and there's patio dining as well. At night, the unusual underwater lighting is nothing short of breathtaking. The gourmet kitchen turns out such goodies as escargots pernod, along with really superb seafood dishes, and the wine list is extensive. Prices are "gourmet" as well ($14.95 and up). Open from 7 a.m. to 11 p.m., with piano music nightly and dancing on weekends. Best reserve at dinner.

Not cheap, but definitely worth the price is Sunday brunch or dinner any day of the week at the **Pigeon House Patio,** 303 Whitehead St. (tel. 294-1034). Outside dining is in a lovely, shady garden patio or on a secluded deck in the rear. Indoors, one dining room is fresh green and white, the other a sunny yellow. As for the food—ahhh! It's highlighted by unusual combinations of local seafood and out-island dishes, plus continental and American specialties. Try the shrimp Cayo Hueso (broiled, bacon-wrapped shrimp on Bahamian rice with cheese sauce) or Caribbean curry. Dinner from 4 p.m. to 2 a.m. (piano bar from 9 p.m. to 2 a.m.); prices begin at $12.95.

The **Half Shell Raw Bar** at the foot of Margaret St. (at the harbor next to the turtle kraals) has a decided dockside air, and the specialty is oysters and clams opened to order in the open-air raw bar. This *very* informal place also serves stone crabs, conch chowder, conch fritters, and hickory-smoked fish in the dining room, along with wine and beer. Prices are moderate, and this is a "don't miss." Open 11:30 a.m. to midnight, except on Sunday, when they open at noon.

Two excellent haunts for lobster lovers are the **A & B Lobster House,** 700 Front St. (tel. 294-1500), open from 5 to 10 p.m. every day except Sunday, and the **Old Island Lobster House,** 2516 N. Roosevelt Blvd. (tel. 294-4951), open every day from 5 to 10 p.m. Prices are slightly above moderate at both.

Cuban

Both **El Cacique,** 125 Duval St., and **La LecHonera,** 900 Catherine St., dish up native Cuban dishes at budget prices. You'll find the usual pork, black beans, fried plantains, and Cuban bread, but take my word for it and try the Cuban-mix sandwich (both places serve it) that combines ham, pork, salami, cheese, and pickles and is accompanied by that strong, aromatic Cuban coffee.

AND THE BARS: Key West bars have been famous for years, and you'll know why after just one night (or afternoon, for that matter) of bar hopping— they're great, all of them, with a lively informality that turns cocktail hour into a party, whenever it happens to fall.

You won't want to miss **Sloppy Joe's,** 201 Duval St., "Papa" Hemingway's favorite hangout. Many a day the husky Ernest could be found working away at a corner table in the bar (whose doors open to the sidewalk), his manuscript pages held securely by a beer-mug paperweight to protect them from the breeze from ceiling fans and wafting in from outdoors. It's all there just as it was then, except that now there are Hemingway mementos all over the place, including a sailfish that the writer landed and proudly hung (it was a rare night when that happened, according to all accounts).

Another Hemingway favorite was The Oldest Bar, at 428 Greene St., but don't look for it by that name—it's now **Capt. Tony's Saloon,** a gathering spot for locals and visitors alike, many drawn by the jazz musicians and other entertainers who show up nightly.

Then, there's Fitzgeralds, 430 Duval St., which combines a genuine old-time saloon environment complete with old movies and live band music, singalongs, and dancing to disco. If you're female, get there on a Thursday— Ladies' Night—when all drinks are free.

Also on Duval St. (no. 224) is the **Bull and Whistle Tavern,** where live entertainment is featured.

TOURS: One of two tours should come *first* (even if you're strictly an on-your-own sightseer). The **Conch Tour Train** takes you on a 1½-hour narrated drive over the entire island, pointing out 60 historical sites and giving a vivid history of Key West. Tours leave daily, 9 a.m. to 4 p.m., from depots at 303 Front St. (Mallory Square), 3850 N. Roosevelt Blvd., and Duval and Angela Sts. (tel. 294-5161). Fare is $5 for adults, $2.50 for ages three to 11. No need to reserve, just show up and hop aboard one of the open-air motorized trams. The **Old Town Trolley,** 1910 N. Roosevelt Blvd. (tel. 296-6688) is styled after those in San Francisco and also takes in the historical highlights of Key West. In addition, your ticket entitles you to discount coupons to a dozen sightseeing attractions. You can buy your ticket at several leading motels around the island and board at any point, hopping off to use those discount coupons to take in something en route, then reboarding when the next trolley comes along.

The glass-bottom boat *Fireball* departs from the northern end of Duval St. on two-hour cruises over living coral reef, with an informative narrative about the formations. Adults pay $8; children under 12, $3.50. Call 296-6293 for reservations and schedule.

Miss Key West sails from 6 Duval St. (across from the Pier House Motel) on 1¼-hour harbor cruises with a sunset cruise featuring live island music during the summer. Fares are $6 for adults, $2.50 for ages ten to 18, 95¢ for ages four to nine. Add $1 for the sunset cruise, and you can call 296-8865 for reservations and sailing times.

You can experience the thrill of being at sea under full sail aboard the *Young America* within the Florida Barrier Reef. The three-hour cruises leave twice daily (except Tuesday) from Pier A of the Truman Annex at Greene and Front Streets, and there are sunset cruises, as well as late-night cruises each full moon. Delightful! And fares are only $15 for adults, $5 for children. For schedules and reservations, call Tall Ship Adventure, P.O. Box 4526, Key West, FL 33040 (tel. 294-8558).

To visit *Fort Jefferson* on Dry Tortugas, the massive hexagonal-shaped fortress which confined the heroic Dr. Mudd (who was imprisoned for setting John Wilkes Booth's leg after the assassination of President Lincoln) for so many years, call the Key West Seaplane Service at 294-6978. It's a thrilling flight, during which a magnificent view of the waters and islands surrounding Key West is yours all the way.

THINGS TO SEE AND DO: Make your very first stop the **Key West Chamber of Commerce,** 402 Wall St. (tel. 294-2587).

Sightseeing by bike or moped is certainly *the* way to go, as I said, and there are several places in town. Look for bikes at Ugly Duckling Rent-a-Bike, 1110 Truman Ave. (tel. 294-1073), for moped at Moped Hospital, 601 Truman Ave. (tel. 296-3344). There's no license or insurance required with the neat little motorized bikes, and you don't have to wear a helmet.

The **Audubon House,** 205 Whitehead St. at Green, was the first of Key West's historic houses to be restored and opened to the public. It was built by Capt. John H. Geiger, a "wrecker" who entertained John J. Audubon there in 1832 when he was studying birdlife on the Keys. Period furnishings re-create that era, and the famous Double Elephant folio *Birds of America* is on display. It's open every day from 9 a.m. to noon and 1 to 5 p.m., and admission is $1.50 for adults, 50¢ for ages six through 12.

The **Hemingway House,** 907 Whitehead St., is a Spanish Colonial house of native rock dating from 1851 that Nobel Prize winner Ernest Hemingway bought in 1931 and owned until 1961, one of his most productive writing periods. When he was in residence, there were some 50 cats here, and their descendants (at least, some of them) are still on the grounds. In fact, there is a cat fountain Hemingway constructed from a Spanish olive jar and a plumbing fixture he found at Sloppy Joe's. The house is very nearly the way it was when he lived there, filled with treasures he brought back from Spain, Africa, and Cuba. Admission is $2 for adults, $1 for children, and hours are 9 a.m. to 5 p.m.

On the south side of the island (S. Roosevelt Blvd.), the **East Martello Fort** was constructed in 1861 and now holds an art and historical museum, with displays representing the cigar-making, sponging, fishing, and railroad industries. There's a lookout tower, a moat that is now a botanical garden, and a section of the museum is devoted to writers who have lived and worked in Key West. Adults pay $2.50; children, 50¢; and hours are 9:30 a.m. to 5 p.m. every day. About three-quarters of a mile away, the **West Martello Fort** is now occupied by the Key West Garden Club, and its tropical plants are on display without charge to the public.

Kraal is an Afrikaans word that means enclosure, and down at the foot of Margaret Street, the **Turtle Kraals** are holding pens for some of the largest turtles in captivity, including the hawksbill and loggerhead. There are also sharks, rays, moray eels, and tropical fish here, as well as an old cannery that is now a museum and a tower over 500 feet high for a breathtaking view of the harbor. And nearby are the shrimp-boat docks (which don't charge for strolling!). The Kraals (pronounced like "corrals" said very fast) are open every day from 9 a.m. to 6 p.m. and cost $2.50 for adults, $1 for children.

If fishing is your thing, the place to go is **Garrison Bight,** a sheltered cove about midway up the island's north shore (U.S. 1 runs alongside), where you'll find the city's charter docks and both bay and deep-sea boats for hire, with or without a guide. If you're not fishing yourself, it's fun to come down about 4 p.m. to see the boats return with happy and unhappy tourists aboard, depending on the day's catch.

Tennis players will find free courts at **Bayview Park** (close to the geographical center of the island) and near the ocean at **County Beach.** They're all concrete with compo surfacing, and they were very well maintained when I was there.

Of course, the one thing you *must* do at least once during your stay is go down to **Mallory Square** at sunset. It's a ceremony, and people who've lived here for years still observe the ritual. The great cumulus clouds seem to catch fire, then when the fiery red sun drops (very suddenly) into the sea, they quickly burn out to a purple gray. There's a cheer from those in the square and a great feeling of camaraderie among the crowd, which is likely to be composed of every age, at least two or three musical groups, and handicrafters spreading their wares out for inspection on the ground.

The sun*rise* is rather spectacular at Key West, too, and the best place to watch it is from the **White Street Pier,** where you'll meet fishermen and dock workers getting out early.

3. The Everglades

Third largest of our national parks, the **Everglades National Park** (c/o Superintendent, P.O. Box 279, Homestead, FL 33030; tel. 305/247-6211) measures some 1½ million acres (about the size of Delaware), and it is the largest subtropical wilderness still existing in North America. Half land, half water, the Everglades' highest points are no more than eight feet above mean sea level, and even the bay bottoms are no more than 16 feet below that level. In short, it is a shallow, swampy, very flat area that is the only sanctuary left for many North American species of birds and animals. This is the only place in the country, for example, where the Cape Sable sparrow and the great white heron are still extant. The manatee (sea cow) and crocodile are protected here, and an occasional Florida panther can still be seen. Alligators, sea turtles, and snakes of every ilk are quite common within the preserve. Vegetation is much like that of Cuba and the West Indies, with six species of palm, ferns, orchids, air plants, and everywhere the mangrove—some as high as 75 feet in the Shark River forest areas. Much of the parkland is covered with sawgrass, a tough plant with barbed blades and razor-sharp edges that can grow as high as ten feet.

The road through the park begins at the Visitor Center 12 miles southwest of **Homestead** on Fla. 27 and runs 38 miles southwest to **Flamingo.** There are exhibits, orientation programs, and detailed maps and other information at the center. A $2-per-car entrance fee is charged, which covers all occupants until noon of the following day, and you can leave through any exit.

Inside the park, you'll find clearly marked interpretive trails and raised boardwalks leading out over the swamp. But you won't find food for sale until you reach Flamingo, and that 50-mile drive will take much longer than you expect, so best stock up with picnic provisions or snacks. Another thing: Fire is one of the most dangerous hazards in the Everglades, and smoking is absolutely *out* except in designated areas. And pets must be kept on leash at all times. Also, remember that the creatures you see are *wild:* by no means try to feed them, and keep as much distance as possible between you and the alligators!

Continuing on the main road, you'll come to the **Royal Palm Visitor Center,** where the Anhinga Trail and the Gumbo Limbo Trail lead off into the wilderness. About two miles farther along, there are campgrounds ($5 a day), picnic facilities, and trails at **Long Pine Key.** A little over eight miles on is **Pa-hay-okee Overlook,** where you can park your car and follow an elevated trail to a high platform overlooking the Shark River Basin. From here to **Flamingo,** there are several other boardwalks into mangrove forests and mahogany groves. At Flamingo, which is on the tip of the mainland at Florida Bay, there's a motel (see "Where to Stay"), restaurant, campgrounds ($4 a day per walk-in site), picnic facilities, service station, post office, marina, sightseeing, and fishing boats, canoes, and interpretive programs. Facilities for tents, campers, and motorcoaches cost $5 per day, with no electrical or water hookups. Spaces are limited, so don't plan to stay overnight without checking before you enter the park. Flamingo is the end of the line, and you must retrace the same ground leaving. However, nothing stays the same very long in the Everglades, and you'll see subtle changes on the return trip—different animals appearing, perhaps, or shadings of light in the afternoon that differ from those in the morning.

At **Shark Valley,** about 35 miles from Miami Beach on U.S. 41, the Tamiami Trail (see Chapter XV), there are open-air tram rides on the 15-mile loop road, but no private cars are allowed. It's along this route that you'll see Miccosukee Indians, as much at home in the Everglades as the wild creatures. All along the way are Indian villages, some of which are open to visitors for a small fee. Notice, too, the flood-control stations on the side of the highway and the canals and levees constructed by the South Florida Water Management District to protect some 18 counties from flood and drought. There are airboat ride stations, as well, most operated by Seminoles; while they can't take you into the park itself, since airboats are prohibited, a ride through the Everglades areas north of the highway can be quite exciting.

When you reach the Shark Valley entrance turnoff, you'll see the **Miccosukee Indian Restaurant** (P.O. Box 440021, Tamiami Station, Miami, FL 33144), and that's the last chance you'll have to buy food until you emerge from the park, since there is not even a settlement at the end of this trail. When you get to Shark Valley itself, the 15-mile loop road is closed to private vehicles, but there's an open-air tram on which you're given a two-hour tour, with a 30-minute stop midway at a 40-foot observation tower. Adults pay $2; children, $1. The Shark Valley route, while not nearly so long as the main road to Flamingo, does give you a representative glimpse of the Everglades without consuming an entire day to get it. If you're hooked by this introduction, you can return to Homestead and set out on the longer route.

WHERE TO STAY: For dyed-in-the-wool nature lovers and adventurers, a drive through the Everglades or a one-day exploration just isn't enough. Well, way down at the southernmost point on the continental U.S., where Florida's west coast curves eastward to the Keys, the **Flamingo Inn** vacation resort, Everglades National Park (tel. 813/695-3101 or 305/253-2241), is a haven for those hardy souls, as well as for fishermen or families who want to *really* get away from it all. Managed by Restaurant Associates, Inc., the Flamingo Inn has the only overnight accommodations actually inside the park. You can have a room in the motel itself (all rooms have picture windows and modern furnishings) or choose a fully equipped housekeeping cabin, or tie up in your own boat (up to 60 feet) at one of the 100 rental slips in the marina.

From here you can take **Back Country Cruises** to Coot Bay, Buttonwood Canal, Tarpon Creek, and Cape Sable; or the **Wilderness Tram** that travels the Snake Bight Trail for a close-up view of Everglades wildlife (see "Things to Do," below). Or you can go it alone by renting a canoe or outboard motorboat and a complete camping outfit for a day or so in the back country—there are marked water trails and maps to guide you into the wilderness and back out. If fishing is your game, there's a free boat ramp if you bring your own, as well as charter boats captained by guides who know how to find the tarpon, snook, redfish, sea trout, snapper, and other fish that abound in these waters. But be sure to reserve such equipment at the same time you book at the inn to avoid disappointment.

As for the inn itself, it has a pool, a recreation area, gift shop, and a very good restaurant with a wide range of entrées and prices, and they'll even cook those fish you had such a good time catching. The Park Service maintains a **Visitor Center and Museum** close by the gift shop, staffed by professional naturalists. Rates for double-occupancy rooms start at $37 (summer) and $50 (winter).

Not in the park, but at nearby Everglades City, the prestigious **Rod and Gun Lodge,** P.O. Drawer G, Everglades City, FL 33929 (tel. 813/695-2101), has been an exclusive sportsmen's hideaway for more than 80 years. The rambling, two-story inn of white cypress wears the air of a country club, albeit a warm, comfortable one, with cypress walls, fishing trophies, wooden overhead fans, deep pile carpets, and guest rooms furnished in the utmost comfort. Fishing is the primary drawing card to most guests, but exploring the Everglades comes in a close second. The lodge is open year round, and rates for doubles range from $55.

Also at Everglades City, the **Captain's Table Lodge and Villas,** P.O. Drawer B, Everglades City, FL 33929 (tel. 813/695-4211), features an exceptional restaurant, regular motel rooms, one-bedroom villas, and two-bedroom apartments. There is a marina, tennis courts, and a heated pool; and they can arrange guides for Everglades tours. Prices start at $35 in summer, $45 in winter.

THINGS TO DO: At Flamingo, boat trips cost $8 for adults, $4 for ages six through 12. You can also rent houseboats here (write **Everglades Park Catering, Inc.,** Flamingo, FL 33030).

From Everglades City, on Fla. 29 just south of U.S. 41, near the west coast of Florida, sightseeing boats and charter boats for fishing leave at regular intervals from 9:30 a.m. to 4:30 p.m.; fares range from $5 to $8 for adults, children half that. For information and reservations, contact **Sammy Hamilton,** P.O. Box 119, Everglades City, FL 33929 (tel. 813/695-2593).

For complete details on any *specific* plan you'd like to make for an Everglades visit, write: Superintendent, Everglades National Park, P.O. Box 279, Homestead, FL 33030.

A SPECIAL WAY TO SEE THE EVERGLADES: You can actually make the 'Glades your home for an entire week by joining a **North American Canoe Tour** (contact: David A. Harraden, 65 Black Point Rd., Niantic, CT 06357; tel. 203/932-2504 weekdays, 203/739-0791 weekdays). Groups of six to ten meet in Naples, then journey to Everglades City to launch canoes, beginning a 109-mile journey through backwater bays, a mangrove forest, Alligator Creek, Shark River, and a lot more before the week ends at Flamingo. It's seven days of the most intimate association with nature, and nights are spent at campsites with intriguing names like Camp Lonesome, Canepatch Campsite, and Willy Willy. There are 12 trips each year (planned during the winter and early spring, January to April), and you must be over 16 to participate (under 18, and you'll need parental consent). NACT furnishes all equipment and food, as well as transport between Naples and the Everglades. Contact them at the above address for schedules and reservations.

Chapter XVIII

THE GULF COAST OF FLORIDA

1. Fort Myers
2. Sarasota
3. St. Petersburg–Tampa

THE WEST COAST OF FLORIDA, on the shores of the Gulf of Mexico, is considered by many to be the best of all possible Florida worlds. Beaches more tranquil than those along the East Coast's Atlantic, metropolitan centers that offer entertainment, culture, and convenience without Miami's hurly burly, and the old-world flavor of Tarpon Spring's Greek settlement plus the Cuban accent of Ybor City in Tampa combine to give a gentler air to this part of Florida's vacationland. Those who live here point with pride—and a hint of smugness—to the fact that Floridians from Miami and other points east vacation regularly at Naples, Venice, and Sarasota.

1. Fort Myers

More than 70 varieties of palms line Fort Myers's streets, making it one of the loveliest towns on the Gulf Coast. Thomas Edison came in 1885, fell in love with the place, and returned every winter for nearly half a century, living and working on a 14-acre riverside estate.

Situated some 15 miles up the broad Caloosahatchee River, Fort Myers is connected to its beaches and offshore islands by two bridges and causeways. On seven-mile-long **Estero Island**, Fort Myers Beach is only three blocks across at its widest point, with the gulf on one side, Estero Bay on the other. Its hotels, motels, restaurants, and shopping centers are set in wooded plots that (except for the busy intersection where San Carlos Blvd. from town joins Estero Blvd. at the beach) reinforce the tropical island atmosphere. It's a relaxed, family-oriented beach resort, although nighttime entertainment in restaurants and lounges often carries on until quite late.

Sanibel and **Captiva Islands**, across a toll bridge ($1.50 each way) at the end of McGregor Blvd., are in the path of gulf tides that wash ashore interesting, and sometimes rare, shells. One of my earliest Florida memories is of running through a mosquito-laden thicket from the one paved road on Sanibel to reach the wide sand beach and walk in undisturbed pleasure at the water's edge, watching the shell harvest of each new wave. Today, the mosquitos are practically all gone, thanks to an effective pest control program, paved roads lead all over the island, and resort communities and private residences have appeared in such numbers that those beaches are seldom, if ever, deserted. Crowded they're *not*, however, and "shelling" is still a delight, drawing Sunday wave-watchers from nearby towns.

Incidentally, those tiny, many-colored clams you'll see burrowing into the sand here and on almost all Gulf Coast beaches are coquinas, sometimes called "butterflies" because that's what they look like when the shell opens up to form two "wings." People hereabout make a delicious coquina chowder, but it requires a *lot* of time and effort. Chances are you'll pick up at least one or two with the clam still alive inside, and be warned—there'll be an ungodly stench if you leave them around for long. You can clean them one of two basic ways: boil them rapidly for about five minutes and pick out the insides with a fork, or freeze the shell and the little critter's remains will slip out easily when it's defrosted. If there's still an odor, soak the shells overnight in alcohol.

Sanibel is also the site of the **"Ding" Darling Wildlife Refuge**, a five-mile, unspoiled mangrove swamp and uplands area that takes about half an hour to drive through, unless you loiter (and I'll bet you do!) to observe the native and migratory birds which have found a sanctuary here.

Fishermen most often go after tarpon in the waters off Fort Myers, and there are plenty of charter boats with experienced guides. Pier fishing is fun too, though, and Fort Myers Beach has a free 600-foot public pier out into the gulf for fishing or just watching.

WHERE TO STAY: Fort Myers Beach, Sanibel, and Captiva Islands are ideal vacation headquarters, all just a short drive away from sightseeing attractions, with the sparkling waters of the Gulf of Mexico right out front for a dip before and/or after your stint behind the wheel. Fort Myers Beach offers the widest variety of accommodations, but the other two islands also offer some nice ones.

Fort Myers Beach (Estero Island)

The **Holiday Inn**, 6890 Estero Blvd. (tel 813/463-5711), is at the southern end of the main drag, but close enough to the center of things to be convenient. Its 103 luxuriously furnished rooms, efficiencies, and apartments all have pool or gulf views (some have both), and there are tennis courts, a miniature golf course, and shuffleboard. The Sunset Dining Room, overlooking the pool with the gulf beyond, serves all three meals at moderate prices, with a pretty good wine list. There's entertainment and dancing most nights in the lounge. It's a restful place, with beautifully landscaped grounds and a 540-foot white-sand private beach. From December 15 to April 30 doubles start at $81 (gulf-front apartments at $97), and then drop. Children under 12 stay free in same room with parents.

Closer in, the **Buccaneer**, 4864 Estero Blvd. (tel. 813/463-5728), is a particularly attractive motel on the gulf side. Here all units are efficiencies (with full kitchens) with two double beds at surprisingly moderate prices. And to make housekeeping even easier, they've provided a coin-operated washerette right on the premises. There's a pretty pool surrounded by palms, a sundeck, shuffleboard, and even a barbecue grill for outdoor cooking. Golf courses and tennis courts are not far away. No restaurant, but some excellent ones very close at hand. You can rent by the day ($29 to $38 May 1 to December 14, $50 to $68 December 15 to April 30), and if you stay as long as seven days, there's a discount. Children under four stay free.

One of the oldest, most atmospheric hotels on the beach is the **Pelican**, 3040 Estero Blvd. (tel. 813/463-9255). It began as a honeymoon hideaway aboard a beached two-story houseboat in the early 1900s, when "Ma" Turner cooked for her guests by kerosene lamps in the galley. It grew, as all good things do, and served as an officers' barracks for Page Field personnel during World War II. Garrett and Esther Reasoner took over from "Ma" in the '50s, and their children carry on the place today. Its age doesn't show once you step inside the plain wooden buildings that make up the small complex. All rooms, efficiencies, and cottages are completely modern, and each is tastefully decorated, with a very homey air. Most of the hotel rooms don't have private baths, only a lavatory each, but there are centrally located showers and baths. Buz and Ann Reasoner have created a real home away from home for vacationers in this old hotel, and even the three meals a day (at the Pelican Restaurant, about which more below) under their American Plan rates have that special, cared-for flavor. Those American Plan rates are mandatory from November 1 to May 1, when bookings are taken by the week only, starting at $290 single, $390 double, for rooms; $320 single, $420 double, for cottages. European (no meals included) daily rates, May to October, start at $25 and $30. Don't expect to get in, though, unless you reserve months in advance—they have scores of regulars who book from year to year.

Sanibel Island

Beachview Cottages, Box 181, Sanibel Island, FL 33957 (tel. 813/472-1202), is located on West Gulf Dr., and has 22 air-conditioned cottages with kitchens and some studios. There's a pool, and a restaurant close by. During winter months, there's a four-day minimum stay, and rates run from $50 up for studios and from $75 up for cottages. Lower rates other months.

The two-story **Casa Ybel**, 2255 W. Gulf Dr., Sanibel Island, FL 33957 (tel. 813/472-3145), has 80 kitchen units, some with one bedroom, others with two. There's a pool, wading pool, and whirlpool, as well as the Thistle Lodge restaurant. Winter rates are $140 for one-bedroom units, $175 for two; all rates are lower other months.

Captiva Island

If it's peaceful seclusion you want, with recreational facilities that are endless, **South Seas Plantation Resort** (tel. 800/237-3102) has it all for you. Scattered within the 330-acre site of a pre-Civil War lime and coconut plantation, at the end of Captive Island, are some 520 villa accommodations in the luxury class. There are tennis and marina villas, beach and bayside villas, and even beach homes and cottages. The Plantation House offers 20 individual rooms. Add to this a nine-hole golf course surrounded by the Gulf of Mexico on three sides, 20 tennis courts, 16 swimming pools, a beautiful yacht harbor (suitable for boats up to 120 feet), windsurfing, sailing, jet skis, two miles of private beach, and charter fishing; and there isn't much more you could wish for during the daylight hours. After the sun goes down, the Ship's Lantern Lounge serves up exotic tropical cocktails, and the King's Crown Restaurant, replete with warm dark woods and teardrop chandeliers, has taste-tempting seafood, gourmet cuisine, and sumptuous desserts. South Seas also has Chadwick's Restaurant, with an Old Florida decor, regional food specialties, and nightly entertainment in the Atrium Lounge. Cap'n Al's dockside pub is a real favorite of most guests—a lovely harbor and marina view, plus good food.

As I said, everything reeks of luxury, as do the prices. Seasonal rates for the wide array of accommodations start at $70 for the Plantation House, $80 for Tennis Villa one bedroom, $95.00 for Bayside Villa one bedroom, $110.00 for one bedroom Beach Villas (double occupancy rates).

WHERE TO EAT: Again, the beaches have a lot to offer; you can eat well and never venture to the mainland. Some landbound exceptions, however, are included in this listing.

Fort Myers Beach (Estero Island)

The **Pelican Restaurant**, 3040 Estero Blvd. (tel. 463-9255), which began life in "Ma" Turner's galley, has gone on to be one of the best around, and people drive relatively long distances to eat here. Crossing an outside wooden plank deck, you step first into the Pegleg Lounge, a cozy place sporting an old wooden sign with the legend: "Sailors Rest, Miss Sally Small, Prop. Miss Small Can Accommodate up to 14 Sailors Per Night." By all means tarry long enough to see the model of an 1879 tea clipper that hangs over the bar and the kegs and baskets and other dockside memorabilia piled around the walls. Once you are inside the rather small dining room, with its walls of windows to the gulf, manager Phil Reasoner will see to it that you understand the reason the place is so popular. If you order one of the many seafood entrées, you can be sure it will be fresh—the Reasoner family has its own boats which supply the restaurant. As for beef specialties, they also have their own butcher to assure good cuts from prime meats. And everything is cooked to order. Prices are moderate: the native seafood platter, for instance, is $10.95; boiled native stone crab claws, $8.95. You really should eat here at least once—and make it early in your visit so you will have time to come back. Open 5 to 10 p.m. for dinner (year round).

Ye Olde Holmes House Gourmet Restaurant, 2500 Estero Blvd. (tel. 463-5519), is just that, a gourmet restaurant serving continental specialties like chicken cordon bleu and crabmeat Monaco. But don't think that's all: the menu runs ten pages long! Seafood, beef, Italian dishes—you name it and it's probably there. And all dishes are excellently prepared. There are two salad bars, exotic coffees, desserts you'll wish you'd saved room for, and a complete cocktail and wine service. Located in one of the oldest residences on the beach, Ye Olde Holmes is open from 5 to 9:30 p.m. on weekdays, 5 to 10 p.m. on weekends, and prices are surprisingly moderate (starting at $9.95).

A Fort Myers Beach friend sent me to **Charley Brown's,** 6225 Estero Blvd. (tel. 463-6660), saying, "This place is a real treat." Well, I found she hadn't exaggerated in the least—it *is* a treat. In a waterfront setting (the enclosed-porch/dining room named Snoopy's overlooks the water), Charley Brown's serves excellent seafood, steak, and other beef dishes (like kebabs and prime ribs), amid lots of greenery. Service is as outstanding as the food, and there's an assortment of special drinks from the bar (try their house special, the Dirty Mouse). Prices on the semi à la carte menu range from $7.95 to $13.95, with children's plates in the $3 to $3.75 range. Hours are 5 to 10 p.m.

Sanibel Island

Scotty's Pub, 1223 Periwinkle Way (tel. 472-1771), is about as homey and informal as you can get, decorated with what can only be described as nostalgic junk (which may account for its slogan: "the most peculiar great restaurant on Sanibel Island"). Peculiar or not, Scotty's food is good and the price is right. Especially tasty is the Sanibel clam chowder, at 95¢ a cup. The whimsical menu also includes oysters MacIntyre and chicken MacGregor (deboned "chest" of a thoroughbred chicken—that's right, "chest," for as Scotty says, this is a *family* restaurant!). Lunch is served 11:30 a.m. to 2 p.m. in winter only; dinner, year round, 5 to 9:30 p.m., and the lounge is open from 5 p.m. to 2 a.m., and prices are moderate.

The **Cafe Orleans,** 1473 Periwinkle Way (tel. 472-5700), is the perfect place for breakfast, lunch, or dinner. Marty (it's a "she") and John Vroman-Vrolyk are island-lovers from way back and came here from Puerto Rico. Their breakfasts have become famous and they have a wide offering of early a.m. dishes. I found, in fact, the best eggs Benedict this side of New York in this small island restaurant (they're called Kay's Delight on the menu and come topped with a special piquant sauce far better than the usual bland hollandaise). Besides the omelets, french toast, waffles, etc., there's a long list of sandwiches, homemade soups and chowder, and an extensive wine list. Breakfast is 7 a.m. to 2 p.m., lunch from 11 a.m. to 2 p.m., dinner 6 to 9:30 p.m. year around. Closed Monday.

Fort Myers and Vicinity

Located in two of Fort Myers's old Victorian homes, connected by a beautiful garden courtyard and country kitchen, **The Veranda,** Second and Broadway (tel. 332-2065), is a treat to visit—and the food's good, too. Furnishings are authentic antebellum antiques, and there's a huge old wooden bar, porches, and that courtyard for alfresco dining. The menu features seafood specialties like shrimp Marteuo, veal dishes, and special desserts at prices a little above moderate (starting at $8.50). There's entertainment every night in the lovely lounge, which opens at 11 a.m. The restaurant serves lunch from 11:30 a.m. to 2:30 p.m. ($4 to $8) and dinner from 5:30 to 11 p.m.

Smitty's has been a Florida west coast institution for over 20 years (you'll find one at Venice and Port Charlotte as well as in Fort Myers). In Fort Myers, **Smitty's,** 2240 W. 1st St. (tel. 334-4415), specializes (as do all three) in custom-aged western beef and superb fresh, hand-breaded seafood. All breads and pastries are home-baked, and desserts like Key lime pie and brandy Alexander cream pie are scrumptious. Dress is casual in Dollison's Lounge, where you can sip in comfort to enjoy live entertainment—a little more "dressy casual" in the Beef Room. Hours are 11 a.m. to 10:30 p.m. (on Sunday from noon to 9:30 p.m.) and prices run from $7 to $15.

NIGHTLIFE: It's mostly in the lounges of motels or restaurants—this is not nightclub territory.

For dancing, there's the **Celebrity Lounge** in the **Sheraton**, 8900 S. Tamiami Trail (tel. 936-4300), or the **Sunset Room**, Holiday Inn at Fort Myers Beach—see "Where to Stay."

Entertainment goes on nightly in the **Celebrity Lounge** (see above); the **Likeke Lounge** of the **Holiday Inn** at Fort Myers Beach; the **Pago Pago Lounge** of the **Holiday Inn** in town, 2066 W. 1st St. (tel. 334-2123); and **The Veranda** (see "Where to Eat").

THINGS TO SEE AND DO: Beach things top the list at Fort Myers and its islands—swimming (and the beaches are safe, with few strong tides to worry about), fishing from pier, surf, or boat, shelling (especially on Sanibel and Captiva Islands), or just plain toasting on the palm-fringed sands.

The **Shell Factory**, four miles north on U.S. 41, has an eye-popping display of shells from all over the world in a large building that houses a museum of rare shells, shellcraft and art supplies, aquarium displays, glass blower, candlemaker, gourmet department, a gift shop, and a snackbar. A lot of the shells are on sale, and there's no admission charge. Open from 8 a.m. to 7 p.m.

The **Thomas A. Edison Home**, 2350 McGregor Blvd., was prefabricated in Maine and shipped down by schooner. The inventor spent his winters here for almost 50 years, and his furnishings are still here, as is his laboratory, still intact (and some of his early lightbulbs have been burning 12 hours a day ever since he made them!). The guided tour includes the lab and workshops, the house, a museum of Edison's inventions, and the 14-acre botanical gardens filled with tropical trees and plants. Hours are 9 a.m. to 4 p.m. except Sunday, when they are 12:30 to 4 p.m. Admission is $3 for adults, $1 for ages six through 17.

At the **City Yacht Basin**, foot of Lee St., you can board the *Sun Coaster* for a three-hour narrated ride either up the Caloosahatchee right to the edge of the Everglades or through the Intracoastal Waterway. Both are informative, fascinating looks at Florida wildlife. The fare is $6 for adults, $3 for ages three through 11, and departure times change seasonally, so call 334-7474 for schedules and reservations.

Nature lovers will want to visit **Corkscrew Swamp Sanctuary,** on Rt. 6, Sanctuary Rd. (tel. 813/657-3771), between Fort Myers and Naples, to the south, where a mile-long boardwalk winds through lush tropical growth, cypress trees, and aquatic plants. Storks, alligators, and other animals live here in abundance. It's open daily from 9 a.m. to 5 p.m., and admission is $3 for adults, $1 for students, free for those under 12.

From early November to mid-May, you can leave civilization behind for five days aboard the *Lazy Bones,* a unique shanty boat that offers cruises for 16 passengers on the Orange and Caloosahatchee Rivers to Lake Okeechobee (leaving from the Orange River dock seven miles east of Fort Myers). The *Lazy Bones* stops for exploring with swamp buggy and air-boat rides. The cost for five days is $350 per person, based on double occupancy. Cabins, three homecooked meals a day, and all side trips are included in the price. For details and reservations, write: Cap'n Stan, Shanty Boat Cruises, Rt. 29, Box 434/P, Fort Myers, FL 33905; tel. 813/694-3401.

READER'S SUGGESTION: "In a spate of ecological consciousness, Sanibel environmentalists are urging shell harvesters to leave live shells on the beach. It seems that even the mollusks are endangered by civilization, with the prettiest species being collected so fast that they have no chance for propagation" (S. Reifler, Clinton Cove, N.Y.).

2. Sarasota

There have been "tourists" in Sarasota from as far back as the early 1700s, when Cuban fishermen set up camp along the gulf shores here and established a brisk trade with local Indians. Indians of one tribe or another (there were several) had known about the sunny climate and bountiful waters for longer than that—20,000 years longer, recent archeological finds reveal. The Spanish (tourists of a sort themselves) had been through in the 1500s (Hernando de Soto landed on Longboat Key in 1539), and pirates sailed in and out of the bays and bayous for years; Jose Gaspar Gasparilla, one of the most notorious, made his headquarters in nearby Charlotte Harbor. Tourism really took off, however, during the land boom years of the early 1920s, faltered, then ceased when the boom became a fizzle. But John Ringling, when he moved his circus's winter headquarters down in 1927, brought economic salvation in the form of a huge construction and maintenance payroll. Not content with investing in a multimillion-dollar estate for his private residence, Ringling also interested himself in all sorts of civic improvements, building the Ringling Causeway and putting hundreds of thousands of dollars into local colleges and artistic institutions. His legacy to the city and the state was enormous, for he left an immense personal fortune, that impressive home, and a priceless art collection housed in its own magnificent museum, all of which play their part in drawing today's tourists—many of whom, like Ringling, find the climate (both weatherwise and culturally) so agreeable they stay on to become Sarasota's most enthusiastic residents.

The natural blessings that make Sarasota so appealing to natives, tourists, and tourists-turned-residents are many. The city, from its gracefully curving waterfront, looks across Sarasota Bay to long, narrow islands, or keys, and beyond to the blue waters of the Gulf of Mexico. Brilliantly colored bougainvillea, hibiscus, azaleas, and flame vines blaze in the shade of assorted palms and pines, and more color is reflected in bay and gulf waters when the run rises and sets in startling splendor. In such a setting, the arts—in many forms—have bloomed, too, to such a degree that Sarasota has become the virtual "culture capital" of Florida. Artists, writers, artisans, actors, and circus performers (artists of another stripe) make this their permanent home and seem to flourish. True, this is resort country, yet its attractions don't wane with the seasons, and all year long sun and sand must compete with concerts and theater and galleries and museums for the tourists' time and attention.

The city's physical beauty is evident in almost every quarter (except perhaps on the shopping-center-and-service-station-bordered stretches of the Tamiami Trail north and south of town). Downtown Sarasota creates a lasting first impression with beautifully landscaped Bayfront Drive and **Island Park,** a small island man-made from bay bottom sand and filled with native plantings that provide a serene setting for boats of all description docked at Marina Jack.

Bayfront Drive takes the visitor across Ringling Causeway, past **Bird Key** (once the home of Henry Ringling North and now an exclusive residential community and yacht club) and onto **St. Armands Key.** Ringling's influence is once more felt on this pretty, circular island, for it was he who first laid out the tropically landscaped park at its center, and the statues it now holds came from his private collection. Around the park, on a circular drive, shops, restaurants, art galleries, and boutiques have gabled windows, striped awnings, and wrought-iron grillwork that impart a European air. Due west from St. Armands Circle is **Lido Key,** with its string of resort hotels, half-mile-long public beach (which, in true Florida style, also has a swimming pool), and imaginative children's playground. A turn north at St. Armands Circle takes you to **Longboat Key,** via a humpback bridge to Lido Shores, site of some striking (and expensive) waterfront homes, then across a concrete-and-steel bridge to the Longboat Key Golf and Country Club. It stands on land which Ringling once thought would hold an ultra-luxury hotel, the Ritz, which would bring even more wealth into the Sarasota area. This was one dream, however, that failed, and construction was halted just 60 days before the scheduled completion date.

Just south of Lido Key lies **Siesta Key,** a beach community more casual than Lido or Longboat, with vacation resorts and private homes nudging each other in groves of peppertrees, mangrove, palms, and pines. This key, with unspoiled, virtually wild northern and southern edges, has attracted scores of artists and writers, drawn by its charm and the seclusion they're able to find here. Siesta Key Public Beach stretches along the gulf shore, with grills and picnic tables, a large children's playground, and all-weather tennis courts. Turtle Beach, on the southern tip, is narrow, but has an "untouched by human hands" kind of beauty. Human hands have, however, added grills and both open and sheltered picnic tables, but in a manner that has enhanced, not spoiled, nature's creation.

Away from the water, there are those Ringling museums, a 28-acre Civic Center with an auditorium, recreation club, art association, library, community house, 40 shuffleboard courts, seven lighted tennis courts, and 15 bowling alleys. And downtown, historic **Mira Mar Plaza** is a one-block-long shopping mall (on Palm Avenue) of graceful arches, wrought-iron balconies, and lovely little gardens.

WHERE TO STAY: It goes without saying that accommodations right on the gulf will cost you more. What *should* be said, however, is that Sarasota has many very desirable motels with lower rates than those on the beachfront which are really *more* convenient to sightseeing attractions. So it becomes a question of priorities. In any case, the drive to a gulf beach from any of these motels on the Tamiami Trail (that's U.S. 41) will be no more than 10 or 15 minutes.

Not on the beach, but definitely the most elegant place in town, is the **Hyatt Sarasota,** 1000 Boulevard of the Arts (tel. toll free 800/228-9000, or 813/366-9000), at Watergate Center just across from Van Wezel Performing Arts Hall. It soars 12 floors above Sarasota Bay and is a tower of modernity, with soft shades of browns, beige, blues, and muted reds setting off high glass lobby windows, with wood used lavishly in combination with aluminum to create a striking effect the minute you walk inside the door. Its 297 rooms are decorated in contemporary furnishings of the luxury sort, with oversize beds. Peppercorn's Restaurant, with colorful tablecloths and fresh plants on the table, looks out over the water and serves outstanding meals from breakfast through dinner which draw a big local following. The Horse and Chaise Lounge has entertainment and dancing in an elegant setting. The Boathouse, built on stilts over the lagoon, is a casual, friendly place to eat or drink (or both) at watered-down prices, and may be reached by boat (as well as by foot over the wooden walkway from the hotel lobby). There are tennis courts a short distance away, and golfers have guest privileges at some 16 local courses. Other extras include a heated pool, plus sail and power charter boats. And if you arrive in Sarasota aboard your own boat, the Hyatt House has a private marina which will accommodate it. Double-room rates start at $90, year round. Children with their parents are free up to the age of 18.

Over on Lido Beach, the **Coquina on the Beach,** 1008 Ben Franklin Dr. (tel. 813/388-2141), has large, airy rooms with tropical furnishings, completely equipped kitchenettes, private balconies or patios (some are screened), and a heated pool with hydrotherapy jets. This is a small (less than 50 units), very friendly motel directly on the gulf (their private beach has thatched shade shelters), with recreation facilities that include sailboats, shuffleboard, picnic tables, and an outdoor grill. Rates are $74 and up during the winter season (January 26 through April 30), lower other months.

Every room has a gulf view at the **St. Armand Inn,** 700 Ben Franklin Dr., Lido Beach (tel. 813/388-2161), seen through large picture windows or from private balconies. Rooms are quite large, with contemporary furnishings. There's a restaurant, cocktail lounge, children's play area, badminton, and volleyball. The heated pool is king-size (should you happen to tire of the 350-foot private beach), and there's a sundeck. Seasonal rates for double rooms peak at $68 and up during winter months.

There are eight units for the handicapped at the **Silver Beach Resort,** 4131 Gulf of Mexico Dr. (tel. 813/383-2434), five miles north of the Longboat Key Bridge on Fla. 789. Rooms are exceptionally nice, some with oversize beds. It's directly on the gulf and has a heated pool, shuffleboard, Ping-Pong, picnic tables, a putting green, and grills (there's a restaurant across the street). There is also limo and taxi service to the airport. During the February to April season, double rooms are $56 (kitchen units, $62), with lower rates from May through January.

A modestly priced motel at Lido Beach, the **Surf View Motel,** 1121 Ben Franklin Dr. (tel. 813/388-1818), is across the street from the gulf, and has rather small, but cozy, rooms, nicely furnished with modern appointments. There's a warm, friendly atmosphere here, plus personalized service, a heated pool, shuffleboard, and beach privileges. Both one- and two-room efficiencies are available (some with two baths) at rates that start at $32 (one room) during the summer season and $50 from February through April.

The **Best Western Royal Palms Motel,** 1701 N. Tamiami Trail (tel. 813/365-1342), is a motel with budget rates, large, comfortable rooms and efficiency units, a heated swimming pool, shuffleboard, a restaurant next door, and free coffee in rooms. During the winter season, doubles start at $32, in summer, $25. Efficiencies are $3 more. Children under 12 stay free and cribs are furnished without charge.

On U.S. 41 South, the **Cabana Inn,** 2525 S. Tamiami Trail (tel. 813/955-0195), also has budget prices for quite nice rooms, and children under 12 stay free. Rooms all have dressing areas and some have extra washbasins. There's a pool and lounge with entertainment and dancing Tuesday through Saturday. Winter rates for doubles begin at $40, dropping in the summer.

Bed and Breakfast

The bed-and-breakfast trend that is beginning to spread across the country has finally reached Florida's west coast. **Florida Suncoast Bed and Breakfast,** P.O. Box 12, Palm Harbor, FL 33563 (tel. 813/784-5118), under the able direction of Carol Hart, lists over 60 guest homes in the Suncoast area, all close to gulf beaches, golf courses, tennis courts, and Florida attractions such as Disney World, Tampa, St. Petersburg, Cypress Gardens, and many others. All undergo rigid inspection by Mrs. Hart, some have swimming pools or spas, most have patios and/or courtyards, and many offer cooking and barbecue privileges. Babysitting and laundry privileges are also available at some. Continental breakfasts are always served, and additional meals can sometimes be arranged, if you wish. A delightful way to set up a home base in Florida in a real home! Mrs. Hart will send you a questionnaire to be completed before your arrival, then try to match up B&B locations with your expressed preferences. She'll also meet you at the Tampa International Airport if necessary. Doubles run $25 to $40.

Campgrounds

From the junction of I-75 and Hwy. 780 (Fruitville Rd.), go one mile east on Hwy. 780 to the **Sun N Fun RV Resort,** which has over 1050 spaces in a semi-wooded, grassy suburban park. Most are full hookups; there are LP gas, flush toilets, showers, laundry, restaurant, recreation hall, recreation room, pavilion, swimming pool, boating (no motors), lake fishing, mini-golf, planned group activities, 18 shuffleboard courts, horseshoes, volleyball, and local tours. Adults only; open all year. Rates start at $13. For full details and reservations, write them at 7125 Fruitville Rd., Sarasota, FL 33582 (tel. 813/371-2505).

The **Sarasota Lakes Camping Resort,** 1699 DeSoto Rd., Sarasota, FL 33580 (tel. 813/355-8585), has 298 sites, all with full hookups. You can reach them from Exit 40 on I-75. All roads are paved, including sites, with concrete patios and picnic tables and individual yard lights. There are LP gas, flush toilets, a laundry, store, recreation hall, shuffleboard, swimming pool, and tennis courts. Rates start at $10 for two, depending on the season.

WHERE TO EAT: Sarasota's good eating places are spread all over the place, from St. Armands Key to downtown to the Tamiami Trail (both north and south). For convenience, I'll group my favorites by location.

Around the Circle on St. Armands Key

For the past five years, Titus Letschert, a native of Austria, and Norbert Goldner, who hails from Berlin, have turned out such consistently good food at **Cafe L'Europe,** 431 Harding Circle (tel. 388-4415), that they've collected the *Holiday* Award for excellence for several years running. The cuisine (under the direction of chef George Lafontaine) is continental, with such specialties as brandied duckling Cafe L'Europe, coq au vin, and veal cordon bleu, and so is the decor. The cafe is completely charming, with its four dining rooms accented by pink brick, arches, antique Italian tile, and lots of greenery. Lunch is served from 11:30 a.m. to 3 p.m., dinner from 5:30 to 11 p.m. (Sunday from 6 to 10 p.m.), and if the crowds I encountered are usual, as I understand they are, reservations are a good idea. Entrées run $8.95 to $18.95.

The **Columbia Restaurant,** St. Armands Circle (tel. 388-3987), is the Sarasota branch of its famous Tampa (Ybor City) parent. This was one of the first fine restaurants on St. Armands and has been voted one of Florida's top restaurants by *Florida Trend Magazine* for several years. The decor is classical Spanish, as is the cuisine. Paella is the dish most asked for here, but my own favorite is the black bean soup—I could make a meal of it, and did once. In the Patio lounge, a cool oasis of Tiffany lamps, green plants, and cozy seat groupings, there's dancing to a lively Latin group. The Columbia opens for lunch at 11 a.m., serves dinner until 11 p.m. (on Sunday from 1 to 11 p.m.), and the lounge stays open until 2 a.m. every day. Prices are in the $6 to $16 range, with a children's menu for less.

Downtown Sarasota

I've been going to **Marina Jack's,** Marina Plaza, Island Park, right on the city's waterfront (tel. 365-4232), almost as long as I've been going to Sarasota, and I've suffered through at least one change of ownership, with differing levels of competence in the kitchen. But the setting for this place is so gorgeous that I'd munch on a hot dog happily just to sit and view the comings and goings in the boat basin or to see a boat pull up and dock right outside so its crew can come in to eat. The present owner (since 1979) has things shipshape once more. The food is good, the view even better than I remembered, and the guitar music downstairs in the cozy Deep Six Lounge a perfect way to end the evening. Do treat yourself to a hour or two here—daytime, at sunset, or after dark when the lights on the water are dreamy. There's a large menu, mostly seafood, and prices for complete dinners start at $7. I had the seafood platter, and it was delicious. Open daily from noon to 10 p.m.

At the Forest Lakes Golf Club, 2 blocks north of Webber, **The Rainforest,** 2401 S. Beneva Rd. (tel. 921-7979), is a relaxed place with lots of greenery and good food at moderate prices. Specialties of beef (with prime ribs as specialty), seafood, veal, chicken, and duck run $6.99 to $13.99. There's also a very good Sunday brunch (11:30 a.m. to 2:30 p.m.) for $5.50. There's dancing in the lounge nightly except Monday from 8:30 p.m. to 1:30 a.m. Dinner hours are 5 to 10 p.m., lunch from 11:30 a.m. to 2:30 p.m., seven days a week, and dress is casual to dressy.

Locals flock to the **Sawmill Inn,** 33 Crossroads Shopping Center—that's U.S. 41 South and Bee Ridge Rd. (tel. 366-7292), and for good reason. Seafood, steaks, veal, and chicken specialties are moderately priced, and the rustic decor (brick walls, raw wood, etc.) creates a casual, relaxed atmosphere. Prices are in the $6.95 to $14.95 range for dinners that include entrée, salad bar, potato or fresh vegetable, and beverage. Lunch is served Monday through Friday from 11 a.m. to 2:30 p.m., dinner from 4:30 to 11 p.m. Monday through Thursday, until midnight on Friday. Saturday, hours are 4:30 p.m. to midnight, on Sunday from 5 to 10 p.m. Daily dinner specials served before 6 p.m. can run as low as $6.50.

The **Old Heidelberg Castle,** 3rd St. and Washington Blvd. (tel. 366-3515), is another Sarasota institution. It's a fun place, specializing in German food (American dishes and seafood, also), a continuous show, and dancing to a Bavarian band, and you'll see all age groups out on the floor. The atmosphere is that of a Munich beer hall, with menu specialties like wienerschnitzel, sauerbraten, and fresh pig's knuckles. Complete dinner prices start at $7.95. Lunch is served from 11 a.m. to 2:30 p.m., dinner from 4:30 p.m. until everybody goes home (Sunday, it's 4:30 to 11 p.m.). Happy Hour is 4 to 6 p.m. with low, low prices for drinks.

On the South Tamiami Trail

About 18 miles south of Sarasota on the Tamiami Trail (U.S. 41), you'll come to Venice and the small, cozy, and elegant Mont Peliano, 102 E. Shamrock Blvd., Venice (tel. 485-5737). It's hard to say which is more outstanding here, food or service—let's just say that they complement each other superbly. The continental cuisine features specialties like chicken cordon bleu, tournedos Jeanette, and shrimp pernod, which are beautifully served by the well-trained staff in a lovely garden setting. Prices are surprisingly moderate—$6.95 to $11.50 for complete dinners. Hours are 4 p.m. to midnight, and because of its popularity locally, reservations are a good idea.

You'll also find one of the **Smitty's** in Venice (see "Where to Eat" in Fort Myers) at 133 S. Tamiami Trail, Venice (tel. 488-2601), open 11:30 a.m. to 2:30 p.m. for lunch, 4:30 to 10 p.m. for dinner (noon to 9 p.m. on Sunday).

NIGHTLIFE: Entertainment and dancing in the various restaurants and lounges around Sarasota make up most of the after-dark activity. Besides **Old Heidelberg, Marina Jack's,** and **Columbia,** all mentioned under "Where to Eat," there's country music at **Shannon's Way Pub,** 3904 Tamiami Trail, jazz and soft rock at **Playground South,** 1927 Ringling Blvd., and the **Moonraker Lounge** of the Holiday Inn North, 8221 N. Tamiami Trail. On Longboat Key, listening and dancing music is in the **Shipwreck Lounge** of the Holiday Inn, 4949 Gulf of Mexico Dr., and the **Tree House Lounge** of the Longboat Key Hilton, 4711 Gulf of Mexico Dr.

THINGS TO SEE AND DO: Many of Sarasota's sightseeing attractions are strung along the North Tamiami Trail (U.S. 41), from about 27th St. all the way to the airport. The Civic Recreation Center, which includes Van Wezel Performing Arts Hall, is just off the Trail, on the bayfront, between 6th and 4th Aves. Bayfront Drive (still part of that Tamiami Trail) runs along the water's edge and past the city marina, headquarters for many charter fishing boats.

Theater

The **Asolo** (pronounced "AH-slow") **State Theater Company of Florida** stages a repertory of seven plays from mid-February through Labor Day in the Asolo Theater in the **Ringling Museums** (tel. 355-2771). The theater itself is a treat (see "Sightseeing"), and performances are usually of top quality—in fact, several of our leading Broadway stars have done a repertory stint here before going on to fame. Curtain time is 8:15 p.m. every night except Monday, and there are matinees Wednesday through Sunday at 2 p.m. Prices for evening shows range from $9 to $14; matinees, $6 to $14.

The enthusiastic (and very good!) **Players of Sarasota** have a year-round schedule of drama, comedy, and musicals, staged in their own 500-seat theater on 9th St. between Cocoanut and the N. Tamiami Trail (tel. 365-2494).

The concert season at **Van Wezel Performing Arts Hall,** 777 N. Tamiami Trail (tel. 953-3366), runs from September through June (with occasional midsummer specials) and includes concerts, ballet, plays, films, and lectures. Call them to see what's scheduled and what prices are when you're in town.

The Asolo Opera Company presents opera (most are in English) at their new, 1000-seat home in downtown Sarasota, 61 N. Pineapple Ave. (tel. 366-8450), from January through March, with tickets in the $12.50 to $25 range.

Sightseeing

Even if you're a confirmed beach bum and sightseeing isn't on your agenda, *do* plan to take time out for the **Ringling Museums.** They have to be seen to be believed, and you'll get far more than your $4.50 worth! The mansion (named Ca' d'Zan, which means House of John in Venetian dialect) was built by that master showman, John Ringling, for his Mable in 1925. He spent more than $1,500,000 and patterned it after the Doge's Palace on the Grand Canal in Venice. By the time he died in 1936, he'd amassed a priceless art collection, built a magnificent museum to house it on his estate overlooking the gulf, and arranged to leave estate, mansion, museum, and his personal fortune to the State of Florida. The elaborately furnished home is just as he lived in it, complete with $50,000 Aeolian pipe organ and gold bathroom fixtures. The museum holds one of the largest Rubens collections in this country, along with art of the 17th, 18th, 19th, and 20th centuries (the classical marble building, with columns, arches, and courtyard, is worth seeing for itself alone). The state has added a **Museum of the Circus,** a treasurehouse of Ringling Bros. Circus memorabilia, and the **Asolo Theater,** an original 1798 Italian theater that was taken, piece by piece, from the castle of Catherine Cornaro at Asolo near Venice, Italy, and reassembled in a building of its own next to the Museum of Art. Now, is *that* a bargain at just $4.50! Ages six to 12 pay $1.75. Hours are 9 a.m. to 7 p.m. Monday through Friday, until 5 p.m. on Saturday, and Sunday hours are 11 a.m. to 6 p.m. And children under six are admitted free with an adult.

The **Glass Blowers,** 5230 N. Tamiami Trail, don't charge for their exhibitions of colored glass and lead crystal being transformed into exquisite art forms, but there *is* a gift shop where you can purchase the end results if you wish. It is open every day except Sunday from 9:30 a.m. to 5 p.m.

Nostalgia buffs will delight in **Bellm's Cars & Music of Yesterday,** 5500 N. Tamiami Trail, with its 170 antique, classic, and racing cars, and 1400 antique music boxes and turn-of-the-century arcade. They've all been expertly restored to working order and their original splendor, and it's a real treat to hear hurdy-gurdies, calliopes, and nickelodeons tinkling away. There are hourly guided tours from 8:30 a.m. to 6 p.m. Monday through Saturday, Sunday from 9:30 a.m. Adults pay $4.50; six through 16, $2.

There are two outstanding gardens open to the public in Sarasota. The **Jungle Gardens,** 3701 Bayshore Rd.—that's two miles north of the city center on U.S. 41, then two blocks west on Myrtle St.—has formal gardens also, but the real feature is the 16-acre wild jungle laced with winding trails through more than 5200 varieties of palms, tropical plants, and flowering shrubs—an ecologist's delight! The wildlife includes monkeys, alligators, leopards, flamingos, waterfowl, emus, parrots, and macaws. And there's a "Jungle Bird Circus" with performing birds as well as a reptile show featuring alligators and snakes. The gardens are open from 9 a.m. to 5 p.m. every day, with admission charges of $4.50 for adults, $2.50 for ages six to 16, free for those under five.

The **Marie Selby Botanical Gardens,** 800 S. Palm Ave., at the corner of U.S. 41 at downtown Sarasota bayfront, is the world's only botanical garden devoted to epiphytic "air" plant research and display. It is the Orchid Identification Center of the American Orchid Society, the International Bromeliad Identification Center, and houses the world's largest gesneriad collection, as well as Florida's finest display hibiscus. A Tropical display house features exotic tropical blooms in a rain-forest setting, and there's a museum devoted to botany and the arts. There's a trellis walk, waterfall, and winding paths through tropical plantings around the ten-acre peninsula. The gardens, as well as the plant, book, and gift shops, are open every day except Christmas from 10 a.m. to 5 p.m. Admission is $3.50, free to under-12s when accompanied by an adult.

A Day in the Country

Seventeen miles east of Sarasota on Fla. 72, the **Myakka River State Park** is an outstanding wildlife sanctuary, with more than 225 identified bird species, deer, raccoon, otter, bobcats, and large rookeries. There's a bird walk along the lake, or you can rent a bike, take a guided boat tour or the train tour. There is picnicking at two designated areas, a snackbar, nature museum, boat rentals, campsites, and cabins that rent for varying daily and weekly rates. If you want to do more than just look around, call 813/924-1027 between 8 a.m. and 5 p.m. for specific information, current rates, and reservations of any of the available facilities. Or write: MYAKKA River State Park, Rt. 1, Box 72, Sarasota, FL 33583.

Sports
Golfers will pay $34 to cover both greens fees and cart at **The Meadows Golf Club,** 3101 Longmeadow (tel. 371-1100), 2½ miles east of U.S. 301. Play is challenging on the Francis Duane-designed 18-hole course, and the scenery is picturesque. There are shady, tree-lined fairways at the **Foxfire** course, 7200 Proctor Rd. (tel. 921-7757), six miles east of U.S. 41 at Proctor and Clark Roads, and during the summer you can play as long as you like after 3 p.m. for a flat $8 fee.

There are public tennis courts at **10th St. and U.S. 41; Gillespie Park,** 8th St. and Gillespie; **17th St. and Tuttle Ave.; Bee Ridge Park** on Wilkinson Road; on **Siesta Beach;** and at the **Newtown Community Center** at Myrtle Ave. and U.S. 301.

3. St. Petersburg–Tampa
Tampa Bay, where it bites into the mainland of Florida's west coast, creates a long, wide peninsula on the gulf side that is dominated by St. Petersburg and a smaller, narrow one jutting out into the bay itself that holds Tampa and, at its very tip, MacDill Air Force Base. Together, they comprise what is commonly called Tampa–St. Pete by natives, or the Greater Tampa Bay Area by the more scholarly. By whatever name, this is a section rich in history, blessed by a subtropical climate, and so "healthy" that the American Medical Association pronounced it an excellent place for preventive-medicine living.

That AMA pronouncement almost did St. Petersburg in—after, of course, promoting a tremendous boom when hundreds of retiring couples chose this as their "last resort." So welcomed were the aging immigrants at first that rows of green benches were put up all along Central Avenue to provide convenient resting places, and curbs had ramps for wheelchairs or cane-carrying citizens. The population swelled with elderly residents, and one day the city fathers woke up to the fact that their senior-citizen image was beginning to hurt the town's long-range growth. A vigorous attack was launched to publicize the youthfulness of the majority of its residents (as well as the activeness of its elders) and the green benches disappeared. Pushing its "Sunshine City" label, St. Petersburg lured new industry and upgraded resort facilities along the string of offshore islands called the Holiday Isles (that's St. Petersburg Beach, Treasure Island, Madeira Beach, Redington Beach, Indian Rocks Beach, and Belleair Beach), with the result that young, old, and middle-aged mingle happily here today.

The beaches are connected to the mainland by the free St. Petersburg Beach Causeway, and Pinellas Bayway which charges a 30¢ toll. Gulf Boulevard runs the length of the Holiday Isles. Getting around St. Petersburg itself is fairly easy if you remember that all avenues, terraces, and places run east and west, streets and ways run north and south, and Central Avenue is the north-south dividing line. There is a very good bus system for the city and suburbs, and the **St. Petersburg City Transit Company** will furnish route information if you call 893-RIDE. The island communities are served by **Gulf Beach**

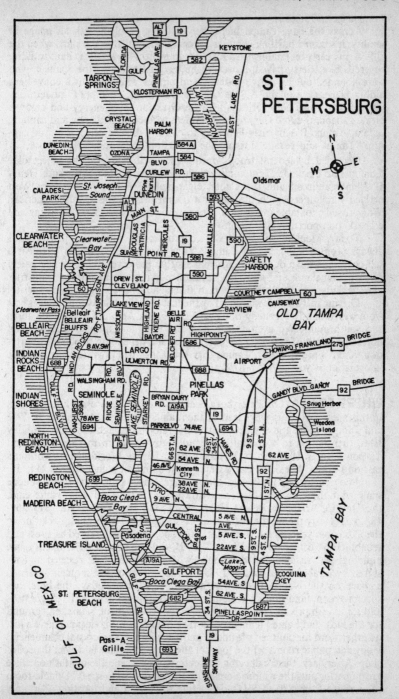

ST.
PETERSBURG

Transit (tel. 896-2655).

Across the bay, Tampa has never had any problem with an image of senility; it's been a bustling commercial center almost from the start, when the U.S. Army early on established a fort here to protect the strategic harbor. Long before U.S. settlers arrived, however, the bay had attracted the Spanish, who were hounded out by native Indians, and pirates who found it a convenient hiding place. One of those, Jose Gaspar Gasparilla, prompts a modern-day festival that rivals New Orleans's Mardi Gras for sheer energy and color: a pirate galleon, the *Jose Gasparilla,* complete with costumed crew and captain, sails up Tampa Bay in early February to end five days of celebration to "capture" Tampa and parade through the streets on fantastic floats.

Occupied by federal troops during the Civil War and the object of a Confederate blockade, Tampa nevertheless flourished, and when both Henry B. Plant's railroad and the Cuban cigar-making industry from Key West arrived simultaneously in the 1880s, it boomed. Even the Spanish-American War proved profitable for Tampa, when it was made a primary outfitting and embarkation port for U.S. troops.

Today, MacDill Air Force Base continues the military emphasis that's always been so important in Tampa; Ybor (pronounced "EE-bo") City is a self-contained town of Cuban cigarmakers that preserves the color and gaiety of their homeland; and although vacation pursuits are important, industries like the Anheuser-Busch Brewery provide an enduring commercial prosperity.

Driving in Tampa is simplified by the fact that Florida Avenue divides east from west, John F. Kennedy Boulevard and Frank Adamo Drive divide north and south, numbered avenues run east and west, and numbered streets run north and south. If you want to park the car and depend on public transportation (and it's pretty good), **Tampa City Bus Lines** will provide route and fare information if you call 251-1078.

WHERE TO STAY: St. Petersburg Beach is the perfect vacation headquarters in this area. Two causeways lead to the mainland and sightseeing in St. Pete and Tampa, while a lovely beach drive goes north through the other Holiday Isles, then across to a coastal mainland highway on up to Clearwater and Tarpon Springs. If you're in the mood for it, Disney World is just two hours east on I-4 and Weeki Wachee's water show about an hour north on U.S. 19.

Looking for all the world like a huge, pastel-pink strawberry sundae sculpted in the shape of a Moorish castle and set in a dish of sugar-white sand, the **Don CeSar Beach Resort Hotel,** 3400 Gulf Beach Blvd. (tel. 813/360-1881), is clearly the most elegant place to stay on the beach. Built back during the '20s boom years, it lay vacant after the boom subsided, served as a rest and rehabilitation center during World War II, did a stint as a government office building, was vacated and threatened with demolition, was rescued and restored by local citizens, and in 1975—perhaps its proudest moment—earned a place on the National Register of Historic Places! Today, the hotel has spacious rooms and suites with sumptuous furnishings (some with refrigerators and some with private balconies), a heated pool, whirlpool, sauna, playground for the kids, and lighted tennis courts. The high-ceilinged, elegant (there's just no other word for polished tile floors, marble columns, and crystal chandeliers) lobby and public rooms set the tone for the two restaurants and even the coffee shop. After dark, there's dancing and entertainment, and the old-fashioned ice cream parlor puts the whipped cream on the sundae, so to speak. Double-room rates range from $80 to $100, depending on season and location. Certainly above the moderate level, but not at all out of line for this kind of old-style beach luxury.

Directly on the gulf, with its own stretch of private beach, the **Holiday Inn**, 5300 Gulf Blvd. (tel. 813/360-6911), has exceptionally well-decorated rooms with oversize beds and resort-style furnishings, with gulf-front or poolside efficiencies and king-size "leisure rooms" also available. The pool is freshwater and heated, and both food and beverages are available poolside. Up in the rooftop restaurant, the view of the gulf and Boca Ciega Bay makes dining (or cocktailing in the Galleon Lounge) a spectacular sort of thing. The kids will stay busy in the game room when they tire of the beach, and there are sail and paddle boat rentals. Double rooms start at $72 in winter, then drop.

Farther north, the **Bilmar Beach Resort**, 10650 Gulf Blvd., Treasure Island, FL 33706 (tel. 813/360-5531), has 175 units in eight-, four- and three-story buildings strung directly along the gulf. Some have private patios, others have balconies, and many have refrigerators. All are spacious and nicely decorated in beach colors. There are two pools, miniature golf, golf privileges at a nearby course, and tennis courts. There's also a lovely dining room, entertainment in one of the two lounges, and a babysitter service so you can enjoy them. Double rooms cost $65 and up in winter, considerably less in summer.

The **Colonial Inn**, 6300 Gulf Blvd. (tel. 813/367-2711), is a large, white-columned motel with some 200 rooms and 100 efficiencies set on spacious grounds. The colonial motif is carried out with wrought-iron balconies on the second story. Both deep-sea and freshwater fishing boats are available nearby, or you can stay right on the grounds and use the private beach, heated swimming pool, and shuffleboard courts. Average-size rooms have traditional furnishings, the Surrey Dining Room is contemporary in decor, and the bar has a nautical theme. A complete floor show is presented nightly in the on-premises nightclub (with dancing, also), and card players will find a special room for them on the mezzanine. Depending on location, double rooms run from $60 up in winter, lower in summer months.

Set on 200 feet of beachfront, the **Buccaneer Resort Motel**, 10800 Gulf Blvd., Treasure Island, FL 33706 (tel. 813/367-1908), serves a complimentary breakfast. Rooms are spacious, stylishly decorated, and open onto a covered ground-floor verandah on the second-floor balcony verandah. Besides the beautiful pool, there's shuffleboard, a cardroom, and tables and umbrellas on the beach lounging area. Nearby, you'll find tennis, golf, and charter fishing. Rates for doubles are $32 and up in winter, lower in summer.

You can opt for the usual double room or a villa apartment (which will accommodate up to four) at **The Alden**, 5900 Gulf Blvd. (tel. 813/360-7081). Most of the rooms and apartments have either white-railed private balconies or patios, affording real privacy. Recreation facilities include two heated pools, lighted tennis courts, game room, cookout facilities, and of course, that gulf beach. Furnishings in all facilities are modern, with lots of bright colors used in decorating. The rates are a modest $45 in winter for double rooms, $60 and up for the fully equipped villa apartments.

Not directly on the gulf, but convenient to it, are two members of the dependable **Days Inn** chain: one in Tarpon Springs (U.S. 19 at Lake Tarpon—address is 816 U.S. 19S P.O. Box 786, Tarpon Springs, FL 33589; tel. 813/934-0859), with double rooms at $30.88; and the other in North St. Petersburg (9359 U.S. 19N; tel. 813/577-3838), charging $34.88 for doubles.

WHERE TO EAT: Good restaurants, in all price ranges, are strung up and down the Holiday Isles and as far up as Clearwater and Tarpon Springs. St.

Petersburg and Tampa, of course, have their share, but my theory is that most of your time will be spent nearer the shore, so we'll head there first.

St. Petersburg Beach and Holiday Isles

On the Treasure Island Causeway at Gulf Blvd., **Gigi's** (tel. 360-6905) is one of a South Florida chain. In a setting of red carpets, wood-paneled walls with lots of arches, and stone fountains, Gigi's serves good Italian dinners (and if the large menu skipped anything, *I* didn't spot it) and pizza. Wine is available by the glass, carafe, or bottle. Lunch is relaxed, and at dinner the ambience is enhanced by candlelight. Prices are moderate. It opens at 11 a.m., closes at 11 p.m.

Farther north on the beach, at Redington Shores (one mile north of the bath club), the **Red Cavalier,** 17855 Gulf Blvd. (tel. 393-8741), begins its swashbuckling theme right in the entrance, where there's a mini-gallery of paintings portraying cavaliers through the ages. Inside the informal, comfortable dining room—with its wall of windows and high, peaked ceiling—there's a menu featuring Danish lobster tails, top sirloin, prime ribs, and fresh seafood, all at moderate prices (beginning at $6.75). If you're an "early bird," and come between 4 and 6 p.m., prices go down to $5.50 (as they do from 1 to 4 p.m. on Sunday). The Bonfire Lounge, in an Olde English setting, has a Happy Hour from 4 to 6 p.m. and entertainment every night except Sunday and Monday. Doors open every day of the week at 4 p.m. (1 p.m. on Sunday).

Indian Rocks Beach is home to the famous Tiki Gardens (see "Sightseeing") and **Trader Frank's Restaurant and Lounge,** 19601 Gulf Blvd. (tel. 595-2567). Here Jo and Frank Byars have created a little corner of Polynesia, and the cuisine carries out that theme with specialties like hula tail shrimp at dinner, with even lunchtime hot dogs and hamburgers dressed up with a little pineapple and Polynesian "Kikiki" labels. It's a fun, informal place for lunch or dinner, or cocktails in the Wiki-wiki Lounge (try a Tiki Typhoon or Hawaiian Sunset, just for kicks), all served by sarong-clad waitresses, at prices much more moderate than the somewhat touristy surroundings would lead you to expect (starting at $7.50 for dinner, $3.75 for lunch). If the Tiki Gardens are on your sightseeing agenda, then Trader Frank's should be on it for lunch or dinner. Hours are 11:30 a.m. to 4:30 p.m. and 5 to 10 p.m. seven days a week.

There's nothing the least bit "touristy" about **Charlie's Oyster Shucker,** 677 75th Ave., on the gulf in St. Petersburg Beach where 75th Ave. dead-ends into Sunset Way. "Beachcomber" more nearly describes the atmosphere, although it's a little more than the shack that term implies. When I first came across it, quite by accident, I thought it must be a hangout for the younger set, but as I sat in a booth and ate my shrimp steamed in beer (out of this world, for $3.50), I watched people of all ages join the blue-jeans-and-T-shirt crowd at the counter, around the pool tables, or on the outside deck overlooking the water. There was a relaxed, casual banter between waitresses and patrons and a continuous turnover as singles and couples wandered in, ate ample portions of raw oysters and other seafood, joined in the informal conversation that seemed to include anybody within listening range, then left as newcomers came through the screened door. Leta and La Verne Hunter, who started this budget-priced place in 1975, have turned the plain wooden building that has its own dock (boats came and left as I ate) into the sort of beach eatery that I thought had disappeared from the face of the earth. Good, plain seafood at prices anyone can pay, in an atmosphere that exactly fits its locale. There are sandwiches and hot dogs on the menu, too (like a deep-fried grouper sandwich with chips, at $2.75), and the German potato salad (60¢ for a large portion) was so good I had seconds. Highest price on the menu is $4.50 for the combination platter of shrimp and beef ribs. The place is open from 11 a.m. to 2 a.m. (1 p.m. to midnight on Sunday), making it an excellent "drop in" spot. Beer can be had by the glass, pitcher, bottle, or can, and soft drinks, lemonade, iced tea, and milk are also available.

In Clearwater

Just a hop, skip, and a jump north of the Holiday Isles, Clearwater has a restaurant that has become famed throughout the state since it started in a modest manner back in 1957. The **Kapok Tree Inn,** 923 McMullen Booth Rd., takes its name from the gigantic tree that came from India as a seedling and now is the focal point of the restaurant. Like the tree, that small inn has grown into a huge, rambling establishment, with a garden-palace-theater sort of environment that brings to mind the Tivoli outside Rome or the other one in Copenhagen—or a combination of the two! The Chandelier Room, Grand Ballroom, and Florida Room are among eight spectacular dining spaces. The gardens, full of plants and fountains and sculpture, are a special treat. The menu is almost as large as the restaurant, and prices are just above budget (dinners begin at $6, run to $11). Corn fritters come with complete dinners of chicken, shrimp and other seafood, steak and other beef dishes. The Kapok Tree is more like an experience than a restaurant. Call 726-4734 to check seasonal hours and reserve.

Tarpon Springs

A day at Tarpon Springs wouldn't be complete without Greek food. In fact, lunch at the Plaka Restaurant followed by an afternoon of browsing, a sponge-boat trip, or the Spongeorama show (see "Sightseeing") and then dinner at Louis Pappas's elegant restaurant is a day a traveler's dreams are made of!

The **Plaka,** 769 Dodecanese Blvd. (tel. 934-4752), is a marvelous little Greek restaurant that seats only 46 in the vine-trellised dining room. Ted and Goldie Varas call their gyro (that's ground beef with herbs and spices wrapped in pita bread with onions, tomatoes, and sadziki sauce) the "Greeks' answer to McDonald's," and sell it for $2.50. The special Greek salad is all it should be, with lettuce, tomatoes, onions, green pepper, feta cheese, beets, cucumbers, Greek olives, Greek peppers, and anchovies, accompanied by bread and butter —for $1.85. A glass of retsina, the wine of Greece, at $1, makes it a lunch to remember. The Plaka used to be a Greek pastry shop, and the delicacies are still made for Ted and Goldie by a local pastry shop from recipes brought over years ago. They, and all other items on the menu, can be bought to take out.

Louis Pappas' Restaurant, 10 W. Dodecanese Blvd., at the corner of Alt. U.S. 19 and Anclote River (tel. 937-5101), is a completely different kind of Greek restaurant. On the Anclote riverfront right where you turn to go down to the sponge docks, it is as much museum as restaurant, although the food is first-rate. Doric, Ionic, and Corinthian designs are worked into the architecture and decor, with Greek lamps dangling over tables, statues scattered about, a lifesize, three-dimensional mural of the *Death of Hector,* and green plants adding a touch of garden atmosphere. It's a large place, and even has docking facilities for those who come by water. The menu, which features Greek salad, has seafood, of course, alligator steak, kalamarakia (that's squid), moussaka, and prime ribs and steak. Dinners start at $7, and you get a lot of Greek elegance as well as good food for the moderate prices.

St. Petersburg

Just across the Sunken Gardens (see "Sightseeing"), **Bradford's Coach House**, 1900 4th St. N. (tel. 822-7982), creates a restful Olde English setting with old brick and stained glass. It's been here since 1934 and is dearly beloved by the natives (much more so than the newer branch at 132 2nd St. N., which has a "restaurant modern" atmosphere). The menu features prime ribs, choice steaks, frog legs, and seafood, all at moderate prices (beginning at $3.50 for lunch, $5.95 for dinner). There are five separate rooms, including a lounge with entertainment in the evening. It's a good idea to reserve at this popular spot.

Aunt Hattie's, 625 1st St. S. (tel. 822-4812), has a sort of Disney World air, with waitresses in candy-striped uniforms and perky caps, and a spanking-clean, bright, and cheerful decor. "Aunt Hattie" started back in 1939 with a little country kitchen in a very small building, but her good cooking and moderate prices have resulted in this rather large (it seats 200), always crowded restaurant. Salads, chicken, beef, and a limited number of seafood dishes make up the menu, desserts are homemade and good, and the whole family can eat without putting a hole in the budget. Hours are 11:30 a.m. until 9 p.m.

Tampa

The restaurant in Tampa is the **Columbia** (tel. 248-4961), in Ybor City at 22nd St. and 7th Ave. Covering an entire city block and seating more than 1500 people, the Columbia was called "the finest Spanish restaurant in the world" by the Spanish government some years ago. The restaurant started back in 1905 and has grown to include 11 dining rooms and three Latin revues every night. The interior can only be called splendid, with lots of decorated tile, arches, iron grillwork, paintings, and porticoes. Jose Greco-type waiters seem to have been created to match the setting. Specialties are, of course, Spanish, with paella and black bean soup leading the list. Dinner can run anywhere from $8.95 to $19.50, and you'll dine to the music of strolling violinists. Open from 11 a.m. until midnight every day of the year, and in spite of its size, best reserve.

There's a good Italian restaurant in the **Holiday Inn West: Ristorante Mama Mia**, 4732 N. Dale Mabry Hwy. (tel. 877-2489), sits you down in native "areas"—a sidewalk cafe, cantina, groceria—to enjoy classic Italian food that some folks claim is the best in the state. The ceremonial donkey cart that serves as a free, unlimited, do-it-yourself antipasto, sits on a colorful *carnevale* wagon, and loaves of just-baked bread complete the before-dinner scene. Specialties here include osso buco, braciole, shrimp parmigiana, and, naturally, spaghetti, served here with a very special meat sauce. Desserts are great—baba au rhum, biscuit tortoni, and other Italian sweets. Prices are moderate, and doors open at 5 p.m. every day, with service until 11 p.m.

NIGHTLIFE: Typical of the after-dark activity in this area are: the revolving **Bali Hi Lounge** at the top of the **St. Petersburg Beach Hilton Inn**, 5250 Gulf Blvd. (tel. 360-1811), where entertainment and dancing go on until 2 a.m. every day and the **Kon-Tiki Supper Club** in the **Hawaiian Inn**, 6200 Gulf Blvd., St. Petersburg Beach (tel. 367-1902). These are only examples—almost all major hotels and motels and many leading restaurants and lounges feature some form of entertainment in the evening. Check local newspapers or *Guide* for current goings-on.

THINGS TO SEE AND DO: The biggest attraction along this stretch of the Gulf Coast is the beach and related sports. However, if you can take just so much sun and sand and water, there's plenty to keep you otherwise occupied.

Tours

Gray Line buses, c/o Gulf Coast Motor Line, P.O. Box 145, St. Petersburg, FL 33731 (tel. 822-3577), tour St. Pete and the surrounding territory, with varying departures and prices.

Over on St. Petersburg Beach, the **Capt. Anderson** sails from the pier behind Dolphin Village Shopping Center, 4901 Gulf Blvd. (tel. 360-2619), every Tuesday, Wednesday, Friday, and Saturday on dinner-dance cruises. The cruise lasts from 7 to 10 p.m., and the $15.50 (adult) and $13.50 (children) fare includes dinner and entertainment. There are daytime sightseeing cruises Tuesday through Saturday from 2 to 4 p.m., and these cost $4.50 for adults, $2.50 for children.

Theater

The **Showboat Dinner Theatre,** 3405 Ulmerton Road (tel. 576-3818 or 223-2545), brings Broadway productions to St. Petersburg every night except Monday, and matinees are staged Wednesday and Saturday. Decorated in turn-of-the-century fashion, the theater is a plush reproduction of a Mississippi River showboat, and your ticket includes dinner and show. Call to check scheduled productions, current prices, and to reserve.

The **Country Dinner Playhouse,** 7951 Gateway Mall, 9th St. N., St. Pete (tel. 577-5515), also brings Broadway stars to town in first-rate shows. Admission covers buffet dinner and the show.

Fishing

All sorts of fish lurk in these waters, and catches of 40 to 50 head are not unusual when a particular species is in season. Among those that lure the boats out again and again are pompano, whiting, sheepshead, trout, kingfish, drum, flounder, mackerel, and redfish—that's not a complete list, by any means. If pulling them in is what makes you happy, you'll find a charter-boat center at **Madeira Beach,** 13201 Gulf Blvd., just half a mile north of John's Pass Bridge. Call 397-3311 for rates and charter info—or better still, run out there and look them over.

Golf

Golfers won't have to look far for courses—they're all over the place. Four of the many that are open for public play are: the **Clearwater Golf Park,** 1875 Airport Dr., in Clearwater (tel. 447-5272); the **Glen Oaks,** in Clearwater at 1345 Court St. (tel. 446-7275); the **Mid City Par 3,** in St. Petersburg at 3001 13th Ave. N. (tel. 895-5214); and the **Pasadena Golf Club** at 1600 Royal Palm Ave. S. in St. Petersburg (tel. 341-3641). Greens fees and cart costs vary, and reservations should be made as far in advance as possible.

Tennis

The **St. Petersburg Tennis Center,** 650 18th Ave. S. (tel. 894-4378), has a clubhouse and 19 courts open to the public. On Treasure Island, the **Paradise Island Tennis Club,** 10315 Paradise Blvd. (tel. 360-6062), has 21 courts, six lighted, and the clubhouse is open to the public. In Clearwater, the **Bayfront**

Municipal Courts are at 3 Pierce St., with nine courts and metered lights—no reservations.

Sailing

You'll find sailing instruction, sailboat rides on Tampa Bay, charter sailboats, and sightseeing cruises at the **Municipal Marina**, 300 2nd Ave. SE, St. Pete.

Sightseeing

The **St. Petersburg Chamber of Commerce** may be contacted at P.O. Box 1371, St. Petersburg, FL 33731 (tel. 813/821-4069); the **Greater Tampa Chamber of Commerce** is at P.O. Box 420, Tampa, FL 33601 (tel. 813/228-7777).

If you stay at St. Petersburg Beach, you can't miss the **London Wax Museum** at 5505 Gulf Blvd. (across the street from the gulf side). And you really *shouldn't* miss it—as my grandmother used to say, "it's a curiosity." Every single one of the more than 100 lifesize wax figures was created by Louis Tussaud in London (the very best in this field). Historical figures are here, there's a chamber of horrors that will give you the creeps (and a thrill!), and the kids will love such storybook characters as Sleeping Beauty, Little Miss Muffet, and Red Ridinghood. There's an ice cream parlor and video game room, as well. Admission is $3 for adults, $1.50 for ages four through 12; it opens at 9 a.m. with varying closing times (usually between 5 and 7 p.m.) every day except Sunday, when it opens at noon.

North of St. Petersburg Beach, at Indian Shores, the **Tiki Gardens** (19601 Gulf Blvd.) are landscaped with tropical plants, birds, temples, and statuary, creating a South Seas environment that's enchanting. Ten shops offer imports and there's a Polynesian restaurant, Trader Frank's (see "Where to Eat," above). Garden tours ($2 for adults, $1 ages three through 12) run from 9:30 a.m. to 10:30 p.m.

If you've ever heard of St. Petersburg's famous "Million Dollar Pier," don't look for it now. It stood for some 40 years at the foot of 2nd Ave. NE, jutting out into Tampa Bay, but in recent years it's been replaced by a **Municipal Pier** that holds a sort of upside-down pyramid. The five-level complex holds 19 ethnic-oriented shops, restaurants, a cocktail lounge (fun place to watch the sailboats below), and an observation deck (great at sunset!). The view of the bay and the harbor with its hundreds of yachts is fantastic and the shops are fun.

Docked at the Pier is H.M.S. *Bounty,* the authentic replica of the famous ship that Metro-Goldwyn-Mayer had made in Nova Scotia (from the original blueprints on file in the British Museum) for their epic *Mutiny on the Bounty.* Even the setting seems authentic, for the Vinoy Basin at the pier has been turned into a bit of Tahiti to surround the ship. On board, the recorded voices of Charles Laughton as Captain Bligh and Clark Gable in his role of Fletcher Christian bring the true-life drama into focus as you roam the decks. This little bit of history come alive is open from 9 a.m. to 10 p.m. every day, and admission is $3.50 for adults, $1.75 ages four through 12.

One of Florida's most beautiful tropical gardens is at St. Petersburg. **The Sunken Gardens,** 1825 4th St. N., are open every day from 9 a.m. until 5:30 p.m., and it's not inconceivable that you could spend an entire day wandering through the pathways past native Florida trees and exotic plants that have been transplanted here from all over the world. And wildlife is here, too, in the walk-through aviary with its hundreds of colorful birds, monkeys, and even

African pygmy goats. Well worth the $4.50 admission ($2.50 for ages six through 12).

Maybe it's not strictly a sightseeing attraction, but if you come to St. Petersburg from any route other than U.S. 19 South and miss the **Sunshine Skyway,** it's worth a trip out to see the series of bridges and causeways that stretch some 15 miles across lower Tampa Bay to the Bradenton side. Cross the four-mile-long main Skyway Bridge (it stands about 15 stories above the water) for a 50¢ toll, or stop short of it in one of the recreation areas, where there are facilities for fishing, picnicking, and swimming.

In Tampa, don't miss **Ybor City,** the famous Latin section founded in 1886 by Vicente Martinez Ybor after Tampa's Board of Trade made the cigar makers of Key West an offer they couldn't refuse to move their industry north to this area. The two-mile-square area, bounded by Nebraska Ave., 22nd St., Columbus Drive, and East Broadway, is a self-contained Cuban "city," loaded with cigar factories and Latin charm that spills out from stores and restaurants. Building facades with ornate grillwork and old brick walls, garden patios, sidewalk cafes and art displays—but most of all, the infectious gaiety of the people who inhabit this place—combine to create an atmosphere so authentic the complex has been recorded in the National Register of Historic Places. Lots of little Cuban eateries and the famous Columbia Restaurant (see "Where to Eat") are here.

Another "don't miss" in Tampa is the **Dark Continent,** 3000 Busch Blvd. (tel. 988-5171), Busch Gardens Tampa, on Fla. 580, 2½ miles east of its junction with I-75 (you'll see the Busch Blvd. exit). This 300-acre park with its turn-of-the-century African theme has the largest collection of mammals, reptiles, and birds in North America, including a 160-acre veldt, the Serengeti Plain, where more than 500 head of big game roam free. You can view it from steam train, monorail, or skyride. Also, Moroccan shopping bazaar, magic performances, and trained animal shows; *African Queen* boat cruise, Python thrill ride, Swinging Vines, Monstrous Mamba, log flume, and games area; Anheuser-Busch brewery tour; bird gardens with trained bird shows; Bengal tiger exhibit; food facilities including the Old Swiss House restaurant; and travel park for overnight camping. Timbuktu is patterned after the mystical city of the 16th century with more rides, dolphin show, and 1200-seat Festhaus restaurant. Open daily from 9:30 a.m. to 6 p.m. with extended summer hours to 10 p.m. One admission includes all, $11.50. Children three and under, free. Parking $1 per vehicle.

Adjacent to the Dark Continent is **Adventure Island,** a 26-acre water park with 300-foot body flumes, wave pool, main pool, kiddie pools, 60-foot speed slide into a pool, picnic areas, and food facilities. Admission and parking are separate from the Dark Continent; $7.35 ages three and up.

Tarpon Springs

I'm always a little afraid to go back to Tarpon Springs (about 30 miles north of St. Petersburg on Alternate U.S. 19) for fear the colorful old Greek settlement will have changed. Well, to be honest, it *has* changed since I first discovered it back in the early '60s, but the changes haven't spoiled its charm, and the crowds of tourists all seem to take on the relaxed, hospitable personality of hardy Greek sponge divers who built the community on the Anclote River and its bayous. They came here after a dismal attempt to establish themselves among the sponge divers of Key West (they were "invited" to leave by the Key Westers and after a period of what amounted to war, they moved here—a happy choice, as it turned out). The **Chamber of Commerce** is at 528 East Tarpon Ave. (tel. 937-6109).

Strolling Dodecanese Blvd. along the sea wall, watching the sponge boats (decorated with Greek symbols), browsing through the curio shops, stopping for lunch (see "Where to Eat") in a friendly Greek restaurant, attending the sponge auctions in the courtyard of the **Sponge Exchange** (Tuesday and Friday mornings), taking in the **Spongeorama Exhibit Center,** 510 Dodecanese Blvd. (tel. 937-4111), and roaming through the re-created Greek village within its confines (it's open from 10 a.m. to 5 p.m. and costs $1 for adults, 50¢ ages five through 11), or just walking from the sound of one Greek record to another and playing Zorba in my mind—all make this a magical place for me, and it gets better every time I go back. Of course, there are other things to see here, too—like the magnificent Byzantine-style **St. Nicholas Greek Orthodox Cathedral** at 36 N. Pinellas Ave. There's no fee to visit the church, but you must be "properly attired." But the highlight of every visit for me is the 25-minute trip on a **sponge boat** down the Anclote River toward the gulf, where a diver goes over the side, submerges, and comes up holding a newly picked sponge (I always wonder if he took it down with him). This little bit of fantasy romance costs $3.50 ($2 for children under 12), and you get the boat at the sponge docks at 810 Dodecanese Blvd.

I've never managed to be at Tarpon Springs for the **Festival of Epiphany** on January 6 when the priest blesses the waters, young boys dive for a golden cross, everybody joins in the parade through town wearing traditional Greek costumes, and the whole town joins in a night of revelry, with banquets, native dancing, and high spirits. Someday, I promise myself, I'll make that event. In the meantime, Tarpon Springs is the highlight of every visit I make to this part of Florida's Gulf Coast and it's bound to be a delight to any tourist.

READER'S SUGGESTION: "**Innisbrook Resort,** P.O. Box 1088, Tarpon Springs, FL 34286 (tel. 813/937-3124), is all you could ask for if you're looking for a complete sports resort in a semi-tropical climate. There are marvelous golf courses, tennis courts, racquetball courts, no less than five swimming pools, and three clubhouses with excellent restaurants. Accommodations are in really luxurious condominiums. They're less than a half-hour from the Tampa airport, and they'll arrange to meet your plane. Our best recommendations" (Mrs. S. Debnam, Virginia Beach, Va.).

Weeki Wachee Spring

About 60 miles north of St. Petersburg on U.S. 19 (at its intersection with Fla. 50), is a "mermaid show" that makes the drive worthwhile. Weeki Wachee Spring, Brooksville, FL 33512 (tel. 904/596-2062 or 904/596-2007), is actually the source of a river that runs 12 miles to the Gulf of Mexico, producing more than 168,000,000 gallons of water a day, and so deep that they've measured only as far as 137 feet down and don't know how much farther it is to the bottom. Well, around this natural wonder, there's a million-dollar auditorium where up to 500 people can watch underwater ballet, comedy, and acrobatics through 19 *very thick* plate-glass windows. When the show is over, you can go on the Wilderness River Cruise down the Weeki Wachee River, where an Indian trading post, Seminole Indian animal traps, and lots of wild animals can be seen on shore. The whole thing costs $6.50 ($4.50 for ages three through 11), and—you should pardon the pun—it's one whale of a show! Hours are 9 a.m. to dusk.

Chapter XIX

ALONG THE GULF FROM FLORIDA TO NEW ORLEANS

1. Florida's Panhandle (Panama City)
2. Mobile, Alabama
3. Mississippi's Gulf Coast (Pascagoula and Biloxi)

THE QUICKEST WAY TO DRIVE to New Orleans from Florida's west coast is north from St. Petersburg via U.S. 19 to where it intersects with I-10 just beyond Capps, then follow I-10 all the way across. That's if you're in a hurry. Be warned, however, that you'll miss some of Florida's most glorious beaches, a great deal of worthwhile sightseeing, and you won't even get a *glimpse* of the gulf.

A far more interesting and scenic alternative is that offered by U.S. 98, which branches off U.S. 19 at Perry, to Panama City (through Apalachicola and Port St. Joe), then on through Pensacola to Mobile, Alabama. A short stretch of I-10 from Mobile leads west to U.S. 90, which follows the Mississippi Gulf Coast through Pascagoula, Biloxi, Gulfport, and Bay St. Louis to New Orleans. As I said, this route is *not* the one to follow if you're in a hurry—but there are few more delightful drives than this in the entire Southeast, especially if you allow overnight (or longer) stops along the way. My heartiest recommendations go to stops in Panama City and Mobile or Pascagoula (they're so close to each other you'll probably want to choose one or the other, not all). Biloxi is another popular resort that offers an attractive alternative to Pascagoula. In this chapter, then, you'll find accommodations, restaurants, and sightseeing tips for each of these waystops—and I *hope* you won't opt for that quick I-10 drive!

1. Florida's Panhandle (Panama City)

Where Florida's Gulf Coast curves under the top of the state, the 108-mile stretch of pure white sand beach, with an offshore formation that makes for good surf, has been dubbed the "Miracle Strip." More than a dozen resort areas bloom between Panama City and Pensacola, Florida's last outpost before the Alabama border. Although temperatures here range as much as ten degrees lower than those farther south in the state, beaches are pretty well populated year round, and they have become a mecca for students from neighboring Alabama and Georgia during school holidays. Indeed, many residents from those states weekend along this coast regularly. It's a summer "season" in these parts, and like the St. Augustine area, bargain rates are charged in the winter.

Along the coast, history has seen five national flags fly triumphantly, although some for a remarkably short period. Pensacola, for instance, changed hands some 17 times before it settled down as a permanent part of the U.S.! Inland, around Tallahassee, the terrain changes to rolling hills, great oaks hung with Spanish moss, and crystal-clear lakes, with pre-Civil War mansions lending an Old South air.

For the tourist, the beaches unquestionably hold the greatest attraction. To "do" those, as well as such area sights as Tallahassee's beautiful gardens, Pensacola and its U.S. Naval Air Station, we'll base at Panama City. From here, Tallahassee and Pensacola are each two hours away.

YOUR PANAMA CITY BASE: Situated on St. Andrew Bay, just off the Gulf of Mexico, Panama City began life in 1765 as a sleepy little fishing village (the Spanish were there in the 1500s but soon moved on). Today, its deepwater harbor and $7-million marina, at the foot of Harrison Ave., make it an important industrial center as well as a thriving resort city. A little to the west, directly on the gulf, Panama City Beach's *only* business is pleasure—and vacationers find it in full measure along a near-perfect strand of white sand. Accommodations are plentiful and less expensive, generally, than those in South Florida. Southeast of the city, at the end of Fla. 392, St. Andrew State Recreation Area is a 1063-acre point of land dividing St. Andrew Bay from the gulf. Wide beaches and high dunes make it an attractive area for protected swimming, picnicking, fishing, and boating.

Where to Stay

At the beach—that's the logical place for vacationers to stay, and that's where you'll find the following accommodations, either directly on the gulf or not far away.

The **Sandpiper-Beacon Motel**, 17403 West U.S. 98 (tel. 904/234-2154), is a family-oriented motel right on the gulf, with a wide variety of accommodations: rooms with refrigerators, some with complete kitchens, some efficiencies (no oven), and two- and three-room combinations. Furnishings are modern and colorfully decorated. In addition to two outdoor heated pools, there's one indoors, and there are sailboat rentals available. The dining room, open for all three meals, is moderately priced (another convenience for families). Doubles here range from a low of $27 in winter to $47 in the summer.

The smaller **Sea Aqua,** 17643 West U.S. 98 (tel. 904/234-2163), also has kitchens (about $5 above regular rates) and nice, well-furnished rooms on the gulf. No restaurant, but there's one just a block away. Double rooms are $42 to $50 in summer, lower in the fall and winter.

Private patios and balconies are features of most rooms at the **Fiesta,** 13623 West U.S. 98 (tel. 904/234-2179), and their units with kitchens will accommodate up to six people (they're large efficiencies, not apartments). Decor is bright, with a slight "south of the border" accent, and there's a pool as well as the gulf out front. The nearest restaurant is a quarter-mile away— well within walking distance. Rates during the summer run $40 and up for doubles, $60 and up for kitchen units; both are much lower other months.

Facing the bay, the **Holiday Lodge,** 6400 West U.S. 98 (tel. 904/234-2114), has a fishing dock, marina, rental sailboats, and charter boats available. The pool has food and beverage service. Rooms are average size, with modern furnishings, and the dining room stays open quite late, as does the lounge (which has dancing and entertainment during the season). Double rooms here run $42 to $48, with a slight reduction during the off-season.

Budget travelers will find a *Days Inn and Lodge* near the beach, 4810 West U.S. 98 (tel. 904/769-4831), with both spacious, bright rooms and the complete kitchen units this chain features. There's a pool, and the restaurant is open from early morning until 9:30 p.m. Double rooms are $42.88 from May 1 through Labor Day, less other months; kitchen units are $44.88 in season, with a reduction off-season.

WHERE TO EAT: Right on the waterfront in Panama City, the popular, chef-owned **Capt. Anderson's Restaurant,** 5551 N. Lagoon Dr. (tel. 234-2225), is a relaxed, pleasant dining spot with reasonable prices. In a glass-walled dining room with nautical decor, the menu features gulf seafood, as you'd expect, plus charcoal-broiled steaks, which are excellent—as are the rolls and breads, all baked right there. Background music makes it even nicer. Prices are in the $7.98 to $18 range. It is open from 4 to 10:30 p.m. every day except Sunday.

Out at the Treasure Island Marina, the **Treasure Ship,** 3605 Thomas Dr. (tel. 234-8881), is a magnificent replica of a 1690 Spanish galleon, built on the shores of the Grand Lagoon. Modeled after the *Golden Hind,* Sir Francis Drake's flagship, the Treasure Ship towers 135 feet above ground, and a variety of restaurants, lounges, and bars occupy its four levels. The truly lavish "Top of the Ship" is a gourmet dining room, with superb food and a very good wine list. Reservations are an absolute must here, and prices on the à la carte menu average $12.50 for entrées. On Level 3, the "Captain's Quarters" has dancing and live entertainment, with an outside Captain's Walk for enjoying the sunset or stargazing. Another, moderately priced Main Dining Room is walled with glass to give a splendid panoramic view of the lagoon. Informality reigns both at the Main Deck Bar (on Level 3) and the Wharf Galley (Level 1), where drinks and light foods are served. Evening entertainment is in The Brig (Level 1). There's also an Italian restaurant (A Bit of Italy, Level 3), a game room, and a gift shop aboard as well, making this a unique family center. Lunch is served from 11:30 a.m. to 2:30 p.m.; dinner from 4 to 10:30 p.m. Some areas close during winter months, so you may wish to call ahead.

One of the most useful restaurant tips I can pass along is to tell you about **Carlo's Charcos,** Thomas Dr. across from the Sheraton Motor Inn (tel. 234-

0174). Not elegant, but attractive, with a friendly staff, and pizza, steaks, seafood, and breakfast served 24 hours a day from May 15 through Labor Day, 8 a.m. to 10:30 p.m. the rest of the year. It's a great place to drop in casually whenever the need for food nudges you, and at prices that range from $1 for salads to $3.50 for a nine-inch pizza to $7 for a T-bone steak, you can afford to indulge.

In Pensacola

The chef-owned **Driftwood,** 27 W. Garden St. (tel. 433-4559), carries out the beachcomber motif in decor and cuisine. Its seafood specialties come mostly from local waters, and everything comes to table piping hot and deliciously prepared (including the steaks that are also featured on their menu). Prices run from $5 to $7 at lunch, $9 to $17 at dinner. Hours are 11 a.m. to 3 p.m. and 5 to 10 p.m. (dinner only on Saturday, closed Sunday).

There's both a dining room and a separate oyster bar at **The Oyster Bar,** 709 N. Navy Blvd. (tel. 455-3925), where the local seafood is excellent. Informality and moderate prices are the keynotes here. I especially liked the place at lunch—it was busy but friendly and efficient. It's open every day except Tuesday from 11 a.m. to midnight, with lunches in the under-$5 range, dinners from $4.95 to $9.50.

In the Seville Square area, an absolute "don't miss" is **Seville Quarter.** A local businessman, Robert Snow, began putting together a dining and entertainment complex in a block of historic old buildings at 130 E. Government St. some years ago. Enlisting the aid of master construction supervisor Robert Pugh, he has restored interiors into **Rosie O'Grady's Good Time Emporium,** a Gay '90s spot that features Dixieland jazz; **Lili Marlene's,** with a World War I aviator's pub atmosphere and entertainment; the **Palace Oyster Bar,** featuring seafood, gumbo, and one of the grandest bars I've seen in years; **Coppersmith's Galley,** a turn-of-the-century dining room; **Apple Annie's Courtyard,** featuring drinks and country and bluegrass music; **End o' Alley Bar,** tucked away in a gas-lit, Victorian courtyard complete with fountain; and **Phineas Phogg's Balloon Works,** where disco and boogie rule supreme. The place is an unforgettable experience, and I found it hard to tear myself away for the sightseeing on my list. The Palace and Apple Annie's are open for lunch from 11:30 a.m., and Coppersmith's serves dinner from 6 to 11 p.m. Hours and entertainment vary at the other spots, so call 433-7436 for current goings on. The Quarter is open seven days a week and after 7 p.m., there's a $3 admission charge to the complex.

There is also a **Morrison's** here, in the Town & Country Mall on U.S. 29, which serves from 11 a.m. to 8 p.m. with the usual good food dished up by this chain. They have a fried fish almondine (not usually found in cafeterias) that I found delicious.

THINGS TO SEE AND DO: Around Panama City, water-related activities dominate the scene. There are the beaches, of course, and the Intracoastal Waterway draws boaters (you'll spot numerous public boat ramps). Fishing seems to be the main preoccupation with both visitors and residents, and just a few of the fishing piers open to the public are those at **St. Andrew State Recreation Area,** the **County Pier** on U.S. 98 West, and **Hathaway Bridge,** also on U.S. 98 West. There is very good bass, bream, and perch fishing at the **Dead Lakes State Recreation Area,** 30 miles east on Fla. 22, then north on Fla. 71.

From early May through mid-September, you can bet the dogs at the **Ebro Dog Track** (about 15 miles north of Panama City on Fla. 79). No minors, of course, and admission is $1. Races start at 8 p.m. every night except Sunday.

Golfers can play at the **Signal Hill Country Club,** W. Thomas Drive and Fla. 392 (tel. 234-5051), or the **Colony Golf Club,** 112 Fairway Blvd., just off U.S. 30A (tel. 234-6586).

At **Anderson's Pier,** Thomas Drive at Grand Lagoon (tel. 234-3435), you can charter deep-sea fishing boats, reserve for the boat trip out to **Shell Island** ($3.50 for adults, $1.75 for children), or join sightseeing and dinner cruises. Call for days and hours, which vary. Deep-sea fishing charters are also available.

Kids will love the coal-burning steam engine at **Petticoat Junction,** ten miles west on U.S. 98 at Long Beach Resort. The amusement area, with many other rides, is open from March 15 through Labor Day from 2 to 11:30 p.m. Admission is free to the park, and you can purchase a combination ticket for $6.50 which covers all rides or pay individually (rides from 60¢ to $2).

In Tallahassee

Contact the **Chamber of Commerce,** 100 N. Duval St., P.O. Box 1639, Tallahassee, FL 32302 (tel. 904/224-8116).

When the first legislature convened in Tallahassee, it met in a log cabin. That was 1824, and since then, Tallahassee has built an impressive capitol building around the 1845 structure that replaced that log cabin and has grown and prospered on the business of government.

The 22-story State Capitol building, on Monroe St. and Apalachee Parkway, sits atop Tallahassee's highest hill, towering above the city. Tours are conducted free of charge from 8:30 a.m. to 4:30 p.m. weekdays, 9 a.m. to 4:30 p.m. on weekends except for major holidays. The Old Capitol, on S. Monroe St., is a classically simple building with columned porticos and a massive dome. Restoration is now underway, after which it will again be open to the public.

Five miles northeast of the center of the city, on U.S. 319, the **Maclay State Gardens,** 3540 Thomasville Rd. (tel. 893-4232), cover 308 acres which were once part of a private estate. The gardens cover 25 acres, with one of the South's finest collections of azaleas and camellias, and there is a picnic area on the lakeshore. The mansion on the grounds, with some rooms restored, is open January through April. The gardens open at 9 a.m. and close at 5 p.m., and entrance fees are 50¢ per person May through December, $1.50 per adult and 75¢ per child January through April.

In Pensacola

This important seaport that means "navy" to many an ex-enlisted man and officer, changed its national allegiance a total of 17 times; and the town itself moved once, over to Santa Rosa Island, as Spanish, French, English, Confederate, and Union governments fought over it. Since 1914, however, when the U.S. Navy located its **Naval Air Station** here because of the abundance of clear flying days, there has been no question of its nationality.

You can tour the air station on your own in your car, and sentries have free guide maps at the entry gates (it's southwest of town, and you won't have any trouble finding it—just follow the crowd).

In the city, go by the **Pensacola Historical Museum** (405 S. Adams St. at Zaragoza St.) and pick up a free booklet and walking tour guide for historical buildings and shops in **Seville Square** (E. Government and South Alcaniz Sts.). There are interesting old homes and churches and even an oldtime sawmill, all open free to the public, in this park that commemorates the Spanish-English period of Pensacola's history. And don't forget to stop by Seville Quarter (see "Where to Eat"). The museum is open every day except Sunday.

2. Mobile, Alabama

Alabama's only seaport, Mobile sits near the head of Mobile Bay on the west side of the Mobile River. Approaching from the Florida coast, you'll get a close look at the docks that are the lifeblood of the busy port, but don't for one moment be misled into thinking that you're approaching an industrial center and nothing else. The Old South is alive and well in this gracious city, even in the center of town, where proud old homes trimmed with iron-grillwork balconies line streets fanning out from Bienville Square.

Mobile, like the southern belle she is, over the years has flitted from one national admirer to the other, with the flags of France, England, Spain, the United States, and the Confederacy fluttering overhead at one time or another during her long history, which began in 1702. It wasn't until federal troops occupied the city on April 12, 1865, and firmly implanted the Stars and Stripes that Mobile settled down to a life of constancy in her national identity.

Today, in addition to the shipping, there's one of the largest drydock and shipbuilding centers on the gulf located here. In addition, industry encompasses chemicals, steel, petroleum refining, food processing, and pulp and paper production. All of which makes Mobile a fascinating mixture of old and new—and during Mardi Gras (the two weeks preceding Lent), her French heritage takes over, with mystic society parades each evening that rival those of New Orleans.

WHERE TO STAY: The city itself offers much sightseeing, along with accommodations that afford both comfort and convenience. However, there is a nearby spot—Point Clear—which combines a resort atmosphere with sightseeing just a short drive away.

In Mobile

The **Malaga Inn,** 359 Church St. (tel. 205/438-4701), is a small, utterly charming hotel consisting of restored 1862 twin town houses, with a garden courtyard and fountain. Many of the original furnishings are in evidence in public rooms. Guest rooms are nicely furnished, many with oversize beds. There's a pool and an excellent restaurant (see "Where to Eat"). You really can't do better if the graciousness for which the South is noted is what you're after. Double rates start at $45, and all rates increase slightly during Mardi Gras.

The **Best Western Admiral Semmes,** 250 Government Blvd. (tel. toll free 800/528-1234, or 205/432-4441), is a large, attractive motor hotel conveniently located to downtown. Rooms are spacious and decorated in above-average motel decor. There's a pool, restaurant, and lounge. Doubles run from $40 to $45, and children under 18 stay free with parents.

More moderately priced accommodations (though of very high quality) are to be found at the **Days Inn,** 3651 Government Blvd. (tel. 205/666-7750), where doubles begin at $30.88.

In Point Clear

Halfway down Mobile Bay, 23 miles east of Mobile on U.S. 98, Point Clear has been a resort area for Southerners since shortly after the Civil War. The

Marriott's Grand Hotel, Point Clear, AL 36564 (tel. 205/928-9201), carries on today, and the key word here is luxury. From the warm, awe-inspiring lobby that rises two stories high, is centered by a huge fireplace, filled with brass, porcelain, and antiques, and paneled and beamed by cypress, to the cypress-paneled rooms and cottages, quiet elegance holds sway. The dining room makes each meal an experience, especially if you get there early enough to sit next to the glass-walled end that overlooks the bay. As for facilities, there's a little bit of everything: a 27-hole championship course, deep-sea fishing, sailing, water-skiing, a pool and a beach area, bowling on the green, shuffleboard, skeet and trap shooting, a recreation hall, dancing and entertainment in the Bird Cage cocktail lounge, and if you have a favorite activity I've left out, it's probably there, too. There's free bus service to the Mobile airport, and the hotel will arrange sightseeing tours. The Grand Hotel operates on a modified American plan (breakfast and full-course dinner included in rates), and offers rooms in the main building, the Bay House, and cottage units for two to eight persons. Rates, per person, for double occupancy range from $88 to $94. They offer a wide variety of golf and family package plans. No pets.

WHERE TO EAT: At Point Clear dining is pretty well restricted to the Grand Hotel listed above (however, that's no handicap, since it is well above average). In Mobile, you'll find restaurants galore—here are my favorites:

The **Malaga Inn,** 359 Church St. (tel. 433-5858), features gracious dining in a Spanish setting. There's background music, and jacket and tie are a must in the evening. Specialties here include escalopes de veau au parmesane, lump crabmeat pestalozi, and steak peperonata, as well as other continental dishes, all exceptionally well prepared and served. The dining room is open for all three meals (7 a.m. to 10:30 p.m.), with breakfast running $2.45 to $6; lunch, $2.95 to $8.95; and dinner, $7.95 to $29.95. Closed Sunday and holidays.

Constantine's, 271 Azalea Rd. (tel. 343-0600), has been in Mobile since 1934 (though not at this same location), run by the same family, and so *well* run that when I was an Alabama resident years ago it was a foregone conclusion that any trip to Mobile meant dinner there. Their specialties are prime ribs, steak, and—best of all, in my opinion—fresh gulf seafood. They serve lunch and dinner at moderate prices: lunch, $3 to $5; and dinner, $6.75 to $15.75 (children's plates from $3). Hours are 11:30 a.m. to 2 p.m. and 6 to 10 p.m., and dress is casual.

Wintzell's Oyster House, 605 Dauphin St. (tel. 433-1004), prides itself on serving oysters "fried, stewed & nude;" but other seafood dishes come to table just as tasty as the bivalves. This is a casual, friendly place for lunch or dinner, and very popular with locals. Hours are 11 a.m. to 9:45 p.m., and prices run from $3 to $14, with children's plates at $2.50.

THINGS TO SEE AND DO: The Tourist Information Center is at 451 Government St. (tel. 205/433-6951).

For a look at a classic "Old South" mansion, visit **Oakleigh,** 350 Oakleigh Pl. at Savannah St. It was built by slaves between 1833 and 1838, and bricks for the first floor were handmade right on the premises. The Historic Mobile Preservation Society has restored the house to its pre-1850 period, complete with authentic furnishings. There's an interesting display of Civil War artifacts and Mardi Gras memorabilia. Oakleigh is open from 10 a.m. to 4 p.m. Monday through Saturday, 2 to 4 p.m. on Sunday; and admission is $3 for adults, $2 ages 12 through 18, $1 ages six through 11. Closed major holidays.

The **Richards–DAR House,** 256 N. Joachim St., is a restored Italianate town house built around 1860. It holds period furniture and has a lovely curved, suspended staircase and elaborate ironwork. It's open 10 a.m. to 4 p.m. Tuesday to Saturday, 1 to 4 p.m. on Sunday, closed major holidays. Admission is $2 for adults, 50¢ ages under 12.

There's a free **Fine Arts Museum of the South** on Museum Drive on the south shore of the lake in Langan Park featuring antiques, crafts, paintings, and prints. Hours are noon to 5 p.m., Wednesday through Sunday.

About one mile east of Mobile via Bankhead and George C. Wallace Tunnels on Battleship Parkway (U.S. 90), the battleship U.S.S. *Alabama* is moored as a memorial to World War II servicemen from Alabama. Tours, from 8 a.m. to sunset, cost $3.50 for adults, $1.50 ages six to 11. Also in the memorial park are the submarine U.S.S. *Drum* and World War II aircraft.

One of Mobile's most spectacular showplaces is about 20 miles southwest (via U.S. 90 or I-10 and Bellingrath Rd.) near Theodore. On more than 800 acres, the **gardens** were developed with the help of French, English, and American landscape architects, and in addition to the 70 varieties of native trees, there are 250,000 azalea plants (200 varieties), gardenias, camellias, roses, water lilies, dogwood, and hydrangeas. The **Bellingrath home** holds collections of Dresden and Meissen porcelain, china, crystal, and Oriental rugs, and is furnished with antiques. Plan plenty of time for your visit so you can enjoy the many wooded walks through the gardens. Hours are 7 a.m. to dusk; admission is $3.60 for adults, $1.80 ages six through 11 for the gardens, $4.50 more for the home, which is open to limited numbers at one time from 8 a.m. to 5 p.m. No matter what time of the year you come, you can be sure something will be blooming at Bellingrath. If you're passing by and want to stop, there's a restaurant at the entrance, as well as kennels for pets of owners who want to tour the gardens.

3. Mississippi's Gulf Coast (Pascagoula and Biloxi)

The 65-mile Mississippi Gulf Coast is a traveler's paradise. Along with the world's longest man-made beach (hurricanes have devastated the beaches time and again, but constant maintenance keeps them intact most of the time), you'll find the coast drive edged by modern hotels, one lovely old home in Pascagoula that's become an inn, countless fine restaurants, and gracious homes. The history of the region is rich in Spanish and French domination, and Mardi Gras is a big event all along the coast. As for scenery, it is breathtakingly lovely (between, that is, the commercial clusters dotted along the way). This is a short drive, but it's one you'll want to make leisurely, and for that reason, I'm including accommodations and restaurants in two of the most popular stopping points, as well as sightseeing tips at each. The only problem you're likely to encounter is deciding *where* to reserve, for there are hundreds of first-rate hotels and motels along the coast. But, *do* reserve ahead if you can, for during the summer season it is quite possible to find almost every room booked, especially on weekends when residents of Mississippi and its neighboring states head for the gulf.

PASCAGOULA: This shipbuilding center dates back to 1718, and its colorful history even further back. Long before the advent of white men in Mississippi, the peaceful Pascagoula Indian tribe lived here, and when a young warrior fell in love with a princess from the fierce Biloxi tribe and spirited her away, the Biloxis went on the warpath. Finding themselves outnumbered and outfought, the Pascagoulas (so the legend goes) walked into the river holding hands and chanting a song of death until the last voice was hushed by the dark waters. Only a romantic legend? Perhaps. Still, there is, to this day, an unexplained singing sound plainly heard in late summer and autumn months in the stillness of Pascagoula evenings, and it seems to come from the river—scientists have never come up with a satisfactory reason for the singing!

Where to Stay

Nearly as romantic as the legend of the Singing River, is **Longfellow House,** 3401 Beach Blvd. (tel. 601/762-1122). Once named "Bellvue," the main house was built in 1850 by slave traders from New Orleans. Since then, it has been a girl's school (run by a headmaster who turned out to be something of a rascal), fallen into the hands of wealthy Northerners who had a penchant for drink, become the property of a sea captain, and finally the happy home of a plantation owner and banker and his family. Somewhere along the way, Henry Wadsworth Longfellow was supposed to have stayed here, and some say he wrote "The Building of the Ship" during his visit.

Today, the house itself is used only for the dining room (a lovely, sunny room looking out over wooded grounds), the popular lounge (which has entertainment and is always filled with locals as well as guests), offices of the inn, and private parties in the upstairs rooms. Guest rooms are in one- and two-story cottages scattered along pleasant walkways through vast lawns and planted gardens. Rooms are much larger than most luxury hotels, and nicely furnished, either opening onto or overlooking the landscaped grounds. There's a pool, golf, tennis, racquet ball, shuffleboard, sailing or boating, and charter-fishing trips can be arranged. For all the feeling of elegance and pampering by the friendly staff, rates are a surprisingly low $45 for doubles, $52 for a cottage that will accommodate four.

In a more modern vein, the **La Font Inn,** on U.S. 90 East (tel. 601/762-7111), is a large, pleasant motel just off the highway, with spacious rooms overlooking the pool, steam baths in some rooms, and oversize beds in many. A lifeguard is on duty at the pool in summer, and there's a playground and wading pool for the young folk. The dining room is reasonably priced and very popular with natives. Doubles here start at $40.

Where to Eat

The **Longfellow House dining room** serves three meals a day, and at lunch or dinner you're likely to see a host of Pascagoula regulars who have come to rely on the excellence of the food here. Specialties include crab or shrimp served in cream and cheese sauce flavored with wine, fresh gulf flounder stuffed with shrimp and crabmeat dressing, and baked spring chicken. The menu is semi à la carte (salad and potato come with several entrees), and prices run from $7.95 to $15.95 at dinner. A wide selection of sandwiches and salads is available at lunch at moderate prices. The dining room itself is a relaxed, garden-type room, with fresh flowers, lots of greens and yellows, and windows looking out over the grounds. Breakfast is served 7 to 11 a.m., lunch from 11:30 a.m. to 2 p.m., and dinner from 6 to 11 p.m.

At the **La Font,** Sunday dinner is an event, with a fixed-price menu ($9 for adults, $5.50 for children) that features baked ham with wine sauce, fresh crabmeat Newburg, veal scallopine, and roast leg of lamb. Vegetables are really fresh and nicely prepared, and the price includes five courses. Other times, dinner prices run $7.95 to $17. Breakfast hours are 6 to 10 a.m., lunch from 11 a.m. to 2 p.m., dinner from 6 to 10 p.m.

Things to See and Do

First of all, if you want to become a true believer in that old Indian legend, try to go down to the **Pascagoula River** (two blocks west of the courthouse) on a hot summer evening just about twilight. You'll hear it faintly at first, then experience the odd sensation of hearing the humming sound swell in volume and seem to come closer to where you stand. The strangest thing of all is that although you *know* it is very near—almost underfoot—you are totally unable to pinpoint exactly where it comes from. It seems to come from any point to which you direct your attention. Go; then I *dare* you to pay any heed to scientists who say it *may* be sand scraping the hard slate bottom of the river!

Five blocks north of U.S. 90 or eight miles south of I-10, the **Old Spanish Fort,** 4602 Fort St., was built in 1718 by the French, later captured by the Spanish. Said to be the oldest fortified structure in the Mississippi Valley, its walls are of massive pine timbers held together with a mixture of oyster shells, mud, and moss. It's open daily from 9 a.m. to 4:30 p.m. except major holidays, and admission is $1 for adults, 50¢ for children.

Two interesting sightseeing destinations are inside the old **L & N Railroad Station** at Magnolia and Railroad Sts. Mississippi crafts are on display at the **Senior Craft Shop,** where needlework, quilts, jewelry, toys, and ceramics made by senior citizens of Pascagoula and vicinity are featured. Original paintings, pottery, and prints by area artists are in the **Old Gallery.** There's no charge to visit either—the gallery is open 11 a.m. to 3 p.m. Monday through Friday; the Craft Shop from 10 a.m. to 4:30 p.m. Tuesday through Saturday. Both are closed on holidays.

BILOXI: This is one of the prettiest towns along the gulf, with Spanish moss trailing from tall trees and magnolias, camellias, roses, and crape myrtle lining its streets. On a peninsula, with 25 miles of coastline, Biloxi first became a resort about the mid-19th century, when inland cotton planters discovered the pleasures of the shore. The only industry that intrudes is the seafood industry, and hundreds of shrimp boats operate out of the town. In early June, there's a Shrimp Festival that culminates in the beautiful Blessing of the Fleet ceremony. Ship Island, 12 miles across Mississippi Sound, was the landing place for seagoing vessels (the sound itself is shallow) in the early days of settlement and was the first glimpse of their new home for some 80 "casket girls" sent over by the French government to marry the settlers (everything they owned was packed in small, wicker "caskets," hence the name.)

Where to Stay

To my mind, the most elegant place to stay in Biloxi is the **Broadwater Beach,** P.O. Box 127, Biloxi, MS 39533 (tel. 601/388-2211 or toll free 800/647-3964). Set in 33 acres of landscaped, wooded grounds, it offers lighted tennis courts, two 18-hole golf courses, a putting green and driving range, lawn games, Ping-Pong, and two pools plus a wading pool. Rooms are large and brightly decorated, and for sheer luxury, there are cottages scattered about the grounds. Doubles run $65 to $80, cottages considerably more.

The **Royal d'Iberville,** 3420 W. Beach Blvd. (tel. 601/388-6610), also has large rooms, many with balconies, extra basins in separate dressing rooms. There's a split-level swimming pool, lighted tennis, and golf privileges at nearby courses. The dining room is above average, and the lounge has dancing and entertainment. Doubles are $56 to $65.

More moderate in price, and quite nice, is the **Beach Manor Motel**, 325 E. Beach Blvd. (tel. 601/436-4361). There's a sundeck overlooking the gulf, and a lounge that has live entertainment and dancing. There are kitchenettes as well as nicely appointed rooms. Doubles are $32 and up on weekdays, $40 and up on weekends and holidays, and kitchenettes run $7 more.

Where to Eat

In a converted house and slave quarters built in 1737, **Mary Mahoney's Old French House**, 138 Rue Magnolia (tel. 374-0163), oozes charm, with fireplaces, antiques, a patio for cocktails, and courtyard dining. Of course, you can't eat charm, and at this place the food measures up to its surroundings. Try the lobster George or the red snapper. Semi à la carte prices range from $4 to $7 at lunch, $7 to $15 at dinner. Hours are 11 a.m. to 10:30 p.m. every day except Sunday and Christmas. It's a good idea to reserve.

White Pillars, 100 Rodenburg Ave. at West Beach (tel. 432-8741), is in a restored southern mansion set back from U.S. 90. Gourmet cuisine stars here, with specialties such as eggplant Josephine, trout en papillotte, and trout Florentine. In addition to the main dining rooms, there's enclosed patio dining, and entertainment and dancing. Hours are 6 to 11 p.m., and it closes on Sunday and major holidays. This is another place reservations are in order. Prices are in the $13.50 to $19.50 range.

For more casual dining at family-oriented prices, you can't do better than the **Sea 'n Sirloin**, 3455 W. Beach Blvd. (tel. 388-6387). It's a big place right on the water, with wide windows to let you enjoy the view as well as the food. The à la carte menu has shrimp boiled in the shell, oysters on the half-shell, fried crab claws and a host of other seafoods at moderate prices, with $16.95 the top price (for the sea 'n sirloin special—sea being lobster stuffed with crabmeat). But perhaps the best buy on the gulf is the buffet served six days a week here. The price is just $5.95 on weekdays, $6.95 on Sunday, and $7.95 on holidays. This is definitely a place to bring the family! Hours are 11 a.m. to 10 p.m., seven days a week.

Things to See and Do

Contact the **Chamber of Commerce** at P.O. Drawer CC, Biloxi, MI 39533 (tel. 601/374-2717).

If you're a Civil War buff, you'll want to visit **Beauvoir**, the home of Jefferson Davis for the last 12 years of his life. Some years after his release from a Federal prison, the former Confederate president came south and, among other things, wrote *The Rise and Fall of the Confederate Government*. After his death, Beauvoir was used as a home for Confederate veterans, and in 1941 turned into a Confederate shrine. On the 88-acre grounds are the home, the little white pavilion Davis used as his library and study, a guest cottage, a museum, and the Confederate cemetery. It's five miles west of Biloxi on U.S. 90 (W. Beach Blvd.), and open daily except Christmas from 8:30 a.m. to 5 p.m. Admission is $3.50 for adults, $2.75 for over-65s and military personnel, $1 ages seven to 12, and $1.50 ages 13 to 17.

Not far from Beauvoir is the **Biloxi Lighthouse**, built in 1848 (on W. Beach Blvd.—U.S. 90—at the foot of Porter Ave.). During "that" war, when federal forces were approaching, the intrepid lady lighthouse keeper climbed to the top, removed the lens, and buried it. Still, when Lincoln was assassinated, the citizens of the town painted the entire structure black. It's white now, and automated (but for some 62 years, the light was faithfully tended by a mother-and-daughter team).

At the lighthouse, you can catch the **Shrimp Tour Train,** an open trolley that leaves six times a day for a sightseeing trip to historic points and such modern attractions as Keesler Air Force Base. Fares are $3 for adults, $1.75 for military personnel, and $1.50 ages three through 12. Phone 432-0523 to confirm departures.

Chapter XX

INTRODUCTION TO NEW ORLEANS

1. By Way of Background
2. Traveling to New Orleans
3. Traveling Within New Orleans

AMONG AMERICAN CITIES, New Orleans reigns supreme in my affections. I say that without reservation (although with a slight apology to New York City) and with the knowledge that many thousands share my love for this lively, lovely old city. From her beginnings, she has had room for all comers and a gracious welcome for those just passing through. You could love her for that alone, but there's much, much more to beguile you in the Crescent City.

There's all that history, of course, and when you walk the narrow streets and see old, old buildings trimmed with fancy ironwork—not set aside as sterile museums, but as functional today as when they were built (even though the functions have changed)—it almost seems that long skirts and frock coats should be passing rather than blue jeans and sweatshirts. It doesn't take much imagination to picture Gen. Andrew Jackson deep in conference with pirate Jean Lafitte over a table at the Old Absinthe House. Or to see with the mind's eye calico-clad black women swaying through the streets hawking sweet pralines as they balance on their heads huge wooden bowls filled with the sugary treats. Then, just around a corner, there's the brassy sound of jazz or the low moan of the blues spilling out into the streets and you know it's the 20th century and this city is anything *but* lost in its past.

There's a vitality about New Orleans that keeps her eternally young, never mind the accumulation of years. She draws the young like a magnet while holding the old close to her heart. I'll not soon forget the night in Preservation Hall when a very young Swedish clarinet player sat in with men who've been playing jazz since it began, and all were comfortable and happy in the music they made together. I guess you could say there's no generation gap in New Orleans. You see that around Jackson Square, too, where artists of all ages sit at their easels painting and sketching with varying degrees of expertise, at ease with life and each other. Or at the Cafe du Monde across from the square near the old French Market, where New Orleanians and visitors alike congregate for strong, hot café au lait and beignets (that's pronounced "baan-yaas" and they're a cross between a doughnut and a cruller, liberally sprinkled with powdered sugar—absolutely delicious!) at all hours of the day and night, young and old rubbing elbows happily.

And if New York is a "melting pot," New Orleans is more a "melding pot," for there's a soft blending of race, color, nationality, and accent—everything and everyone seem to come together here in terms of interests that unite rather than spawn conflict. The explanation, of course, lies in the city's long history of widely different groups who met headlong in combat, only eventually to join hands in mutual enterprise.

1. By Way of Background

Founded in 1718 by Sieur de Bienville, the strategically located settlement was named for the then Regent of France, Duc d'Orléans. Around the Place d'Armes (now Jackson Square) streets were laid out and rude huts built in what we know as the French Quarter, or Vieux Carré (it means Old Square and is pronounced vew-ka-ray). Government buildings and a church were added, and one of the most successful promotion campaigns in history drew shiploads of settlers from Europe, Africa, and the Caribbean—merchants, royalty, exiles, criminals, slaves—all expecting to find a paradise on earth. Whatever their reactions when they arrived to find swampy land, mosquitoes, and the rawness of frontier life, they stayed on to implant the niceties of European culture adapted to New World circumstances. Ursuline nuns came in 1727 and were soon importing "casket girls" (poor, but "nice" French girls who brought their belongings in casket-like trunks) to wed settlers and provide "respectability"—or so the nuns hoped, although one could, and still can, find "respectability" defined in many different terms in New Orleans!

As the little colony grew and prospered, it reflected much of the gaiety and fashion of the French court as practiced by aristocrats who arrived in ever-increasing numbers. Descendants of this privileged class were the original "Creoles," although with time the name has come to mean well-to-do French-speaking natives of mixed French and Spanish ancestry. It also offered refuge to Acadians from Nova Scotia, most of whom soon moved out to become farmers and trappers (ancestors of present-day "Cajuns," who still speak French in their own peculiar style), and was a welcomed shore leave for seafarers who added their own dash of spice to the color and growing sophistication of the city.

In 1762, New Orleanians woke up to find that their king, Louis XV, had given Louisiana, along with its residents, to his cousin, Charles III of Spain, beginning a period of hostility and revolution on the part of Frenchmen who bitterly resented the new rule. It wasn't long, however, before Spanish and

French were intermarrying and the city took on yet another hue. After two disastrous fires in 1788 and 1794 which left most of New Orleans in ashes, a proud new town began to emerge, much of it erected in the Spanish style of brick and plaster buildings with many arches, courtyards, balconies, and, of course, attached slave quarters. Tile markers at every corner still list the old Spanish street names.

By this time, New Orleans was a prize much desired by the English and Americans, and the French government also wanted it back. Governor Carondelet surrounded the city with five forts connected by a strong city wall (which, significantly, had cannons pointing both inside and out!), but in 1800 it was quietly given back to France, which held control until 1803, when Napoleon sold all of Louisiana to the United States for $15,000,000, a move natives viewed with horror, since all Americans were considered barbarians. Americans, when they found no welcome in the warm-blooded Vieux Carré, set to work building their own New Orleans "uptown" north of Canal Street. Splendid homes began to appear in what is now the Garden District and their commercial section took on a boomtown air. Since "downtowners" desperately needed some of that uptown Yankee money, and since the newcomers found themselves drawn to the vitality and warmth of downtown, and because everyone joined in a constant battle against hurricanes, yellow fever epidemics, and floods, a spirit of unity gradually developed between the two sections. And when Andrew Jackson called for volunteers from every segment of New Orleans citizenry to protect the city from British attack in 1814, some 5000 responded. With cannon and ammunition supplied by the pirate Jean Lafitte, they soundly defeated 8500 seasoned British troops, saving the city and the Mississippi for the U.S., and emerging with a confidence that was largely responsible for the most prosperous and glamorous era yet known in the delta city.

Increasingly wealthy cotton and sugarcane planters built mansions upriver and maintained luxurious town houses in New Orleans, making frequent visits to attend festivals, parades, opera, theater, banquets, and spectacular balls (some, the "Quadroon Balls," were held solely to introduce beautiful mulatto girls to the gentry as possible mistresses), or to patronize opulent gambling halls and resplendent "bawdy houses." Hardworking Irish and German immigrants poured in, along with Italians, all of whom added bits of culture and tradition to the already exciting milieu. For a time, New Orleans was the richest city in the country, and its citizens enjoyed a truly exotic existence.

The Civil War ended all that and the town went through a bitter period of Reconstruction from the time federal troops marched in during 1862 until they finally left in 1877. Since then, although some of its flamboyance is gone, New Orleans has clung to its unique heritage, learned about drainage and epidemic control, given birth to American jazz, and most of all, retained an enthusiasm for fun in almost every form that is simply not equaled any other place. Today's visitor will find the French Quarter still marked by its original "downtown" settlers' architecture and lifestyle, "uptown" still vibrating with Yankee business enterprise, and the combination one of the friendliest, heart-warming cities in the world. Incidentally, natives pronounce it "New ORL-yons"!

NEW ORLEANS CLIMATE: Light-weight clothing is all you'll need in New Orleans most seasons, for the average mean temperature is 70°, and I have found that a medium-weight raincoat will usually provide enough warmth any time; although during winter months, you might want to carry along a somewhat heavier coat, since it can get down to the high 50s. With a total annual rainfall of 63 inches, the city can be damp and it's a good idea to have an umbrella and that raincoat handy.

TELEPHONE AREA CODE: When telephoning to New Orleans, the area code for all sections of the city is 504.

2. Traveling to New Orleans
New Orleans is a "gateway" city, and as such has entry transportation of almost every kind available.

BY AIR: There are no fewer than 18 airlines serving New Orleans from within the United States and from South America: Eastern, Delta, Pan Am, Republic, Texas International, Continental, Aviateca, TACA International, SAHSA Servicio Aereo de Honduras, Aeromexico, American, Jet America, Lacsa, Ozark, Royale, Southwest, TWA, USAir, and Northwest Orient.

BY TRAIN: Amtrak has runs to New Orleans from both coasts and Chicago, and no fewer than *seven* tour packages that make New Orleans a bargain as well as a joy. They will also be offering good-value World's Fair tours during 1984.

BY BUS: Greyhound and Continental Trailways serve New Orleans, as do Southeastern Stages, Texas Bus Lines, Sun Valley Bus, Oklahoma Transport, New Mexico Transport, Gulf Transport, Arrow Coach, ABC Coach, Illini-Swallow Lines, Central Texas, and Transportes del Norte.

BY CAR: From Picayune, Mississippi, you can travel I-59 to New Orleans; from Baton Rouge, U.S. 61; and from Biloxi, Mississippi, or the west coast of Florida, I-10.

3. Traveling Within New Orleans
The first thing that must be said about traveling around New Orleans is don't do anything or go anywhere until you've stopped by the **Visitor Information Center** at 334 Royal St. (tel. 504/566-5011) in the French Quarter. Operated by the Greater New Orleans Tourist and Convention Commission and the Louisiana Tourist Development Commission, the center is a veritable fount of information; they have excellent maps for walking or driving tours, booklets on restaurants, accommodations, tours, special attractions, and just about anything you could want to know. And they'll give you a cup of that good New Orleans coffee while you orient yourself. The staff is multilingual, as befits this city of so many accents, and as friendly as any you're likely to meet.

GETTING YOUR BEARINGS: The layout of New Orleans is fairly simple, and getting around is not at all difficult. The historic **French Quarter** (Vieux Carré), where the city began, lies in a 13-block-long area between Canal St. and Esplanade Ave. Directions are apt to be given by New Orleanians as "riverside" or "lakeside" (referring, of course, to toward the Mississippi River or toward Lake Pontchartrain), and in that context, North Rampart St. is the "lakeside" boundary, the Mississippi the "riverside." "North" or "South" on street names simply refers to north or south of Canal St., although most streets change their names when they cross Canal. As for building numbers, they start at 100 on both sides of Canal, and at 400 in the Quarter at the river (that's because four blocks, already numbered, of the original settlement were lost to the river before the levee was built). Jackson Square is at the very heart of the Quarter, facing Decatur St. "riverside" and Chartres St. "lakeside," bounded on one side by St. Ann St., by St. Peter St. on the other. Across Decatur St. from the square is pretty little Washington Artillery Park, with its splashing fountain, back of which the elevated Moon Walk (named for Mayor "Moon" Landrieu), complete with benches and hanging lanterns, runs along the riverfront.

The business district is directly above Canal St. from the French Quarter, and toward the lake. The lovely **Garden District** is bounded roughly by St. Charles Ave., Magazine St., and Jackson and Louisiana Aves. Farther along St. Charles Ave., you'll find Loyola and Tulane Universities, and Audubon Park. "Fat City" can be reached via Veterans Highway to Causeway Blvd.—its other boundaries are West Esplanade and Division St. Lake Pontchartrain lies out Canal St. to West End Blvd. or Pontchartrain Ave.

The 1984 Louisiana World Exposition (known locally—and in this book— as the World's Fair) is situated on an 82-acre site stretching along the Mississippi immediately adjacent to the central business district, near the foot of Canal Street. The main entrance is on South Front Street, near its intersection with Girod, and you'll know it by the spectacular entrance gates.

BY CAR: Thrifty, National, Hertz, Avis, Budget, Econo-Car, and Dollar Rent-A-Car car rentals are available both within and near the airport. The driving tour detailed on the Visitor Center map can't be beat if you plan to spend much time behind the wheel.

BY BUS: From that same Visitor Information Center, you can pick up a copy of "Where to Find It in New Orleans," a map and guide which shows all bus routes, clearly marked with bus numbers. All bus fares are 60¢ except expresses, which are 65¢.

A very special bus ride if your feet really aren't up to a walking tour of the French Quarter is the **Vieux Carré Minibus.** This quaint little transit line leaves Canal and Bourbon Sts. from 6 to 9:30 a.m. and 4 to 6 p.m. on weekdays; or you can board at Bourbon and Iberville 9:30 a.m. to 4 p.m. and 6 p.m. to 12:30 a.m. weekdays, all day on Saturday, Sunday, and holidays. It'll cost you just 60¢ to see all of the French Quarter in comfort, although I personally recommend the hoof-it route.

A TOUR BY TROLLEY: No matter how else you see New Orleans, reserve at least an hour and a half to ride the famous old **St. Charles streetcar** (which, incidentally, has been named a National Historic Landmark). The trolleys run 24 hours a day, at frequent intervals, and the fare is 60¢. You can pick up an all-day, unlimited-rides pass from **The Streetcar Store,** 111 St. Charles Ave. (tel. 524-2626), for $4.50, and for another $6, have their invaluable **Streetcar Guide to Uptown New Orleans,** which identifies attractions by car-stop number and gives you tons of information about each stop. Then, for the most complete look at "uptown" along the historic old avenue, board at Canal and Carondelet Sts. (just across Canal St. from Bourbon Street), sit back, and look for landmarks in this part of town. Lafayette Square is at the 500 block of St. Charles, and just across from it, the 1840s Gallier Hall, which was the seat of the city's ruling fathers for 100 years.

At Lee Circle, a little farther on, you'll see a huge statue of the general (Robert E., that is), and from here on, it's fun to watch the homes that line the street as they change from Greek revival architecture to Victorian to early 1900s. From Jackson Ave. on, the houses are surrounded by gardens, not the other way around as in the Quarter, giving rise to the "Garden District" name of this area of huge mansions built before the Civil War. Loyola and Tulane Universities are located at the 6000 block, across from Audubon Park with its huge old live oaks, zoo, lagoons, children's amusement park, tennis courts, and a municipal golf course. The park extends all the way to the levee at the Mississippi and is a worthwhile stop if you have the time—you can always catch the next trolley for the remainder of the ride up St. Charles.

The ride back to your beginning point will cost another 60¢, and I like to change sides on the return trip to see all the things I missed going out. This is without a doubt the best $1.20 buy in New Orleans.

BY HORSE AND CARRIAGE: Who could resist the authentic old horse-drawn carriages that pick up passengers at Jackson Square? Drawn by horses suitably adorned with flower-and-ribbon-trimmed straw hats, the carriages cover 2¼ miles of the French Quarter, with drivers giving a nonstop monologue on the historic buildings along the way. They operate from 9 a.m. to midnight in good weather, and the cost is either $6 or $7 (I paid $7, but was quoted the lower price by another driver, so it might pay to shop a little), with those under 12 paying half-fare.

BY FERRY: One of New Orlean's nicest treats is absolutely free. It's the 25-minute ferry ride across the Mississippi from the foot of Canal St., and it's a joy whether you go by day for a view of the busy harbor or at night, when the lights of the city reflect in the mighty river. It takes 25 minutes for each crossing, so be sure to allow about an hour for the round trip. It carries car and foot passengers, in case you want to do some West Bank driving between trips.

BY FOOT: Within the French Quarter and the Garden District, there simply is no better way to get around than by foot and the Tourist Commission, 334 Royal St. (tel. 566-5011), has a very good walking tour map. Distances are not difficult to manage, and only by ambling can you really see the charm of both places. In the Quarter, glimpses of lovely patios and courtyards come one after another as you stroll the narrow sidewalks, and you can stop to listen to live jazz pouring from the open doorways of several saloons that have nonstop music most of the day. In the Garden District, walking permits you to drink in the beauty of formal gardens that surround the mansions. See the listing below for two excellent guided walking tours.

TOURS: Friends of the Cabildo (tel. 523-3939) is a nonprofit, volunteer group that sponsors a two-hour guided walking tour of the French Quarter, leaving from the Presbytere, 751 Chartres St. at 9:30 a.m. and 1:30 p.m. Tuesday through Saturday except holidays. You'll be asked for a $5 donation ($2.50 for ages 13 to 20—free for those 12 and under), and no reservations are necessary; just show up, donations in hand.

Three different walking tours are conducted by the Jean Lafitte National Historical Park Information Center, 527 St. Ann St. (tel. 589-2636), at no charge at all. The "History of New Orleans" tour is a 1½-hour walk through the French Quarter, with an informative historical narrative; the two-hour "City of the Dead" walk is a tour of St. Louis Cemetery No. 1 and includes a commentary on the historical development and social customs of the burial system in the city; and you take potluck with the 1¼-hour "Odds and Ends" tour, which might explore French Quarter legends, the history of jazz, the haunts of Jean Lafitte, or almost any other intriguing facet of New Orleans. Call ahead for days and hours scheduled.

Gray Line Tours, 108 University Pl. (tel. 525-0138), has City Tours ($13), a Plantation Tour ($26, includes all entry fees), and an After Dark Tour ($28) that includes three nightclubs, drinks, gratuities, and cover charges. They'll call for and deliver you to selected hotels.

Destination Unlimited, P.O. Box 56187, New Orleans, LA 70156 (tel. 821-5200), provides a nighttime tour that begins with dinner in the elegant revolving rooftop restaurant, the Vendome, at the Hyatt Regency Hotel, then takes in floor shows at the Fairmont supper club, Chris Owens' 809 Club, and the Blue Angel. All expenses are included in the fee.

Adventure Louisiana, 636 St. Ann St. (tel. 523-2906), has a unique Voodoo Tour for lovers of the occult. You'll see the only voodoo museum in the U.S., a voodoo church, Congo Square, the house and tomb of voodoo queen Marie Laveau, and stop for refreshments at the Voodoo Lounge. The charge includes all admissions and refreshments. This same outfit also offers two other unusual and interesting tours: the 6½-hour Plantation Glamour (the charge covers drinks, admissions to historic old plantations, and dinner in a restored slave dwelling); and the eight-hour Bayou Wilderness Tour (a trip deep into the bayous to visit quaint old Cajun villages, with a stop at a restored Cajun cabin from the old days and a Cajun-style seafood dinner). Call for current prices and reservations.

If the horse-drawn carriages represent romance on land, they are matched on the river by several oldtime steamboats that leave from the foot of Canal St. for **river cruises.** The S.S. *President* (tel. 586-8777) has been hauling visitors around the harbor since 1933 and is the largest and oldest side-wheel steamboat in America. There are five spacious decks, food and beverages at moderate prices and glamorous moonlight dance cruises from 10 p.m. until midnight.

The gracious *Natchez* (tel. 586-8777) is the newest of the stern-wheelers and leaves from the Toulouse St. Wharf for 2½-hour "up and down the Mississippi" cruises. Facilities include both snackbars and dining rooms, as well as cocktail lounges. Adults pay $8.50; children six to 12, $4.25, with those under six traveling free.

The delightful *Cotton Blossom* zoo cruises leave the Canal St. dock daily, and you can purchase either round-trip or one-way tickets (perhaps returning by the St. Charles streetcar), both of which include admission to the zoo. Adults pay $9.50 round trip, ages three through 15, $4.75; one-way fares are $7.50 and $3.75. You'll find food and beverage services aboard. Call 586-8777 for schedules and reservations.

There's a daily bayou cruise aboard the *Bayou Jean Lafitte,* departing the Toulouse St. wharf at 11 a.m. and returning at 4 p.m. Tickets are $11.50 for adults, and $5.75 for ages six to 12. Call 586-8777 for reservations.

Note: As we go to press, there are no scheduled special cruises for the World's Fair, but they are almost surely on the drawing boards. If you plan to visit the city during that event, contact in advance, New Orleans Steamboat

Company, 2340 International Trade Mart, New Orleans, LA 70130 (tel. 504/ 586-8777), for information on any additional cruises operating then, as well as those listed above.

Chapter XXI

NEW ORLEANS HOTELS AND RESTAURANTS

1. Hotels, Motels, and Guest Houses
2. Restaurants

TRUE TO HER HERITAGE of hospitality to the traveler, New Orleans today is lavish in her offering of accommodations and cuisine. No matter what the budget, taste, or style, the Queen City is certain to have at least one establishment that fits the bill exactly.

1. Hotels, Motels, and Guest Houses

In the years that had elapsed since my last visit to New Orleans, hotels and motels had sprung up all over the place, and I almost dreaded going back—I couldn't bear the thought of the French Quarter being defaced with highrise, modern monstrosities, no matter how luxurious inside or how much easier they made a stay in the city. I needn't have worried: everything within the Quarter has been kept to the same style as the historic old buildings lining the streets, and it is sometimes difficult to tell if a "new" hotel has been built from scratch or simply placed inside, the shell of one of the gracious old buildings. The older hotels are still there, even more comfortable and elegant than I remembered, and the motor hotels do away with that ever-present problem, parking. As for the guest houses, they are a different breed in New Orleans, for instead of the slightly frayed rooms that usually go with the name, many of those here are furnished with antiques and presided over by people who love the city and want their guests to do the same, making them "hosts" in the true sense of the word. In short, accommodations in New Orleans, no matter what the price range, are likely to give the visitor more than just a place to lay a weary head.

As we go to press, the biggest lodging news in New Orleans is the spate of new hotel construction underway in anticipation of the 1984 World's Fair. The additional accommodations have been sorely needed for some years and should ease the housing situation tremendously. While most have not been completed at this writing, it *is* possible to give you names, addresses, and telephone numbers, with a brief description in some cases. All are located outside the French Quarter, and many are within easy walking distance of the fairgrounds.

Before listing recommendations in the various sections, I should warn you that even with the thousands of new rental rooms in New Orleans, there are times when there isn't a bed to be had. The summer months are crowded, making advance reservations an absolute must, and as far in advance as possible, please. If you're planning to come to the city during a holiday, to attend the World's Fair, or at Mardi Gras time (it begins soon after Christmas, when the Carnival season opens and lasts until "Fat Tuesday," the last day before Lent), it isn't an exaggeration to say you should reserve as far in advance as possible, and in the case of Mardi Gras, as much as a year ahead! There is always the chance, of course, that you'll run across a cancellation and be able to book at the last minute, but that chance is remote, to say the least. A good time to visit if you want to miss crowds and hard-to-find lodging, is in the month immediately following Mardi Gras or in the fall months, when weather is mild enough to be comfortable and the streets are not nearly so thronged as at other times.

As I've stated throughout this book, the prices quoted are as of the time of writing and subject to change. Another thing you should know is that *all* prices go up for holidays and Mardi Gras.

IN THE FRENCH QUARTER: For my money, the *only* place to stay in New Orleans is in the Quarter—it is the very heart and soul of the city, pumping life and vitality into its own confines and beyond. There's a concentration of accommodations that should make it possible (except, of course, during Mardi Gras or the World's Fair) for you to find the type of hotel that suits you in the price range you want if you book far enough in advance.

Hotels

The French Quarter's largest, and one of its oldest, hotels has been family operated by three generations of Monteleones. Covering almost the entire 200 block of Royal St., the 600-room **Monteleone Hotel**, 214 Royal St. (tel. 504/523-3341), seems to keep growing and expanding over the years without losing a trace of the charm that has been a trademark since its beginning. Rooms cover the whole decor spectrum, from luxurious, antique-filled suites, to more modern, very comfortable family rooms. The trellis-trimmed, green and white Le Cafe restaurant is a favorite among native New Orleanians, and the Carousel Bar, which slowly revolves under its red and white striped canopy, also draws the locals. Up on top, the fabulous Sky Terrace has to be seen to be believed: there's a heated swimming pool, a putting green, the 9-to-5 Bar and the exquisitely elegant Sky-lite Lounge, really a rooftop club that features top-notch live entertainment, such as the famous "Dukes of Dixieland." This is, for my money, the "Grand Old Lady" of New Orleans hotels and well worth the more-than-modest prices. Rates begin at $85 and range to $125 for double occupancy.

Much newer, but very elegant, is the **Royal Orleans**, 621 St. Louis St. (tel. toll free 800/223-5757, or 504/529-5333), considered by many as "the" place to stay. The rooms and public rooms here reflect the same old-world style as does the outside, with its New Orleans grillwork. Guest rooms, too, are sumptuously furnished, with many extra touches, like a "goodnight mint" and beds turned down at night. You can dine informally in the Cafe Royale's garden setting or go gourmet in the classic Rib Room. The Touche Lounge is a sidewalk cafe by day, a cozy gathering place at night. In the Esplanade Lounge, there's soft music after 8 p.m. Doubles here are in the $100 to $150 range.

Yet another luxury hotel in the Quarter is the **Royal Sonesta**, 300 Bourbon St. (tel. 504/586-0300), also adorned with those lacy New Orleans balconies. It's large, with some 500 rooms, many of which have elegant period furnishings and overlook inner patios or the pool. Begue's, the elegant restaurant, serves daily buffets by day and continental and creole cuisine by night. Light meals and snacks are available in the Greenhouse, an indoor-outdoor cafe featuring soups, salads, crêpes, and creole specialties. Best of all, it's right smack in the middle of Bourbon St. action. Doubles here begin at $95.

Still in the luxury class, but quite different in style, is the small, European-style **Maison de Ville**, 727 Rue Toulouse, (tel. 504/561-5858), built in 1742. In addition to gem-like rooms, some furnished with antiques, there are cottages available, one of which was John Audubon's residence when he was painting *Birds of America* in the 1820s. The very personal service here includes a breakfast of fresh orange juice, croissants, steaming chicory coffee, which you may have in your room, or on the patio, or in the parlor, and complimentary sherry and port served in the afternoon and evening. Morning and evening newspapers are delivered to your room and that almost-vanished shoe-polishing service is available—just leave them outside your door at night and notify the desk. Double occupancy rooms begin at $95, suites at $180, and cottages at $250.

The sophisticated elegance of the **St. Louis**, 730 Rue Bienville (tel. 504/581-7300), makes this a very special place, with a decided European flavor. The courtyard, with its huge marble fountain, antiques, and gilt-framed oil paintings are indicative of the luxury you'll find in guest rooms. Some rooms have private balconies overlooking the courtyard. Doubles run from $110 to $160, with suites starting at $180. Children under 12 are free with parents.

The **Bourbon Orleans**, 717 Orleans St. (tel. 504/523-5251), is a member of the Ramada chain but with no trace of the "plastic modern" so often found in chain hotels. Instead, rooms are done in a warm, almost plush decor. There is a refrigerator and sink in every room, a pool, and babysitter service. Double rooms run from $65 to $90.

The lovely **Place d'Armes Hotel**, 625 St. Ann St. (tel. 504/524-4531), has one of the most magnificent courtyards in the Quarter, as well as the largest swimming pool. Rooms are homey, many of them wallpapered and all furnished in traditional style. The Carriage Cafe is Parisian coffeehouse style and serves breakfast and lunch at moderate prices. The just off Jackson Square location makes sightseeing a breeze. Bedrooms start at $75 double occupancy, and one-bedroom suites are $140 and up.

Motels

Right in the heart of everything is the **de la Poste Motor Hotel,** 316 Chartres St. (tel. 504/581-1200). The 100 rooms are all spacious and comfortable and most either overlook the Grande Patio and pool or face onto one of the more interesting French Quarter streets. The courtyard, incidentally, has a magnificent staircase leading up to a second-level outdoor patio. Parking is free, there's a babysitting service, and children under 12 pay nothing when occupying the same room as parents. Double occupancy rooms begin at a stiff $85, but location, accommodations, and service all qualify as deluxe.

The **Inn on Bourbon Street,** 541 Bourbon St. (tel. 504/524-7611), sits on the site of the 1859 French opera house, the first one built in the U.S., which burned to the ground in 1919. It's hard to tell, however, that the present building hasn't been here for just that many years, so well have the planners integrated its design into New Orleans traditional architecture. All rooms have a Deep South decor and oversize double beds, and some have balconies overlooking Bourbon St. There's a pancake parlor that serves around the clock, the Beef'n Bourbon dining room, and the Cabaret Toulouse with continuous entertainment. Prices here hinge on whether or not your room faces Bourbon St. and has a balcony. Doubles without same begin at $75.

A restored row mansion and a macaroni factory have been combined to create **Le Richelieu Motor Hotel,** 1234 Chartres St. (tel. 504/529-2492). The folks here are proudest of their VIP suite, which has three bedrooms, a super kitchen, and even a steamroom—and which goes for $300 a night! But the "ordinary" guest rooms I saw were all exceptionally nice and *much* less expensive (doubles begin at $65). The large courtyard holds a pool, where you lunch poolside. Most rooms have balconies and all overlook either the French Quarter or the pool and courtyard.

There are no fewer than *five* patios—each one a real jewel—at the family-owned **Provincial Motor Hotel,** 1024 Chartres St. (tel. 504/581-4995). The 1830s building has kept its high-ceilinged rooms, and each one is decorated in a distinct style with imported French and authentic Creole antiques. My favorite holds a huge carved mahogany double bed with a high overhanging canopy topped with a carved tiara. Gaslights on the patios and the overall feeling of graciousness make this one a real delight, a tranquil refuge from the rigors of sightseeing or nighttime revelry. Rates run $65 and up for a double-occupancy room.

A bit out of the center of things, but close enough to be convenient, the **Landmark French Quarter,** 920 N. Rampart St. (tel. 504/524-3333), is built around a large courtyard which focuses on the pool. All rooms open onto long, outer balconies that run the length of each wing, affording pleasing courtyard or street views. The attractive sidewalk cafe lets you drink or dine poolside. Rates here begin at $65 for double occupancy.

The **Chateau Motor Hotel,** 1001 Chartres St. (tel. 504/524-9636), is one of the best buys in town, both in terms of comfort and just plain charm. Its flagstone-paved courtyard is bordered by an awning-covered cafe, where breakfast or lunch may be taken in the out-of-doors and the classic statuary and fountains add a continental touch. There are some four-poster beds as well as bed-living room combinations. Parking is free. Doubles here begin at $55.

The **Best Western French Market Inn,** 501 Decatur St. (tel. toll free 800/528-1234, or 504/561-5621), is just two blocks from Jackson Square, in a historic building restored to its former beauty. Rooms, which face the lovely tropical patio or views of the Quarter, are individually decorated, many with exposed brick walls. Rates for doubles range from $65 and up, and include complimentary coffee and morning newspaper.

Guest Houses

I met Mrs. Junius Underwood, proprietor of the **French Quarter Maisonnettes**, 1130 Chartres St. (tel. 504/524-9918), over morning coffee—hers, not mine. When I apologized for the intrusion, she quickly assured me, "I haven't had a hot cup of coffee in years, but I don't mind, I'd much rather chat with my guests." This gracious lady presides over an 1825 mansion that you enter through a wide carriage drive paved with flagstones leading to the plant-filled courtyard with its three-tiered fountain. Most rooms open onto the courtyard and each is comfortably furnished and has its own private bath. The location is a sightseer's dream: across the street is the historic Beauregard House, next door is the original Ursuline Convent built in 1734 and said to be the oldest building in the Mississippi Valley, and just a few blocks away is the old French Market, so handy for coffee and beignets to begin or end the day. Best of all, there's Mrs. Underwood, whose thoughtfulness toward guests extends to furnishing a privately printed brochure containing tips on dining, sightseeing, shopping, and almost anything else to make your visit more entertaining and comfortable, all gleaned from her intimate, longtime association with New Orleans. And there's Jesse, who has worked here for years and whose pleasant personality and always-cheerful assistance adds immeasurably to your stay. Rates run $40 and up, and there is parking for a slight fee.

Jim Weirich and Don Heil have opened their lovely old home at **623 Ursulines St.** (tel. 504/529-5489). Centered around a courtyard that holds blooming orchids, azaleas, crape myrtle trees, and magnolias, are four suites in old slave quarters. All are thoroughly modern and have a bedroom, living room, and private bath. There are three suites of comparable size in the main house. Rates begin at $46 for double occupancy.

Down on the *quiet* end of Bourbon Street, the **Lafitte Guest House,** 1003 Bourbon St. (tel. 504/581-2678), is in a residential neighborhood, yet close enough to the action for easy walking. The three-story brick building, adorned with balconies on the upper floors, was built in 1849, and the restoration has retained marble fireplaces and 14-foot-high ceilings. Furnishings are a mix of antiques and modern upholstered furniture. A telephone in each room and a continental breakfast are included in rates, which begin at $68.

The **Lamothe House,** 621 Esplanade Ave. (tel. 504/947-1161), was built in 1800 and is largely furnished with antiques. The pretty flagstone courtyard has flowering plants, banana plants, and a small fish pond. There is free parking on the premises, color TV, and AM/FM radios in each room. Rates for doubles on the courtyard or balcony begin at $65 and include a Creole breakfast.

The **Hotel Villa Convento,** 616 Ursulines St. (tel. 504/522-1793), is really a small inn that is run much like a guest house by the Campo family. The 24 rooms in the restored Creole townhouse are luxuriously furnished and have full baths, TV, and telephones. Some face onto the patio, others have balconies, and there's a small, cheery breakfast room just off the lobby where orange juice, coffee, toast, and sweet rolls make up the continental breakfast. The central courtyard features a three-tiered fountain and tropical plants. Doubles here begin at $40, with suites running $95 and the unusually attractive loft rooms at $60.

A French Quarter Hostel

L'Auberge Hostel and Guest House, 717 Barracks St. (tel. 504/523-1130), is not your usual hostel, and just barely misses being a full-fledged guest house. Nancy Saucier has converted a classic "double shotgun" Creole house into accommodations that fit each category. There are five single beds in one side (you may, for instance, share a bedroom as in a hostel), and kitchen and bath are shared by all guests. The other side contains sleeping space for six, and may be rented alone (there's a private kitchen and bath) or as hostel-type space. Also, it is possible to rent either side exclusively if you have a family or large group. The rooms are furnished with antiques, there's a patio to use for cook-outs, and Nancy has bicycles for hire—a perfect way to get around the French Quarter. Rates run from $30 for one upward to varying rates, depending on how many share room, location, etc. For one entire side, rates are $125. Nancy doesn't take reservations, but if readers of this book will telephone a day in advance of arrival, and mention the book by name, she will hold space if it is available.

READER'S SUGGESTION: "We stayed at the Burgundy Inn, 911 Burgundy St. (tel. 504/524-4401). The rooms were small, but very quaint and clean. Right in the heart of the French Quarter" (P. Crespo, Panama).

OUTSIDE THE QUARTER: Convenience based on special interests may well lead you to prefer accommodations outside the Quarter, and there is a wide variety from which to choose.

Hotels

The **Pontchartrain Hotel,** 2031 St. Charles Ave. (tel. 504/524-0581), is as elegant as its Garden District location. Rooms are beautifully furnished, many with service bars; service is so polished you'll feel pampered (for example, your bed is turned down at night and nightclothes laid out); and the gourmet cuisine of the Caribbean Room is internationally known. Everything in this 50-year-old New Orleans institution is in the continental tradition, and "deluxe" is the only word that fits. Prices, too, fall into that category, with double rooms beginning at $95.

The luxurious **Fairmont Hotel,** University Place (tel. 504/529-7111), is just one block from the French Quarter. The famous Sazerac Restaurant is sheer elegance; some of the best shows in town are featured in the Blue Room; and the Sazerac Bar is open mornings as well as evenings. Rooms are plush, with elegant modern furnishings. Prices are, of course, also in the luxury range, with a $100 beginning rate for double occupancy.

Le Pavillon, Poydras and Baronne Sts. (tel. 504/581-3111), is a lovely small hotel with a French château air. You enter under Corinthian columns supporting a high porte-cochère and into a lobby with marble stairs and floors and decorated with statuary and elegant wall hangings. Furnishings are in the French style, with warm sun colors punctuated by cooler sea tones. There's a rooftop pool and a lounge with entertainment and dancing. And best of all, Le Pavillon is very convenient to the French Quarter. Doubles here start at $100.

Over on the riverfront (in an area some are now calling the "River Quarter"), the **New Orleans Hilton,** Poydras St. at the Mississippi River (tel. 504/561-0500), radiates such New Orleans character that it's hard to believe it is a relative newcomer on the scene. This *is* a modern, highrise hotel all right, but inside the public rooms are warm with shades of tea roses and emerald green and lots of mahogany paneling. And the food and entertainment reflect the Crescent City perfectly, as do the hospitable and efficient staff. That consummate New Orleanian, Pete Fountain, entertains in his own club here. Guest rooms are unusually spacious, many with river views (others overlooking the cityscape). Doubles are in the $95 to $125 range, and the luxurious suites start at $175.

The **Avenue Plaza Hotel,** 2111 St. Charles Ave. (tel. 504/566-1212 or toll free 800/535-9575), exudes graciousness from the moment you enter the mahagony panelled lobby with its large fireplace. All 100 rooms have a wet bar, coffee maker, fridge, TV, and clock radio and all are furnished quite nicely. There's a cheerful, window-lined dining room looking out onto St. Charles Avenue, a courtyard pool and a rooftop sun deck and physical fitness area. Doubles begin at $90.

The **Sheraton New Orleans,** 500 Canal St. (tel. 504/525-2500 or toll free 800/334-8484), rises 49 stories, with some 1200 rooms, including 175 very posh accommodations in the luxurious Tower Section. Rooms are beautifully furnished, there's a heated outdoor pool, tour booking service, and entertainment in the lounge every night except Sunday. Double rates begin at $106, but there are some extremely attractive package deals available.

The **St. Charles Hotel,** 2203 St. Charles Ave. (tel. 504/529-4261), is right on the trolley line, and a ten-minute ride takes you to the French Quarter. The hotel itself is in the beautiful Garden District. Rooms are unusually spacious, they have a restaurant and lounge, and the staff is both friendly and helpful. Rates start at $58 for doubles.

About Those New Hotels

Construction is at various stages of completion on the bevy of new hotels in New Orleans, with late-summer or early-fall opening dates in 1983 projected. In the absence of specific information on these hostelries, however, I will simply list two of the deluxe hotels and two in the more moderate price range. By the end of 1983, telephone numbers should be available through New Orleans operators so that you may contact the ones that have special appeal.

The **Iberville Hotel,** 365 Canal St., New Orleans, LA 70130, is one of the exclusive Trusthouse-Forte properties and promises to be in the deluxe price range, with luxurious accommodations.

Another in the deluxe class is the **Hotel Inter-Continental,** 444 St. Charles Ave., New Orleans, LA 70130, and plans call for a gourmet restaurant on the premises as well as rather complete exercise rooms.

A new **Ramada Inn** is planned at 1732 Canal St., New Orleans, LA 70157, that will undoubtedly have rates that are moderate by New Orleans standards.

In Metarie, the new **Holiday Inn-Crowne Plaza** is at 3445 N. Causeway Blvd., Metarie, LA 70002, and should be ready for occupancy by early 1984.

Motels

The **Quality Inn Midtown,** 3900 Tulane Ave. (tel. 504/486-5541), is just minutes away from the Quarter, and rooms are nicely decorated, above average in size for this price range. There's a gourmet restaurant, a lounge with live entertainment, and free off-the-street parking. Doubles begin at $48.

The **Holiday Inn-East Highrise,** 6324 Chef Menteur Hwy. (tel. 504/241-2900), is northeast of the city at the junction of U.S. 90 and I-10. Rooms are typical of this chain (i.e. attractive and comfortable), there's a pool, dining room, and entertainment in the lounge except on Sunday. Doubles are in the $48 to $55 range. In the other direction, the **Holiday Inn-Gretna,** 100 West

Bank Expressway (tel. 504/366-2361), offers attractive rooms just across the river from the city. There's a pool, dining room, and a lounge with entertainment on Friday and Saturday. Doubles run $43 to $50.

Located two miles from the airport and 14 miles from the French Quarter and Superdome is the 371-room **Days Inn-New Orleans Airport,** 1300 Veterans Blvd., Kenner, LA 70062 (tel. toll free 800/241-3400 or 800/325-2525). There are the usual above-average rooms with two double beds, some lodge accommodations with kitchens, a pool, restaurant, and a laundry. Also, transportation to and from the airport. Budget prices begin at $35.88.

Guest House
Right at the edge of Audubon Park, the **Park View Guest House,** 7004 St. Charles Ave. (tel. 504/861-7564), is an old Victorian home—it's on the National Register of Historic Landmarks—with comfortable rooms at bargain prices. There's a large lounge (with a lovely stained-glass window) and dining room where a complimentary continental breakfast is served. Most rooms have private baths, and those that don't only share with one other room. Double rooms cost $40 to $50 per day. This location is especially convenient if you plan to visit Tulane, Loyola, or Dominican Universities.

Campgrounds
KOA New Orleans East, Rt. 1, Box 335E, Slidell, LA 70458 (tel. 504/643-3850), has 130 campsites (for tents and trailers), a pool, store, LP gas, playground, laundromat, and picnic facilities, and will arrange tours. To reach it, turn east off I-10 at L.A. 433 and drive half a mile. Rates are $11.

KOA New Orleans West, 219 S. Starrett Rd., River Ridge, LA 70123 (tel. 504/467-1792), has large, shaded sites for both tents and trailers, a pool, store, laundromat, and tour arrangements. To reach it, take I-10 to Williams Blvd., then south 2½ miles to Jefferson Hwy. and left three-quarters of a mile. Rates are $12.

2. Restaurants
Just as her people are a mixture of many cultures, New Orleans's cuisine reflects a rich blending of much of the world's cooking. As a well-known New Orleans cook once wrote, the food is "grandchild to France, descendant to Spain, cousin to Italy, and also is full-fledged southern." That just about says it, except that she might have added the West Indies and American Indians to the gastronomic ancestry.

The "haute cuisine" and provincial French recipes brought to the New World by early settlers fast acquired the flavorings of native herbs and filé (ground sassafras leaves) used by local Indians, the Spanish saffron and peppers that arrived a little later, West Indian vegetables, spices, and sugarcane, and African influences that survived the slave-boat voyages and made their way into white kitchens as black women took over much of the cooking. Out of all this came a distinctive Creole cuisine found only in New Orleans. Italian touches came later, adding another dimension to the city's tables, and dishes from the American South were retained virtually intact.

Along with their love of the exciting combinations—and they are endless —that resulted from this "stew" (or perhaps "gumbo" is a better word) of international cooking, the people of New Orleans have inherited an appreciation for fine service in elegant surroundings and have acquired a sense of fun that permits gourmet dishes to appear in the plainest of settings and the plainest meal of boiled crawfish or red beans and rice to come to table in the fanciest of eateries. And no matter where a meal begins, it is likely to end down in the French Market over café au lait and hot beignets.

If you're in the mood for that perfect service and posh setting, you'll find it at your elbow. Or if taste and budget call for simpler dining, that, too, is never far away. "Downtown" in the French Quarter or "uptown" in the newer part of town, good eating is an integral part of any visit to New Orleans.

FRENCH QUARTER DINING: The city's best—certainly the most famous —restaurants are right here. Read on.

The Top Restaurants

Who hasn't heard of **Antoine's,** 713 St. Louis St. (tel. 581-4422), and dreamed of at least one meal in this legendary restaurant that has been run by the same family for more than 130 years? Just entering the ironwork-adorned building set the tone, and once inside you're in a world of white tile floors, slowly turning antique ceiling fans, 14 separate rooms that run the gamut from plainness to grandeur—and tuxedo-garbed waiters. As for the food, choose from such classics as oysters Rockefeller, pompano en papillote, chicken Rochambeau, or filet de boeuf Robespierre en casserole; or settle for something simpler from a menu that lists more than 150 selections. To accompany your choice, you have at your disposal one of the richest wine cellars in America. Be sure to bone up on your French before you come, for there's not a word of English on the à la carte menu (or resign yourself to asking for help from the waiters, who can sometimes be quite condescending about it). I must confess to a growing disappointment in this fine restaurant—for years, no matter how high the check or how long the wait for a table, I always left knowing it was money and time well spent. That's not always true these days, sad to say, and you'll have to decide for yourself if a visit to one of America's most famous eating places is, in itself, compensation for overpriced and less-than-perfect meals served by indifferent waiters. Prices are à la carte, and complete dinners run upward of $20 per person. Lunch hours are noon to 2 p.m., dinner from 5:30 to 9:30 p.m. It closes Sunday.

Brennan's, 417 Royal St. (tel. 525-9711), is a longtime favorite with residents and visitors alike. There's just no way to describe their beautiful patio— you have to see it to believe it. "Breakfast at Brennan's" has become internationally famous, and you can breakfast here even in the evening. Only if that's what you have in mind, don't plan another meal that day—you'll want to be able to do justice to the sumptuous dishes listed on a menu that tempts you with items like eggs Hussarde (poached eggs atop Holland rusks, Canadian bacon, and marchand de vin sauce, topped with hollandaise sauce and accompanied by grilled tomato—$13.75) or pompano Pontchartrain amandine (sauteed in butter with grilled almonds, lump crabmeat, and lemon butter sauce—$15.75). Even their omelets are spectacular. You see, this is not your typical bacon-and-eggs breakfast, but breakfast in the old tradition of antebellum days in the Quarter, and if you really want to do it right, order one of their complete breakfast suggestions. Typical is the $16.75 selection, which starts with egg Sardou (poached egg atop creamed spinach and artichoke bottoms, served with hollandaise sauce), followed by quail in burgundy sauce (served over wild and white rice), and topped off by crêpes Fitzgerald (served with a sauce of crushed strawberries flamed in maraschino) and hot chicory coffee. Brennan's is open every day from 8 a.m. to 2:30 p.m. and 6 to 11 p.m.

When I put together the first edition of this book, I made the sad decision to omit any mention of **Arnaud's,** 813 Bienville St. (tel. 523-5433). The kitchen had deteriorated into nothing short of a mess, and although I had loved the place over the years, it simply could not be recommended at that time. Well, on my return to New Orleans to update the last edition, I found myself sharing the excitement of New Orleans friends at what has happened at Arnaud's—under the new direction of Archie Casbarian, not only has the interior been restored to its former grandeur, but the *food* is once again worthy of the praise it once knew. The restaurant was built in 1918 by a Count Arnaud, and Mr. Casbarian has retained the original menu specialties, along with exciting new dishes created by Claude Aubert, a Frenchman with outstanding credentials. Try shrimp Arnaud, oysters Bienville, crabmeat imperial, trout amandine, or pompano en croûte, at prices that range from $9.95 to $19.75 on the à la carte menu, and any or all of them are *certain* to reach your table in a state of pure perfection. This has been a favorite place to eat, especially during Carnival season, with locals for years, and now it is reclaiming their devotion. Especially popular is the jazz brunch on Sunday from 10 a.m. to 2:30 p.m. and the Richelieu Bar anytime. Hours are 11:30 a.m. to 3 p.m. for lunch, 5:30 to midnight for dinner.

Also Good

One of the loveliest of French Quarter restaurants is the **Court of Two Sisters,** 613 Royal St. (tel. 522-7261), where you can dine outside in a court-yard filled with flowers, fountains, and low-hanging willows or in the Creole Patio Room. Creole and French cuisine are the specialties here, and if you fall in love with their original-recipe lemon-lime sauces, they'll sell you some to take home. You'll know you've found a friendly establishment from the very first, for a sign just inside the door lists their hours as: "Jazz Buffet 9 a.m.-3 p.m., Dinner 5:30-11 p.m. Browsing 3:30-5 p.m. Have a nice day!" You can accept the invitation to browse and enjoy a cocktail in the courtyard while you're about it. Reservations are necessary for dinner, which features such delicacies as shrimp Toulouse, crabmeat Rector, and sirloin tips à la Creole. Prices at dinner for a complete meal start at $20.50, and à la carte prices run $12.50 to $19.50. Other meals are lower. In their **Ye Olde Court Tavern,** 614 Rue Bourbon, you'll find drinks and an excellent revue called "+ Mo' Jazz."

Don't worry about reservations at **Galatoire's,** 299 Bourbon St. (tel. 525-2021)—they don't accept them. So, unless you take a tip from the natives and go to lunch before noon or dinner before 6, you'll stand in line outside along with everyone else. It's worth a wait to eat in this family-run restaurant that serves possibly the best fish dishes in town. Try the trout Marguery (with shrimp in a lovely white sauce). Prices are in the $6.50 and up range on the à la carte menu. It's open 11:30 a.m. to 9 p.m. Tuesday through Saturday, noon to 9 p.m. Sunday; closed Monday.

The elegant **Andrew Jackson Restaurant,** 221 Royal St. (tel. 529-2603), is decorated with crystal chandeliers, a lifesize wall sculpture of Andrew Jackson, and a marble fireplace which once was part of the Paris Opera House. There are some very good seafood specialties, as well as veal and beef dishes, but I especially like the entrecôte of chicken Rochambeau Rachel (broiled ham in mushroom and wine sauce topped with tender chicken breasts sauteed in toasted crumbs and enveloped in béarnaise sauce—makes me hungry just remembering!). Expect to pay $10.25 and up, more for the complete dinner. Lunch is served from 11 a.m. to 2:30 p.m. Monday through Friday, dinner from 5:30 to 10 p.m. every day of the week.

Moran's **Riverside Restaurant**, 44 Market Place (tel. 529-1583), is surely one of the most *romantic* places to eat in the French Quarter—it sits atop the Bazaar Building of the renovated French Market complex and affords sweeping views of both the market and the river. The dining room is done in low-keyed elegance, with a window wall facing out to the river and soft lighting. The cooking is French-Italian (with homemade pasta), and specialties include seafood, chicken, lamb, veal, and steak. I especially like the lemon-butter sauce on shrimp scampi "Don Josey," but almost any dish is likely to have you raving. Outstanding on the dessert list is their amaretto parfait. Prices range from $11 to $20 on the à la carte menu, and hours are 6 to 11 p.m., with reservations absolutely necessary most nights.

Just across from the French Market, the **Cafe Sbisa**, 1011 Decatur St. (tel. 561-8354), is much favored by the artistic crowd in New Orleans, with some of her best writers and painters showing up regularly. It's easy to see why, when you enter the casually elegant cafe with its ceiling fans, potted greenery, tile floor, and endless mirrors. The atmosphere is relaxed, and the food is exceptional, with seafood specialties like smoked fish, swordfish, mussels, salmon, clams, and a very good bouillabaisse. Lamb, duckling, and steaks are also good. Prices run from $10 to $19, hours are 6 to 11 p.m. Tuesday through Thursday, 'til midnight Friday and Saturday. Sunday features a champagne brunch from 10:30 a.m. to 2:30 p.m. and dinner from 6 to 10 p.m. Closed Monday.

Very Reasonable and Very Good

One of the delights of exploring New Orleans's French Quarter is discovering the many small, inexpensive places to eat, some just as exciting as the better-known restaurants. What you'll find here is sort of a thumbnail sketch of some of my own favorites. But do explore on your own and let me know about your special "finds."

K-Paul's Louisiana Kitchen, 416 Chartres St. (tel. 524-7394), may *look* like any other rather plain cafe-style eatery, but just wait till your order arrives! The chef and co-owner (Paul Prudhomme) presents mouthwatering Louisiana specialties here, just as he once did at the award-winning Commander's Palace (see below). The only difference is the decor and the price. You just won't believe prices of $7 to $15 for duckling étoufée or shrimp Bayou Teche or . . . well, any one of a dozen or so superb dishes. And if you're going to try red beans and rice anywhere while you're in New Orleans, make *this* the place. Incidentally, there are daily specials between 11 a.m. and noon that go for $4 to $5, and they also have very good po-boy sandwiches. Hours are 11:30 a.m. to 2:30 p.m. and 6 to 10 p.m. Monday to Friday. (Give that friendly staff a greeting from me when you drop in—they managed to convert me from "customer" to "friend" in the course of just one meal.)

Molly's, 732 Toulouse St., is an Irish bar and restaurant I discovered during a rainy day in the heart of the Quarter when I ducked in for an Irish coffee and stayed to enjoy a dozen fried oysters, french fries, and salad for just $5.50, and I never had better anywhere else in the city. That says a lot for the kitchen here, especially since there is a very wide variety of offerings on the menu. It's open 24 hours a day and a great place to watch all sorts of New Orleans types, as well as tourists who find it as I did. Breakfast is served at any hour, which makes it a special favorite of night owls who have a taste for bacon and eggs after a night on the town. For a special treat, order Irish coffee—the best I've had outside the Emerald Isle.

Jim Monaghan, original owner of Molly's (he's since sold it), is now a leading citizen of Decatur Street, with three very good eating establishments, and boundless enthusiasm for the restoration of what had become a very seedy part of the Quarter. **Molly's at the Market,** 1107 Decatur St. (tel. 581-9759), serves breakfast all day, and the extensive lunch and dinner menus offer American, Italian, and Irish dishes for under $6. So fond am I of Molly's that I find myself heading in that direction almost any time hunger pangs strike. Good food and reasonable prices, too, at the **Backstage Restaurant,** 1109 Decatur St. (tel. 523-9403), and a special brand of drink and New Orleans merriment at **Bonaparte's Retreat,** 1007 Decatur.

The **Original Melius Bar,** 622 Conti St. (tel. 523-9292), is an attractive, rather large place with lots of exposed brick, dark wood, and overhead fans. It's a great lunch favorite of lawyers, bankers, and, surprisingly, waiters from some of the more elegant restaurants in the neighborhood. A sample price here is $3.50 for red beans and rice. Lunch is from 11 a.m. to 3:30 p.m. but it stays open until 2 or 3 a.m. for drinks. On Wednesday, there's draft beer for 50¢ a glass after 8 p.m., and Wednesday through Saturday there's dancing in the back room.

Over on Jackson Square, the **Cafe Pontalba,** corner of Rue Chartres and Rue St. Peter, is an old-fashioned, tiled-floor, high-ceilinged cafe with doors that are left open to the street. It's generally full, but the busy atmosphere is part of the charm, and the menu is both extensive—from burgers to seafood to Creole—and moderate to cheap. This is also a good foot-resting, elbow-bending stop, and if there's a drink they don't serve—alcoholic or otherwise—I couldn't think of it.

The **Napoleon House,** 500 Chartres St., is at the corner of Chartres and St. Louis Sts., and is so named because at the time of the "Little Corporal's" death there was actually a plot ahatching in this 1797, National Landmark house to snatch him from his island exile and bring him back to New Orleans. The third floor was added expressly for the purpose of providing a home for him after the rescue. It wears its history well and with dignity; there is a limited menu of po-boys, Italian muffuletta sandwiches, and pastries ($2 to $3.50); and the jukebox plays only classical music! This is Dick Cavett's favorite New Orleans haunt, as well as a very popular spot with residents. Hours are 11 a.m. to 1 or 2 a.m.

A real favorite with locals, the **Port of Call,** 838 Esplanade Ave. (tel. 523-0120), is a cozy, pub-ish sort of place (lots of wood) with probably the best hamburgers and steaks in town. Pizza is also on the menu, as well as a dish I *really* liked, mushrooms in wine. Prices can run anywhere from $4 to $16, depending on your culinary mood (hamburger or steak), and because it's always packed at regular lunch and dinner hours, I like to drop in during off-hours (or sometime after 7 p.m., when neighborhood residents get together at the bar to relax). Hours are noon to 1 a.m., with food service until around midnight.

Tujague's, 823 Decatur St. (tel. 525-8676), was established in 1856 to feed the husky butchers in the French Market, and it hasn't really changed much since then. It's a favorite with New Orleanians, who seem to mind not at all that there's no menu, or even a choice of food—the only question you'll be asked is "Do you want a cocktail?" and then you're served whatever the books are dishing up. Never mind, it will most likely be a regional specialty, and it most certainly will be delicious. Best of all, your dinner bill will run well under $11. This one is a real experience—definitely *not* a tourist trap. If you're timid, call ahead to check the day's specialty.

The **Coffee Pot,** 714 St. Peter St. (tel. 523-8215), has been known for its breakfasts (which are served all day) since the 1940s. And what a breakfast you can put together from the large menu! Omelets come with just about everything you can think of—oysters or shrimp, chicken livers, red beans, ham and cheese, and there's even a "soul food" creation. Eggs Benedict, eggs creole, pancakes (strawberry, pecan, and sliced apple are just a few of the varieties), biscuits, and fresh fruit juices are all here. In addition, there are lunch or dinner dishes such as country steak, a Gulf Coast seafood platter, red beans and rice with smoked sausage, and a dozen others for prices of $3.50 to $9, and a large selection of po-boys. Desserts are homemade and delicious (try Cousin Pearl's bread pudding or a fruit cobbler). And true to its name, the Coffee Pot offers some 20 varieties of coffee at $2 each (all are beefed up with alcoholic additives). They believe in the old Turkish proverb: "Coffee should be black as Hell, strong as death, and sweet as love." Hours are 8:30 a.m. to 10:30 p.m.

Jackson's Place, 1212 Royal St. (tel. 522-4468), is a small, friendly neighborhood place with brick floors, white walls trimmed in soft rose, ceiling fans, plants in the window, and framed artwork hung about. Gary Jackson and Glenn Watson offer mainly Creole food here, at budget prices of $2 to $4. The menu changes slightly every day, but usually you can count on finding red beans and rice with sausage, seafood gumbo, jambalaya, and the like, and you really should save room for their excellent bread pudding. A friend told me about this place, with the comment, "It's like eating in someone's home," and I couldn't agree more.

In the French Market

You'll find the **Cafe du Monde,** across from Jackson Square, absolutely habit forming! More than once, I found myself headed back across the Quarter to sit at one of the little round tables for a spell of people-watching and a steaming cup of café au lait (strong chicory coffee laced with hot milk) and the indescribably good beignets. Except for milk, that's all they serve, but a $1.20 order (for three of the doughnuts and coffee) is filling enough to serve for breakfast or a light lunch. New Orleanians have been coming here for years—it's open around the clock—and visitors flock back again and again. Besides your fellow customers, there's all of Jackson Square, with the horse carriages lined up across from the cafe, spread out before you, as well as shoppers headed for the French Market a little farther along Decatur St.

Other reasonably priced eating places in and near the Market include **Delerno's French Market Po-Boy, Inc.,** 1012 Decatur St.; the **Cafe Maison,** in the Market itself and serving café au lait, beignets, and omelets; and **Jonah's Deli,** a small, New York-style deli inside the Marketplace at 1015 Decatur St.

For Your Sweet Tooth

When that craving for something sweet hits you, my best advice is to head for **Croissant d'Or,** 617 Ursulines St. (tel. 524-4663). It's an old-fashioned, light, and cheerful place with tiled floors, ceiling fans, and a bakery case across one side that will send you into fits of indecision—the array of gorgeous goodies is staggering. Maurice Delechelle is the master baker here, and his kitchen turns out galettes bretonnes (butter cookies), pain au chocolat (chocolate bread), cygne swan (an eclair in the shape of a swan filled with whipped cream), croissants, brioches, and all sort of Danish pastries. Prices start at 55¢ and hours are 8 a.m. to 5:30 p.m. seven days a week.

When you're in the Jackson Square area, look for tiny **La Marquise** at 625 Chartres St., also run by Mr. Delechelle, with the same mouthwatering offerings and a small outdoor courtyard for diners.

OTHER LOCALES: Moving out of the French Quarter, you'll find you can eat surprisingly well elsewhere in this city:

Award Winning

Since it opened in 1948, the **Caribbean Room** in the elegant **Pontchartrain Hotel,** 2031 St. Charles Ave. (tel. 524-0581), has won a list of culinary awards as long as your arm, and it really epitomizes New Orleans cuisine at its finest. The decor, like that of the rest of the hotel, is refined (almost understated) luxury. As for service—well, impeccable and solicitous come to mind. Their French and Creole kitchen turns out specialties like shrimp saki and backfin crabmeat with a lovely creamy, rather tart house dressing (actually, it's a combination of two, mustard and French) that have made fans of Artur Rubinstein, Gerald Ford, Mary Martin, and a host of other celebrities. Dinner prices, while high ($14 to $20 for entrées), are certainly not exorbitant for such attention to detail in both food and service, and luncheon is quite reasonable. Reservations are advisable for both lunch (noon to 2 p.m.) and dinner (6 to 9 p.m.).

Very Good

The unusual, rather grand blue-and-white building at the corner of Washington Ave. and Coliseum St. was built as a restaurant in 1880 by Emile Commander, and **Commander's Palace** (tel. 899-8221) has been a favorite of New Orleanians ever since. The patio, fountains, lush tropical plants, and soft colors are a perfect backdrop for Creole specialties. If you're a jazz buff, don't miss their famous Jazz Brunch (on Saturday and Sunday from 11 a.m. to 2 p.m.), where Dixieland is played by jazz greats. Brunch prices begin at $9.75, dinner at $19, and both menus are table d'hôte. Weekday lunches are à la carte from $7.50.

You'll find the **Bon Ton Cafe,** 401 Magazine St. (tel. 524-3386), absolutely jammed at lunch with New Orleans business people, and at dinner you'll be seated *only* if you have reservations. Such popularity is certainly well deserved, and Al Pierce, its owner, is well qualified to have earned it. He grew up on the banks of Bayou Lafourche, learned Cajun cooking from his mother, came to New Orleans in 1936, bought the Bon Ton in 1953, and since then has been serving up seafood gumbo, crawfish bisque, jambalaya, crawfish omelet, and other Cajun dishes in a manner that would make his mother proud. This is a small, utterly charming place, and one not to be missed if you want to sample true Cajun cooking (it's more subtle than Creole, and makes use of shallots, parsley, bell peppers, and garlic). Hours are 11 a.m. to 2 p.m. and 5 to 9:30 p.m. Monday to Friday. Prices run $6.50 to $13 at lunch, $14 to $18 at dinner.

Corine Dunbar's, 1617 St. Charles Ave. (tel. 525-2957, or 525-0689) is in an elegant antebellum home furnished in antiques. The distinctively Creole cuisine features old family recipes like oysters Dunbar and banana puffs. Service is beautifully gracious, and as is fitting, coat and tie are requested at dinner. Prices run from $13 for lunch to $20 for complete dinners. Lunch hours are noon to 2 p.m. and dinner is from 6 to 9:30 p.m. Tuesday through Saturday. This is another place where reservations are an absolute necessity.

Good—and Easy on the Budget

Lido Gardens, 4415 Airline Hwy., Metaire (tel. 834-8233), is the kind of local restaurant you're likely to have a New Orleans friend tell you about. It's been a favorite with residents for years, and on *my* first visit, it became an instant personal favorite. In a low, roadside building, Lido Gardens is a friendly, relaxing restaurant serving some of the best Italian cooking hereabout. There are red-checked tablecloths, a wishing well (hung with wine bottles) in the center of the room, and various members of the Mongiat family waiting to make you feel at home. The pasta dishes are superb (my Italian friend insists the lasagne is the best he's ever eaten away from home), and veal dishes come in a number of traditional recipes, including piccata, Milanese, scalloppini, Parmigiana, salt-n-bocca, and the marvelous involtini (prosciutto and cheese rolled in veal and simmered with butter, wine, and rosemary). Prices run from $7 to $12. They're open every day except Sunday: lunch from 11 a.m. to 2 p.m. (no lunch on Saturday), dinner from 5 to 9 p.m. Monday to Thursday, until 10 p.m. Friday and Saturday.

Kolb's, 125 St. Charles St. (tel. 522-8278), just across Canal St. from the Quarter, is the oldest and largest German restaurant in New Orleans. Its European manner and very moderate prices keep it humming from 11 a.m. to closing time at 10 p.m. Residents are particularly fond of Oktoberfest here (every October) and make reservations as much as a year in advance. German dishes, as you might guess, are featured, but there are local specialties as well, and complete-meal prices start at $4.95.

The **Camellia Grill,** 626 Carrollton Ave. (tel. 866-9573), is another locally popular restaurant, serving omelets, sandwiches, salads, and desserts at moderate prices. It's on the trolley line near the Riverbend Shopping Center, and prices are in the $1.95 to $4 bracket.

A fun place to eat (it's furnished with unusual antiques, Tiffany lamps, stained-glass windows, and even an old trolley!) at very little cost is **The Old Spaghetti Factory,** 330 St. Charles St. at Poydras (tel. 561-1068). Complete meals of steaming spaghetti and your choice from a selection of seven marvellous sauces start at a very modest $3. You can really make this an entertaining evening or afternoon before or after eating by having your picture taken in Victorian costumes or sipping cocktails at the fabulous old brass-railed mahogany bar. Open every day from 11:15 a.m. to 10 p.m. (11 p.m. on Friday and Saturday).

Out of Town

About 30 minutes' drive on U.S. 90 west of the city, past Avondale, there's a plain plywood building with a shell front painted white that holds one of the area's best restaurants. **Mosca's** (P.O. Box 52403, New Orleans, LA 70152; (tel. 504/436-9942) was started in 1946 by Lisa and Provino Mosca, and since their death, son Johnny and daughter Mary have carried on their unique style of cooking that combines elements of Italian and local Creole cuisine. If an evening in the countryside appeals to you, by all means make the drive and try dishes you'll find nowhere else. I can especially recommend the Italian crab salad (they use vinegar to flavor the crab and pickle the vegetables—delicious!) at $5.75 for an appetizer portion. And Mosca's Italian oysters are a treat, even at $14.50. Other specialties are quail with wild rice and roasted potato, squab and cornish hen, also with wild rice and potato, and chicken cacciatore (you get the whole chicken) at prices of $12 to $18.95. Everything is prepared to order, and a wait of 40 minutes is sometimes necessary. As you can see, prices aren't cheap, and they accept no checks or credit cards, but for a real dining experience, Mosca's can't be beat. Since hours sometimes vary, best call ahead.

READER'S SUGGESTION: "Out in the Lake area, the food is excellent and reasonable at **Poldi's,** 6940 Martin Dr. (exit off I-10 at Morrison Rd.). The lunch menu is smaller than the dinner menu, however, lunch is exactly half the price of those same meals on the dinner menu" (P. Hebert, DeRidder, La.).

Chapter XXII

NEW ORLEANS: THINGS TO SEE AND DO

1. Seeing the Sights
2. Nightlife
3. Festivals
4. The Sporting Life
5. Shopping

AN ENTIRE BOOK could be written on things to see and do in New Orleans—it's a city that cannot be seen or fully enjoyed hurriedly. And no matter how carefully you plan your time, you're certain to get back home and realize you've missed at least one thing you should have seen or done. People who live here will tell you that the only thing to do is move and settle in to a lifetime of learning the city, and there are many tales of people who've come here "on a lark," as one man put it, and stayed on for years. But, since that isn't possible for you and me, I'll do my best to give you a list, and you'll surely have your own by the time you've been in New Orleans a day or so.

I'd like to point out again, however, that *no one* should set out to see the city without first stopping by the **Tourist Commission** at 334 Royal St. (tel. 566-5011). Both the walking- and driving-tour maps they provide are circular tours, easy to follow, and so informative they are mini-courses in New Orleans history and culture. Two days, one for walking, the other for driving, set aside for these tours at the beginning of your stay will give you the best introduction to this grand old city.

In the meantime, here are my personal suggestions:

1. Seeing the Sights

AROUND THE FRENCH QUARTER: Because of the wealth of sightseeing in this small area, I've divided my list into categories which I hope will be more helpful to you in deciding just what you'd like to see first. Since there are so many of them and they are so lovely, let's start with—

KEY TO THE NUMBERED REFERENCES ON THE FRENCH QUARTER MAP: 1. Old Bank of Louisiana; 2. Old Bank of the U.S.; 3. Old La. State Bank; 4. N.O. Court Building; 5. Casa Faurie; 6. The Hermann House; 7. Maison Seignouret; 8. Merieult House; 9. Casa de Comercio; 10. Court of Two Lions; 11. LeMonnier House; 12. Maison de Flechier; 13. Maison LeMonnier; 14. Spanish Arsenal; 15. Pirates Alley; 16. Cathedral Garden; 17. Salle d'Orleans (Orleans Ballroom); 18. Pere Antoine's Alley; 19. The Presbytere; 20. St. Louis Cathedral; 21. The Cabildo; 22. Jackson Square; 23. Pontalba Buildings; 24. 1850 House; 25. The French Market; 26. Old Ursulines Convent; 27. Beauregard House; 28. Soniat House; 29. Clay House; 30. LaLaurie House ("The Haunted House"); 31. Thierry House; 32. The Gallier House; 33. Lafitte's Blacksmith Shop; 34. The Cornstalk Fence; 35. Miltenberger Houses; 36. "Madame John's Legacy."

Historic Homes

The classic New Orleans home is built around an open courtyard or patio, frequently centered with at least one fountain. Besides being a feast to the eye, these restful oases provided a gathering place for families and served as natural air-conditioning systems in the steamy summers.

On Royal Street: 631 is the second-oldest building on this street and was the residence for a time of the famous singer Adelina Patti, who gave the 1777 house its name of **Patti's Court.** The house at 640 was built in 1811 and was the city's first "skyscraper." The most notable occupant, however, was Antoine Alciatoire, who took up residence in 1860 and operated a boarding house whose food became so famous that it led to his opening a restaurant, the same one his family still runs today, Antoine's. The **LaBranche Home,** at 700, has some of the loveliest lace ironwork in the city (stand across the street for the best view). 900, 906, and 910 are the **Miltenberger Mansions,** built by a wealthy widow in 1838 for her three sons, and splendid indeed.

The **Gallier House** at 1132 was the home of the talented architect responsible for many of the fine old homes in the French Quarter. It is open to the public and you can see it restored to its original 1860 state for a fee of $2.50 for adults, $2 for children five to 11, and no charge for those under five. Hours are 10 a.m. to 5 p.m., with the last tour at 3:45 p.m.

Go by to see 1140 in daylight, otherwise you may hear ghostly moans or the savage hissing of a whip or catch a glimpse of a small black child walking on the balcony! The story behind this haunted house, built in 1831, is a New Orleans horror tale: The very beautiful and socially prominent Delphine LaLaurie lived here and entertained lavishly, until a night in 1834 when fire broke out and neighbors crashed through a locked door to find seven starving

THE FRENCH QUARTER

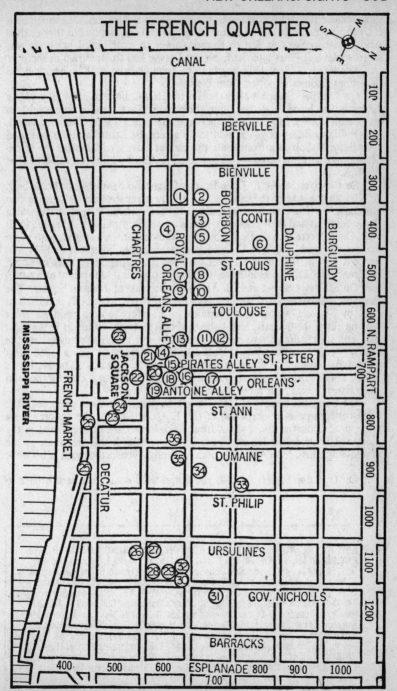

slaves chained in painful positions, unable to move. After rescuing the prisoners, the citizens turned on Madame LaLaurie and her family, but they dashed away in a carriage and fled to Europe, never to return until her body was returned several years later and, even then, she had to be buried in secrecy.

The Italian villa at 1315 was built by John Gauche in 1856, who had the cast-iron balconies imported from Germany.

On Bourbon Street: 624 is the **Fortin House,** built in 1834 by a young doctor for his bride. Walk back into the patio and you can see how neighbors often built connecting doorways between their courtyards. The very small, cottage-like building at 941 is said to be where the Lafitte brothers operated a blacksmith shop as a front for a prosperous slave trade. Notice the brick-between-posts construction—this is one of the few buildings of the type that survives.

On Chartres Street: 617, the **Bosque Home,** is a Spanish-style home built in 1795. In the rear of the carriageway are three separate patios opening one into the other. The **Beauregard House** at 1113 is a "raised" Creole cottage with Doric columns and twin stairways with wrought-iron railings. After the Civil War, Confederate Gen. P. G. T. Beauregard lived here in a rented room while looking for work. Novelist Frances Parkinson Keyes bought it in 1944 and restored it as her winter residence. It is open to the public for a fee of $2.50; children under 12, 75¢. Hours are 10 a.m. to 4 p.m. (last tour begins at 3 p.m.).

On St. Peter Street and St. Ann on either side of Jackson Square: The **Pontalba Apartments,** 16 row houses on each street, were built in 1850 and 1851 by Micaela Almonaster Pontalba in an effort to stop residents from moving out of the Quarter. Said to be the first apartment buildings in the U.S., they hold fascinating shops on the first floor and luxury apartments on the upper. On the St. Ann side, 525 has been restored as a typical 1850 New Orleans dwelling. At 547 St. Ann, at the corner of St. Ann and Chartres, there's a very fine historical research library on Louisiana history. (See "Parks and Amusement Areas" for more about Jackson Square.)

On Dauphine Street: 430, the **Pierre Cottage,** is another example of the brick-between-posts construction of the 1700s. Bricks for the building were made in the courtyard and shells from Lake Pontchartrain were used in the mortar. The **Audubon House,** a small cottage at 511, was the home of the famous naturalist, John Audubon, and his family when he did much of his work here.

On Dumaine Street: At 632, you'll find what some historians believe to

KEY TO THE NUMBERED REFERENCES ON THE "FRENCH QUARTER AND ENVIRONS" MAP: 1. The Old U.S. Mint; 2. The Gauche House; 3. St. Louis Cemetery No. 1; 4. Our Lady of Guadeloupe Church; 5. Mayor Pitot House; 6. The Blanc House; 7. New Orleans Museum of Art; 8. City Park; 9. Dillard University; 10. Lakeshore Drive; 11. Southern Yacht Club; 12. Metairie Cemetery; 13. Notre Dame Seminary; 14. Old Carrollton Courthouse; 15. St. Mary's Dominican College; 16. Audubon Park; 17. Tulane and Loyola Universities; 18. The Latter Memorial Library; 19. Academy of the Sacred Heart; 20. The Short House; 21. The Robinson House; 22. The Musson House; 23. The Morris House; 24. The Brevard House; 25. The Payne House; 26. The Johnson House; 27. Lee Circle; 28. Confederate Memorial Museum; 29. St. Patrick's Church; 30. Lafayette Square; 31. Gallier Hall; 32. Superdome; 33. Customs House; 34. Rivergate Exhibition Center; 35. International Trade Mart.

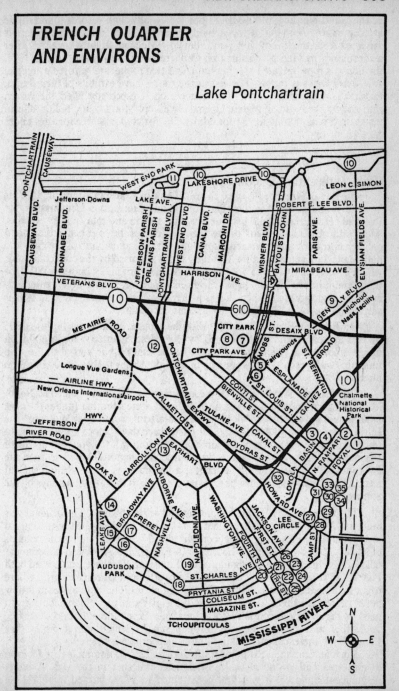

FRENCH QUARTER AND ENVIRONS

Lake Pontchartrain

be the oldest building in the Mississippi Valley, although records found in the last few years reveal that it was actually *rebuilt* in 1788, using some materials salvaged from the fire of that year. Named **"Madame John's Legacy,"** after a short story by George Washington Cable referred to it by that title in 1874, the house is now operated as a museum, and two rooms are restored as typical 1830 New Orleans rooms. The rest of the rooms have exhibits of furnishings, textiles, and decorative arts from that period. I especially liked the woven things from the Acadian region. Open daily except Monday and holidays from 9 a.m. to 5 p.m., admission $1 for adults, 50¢ for students, free for ages under 12.

Other Interesting Buildings

On Royal Street: 334, once the old Bank of Louisiana, built in 1827, is now the home of the **New Orleans Tourist and Convention Commission.** As I've said before, this should be your very first stop in any tour of New Orleans. At 339, the 1800-built **Bank of the U.S.** was one of the four banks that stood on each corner of this intersection, making it the financial hub of the city. 400 houses the **Louisiana Wildlife Museum,** but is still used by the civil courts, for which it was built. 417 was once the Casa Faurie, originally built (in 1801) for the grandfather of Edgar Degas, the French painter. It saw much entertainment on a grand scale when it was a private residence, and the tradition is carried on today at **Brennan's,** its present occupant.

On Bourbon Street: The **Old Absinthe House,** at 238, was built in 1806 by two Spaniards and is still owned by their descendants. When prohibition officers closed the place during the '20s, the marble bar and absinthe drip fountains were rescued and wound up in the **Old Absinthe Bar,** at 400 Bourbon Street.

On Chartres Street: The **Napoleon House,** at 500, was planned as Napoleon's refuge after an ill-fated rescue plot. Jean Lafitte's brother (under the alias Dominique You) had been hired to captain a trim racing boat and spirit the Little Corporal away. Alas, Napoleon died three days before the boat was to sail from New Orleans; there are some in town who will tell you that his death was not a natural one, but that he was murdered when his captors learned the not-too-well-kept secret. Stop in here for a few minutes of classical music and refreshment and you'll almost be transported back to those exciting days by the atmosphere.

The **Cabildo,** at 701, has had a long and varied history. The original was built in 1769 by the Spanish, burned in 1788, was replaced then burned again in 1794, and the present building, completed in 1795, incorporates the remains of its two predecessors. It has housed both French and American government offices, been the scene of the signing of the Louisiana Purchase, and hosted both Pierre Lafitte (as a criminal in jail) and Lafayette (as a visiting celebrity whose royal treatment contrasted vividly to that of Lafitte). The state museum it now holds reflects all this and much more of the city's history (Napoleon's death mask is here). Admission is $1 for adults, 50¢ for children 12 and over, free under that; and it's open Tuesday through Sunday from 9 a.m. to 5 p.m. (See "Tours" for the excellent walking tour which originates here.)

You can't miss the **St. Louis Cathedral,** at 721—it dominates the Jackson Square area and is one of the most famous churches in the U.S. A really magnificent building, it was first constructed in 1724, burned in that 1788 holocaust, and rebuilt in 1794. "Uptown" Americans used to say that God spoke only in French here! There are free guided tours from 9 a.m. to 5 p.m. Monday through Saturday, 1 to 5 p.m. on Sunday.

Pirate's Alley, which runs between the Cabildo and the cathedral, was supposedly used by buccaneers even before the alley was cut and officially named Ruelle d'Orléans, Sud. On the other side of the cathedral, **Père Antoine's Alley** was named for a priest much loved for his good works. In **St. Anthony's Garden** behind the cathedral, many a duel was fought by hot-blooded Creole gentlemen over the "honor" of beautiful mulatto women at the Quadroon Balls.

The **Presbytère,** at 713, was meant to be the rectory for the cathedral and is a twin architecturally to the Cabildo. It served instead as a courthouse until 1911, when it was taken over by the **Louisiana State Museum.** If you pay the small admission fee (same as for the Cabildo), you'll see not only some very fine formal art, but very lively folk and native art as well.

On the site of the Old Ursuline Convent, the **Archbishop Antoine Blanc Memorial** is located at 1112 and includes the oldest building in the city, erected in 1752. For its first 74 years, it was the convent of the Ursuline nuns, then the residence of the archbishops for the next 74 years. Currently, it is the home of the Archdiocesan Archives, and part of the premises are open to the public on Wednesday afternoons only.

At 1116, the **Ancient Chapel** of the Archbishops was erected in 1845. It served as the house of worship for French, Spanish, Irish, German, and Italian immigrants, and is now Our Lady of Victory Chapel and the National Shrine of St. Lazarus, open for daily mass.

On Orleans Street: 717 was the site of those famous (or infamous!) Quadroon Balls, begun in 1838, at which ambitious mothers would trot out their loveliest mulatto daughters in the hope they'd be chosen by a "gentleman" as his mistress and set up in one of the small cottages over on Rampart St. When a "free man of color," Thomy Lafon, bought the building in 1873 for the Negro Sisters of the Holy Family, the ballroom became a chapel for their orphanage. Today, it's the Bourbon Orleans Ramada Hotel.

On St. Peter Street: The best time to go to **Preservation Hall** (726) is at night, when the place is filled with some of the best jazz in the Quarter, but a daytime stop will give you an intriguing look through the big, ornate iron gate at a lush, tropical courtyard in the back. **Pat O'Brien's** now occupies what was known as the Maison de Flechier (718) when it was built for a well-known planter in 1790. **Le Petit Theater,** the oldest nonprofessional theater in the country, has been at 616 since 1922, but the Spanish-style building has had such widely diverse tenants as cafes, bars, and the first bishop of New Orleans.

On Decatur Street: The **U.S. Customs House** (100) was begun in 1847 on the site of old Fort St. Louis, but it wasn't completed until 1913.

Stretching down Decatur St. (800, 900, 1000), on the river side, is the **Old French Market,** which has been a marketplace since Choctaw Indians traveled to the riverbank here to peddle their wares. The Spanish erected a market building, but when it was destroyed by a hurricane in 1812, it was replaced the very next year by the Butchers' Hall (that's the building closest to Jackson Square), and two more were added in 1822 and 1872. Still growing, the Market was given a fourth building as recently as 1975. There's much restoration going on to spruce the place up, but what you'll most likely want to do here is just wander through the market stalls piled high with fresh fruits and vegetables that make you hungry just to see them and stop by the praline shops for a nibble of candy you can see being made. This is one of my favorite places in the city, and I warn you, be sure to allow plenty of time—you won't want to leave.

If you've ever harbored a secret desire to see that **Streetcar Named Desire,** you'll find it behind the **Old U.S. Mint** at 1300 (just behind the French Market), restored to its original 1906 style. The mint was constructed on the site of Fort St. Charles and operated until 1910. On Saturday and Sunday, a public **flea market** is held in its shadow—great fun.

BEYOND THE QUARTER: The "American" sections of New Orleans are pretty spread out, but you can see them easily using public buses or, in the case of the Garden District, the St. Charles trolley.

The Garden District

The Garden District is so called because of the lavish formal gardens that were the pride of wealthy planters who built the lovely "town" mansions you'll see along St. Charles Ave. and the numbered streets that cross it. A ramble through the pleasant streets will be a highlight of your trip if you try to imagine the interiors of these large homes with their colonnaded "galeries" and iron- work balconies. If you could peep inside (and you can at certain times of the year—see "Festivals," below), you'd be treated to a decor of ornate moldings, mahogany banisters, and mantels of rosewood or Italian marble, winding stair- cases, crystal chandeliers, and priceless antiques—the "uptown" Americans were determined to equal, if not outdo, those snooty French aristocrats in the Quarter, and they certainly came close!

But before you get to the residential section, be sure to stop by **Gallier Hall,** 524 St. Charles Ave., completed in 1850 as the city hall of the American section. It was designed by Gallier (who, significantly, was the architect of so many memorable Quarter homes), and it is here that Mardi Gras comes to a climax each year with the crowning of the Carnival King and Queen.

Also, take time to go by **Lee Circle,** which stands in the middle of St. Charles Ave. a little above Gallier Hall. Planned as the Place du Tivoli in 1806, it was a cultural center and had a children's merry-go-round in the middle until 1884, when the general's statue was erected (Yankees please note—he's facing north!).

The residential section of the district begins just after Felicity, and on First St., look especially for 1134 (Confederate President Jefferson Davis visited here often and died while a guest in 1889), 1236, and 1239. 1427 Second St. was built in 1845 and was moved to its present location from a nearby plantation. On Third St., notice (you really can't help noticing!) 1331, 1415, and 1417; and on Fourth, 1241 and 1448. On Seventh, 1221 and 1215 were twins when they were built as wedding gifts for two sisters, but as you can see, they've taken on individual personalities with modifications over the years. George W. Cable lived at 1313 Eighth, and entertained such famous writers as Mark Twain and Joel Chandler Harris (he wrote the Uncle Remus stories) in the house that was built off the ground to prevent flood damage and (so he thought) yellow fever.

St. Charles Avenue itself makes interesting touring, and the trolley ride is a comfortable way to go. (See "Tours") Look for the **St. Charles Christ Church Cathedral** (2919). This is the fourth structure since 1805, and even it has suffered the loss of its tall steeple in a 1915 hurricane.

The home at 2926 has a gallery for every room, and the 12-inch space between inner and outer walls made for comfort year round. The exclusive **Orleans Club** (a private social and cultural women's club) now occupies 5005 St. Charles, but it was originally built in 1868 by a Colonel Lewis as a wedding gift for his daughter. A World War II hero is honored by the gift to the city by his family of the **Milton Latter Memorial Library** at 5100 St. Charles.

The largest Catholic university in the South, **Loyola,** is at 6363 St. Charles, and close by, at 6823, is **Tulane,** with its medical school that dates back to 1834. There's another campus downtown, but this is where it all began. Another school going back to the 1800s is **St. Mary's Dominican College** (it's across the avenue from the other two), a girls' school in an ornate white wooden building with outside balconies running the length of each floor.

Audubon Park has an entrance on St. Charles also ("See Parks and Amusement Areas," below).

Carrollton

In 1812, a tiny settlement sprang up around Gen. William Carrollton's camp at the very end of St. Charles Ave., and it grew into a thriving town with a resort hotel and a railroad depot (for the streetcar line). The levee to control the Mighty Mississippi displaced both hotel and depot, but the area continued to grow. The school you'll see at 719 South Carrollton was the Carrollton Courthouse from 1855 to 1874, but the best reason for going out there today is to see **Riverbend,** a really charming section of homes that have been transformed into a shopping area. To reach it, turn right off Carrollton Ave. at Burthe, then left on Dublin.

Bayou St. John and Lake Pontchartrain

When Bienville chose New Orleans's location, it was partly because Bayou St. John and Lake Pontchartrain provided a sort of back door that made for easy defense. To retrace what had begun as an Indian route long before there were Frenchmen here, start near the Old Mint in the French Quarter and walk (or drive) down Esplanade Ave., one of the quietest and prettiest in the Vieux Carré, to Rampart St. Turn left and you'll be following the line of the wall (or ramparts) that connected three forts on this northern border of the original city. There is no trace of either wall or forts today, but you will come to **Congo Square** (now known as Beauregard Square), a quiet park that began as an Indian camp, but was given over by the city fathers as a gathering place for slaves on Sunday afternoons to sing and dance and "let off steam" so that, hopefully, the secret voodoo ceremonies would be reduced, or at least be brought out in the open. Unfortunately, not only did the meetings continue among slaves and even attract prominent French residents, but Congo Square became the scene of wild, sensual dancing accompanied by beating drums, fights precipitated by heightened emotions, and a source of fascination for as many as 2000 spectators who would congregate to watch the dancing until a 9 o'clock cannon boomed curfew for all slaves.

Just behind the square, you'll see the **Municipal Auditorium** and **Theatre of the Performing Arts,** where the unique New Orleans "art" of Mardi Gras balls is practiced.

At Bienville, turn right again onto **Basin Street** (you remember that street, of course, as the birthplace of jazz), which used to be the main drag of Storyville, a red-light district that held so many houses of ill-repute that a "Blue Book" was actually compiled advertising the charms of over 700 prostitutes and the "sporting palaces" that flourished along with fancy saloons! It flourished as a wide-open den of iniquity from 1897, when Alderman Sidney Story attempted to clean up the French Quarter by moving sin outside, until 1917, when the U.S. Navy complained about the bad effect of so much vice in such proximity to our wartime servicemen. (Actually, it was the secretary of the navy who requested that the district be closed down—not a single complaint was recorded as coming from the troops.)

In the 400 block of Basin St., you'll find the first of New Orleans's "Cities of the Dead," inhabited by above-ground tombs: **St. Louis Cemetery #1** (#2 is behind a housing project on St. Louis, and #3 is further out Esplanade). The city's low, just-above-sea-level location made burial in above-ground vaults a necessity. Often the outer walls of cemeteries would be made up of rows of attached vaults stacked one above the other, while vaults inside the walls formed "streets," giving the appearance of a miniature city. If you feel in need of a little help from that Queen of Voodoo, Marie Laveau, look for her grave. Faithful believers have marked it with crosses, and some say that even now a "gris gris" (which is pronounced "gree gree" and might be anything from a string around a bone to a doll stuck with pins) left overnight there and then placed on the doorstep of the person you want to influence will absorb the power of this "free" mulatto woman who—for a small fee, of course—worked miracles for New Orleanians, black and white, rich and poor, for nearly 70 years.

Turn right on Toulouse, then left on Rampart. On your right, you'll see the **Quadroon Quarters,** the small cottages maintained by Creole gentlemen for their mistresses and the children they fathered. Looking at them gives rise to a wonder that these were such prized positions among mulattos—until you remember that along with "mistress" went the title "free"!

At Esplanade, turn left and go about 20 blocks (you'll need a car for this expedition) to Moss, then turn left and follow the banks of **Bayou St. John,** which formed a lake-to-river link by means of an old Indian trail that led from bayou to the Mississippi. On this side of the bayou there are several old plantation homes built in the 1780s and early 1800s, the most notable of which is the **Pitot House,** 1440 Moss St., home of Mayor James Pitot, which is open to the public only on Thursday (11 a.m. to 4 p.m.; $2 for adults, $1.50 for children; groups may arrange visits at other times by calling 482-0312). It is a typical West Indian plantation house, with wide galleries on three sides and large columns supporting the second-floor—interesting to see from the outside if you should happen to drive out on, say, a Monday.

You'll have to return to Esplanade to cross the bridge and take the first left turn onto Wisner Blvd., which runs along the other side of the bayou. The entrance to **City Park,** with its famous old dueling oaks and the **Museum of Art** (see "Parks and Amusement Areas" and "Museums," below) is on Esplanade before you make the turn. Stay on Wisner (past some very grand modern homes) until you reach Robert E. Lee Blvd., turn right to Elysian Fields Ave., and then turn left. The **University of New Orleans** will be on your left, and the **Pontchartrain Amusement Park** directly in front of you (see "Parks and Amusement Areas").

Now turn left onto Lakeshore Drive. **Lake Pontchartrain** is some 40 miles long and 25 miles wide, and the bridge that goes across is the longest in the world. (There's a $1 toll to cross it.) You'll pass the **Mardi Gras fountain,** with plaques of Mardi Gras krewes around its base, and come to the **Coast Guard Lighthouse** at West End, a tiny park in the midst of marinas, an old fishing village, **Bucktown,** and the **Southern Yacht Club,** the second oldest in the country. It's easy to spend time in this charming spot, and if you can time your trip out for late afternoon, you'll see the Mardi Gras fountain beautifully lighted in Mardi Gras colors of purple, green, and gold after dark on the drive back.

Other Points of Interest

The site of the Battle of New Orleans is now **Chalmette National Histori-cal Park,** on St. Bernard Highway. To get there, take Rampart St. and stay to the left as it becomes St. Claude, which will, in turn, become St. Bernard Highway. It was out here in a cane field that Gen. Andrew Jackson pulled together a ragtag army made up of Creoles, "free men of color," Indians, and Americans (Kentucky and Tennessee soldiers, mostly) with a few Germans and Acadians, to man the rampart he'd put up from the river to a nearby swamp. With cannon, flints, and gunpowder supplied by Jean Lafitte (and also a goodly number of his privateers), they repulsed a massive British head-on attack on January 8, 1815, with over 2000 enemy casualties (285 killed), with only a few casualties themselves. The British retreated, but remained in camp for ten days before they went back to their ships and sailed away. The irony is, of course, that the Peace of Ghent treaty ending the war had been signed (although not ratified) a full two weeks before the bloody encounter!

To sports fans, New Orleans means the **Superdome.** It's at the 1500 block of Poydras St., not far from the French Quarter. The largest building of its kind in the world, looking for all the world like a grounded saucer, it seats some 80,000 people. Tours are conducted daily from 9:30 a.m. to 4 p.m. Call 587-3663 for information.

The **Rivergate Exhibition Center,** at 4 Canal St., is another modern giant of a building, although it isn't nearly as huge as the Superdome. Its next-door neighbor, the **International Trade Mart** at 2 Canal St., is even closer to the river and has an observation deck that you can reach by inside or (for the more stouthearted) outdoor elevators. The trip up on the outside costs $2.50 for adults, $1.50 for children under 12. The view up there is spectacular—the busy harbor traffic, the French Quarter, the rest of the city stretching beyond, all are breathtakingly beautiful from 31 stories up. And two flights further up, you can watch it unfold in comfort from the **Top of the Mart** revolving cocktail lounge (see "Nightlife").

"Fat City" is a collection of discos, restaurants, lounges, and shops that developed in an affluent section of modern apartment buildings. It is bounded roughly by Veterans Highway, Causeway Blvd., West Esplanade, and Division St., and draws many locals when French Quarter nightlife palls.

PARKS AND AMUSEMENT AREAS: Down in the French Quarter, lovely **Jackson Square** serves as a focal point for artists and craftsmen who set up shop outside the iron railings. But it wasn't always like that. Back in 1721, the square was a dusty drill field (the French called it Place d'Armes and it was Plaza de Armas to the Spanish). It was the Baroness Micaela Pontalba, the same one who built the apartments on each side, who transformed it by putting up the fence, planting it like a garden, and installing benches so it could be enjoyed as a park. That was in 1851, and the present name was bestowed in 1856, when the impressive Andrew Jackson statue was added. That statue, incidentally, is by Clark Mills and was the first equestrian sculpture to be made with more than one hoof unsupported.

Audubon Park, with an entrance on St. Charles Ave. across from Tulane University and another on Magazine St., is one of the prettiest spots in New Orleans. The oaks here turn walkways into covered alleys, and there are wind-ing lagoons, fountains, and statuary, as well as a very nice zoo. As far as *I'm* concerned, this park (once part of plantation) is complete enough with the trees and paths and a general atmosphere of peace and quiet. But if you're looking for recreation facilities, they're here, too. There's an 18-hole golf course, picnic facilities, tennis courts, a swimming pool, horseback riding, and bike rentals. For full details, call 861-2537.

City Park, at the end of Esplanade and the beginning of the City Park Ave., was also once part of a plantation. Look for the **New Orleans Museum of Art**—just to the left you'll see those ancient old oaks under which men of honor settled their disputes in the late 1700s and early 1800s (remember all those old movies with the dueling scenes at dawn?). **Children's Storyland,** Victory Drive across from the tennis courts, is an enchanted place for youngsters, with Mother Goose characters in papier-mâché. This park is really beautifully landscaped, and has *four* golf courses, boating lagoons, tennis courts, horseback riding, a miniature train, and an amusement area with carnival rides for children.

Out on Lakeshore Drive at Elysian Fields Ave., the Pontchartrain Beach Amusement Park is a 1928-style New Orleans institution. It's open only from the last weekend of March until Labor Day, from 5 p.m. to midnight, noon to midnight on weekends, but it's usually jumping, with over 100 rides, live stage shows, and there's usually a comedy high-diving show.

MUSEUMS: Many of the museums in historic homes and buildings have already been described, but here are some more that you won't want to miss.

The **Historic New Orleans Collection,** at 533 Royal St., is in a 1792 structure that is really two houses. When the original was turned into a small hotel in the 1880s, the owners built a separate house across the back of the courtyard so the family could come and go in privacy. In the original, or Merieult House, the collection features maps, prints, photographs, and the like, adding up to a remarkable library of Louisiana history. In the newer section, the Trapolin House, beautiful antique European, Oriental, and American furniture and accessories are displayed. Guided tours begin on the hour and half hour; adults pay $1; children, 50¢. It's open Tuesday through Saturday (except holidays) 10 a.m. to 5 p.m.

The **New Orleans Museum of Art** is on LeLong Ave. in City Park, and is housed in a building that is, itself, a work of art. The neoclassic, columned main building is a beauty, inside and out. The Delgado Great Hall on the first floor leads to a branched staircase at the back that rises to a mezzanine overlooking the hall. Beautiful! And the art inside does justice to its housing.

The museum's permanent collection includes works from the Kress Collection of Italian Paintings, and galleries of contemporary, Oriental, and African art, and portrait miniature paintings. In addition to its permanent collection, the museum often schedules major international exhibitions. General admission charges are $1 for children (three to 17) and senior citizens (over 65), $2 for adults (18 to 64); museum members are admitted free at all times. The museum is open from 10 a.m. to 5 p.m. Tuesday through Sunday, and closed Monday and all legal holidays. Additional information about special exhibition hours and fees may be obtained by calling the Public Relations Office, 488-2631.

There's no charge to view the more than 500 dolls from 40 countries in the **Cabrini Doll Museum** at 1218 Burgundy St. in the French Quarter. All kinds of dolls are here and all are handmade of wood, china, bisque, wax, and even cornshucks. I was especially intrigued by the French fashion dolls made for the purpose of showing American buyers the latest French styles. Lifesize dolls are posed in schoolroom and other lifelike settings, and there are miniature furniture pieces made as sales models by cabinetmakers. They're all housed in an old Creole cottage with brick floors, exposed cypress beams, and a two-story detached kitchen behind the patio. Hours are 1:30 to 6 p.m. Monday through Friday, 9:30 a.m. to 5 p.m. on Saturday. It is sometimes closed, so you may want to call 524-9919 before going.

The **Confederate Museum,** at 929 Camp St., was established in 1889, close enough to the end of the Civil War for many donations to be in better condition than is sometimes true of museum items. You'll find battle flags, weapons, personal effects of Confederate President Jefferson Davis, part of Robert E. Lee's silver camp service, and many portraits of Confederate military and civilian personalities. A series of detailed pictures traces Louisiana's history from secession through Reconstruction. There's a $1 charge for adults, 50¢ for students, 25¢ for children under 12. Open Monday through Saturday from 10 a.m. to 4 p.m.

On the 31st floor of the International Trade Mart, 2 Canal St., the **Louisiana Maritime Museum** is in a glass-enclosed area overlooking the river and the city. There are charts, ship models, paintings, and a host of other items connected with shipping. But what I liked best was the old steamboat furniture—shades of Mark Twain! There's also an interesting slide presentation on Louisiana history. You can visit Monday through Saturday, 9 a.m. to 4 p.m., for a $2 fee for adults, $1 for children under 12.

The **Louisiana Wildlife Museum,** 400 Royal St., is in the Louisiana Wildlife and Fisheries Building that fills an entire block between Royal and Chartres, Conti and St. Louis. The exhibits are primarily of Louisiana animal and bird life, and some of the specimens are incredibly beautiful. No charge to see them, 9:30 a.m. to 4:30 p.m. Monday through Friday.

If you *really* want to see what went on down in Louisiana from the discovery of the lower Mississippi River by LaSalle in 1699 until the beginning of this century, there's no better place to do it than the **Musée Conti** at 917 Conti St. (tel. 525-2605). The 31 tableaux, with 144 lifesize wax figures, are historically accurate and beautiful to see. There's also a just-for-fun Haunted Dungeon, with 23 figures (like Dracula, Frankenstein, and the Wolf Man) in ten settings. Admission is $3.50 for grownups, $2.25 for ages 13 to 17, $1.25 for ages six to 12, free for under-sixes with adults. Open daily at 10 a.m. except Christmas and Mardi Gras Day.

In the early 1970s, two New Orleans brothers, Charles and Jerry Gandolfo, found a real voodoo priest living in a small town near New Orleans. When he offered to donate artifacts to a museum for the religion and act in an advisory capacity, they went to work and established the **Voodoo Museum** at 636 St. Ann St. The collection has grown to include not only potions, charms, paintings, and photographs from the New Orleans area, but also items from Haiti, South America, and Africa as well. They even sponsor an exotic dance and musical group that performs locally (although not at the museum) the snake dances and fire dances that once went on in and around New Orleans. The gift shop sells all sorts of voodoo items—maybe you'd like to pick up a special potion or two to test the power of gris gris for a "spell" of your own! The cost to get in is $3 for adults, $2 for students, $1 for children. It's open every day from 10 a.m. to midnight.

2. Nightlife

JAZZ: The joyous, soul-lifting music form that is jazz grew out of the anger, fear, love, joy, pride, back-breaking toil that filled the emotional lives of blacks in New Orleans from the days of slavery up to the advent of "Storyville."

When the restricted area around Basin St. opened up highly competitive bordellos, saloons, and nightclubs, black musicians moved their vibrant, expressive music inside from street corners to provide entertainment for paying customers, and it wasn't too long before it began showing up in the white man's world of college campuses, riverboats, "respectable" nightclubs, and restaurants. New Orleans-born masters of the art, such as Louis Armstrong and "Jelly Roll" Morton, left Storyville and moved upriver to St. Louis and Memphis, and eventually carried their music to Chicago, New York, and the West Coast. Others—"Papa" Celestin, Bunk Johnson, and Sweet Emma Barrett, to name just a few—stayed on in New Orleans, keeping the free-spirited music alive at the scene of its birth.

Today, jazz permeates the French Quarter, with black and white, newcomers and oldtimers joining together to keep it filling the air at all hours of the night and day. As for those oldtime jazz funerals, you can still occasionally see one, the jazzman being escorted to his final resting place by a band playing sorrowful dirges, followed by "second liners" (shuffling, hand-clapping mourners). It's on the return trip, after the departed has been "freed," that the mood turns lively and the mourners really get into the "liberate" swing of things.

Strictly Jazz

Jazz in its purest form is found at **Preservation Hall,** 726 St. Peter St., unaccompanied by such refinements as air conditioning, drinks, or even (unless you get there *very* early) a place to sit down. The shabby old building offers only hot, foot-tapping, body-swaying music, played by whatever top professionals happen to be in town on a particular night. And nobody seems to mind the absence of those other refinements—the place is not only packed, its windows are filled with faces of people who stand on the sidewalk for hours just to listen! After one night, I was hooked.

Part of the fun is never knowing who will be there—the place holds a special spot of affection in the hearts of jazzmen, and some of the greatest drop in to play when they're in town. Another part is knowing that no matter who's sitting in, they'll all be good and they'll have as good, if not better, a time as their enthusiastic audience. The whole atmosphere is one of an informal jazz session, and even the younger generation—there are lots of fascinated children every night I go—joins in the spirit of things. Admission is an unbelievably low $2, and if you want to sit on one of the much-sought-after pillows right up front or the couple of rows of straightbacked chairs just behind them, get there at least 45 minutes before doors open at 8 p.m. Otherwise you stand. The music goes on until 12:30 a.m., with long sets being interrupted by ten-minute breaks and the crowds continually changing as parents take children home at bedtime and sidewalk listeners move in to take their places. Oh, yes, they have a marvelous collection of jazz records on sale, some of them hard-to-find oldies.

Pete Fountain, the clarinetist, has moved out of the French Quarter (but not far away) to the **New Orleans Hilton** at Poydras St. and the Mississippi River. The somewhat plush interior—gold chairs and banquettes, red velvet bar chairs, white iron-lace-railinged gallery—sets the mood of the popular nightspot. Pete performs at 10 p.m. on Tuesday, Wednesday, Thursday, and Friday, at 9 p.m. on Saturday. The club (named simply **Pete Fountain's;** tel. 523-4374 or 523-3105), is closed Sunday and Monday. There's an $18-per-person cover, for the show and one drink. Call for reservations.

Dukes of Dixieland's Duke's Place, the rooftop lounge of the **Monteleone Hotel,** 214 Royal St. (tel. 581-1567), is open from 5 p.m. to 2 a.m. every night except Sunday. But to catch the Dukes of Dixieland and other jazz greats, plan to be there at 9:30, 10:30, and 11:30 p.m., or for the last show at 12:30 a.m. The music is always top-notch and there's a sweeping view of the Mississippi, the French Quarter, and the Canal St. business section. It's a good idea to make reservations.

The Famous Door, 330 Bourbon St., is not a club in the strictest sense, just a good place to hear live jazz—even from the sidewalk, since doors on both sides are left open—almost any time of day. There's always someone on the bandstand, since they use alternating groups and keep the music going.

Maison Bourbon, 641 Bourbon St., also opens its doors to the sidewalk and employs three bands every day to play from 11 a.m. to 2 a.m. Owners John Keifer and Albert St. Germaine have added a plus for jazz lovers by recording the sessions so that you can spin at home the music you heard live. Incidentally right next door, Cap't Al's Seafood House features fresh seafood at moderate prices, and the longest oyster bar in New Orleans.

Down by the river, **Tipitina's,** 501 Napoleon Ave. (tel. 899-9114), is an old bar with a stage at one end that seems to draw jazz, blues, and reggae musicians like a magnet. It's anything *but* elegant, but you're likely to hear the best music in town here, especially late at night. There's a dance floor, too, so if you're so inclined you can move with the music. Depending on who's on stage, there's no charge or up to an $8 cover charge. Open seven days a week, as is their Creole restaurant (5 to 10 p.m.), and Sunday through Wednesday, the music starts as early as 9:30 p.m.

Other Nightspots

Pat O'Briens, at 718 St. Peter St. (tel. 525-4823), has been famous for as long as I can remember for its gigantic rum-based Hurricane drinks, served in 29-oz. hurricane-lamp-style glasses. But it's equally well known for the good entertainment offered in one of the most beautiful patios in New Orleans and the lounge that features at least four entertainers nightly. There's a neighborhood air about the place and the singalongs will quickly make you feel at home with everybody else there. There are three bars here; the main bar opens 10 a.m. to 4 a.m., the patio bar from 11 a.m. to 4 a.m., and the lounge from 2 p.m. to 4 a.m. (5 a.m. on Friday and Saturday). There's no minimum, no cover.

Chris Owens Club, at the corner of Bourbon and St. Louis Sts., features who else but Chris Owens, a very talented singer and dancer, in a one-woman show of jazz, popular, and blues music. Between shows, there's dancing on an elevated dance floor and electrifying light and sound everywhere. There's no cover, but the $6 admission covers the show and there's a one drink minimum. Showtime is 10 p.m. and midnight Monday through Saturday. Reservations are a good idea (tel. 523-6400). The club is closed Sunday.

If it's supper club entertainment you're in the mood for, some of the biggest names in show business (for example, Ella Fitzgerald, Joel Grey, and Carol Channing) are booked into the **Fairmont Hotel's Blue Room** (University Place; tel. 529-4744). Performance times change occasionally, but are usually 9 and 11 p.m.; and the price of the show alone varies from $10 to $20. Dinner and drinks are extra, but not required. Call for reservations.

The revolving lounge at the top of the International Trade Mart (2 Canal St.), appropriately called the **Top of the Mart** (tel. 522-9795), offers musical entertainment nightly. The everchanging view is part of the fun—you move three feet per minute and make the full circle in 90 minutes. It's open 10 a.m. to 2 a.m. Monday to Friday, 11 a.m. to 3 a.m. Saturday and 4 p.m. to midnight Sunday.

For disco, try **Rainforest** in the **New Orleans Hilton Hotel, 2 Poydras St.** and the Mississippi River (tel. 561-0500). Drinks are reasonable here, and the decor is sensational, with lots of flashing lights, smoky mirrors, and even—believe it or not—a periodic rainstorm, complete with thunder. Dress is casual, and sometimes very colorful, depending on the crowd. A fun place to go if you like this kind of thing.

On the Sexy Side

Two of the famous female-impersonator clubs in New Orleans are the **Gunga Den,** 325 Bourbon St., which presents a "Powder Puff Review," and the **Silver Frolics,** 427 Bourbon St., with the "Me o My" show. If it's strip shows you want, you'll find them right along this part of Bourbon St.

Theater and Cabaret

The **Beverly Dinner Playhouse,** 217 Labarre Rd. (tel. 837-4022), presents Broadway and Hollywood stars in outstanding productions in an Old South mansion that was, during the '40s, an opulent gambling casino and supper club where such greats of the entertainment world as Judy Garland, Sophie Tucker, and Rudy Vallee made regular appearances. Then it stood shuttered and weed-choked until the '70s, when it was reopened and restored to its former elegance. Prices range from $14 to $24.50, and include dinner, the show, and tax. There's an extensive wine list, and cocktails. The lounge opens at 6 p.m., the dining room and buffet open at 6:30 p.m., and curtain time is 8:30 p.m. The playhouse closes Monday, but has a noon buffet and matinee on Sunday. Reservations are a must.

The oldest nonprofessional theater troupe in the country, **Le Petit Theatre,** 616 St. Peter St. (tel. 522-1954), periodically puts on plays that rival the professionals in excellence. Check when you're in New Orleans to see if they're in production.

Also check to see if the University of New Orleans **Theatre by the Lake-front** has anything going on. Their productions are first-rate, many of them by Tennessee Williams (who had a home here), and prices are a low $5, with students paying only $2.

3. Festivals

MARDI GRAS: This is the festival of festivals in New Orleans! It has been celebrated along the banks of the Mississippi since Bienville arrived in 1699, and many residents prepare for it all year long, designing costumes and floats and planning the elaborate balls. To get the most out of any Mardi Gras visit, arm yourself (I urge this strongly) with the handy **New Orleans Mardi Gras Guide** published by Arthur Hardy, P.O. Box 8058, New Orleans, LA 70182. It costs $2.95, postpaid, and is invaluable. If you don't write ahead, look for it on newstands.

The Carnival season actually opens shortly after Christmas, as "mystick krewes" begin to hold their more than 60 masquerade balls. Festivities pick up momentum as Shrove Tuesday (Mardi Gras means literally "Fat Tuesday"), the last day before Lent, approaches. Street parades start about ten days before Mardi Gras Day, and they are a sight to behold, with satin-covered horses, the beat of drums in the streets, masked crowds shouting the traditional "Throw me something, mister," the mad scrambling for beads and "doubloons" as those on the floats respond to the cries, the colorful, noisy blending of music and nonsense and just plain fun. When the big day finally arrives, the Mystick Krewe of Comus—the first carnival organization and the one that introduced street parades—holds its glittering parade, along with the krewes of Rex and Zulu, and everything comes to a happy climax at the grandest of all the balls, reigned over by the King and Queen of Carnival. Then it's all over until the next year, and New Orleanians repair to their homes to begin planning for bigger and better things when Mardi Gras comes around again.

Literally thousands of outsiders pour into New Orleans for what is really the city's "family party," and they are warmly welcomed by its citizens. But rooms are scarce as hens' teeth and prices jump astronomically. Still, it is a *very* special occasion and everyone should participate at least once before departing this earth. When your turn comes, be sure to plan as far ahead as you can (a year isn't too long) and leave your inhibitions at home—there's no place for them in the revelry of Mardi Gras!

THE NEW ORLEANS JAZZ AND HERITAGE FESTIVAL: For at least two weekends (and a *full* week between) in late April or early May of each year, jazz, folk, gospel, Cajun, and popular music take over the city. There are concerts indoors and out, parades, and displays of Louisiana foods and crafts. It's another carnival, and it draws internationally known musicians to join those already on the scene for the season of fun, food, and good music. For dates and specific information, write: The New Orleans Jazz and Heritage Festival, P.O. Box 2530, New Orleans, LA 70176, or call 504/522-4786.

SPRING FIESTA: Since 1947, the Spring Fiesta has opened on the first Friday after Easter and continued for 19 days of touring plantations, Vieux Carré and Garden District homes, and other showplaces in the area. Many are open only during this period, and visitors are conducted on the two- to three-hour city tours by costumed hostesses. Plantation tours take a full day. There's a beautiful "Patios by Candlelight" tour, a "Night in Old New Orleans" parade, an art show, a festival of flowers, and a historical pageant. For tour information and reservations (which are a must), write the Spring Fiesta Association, 529 St. Ann St., New Orleans, LA 70116, or call 504/581-1367.

THE FOOD FESTIVAL: Once a year, in early July, New Orleanians celebrate their love of good eating with a smashing food festival. Just about every chef in the city participates by preparing an array of specialties that you just have to see to appreciate its scope! Some are literally works of art, others picture-pretty dishes of humble, everyday foods. And best of all, you can sample most of them, portions costing anywhere from 25¢ to $1. Festivities include spaghetti-eating contests, special river cruises, musical performances, and lots more. To top it all off, there's a final grand gourmet dinner party. You can get details by writing the New Orleans Food Festival at P.O. Box 2410, New Orleans, LA 70116 (tel. 504/522-7273).

4. The Sporting Life

FOOTBALL: That palatial **Superdome** is the scene of all home games for the New Orleans Saints football team. Call 525-8573 for ticket information.

HORSE RACING: The "Sport of Kings" has always been a favorite of New Orleanians, and there's racing at the **Fair Grounds**, 1751 Gentilly Blvd. (tel. 944-5515), from November to late March. It's the third-oldest track in the U.S., and admission to the grandstand will cost you $1, to the clubhouse (and you should call for reservations) $3.

TENNIS: There are public tennis courts at both **City Park** and **Audubon Park,** and hourly rates are low. They're usually pretty crowded during summer months, so it's a good idea to call Audubon at 861-2537 and City Park at 482-2230 to check on availability before making the trip.

GOLF: Both parks also have public golf courses, and to reserve starting times and check on the reasonable greens fees, call 283-4324 for City Park courses, 861-9511 for Audubon.

5. Shopping

Like everything else in New Orleans, shopping is fun. And you can find almost anything your heart desires—if you can't find the article, you can find someone to make it for you! The place is loaded with craftsmen and artisans in almost every conceivable material: cast iron, wood, leather, fabric, brass, plastic, and precious metals. You can even have one of those marvelous oldtime overhead fans shipped back home. The following listing of shops is far from complete, but if you don't see something here that particularly interests you, be assured that you'll find it when you get there.

ANTIQUES: Boyer Antiques—Dolls & Buttons, 241 Chartres and 404 Chartres, has the usual assortment of antiques, plus an enchanting collection of old dolls and doll furniture. Open 9:30 a.m. to 5 p.m. Monday to Saturday. You'll find all sorts of miniature soldiers and military antiques at **Le Petit Soldier Shop, Inc.,** 528 Royal St., as well as antique helmets, swords, books, and prints. Open 10 a.m. to 5 p.m. Monday through Saturday. **The London Shop, Inc.,** in a lovely old building at 115 Chartres St., has a wonderful assortment of English and continental furniture, porcelains, paintings, and accessories. Open 9 a.m. to 5 p.m. Monday through Saturday (closed on Saturday from June to Labor Day). Antique weapons are the specialty at **James H. Cohen,** 319 Royal, who advertise that they "buy, sell and horse trade."

ART GALLERIES: At **Nahan Galleries,** 540 Royal St., you can watch ceramic tiles being hand-painted in the shop, but they specialize in important, signed graphics by Chagall, Miro, and Calder (among others), and are world-wide representatives for important international artists such as Max Papart, Paolo Boni, etc. Open 9:30 a.m. to 5:30 p.m. seven days a week. For limited edition graphics and jazz posters, try **Lorenzo Bergen Galleries** at 730 Royal. Open from 10 a.m. to 7 p.m. daily.

ARTS AND CRAFTS: In addition to a huge selection of ready-made wooden items (toys, furniture, clocks, boxes, art objects, cooking utensils, etc.), **Out of the Woods,** 812 Royal St., will custom-make articles. Open every day from 10 a.m. to 6 p.m.

BRASS & COPPER: You won't believe the sheer number of items at **The Brass Menagerie,** 524 St. Louis St.! They have everything from chandeliers and lanterns to bathroom faucets to brass locks to antique doorknobs to bathroom fixtures to whatever else you can name. They specialize in antique, period, and contemporary fine, solid-brass hardware. They're open 9 a.m. to 5:30 p.m. Monday through Friday, 10 a.m. to 5 p.m. Saturday. Another shop crammed full of brass treasures is the **Brass and Copper Shop,** 541 Chartres St. Pots, pans, and bric-a-brac galore. Open 10 a.m. to 5 p.m. seven days a week.

CANDIES AND PRALINES: Once you taste New Orleans pralines, you'll want to take some home. And if your bags are already filled, most shops will mail them for you. One of my favorites among the many praline shops is **Aunt Sally's,** in the French Market at 810 Decatur. You can watch skilled workers fashioning the goodies, so you know they're fresh when you get them. The shop also carries souvenirs and imported gifts, and they'll ship anything you buy. Open 8 a.m. to 6 p.m. every day. **Laura's Praline Shoppe,** 115 Royal, has been in business since 1913 and makes all kinds of candies, pralines, and jellies, as well as hand-dipped chocolates. Also, all Creole condiments. Open 9 a.m. to 10:30 p.m. daily.

CLOTHING: Women shoppers will find sophisticated clothes at **Lilly Pulitzer,** 530 Wilkenson, and their menfolk and children can shop here as well. **Meyer the Hatter,** 120 St. Charles St., has been topping New Orleans males for over 80 years, and carries such leading names as Dobbs, Stetson, and Borsalino. Open 9:30 a.m. to 5:30 p.m. Monday through Saturday.

An outstanding women's shop in the Quarter is **Donnis Boutique,** 500 St. Peter St., across from Jackson Square, featuring classic styles as well as innovative new fashions "For interesting women with interesting minds."

DEPARTMENT STORES: The **Maison Blanche** department store at 901 Canal is world famous for quality and luxury goods. This is good browsing country, and it is open from 10 a.m. to 5:45 p.m. Monday through Saturday, staying open until 8:30 p.m. on Thursday. There are also branches in Metairie, the Clearview Shopping Center, and the Westside Shopping Center in Gretna. **D. H. Holmes Company, Ltd.,** 819 Canal, is another longtime New Orleans favorite. Incidentally, its restaurant and cafeteria have very good food at very reasonable prices.

FANS: Because I'm an incurable romantic, I can't think of a better cooling system (no, not even air conditioning!) than those slow-turning ceiling fans you see all over the South. So it was a real treat to see the marvelous old restored specimens at **The Fan People,** 1137 Dante St. in the Carrollton area—you can get there by trolley. Not all the fans are old; they have some very contemporary examples, but I'd opt for one of the Victorian models. You might be interested to know that prices start at around $150. Not far away from this shop is another which also has a large collection of fans, the **White Pillars Emporium,** at 8312 Oak St. in the Carrollton section.

FOODS: If you want to try your hand at making those scrumptious beignets, you can buy the mix at the **Cafe du Monde's** retail store, 805 Decatur St., and to make it complete, do get a tin of their famous coffee. Open 10 a.m. to 5:30 p.m. Monday through Saturday, 10 a.m. to 1 p.m. on Sunday.

GIFT SHOPS: There are literally hundreds of gift shops in New Orleans. Herewith, some of the ones I found most attractive. The **Pontalba Gift Shop,** 801 Decatur St., has one of the widest varieties of gifts I ran across. Their handmade New Orleans dolls are a delight, as are the cut glass and custom-made jewelry. Some items are costly, many quite reasonable, and the usual souvenirs at lower prices are also on hand. It's open seven days a week from 9 a.m. to 5:30 p.m.

THE MARKETPLACE: Even if you're not shopping, don't miss browsing here. The Marketplace is located inside an old warehouse across from the French Market at 1015 Decatur St. It is composed of small shops lining a brick walk, and besides the fascinating display of wares, there is usually some sort of entertainment going on (a slate hanging outside tells about the scheduled activities). You might see craft demonstrations, jugglers, magicians, or listen to local musicians. **"The Loft"** upstairs holds mostly crafts and handmade items, and you frequently see someone making one of the articles to be sold. It is open seven days a week from 10 a.m. to 8 p.m.

PIPES: Because I'm a pipe smoker (no letters, please—women have been smoking pipes for centuries!), I was intrigued by Mr. Edwin C. Jansen's Ye Olde Pipe Shoppe, 306 Chartres St. The shop was established in 1868 by Mr. Jansen's grandfather, August, and in addition to the present, third-generation owner's briar pipes that he handmakes, there is a great collection of antique pipes put together by his father and grandfather.

RIVERBEND SHOPPING AREA: If you're a true shopper, give yourself a treat and ride the trolley out to this beautiful old section that has been turned into a shopping area with charming little boutiques, art galleries, and arts and crafts shops. Get off the trolley just as it turns from St. Charles Ave. onto Carrollton Ave.

Chapter XXIII

NEW ORLEANS: 1984 LOUISIANA WORLD EXPOSITION

1. The Site
2. Entertainment
3. The Practicalities

EXACTLY ONE HUNDRED YEARS from the date of its last spectacular Exposition (the Louisiana Cotton Exposition of 1884), New Orleans will host the **1984 Louisiana World Exposition** from May 12 to November 11, 1984. That's its *official* name—the familiar term is "World's Fair," and with good reason, since it will be the only such event registered for that year with the Bureau of International Expositions.

The Fair's theme is a fitting one for New Orleans: "The World of Rivers—Fresh Water as a Source of Life." And, indeed, the mighty Mississippi has been the source of New Orleans's life from the very beginning. From the time it served native Indians as the site of an important trading post to today's busy harbor (which sees more than 5000 cargo ships, flying the flags of all nations, dock here in the course of a year), the Mississippi has been the heartbeat of the city. As a highway for exploration, it has figured, as well, in the physical development of the entire country. Its grasp on the human imagination has found expression in music, art, poetry, and legends. As "King Cotton" was celebrated in the 1884 Exposition, so the Mississippi will reign over *this* celebration.

On an international scale, major rivers of the world such as the Amazon, Thames, Seine, Rhine, Congo, Danube, Nile, and Ganges will be recognized as the destiny-shaping forces they represent for the world's civilizations. With the United Nations having declared a goal of clean drinking water and adequate sanitation for the globe by 1990, the Fair's theme will focus on efficient freshwater management as well as the historical significance of the world's waterways.

New Orleans, however, with its inborn flair for celebrations of all kinds, will lend its own special flavor to the theme, and if you have never been able to manage a Mardi Gras attendance, you can count on a taste of its exuberance during the Fair. And it goes without saying that this city will see to it that your Fair experience includes all facets of its marvelous and unique cuisine.

The realities of publishing and a mid-1983 deadline for this book prevent my giving you as much *specific* information as I would like. What I *can* do, however, is outline the plans and projections that are already being implemented, give you ticket prices and an overall view of what to expect.

1. The Site

Some 82 acres stretching along the riverfront in the old warehouse district of downtown New Orleans have been revitalized and converted into a Fair site especially well suited to demonstrate the importance of the river to the city. Crumbling old buildings that had for decades seen minimal use have been rehabilitated and begun a new and useful lifespan. With commendable foresight, planners have brought much of this riverfront area back to a status of permanent use for long after the time when the Fair becomes history. For example, the 15-acre Convention Hall is already accepting 1985 bookings from groups that have been cramped for exhibition space when planning New Orleans meetings. And the warehouses will, after the Fair, remain as a new complex of shops and restaurants.

Your first glimpse of the fairgrounds may well be from Canal Street, looking toward the river. Flags, balloons, music, and entertainers will direct you to a part of the Rivergate Convention Center, which has been transformed into a sort of giant foyer for the Canal Street entrance. The actual entrance gate is at the intersection of Front and Girod Streets and is set off by massive figures straight off Mardi Gras floats.

Once inside, visitors will view the 2300-foot-long **Wonderwall** that runs along this axis of the grounds. It is a fascinating, fanciful structure that holds a meandering water-course, fountains, pools, sculpture, concession areas (including amusement centers such as video game rooms), and continuous entertainment of one sort or another. It serves to link the Louisiana Pavilion with the row of warehouse buildings that have been converted to shops and restaurants, as well as to set the festive mood of the entire Fair.

A winding stream and walkway will lead you into the **Louisiana Pavilion,** from which other pathways lead to exhibits of various states, as well as leading corporations.

From the Louisiana Pavilion, you can reach major riverfront spaces such as the International pavilions, amphitheater, and waterborne exhibits by way of a series of stairs and bridges that link up to a wide promenade on the river's edge. While all international participants have not, at this writing, clearly defined their exhibitions, one major attraction which *is* definite is the stunning array of art treasures from the Vatican.

The 1.5-acre **Watergarden** is south of the Louisiana Pavilion and was created to demonstrate the recreational use of fresh water. Thus, you'll find all sorts of watergames (some educational as well as just plain fun) in a jewel of a setting. The south pool is peopled by mythical water beasts that emerge when visitors operate special valves, and there's an "orchestra" of whistles, toots, drums and cymbals whose sounds bubble forth from fountains as you "conduct" to create your own water music.

The amusement area will hold a ferris wheel and various other rides and games to keep the kiddies occupied (unfortunately, at press time details are sketchy as to their exact nature)—but perhaps the best news of all to those of us who have tramped around World's Fairs in the past, there will be a monorail to transport you from one area to another when the feet begin to ache.

2. Entertainment

Unlike many other world's fairs, the 1984 event in New Orleans draws from a great pool of natural entertainment resources that are indigenous to the city. It is *normal* for New Orleans to have great resident entertainers and to attract the best of those who live elsewhere. With an average influx of more than 7 million tourists annually, top entertainment is always on tap—the additional visitors attracted by the 1984 World's Fair will simply mean there will be even more. Rest assured that wherever you are during the Fair—on the grounds, sightseeing in the French Quarter, or roaming about the city's environs—you will not lack for entertainment.

As for the fairgrounds itself, you will encounter three stages for performances in the Wonderwall, floating stages in lagoons and pools, mobile stages dispatched to any attraction that has a long line of people waiting to be admitted, a 5500-seat amphitheater on the riverfront, a more intimate Victorian-style theater for drama, and twice a day, a miniature Mardi Gras parade will pass through the grounds complete with bands, floats, costumed revelers, and doubloons and trinkets to be thrown just as in the real thing.

Those stages will hold just about every type of entertainment you can imagine: musicians, magicians, jugglers, mimes, puppet shows, medicine shows, and hurdy-gurdy music, and one will even feature a calliope. All will be free and spread out before you like a great buffet from which you may pick and choose that which appeals to you most.

And the music! New Orleans is, of course, the jazz capital of the world, and for these six months the fairgrounds will resemble a continuous jazz festival, with internationally acclaimed performers joining local talent to play that brand of music in all its forms, from the basic sound of Dixieland to the more complex and powerful rhythms of today's jazz. You will find it concentrated in the Jazz and Gospel Tent, and there will be plenty of spicy regional foods like jambalaya, red beans and rice, and crawfish to help you get in the Louisiana mood.

Nor is the music confined to jazz: you'll hear everything from classical to rock-and-roll to country/western to—well, you name it, and you'll find it being played somewhere on the fairgrounds. The music of Louisiana's lively Cajuns (which reflects the basic philosophy of *"Laissez les bon temps rouler,"* or "Let the good times roll"), will be there in an authentic setting with the traditional "dogtrot" house for working craftsmen, a cookhouse like you'd find out in the bayous, a boat building shed, and many other everyday items of the culture. No charge above your admission ticket.

Caribbean sounds, which came to New Orleans centuries ago with the people of the islands, will ring through the **Spanish Plaza** right on the riverfront. There will be steel bands, street entertainers, and dancers in colorful island costumes, a pirate ship, and an open invitation for viewers to join in the dancing. Sidewalk cafes will serve cool drinks and Caribbean foods. All this at no additional charge.

The **Classical Concert Series** will bring to the amphitheater stage some of the world's greatest symphonic orchestras, performing under the batons of conductors whose names are legendary. As this is written, a definite schedule of performances has not yet been established, but you can call ahead (see the telephone number at the end of this chapter) to see who will be appearing during your visit. Amphitheater events (in the evenings) will be the only place at which you will pay an additional charge.

At one point during the six months of the Fair's run, the **World Youth Symphony,** made up of talented young musicians of professional caliber between the ages of 18 and 24, will present a concert series under the direction of Eduardo Mata, music director of the Dallas Symphony and artistic advisor to the National Opera of Mexico. These concerts will probably take place in the amphitheater at a small additional charge.

You'll find the lovely **World Theatre,** with its look of a grand house in the Victorian era, inside the centrally located Great Hall. It will hold some 1200 seats and will present outstanding theater from all over the world. Chinese illusion theater, mime, black theater, kabuki, and international comedy will all be represented. Young theater-lovers will want to see at least one performance in the World Festival of Theater for Young Audiences series, with twelve theatrical companies from six continents acting out plays which, for the most part, have never been seen in the U.S. before. They'll be presented in June, and are an excellent way for children to experience cultures different from their own.

Over on the river, the amphitheater will be busy both day and night. Plans now are to have daytime performances at no additional charge, but to charge a small admission fee in the evenings. Events will include world-class performances of everything from Paganini to rock, ballet to Beethoven, country singers to concert pianists.

Also on the riverfront, a giant **Aquacade** (shades of Esther Williams!) is planned, the first in this country since Billy Rose's Aquacade at the New York World's Fair in 1939. Beautiful girls in lovely swimsuits will dive into an elliptical tank and surface in fabulous gowns and tiaras to dance a graceful water ballet. Unless plans change, the show will go on ten times a day, seven days a week, for the entire six months.

If your artistic interests are centered on paintings, films, crafts, or other visual arts, you will want to take in the **Artworks '84** exhibits in the Federal Fibre Mill building. A little like the SoHo section of New York City, it will hold a conglomeration of painters, sculptors, glass blowers, weavers, potters, photographers, and filmmakers—you'll actually be able to see an artistic concept take shape as the artist or craftsperson executes a finished work. Look also for the winning entry in the First International Water Sculpture Competition, sponsored by the Louisiana World Exposition in 1983, which may be with the Artworks exhibits or elsewhere on the grounds (plans are not definite at this writing).

Besides all this, there are all sorts of maritime galas planned over on the river: Memorial Day, Independence Day, Navy Day, Labor Day, Columbus Day, and Veterans Day—all will have special ceremonies there, with naval vessels of the U.S. and allied countries, sailing ships, cruise liners, fishing boats, and paddlewheel steamers taking part. Everyday waterborne traffic on a working river always inspires an excitement all its own, and the special events are bound to prove fascinating.

And, of course, there are the fireworks. No World's Fair would be complete without them, and New Orleans has outdone herself in this respect. A dazzling spectacle of fireworks will be launched each night from a barge out on the Mississippi River, and they've been carefully choreographed to burst with the beat of music coming from the shore. The grand finale of sound, light, and music is truly thrilling.

There will undoubtedly be much more in the way of entertainment as plans are finalized, and certainly national, international, and state pavilions will provide their own unique appeal. You should be able to obtain detailed information on all events by early 1984 (see below for address to contact).

3. The Practicalities

Once you've decided when you will be coming to the 1984 Louisiana World Exposition, the first order of business is deciding how you'll get there and where you will stay. Information on getting to New Orleans is included in Chapter XX and accommodations are outlined in Chapter XXI. However, it should be pointed out that there will be many attractive package tours put together especially for those coming to the World's Fair—Amtrak, Trailways and Greyhound, and the airlines will all undoubtedly have special deals that can save you a great deal of money as well as the trouble of making your own arrangements. Several leading national tour companies have also announced their intentions to offer such deals.

My personal inclination—and it is a strong one—is usually to travel on my own, making my own reservations, time schedule, etc. In this particular case, though, my recommendation—and it is just as strong—is to consult your travel agent to see what is being offered and when. With a projection of more than 11 million visitors to New Orleans within the six months' life of the Fair, bookings may be hard to come by, indeed, and a package special may well make your visit during that time much less trouble and much less expensive.

If you drive, there will be parking lots especially for World's Fair visitors, as well as shuttle bus service to and from the grounds. My best advice, however, is to make use of the excellent public transportation that will be provided and leave your car parked at your hotel. You'll save time in the long run, and it's an easy matter to find out about bus transportation from your accommodations to the fairgrounds: simply call 586-2192.

Inside the fairgrounds, your entrance ticket entitles you to unlimited rides on the monorail.

TICKET PRICES: A one-day admission ticket will cost $15 for adults (ages 12 to 54), $14 for ages four to 11 and 55 and over. The two-day tickets will run $28 and $26.

Each ticket entitles you to unlimited ridership around the site on the monorail, as well as entry to all pavilions, exhibits, and regularly scheduled entertainment.

By December of 1983, season tickets will be offered that will allow unlimited attendance at the Fair. Prices have not been set as we go to press, but you can get details by contacting the address below.

FOR MORE DETAILS: For more detailed information than is available to us at this time, you can contact (after November 1983): Sales Department, Louisiana World's Exposition, P.O. Box 1984, New Orleans, LA 70158 (tel. 504/566-1984).

NOW, SAVE MONEY ON ALL YOUR TRAVELS!
Join Arthur Frommer's $25-A-Day Travel Club

Saving money while traveling is never a simple matter, which is why, over 21 years ago, the **$25-A-Day Travel Club** was formed. Actually, the idea came from readers of the Arthur Frommer Publications who felt that such an organization could bring financial benefits, continuing travel information, and a sense of community to economy-minded travelers all over the world.

In keeping with the money-saving concept, the membership fee is low—$14 (U.S. residents) or $16 (Canadian, Mexican, and foreign residents)—and is immediately exceeded by the value of your benefits which include:

(1) An annual subscription to an 8-page tabloid newspaper *The Wonderful World of Budget Travel* which keeps you up-to-date on fastbreaking developments in low-cost travel in all parts of the world—bringing you the kind of information you'd have to pay over $25 a year to obtain elsewhere. This consumer-conscious publication also provides special services to readers:

Travelers' Directory—a list of members all over the world who are willing to provide hospitality to other members as they pass through their home cities.

Share-a-Trip—requests from members for travel companions who can share costs and help avoid the burdensome single supplement.

Readers Ask . . . Readers Reply—travel questions from members to which other members reply with authentic firsthand information.

(2) The latest edition of any TWO of the books listed on the following page (except for *The Adventure Book,* which is available at only $7.50 to members).

(3) A copy of *Arthur Frommer's Guide to New York.*

(4) Your personal membership card which entitles you to purchase through the Club all Arthur Frommer Publications for a third to a half off their regular retail prices during the term of your membership.

So why not join this hardy band of international budgeteers NOW and participate in its exchange of information and hospitality? Simply send $14 (U.S. residents) or $16 U.S. (Canadian, Mexican, and other foreign residents) along with your name and address to: $25-A-Day Travel Club, Inc., 1230 Avenue of the Americas, New York, NY 10020. Remember to specify which *two* of the books in section (2) above you wish to receive in your initial package of members' benefits. Or tear out this page, check off any two books on the opposite side and send it to us with your membership fee.